MW00650409

Core Knowledge® Grade 2

Teacher Handbook Series
Grade 2

Edited by E. D. Hirsch, Jr.
and Souzanne A. Wright

Core Knowledge® Foundation
Charlottesville, Virginia

Photography Credits

© Marcel & Eva Malherbe/The Image Works: 132
© Fujifotos/The Image Works: 139
© North Wind Picture Archives: 147
© Paul Souders/CORBIS: 152
© North Wind Picture Archives: 179
Private Collection, © Christie's Images Ltd. All Rights Reserved: 184
© Hulton Archive/Getty Images: 196
© Underwood and Underwood/CORBIS: 214
© Rod Planck/Photo Researchers, Inc.: 226
© Gerhard Gscheidle/Peter Arnold, Inc.: 265
© Bill Lai/The Image Works: 285
State Archives of Michigan: 458
© Bettmann/CORBIS: 460

Published by Core Knowledge® Foundation

Library of Congress Cataloging-in-Publication Data
Grade 2 Teacher Handbook
Edited by E. D. Hirsch, Jr. and Souzanne A. Wright—1st ed.
p. cm.—(The teacher handbook series)

ISBN 978-1-890517-74-8
2005920257

Copyright © 2005 by Core Knowledge® Foundation
All Rights Reserved

PRINTED IN CANADA
10 9 8 7 6 5 4

2014; Fourth Printing
First Edition

Requests for permission should be directed to:
Core Knowledge Foundation
801 East High Street
Charlottesville, VA 22902
Telephone: (434) 977-7550
Fax: (434) 977-0021
E-mail: coreknow@coreknowledge.org
Home page: www.coreknowledge.org

"Core Knowledge™" is a trademark of the Core Knowledge Foundation.

This book is dedicated, gratefully,

to

the hard-working Core Knowledge second-grade teachers
who have gone for so long without this book.

A Note to Teachers

This book is addressed to, and intended to be read by, Grade 2 teachers. When Core Knowledge was first used in the classroom, some topics in the *Core Knowledge Sequence* sent teachers scrambling to the library. Many teachers spent hours consulting encyclopedias and looking for other reliable sources of information on topics they were asked to teach—topics they had not studied in college or education school. Now, with the development of the *Core Knowledge Teacher Handbooks,* Core Knowledge teachers will have a single, reliable source that gives them not only the background knowledge they need but also valuable teaching tips and review strategies. We hope this handbook will be useful for teachers seeking to build on their foundation of knowledge, whether or not they teach in the growing network of Core Knowledge schools.

If you are interested in learning more about the Core Knowledge curriculum and the work of the Foundation, please contact us for more information: 801 East High Street, Charlottesville, VA 22902; (434) 977-7550; coreknow@coreknowledge.org.
On our website (www.coreknowledge.org), you will find an online bookstore, lessons created by teachers in Core Knowledge schools, and other supporting materials developed by the Foundation.

Acknowledgments

This series has depended on the assistance of more than 100 people. Some of those named here already know the depth of our gratitude; others may be surprised to find themselves thanked publicly for the assistance they gave quietly and freely. To all helpers named and unnamed, we are deeply grateful.

Editor-in-Chief of the *Teacher Handbook Series:* E. D. Hirsch, Jr.
Editor and Project Director: Souzanne A. Wright

Core Knowledge Reviewers: Linda Bevilacqua, Matthew Davis, and Cyndi Wells
Resources Coordinator: Rob Hewitt
Assessments Writer: Margarete C. Grove
Expert Reviewer Coordinator: Elizabeth B. Rasmussen

Experts on Subject Matter: Louisa Moats (language arts); Fritz Gritzner, Wilfred McClay, Sterling Stuckey (history and geography); Lucien Ellington (history and geography–Asian and Japanese history); Jenny Strauss Clay (history and geography–Greek history); Thomas Thangaraj (history and geography–Hinduism); Kristin Onuf (visual arts); Diane Persellin (music); Wayne Bishop (mathematics); Louis Bloomfield (science)

Contributing Editors (across all grades): Matthew Davis; E. D. Hirsch, Jr.; Susan T. Hitchcock; Michael J. Marshall; Elizabeth B. Rasmussen; Charles J. Shields; Souzanne A. Wright

Contributing Editors (specific subject): Sandra Stotsky (language arts); Fritz Gritzner, Sheldon Stern (history and geography); Bruce Cole (visual arts); David Klein (mathematics); Martha Schwartz (science)

Contributing Writers: Mary Epes, Gail B. Hedges, Mary Yarber (language arts); Hendrik Booraem, Michael Chesson, Fritz Gritzner, Mary Beth Klee, Luther Spoehr (history and geography); Jody Shiffman (visual arts); David Klein (mathematics); Roberta Friedman, Steve Lund, Martha Schwartz, Stephanie Trelogan, Lynn Yarris (science)

Advisors on Elementary Education: Linda Bevilacqua; Margarete C. Grove; Becky Poppe; Elizabeth B. Rasmussen; Cyndi Wells; Souzanne A. Wright

Teachers: Special thanks to the teachers—too many to list here—who have offered their suggestions during focus groups at our national conference

Development House: Brown Publishing Network, Inc.

Benefactor: The Walton Family Foundation

Our grateful acknowledgment to these persons does not imply that we have taken their (sometimes conflicting) advice in every case, or that each of them endorses all aspects of this project. Responsibility for final decisions rests with the editors alone. Suggestions for improvements are always welcome. We thank, in advance, those who send advice for revising and improving this series.

Contents

Introduction

About These Books

The Core Knowledge Foundation has written this *Teacher Handbook* to help you teach the Core Knowledge curriculum for Grade 2. The handbook is based on the *Core Knowledge Sequence.* The *Teacher Handbook* complements the *Sequence,* so using them together is easy. The *Sequence* outlines the specific topics to be taught in the six subject areas, then the *Teacher Handbook* expands on every topic listed. It's as though the *Sequence* topics are links on a website, and the handbook is the content behind each link.

The *Teacher Handbook* is a rich resource that provides essential background information about language arts, history and geography, visual arts, music, mathematics, and science. It identifies what children should have learned in previous grades and what they will learn in future grades. It defines crucial vocabulary words, points out cross-curricular connections, offers teaching and review suggestions, and lists titles of books and website addresses as resources for you and your class.

I. American Government: The Constitution

The Big Idea

The United States is founded on the principle of consent of the governed as stated in the opening phrase of the Constitution, "We the people."

Remember that each subject you study with children expands their vocabulary and introduces new terms, thus making them better listeners and readers. As you study historical people and events, use read alouds and discussions to build children's vocabularies.

The items in bold relate to the content in Grade 2. In discussions with children, use terminology such as "long, long ago" to set this information in time.

- **1776** Declaration of Independence
- **1777** Adoption of Articles of Confederation by Congress
- **1781** End of Revolutionary War

What Students Need to Learn

- **The government of the United States is based on the U.S. Constitution, the highest law of our land.** ❶
- **James Madison is known as the "Fatherof the Constitution."** ❷
- **Government by the consent of the governed: "We the people"** ❸

What Students Will Learn in Future Grades

In future grades, students will review and extend their learning about the U.S. Constitution.

Grade 4

- from the Declaration of Independence to the Constitution: making a new government
- Constitution of the United States: Preamble, separation and sharing of powers, limitations, Bill of Rights
- national, state, and local levels and functions of government

American History and Geography

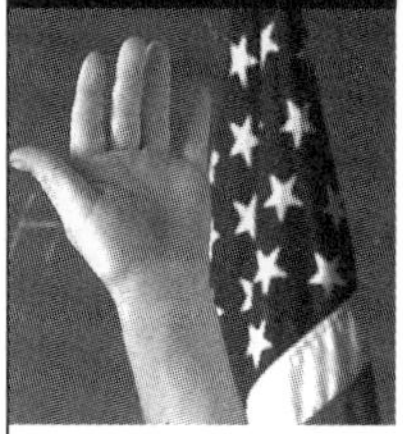

2

AMERICAN HISTORY AND GEOGRAPHY

TEACHERS: The study of American history begins in grades K-2 with a brief overview of major events and figures, from the earliest days to recent times. A more in-depth, chronological study of American history begins again in grade 3 and continues onward. The term "American" here generally, but not always, refers to the lands that became the United States. Other topics regarding North, Central, and South America may be found in the World History and Geography sections of this Sequence.

I. American Government: The Constitution

TEACHERS: Through analogies to familiar settings—the family, the school, the community—discuss some basic questions regarding American government, such as: What is government? What are some basic functions of American government? (Making and enforcing laws; settling disputes; protecting rights and liberties, etc.) Only basic questions need to be addressed at this grade level. In fourth grade students will examine in more detail specific issues and institutions of American government, including, for example, the separation of powers, and the relation between state and federal government.

History and Geography

- American government is based on the Constitution, the highest law of our land. ❶
- James Madison, the "Father of the Constitution" ❷
- Government by the consent of the governed: "We the people" ❸

II. The War of 1812

- President James Madison and Dolley Madison
- British impressment of American sailors
- Old Ironsides
- British burn the White House
- Fort McHenry, Francis Scott Key, and "The Star-Spangled Banner"
- Battle of New Orleans, Andrew Jackson

III. Westward Expansion

TEACHERS: Students will study Westward Expansion in greater depth and detail in grade 5. Second grade teachers should examine the fifth grade guidelines to see how these topics build in the later grade. It is recommended that second grade teachers keep their focus on the people and events specified here, and leave for fifth grade the figures and ideas specified for that grade.

In the sections that follow, you will be introduced to the key elements of the handbook, step-by-step. Our purpose is not only to guide you through the handbook, but also to introduce you to some other key resources and help you to teach the Core Knowledge curriculum to your class.

Organization of the Handbook

Both the *Sequence* and the *Teacher Handbook* are divided into six subject areas: language arts, history and geography, visual arts, music, mathematics, and science. Then each of these subjects is divided into sections.

Subject Opener

▸ *Percentage Guidelines*

The first page of every subject includes a brief outline of the subject matter and suggested percentages of time you might choose to allot to teaching each section.

▸ *Introduction*

The introduction to each subject area gives a summary of the topics covered in this subject. Written in essay style, it summarizes upcoming content and often suggests the importance of certain topics to your children.

Sections

Some sections in the handbook can be taught as individual units that last a few weeks; others are better taught by weaving them in throughout the year. Although the *Sequence* and the *Teacher Handbook* have specific sections on reading and mathematics, it is expected that both will be taught on an ongoing basis throughout the year. Most Core Knowledge teachers spend a few weeks teaching the material on "Westward Expansion." On the other hand, many teachers prefer to spread out the stories and poems in Language Arts and the songs in Music throughout the year. This "stretched-out" approach allows you to match poems about the seasons with the Science section on the four seasons, and so on. The same strategy will work with the science biographies, which can be paired with the science topics they illustrate; for example, Anton van Leeuwenhoek with the human body and Elijah McCoy with simple machines.

▸ *Section Opener*

Each section in the *Teacher Handbook* begins in the same way.

• *The Big Idea* contains the central idea of the section.

• *What Students Should Already Know* outlines what children *should* have learned in previous grades if they have been in Core Knowledge classrooms. You may wish to assess how much of this content they already know and how much they still need to learn.

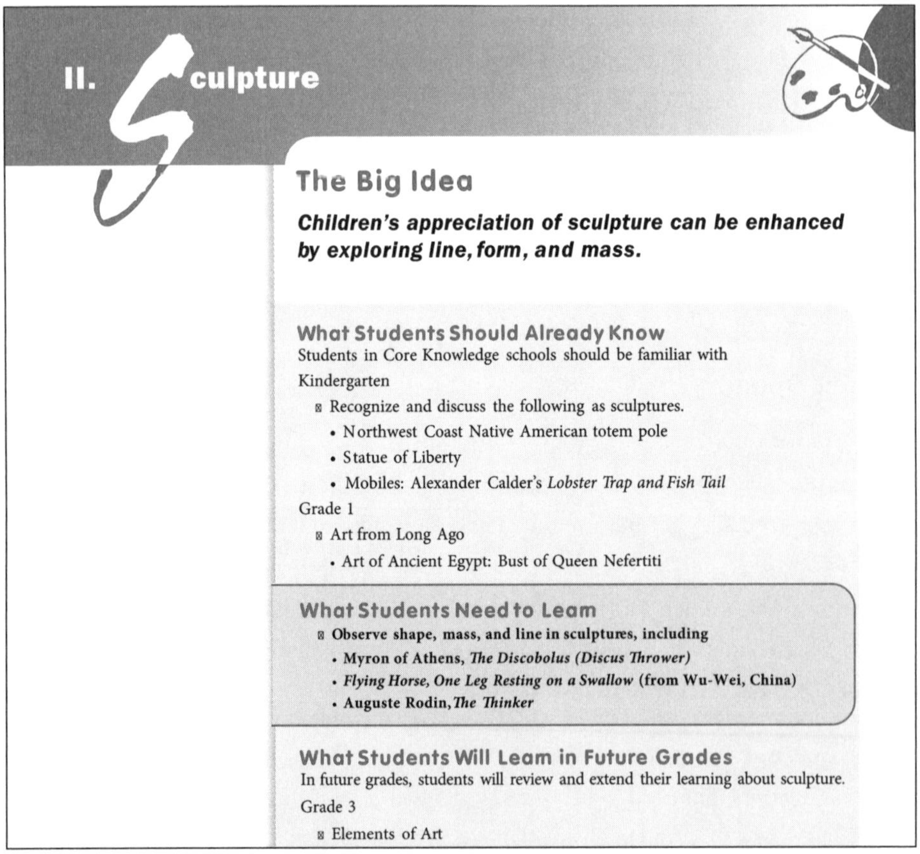

II. Sculpture

The Big Idea

Children's appreciation of sculpture can be enhanced by exploring line, form, and mass.

What Students Should Already Know

Students in Core Knowledge schools should be familiar with

Kindergarten

- Recognize and discuss the following as sculptures.
  - Northwest Coast Native American totem pole
  - Statue of Liberty
  - Mobiles: Alexander Calder's *Lobster Trap and Fish Tail*

Grade 1

- Art from Long Ago
  - Art of Ancient Egypt: Bust of Queen Nefertiti

What Students Need to Learn

- **Observe shape, mass, and line in sculptures, including**
  - **Myron of Athens, *The Discobolus (Discus Thrower)***
  - ***Flying Horse, One Leg Resting on a Swallow* (from Wu-Wei, China)**
  - **Auguste Rodin, *The Thinker***

What Students Will Learn in Future Grades

In future grades, students will review and extend their learning about sculpture.

Grade 3

- Elements of Art

• *What Students Need to Learn* presents the learning goals for the section, adapted from the bulleted items in the *Core Knowledge Sequence.* Sometimes, the *Sequence* goals are summarized in the handbook, so it's a good idea to compare the handbook learning goals to the *Sequence* as you plan your lessons. Note that if a topic has already been introduced in a previous grade and is a repeated learning goal, it is listed only once under *What Students Should Already Know.*

• *What Students Will Learn in Future Grades* provides a glimpse of topics that Core Knowledge teachers will cover in the grades ahead. You may recognize opportunities for joint projects involving children in different grades. For example, in Core Knowledge schools, children learn about the Civil War in Grade 2; then again, in more detail, in Grade 5. Some teachers use the Civil War as a theme to tie classrooms together, with fifth-grade "experts" helping teach second graders.

Vocabulary

The next two sections list vocabulary words. Core Knowledge is, among other things, an ambitious vocabulary-building program. It is based on the idea that children learning to read need to do more than just sound out words. They also need to recognize the words they are sounding out and rapidly *comprehend* them. Children who are limited by small vocabularies are likely to encounter difficulties in reading comprehension in later grades, even if they have good decoding skills. Consequently, it is almost impossible to overestimate the importance of building vocabulary in the early grades.

II. Sculpture

Materials

Art Resources

Myron of Athens, *The Discobolus (Discus Thrower)*

Flying Horse, One Leg Resting on a Swallow

Auguste Rodin, *The Thinker*

Instructional Master 30

Looking at Sculpture, p. 255

decorative object, p. 254

supplemental art prints, p. 254

frisbee, p. 256

number line, p. 258

paper for sculpture, p. 258

modeling clay, p. 258

styrofoam, p. 258

a cup of water for each child, p. 258

sports magazines, p. 259

Vocabulary

Student/Teacher Vocabulary

form: an element of design that is three-dimensional and encloses volume (S)

mass: the quantity of matter an object contains (S)

negative space: the space defined by the positive elements (shapes in two-dimensional art, forms in three-dimensional art); sometimes referred to as "empty space" (T)

patina: a green film resulting from oxidation that is typically found on copper or bronze (T)

sculpture: a three-dimensional work of art (that may be carved, modeled, or assembled (S)

shape: a two-dimensional enclosed area (S)

Domain Vocabulary

Sculpture and associated words:
carve, balance, position, pose, in the round, high relief, low relief, proportion, form, volume, organic, perspective, gravity, tension, motion, expression, representation, illusion, sculptor, enclosed area, three-dimensional versus two-dimensional, 360 degrees, height, width, depth, relationship, statue, public art, media, metal, balance, freestanding sculpture, function, spiritual, ritual, decorated, represent, subject matter, pole, lifelike, form, chisel, mallet, hammer, marble, stone, wood, clay, metal, wax, plaster, cast, bronze, plus words that describe the sculptures, e.g., discus, competition, galloping, gaze, etc.

This handbook helps you teach vocabulary in several ways. First, the background information on each topic will enhance your own understanding. Second, each section of the handbook also defines a number of challenging words—unusual words, technical terms, and words that need to be precisely defined. These words are identified with either an (S) or a (T). An (S) means that students should learn this word, so words marked (S) are good candidates for repeated use and explicit vocabulary work. A (T) means that the word is important for teachers to know but not one that children are expected to master. Of course, you always have the option of including (T) words in your instruction, thus exposing children to a richer vocabulary.

Domain Vocabulary

The handbook also includes a section called Domain Vocabulary. A domain is simply an area or field of knowledge, such as maps, planets, or Native Americans. Domain Vocabulary is a collection of words you are likely to use while talking about that topic with children. If you were teaching the Grade 2 unit on seasonal cycles and discussing seasons and life processes, you might use words like *sprouting, hatching, growth, ripening, migration, dormancy,* and *hibernation*. Sometimes you might use the words often enough that children could eventually add them to their own working vocabularies. Other times, you might use the words only once or twice in passing. This might not be enough for children to master the word, but it will provide a base on which they can build if they encounter the word later.

You don't need to use all the words under Domain Vocabulary; think of them as a bank of words you can draw upon—in large or small amounts—that will enrich your classroom discussions and help your children become better readers because you are strengthening and building their vocabularies. For more details on teaching vocabulary, please refer to Supplemental Essay #3 on pp. 55–57.

Materials

To help you plan your lessons, a list of Instructional Masters, Art Resources, Text Resources, and teaching materials used in the section is found here.

Cross-curricular Connections

This section provides suggestions of material from other subject areas that might be incorporated into the current unit of study you are teaching.

II. Poetry

Cross-curricular Connections

History and Geography	Music
American: Westward Expansion Native Americans **American: The Civil War** • Harriet Tubman • President Abraham Lincoln	**Songs** • "Follow the Drinking Gourd"

Main Text

The larger column of text provides you with background information about specific subjects. Since none of us are experts in all topics, this information is useful as a refresher course on a given topic. The more background you have as a teacher, the better able you will be to guide children's learning.

What Teachers Need to Know

Background: Why Study Poetry?

This section offers a selection of poems by favorite 19th- and 20th-century writers. The purpose of this section is to help children appreciate the genre of poetry, build vocabulary, delight in the play of language, and perhaps become familiar with literary devices, such as alliteration, rhyme, rhythm, and imagery. As you teach this section, you may want to read with your class many more grade-appropriate poems by the same poets or by different poets.

Although some second graders may be able to read these poems on their own, we encourage you to read these poems aloud. Listening to poetry helps children develop an awareness of language that will help them become better writers and readers. By listening closely, by repeating certain lines or phrases

Teaching Idea

Before you begin teaching poetry, check that children in your class are able to differentiate between poetry and other forms of literature they may know. Ask them to name their favorite poems and poets. Invite volunteers to recite any poems or passages from poems they might know by heart.

60 *Grade 2 Handbook*

Teaching Ideas

The Core Knowledge Foundation does not require teachers to follow any particular teaching strategy when teaching the topics in the *Sequence.* The teaching ideas in the margins and the cross-curricular connections are only *suggestions.*

However, it is worth keeping in mind the ways in which children learn. Children learn through a process of building schemas and connections based upon prior knowledge. Children can build these schemas only through connecting their current experiences with previous ones. In other words, prior knowledge is the base, or foundation, on which new knowledge is constructed.

Review

Near the end of each section are suggestions for review and some classroom discussion questions. These review suggestions do not represent a complete Core Knowledge assessment package. You are strongly encouraged to develop or acquire review and assessment materials of your own.

Just a word on assessing children: The purpose of assessment is not to judge children, or to teach to a test, but to guide instruction. The best kind of assessment goes on regularly, not just at the end of a section. Assessments should include initial assessment, monitoring, and summative evaluation.

For an initial assessment, you as the teacher need to evaluate the prior knowledge that children possess and then provide the experiences they need to learn more. Monitoring goes on while instruction is taking place; it establishes whether a child is moving toward a goal. This kind of assessment can often be informal and might include noting children's participation in class discussions, observing children as they work on an activity or interact with classmates, journal writing, and keeping portfolios of their work. Summative evaluation happens at the end of the section. It determines whether the child has met the goals and learned the content.

To help gauge your children's level of learning, in addition to the materials offered in this book, you will find summative evaluation materials in the *Pearson Learning/Core Knowledge History & Geography* books and in your basal mathematics and reading programs. Your school may also give various state and national tests. All of these evaluative materials can provide you with data about your children's progress.

More Resources

The titles listed below are offered as a representative sample of materials and not a complete list of everything that is available.

For children —

These books are generally intended to be read aloud, though some children may be able to read parts or all of the simpler texts.

- *Listen My Children: Poems for Second Graders* (Core Knowledge Foundation, 2001). Includes all the poems listed in the *Sequence* for Grade 2.
- *A Child's Garden of Verses*, by Robert Louis Stevenson and illustrated by Tasha Tudor (Simon & Schuster, 1999). Hardcover, 72 pages, ISBN 0689823827.
- *Favorite Poems Old and New.* A treasury of over 700 poems, including many old favorites. Available from The Elijah Company, www.elijahco.com or 1-888-235-4524.
- *The Kingfisher Book of Family Poems*, selected by Belinda Hollyer (Kingfisher, 2003). ISBN 0753455579.
- *The Night Before Christmas*, by Clement Clark Moore and illustrated by Douglas Gorsline (Random House, 1975). Paperback, 32 pages, ISBN 0394830199.

For teachers —

- *Rose, Where Did You Get That Red? Teaching Great Poetry to Children*, by Kenneth Koch (Vintage Books, 1990). Kenneth Koch has inspired even children who "hate" poetry. Here is a teaching method that may inspire you as well. Paperback, 416 pages, ISBN 0679724710.
- *The Word in Play: Language, Music, and Movementin the Classroom* (Paul H. Brookes Publishing Company, 2004). The author offers practical, yet creative suggestions for exploring and creating poetry with children. ISBN 1557666164.
- Every Poet.com, www.everypoet.com, contains many links to classic poetry, as does the Poetry Lover's Page, www.poetryloverspage.com.
- Poetry Alive, www.poetryalive.com/pr oducts.html. Poetry Alive sells recording and teacher materials to help you bring poetry to life in the classroom.
- Poetry Teachers.com, www.poetryteachers.com, has suggestions for poetry theater, how to teach poetry, and poetry activities.

Language Arts **69**

More Resources

At the end of each section we list some books, websites, and other resources that may be useful to you in teaching the section, including books for children and teachers.

Lesson Plans

You can use the teaching ideas and the background information in the main text of each section to develop lesson plans.

In many cases, you may not need to write a lesson plan from scratch: you may be able to borrow or adapt an existing lesson. Every year, veteran Core Knowledge teachers present lesson plans at the Core Knowledge National Conference. Hundreds of these lesson plans are available on our website. The lesson plan web pages also contain links to large collections of lesson plans created by various regional groups dedicated to supporting the teaching of the Core Knowledge curriculum, including the Baltimore Curriculum Project and the Colorado Unit Writing Project.

In addition, there are websites that collect or link to lesson plans that are not written specifically for Core Knowledge schools but might be adapted for your use. Internet search engines like Google.com can be very valuable in locating these.

Supplemental Materials

Supplemental materials that go with the handbook include a set of Instructional Masters, a set of Art Resources, and a set of Text Resources.

• The **Instructional Masters** highlight concepts and information from the curriculum. They can serve as worksheets or be turned into transparencies for introducing, teaching, or reinforcing a topic. These worksheets are meant to supplement the worksheets you create to help your children learn in every subject. We have not included any Instructional Masters for mathematics or for reading, because mathematics and reading programs generally come with their own supplementary materials. In the back of the package of Instructional Masters are additional materials for you to use. These include a Venn diagram, T-chart, and K-W-L chart. Instructional Masters are listed under Materials and are reduced and shown next to the topics they support.

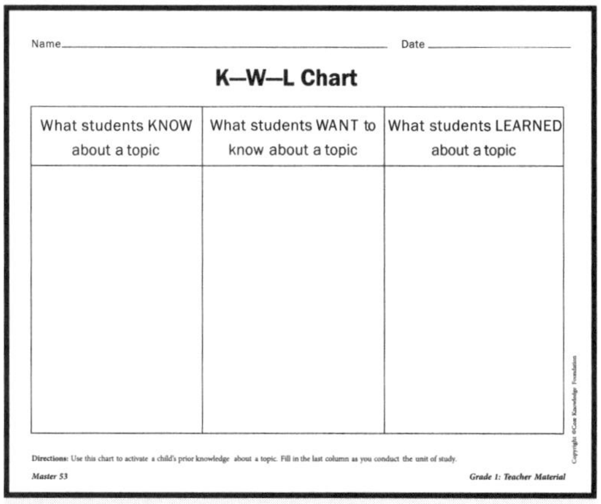
Name______ Date______

K—W—L Chart

What students KNOW about a topic	What students WANT to know about a topic	What students LEARNED about a topic

Directions: Use this chart to activate a child's prior knowledge about a topic. Fill in the last column as you conduct the unit of study.

Master 53 *Grade 1: Teacher Material*

Copyright ©Core Knowledge Foundation

Use Instructional Master 53.

• The **Art Resources** are the works of art listed in the *Sequence,* as well as other important works of art. On the back of each print is a set of Looking Questions to initiate discussion. These same questions are in the main text of the *Teacher Handbook.* Art Resources are listed under Materials, and an icon (art resource 4) appears in the section of the text they support.

• The **Text Resources** include all of the stories and poems in the second and third sections of Language Arts for Grade 2—"Beauty and the Beast," "A Christmas Carol," "The Emperor's New Clothes," and so on, plus additional stories and poems. There are additional read-aloud texts in world history and geography, American history and geography, music, and science. There are lyrics for all the Grade 2 songs listed in the *Sequence,* and sheet music is also provided for seven songs. A list of Text Resources appears at the front of the section, and then an icon (99) appears in the text.

Developing a Yearlong Plan

Once you are familiar with the *Sequence* topics, you should draw up a yearlong plan. The *Core Knowledge K–8 Guide: A Model Monthly Topic Organizer* (informally known as the "monthly planner") shows one of the many possible ways of arranging the Core Knowledge topics to fit in a school year. The Foundation also has the *Core Knowledge Day-by-Day Planner,* which provides an even more detailed and comprehensive map of topics. You may be able to follow one of these planners more or less exactly, or you may need (or prefer) to develop a customized yearlong plan that indicates when you plan to address the various Core Knowledge topics, when you intend to address state standards, and how and when Core Knowledge topics can be combined to help you meet and exceed state standards.

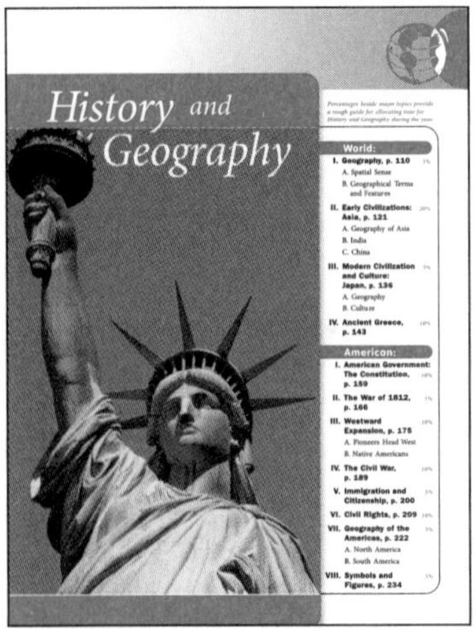

The Core Knowledge topics are intended to occupy about half of your curriculum, or perhaps a little more. This leaves time to teach material covered in the state standards and add topics of local interest. In many cases, Core Knowledge content can be combined with state standards and/or used to enhance state standards. For example, it is often possible to combine a general state standard (e.g., "Learn about significant cultures of the past.") with a specific topic in the *Core Knowledge Sequence* (e.g., Egypt or Mesopotamia). You can find guidelines for state alignments, as well as several completed alignments, on the Core Knowledge website, under "Schools." The Foundation also has consultants who can help you with alignments.

When working on the yearlong plan and during the school year, we strongly encourage you to meet regularly with other second-grade teachers. The first year of Core Knowledge teaching can be a daunting experience, with many new topics to master and fit into the school year. But it is much less daunting when teachers are willing to share ideas and work together to identify resources and develop lessons. Research has shown that the Core Knowledge curriculum is most successfully implemented when teachers have common planning time, both before and during the school year. Teachers report that such teamwork helps ease the workload associated with the first year of Core Knowledge teaching and leads to better classroom units, better relations with colleagues, and an enjoyable learning experience for all.

Core Knowledge Resources for Grade 2

This handbook is intended to be a key resource for you as you prepare to teach the topics in the *Core Knowledge Sequence.* However, it is not the only resource at your disposal. Over the past decade, the Foundation has introduced a number of books and other resources to help teachers teach the Core Knowledge curriculum. Except where noted, the following materials can be ordered from the Foundation by visiting our online bookstore or calling our order line: 1-800-238-3233. Some of the materials are also available in bookstores.

• *What Your Second Grader Needs to Know,* edited by E. D. Hirsch, Jr. Part of the popular Doubleday series, this book (available in bookstores as well as from the Foundation) contains a brief treatment of the subjects in the *Core Knowledge Sequence* for Grade 2. Although the book's primary audience is parents, Core Knowledge teachers have used it for many years. Overall, you will probably find the handbook is more useful to you than the series book, because the handbook is addressed directly to teachers and addresses issues of pedagogy and review. However, the series book contains much material suitable for reading aloud and can be a valuable secondary source of information.

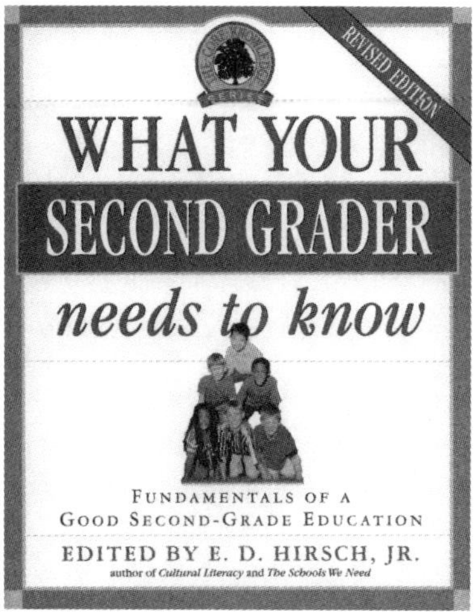

• The Spanish translation of *What Your Second Grader Needs to Know* is particularly useful for families where Spanish is the first language, and for teachers who teach children from these families. This book is available, free of cost, on the Foundation's website.

• *Pearson Learning/Core Knowledge History & Geography* series. These are the only official Core Knowledge textbooks for history and geography. For Grade 2, eleven units are available, covering the history and geography topics listed in the *Sequence* in more detail than the history and geography sections in this book. Each unit includes a black-and-white teacher guide and a small, full-color student book. The teacher guide contains read alouds for you to read to the class, as well as discussion topics, suggested activities, learning masters, and assessment questions. The student books are small pamphlets, easy for young children to handle. They include full-color pictures for children to look at before, during, or after the read alouds, as well as simple captions for illustrations. Although the teacher guide and student book can be purchased separately, they are meant to be used in tandem, with the illustrations in the student book complementing and reinforcing the read alouds in the teacher guide. Whenever a Pearson Learning unit is also a topic in this handbook, the unit is listed under More Resources. The books are described in more detail on the Core Knowledge website but must be purchased from Pearson Learning: 1-800-321-3106.

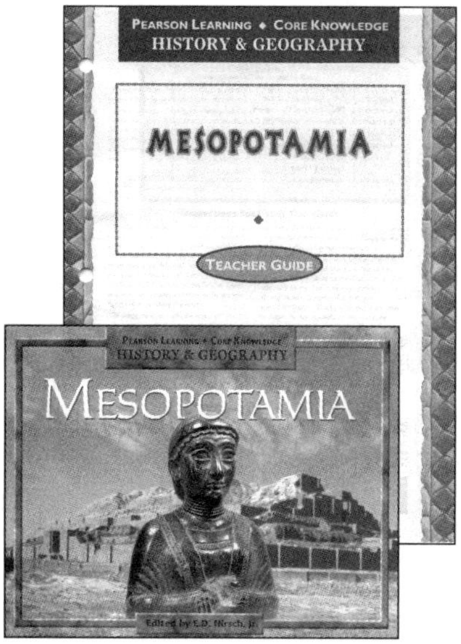

• *Listen My Children: Poems for Second Graders* includes all the poems listed in the *Sequence* for Grade 2.

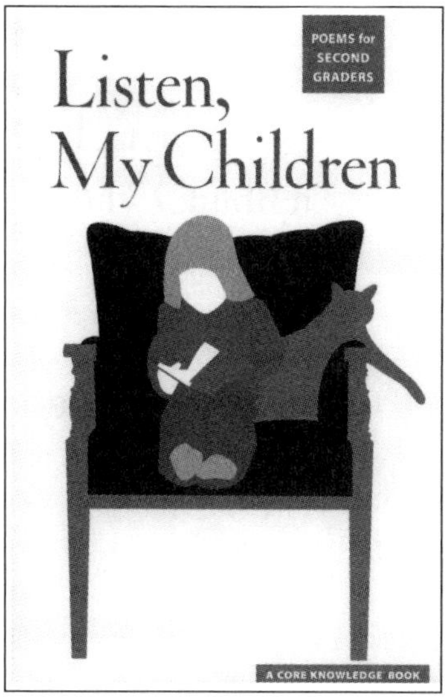

• *Core Knowledge Day-by-Day Planner* is available on individual grade-level CDs and provides a yearlong plan, weekly plans, and daily plans for Core Knowledge, while allowing plenty of room for state standards and other expectations. Additionally, resources and units are streamlined to ease the daunting task of "fitting it all in" in your first year.

• *Core Knowledge K–8 Guide: A Model Monthly Topic Organizer* divides the *Sequence* into monthly installments, showing you one way to cover all topics during the school year. This can be very useful for developing your yearlong plan.

• *The Core Knowledge Music Collection: Grades 1 and 2* is a multi-CD set that includes works listed in the *Sequence* for Grade 2, such as *The Four Seasons.*

Note that earnings from the sale of Core Knowledge books and products go to the nonprofit Core Knowledge Foundation. E. D. Hirsch, Jr. receives no remuneration for editing the series nor any other remuneration from the Core Knowledge Foundation.

Finding Additional Resources

Although this book and other Core Knowledge publications will help you cover many topics in the *Core Knowledge Sequence,* you will also need to use resources from other publishers.

Your school probably already has a reading program and a mathematics program. Some characteristics of a good language arts program are given in Supplemental Essay #1, "Elements of a Good Language Arts Program," on pp. 49–51 in the first section of Language Arts in this book. Your mathematics program should contain many opportunities for practice to ensure that children master the basic skills they will need to move on to more advanced mathematics. The Foundation can provide you with information on reading and mathematics programs that are widely used in Core Knowledge schools.

In addition, we encourage you to enrich and enliven your teaching by sharing outstanding trade books, both fiction and nonfiction, with children. Using trade books in class is a longstanding Core Knowledge tradition, and one that we hope will continue even now that the Foundation is beginning to offer more resources. You will find lists of book titles and websites at the end of each section of this book, although these are only a sampling of what is available.

The Foundation has also published a book and compiled an online database to help teachers locate additional grade-appropriate books and educational materials. The book is *Books to Build On: A Grade-by-Grade Resource Guide for Parents and Teachers.* Published in 1996, this resource guide lists hundreds of books and resources that will help you teach the topics specified in the *Sequence. Resources to Build On (RTBO)* is an online, searchable database designed to supplement *Books to Build On.* The search engine allows you to search for books relevant to second graders and/or to limit your search by topic. *RTBO* is available, free of charge, on the Core Knowledge website.

Remember to explore your school library and local public libraries as sources for books. Many libraries contain hidden treasures. Ask librarians to carry Core Knowledge books, including *What Your Second Grader Needs to Know,* and other books in the series. Search engines and online bookstores can also be tremendously useful when it comes to locating suitable trade books. For example, Amazon.com has an "advanced search" feature that allows you to specify the age level and subject of a book. You can search for books about Abraham Lincoln, architecture, or Buddhism, written for children ages 4–8. Amazon.com also includes published reviews and customer reviews for many books. Search engines like Google.com allow you to find book recommendations from teachers and librarians around the country.

Professional Development

You may have already attended the Core Knowledge "Overview" presentation. This presentation introduces teachers and administrators to the idea of cultural literacy; the nature, aims, and history of the Core Knowledge Foundation; the benefits of implementing the Core Knowledge curriculum; and some of the practical considerations involved in its implementation. If your school has not had an "Overview" session, we strongly recommend that you call the Foundation to schedule one.

After the "Overview" presentation, your next step should be to participate in the Foundation's "Getting Started" workshop to familiarize yourself with the *Core Knowledge Sequence,* the topics it outlines, its unique spiraling nature, and the cross-curricular teaching opportunities it offers. Although you will want to focus most of your attention on second grade, we encourage you to also look at other grades, so you can see what children have learned in previous grades and how the curriculum builds on prior learning. You can use the *Sequence* to get an overview of the curriculum for Grade 2 and the *Teacher Handbook* to get more information about specific topics.

A third professional development workshop, "Developing Core Knowledge Lessons and Assessments," focuses on writing lessons and assessments using this handbook and the *Sequence.*

Beyond the Teacher Handbook: Some Additional Strategies for Success

Although this handbook will provide you with the basic knowledge you will need to teach second graders the Core Knowledge topics, there are many other things you can do to improve your teaching of Core Knowledge. Here are a few strategies we've learned from successful Core Knowledge teachers and schools over the past decade.

• As you teach the Core Knowledge topics, look for ways in which special area teachers—art, music, and physical education teachers; special education teachers; ESL teachers; media and technology specialists; and so on—can enhance and connect with the topics you are teaching. The most successful Core Knowledge schools are the ones where the curriculum is implemented and supported by all key staffers, where the librarian and media specialists use the *Sequence* as a purchasing guide for books and software, and the physical education teachers enhance the classroom content.

• Look for ways to get parents and caregivers involved. Core Knowledge is a popular curriculum with many adults, not only because it is academically rich but also because it is very explicit. If you share the relevant sections of the *Sequence* and/or your yearlong plan with the adults at home, they will know what is happening at school and may be able to help you in various ways. Some may have knowledge of a particular subject that they would be willing to share with the children; others may be willing to talk with children at home about the topics they have been studying at school. The

Sequence and yearlong plan, when shared, can become a link that enables parents, caregivers, and teachers to work together.

• Look for ways to involve local groups and businesses. They may be able to visit classes to talk about topics that relate to what they do, or they may be able to donate services or materials. One Core Knowledge school in Texas contacted a local tile company when the school was preparing to do a unit on mosaics. The tile company offered them thousands of bits of broken tile. The school got its mosaic materials for free, and the company got a tax write-off! With a little creativity you can accomplish a lot.

• Visit our website, www.coreknowledge.org, which contains a wealth of information about Core Knowledge, as well as lesson plans, *Resources to Build On,* and other teacher resources.

• Subscribe to our free electronic newsletter. The newsletter includes stories on Core Knowledge schools, articles by E. D. Hirsch, Jr., and other prominent writers, links to useful websites, and announcements of upcoming events. A subscription box is located on our main web page.

• If you don't have an opportunity to share ideas regularly with other teachers at your school—or even if you do—consider subscribing to Core-net, an e-mail newsgroup for Core Knowledge teachers and supporters. For details on how to subscribe, see the Foundation's website.

• Sign up for additional Core Knowledge professional development workshops. In addition to the "Overview," "Getting Started," and "Developing Core Knowledge Lessons and Assessments" workshops mentioned above, the Foundation also offers several other workshops, including "New Teacher Orientation," "Implementation Analysis," "Summer Writing Institutes," and "Core Knowledge Coordinator and Leadership Institutes." For details, see the website.

• Attend the Core Knowledge National Conference. Held each year in the spring, the conference attracts several thousand Core Knowledge teachers who learn about Core Knowledge, attend lectures on topics in the *Sequence,* and share units. Teachers whose units are accepted for presentation get a discounted registration.

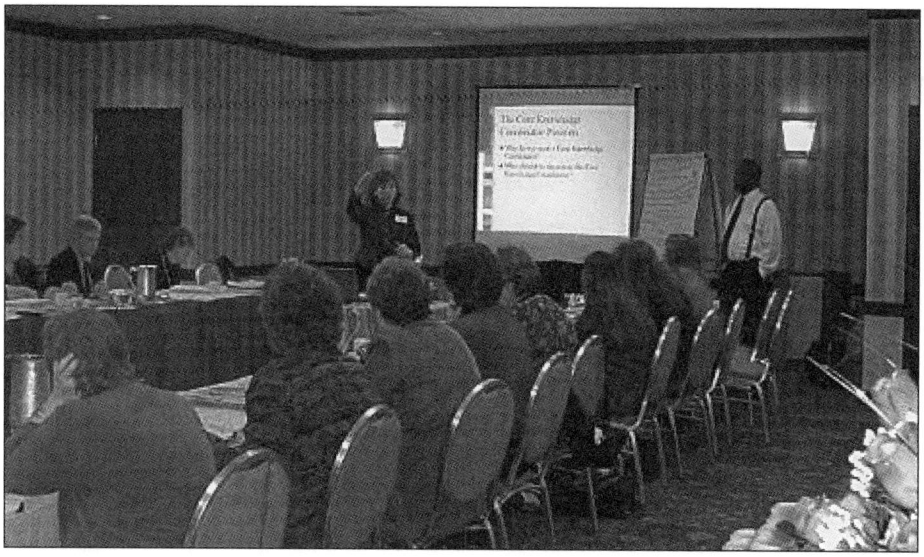

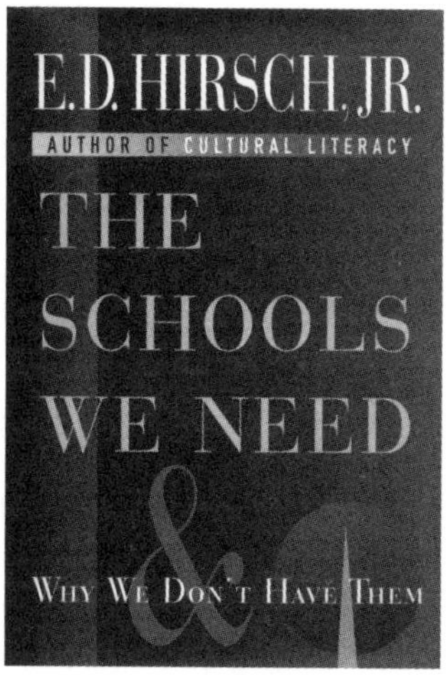

• Learn more about the ideas behind Core Knowledge. Two books by E. D. Hirsch, Jr., *Cultural Literacy* and *The Schools We Need & Why We Don't Have Them,* are available in print form and as books-on-tape from Blackstone Audio. Articles by E. D. Hirsch, Jr. can also be found on the Foundation's website.

• Continue to learn more about a subject in order to better teach it. We realize that all 50 states require teachers to take courses regularly to keep their certification. You may want to consider taking courses not only in pedagogy and educational theory, but also in subject areas like history and science.

Finally, remember that implementing Core Knowledge is not a simple matter of buying materials and following a script. It is an ongoing process, which includes professional development; background reading; individual and group preparation; use of the *Sequence,* the *Teacher Handbook,* and other resources; and the creation of lessons and assessments. Part of the adventure of teaching Core Knowledge consists of finding ways to bring all of these elements together to create successful units. We wish you luck in your own adventure with Core Knowledge, and we hope to see you at conferences and workshops for years to come.

Core Knowledge Foundation
801 East High Street
Charlottesville, VA 22902
Telephone: (434) 977-7550
Ordering line: 1-800-238-3233
Fax: (434) 977-0021
E-mail: coreknow@coreknowledge.org
Home page: www.coreknowledge.org

Language Arts

Follow your reading program for Reading and Writing. Percentages beside other topics are for allocating remaining time.

Language Arts in Second Grade

Language arts includes all aspects of English. Reading, writing, speaking, listening, spelling, and grammar are all considered part of the language arts curriculum.

Second graders will continue to practice decoding, or turning letters of the alphabet into the speech sounds they represent, by reading single-syllable and multisyllable words. By the end of Grade 2, children's decoding skills should become virtually automatic so that the children are able to focus their mental energies on meaning. Fluent decoding skills are essential if children are to make the transition from "learning to read" to "reading to learn."

Children should also be able to produce different kinds of written text, including stories, reports, letters, poems, and descriptions. They should be able to write legibly and should be moving away from phonetic spelling toward conventional spelling. They should also be introduced to basic conventions of grammar and usage (e.g., parts of speech, capitalization, and punctuation).

While learning the basics of reading and writing, children should also have many opportunities to use their listening skills. They should be hearing fiction, nonfiction, and poetry read aloud regularly, and should have opportunities to discuss characters, ideas, events, and words. Children at this age can listen to and understand books that they would have trouble reading themselves, and it is important that they have opportunities to listen to a wide variety of challenging materials, including age-appropriate historical and scientific books. Such listening experiences help children increase their background knowledge and their vocabularies, which in turn help them become better readers.

The literary selections listed in the *Sequence* provide a good starting point for your read-aloud adventures. The poetry selections feature strong rhythms and rhymes, which make them easy to remember and delightful to read aloud. Listening to poems also introduces children to new vocabulary words like *chirping*, *harmless*, and *ruddy*. The stories include many classics that have delighted generations of children, including mythological stories from ancient Greece. By listening to these stories, children will increase their vocabulary and reading comprehension skills, learn valuable lessons about behavior, become familiar with the key parts of a story, and acquire essential cultural literacy. Be sure to supplement your fictional reading selections with non-fictional read-aloud texts, too.

Finally, children will be introduced to some common English sayings and phrases. These, too, are part of cultural literacy. Becoming aware of proverbial sayings and their meanings is especially useful to children from cultures where American English is not the first language, though the experience is pleasurable for native and non-native speakers alike.

I. Reading and Writing

A. Decoding, Word Recognition, and Oral Reading

The Big Idea

Decoding is the act of turning letters into the speech sounds they represent. Decoding skills should become virtually automatic by the end of second grade.

The Core Knowledge Language Arts sequence is intended to complement and/or supplement most basal reading programs. Many basal reading programs teach decoding and encoding well, but neglect the importance of vocabulary development. Check to see whether your basal program teaches vocabulary development across all the content areas (science, mathematics, music, etc.). If it doesn't, be sure to emphasize vocabulary-building activities throughout the curriculum.

What Students Should Already Know

During Kindergarten and first grade, students should have acquired phonemic and print awareness and learned the names of the letters. They should also have learned a large number of the most important letter-sound correspondences in English and a number of sight words, and they should have had numerous opportunities to read simple decodable texts. The details of what they know—e.g., which letter-sound correspondences they know, which sight words, etc.—will depend on the reading program used, as well as other variables.

What Students Need to Learn

- **To accurately decode phonetically regular two-syllable words (e.g., *basket*, *rabbit*)**
- **To use knowledge of letter-sound patterns to sound out unfamiliar multisyllable words when reading (e.g., *caterpillar*, *elephant*)**
- **To recognize and compare the sounds that make up words, and to segment and blend a variety of sounds in words**
- **To accurately read single-syllable words and most two-syllable words including irregularly spelled words, words with diphthongs, words with special vowel spellings, and words with common beginnings and endings**

What Students Will Learn in Future Grades

In Grade 3, students should emerge as independent readers. They should move from "learning to read" to "reading to learn."

I. Reading and Writing

A. Decoding, Word Recognition, and Oral Reading

Vocabulary

Student/Teacher Vocabulary

alphabet: the 26 letters used to write words and sentences in English (S)

blend (noun): a combination of two or more consonant sounds represented by two or more letters, such as *bl* or *nd* in *blend*; blends should be distinguished from digraphs (T)

blend (verb): to combine separate syllables or phonemes into words, such as orally blending the separate syllables *pic* and *nic* to say "picnic," or the sounds /sh/ /e/ /l/ to say "shell" (T)

consonant: a closed speech sound made with obstruction of the air stream. Consonant phonemes are represented by consonant letters, including *b, c, d, f, g, h, j, k, l, m, n, p, q, r, s, t, v, w, x, y, z,* and combinations of letters, such as *th, sh, wh, ch,* and *ng.* (S)

decodable text: printed matter that a child is able to sound out and read independently, based on the letter-sound combinations that he or she has learned (T)

decoding: the process of turning printed letters into sounds and spoken words (T)

digraph: a two-letter combination (grapheme) that represents a single speech sound (*th, wh, ch, sh, ng, ph, gh*) (T)

diphthong: a single vowel sound that slides in the middle and may feel as if it has two parts, e.g., *oi* in *join* (T)

encoding: spelling; the process of turning spoken or heard words into print (T)

fluency: the ability to read a text accurately, quickly, and with understanding (T)

grapheme: a letter or letter combination that spells a phoneme, including combinations such as the *igh* in *fight*, and the *tch* in *blotch* (T)

letter: one of twenty-six written symbols of the alphabet that is used, singly and in combination, to represent phonemes (S)

long vowel: a vowel that is spoken with tension in the vocal cords; long vowel sounds include /ē/ as in beet and /ā/ as in fate. They are often written with the long sign over the vowel: ā, ē, ī, ō, ū. (T)

medial vowel: a vowel sound that comes in the middle of a word, e.g., /ā/ in *grate* (T)

onset: the part of a syllable consisting of the consonant or consonants that come before the vowel, for example, *bl* in *blank* or *b* in *bank* (T)

phoneme: a speech sound that in combination with others distinguishes a word in a language system; the phoneme is the smallest unit of speech sound. The word *bridge* has four phonemes: /b/ /r/ /i/ /j/—the slashes denote a phoneme, not a letter. (T)

phonemic awareness: the understanding that words consist of sequences of smaller, individual sounds (phonemes) and the ability to identify, compare, segment, and blend those phonemes (T)

phonics: the field of study that teaches the predictable relationships between the phonemes (sounds) and the letters that represent phonemes in written language, e.g., the relationship between the letters *ph* and the /f/ sound; also, the system of sound-symbol correspondence (T)

phonological awareness: a more inclusive term than phonemic awareness, phonological awareness includes not only awareness of phonemes but also awareness of syllable sequences, rhyme, alliteration, and stress patterns in words (T)

rime: the part of a syllable that contains the vowel and any subsequent consonants in the syllable, e.g, *im* in *trim*, *eg* in *beg*. A *rime* is not the same thing as a *rhyme*: the former is a linguistic unit while the latter is a kind of word play. (T)

segment (verb): to take words apart into separate syllables or phonemes (T)

short vowel: a lax vowel; short vowel sounds include /ĭ/ as in *bit* and /ĕ/ as in *bet*. Short vowels are often written with a short symbol over the vowel: ă, ĕ, ĭ, ŏ, ŭ. (T)

Vocabulary continued

sight word: a word that does not follow the regular pronunciation rules and so must be recognized by sight (T)

syllable: a unit of spoken language that is organized around a vowel sound. A syllable can consist of a vowel sound alone or a vowel sound with one or more consonant sounds preceding and following. *A-fri-can* and *prin-ci-pal* are words of three syllables. (S)

vowel: an open phoneme that is not a consonant; there are 15 or more vowel sounds in English that are spelled with the vowel letters *a, e, i, o, u,* and y, singly and in combination. Sometimes other letters are included in vowel graphemes, such as *augh, aw, eigh,* and so forth. (S)

Domain Vocabulary

Words associated with phonics and phonemic awareness:
sound, letter, hear, listen, same, different, put together, pull apart, first, next, beginning, end, last, rhyme, word, sentence, letter, alphabet, pronounce, uppercase, lowercase, read, write, spell, capital, capitalize, *plus countless words used in children's reading text*

Materials

Instructional Masters 1a–1b
The Blind Men and the Elephant p. 16

chart paper, p. 16

markers, p. 16

tape recorders with earphones, p. 17

short books to read on tape, p. 17

At a Glance

The most important ideas for you are:

- A child has phonemic awareness when he or she understands that words are made up of sequences of smaller sounds and has the ability to blend, segment, and combine these sounds.
- Acquiring phonemic awareness is a crucial step on the road to reading and writing.
- Decoding is the act of turning printed or written letters into the speech sounds they represent. Decoding is a key component of reading.
- Phonics instruction teaches the associations between letters and sounds. Research indicates that explicit phonics instruction leads to improvement in children's reading achivement. Occasional or "as needed" phonics instruction proves inadequate for many children.
- By the end of second grade, children should have learned all of the most important letter-sound correspondences. They should therefore be able to decode most two-syllable words including irregularly spelled words, words with diphthongs, and words with special vowel spellings.
- Decoding needs to be practiced frequently. By the end of second grade, children's decoding skills should become virtually automatic.
- Automatic decoding skills and fluency are essential to reading comprehension. If a child does not have automatic decoding skills, he or she will exert too much mental energy on the decoding aspects of reading and will not have enough energy left to make sense of phrases and sentences.
- One valuable way of developing and assessing fluency is guided oral reading.

What Teachers Need to Know

A. Decoding, Word Recognition, and Oral Reading

Background: Teaching Children to Read

Literacy is the single most important skill children learn at school because literacy opens the door to all other fields of study. A literate child has the ability to learn about any subject under the sun and the opportunity to participate fully in American political, social, and intellectual life. By contrast, an illiterate child has little hope of becoming a fully enfranchised member of society and will almost certainly face a drastically reduced range of career choices.

As a primary teacher, you must be actively engaged in all aspects of literacy: training children to listen and speak; building oral vocabulary; teaching decoding (translating visual symbols into speech sounds) and encoding (writing); and increasing fluency.

The teaching of reading is complicated by the many elements that have to come together before children can read successfully, and also by the astounding variety of rates at which children master initial reading skills such as decoding.

It is important to remember that reading is not *natural. This may strike many adults—especially those who have never taught young children to read—as an odd statement, because most literate adults have learned to read so well that reading* feels *natural. But the skills required to read and write are not hardwired into the human brain in the same way as the skills required to listen and talk. Humans have a language instinct, but it is an instinct for oral language, not written language. Writing is a recent invention in human history, developed just a few thousand years ago (about 3500 BCE). Many cultures have existed without it. As recently as 200 years ago, many Native American cultures had no mechanism for reading and writing, though they had rich oral traditions. Because reading and writing aren't natural skills, it isn't surprising that they are difficult for a significant percentage of children.*

The basic task of reading is to take a written code and turn it into meaningful speech—in a three-stage process, from sight to sound to meaning. The beginning reader transforms the mute symbols on the page into sounds, then the sounds into words. But each of these translations requires knowledge, and each must happen in working memory very quickly. Working memory (or "short-term" memory) is the "place" in the brain where we put things together and create meaning, where we solve problems and process language. Only a few items can be juggled in working memory at the same time. The leaps in the reading process—from sight to sound, and from sound to meaning—must occur smoothly and quickly. That is why children need to practice decoding until it becomes automatic. If decoding is not automatic and uses too much working memory, there will not be enough mental energy left to make sense of the words being decoded.

Second grade is a crucial year for reading development. During second grade, children should be introduced to any key sound-letter correspondences they have not yet studied, and they should be given many repeated opportunities to practice their decoding skills. Practice is essential if children are to develop the automatic decoding skills they will need to read with understanding in later grades. By the end of second grade, children should be able to read (both aloud and silently) with fluency, accuracy, and comprehension, any story or other text appropriately written for second grade. Such texts include Peggy Parish's Amelia Bedelia *books, and Lillian Hoban's* Arthur *books, among many others.*

It is worth noting that, during second grade, it is especially important that teachers take note of any children who are struggling with decoding skills. It is quite likely that some children will enter second grade without having adequately mastered previously taught skills from Grade 1 and even Kindergarten. Now is the time to identify the specific decoding skills and letter-sound associations that these children have not learned and to provide the remedial help necessary to acquire those skills. Many school systems have reading specialists who can assist the classroom teacher in evaluating children's skills, as well as recommending materials and activities for remediation.

It is also important to note that, although second graders should be beginning to develop independent reading skills, this does not mean that reading aloud by the teacher now becomes unnecessary. On the contrary, listening to stories and non-fictional texts read aloud remains the single most important source of vocabulary and background knowledge for children at this age. Second graders are able to listen to stories they would have difficulty reading, and the vocabulary and background knowledge they pick up from listening to read alouds and discussing them will help them make sense of the texts they read themselves. Therefore, you should continue to read aloud to your children as they develop their independent reading skills.

In third grade, the emphasis in instruction needs to begin to shift from learning to read *to* reading to learn, *but this can only happen if children emerge from second grade with nearly automatic decoding skills, as well as a solid base of background knowledge.*

Sequence, Handbook, and Reading Program

The learning goals listed in this section of the *Sequence* do not represent a complete reading program. Nor are the essays in this book intended to constitute a complete program. Your school should have a reading program that enables children to achieve the decoding goals listed in the *Sequence*.

There are many programs currently available that do a good job teaching the letter-sound correspondences necessary for effective decoding. Some characteristics of a good language arts program are given in Supplemental Essay #1. The Foundation can also suggest some specific reading programs that do a good job teaching decoding and have been used with success in Core Knowledge schools.

What then is the relationship between your reading program, the *Core Knowledge Sequence*, and this book? We suggest that your reading program should serve as your primary resource and should guide your day-to-day instruction, while the *Sequence* and this handbook can be used to increase your background knowledge about reading and help you evaluate and assess your reading program. If your program has shortcomings, you can use the *Sequence* and this handbook to diagnose and, in some cases, correct these shortcomings. For example, many reading programs are better at teaching phonics and decoding than they are at encouraging language and vocabulary growth through reading aloud and discussion. If your basal reading program neglects the importance of vocabulary development across all the content areas (science, mathematics, music, etc.), be sure to emphasize vocabulary-building activities throughout the curriculum. The essays in this book can help you learn how to supplement your reading program so that your classroom combines language enrichment activities with solid skills instruction to lay a solid foundation for successful reading in subsequent grades.

One additional caution is in order. The materials in this section of the *Sequence* should not be thought of as a discrete "unit" that lasts only a few weeks. Rather, children should be practicing their decoding skills daily, throughout the year. Your reading program should devote some time to these all-important skills every day, though probably no more than 30-40 minutes a day is needed. As noted, above, this period of "skills" instruction should be supplemented with frequent reading aloud. The goal is for children to develop strong decoding skills while also building vocabulary and general knowledge by listening to read alouds and participating in discussions. Decoding instruction, important though it is, should never be permitted to crowd out rich oral language experiences like listening to stories and non-fictional books read aloud. For more on the importance of oral language, see Supplemental Essay #2 on pp. 52–54.

Phonemes and Phonemic Awareness

One of the bulleted learning goals listed in the *Core Knowledge Sequence* for this grade is "Recognize and compare the sounds that make up words, and segment and blend a variety of sounds in words."

Comparing sounds, blending, and segmenting are all phonemic awareness skills. By the time children arrive in your classroom, they should already possess phonemic awareness. They should be able to distinguish different sounds, combine sounds, and break a word up into its component sounds. However, since some children may not have mastered these skills in earlier grades, and since the lack of phonemic awareness can be a serious obstacle on the road to learning to read, it makes sense to say a few words about phonemic awareness here.

In order to understand what phonemic awareness is, you have to first know what a phoneme is. *Phoneme* is another word for a sound. You can break a word up into *syllables* (*catcher* → catch-er), and you can break a syllable up into single sounds, or *phonemes* ("catch" → /k/ /ă/ /ch/) The phoneme is the smallest unit in this progression. There are three phonemes or component sounds in the word *catch*: the /k/ sound, the /ă/ sound, and the /ch/ sound. We write phonemes inside back slashes to make it clear we are talking about sounds and not the letters that stand for those sounds. When you say phonemes, you should resist the temptation to add an extra vowel sound; /b/ should not be pronounced "bee" or "buh," but as a clipped /bh/ sound.

When people speak, they combine a relatively small collection of phonemes to make a very large, potentially infinite number of words and sentences. Each language has its own collection of sounds. If you compare Russian and English, for example, you will find that the two languages have many sounds in common, like the /f/ sound, as in *find*. But there are other sounds that Russian has that English does not, and vice versa.

English has more than 40 phonemes. Yet English only has 26 letters to represent these 40-plus phonemes. English solves this problem by combining two or more letters and using the combination to represent a single sound different from the individual letters. Thus, the letters *c* and *h* can be written together to represent the /ch/ sound; /ch/ is a single, distinct phoneme, which is not equivalent to what you would get if you said the /k/ sound that the letter *c* can make followed by the /h/ sound. English also uses single letters to stand for more than one sound. Thus, the letter *a* stands for one sound in the word *pat* and another in the word *paste*.

Letter	Sounds
a	|ā| as in *hate*
	|ă| as in *hat*
c	|k| as in *cat*
	|s| as in *ice*

If there were a simple one-to-one correspondence between letters and phonemes, English would be an easier language to learn to read and write. Since there is not a simple one-to-one correspondence, learning to read and write English can be tricky. A word with five letters might contain five phonemes (*drags*), or four (*happy*), or three (*catch*), and a vowel might be pronounced as one of several phonemes (*pat/paste*). A single phoneme can also be written using different letters. For example, the words *moon* and *true* both contain the phoneme /oo/ but use different letter spellings to represent that phoneme.

You can learn more about English phonemes by looking at the sample phoneme sequence on p. 205 of the *Core Knowledge Sequence*. This chart displays common phonemes and also a sequence of phoneme-letter connections that can be taught in the early grades. You can also learn more about phonemes by reading a good book on the English language, such as *Speech to Print: Language Essentials for Teachers*, by Louisa Moats, or by studying Module 2: "The Speech Sounds of English" in *LETRS (Language Essentials for Teachers of Reading and Spelling)*. (See More Resources.)

Phonemic awareness is the understanding that the sound of a word consists of a sequence of smaller, individual sounds. It is not natural for children to grasp this point, and many young children do not grasp it without explicit instruction. Indeed, studies show that phonemic awareness eludes 25% of middle-class first graders and a substantially higher percentage of children who come from disadvantaged backgrounds.

When a child says "dog," she does not naturally think of this word as a sequence of three separate sounds. She has probably not practiced breaking the word into separate sounds. And why should she? As long as all she wants to do is speak and be understood, there is no reason to do this. Knowing the word as a whole is good enough; there is no need to be able to break it into parts, or to understand that the word is a combination of several discrete sounds. But this all changes when the child needs to learn to read and write using an alphabet. Then the child needs to learn that spoken words are made up of discrete sounds, and that these sounds are represented by letters on the page when the word is written.

Phonemic awareness is an essential step toward learning to read an alphabetic language because it is these elementary sounds, or phonemes, that the letters of the alphabet represent. But phonemic awareness alone is not enough to learn to read. In addition to learning that words are made up of sequences of sounds, children must also learn which letters in the alphabet correspond with which sounds. The study of the relationships between letters and sounds is called "phonics."

Instruction in phonemic awareness is not synonymous with phonics instruction. It is possible to teach phonemic awareness in a strictly oral fashion, without making any reference to printed letters. For example, a child can be asked to listen to and identify spoken words that start with the same sound as *pig*. Or the child might be asked "Which sound is the same in the words *big*, *boy*, and *bell*?" Both of these exercises promote phonemic awareness, because they involve breaking the word up into its component sounds, but neither exercise deals with the correspondence between printed letters and sounds, so neither qualifies as "phonics" instruction.

Phonemic awareness is an essential prerequisite for the study of phonics. Unless the child understands that words can be broken up into strings of smaller sounds, he or she is not likely to benefit from learning letter and sound correspondences.

Recent studies, including the report of the National Reading Panel (2000), have shown that children who have phonemic awareness are more likely to succeed at reading and spelling. Indeed, phonemic awareness seems to be more closely related to learning to read than tests of general intelligence, reading readiness, and listening comprehension. Obviously, this is an important skill to acquire.

Research also indicates that *all* young readers benefit from explicit assistance with phonemic awareness, and a significant percentage of children are critically dependent on it. As a result, phonemic awareness instruction should be emphasized in the early grades. As mentioned above, instruction in phonemic awareness can be delivered orally through language activities that encourage exploring and manipulating sounds. Again, research indicates that these oral activities can have a significant positive impact on both reading and writing.

Phonemic awareness can be taught in 5- to 15-minute segments using games and oral exercises. Phonemic awareness can also be taught in conjunction with phonics, poetry, and other subjects. For example, a discussion of poetry or nursery rhymes might provide an opportunity to talk about rhymes and sounds.

By second grade, most children who have been following a good reading program should have already developed a good sense of phonemic awareness. However, some may not have, and these children are likely to have difficulties learning to read. If you encounter a child who is having difficulty learning to read, lack of phonemic awareness may be the cause of the problem, or at least a significant contributing factor. If your school does not have an early screening program that measures phonological skills, letter knowledge, and early decoding in all children, make arrangements to have the child tested. Consider learning a valid, reliable, scientifically grounded assessment yourself. Recommended tools include Dynamic Indicators of Basic Early Literacy (DIBELS), the AIMSweb assessment system, or the Texas Primary Reading Inventory. (See More Resources.) The *Teacher Handbooks* for Kindergarten and Grade 1 also contain a brief treatment of phonemic awareness that introduces some basic language games that are used to teach phonemic awareness but can also be used to assess whether a child has phonemic awareness. For a fuller treatment of phonemic awareness, consult a good book on phonemic awareness, such as *Phonemic Awareness in Young Children*, by Marilyn Jager Adams, Barbara Foorman, Ingvar Lundberg, and Terri Beeler. (See More Resources.)

Decoding

Decoding is the process of identifying the graphic symbols of print (letters) and translating them into sounds. Whenever we read, we are decoding. Indeed, in one sense *decoding* and *reading* are synonyms. However, there is another sense in which the two words have slightly different meanings. Decoding refers to the process of translating letters into sounds. Successful reading requires good decoding skills, but it also requires the reader to make sense of the words and sentences that have been decoded. Thus, reading for comprehension involves more than just decoding skills. It involves rapid, fluent decoding *plus* possession of sufficient background knowledge and vocabulary to understand the words and sentences being decoded. Thus, it is possible for a child to have strong decoding skills and yet still be a weak reader for lack of adequate background knowledge and vocabulary. This is why many reading experts use "decoding" to refer strictly to translating symbols into sounds, while using "reading" or "reading comprehension" to refer to the larger process of which decoding is a crucial element.

Three of the four bulleted points in the *Sequence* for this section have to do with decoding:

- Acurately decode phonetically regular two-syllable words (for example, *basket, rabbit*).
- Use knowledge of letter-sound patterns to sound out unfamiliar multisyllable words when reading (for example, *caterpillar, motorcycle*).
- Accurately read single-syllable words and most two-syllable words, including irregularly spelled words (for example, *tough, through*), words with diphthongs (for example, the *oy* sound in *boy*), words with special vowel spellings (for example, the *ow* sound in *now* and *clown*, the long *i* sound in *night*), words with common beginnings and endings (for example, the *spr* beginning in *spring*, the *le* ending in *apple* and *riddle*).

The points at which children in your class reach these benchmarks will depend on their prior knowledge and the pacing of the reading program you use. We suggest that you use these *Sequence* guidelines to monitor the progress your children are making with their reading program. If children are not reaching these goals, you may wish to consider changing your reading program.

The key to helping children unlock the code of written English is to help them understand the relationships between individual letters and combinations of letters, and the sounds they make. Your reading program should have introduced a great many of these relationships in Kindergarten and Grade 1. If children do not know the relationships between letters and sounds, they will not be able to meet the goals listed above. In such a case, children should be taught the correspondences they don't know.

By second grade the children in your class should already know many of the key letter-sound relations in English. However, since some of them may not, the sections that follow offer some background information on the alphabetic principle and the reasons why systematic teaching of letter-sound correspondences (phonics) is important.

The Alphabetic Principle

English is an alphabetic language. The alphabet is a code, consisting of 26 letters. An important step in learning how to read in English is for a child to "crack" the code of the alphabet by understanding and using the alphabetic principle. Children may be said to understand the alphabetic principle when they understand two closely related points about our language: 1) sounds are represented with letters and letter combinations; and 2) the letters that represent these sounds are written from left to right.

Before a child can learn how to read, he or she must learn that words are made up of strings of smaller sounds, or phonemes; in other words, the child must have basic phonemic awareness. The child must also be able to match phonemes with graphemes, or the most common spelling units for those sounds. Once children understand the relationship between letters and phonemes, they can figure out how to pronounce or spell a word.

Some beginning readers in English have difficulty understanding the alphabetic principle. One reason for this difficulty is that the child must make the mental leap from a sound to its graphic representation by a written letter. Some children with poor phonemic awareness cannot easily make this connection. Another reason for this difficulty is that letters in English can represent more than one sound. For example, the letter *c* represents a /k/ sound in *cat* but an /s/ sound in *ice*. The letter *a* represents the /xa/ sound in the word *hat*, but if you add an *e* to make *hate*, the same letter represents the /ā/ sound. A third source of problems is that variations in pronunciation exist in different areas of the country. A child who is accustomed to hearing nonstandard English or a language other than English will face greater challenges in acquiring letter-sound relationships and the alphabetic principle.

Phonics

Phonics instruction teaches children the relationship between the letters of written language and the individual sounds (phonemes) of spoken language. Understanding these relationships enables children to read and write. Reading teachers and publishers of reading programs use different terms to describe these relationships, including letter-sound associations, letter-sound relationships, letter-sound correspondences, sound-spellings, sound-symbol correspondences, grapheme-phoneme correspondences, and grapho-phonemic relationships. All of these terms refer to the relationships between written letters and spoken sounds.

No matter which terms are used, the goal of phonics instruction is to help children learn the alphabetic principle and the letter-sound relationships. Knowing these relationships will help children recognize familiar words accurately and automatically and will also allow them to decode new words. Knowing the alphabetic principle contributes greatly to children's ability to read words and sentences.

Key findings from scientific research clearly indicate that systematic and explicit phonics instruction is more effective than nonsystematic instruction or no phonics instruction. The need for explicit phonics instruction is even more critical for at-risk children who, lacking much exposure to reading and writing, have had fewer opportunities to figure out how our alphabetic system works.

Systematic phonics instruction means that phonemes are introduced in a logical order, explained through explicit, guided instruction, and associated with keywords (for example, the phoneme /d/ might be associated with the word *dog*). The children are taught to attend to the phonemes in words, and then to blend the sounds together to make simple words. In a program with an explicit phonics component, letter-sound correspondences are introduced at regular intervals—say, one or two each week. Each day's lesson reviews and builds on what was previously taught.

There is no single "correct" sequence for introducing letter-sound correspondences, though most good reading programs follow a few basic principles, such as introducing short vowels before long vowels, and digraphs before blends. A sample phoneme teaching sequence is presented on pp. 205–209 of the *Core Knowledge Sequence.* You may wish to compare this sequence to the letter-phoneme combinations taught in your reading program. Different reading programs use different sequences, and one unfortunate consequence of this lack of agreement in sequencing is that children moving into your classroom may have learned different sound-letter correspondences than children who have been in your school for several years.

By second grade, no matter what sequence has been used, children should know most of the key letter-sound correspondences. During second grade, they should learn any key letter-sound associations that have not been taught and review the ones they have been taught. They should also be given frequent opportunities to apply their knowledge of letter-sound correspondences by reading decodable text and other simple, age-appropriate stories. If children have gaps in their knowledge of letter-sound correspondences, these need to be diagnosed and corrected through explicit phonics instruction. If necessary, you may wish to use a supplemental phonics program to ensure that children learn the letter-sound correspondences. You may contact the Foundation for the names of some solid comprehensive or supplemental phonics programs.

In some cases, children may need individual tutoring with a reading teacher or volunteer to build up their decoding skills. If your school doesn't have a tutoring program for struggling readers, consider setting one up. Once a tutoring program is in place, parents and neighborhood volunteers can work with children one-on-one while you teach the larger class. This can be a great help in getting struggling readers back on track. There are a number of successful tutoring programs scattered around the nation, including the Book Buddies program. (See More Resources.)

Reading Nonsense Words

Because your reading program is expected to be your primary resource for reading instruction, and because every reading program is different, we have confined ourselves largely to general principles of reading and have limited the number of teaching suggestions in this section. Any particular teaching idea we offered might turn out to be difficult or impossible to combine with the instruction in your reading program. However, there are some widely accepted practices that are worth mentioning because they can be easily combined with just about any program. One such practice involves the reading of nonsense words.

You might wonder why nonsense words are emphasized: would it not make more sense to have children read *real* words? The reason is because nonsense words provide a pure test of a child's ability to map sounds to symbols. If the child is asked to read a known word like *dog*, the child may be able to guess the word from context, or recognize it as a whole word, especially if the child has seen the word in a book. On the other hand, if the child is given nonsense words, like *glup*, or *sherbist*, the only way to figure out the words is to sound them out. For this reason, one way to test your children's knowledge of letter-sound correspondences and ability to decode is to ask them to read nonsense words that incorporate the letter-sound associations they have been taught. A child who has trouble sounding out nonsense words is likely to have trouble reading real words as well.

Fluency

Fluency is the ability to read a text accurately, quickly, effortlessly, and with appropriate expression and meaning. Fluent readers recognize words automatically. They group words rapidly to help them gain meaning from what they read. When fluent readers read aloud, they do so with expression, almost as if they were speaking. In contrast, nonfluent readers read in a more word-by-word fashion. Consequently, their oral reading sounds choppy and plodding.

Eye-movement studies have shown that advanced readers actually scan and focus on nearly every word and word part. They are decoding sounds, but they are doing it so easily and so rapidly that it does not require their conscious attention. This ability to decode fluently, without even being aware of the process, is what enables advanced readers to make sense of what they are reading.

Fluency is important because it provides a bridge between decoding and comprehension. Readers have only a limited amount of attention that they can devote to a cognitive task such as reading. If they expend too much attention and mental energy on the decoding process, they will not have enough left to achieve comprehension. That's why it is important that children become not just adequate decoders, but *fluent* decoders. Only if they can decode fluently will they be able to devote enough attention to making sense of the text they are reading.

Fluent readers expend relatively little mental energy on decoding and so have more energy to focus on the meaning of words, sentences, and paragraphs. They are able to connect what they are reading with what they already know and so are able to understand it. Less-fluent readers must focus most, if not all, of their attention on the mechanics of decoding. Consequently, they have little attention left for comprehending the text. They may be able to read individual words and yet not read them rapidly enough to understand whole sentences. By thc time they reach the last word of the sentence, they have forgotten the first words and the larger context. This is why fluency is so important.

Unfortunately, fluency is sometimes neglected or shortchanged in reading programs, as well as in classrooms. Many teachers have been conditioned to avoid any kind of repetition, rehearsal, or repeated practice. These methods are frequently criticized as "drill and kill." In some subjects, however, repeated practice is crucially important, and a teacher or program that does not allow children sufficient opportunities to practice is in fact doing children a great disservice. Decoding is one such area. Therefore, you should be sure that children have many opportunities to rehearse their decoding skills and move toward fluency.

The phrase "drill and kill" implies that practice kills the spirit, but in fact there is no reason why decoding practice cannot be made enjoyable as well as useful. We should never forget that children take great pleasure in being able to read by themselves, even when this involves reading very simple stories.

Oral Reading

One strategy that has been shown in numerous scientific studies to be useful for building fluency (and also for assessing it) is guided oral reading. In guided oral reading, the child is asked to read a text aloud under the supervision of a better reader. The child may be asked to read several times, either all at once or over a period of days, until a level of proficiency is achieved. The reading is monitored by someone capable of identifying and correcting mistakes. This might be the classroom teacher, a reading assistant, a parent, a community volunteer, or possibly even another child with the necessary skills. When the reader stumbles over a passage or makes a mistake, the monitor asks the reader to go back and read the passage again, decoding the words carefully. Oral reading of this kind has been shown to boost reading scores, but it can cause scheduling issues, since a teacher can only work with one child at a time. For this reason, oral reading is often taught using tutors, parents, and other helpers. Although it may require some planning and recruitment of helpers, it can be well worth your while to make arrangements that will allow your children to participate in frequent guided oral reading.

Fluency instruction for children who are below the benchmark in oral reading fluency is best accomplished with data-based techniques such as repeated readings, alternate oral reading, and progress-monitoring charts that motivate the children. You may wish to reference some scientifically supported techniques mentioned in Module 5: "Getting Up to Speed: Developing Fluency" in *LETRS (Language Essentials for Teachers of Reading and Spelling)*. (See More Resources.)

Teaching Idea

At the beginning of the year, provide a sign-up sheet for parents to come into the room and read with children. You can organize this time in a variety of ways, but make it clear that you need volunteers for this vital activity.

Reader's Theater

A kind of repeated oral reading that is used by a growing number of teachers is "reader's theater." In reader's theater, children rehearse a dramatic script for several days until they can read it with fluency and then perform it. Reader's theater differs from conventional theater in that children *read* their parts rather than memorize

Teaching Idea

Have children practice and perform a dramatic reading of a reader's theater script using Instructional Masters 1a and 1b, *The Blind Men and the Elephant*. Allow children to take turns so that each child has an opportunity to participate. Find or create other reader's theater scripts to use throughout the year.

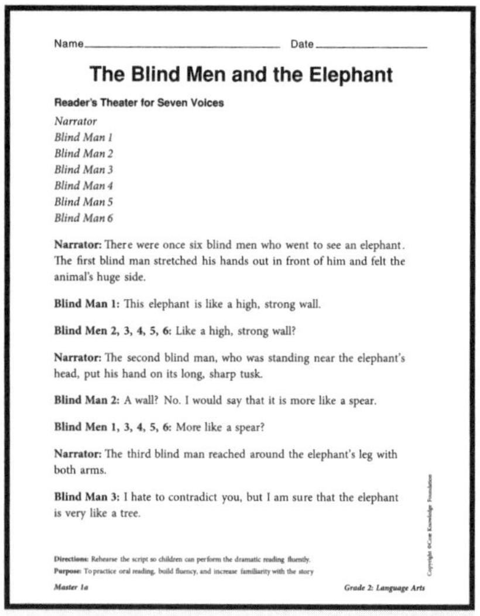

Name________________ Date________

The Blind Men and the Elephant

Reader's Theater for Seven Voices

Narrator
Blind Man 1
Blind Man 2
Blind Man 3
Blind Man 4
Blind Man 5
Blind Man 6

Narrator: There were once six blind men who went to see an elephant. The first blind man stretched his hands out in front of him and felt the animal's huge side.

Blind Man 1: This elephant is like a high, strong wall.

Blind Men 2, 3, 4, 5, 6: Like a high, strong wall?

Narrator: The second blind man, who was standing near the elephant's head, put his hand on its long, sharp tusk.

Blind Man 2: A wall? No. I would say that it is more like a spear.

Blind Men 1, 3, 4, 5, 6: More like a spear?

Narrator: The third blind man reached around the elephant's leg with both arms.

Blind Man 3: I hate to contradict you, but I am sure that the elephant is very like a tree.

Directions: Rehearse the script so children can perform the dramatic reading fluently.
Purpose: To practice oral reading, build fluency, and increase familiarity with the story

Master 1a *Grade 2: Language Arts*

Copyright ©Core Knowledge Foundation

Use Instructional Masters 1a and 1b.

Teaching Idea

Provide children with many opportunities for reading in a variety of ways throughout the day. For example, you may have the children take turns reading a story in Language Arts aloud together. Alternatively, you could group the children and have each read a different part of the History text and then summarize it to the class. Record the children's responses on chart paper for everyone to review.

The Big Idea in Review

Decoding is the act of turning letters into the speech sounds they represent. Decoding skills should become virtually automatic by the end of second grade.

them; also, the scripts tend to be fairly short, and the use of props and staging is kept to a minimum. As a result, the preparation time for a reader's theater script is much shorter than for a conventional theatrical production, and it is possible to do a reader's theater performance as often as once a week, as opposed to once a year. Many children appear to enjoy participating in reader's theater. The activity combines repeated oral reading with a literary or dramatic context that makes the reading experience meaningful and fun. The Core Knowledge curriculum provides many possible starting points for reader's theater scripts. Reader's theater scripts can be based on a poem, a story, a saying, or a dramatic episode drawn from science, history, or art content (e.g., the Battle of New Orleans or the adventures of Florence Nightingale). You can find reader's theater scripts online using a search engine. (Also see More Resources.)

Other Kinds of Reading Practice

In addition to having children read with you or other adults, there are many other kinds of reading activities that may help children become better readers. Children can practice reading using recordings of books, or through choral reading, in which small groups of children read the same passage aloud together. Children can also practice reading together with partners. In partner reading, it can be good to group a stronger reader with one needing improvement.

Sustained silent reading, popular with many teachers, may also make a contribution to the development of reading skills. However, it will be useful only if children are *really* reading, and this can be hard to monitor. The National Reading Panel, which found strong evidence for the effectiveness of guided and repeated oral reading, did not find conclusive evidence to support the effectiveness of sustained silent reading in raising reading achievement. This does not mean that the practice is ineffective, only that its effectiveness has not been reliably and consistently proven.

Remember that there are three main accomplishments that characterize good readers:

- They understand the alphabetic system and can use it to identify printed words.
- They read fluently.
- They have the background knowledge and vocabulary needed to obtain meaning from print.

Review

Your reading program should include materials for reviewing and assessing decoding fluency. In addition, your school should give standardized tests that assess reading and oral language skills.

Below are some ideas for ongoing assessment and review activities. These are not meant to constitute a comprehensive list.

- Core Knowledge poetry provides an excellent opportunity for children to hear different rhyming sounds and to identify other familiar sounds. The Core Knowledge songs also provide an opportunity for children to "sing" different sounds. Use Core Knowledge poems and songs to solidify decoding skills by identifying familiar word and letter patterns in this section.

• Arrange a listening center in your classroom with tape recorders, earphones, and short books. Enlist volunteers to record the stories on tape. Then, have children choose a book and listen to the story while following along with the text. When children have finished, ask each child to summarize the story to a fellow student.

• When arranging a reader's theater, have your class perform the play for fellow second-grade classrooms. After finding short plays to perform, organize a performance schedule for classes on the grade level. The children will enjoy reading their texts and will improve their presentation skills.

• Provide an opportunity for children to read with "book buddies" from an older grade at least once a month. Pair a younger child with an older student, and have them read together. This activity provides time for younger children to interact with older students, and it is also an excellent opportunity for grade levels that share Core Knowledge content (for example, Grades 2 and 5 and the Civil War) to read about that area and learn more together.

More Resources

The titles listed below are offered as a representative sample of materials and not a complete list of everything that is available.

For children —

These books are generally intended to be read aloud, though some children may be able to read parts or all of the simpler texts.

• *Amelia Bedelia Helps Out*, by Peggy Parish (Greenwillow Books, 1976). The main *Sequence* goal for this year is to have children read text appropriate for second grade. This book is specifically mentioned in the *Sequence* as an example and can be used as an evaluation mechanism to find similar books. Paperback, 64 pages, ISBN 038072796X.

• *Arthur's Loose Tooth*, by Lillian Hoban (HarperTrophy, 1987). (See comment under *Amelia Bedelia.*) Paperback, 64 pages, ISBN 0064440931.

For teachers —

THEORY AND RESEARCH

• *The Academic Achievement Challenge: What Really Works in the Classroom*, by Jeanne Chall (Guilford Press, 2002). Paperback, 211 pages, ISBN 1572307684.

• AIMSweb® is a literacy assessment tool available through Core® (The Consortium on Reading Excellence). For more information, go to www.corelearn.com/assess.htm, or phone 1-888-249-6155.

• *Beginning to Read: Thinking and Learning About Print*, by Marilyn Jager Adams (MIT Press, 1994). Paperback, 504 pages, ISBN 0262510766.

• *Book Buddies: Guidelines for Volunteer Tutors of Emergent and Early Readers*, by Francine R. Johnston, Marcia A. Invernizzi, and Connie Juel (Guilford Press, 1998). Paperback, 176 pages, ISBN 1572303476.

• Dynamic Indicators of Basic Early Literacy (DIBELS), is a free screening tool available for download at http://dibels.uoregon.edu. Print version available at www.sopriswest.com.

• *LETRS (Language Essentials for Teachers of Reading and Spelling)* is a professional development sequence for teachers of reading authored by Louisa Moats and available from SOPRIS West at www.sopriswest.com, or by phoning 1-800-547-6747. Topics covered by volume are as follows:

Module 1: The Challenge of Learning to Read

Module 2: The Speech Sounds of English: Phonetics, Phonology, and Phoneme Awareness

Module 3: Spellography: A Road Map to English Orthography

More Resources continued

Module 4: The Mighty Word: Building Vocabulary and Oral Language

Module 5: Getting Up to Speed: Developing Fluency

Module 6: Digging for Meaning: Teaching Text Comprehension

Module 7: Teaching Phonics, Word Study, and the Alphabetic Principle

Module 8: Assessment for Prevention and Early Intervention (K–3)

Module 9: Teaching Beginning Spelling and Writing

• *Making Words: Multilevel, Hands-On Developmentally Appropriate Spelling and Phonics Activities Grades 1–3*, by Patricia M. Cunningham and Dorothy P. Hall (Good Apple, 1994). Paperback, 178 pages, ISBN 0866538062.

• *Phonemic Awareness in Young Children*, by Marilyn Jager Adams, Barbara Foorman, Ingvar Lundberg, and Terri Beeler (Paul H. Brookes, 1997). Some theory, but heavy on practical, game-like activities. This resource is useful at second grade only as a remedial reference for children who didn't master these skills in Kindergarten and Grade 1. Spiral-bound, 208 pages, ISBN 1557663211.

• *Phonics They Use: Words for Reading and Writing (3rd edition)*, by Patricia M. Cunningham (Addison Wesley, 1999). Paperback, 196 pages, ISBN 0321020553.

• *Preventing Reading Difficulties in Young Children*, edited by Catherine Snow, Susan Burns, and Peg Griffin (National Academy Press, 1998). Hardcover, 448 pages, ISBN 030906418X. (See comment under *Starting Out Right.*)

• *Road to the Code: A Phonological Awareness Program for Young Children*, by Benita A. Blachman, Eileen Wynne Ball, Rochella Black, and Darlene M. Tangel (Paul H. Brookes, 2000). (See comment under *Phonemic Awareness in Young Children*). Spiral-bound, 416 pages, ISBN 1557664382.

• *Speech to Print: Language Essentials for Teachers*, by Louisa Moats (Paul H. Brookes Publishing, 2000). Paperback, 288 pages, ISBN 1557663874.

• *Starting Out Right: A Guide to Promoting Children's Reading Success*, by Susan Burns, Peg Griffin, and Catherine Snow (National Academy Press, 1999). This resource provides background knowledge about the early reading process. Paperback, 182 pages, ISBN 0309064104.

• "Teaching Reading Is Rocket Science," by Louisa Moats, in *American Educator* (American Federation of Teachers, June 1999).

• The Texas Primary Reading Inventory (TPRI) includes both screening and inventory sections at all levels. For more information, go to www.tpri.org. The kits can be purchased through the Texas Education Agency (TEA) through a special website, www.txreadinginstruments.com, or by phoning 1-800-758-4756.

• *Why Our Children Can't Read and What We Can Do About It*, by Diane McGuinness (The Free Press, 1999). Paperback, 400 pages, ISBN 0684853566.

• *Words Their Way: Word Study for Phonics, Vocabulary, and Spelling Instruction (3rd edition)*, by Donald Bear, Marcia Invernizzi, Shane Templeton, and Francine Johnston (Prentice Hall, 2004). Includes instructional pages and an interactive CD. For more information, go to www.prenhall.com/bear. Paperback, 464 pages, ISBN 0131113380.

• Compact for Reading, www.ed.gov/pubs/CompactforReading/index.html, is a project of the U.S. Department of Education that offers a Home-School Links Reading Kit for Kindergarten through Grade 3.

• The Report of the National Reading Panel, *Teaching Children to Read: An Evidence-Based Assessment of the Scientific Research Literature on Reading and Its Implications for Reading Instruction,* summarizes the results of a comprehensive examination of what reading research tells us. Available online at www.nichd.nih.gov.

PHONICS BACKGROUND KNOWLEDGE

• *Phonics, Phonemic Awareness, and Word Analysis for Teachers: An Interactive Tutorial (Seventh Edition)*, by Robert Wilson, Mary Ann Hall, Donald Leu, and Charles Kinzer (Prentice Hall, 2000). Spiral-bound, 122 pages, ISBN 0130181714.

READER'S THEATER

• *On Stage: Theater Games and Activities for Kids,* by Lisa Bany-Winters (Chicago Review Press, 1997). Paperback, 171 pages, ISBN 1556523246.

• *Social Studies Readers Theatre for Children: Scripts and Script Development*, by Mildred Knight Laughlin, Peggy Tubbs Black, and Margery Kirby Loberg (Teacher Ideas Press, 1991). Paperback, 189 pages, ISBN 0872878651.

I. Reading and Writing

B. Reading Comprehension and Response

The Big Idea

Reading comprehension depends on listening comprehension as well as fluent decoding skills.

What Students Should Already Know

Students in Core Knowledge schools should be familiar with

- how to listen to and discuss a wide range of fictional and non-fictional read-aloud stories
- how to read simple "decodable" text
- how to notice their own difficulties in understanding text
- how to make, justify, and reflect on predictions about what will happen next
- how to retell a story in their own words
- how to reply to *what*, *where*, and *when* questions about fiction and non-fiction texts
- how to understand and follow oral and written instructions
- how to distinguish fantasy from reality

What Students Need to Learn

- **How to listen and read independently with comprehension**
- **How to reread sentences for clarification**
- **How to recall incidents, characters, facts, and details of stories and other texts**
- **How to discuss similarities in characters and events across stories**
- **How to gain answers to specific questions from reading non-fiction materials, and interpret information from simple diagrams, charts, and graphs**
- **How to give plausible answers to *how, why,* and *what if* questions in interpreting texts, both fiction and nonfiction**
- **How to explain and describe new concepts and information in their own words**
- **Demonstrate familiarity with a variety of fiction and non-fiction selections, including both read-aloud works and independent readings**

What Students Will Learn in Future Grades

In Grade 3, students should be independent readers. They should go from "learning to read" to "reading to learn." They will gain exposure to longer books, including "chapter books." They will also learn to use a table of contents, an index, and a dictionary.

Materials

plain chart paper, p. 21

simple book report forms for the children to complete at home, p. 25

sentence strips, p. 25

sentence strip holder, p. 25

chart paper with graph boxes, p. 25

individual pieces of graph paper, p. 25

Vocabulary

Student/Teacher Vocabulary

fiction: an invented story that comes from a writer's imagination (S)

nonfiction: a true story that is based on facts (S)

prediction: a guess about what is going to happen next (S)

Domain Vocabulary

Words associated with reading and language comprehension:
first, next, then, ending, character, setting, plot, fantasy, title, author, illustrator, what, where, why, when, what if, directions, instructions, steps, realistic, story, retell, understand, *plus words—hopefully many thousands of them—that children hear during read alouds*

At a Glance

The most important ideas for you are:

- Listening comprehension can only take place if a child has adequate vocabulary and background knowledge to understand what is said.
- Reading comprehension can only take place if a child has adequate listening vocabulary and background knowledge to understand what is said, plus fluent decoding skills.
- You should be actively building children's oral vocabulary and general knowledge while they are learning to read. The best way to do this is by reading aloud to them frequently and encouraging them to discuss what they have heard.
- Your read-aloud selections should include non-fiction selections, as well as fantastic and realistic fiction.
- Children love to hear favorite stories repeated, and it is useful to give them repeated exposures to favorites.
- Second graders should be able to respond to *who, what, when, where, why,* and *what if* questions about incidents, characters, facts, and details in stories and non-fictional works. They should also be able to discuss similarities between stories.
- Reading comprehension should not be thought of as a "unit" that lasts a week or two, but as a skill that develops gradually, all year long, as children listen to stories and read on their own.

What Teachers Need to Know

B. Reading Comprehension and Response

Background: Listening and Reading Comprehension

In order to understand spoken language or a story read aloud, a person needs to be familiar with most of the words being used. That is to say, oral comprehension depends on background knowledge and vocabulary.

In this sense, reading comprehension, especially in the early grades, depends on listening comprehension, that is, on the background knowledge and vocabulary that children have acquired through everyday experiences and while listening to read alouds. If a child can't understand words when spoken, he or she will not be able to understand them when written, either. As noted in the previous section of this chapter, reading also requires additional skills, including the ability to decode. But comprehension is the reason for reading. If readers can "decode" or "say" the words on a page but do not understand what they are reading, they are not really reading. Comprehension can only take place if a child has mastered phonemic awareness and decoding skills at an automatic level, and if the child has a broad base of oral vocabulary and general knowledge.

You might be tempted to conclude that children who can decode rapidly are well on their way to achieving comprehension. But actually, that's only partly true. We have all had the experience of watching a child decode the words in a sentence accurately only to look up with a bewildered expression because the sense of the words didn't "sink in." A complex skill like reading is composed of both procedural elements like decoding and content elements like vocabulary knowledge. Text can be colorful, informative, and engaging, and children can take a delight in hearing it read aloud or examining pages of print. But if they lack vocabulary and background knowledge, they can barely take the first step toward understanding what they're supposedly reading. After all, how can they understand a history book about buffalos, a song about the Erie Canal, or a science story about magnets, if they don't understand the words buffalo, canal, or magnet? Second graders need constant opportunities to build their background knowledge and vocabularies.

In second grade, when many children are still learning to read, the best way to provide children with background knowledge and vocabulary that will improve their reading comprehension is to feed them a steady, rich diet of oral language. Read aloud to them at least 20–30 minutes every day, preferably more—and don't confine your reading to fiction. Include non-fiction readings on history, science, music, and art topics in the Core Knowledge Sequence, as well as other domains of knowledge, such as cooking, sports, clothing, furnishings, nature, and so on. Printed books contain many words that are rarely used in daily speech—and this is true even of children's books. What's more, books on different subjects contain different kinds of words. Children will learn one set of words from a story about the War of 1812 and another very different set from a story about insects. Every domain has a vocabulary of its own, and by learning something about a number of domains, children can

Teaching Idea

Writing topic-related words on chart paper and posting them around the room will give the children a "bank" of words that they can use when writing about units of study.

begin to accumulate the broad range of background knowledge they will need to become good readers later.

In addition to reading to children, you should give them frequent opportunities to discuss the stories and books they have heard. While reading a story, you can stop just before a key moment and ask children to predict what might happen next and to say why they think so. If they are confused during the read aloud, you can model strategies for clarification: you might ask questions to expose and clarify the confusing issues, or you might go back and reread the confusing sentences. When children see you model these practices, they are more likely to use them in their own, independent reading.

After the read aloud, invite children to identify any parts that confused them and ask questions about elements they did not understand. Children should be encouraged to talk about the reading and answer who, what, why, where, when, *and* what if *questions, such as "How does Beauty feel about the Beast at first? Why do her feelings change?" They should be able to recall incidents, characters, facts, and details of the stories and books they have heard read aloud. Children should be prepared to discuss any predictions they may have made before or during the reading: Were they right or wrong? Why? Try to ask "open questions," questions that cannot be answered with a yes or no, or with only a few words, but require children to formulate sentences of their own. Whenever it makes sense to do so—for instance, when asking* who *or* why *questions—encourage children to answer in complete sentences.*

By second grade, children should be able to retell stories they have heard and explain concepts they have studied in their own words. They should be able to make connections between a story they have just heard (or read independently) and another story with a similar plot, character, or theme that they heard or read earlier in the year. For example, they might connect one of the Greek myths they hear with another one, or the story of Demeter and Persephone with "How the Camel Got His Hump" (both stories are "pourquoi stories," which explain why something is the way it is). You can help children make connections of this sort by grouping read alouds with similar themes or subjects together in your yearlong schedule.

You should also work to promote vocabulary growth. You can do this through frequent reading aloud and also through guided vocabulary study. If there are interesting words in a story you have read, explain the words; offer examples, synonyms, and antonyms; and show children how these words can be used in sentences. Look for opportunities to use the words again in later discussions, and invite children to try to use the words in sentences of their own. For example, if the word distressing *occurs in a story, you might begin with a simple explanation: "Something distressing is something that upsets you." Then give some examples: "You might be distressed if you got a bad grade in school or if you broke one of your favorite toys." Finally, give the children a chance to use the word themselves using a structured response, like this: "I'm going to name some things; you tell me if you would find them distressing, and be sure to tell me why or why not: breaking your finger, eating spinach for dinner, eating pizza for dinner, etc. What are some other things that might make you feel distressed? When you answer, say 'I would be distressed if . . .' " Engage in vocabulary-building activities like the ones suggested in the*

Teaching Ideas *in this handbook, and in the brief Supplemental Essay # 3 on building vocabulary on pp. 55–57. We also recommend the kind of rich vocabulary instruction contained in Beck, McKeown, and Kucan's* Bringing Words to Life. *(See More Resources.)*

Reading and discussing stories with children is like putting money in the bank. Instead of dollars and cents, your deposits are words and bits of background knowledge. As children listen to stories and non-fiction selections and discuss them, they will be constantly adding new words and ideas to their "bank." When they are asked to begin reading longer texts on their own, they will have a rich bank of words and knowledge to draw on.

Customizing Your Reading Program or Basal Reader

Many second graders spend time listening to stories from basal reader programs. Sometimes these stories are rather dull and do not press beyond the world children already know. For example, the stories might focus on household pets or a trip to the grocery store. Often, the suggested discussion questions are merely recall questions, e.g., "Where did the family go to buy food?" While the accompanying worksheets that try to link thinking skills with comprehension may be plentiful, often the content itself is neither challenging nor memorable, and does little to expand a child's background knowledge and vocabulary in a coherent fashion.

Compounding the problem, language arts has come to occupy the largest time slot in many primary classrooms, drastically reducing the time available for other curricular areas. In some states, language arts takes up half the day in the early grades, while other subjects, like science, history, art, and music, are squeezed into the afternoon, or, worse yet, squeezed out of the curriculum altogether. This means that many children are not being exposed to the kind of wide-ranging content they will need to emerge as strong readers, capable of comprehending books and newspaper articles.

If the read-aloud stories in your basal reader are not challenging in terms of content, you should think about replacing some or all of them with lively read-aloud trade books. If the read alouds in your program are few and far between, or are exclusively fiction, you should try to supplement them with additional readings, including nonfiction. You might begin with the stories and poems from the *Core Knowledge Sequence*, plus non-fiction read-aloud selections on Core Knowledge history, science, art, and music topics. You can also add favorites of your own.

Young children often like to hear stories more than once. It's a good idea to repeat at least some of the stories you read a second time, and possibly even a third time, as children will be able to learn words and spot details that they missed during the first reading. Try to balance the need to introduce them to new subjects and stories with their desire to hear old favorites again and again.

Research indicates that children are more likely to learn a particular word if they are given multiple exposures to the word. One way to increase the likelihood of children getting multiple exposures is to try to stay on the same general topic for several days, possibly for a week or two. As you arrange a program of read alouds for your children, think about how you might group the books and stories you intend to read aloud into related subjects. For example, you might read a set of stories about Iktomi, a set of readings about westward expansion, and a set on

Teaching Idea

Send home a weekly newsletter sharing the highlights of the week. Instruct parents or caregivers to read the newsletter together with their child and to write a note stating what the child enjoyed learning most. They should send the note to school with their child, and you and the child can discuss it. This is a good way to help the child understand that print conveys meaning and a way to involve parents and caregivers in their child's learning.

Teaching Idea

Encourage children to become "word collectors." Model this behavior by calling attention to new or interesting words; giving children new words to describe what they are doing or learning; rephrasing children's remarks; praising children who try out new words; playing word games; and adding words to a Word Wall.

insects. Within each set of read alouds, children might get multiple exposures to several key words in each domain. From the cluster of read alouds about insects, for example, they might get several exposures to words like *wing, shell, molt, larva*, and *metamorphosis*.

Teaching Idea

Give oral language homework that builds on topics discussed in class. For example, after you read aloud a story or non-fiction text in the classroom, give children the assignment of retelling the story or describing what they learned to their parents or caregivers at home. This kind of homework requires clear and consistent communication between teachers and parents or caregivers. A simple note can do the trick: "Today we started studying ancient Greece. We will be learning about gods, goddesses, and the Olympic Games. At dinner tonight, your child may have a lot to tell you about ancient Greece."

Teaching Idea

Maximizing children's exposure to new words takes planning. Here are some ideas:

- **Reflect on and note new vocabulary words that can be introduced to children; consider the themes, topics, books, and stories that you're teaching.**
- **Post these words in the classroom as a reminder to yourself.**
- **Include new vocabulary words in parent communications.**
- **Start a child-generated Word Wall. Let the children know how excited you are when they discover new words.**
- **Play word association games using new vocabulary.**

Reading to Learn

One of the bulleted points in the *Sequence* for this grade is:

- Gain answers to specific questions from reading non-fiction materials, and interpret information from simple diagrams, charts, and graphs.

This learning goal is closely connected to the overall goal for Grade 2, which is to have children reading with fluency by the end of the year, so that in third grade (if not sooner) they can make the all-important transition from "learning to read" to "reading to learn."

In second grade, many children may be limited in terms of the books they can read independently, but you can still model for them how it is possible to use books as sources of information to answer questions they might have. Instruction of this sort can be combined with many topics in the *Core Knowledge Sequence*. For example, if your children have been learning about ancient Greece in History and Geography, you could find several easy books on various topics relating to ancient Greece, show them to children, and ask questions like "Which one would you read if you wanted to learn about the Olympics?" Then you can read the book aloud to children and talk about whether it answered their questions, and if they have new ones. You can repeat this for different subjects until children begin to learn that books can be selected and read as sources of information. As the year goes on, your more advanced readers may be able to select and read books on their own.

You can apply the same approach to introducing children to diagrams, charts, and graphs. Again, this can be easily combined with other subject areas. For example, in connection with the unit on Westward Expansion and Native Americans, you might present children with a simple chart showing how the number of buffalo decreased over the years. From an exercise of this sort, children learn chart-reading skills while also deepening their knowledge of an important historical topic.

Monitoring Comprehension

Although you will want to have frequent read-aloud experiences in which the entire class participates, you should also look for opportunities to listen to each child reading aloud individually. Although this can be complicated from a logistical point of view, it is the best way to see how well a child is reading and where he or she might be encountering difficulties.

As you listen, make notes on the child's fluency and knowledge or lack of knowledge of particular letter-sound correspondences, but also monitor comprehension to be sure the child is getting the "message." If the child displays a lack of comprehension, show him or her how to go back and read sentences that were not understood. This sort of comprehension monitoring can be combined with the oral reading practice for fluency discussed in the previous section.

Review

The Big Idea in Review

Reading comprehension depends on listening comprehension as well as fluent decoding skills.

Below are some ideas for ongoing assessment and review activities. These are not meant to constitute a comprehensive list.

- Schedule a library time with the media specialist in your school. Each week, make a visit to the library, and help children select both fiction and non-fiction books to read for the week. If you do not have a library in your school, many public libraries will allow teachers to check out a collection of class books for the room. Schedule time in the classroom to have a book review when children can share the book that they read, summarize it for the class, and talk about whether or not they liked it. You may want to highlight a different aspect of the book each week. For example, one week may be focused on characterization, when the children discuss and describe the main characters. This activity encourages children to describe concepts from a book in their own words.
- Book report forms provide an opportunity for children to read at home and then present the report to the class. You may make up simple forms for children to complete that highlight different aspects of both fiction and non-fiction books. For example, children can write sentences about the beginning, middle, and end of a story. One popular method is to have children write a sentence based on the framework, "Somebody, Wanted, But, So." The child writes sentences about a story or book based on the words as an organizer. The first sentence would be about the "somebody" in the book. The second sentence would tell something that the character "wanted." Then, the child writes a sentence about the plot twist ("but"). Finally, the child writes about the conclusion of the story ("so").
- During the study of Core Knowledge content, share non-fiction books with children. Encourage children to write questions that they would like answered before you read the book together. Have each child write a question on a sentence strip, and then you can post these questions in a sentence strip holder or on the board tray. While reading the book, encourage children to listen for the answers. You can then have them write the answers to the questions and post them in the room for future reference. This activity is particularly helpful when studying science topics. A K-W-L chart (included in the back of the package of Instructional Masters) can also be used as a resource for teaching nonfiction.
- Make simple crossword puzzles with children that allow them to find the definitions of words and place them in puzzles. These crossword puzzles work well with non-fiction text to help define words, but you can also use them with fiction texts to identify elements of plot in a story (characters, setting, facts, and details from the plot). You can make a class crossword on graphing chart paper or provide children with individual pieces of graph paper to make their own puzzles to trade with other children.
- Using texts from this section, have children think about what would happen if another character were introduced into the story or if the story happened in another setting. Pick a story, read it as a group, and have children write part of the story in another setting. They can describe what would happen in the story and then illustrate their text. Share these alternative settings with the class. You may also use this activity to have children write an alternative ending to a story.

• As a class, discuss the similarities and differences in fiction and non-fiction texts. Use chart paper to record the similarities and differences in a Venn diagram. Ask children to vote on whether they enjoy fiction or non-fiction stories most, and record the vote on the chart. Then, ask the children to write about their favorite story or book that they have read. This activity could be incorporated into the weekly book sharing time by having the children actually sort their books into a pile of fiction or nonfiction. Which type of book is the most popular that week?

• Have a weekly book sharing time, when children retell a story they read or share information that they learned about a non-fiction topic. Retelling stories is a good review strategy that will demonstrate children's reading comprehension.

More Resources

The titles listed below are offered as a representative sample of materials and not a complete list of everything that is available.

For children —

These books are generally intended to be read aloud, though some children may be able to read parts or all of the simpler texts.

Any good children's book—fictional or non-fictional—will make a contribution to children's vocabulary and comprehension abilities, either by introducing new words or by providing additional exposure to words they have already encountered. For a list of classic children's stories, see the *Sequence* listings under "Fiction." To find contemporary classics, you might look through the list of Caldecott Award books chosen for their outstanding illustrations (available online and in many bookstores), or visit your local library or bookstore. For non-fiction books, consult the relevant section of this handbook or search *Resources to Build On* on the Core Knowledge website.

For teachers —

• *Cultural Literacy*, by E. D. Hirsch, Jr. Famous for its list of things literate Americans know, this book also outlines the fundamental importance of cultural literacy for reading. Available directly from the Core Knowledge Foundation, www.coreknowledge.org or 1-800-238-3233.

• Several articles by E. D. Hirsch, Jr., are available online: "Overcoming the Language Gap: Make Better Use of the Literacy Time Block" at www.aft.org/american_educator/summer2001/lang_gap_hirsch.html.

"Reading Comprehension Requires Knowledge—of Words and the World" at www.aft.org/american_educator/spring2003/AE_SPRNG.pdf.

"The Latest Dismal NAEP Scores: Can We Narrow the 4th-Grade Reading Gap?" at www.coreknowledge.org/CKproto2/about/articles/readinggap.htm.

• *American Educator* (published by the American Federation of Teachers) has several articles of interest in its Spring 2003 edition: "Reading Comprehension Requires Knowledge—of Words and the World," by E. D. Hirsch, Jr.; "Taking Delight in Words," by Isabel Beck, Margaret McKeown, and Linda Kucan; and "The Early Catastrophe: The 30 Million Word Gap," by Betty Hart and Todd Risley.

• *Bringing Words to Life: Robust Vocabulary Instruction*, by Isabel Beck, Margaret G. McKeown, and Linda Kucan (Guilford Press, 2002). An excellent guide to vocabulary instruction. Paperback, 148 pages, ISBN 1572307536.

• *How to Increase Your Child's Verbal Intelligence*, by Carmen and Geoffrey McGuiness (Yale University Press, 2000). Paperback, 288 pages, ISBN 0300083203.

• *Language and Reading Success*, by Andrew Biemiller (Brookline Books, 1999). Provides teachers with a review of research, theories, and practices on the nature of language and reading, as well as suggestions for focusing on listening comprehension to build vocabulary. Paperback, 64 pages, ISBN 1571290680.

• *Matching Books to Readers: Using Leveled Books in Guided Reading, K–3*, by I. C. Fountas and G. S. Pinnell (Heinemann Educational Books, 1999). Lists several fine books based on their reading level. Paperback, 416 pages, ISBN 0325001936.

• *Vocabulary Development,* by Steven Stahl (Brookline Books, 1999). Paperback, 64 pages, ISBN 1571290729.

• "What Reading Does For the Mind," by Anne Cunningham and Keith Stanovich, in *American Educator* (American Federation of Teachers, Spring/Summer 1998).

More Resources continued

• Caldecott Medal & Honor Books, 1938–Present. Caldecott awards are given to artists of children's picture books judged to be the best of a particular year. Not all Caldecott books are suitable for reading aloud, but this is one place to look for beautifully illustrated stories. Go to www.ala.org/alsc/caldecott.html, and click on the link "Caldecott Medal & Honor Books, 1938–Present."

• *Children's Classics: A Booklist for Parents,* compiled by Mary M. Burns, is an annotated list of perennial favorites, both old and new. Available online at www.hbook.com/childclass1.shtml or as a printable .pdf document.

• The National Center for Literacy, www.nifl.gov, is a government agency intended to serve as a focal point for public and private activities that support the development of high-quality regional, state, and national literacy services.

• The Report of the National Reading Panel, *Teaching Children to Read: An Evidence-Based Assessment of the Scientific Research Literature on Reading and Its Implications for Reading Instruction,* summarizes the results of a comprehensive examination of what reading research tells us. Available online at www.nichd.nih.gov.

The Big Idea

Children can communicate their ideas, thoughts, and feelings by using their knowledge of letter-sound patterns to create many types of written text.

What Students Should Already Know

Students in Core Knowledge schools should be familiar with

- how to write all the uppercase and lowercase letters of the alphabet
- how to write their first and last names
- how to write simple words and messages
- how to produce various different kinds of writing—e.g., stories, descriptions, and journal entries—with spelling accurate enough to enable them to read their own work

What Students Need to Learn

- **How to write in a variety of formats, such as stories, reports, letters, poems, and descriptions**
- **How to make reasonable judgments about what to include in their writing**
- **How, with assistance, to produce written work with a beginning, a middle, and an end**
- **How, with assistance, to evaluate, revise, and edit their work, paying attention to spelling, mechanics, and handwriting in the preparation of final drafts**

What Students Will Learn in Future Grades

In Grade 3, students will continue to practice the writing skills they learned in Grade 2 and will also learn how to gather information from printed sources like encyclopedias, how to follow established conventions in a letter, how to write a topic sentence, and how to organize their writing into paragraphs. They will also build on their knowledge of spelling, grammar, and usage.

Vocabulary

Student/Teacher Vocabulary

description: writing that uses specific words and details to describe a person, place, or thing (S)

draft: a version or stage of a written work; writers begin with first drafts and make changes to end up with a final draft (S)

proofread: to read in order to find and correct mistakes in a piece of writing (S)

revision: the process of changing a draft of a written work; revision literally means "seeing again" (S)

Domain Vocabulary

Words associated with writing:
spell, write, pencil, pen, marker, paper, computer, letter, sound, capital, uppercase, lowercase, space, period, question mark, paragraph, indent, essay, story, beginning, middle, end, next, then, character, plot, left, right, top, bottom, indent, plural, draft, meaning, clarify, improve, add, remove, include, omit, change, mistake, *plus words children use in their own writing*

Materials

chart paper, p. 33

examples of different types of writing, p. 33

colored pencils, p. 33

colored highlighters, p. 33

overhead projector, p. 33

At a Glance

The most important ideas for you are:

- Second graders should be able to form all uppercase and lowercase letter correctly and express themselves comfortably and legibly in writing.
- Children should have frequent opportunities to write and should be asked to produce different types of writing.
- Schools use different handwriting styles. You should use the handwriting models followed by your school.
- Children should understand that written works should have a beginning, a middle, and an end.
- In second grade, children will still spell some words phonetically, but they should begin to move toward consistently conventional spelling. They should also begin to pay attention to grammar and usage. It is important not to overemphasize or underemphasize mechanics and correctness. Whenever possible, try to combine praising children for what they have written with coaching them to further improve their writing.
- Encoding (writing) and decoding are complementary skills. The former involves moving from sounds to symbols, and the latter from symbols to sounds. Writing practice and reading practice reinforce one another.
- Writing should not be thought of as strictly a language arts subject. The Core Knowledge curriculum offers many exciting topics for writing across the curriculum. Children should be encouraged to write about stories and poems they've listened to, as well as about topics they have studied in history, science, art, or music.

What Teachers Need to Know

C. Writing

Background: Keys to Writing

While writing is addressed here as a separate subject, common sense tells us that it is closely connected to decoding and listening, as well as to spelling, grammar, and usage. Decoding and writing are inverse, complementary processes. Decoding involves translating symbols into sounds. Writing involves translating sounds into symbols. It is crucial to teach children to go back and forth on the pathways from sound to symbol and from symbol to sound. Children remember material more effectively when they know it backwards and forwards. Thus, there is a strong connection between the teaching of reading and the teaching of writing, and the two can and should reinforce each other.

Listening to stories and books read aloud is also connected to writing in important ways: it supplies children with information, introduces them to words they can use in their own writing, and provides models for them to imitate in their own writing. As for spelling, grammar, and usage, they provide children with guidelines to make their writing more correct and more understandable to others.

In writing, mechanical and fine-motor challenges can be frustrating for some children. But many of these challenges can be overcome through practice. Make writing a regular part of your curriculum, and make an effort to choose exciting, intellectually stimulating topics for writing so that children learn to take pleasure in expressing themselves in print. Rules of usage and spelling need to be taught, but can be introduced gradually as suggestions to make good writing even better. In this way, the rules can be taught without making children dislike writing.

Getting Started

A good strategy for introducing writing is to look for assignments that will allow children to write about what they know. Even expert writers have trouble writing about subjects they don't know! At the beginning of the year, this might mean having children write about themselves. For example, children might be asked to create an "autobiography" in the form of a letter to a pen pal. Have children include personal information about themselves and their family, interests, places they have traveled, favorite activities, etc. Encourage children to share their autobiographies with the class. This activity also allows children to get to know a little about one another.

As the school year progresses, children will be introduced to many topics in the Core Knowledge curriculum and will have opportunities to write about topics other than themselves. A good strategy is to let writing assignments grow out of reading and listening experiences. For example, if children have been listening to trickster stories about Iktomi, you might encourage them to try to write a description of Iktomi for their parents, or even try to write a trickster story of their own. Writers of all ability levels benefit from having models to follow, and also from having background knowledge about a subject.

Teaching Idea

Practice brainstorming with the class, because some of the children may not be used to accepting all answers without judgement in a brainstorming session. In the beginning of the year, you can practice by brainstorming as a class and then model how to choose information from the brainstorming list for writing. As you practice this method, children will enjoy being able to use their imagination to brainstorm as many options as possible.

Even experienced writers sometimes have difficulty getting started. To help children get started, you might use brainstorming activities to get them thinking. You can do these as a class, in small groups, or with individual children. Once children become more familiar with brainstorming, they can do it in pairs or by themselves. The key to brainstorming is not to censor or analyze any idea. All ideas are worthy of consideration at first. The point is to generate as many ideas as possible, and then sift through them to see which might be worth developing in the written work.

Another helpful strategy for assisting beginning writers is to give them fairly specific prompts and/or parameters. For example, instead of just saying "Write a story," you might give them the first few sentences of a story and ask them to finish it. Or you might say, "Write a story about Iktomi that includes a trick of some kind." Instructions of this sort narrow down the spectrum of possibilities and give young writers enough structure to get started.

As you think about topics for writing, don't forget to consider topics from the other subject areas in the *Sequence*. Writing can and should be a cross-curricular activity. As a Core Knowledge teacher, you have a significant advantage when it comes to teaching writing: the topics in the *Core Knowledge Sequence* provide you with dozens of possible starting points for writing assignments. Some possibilities for this grade would include an explanation of a saying or phrase; a made-up story involving two or more of the Greek gods and goddesses that have been studied; a brief report about an Olympic sport, or a kind of insect; a story in which one of the characters uses one of the simple machines studied in science; a retelling of the story of Francis Scott Key and "The Star-Spangled Banner;" a letter to a relative on "what we learned about China;" a description of one of the artworks that children have studied or of a historical figure; a poem modeled on one of the poems children have read, e.g., "Bed in Winter" (modeled after Robert Louis Stevenson's "Bed in Summer") or "Spider! I'm expecting you!" (modeled after Emily Dickinson's "Bee! I'm expecting you!"); a haiku in connection with East Asian studies; or a limerick after reading Edward Lear's "There Was an Old Man with a Beard." These are just a few possibilities among many. Don't fall victim to preconceived notions about what children can and can't do or about what is "developmentally inappropriate." Core Knowledge teachers consistently tell us that they are astonished at some of the writing their children produce on *Sequence* topics.

Stories: Beginning, Middle, and End

As you read stories with children, use the terms beginning, middle, and end. Ask, "What is happening at the beginning of the story? What happens in the middle? In the end?" Once children are familiar with these terms, you could do a group writing exercise in which the class creates a story with a beginning, a middle, and an end. Give some guidelines and parameters, as discussed above. For example, you might decide to write an Iktomi story or a Greek gods and goddesses story.

Have children discuss what should happen in the beginning, middle, and end of the class story. Take several suggestions and allow them to vote on possible plot turns. Once you have an outline, work with children to actually write the story on chart paper. Model using paragraphs so that the beginning, the middle, and the end all have their own "space." When the story is done, read the story back to the children, emphasizing its three chunks. Invite children to create illustrations for the story.

After doing this kind of group writing once or twice, give children a writing assignment that involves writing a story of their own with a beginning, a middle, and an end. Have them follow the same steps, e.g., making an outline of what will happen in each stage before they start writing. Provide a prompt and some guidelines. Encourage children to use separate paragraphs for the three separate parts. Invite children to share their stories.

Descriptions

All forms of writing are enhanced by lively and accurate description. Description comes from acute observation and a rich vocabulary that can be employed to put what was observed on paper and make it come alive for the reader. During this grade, children are being introduced to key parts of speech, including adjectives, which are important for description. You may wish to combine one or more writing assignments on description with a discussion of adjectives. Remember that description need not be limited to objects in the classroom. Children could also describe animals they have learned about in science, people they have learned about in history, or paintings they have looked at in art.

Revising

One of the most important things children need to learn about writing is the importance of revising. In writing, as in many other things in life, one doesn't always get everything exactly right on the first try. Children need to learn that even good writing can often be made better, but it is also important that teachers convey this message without demoralizing the child by suggesting, or seeming to suggest, that the child's first attempt was insufficient. One way to explain the importance of revision is to explain that even the very best writers revise. In fact, most great novelists go through multiple drafts before their novels are "done." Therefore, revision should not be seen as a punishment for an inadequate first try but as a normal part of the writing process.

Children should be offered frequent opportunites to revise their writing, especially if the work is to be displayed or shared with parents and/or the larger school commmunity. Explain that when we write for ourselves, we may not always feel the need to revise, but when we write for others we want to make our writing as good as it can be. By explaining in advance that a project will be written and then revised, you can make it clear that revision is part of the normal process of writing, and an important opportunity to make a good thing better.

In commenting on a child's writing, always try to praise first and then ask the child if he or she can think of any way the work might be made even better. Allow children to offer suggestions of their own; then, if necessary, add one or two suggestions of your own. Instead of marking up or pointing out everything that's not entirely correct, spend a few seconds thinking of one or two points that would be most useful to the individual child and focus on those. Whenever possible, offer the advice as one writer sharing ideas with another writer, rather than as a superior correcting the faults of an inferior. After modeling this kind of feedback, you will set a tone that will allow children to effectively but humanely critique each other's work in small groups and pair situations.

Teaching Idea

Use the following second-grade Core Knowledge works of art as writing prompts: *The Thinker* (Rodin), *Virgin Forest at Sunset* (Rousseau), *The Starry Night* (Van Gogh), *I and the Village* (Chagall). Conduct a group writing experience with at least one of the artworks before suggesting that children try to write on their own. Possible ideas/ story starters include: "What is the Thinker thinking about? Describe the landscape of the starry night, where it is taking place, and what might happen next," etc.

Teaching Idea

Ask children to look around the classroom and identify an object like a desk, an item on the bulletin board, or a poster on a wall. Write the word on the board. Then have children work in small groups or pairs to come up with words that describe the object. Encourage them to consider qualities like sensory attributes, (e.g., light, color, texture, and odor); category; function; material; etc. Have each group report its work and write their words on the board. Then have children write sentences using the words that describe the object.

Teaching Idea

Look for chances to display children's writing. Post children's work on the walls of the classroom. Have children write letters to parents and caregivers about what they have been studying. Assemble a scrapbook of their writing.

Review

Below are some ideas for ongoing assessment and review activities. These are not meant to constitute a comprehensive list.

- Provide children with a variety of writing examples, and talk about what the most appropriate way to write is based on the purpose of the work. For example, provide children with a situation, and ask them what kind of writing would be the best way to convey information. You may post the situations on a piece of chart paper and ask the class what kind of writing is best. Examples of situations may include: putting together a model car (you would want very specific directions written in order); giving someone special a card (you may want to write a poem or a special saying); or reading an adventure story (you would want the story to be exciting and have interesting characters). Show an example of one kind of writing to the class, and have children try to imitate it before moving on to another kind of writing.
- Before you introduce a writing activity to the class, review the different types of writing and ask children to think about what they want to accomplish with the writing. By doing this before each writing assignment, you are helping children to practice thinking about their writing and how they should prepare. Brainstorm with the class the appropriate components of the assignment for the day.
- Provide examples of writing pieces, and identify with children the beginning, middle, and end. Keep in mind that in many cases, it is possible to draw the dividing lines in different places. Ask children why they think the beginning ends at point A or B. Let the lines become the basis for a discussion of the story, instead of "This is the correct line and that one's wrong." Read these pieces together and have children underline each part in a different-colored pencil or have them highlight each part with a different-colored highlighter. Then, have children practice writing short pieces with a beginning, a middle, and an end. Share these pieces with the class, and then have the class identify each part from the child's writing.
- One way to have children think about their writing is to provide examples from the class for children to read. Encourage children to publish their work and organize a classroom library of writing projects. This library can provide opportunities for children to read and compare their work from throughout the year.
- Provide lessons to children on how to edit their work. Provide each child with a copy of a paragraph that you have written to include mistakes. Go through the piece and have children identify these mistakes while you make corrections on a copy of the piece on an overhead projector. Also identify the beginning, middle, and end of the piece. Once you do this exercise as a group, give children a chance to work individually.
- Find a class in another state or country that would like to have a class of pen pals. Writing letters is an excellent way for children to practice letter writing conventions and grammar concepts, particularly the use of commas and capital letters. Children will also enjoy learning about the culture of another second-grade class.
- You may also practice editing and writing skills by having a morning message written to the class on the board or on chart paper. Have children copy the message

The Big Idea in Review

Children can communicate their ideas, thoughts, and feelings by using their knowledge of letter-sound patterns to create many types of written text.

and correct any mistakes. If you would like to extend this into a journal activity, provide an open-ended response question for children. Provide time to share how to correct the mistakes, and then let children share their journal responses.

• Have children write on a variety of Core Knowledge topics throughout the year. Although a portfolio is no substitute for more rigorous forms of evaluation, gathering a child's writing into a portfolio over the course of the year can be a testimony to what a child has learned in the various subjects, as well as show a child's progress in writing.

More Resources

The titles listed below are offered as a representative sample of materials and not a complete list of everything that is available.

For children—

These books are generally intended to be read aloud, though some children may be able to read parts or all of the simpler texts.

• *The American Heritage Picture Dictionary* (Houghton Mifflin, 2003). Great pictures for each of the 900 entries, many with easy-to-read sentences. Hardcover, 144 pages, ISBN 0618280049.

• *Draw Write Now, Book 6: Animals & Habitats,* by Marie Hablitzel and Kim Stitzer (Barker Creek Publishing, 1999). A drawing and handwriting course for young children. Good cross-curricular connections. Paperback, 64 pages, ISBN 0963930761. Other titles in the multiple-volume series include *Animals of the World, Part II (Savannas, Grasslands, Mountains and Deserts; The Polar Regions, The Arctic, the Antarctic);* and *The United States, From Sea to Sea, Moving Forward.*

• *Nothing Ever Happens on 90th Street,* by Roni Schotter (Orchard Books, 1999). This book is about a child who eventually finds plenty to write about by just observing the everyday events in the neighborhood. Often writers feel they have nothing to write about because their experience is so "ordinary," but it may not be ordinary to others. Paperback, 32 pages, ISBN 0531071367.

• *Punctuation Takes a Vacation,* by Robin Pulver (Holiday House, 2004). Paperback, ISBN 0823418200.

• *Richard Scarry's Best Picture Dictionary Ever,* by Richard Scarry (Golden Books, 1998). "This truly unique word book for children contains over 700 entries, each telling its own separate and complete little story with a setting, plot, and characters, all in Richard Scarry's playful style" (from the publisher). Hardcover, 128 pages, ISBN 030715548X.

• *Scholastic Writer's Desk Reference* (Scholastic, 2001). Covers punctuation, grammar, writing, spelling, and correspondence. Paperback, 312 pages, ISBN 0439216508.

• *A Spelling Dictionary for Beginning Writers (Book 1),* by Gregory Hurray (Educators Publishing Service, 2001). "Contains approximately 1,500 high-frequency words that account for more than 90% of the words beginning writers use. A thematic word bank and a Mini-Thesaurus provide words by category and suggest alternatives for words children tend to overuse in their writing" (from the publisher). Intended for children in Grades 2 through 6, but more advanced writers may make better use out of Book 2 in this series. Available through Educators Publishing Service, www.epsbooks.com or 1-800-225-5750.

• *Start Writing About Things I Do,* by Penny King and Ruth Thomson (Chrysalis Books, 2000). An engaging start to non-fiction writing. Paperback, 32 pages, ISBN 1841382132.

• *Write Away: A Handbook for Young Writers and Learners* (Great Source Education Group, 2002). Also includes a *SkillsBook* providing editing and proofreading practice, and a *Program Guide* for teachers. To order, contact Great Source at www.greatsource.com, or phone 1-800-289-4490.

For teachers —

• *75 Picture Prompts for Young Children,* by Rick Brown (Scholastic, 1993). Paperback, 88 pages, ISBN 0590494082.

More Resources continued

• *Any Child Can Write: An At-Home Guide to Enhancing Your Child's Elementary Education (Fourth Edition),* by Harvey S. Weiner (Oxford University Press, 2003). This resource can be used to involve parents or caregivers in the educational process and their child's writing. Paperback, 366 pages, ISBN 0195153162.

• *Daily Paragraph Editing (Grade 2),* by Kristen Kunkel (Evan-Moor, 2004). Writing across the curriculum. Daily editing assignments with an end-of-the-week writing prompt. Paperback, 176 pages, ISBN 1557999562.

• *The Elements of Style (Fourth Edition),* by William Strunk, Jr., and E. B. White (Pearson Higher Education, 2000). A brief and sensible overview. Paperback, 104 pages, ISBN 020530902X.

• *In Print! 40 Cool Publishing Projects for Kids,* by Joe Rhatigan (Lark Books, 2003). Ideas to spark your imagination. Hardcover, 128 pages, ISBN 1579903592.

• *Solving Writing Problems with Easy Mini-Lessons (Grades 2–4),* by Dolores Hudson (Creative Teaching Press, 1999). Includes lessons on punctuation, generating ideas, developing organization, maintaining focus, improving description, and enhancing word choice. Paperback, 96 pages, ISBN 1574715321.

• *Startwrite* is a computer software program that allows you to create individualized handwriting exercises based on children's dictated stories, spelling lists, or more. Fonts include styles similar to Getty-Dubay Italic, D'Nealian, and Zaner-Bloser manuscript and cursive models. Extremely customizable. Both PC and Mac versions are available. To download a free trial, visit their website at www.startwrite.com.

D. Spelling, Grammar, and Usage

The Big Idea

Correct spelling, grammar, and usage can be learned through direct instruction and also indirectly through reading and writing.

What Students Should Already Know

Students using Core Knowledge should be familiar with

- how to write all 26 letters, uppercase and lowercase, as well as letter-sound correspondences
- how to listen carefully to each of the sounds in a word to help them spell correctly
- how to use periods, question marks, and exclamation points, as well as a few basic rules concerning the use of capital letters
- how to make many singular words plural by adding *-s*

What Students Need to Learn

- **Represent all the sounds of a word when spelling independently**
- **Correctly spell words that contain spelling patterns that have been taught**
- **Begin to use a first dictionary to check and correct spelling**
- **Write legibly on ruled paper**
- **Understand the concept of a complete sentence, and identify subject and predicate**
- **Identify nouns, verbs, and adjectives as parts of speech**
- **Use the comparative (*-er*) and superlative (*-est*) forms of adjectives**
- **Change regular verbs from present to past tense using *-ed***
- **Use the correct present- and past-tense forms for common irregular verbs**
- **Recognize singular and plural forms of widely used nouns**
- **Use capital letters for the first word of a sentence, proper nouns, the pronoun *I*, holidays, months, days of the week, countries, cities, states, main words in titles, and initials**
- **Use commas when writing dates, and city and state names**
- **Use apostrophes in common contractions**
- **Recognize common abbreviations, e.g., St., Rd., Mr., Mrs., Ms., Dr.**
- **Understand what synonyms and antonyms are, and provide synonyms and antonyms for common words**

What Students Will Learn in Future Grades

In future grades, students will review and extend their learning about spelling, grammar, and usage.

Vocabulary

Student/Teacher Vocabulary

adjective: a word that describes a noun (S)

antonym: a word that means the opposite of another word (S)

legible: capable of being read or deciphered (T)

noun: a person, place, thing, or idea (S)

phonetic spelling: spelling that may not be correct in terms of meeting the conventions of English spelling but captures the sounds in a word. Examples of phonetic spelling include writing *sum* for *some*, *mi* for *my*, or *bot* for *boat*. This is also sometimes called "invented spelling." (T)

predicate: one of two necessary parts of a sentence; the part that contains the verb (S)

punctuation: the use of commas, periods, and other marks (S)

subject: one of two necessary parts of a sentence; the part that tells whom or what the sentence is about (S)

synonym: a word that means just about the same thing as another word (S)

verb: a word that expresses action (S)

Domain Vocabulary

Words associated with spelling, grammar, and usage:
spell, letter, sound, period, question mark, exclamation point, comma, apostrophe, same, opposite, correct, incorrect, revise, fix, sentence, beginning, end, capital, capitalize, big, small, space, singular, plural, description, *plus words used or created during spelling and grammar work, e.g.,* rich, richer, richest, *etc.*

Materials

children's dictionary, p. 39
overhead projector, p. 44
index cards, p. 46

At a Glance

The most important ideas for you are:

- Children should be able to correctly spell most of the words they know.
- In second grade, children may still spell some words phonetically. While they may be praised for recording a phonetically plausible spelling, they should also be coached to use the conventional spelling.
- Children should be able to write legibly and should be given frequent opportunities to write.
- Although learning the rules of spelling, grammar, and usage can seem tedious, these rules are worth learning because they enable us to communicate more effectively with one another.
- The spelling, grammar, and usage guidelines discussed in this section should be taught in conjunction with the writing assignments discussed in the previous section.
- Instead of treating this section as a discrete unit, you may wish to explain the various points of usage over a longer period of time as children practice their writing.
- It is seldom adequate to merely explain proper usage. Children should also have opportunities to practice correct usage, both in exercises and in their own writing.

What Teachers Need to Know

D. Spelling, Grammar, and Usage

Background

In order for children to write and be understood, they need to master the rules of spelling, grammar, and usage.

In spelling, a major issue is correct spelling versus phonetic spelling. Phonetic spelling is generally allowed in Kindergarten and Grade 1. By second grade, however, children should be ready to spell more words conventionally. In particular, they should be expected to correctly spell any word that contains spelling patterns they have been taught as part of their reading and writing instruction. Second graders can also begin to use a children's dictionary to check their spelling or use spell check on a word processor.

Children need regular practice in grammar and usage to gain mastery. As always, exposure to correct spelling, grammar, and usage can be a powerful aid in gaining mastery.

Children probably will have already learned some of the rules discussed below. But it is important to review all of the points to be sure that children possess the basic knowledge they will need as a foundation for future study.

Although the basic rules of spelling, grammar, and usage have not always been imaginatively taught in the past, there is no reason why they cannot be taught in a way that is both informative and enjoyable. Well-designed and creative lessons are an important part of the process. Teachers should be mindful when providing corrective feedback that they don't overwhelm and discourage the child. Feedback that is constructive and encouraging can mean the difference between mastery and discouragement, either of which can continue into the higher grades.

Spelling and Legibility

In earlier grades, children have probably used phonetic spelling. Some may continue to use it for certain words in second grade. However, by second grade children need to be learning and practicing conventional spellings. Spelling instruction may be included in your reading program. If not, you can teach spelling through the tried and true method of dictation, in which the teacher reads a word, gives a sentence using the word, repeats the word, and then the children write down the word. For a fuller background on spelling development and instruction, consult the following resources: "Spelling and Language Structure: An Essential Foundation for Literacy," a chapter in *What's Gone Wrong in America's Classrooms;* Module 3: "Spellography" and Module 9: "Teaching Beginning Spelling and Writing" in *LETRS (Language Essentials for Teachers of Reading and Spelling)*; and *Words Their Way: Word Study for Phonics, Vocabulary, and Spelling Instruction.* (See More Resources.)

In testing spelling, use spelling combinations that children have studied in Grade 2 and in previous grades and words that they are likely to recognize. Some typical words second graders should be able to spell include *animal, bright, planet, frog, street, grandmother, tray, town, horse, whale, dream, boat, alarm, bread, march, food,* and *flash.* To this list, you may add important and relatively easy-to-spell words from other Core Knowledge content areas like history and science (e.g., *Africa, coast, Japan, winter, insect,* etc.). Creative activities including spelling bees can capture children's interest.

At some point in this grade, you should introduce children to the dictionary and its uses. Explain that a dictionary can be used to gain an understanding of a word you don't know, but also, in some cases, to check the spelling of a word. For example, if you were not sure whether the word *Africa* is spelled with a *c* or a *k*, but you knew the first few letters, you could look it up in the dictionary. Model this procedure for children, then give them some words and have them "check the spelling" using the dictionary. When children are comfortable with this procedure, you can begin suggesting that they check the spelling of words in their own writing—both during the creation of drafts and during revisions. You can use the writing assignments discussed in the previous section to monitor legibility as well as spelling.

Subjects and Predicates

A complete sentence contains a *subject* and a *predicate.* The subject tells whom or what the sentence is about. It may be

- a person (Harriet Tubman, monster, sister, musician).
- a place (China, home, cafeteria, corner).
- a thing (battle, republic, leaf, guitar).
- an idea (Buddhism, democracy, romance, harmony).

The simple subject is always a noun or pronoun. The complete subject includes the simple subject plus any words or groups of words modifying the simple subject. Consider the following example:

The essence of Plato's philosophy is very simple.

The simple subject is "essence," and the complete subject is "the essence of Plato's philosophy."

The predicate is the part of the sentence that contains the verb. The predicate describes the action of the subject. It shows what the subject *does* or *did, is* or *was.* The predicate includes the verb and all of the words associated with it. These may include a direct object and/or an indirect object, for example. The predicate is underlined in each of the following sentences:

The Statue of Liberty welcomes newcomers to the United States.

Samantha hit the ball over the fence.

The Nile runs through Africa.

In the sentences below, the simple subjects are bolded, and the predicates are underlined. Words in normal print are part of the complete subject but not the simple subject.

James Audubon traveled throughout North America to observe and sketch birds.

The ancient **Greeks** built the Parthenon to honor the goddess Athena.

Patriotic **songs** celebrate America's land, people, and history.

All **squares and rectangles** have four sides .

You may explain subject and predicate to children by extracting examples from selections they've already read. We *don't* recommend that you stop while reading to identify the subject and predicate, because children may lose their train of thought in terms of comprehension of the text. For certain classroom activities and discussion questions, you might also ask children to display their knowledge of grammar by answering your questions using complete sentences.

Nouns

A noun is the name of a person, place, thing, or idea. Two other characteristics of nouns may also be helpful in explaining the concept to children and teaching children to recognize nouns: 1) a noun is often preceded by an article like—*a, an,* or *the*; 2) A noun is a word that can usually be made plural, e.g., one *dog*, two *dogs*.

All nouns are either proper or common and either concrete or abstract. Nouns that name specific persons, places, or things are called *proper nouns*. Jackie Robinson, Tokyo, and China are all proper nouns. Nouns that name a *general* class of person, place, thing, or idea are called *common nouns*. *Concrete nouns* are persons, places, or things you can see and point to, like a tree, an apple, or a musician. The opposite of a concrete noun is an *abstract noun*. An abstract noun is an idea, a feeling, or something else that you can't point to, like freedom or sorrow. Nouns, therefore, have several classifications. For example:

Labor Day: proper, abstract	immigration: common, abstract
Statue of Liberty: proper, concrete	tree: common, concrete

In Grade 2, the emphasis should be on concrete nouns.

Nouns can be singular or plural. A singular noun describes one object; a plural noun describes two or more objects. Most nouns form their plurals by adding the letter *-s* to their singular form:

hamsters, crops, planets, myths, friends, equations, canals, sculptures

Most nouns that end in *s, ch, sh,* or *x* form their plurals by adding *-es* to their singular form:

classes, masses, churches, crutches, dishes, clashes, taxes

Some plural nouns are irregular and can be formed only by a change in spelling:

man, men	child, children	foot, feet
woman, women	tooth, teeth	ox, oxen

Verbs

A verb is a word that is used to express action or being. One good way of finding a verb is to look for a word that can change tense, e.g., "I run every day" can be changed to "I ran every day," or, for the hopeful jogger, "I will run every day." Verbs can change tense. Nouns, pronouns, adjectives, and adverbs can't do this. Once you have used this rule to help you find the verb in a sentence, you can find the subject by asking "Who or what does the verb describe?" In the case of "I run every day," once you identify *run* as the verb, you would ask, "Who runs?" The answer is "I run." So *I* is the subject of the sentence.

In Grade 2, the emphasis should be on action verbs. An action verb expresses action and therefore tells what a noun or pronoun *does*. Here are two examples of action verbs.

A female frog lays about one thousand eggs at a time.

The drummer strikes the kettledrum with a baton.

Regular verbs form the past tense by adding *-ed* or *-d* to their present-tense forms:

talk, talked	walk, walked	love, loved
smile, smiled	ask, asked	trick, tricked

Irregular verbs are irregular in the way their past tense is formed. They change in ways that cannot be predicted, and this lack of a rule can be frustrating for many children. Verbs that are irregular in the way their past tense is formed must be memorized. Some common irregular verbs are listed below:

TO BE
Present: I am, you are, he/she is, we are, they are

Past: I was, you were, he/she was, we were, they were

TO HAVE
Present: I have, you have, he/she has, we have, they have

Past: I had, you had, he/she had, we had, they had

TO SEE
Present: I see, you see, he/she sees, we see, they see

Past: I saw, you saw, he/she saw, we saw, they saw

TO DO
Present: I do, you do, he/she does, we do, they do

Past: I did, you did, he/she did, we did, they did

TO GO
Present: I go, you go, he/she goes, we go, they go

Past: I went, you went, he/she went, we went, they went

TO COME
Present: I come, you come, he/she comes, we come, they come

Past: I came, you came, he/she came, we came, they came

TO RUN
Present: I run, you run, he/she runs, we run, they run

Past: I ran, you ran, he/she ran, we ran, they ran

TO GIVE
Present: I give, you give, he/she gives, we give, they give

Past: I gave, you gave, he/she gave, we gave, they gave

TO SING
Present: I sing, you sing, he/she sings, we sing, they sing

Past: I sang, you sang, he/she sang, we sang, they sang

Although most of these forms will be familiar to children, a handful of them may not be. In some areas of the United States, dialect forms are common in oral speech, so that children might routinely say "I seen," "I done," or "you was." Although these forms are perfectly functional and understandable during daily speech in local contexts, many will consider them ungrammatical and inappropriate, and children who use dialect forms such as these may be looked down on for using them. Children should therefore have the chance to learn the forms that are most widely accepted as correct, so that they can use them in formal situations like job interviews, though they may prefer the dialectical form for everyday situations.

Teaching Idea

Look for ways to reinforce usage points during discussions of stories, poems, and nonfiction. For example, you might reinforce comparative and superlative adjectives by discussing which characters in a story are *smarter* or *stronger* than others, and which is the *smartest* or *strongest* of all. Or, after reading a story, ask children to think of adjectives that describe the main character or characters, or verbs that describe what the characters do in the story.

Adjectives

An adjective modifies a noun or a pronoun. In English, adjectives almost always appear before the nouns they modify. An adjective will answer one of the following questions: How many? What kind? Which one? What color? In each example, the adjective is underlined.

(How many?)	<u>Several</u> kinds of animals hibernate in winter.
	<u>Four</u> chipmunks sleep in the hole in our backyard.
(What kind?)	An <u>equatorial</u> climate is usually very warm.
	The <u>grassy</u> areas of Argentina are called pampas.
(Which one?)	<u>This</u> painting shows an oxbow river in Massachusetts.
	<u>That</u> man near the painting's center is the artist himself.
(What color?)	Send <u>yellow</u> roses to signify friendship.
	<u>Red</u> roses indicate a declaration of love.

You can make comparisons by adding *-er* and *-est* to most adjectives:

early, earli<u>er</u>, earli<u>est</u>

The *-er* form is called the comparative form, and the *-est* form is called the superlative.

Note that not all adjectives form their comparative and superlative forms according to this rule. Some use *more* and *most* instead:

careful, more careful, most careful

Most English speakers learn when to use *-er* and *-est* and when to use more and *most* by hearing the language spoken, but you may wish to point this out if an opportunity presents itself.

Teaching Parts of Speech

Parts of speech may be taught as part of your reading program. If not, you may wish to introduce them as a separate topic, using examples and worksheets. After explaining each part of speech, you can have children circle all examples of that part of speech in a text selection. When they know all three parts of speech, they can circle the nouns, underline the verbs, and put boxes around all the adjectives in a passage.

Once you have given this initial instruction, you can review and reinforce the parts of speech as opportunities present themselves. For example, while looking at a poem you might have children look for the parts of speech that are most important in the poem; or you might have them think of adjectives to describe a painting they are looking at or a historical character they have studied. They could make a list of verbs that describe things people did in a story they have listened too, e.g., "The camel said humph," etc. You could assign a descriptive writing assignment in which children have to use a certain number of adjectives. The possibilities are almost endless.

Whenever possible, look for ways to link the grammar to topics children are studying or to topics that interest them. You might teach tense by having children say what they did yesterday, and then asking them what they would say if they were doing it now or in the future. You can do similar things with comparative and superlative forms of adjectives; e.g., in geography ask, "What's a big state, a bigger state, the biggest state?" or in music have them sing loud, louder, and loudest.

Capitalization

Capitals are used, in general, for the names of *specific* persons, places, and things (proper nouns). There is no need to capitalize *general* persons, places, and things (common nouns) unless they begin a sentence. For example, do not capitalize *father* in "The fathers of the second graders brought the sports equipment to the school camp." But *do* capitalize *father* in "Fathers usually give wise advice." Here are examples of the seven guidelines for capitalization listed in the *Sequence* for this grade:

1. Capitalize the first word of a sentence:

   About three-fourths of your body is water.

2. Capitalize proper nouns. Proper nouns include the names of people; religious, ethnic, and political groups; languages; nationalities; and adjectives derived from them:

   My new dress is made of Chinese silk.

   The Greeks believed that people went to Hades when they died. Jews throughout the world celebrate Passover.

   Doctor Yamada greeted me in Japanese when I telephoned.

3. Capitalize the pronoun *I*:

   Rishi and I read a book about Mesopotamia.

4. Capitalize holidays, months, and days of the week:

   Easter falls on the last Sunday of March this year.

   During their holy month of Ramadan, Muslims fast during the daytime.

   Meet me on Monday or Tuesday to shop for Chanukah gifts.

   Ah, to be Irish on Saint Patrick's Day!

5. Capitalize names of countries, cities, and states:

   Kela brought me olives and grapes from Athens, Greece, for my birthday.

   John's uncle in Provo, Utah, drives a green truck with a ski rack on top.

   Karen will visit Kyoto, Japan, her penpal's hometown.

6. Capitalize the main words in titles. Specific practice on this point varies slightly. We suggest capitalizing the first and last words in a title, as well as all other important words, such as nouns and verbs. Do not capitalize *a, an, the,* or other unimportant words with fewer than five letters:

   Beauty and the Beast, Joan of Arc, Ten Minutes till Bedtime, Bodies from the Bog

7. Capitalize a person's initials:

   Clement C. Moore, E. B. White, Robert E. Lee, Susan B. Anthony

Teaching Idea

Keep a clipping file of simple typos from newspapers and other published materials. Once children have learned the relevant rules, show some examples on an overhead projector, and invite children to fix the mistakes.

Teaching Idea

Many teachers find it effective to start every day by posting a very brief writing sample with several spelling and grammatical errors (thoughtfully selected to provide practice in those skills that are being taught) on the board. The children are expected to copy the writing sample and correct the errors. The teacher then leads the class in a group exercise to discuss and correct the errors.

Rather than try to introduce all of these points at once, you may wish to introduce them one or two at a time over a period of several days. Once children know the rules, you can give them sentences to fix, like this one:

today is tuesday and sarah is going to a show in dallas that has a singer from mexico i know well.

Capitalization can also be practiced during writing and revision.

End Punctuation

There are three kinds of end punctuation, or end marks: periods, question marks, and exclamation points.

The *period* is used to end a statement (a declarative sentence), an indirect question, or a mild command:

Declarative sentence: Susan B. Anthony helped women win the right to vote.

Indirect question: Cesar asked me if I knew that Susan B. Anthony helped women win the right to vote.

Mild command: Keep in mind that women could not vote until 14 years after Susan B. Anthony's death.

The *question mark* follows a direct question (or interrogative sentence):

Has Moesha finished her math homework?

Will she come ride skateboards with us?

The *exclamation point* shows strong emotion or urgency. It is also used for strong commands.

Hurry! You'll be late!

Don't run!

Wow! That's amazing!

Commas

There are many uses for commas. In second grade, only two are emphasized.

1. Use commas to separate the year and the date in complete dates:

   The death of President Kennedy occurred on November 22, 1963.

   When just the month and year are given, use of a comma is optional:

   November, 1963, or November 1963

2. A comma separates the elements in an address:

   Detroit Red Wings, 600 Civic Center Drive, Detroit, MI 48226

Apostrophes

A *contraction* is formed when two words are combined, but a few letters in the middle are left out. The apostrophe goes where the omitted letters used to be. Some examples:

I'm (I am)	you're (you are)	aren't (are not)
he's (he is)	we're (we are)	they're (they are)
aren't (are not)	can't (cannot)	won't (will not)
don't (do not)	shan't (shall not)	doesn't (does not)
didn't (did not)	shouldn't (should not)	wouldn't (would not)
couldn't (could not)	hadn't (had not)	

Abbreviations

An abbreviation is a word that is shortened when it is written down, for example, *Main St.* for *Main Street.* An abbreviation is usually used with a period after it to show that it is an abbreviation and not a whole word. However, some modern abbreviations use capital letters and no periods, like AM and PM. Some common abbreviations are:

St. (Street)	Rd. (Road)	Mr. (Mister)	Mrs. (Mistress)
Ms. (Miss or Mrs.)	Dr. (Doctor)	ft. (foot or feet)	in. (inch or inches)
U.S.A. (United States of America)			

Synonyms and Antonyms

The words *synonym* and *antonym* may not be familiar to children, but the concepts probably are. A synonym is a word whose meaning is almost the same as another word, e.g., *quick* and *fast*, or *mad* and *angry*. An antonym is a word that means the opposite of another word, e.g., *fat* and *thin*, *beautiful* and *ugly*, *rough* and *smooth*.

You may wish to teach synonyms and antonyms near the beginning of the year, since these concepts can be very useful in explaining other words and concepts later on. Antonyms may actually be easier to teach than synonyms. You might give children some examples of paired antonyms, e.g., *sharp* and *dull*, *hot* and *cold*. Then give them a single word that has one or more well-known antonyms and ask them if they can think of an antonym. Finally, ask if children can think of any pairs of antonyms. You can build on this with a simple worksheet, like "match the word to its antonym."

After practicing antonyms for a while, explain synonyms. Go through the same steps as for antonyms: give examples (*happy* and *glad*, *nice* and *kind*, etc.), ask for synonyms for individual words (*tired*, *mad*, etc.), and then for matched pairs. You could also hold a synonym or antonym bee in which pairs or small groups of children compete to name a synonym or antonym to a word you write on the board.

Look for opportunities to talk about synonyms and antonyms as you discuss other subjects. For example, if you have a vocabulary element to your instruction, you can use synonyms and antonyms to introduce and explain new words.

Review

Below are some ideas for ongoing assessment and review activities. These are not meant to constitute a comprehensive list.

- After you have reviewed and practiced the guidelines for spelling, grammar, and usage from this section, have children construct a checklist for each piece of writing. Make sure that they understand their writing must include each of the requirements of the checklist. For example, you may include a requirement to check for capital letters and proper end punctuation. You may also have them make sure they spelled words correctly, and that they used a dictionary where appropriate. Include a requirement to use their best handwriting on final drafts.

The Big Idea in Review

Correct spelling, grammar, and usage can be learned through direct instruction and also indirectly through reading and writing.

• Children may practice the skills included in this section in their writing assignments. Include writing lessons that focus on the specific skills in this section, such as understanding sentence structure or parts of speech. Then, have children practice the skill for the day in their writing assignments. You can build on the skills that children practice by including them in editing checklists and by identifying them in writing and literature as a class.

• You may also begin to use simple peer editing with the class. Children may trade pieces of writing and read them aloud to a partner to check for errors. Each partner can also use the editing checklist to make sure that all areas of spelling, grammar, and usage have been completed.

• Make a class set of flash cards on index cards with a variety of simple nouns, verbs, and adjectives. When children read the words, have them identify the word and its part of speech. You may extend this activity by making a set of cards with words that have to be capitalized and words that do not have to be capitalized. For example, include names of the children in the class, cities, states, countries, and continents. Have children identify whether the word needs a capital letter or not and explain why.

• A "mad lib" is a fun story activity in which children customize a story by filling in nouns, adjectives, verbs, and other parts of speech. Mad libs can be a fun way of solidifying knowledge of parts of speech. Information about mad libs can be found in More Resources and on the Internet.

• Read sentences aloud to children and have them identify whether the sentence needs a period, question mark, or an exclamation point. You can extract sentences from a story children have read. Read the sentence aloud and then have children predict which end punctuation the sentence has. Then, ask children to explain why that punctuation is used. "Is the sentence telling, asking, or exclaiming something?"

More Resources

The titles listed below are offered as a representative sample of materials and not a complete list of everything that is available.

For children —

These books are generally intended to be read aloud, though some children may be able to read parts or all of the simpler texts.

- *The American Heritage Picture Dictionary* (Houghton Mifflin, 2003). Great pictures for each of the 900 entries, many with easy-to-read sentences. Hardcover, 144 pages, ISBN 0618280049.
- *Punctuation Takes a Vacation*, by Robin Pulver (Holiday House, 2004). Paperback, ISBN 0823418200.
- *Richard Scarry's Best Picture Dictionary Ever,* by Richard Scarry (Golden Books, 1998). "This truly unique word book for children contains over 700 entries, each telling its own separate and complete little story with a setting, plot, and characters, all in Richard Scarry's playful style" (from the publisher). Hardcover, 128 pages, ISBN 030715548X.
- *Scholastic Writer's Desk Reference* (Scholastic, 2001). Covers punctuation, grammar, writing, spelling, and correspondence. Paperback, 312 pages, ISBN 0439216508.
- *A Spelling Dictionary for Beginning Writers (Book 1),* by Gregory Hurray (Educators Publishing Service, 2001). "Contains approximately 1,500 high-frequency words that account for more than 90% of the words beginning writers use. A thematic word bank and a Mini-Thesaurus provide words by category and suggest alternatives for words children tend to overuse in their writing" (from the publisher). Intended for children in Grades 2 through 6, but more advanced writers may make better use out of Book 2 in this series. Available through Educators Publishing Service, www.epsbooks.com or 1-800-225-5750.
- *Super Silly Mad Libs Junior: World's Greatest Word Game (Mad Libs Junior),* by Roger Price and Leonard Stern (Price Stern Sloan, 2004). Paperback, 48 pages, ISBN 0843107588.
- *Write Away: A Handbook for Young Writers and Learners* (Great Source Education Group, 2002). Also includes a *SkillsBook* providing editing and proofreading practice, and a *Program Guide* for teachers. To order, contact Great Source at www.greatsource.com, or phone 1-800-289-4490.

For teachers —

- *Daily Oral Language, Grade 2,* by Gregg O. Byers (Carson-Dellosa, 2001). Thirty-six weeks worth of daily, two-sentence lessons that teach grammar, punctuation, and usage. Paperback, 96 pages, ISBN 088724646X.
- *First Language Lessons for the Well-Trained Mind,* by Jessie Wise (Peace Hill Press, 2003). Beginning grammar lessons for the early elementary grades. Paperback, 422 pages, ISBN 0971412928.
- *Grammar and Punctuation, Grade 2,* by Susan Kunze (Evan-Moor, 2002). Teaches sentence punctuation, commas, possessives, plurals, contractions, nouns, and verbs. Includes CD-ROM with animated rule charts, printable practice pages, skills review, and record sheet. Paperback with CD-ROM, 112 pages, ISBN 1557998469.
- *LETRS (Language Essentials for Teachers of Reading and Spelling)* is a professional development sequence for teachers of reading authored by Louisa Moats and available from SOPRIS West at www.sopriswest.com, or by phoning 1-800-547-6747. Presenter's Packs include a presenter's manual, CD-ROM, and additional resources. Topics covered by volume are as follows:

Module 1: The Challenge of Learning to Read

Module 2: The Speech Sounds of English: Phonetics, Phonology, and Phoneme Awareness

Module 3: Spellography: A Road Map to English Orthography

Module 4: The Mighty Word: Building Vocabulary and Oral Language

Module 5: Getting Up to Speed: Developing Fluency

Module 6: Digging for Meaning: Teaching Text Comprehension

Module 7: Teaching s Phonics, Word Study, and the Alphabetic Principle

Module 8: Assessment for Prevention and Early Intervention (K–3)

Module 9: Teaching Beginning Spelling and Writing

- *Phonics They Use: Words for Reading and Writing (3rd edition),* by Patricia M. Cunningham (Addison Wesley, 1999). Paperback, 196 pages, ISBN 0321020553.

More Resources continued

- *Skill Drill Grammar: Black Line Reproducibles, Grades 1–2* (Frank Schaffer Publications, 1999). Covers capital letters in names, dates, and the beginning of sentences; punctuation in sentences, dates, and addresses; and word usage. Paperback, 64 pages, ISBN 076820335X.
- *Spelling: Development, Disabilities, and Instruction,* by Louisa Cook Moats (York Press, 1995). Paperback, 137 pages, ISBN 0912752408.
- *What's Gone Wrong in America's Classrooms,* edited by Williamson M. Evers (Hoover Institution Press, 1998). The "Spelling and Language Structure: An Essential Foundation for Literacy" chapter by Louisa Moats is a good reference on spelling development and instruction. Paperback, 190 pages, ISBN 0817995323.
- *Words Their Way: Word Study for Phonics, Vocabulary, and Spelling Instruction (3rd edition),* by Donald Bear, Marcia Invernizzi, Shane Templeton, and Francine Johnston (Prentice Hall, 2003). Paperback, 464 pages, ISBN 0131113380.
- Compact for Reading, www.ed.gov/pubs/CompactforReading/index.html, is a project of the U.S. Department of Education that offers a Home-School Links Reading Kit for Kindergarten through Grade 3.

Supplemental Essay #1

Elements of a Good Language Arts Program

Reading is the most important skill children learn in the early grades, and successful reading depends not only on good decoding skills but also on vocabulary and background knowledge. It is therefore important that you have a good, comprehensive language arts program in place. In the paragraphs that follow, the Core Knowledge Foundation identifies several key components of a good second-grade program. We then indicate how these components might be combined in a two-hour language arts block.

- A good second-grade program helps children continue to develop their oral language, including speaking and listening skills. Children have frequent opportunities to listen to stories and non-fiction books and are asked to talk about these readings, to ask and answer questions, and sometimes to retell or summarize a story. Children who hear a wide range of fictional and non-fictional read alouds will be able to build vocabulary and increase their reading comprehension skills.
- A good program provides a solid understanding of the basic principle underlying our written language—the *alphabetic principle*: that the sounds we hear in words are represented by letters written from left to right. Individual letters represent specific sounds, and groups of letters may also be combined to form specific letter-sound patterns (such as the letters *ch* in *check*, *chick*, and *chimp*). While there is no single universally accepted sequence for teaching the letter-sound patterns of the English language, a good program will introduce sounds according to a logical sequence, and will introduce nearly all of the letter-sound correspondences by the end of second grade. Whatever sequence a reading program follows, it is important that the instruction be systematically organized to make the letter-sound patterns *explicit* and present them in a way that builds logically and sequentially, *not* in a haphazard or occasional fashion. Phonics instruction is most effective when it is regular, if not daily, with one skill building on another, and with plenty of practice and review.
- A good program will give children regular opportunities to "sound out," read, and write words that correspond to the letter-sound patterns they have been taught. Some schools discourage children from sounding out words and urge them instead to "guess" the words, based on "clues" from pictures or what's going on in the story. This is a serious mistake. Children need to learn a systematic, reliable way to figure out words they don't know, and this can come only from giving them explicit instruction in the code of our written language.
- As children master individual letter-sound patterns and become able to sound out words, a good program provides phonetically controlled reading materials (also known as "decodable text"). By second grade, these stories, written in a controlled vocabulary that corresponds to the letter-sound patterns the children have been taught, should be becoming longer and more complex. While such stories are, of course, not great literature, they are very helpful in teaching children to read, especially in providing the early and tremendously satisfying experience of being able "to read it all by myself." Once children have demonstrated

some success with phonetically controlled reading materials, they should be introduced to and asked to read, with occasional assistance, stories that are not phonetically controlled but are written for beginning readers. In second grade, children should have regular opportunities to practice reading simple books aloud to adults to build fluency.

- A good program includes diagnostic evaluation of those children who still seem to struggle in sounding out words and do not decode automatically. Such assessment pinpoints the precise letter-sound correspondences that have not been mastered so that remedial instruction can be provided.
- A good program recognizes that reading and writing reinforce each other and therefore provides children with many opportunities to communicate in writing and practice handwriting. This means not only having the children copy individual words in a workbook, or write down words the teacher dictates—both of which are valuable practice that should take place regularly—but also occasionally having the children write letters, short stories, captions to pictures, descriptions, poems, and reports. A good program, while recognizing the necessity of phonetic spelling in the early grades, will begin to ensure that second graders are explicitly taught and practice conventional spelling. Morning message, dictation, and journal writing can all be important components of second-grade writing. In addition, the *Core Knowledge Sequence* provides a wealth of topics in history, science, art, and music that can inspire writing assignments in the content areas.
- A good program introduces conventions and rules of capitalization, punctuation, grammar, and spelling, like those described in an earlier section of this book.
- A good program provides a print-rich environment. The ideal classroom surrounds children with written language that is meaningful to them, such as a written listing of the classroom schedule, Word Walls with new vocabulary, etc. These words are not simply "on display," but are regularly referred to by both the teacher and children. Children also have their attention drawn to familiar uses of written language in everyday life, such as signs, recipes, invitations, and announcements of upcoming events.

That, in brief, describes some of what a good second-grade program will do to help *all* children achieve the goal of becoming independent readers and writers. Of the elements listed, some are more likely to be well taught by current reading programs than others. A number of programs on the market now teach phonemic awareness, phonics, and decoding skills well, and the Foundation can give you the names of some programs that are solid in this area. When it comes to oral language, however, there are very few programs that do an entirely satisfactory job. Many reading programs include only a few read alouds, and most contain very little, if any, nonfiction. What's more, most reading programs stick to familiar topics, like families, pets, and school; most do not address topics of the sort found in the *Core Knowledge Sequence*—such as early civilizations, astronomy, and the orchestra—which are essential for building cultural literacy. If your reading program contains few read alouds and little nonfiction, you should be sure to supplement it by finding time to read to your children every day and by supplementing or replacing some of the fictional stories with non-fiction titles.

Scheduling

How might all of these elements be combined and integrated into a daily schedule? There is no one correct answer. However, a good second-grade language arts program might take about two hours of time each day and might allocate teaching time according to the following guidelines:

Skills:

40–60 minutes on skills each day, which might be divided roughly as follows: 25–30 minutes of reading practice and fluency-building work; 10–15 minutes of writing; 5–15 minutes on spelling, grammar, and usage.

By second grade, children should have mastered most of the letter-sound correspondences. However, in order to read words with lower frequency correspondences and conditional correspondences, multisyllabic words, irregular words, words borrowed from other languages, and other oddities, children should continue to study word structure and the relationships between sound, spelling, meaning, and word origin. A well-rounded approach may go by the name of "word study." The goal of such instruction is to engender metalinguistic awareness that will generalize to a love of and interest in words, in addition to a large word recognition vocabulary.

Oral Language:

40–60 minutes of oral language activities each day. These should include at least one read-aloud session per day, preferably two. One read aloud might be fiction or poetry; the other might be a non-fiction read aloud that connects to a topic in the *Core Knowledge Sequence*, e.g., a history or science selection. Read alouds should be followed by discussion, vocabulary work, or other oral language activities.

Supplemental Essay #2

Oral Language: The Foundation of Reading

Traditionally, the overwhelming emphasis in language arts programs in the early grades has been placed on reading, writing, spelling, and grammar, with little instructional time directed to building children's listening and speaking skills. This has been a grave oversight. It is almost impossible to overemphasize the significance of oral language development and its impact upon nearly every aspect of learning. Oral language skills, such as listening and speaking, are necessary prerequisites for written language skills like reading and writing. To fully understand the links between listening and speaking skills on the one hand and reading and writing skills on the other, it may be helpful to conceptualize language arts as follows:

	Receptive Language	Expressive Language
Oral Language	*Listening*	*Speaking*
Written Language	*Reading (decoding + comprehension)*	*Writing (handwriting, spelling, written composition)*

In this chart, the various manifestations of "language" are categorized as either receptive or expressive, and as either oral or written. "Receptive language" is language we take in, process, and (hopefully) understand. "Expressive language" is language we generate or produce. Oral language is spoken language, or speech. Written language is handwriting or print.

Specialists who study normal language development in children have noted the following universal, developmental features:

- Oral language development precedes and is the foundation for written language development. Furthermore, the child's degree of oral language competence is strongly correlated and predictive of the child's facility in learning to read and write and of their overall competence in written language. Said another way, a young child's listening and speaking vocabulary sets immediate boundaries in terms of what a child is able to read and understand. A child with a sparse listening and speaking vocabulary will likewise be limited in understanding what he reads, even if he is successful in decoding the written words.
- Receptive and expressive language do not develop simultaneously or at a parallel pace, particularly in the early stages of development. Especially in oral language, receptive language development generally precedes expressive language: children are able to listen before they are able to speak. Said another way, children need to understand and comprehend language before they are asked to produce it. For example, children need to hear new vocabulary used in meaningful contexts on repeated occasions before they develop an understanding of that vocabulary and then are able to use it in their own language. Likewise, children need many opportunities to listen to narrative descriptions (in adult commentary, books read aloud, and so on) before they can be expected to produce narrative descriptions themselves, either orally or in writing.

Each of these two insights can usefully guide instruction. But let us focus on the first one for a moment. Perhaps the most important sentences are these: "A young child's listening and speaking vocabulary sets immediate boundaries in terms of what a child is able to read and understand. That is, a child with a sparse listening and speaking vocabulary will likewise be limited in understanding what he reads, even if he is successful in decoding the written words." What these sentences point out is the extent to which successful reading depends not only on decoding skills but also on knowledge and vocabulary, which, in the early years, must be gained mostly, if not wholly, through oral language.

The National Reading Panel, a group of experts who reviewed all the scientific research that has been done on reading, made this important point in its final report, published in 2000. The report describes the challenge that still faces a reader, even once the reader has learned to decode: "A reader who encounters a strange word in print can decode the word to speech. If it is in the reader's oral vocabulary, the reader will be able to understand it. If the word is not in the reader's oral vocabulary, the reader will have to determine the meaning by other means, if possible. Consequently, the larger the reader's vocabulary . . . the easier it is to make sense of text."

In other words, to be successful as a reader a child needs to bring at least two things to the table; the ability to decode words, and the ability to recognize and make sense of the words once they have been decoded. If either of these is lacking, the child will not be able to comprehend what is being read.

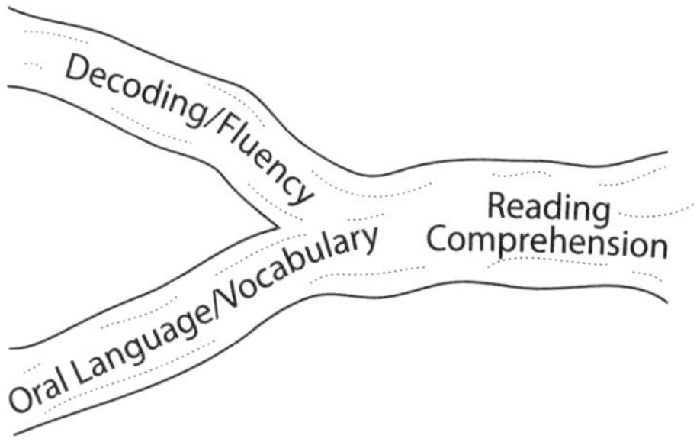

As a second-grade teacher, you should have your eye on the point in the not-too-distant future when children will be asked to switch from listening to reading as their primary means of getting information. This transition from "learning to read" to "reading to learn" is a crucial "bridge" children have to cross if they are going to prosper in the later years of their education, when a great deal depends on being able to read independently with understanding. To ensure that children are able to cross this bridge, you need to teach decoding skills while also enriching the child's oral language skills. You need to train the eye to read print from left to right and to decode fluently, but you also need to feed the ear a steady diet of oral language so the children will be familiar with many of the words their eyes will soon be decoding. The stream of oral language should begin early and should continue at least until children have become effective readers who can read passages of a thousand or more words with relative ease and comprehension. It should certainly continue all the way through second grade.

How can you build oral language skills? One of the most important ways is by reading aloud. You should aim to read aloud for at least 20–30 minutes every day, preferably more, and your readings should include a wide variety of materials—poems as well as prose, and nonfiction as well as fiction. Variety is important because a book on insects or a read-aloud selection on China or civil rights will introduce children to a different set of vocabulary words than a fictional story like "How the Camel Got His Hump." You can use the Core Knowledge topics in science, history, and the arts to guide your selection of non-fiction topics. After each read aloud, children should have an opportunity to listen to and participate in a discussion on the events, characters, words, ideas, or lessons in the story. If regular read alouds in fiction *and nonfiction* are not included in your language arts program, you should supplement your program.

Although listening to stories is vitally important, second graders also need opportunities to develop other basic language skills, such as clearly communicating needs and desires; understanding and giving verbal descriptions of experiences, people, or objects; understanding and giving directions and explanations; and using language to express an opinion or to pretend.

Supplemental Essay #3

How to Build Vocabulary

Because a robust vocabulary is essential for successful reading, it is almost impossible to overstate the importance of building vocabulary in the early grades. Children with inadequate vocabularies will encounter difficulties in reading comprehension in later grades, even if they have good decoding skills. Therefore, beginning in the earliest grades, schools should emphasize building vocabulary as well as teaching decoding skills.

Unfortunately, this does not always happen. In fact, some schools have begun to decrease the amount of time spent on history and science and other subjects in order to increase the amount of time they can spend teaching beginning reading skills (e.g., decoding). This is a well-intended but harmful approach, because the vocabulary words children would have learned in history and science and the arts include many words they will need to become successful readers.

Researchers have established that children learn words gradually, as a result of many exposures. Although a child may say, “I know that word,” or “I don’t know that word,” in fact, knowing a word is not an all-or-nothing matter. There are degrees of word knowledge. Many experts note four stages:

1. The child has never encountered the word.
2. The child has heard the word but doesn’t know what it means.
3. The child has heard the word several times and has some sense of the context in which the word is used, e.g., “It has something to do with food”.
4. The child knows the word and can understand it in speech and writing.

Movement from stage 1 to stage 4 is gradual and may require many exposures.

Researchers have also established that children (and people generally) learn a great deal of vocabulary indirectly, without ever being presented with a definition or doing formal vocabulary work. This can be demonstrated mathematically. A college-bound 12th grader knows between 60,000 and 100,000 words. Experts disagree on the exact numbers, but even if one uses the lower estimates, it means that the child must have learned more than 3,000, and possibly as many as 5,000, words a year, every year since birth. This is many more words than could be taught explicitly in schools. Vocabulary experts suggest that perhaps 500 words can be explicitly taught in school each year, but probably relatively few schools actually succeed in teaching so many words. It is therefore clear that children learn the great majority of words indirectly, or implicitly, by deducing the meaning of a word based on multiple exposures in different contexts, and not through explicit vocabulary instruction.

Since children learn so many words indirectly, one of the most effective ways of building vocabulary is to increase the amount children read and/or hear; research suggests that this may be a more effective way of increasing vocabulary than any specific direct instruction technique. In the early grades, when children are learning to read for themselves, they can take in relatively few words through the eye; their primary channel for learning is still the ear. That is why it is crucial that teachers in the early grades provide children with a steady, rich diet of oral language, including many read alouds.

To ensure that children are exposed to a wide range of vocabulary, read alouds should include not only fiction but also plenty of nonfiction in areas like history, science, and the arts. Each of these subjects introduces children to words, phrases, and ideas that are less likely to be encountered if read alouds are limited to fiction. *This is a very important point: properly understood, vocabulary instruction is not just an "English" or "language arts" topic; it extends across every subject in the curriculum.*

In the past, the most common kind of vocabulary instruction involved giving lists of words to children who could read. Teachers would provide matching dictionary definitions or ask children to find dictionary definitions, and then children would memorize the definitions for a quiz. Researchers now believe this kind of instruction is of limited value. Children often have difficulty choosing appropriate meanings from a dictionary and do not always gain the information they need from dictionary-style definitions. Also, children in the early grades are still learning to read and so can make only limited use of dictionaries.

Children need some explanation of what a word means, but they also need to see how the word functions in various contexts. Most dictionaries address the first need, though not always in a way that is clear to young children. Most dictionaries do not illustrate how words are used, because multiple examples of usage would make the dictionary too large for convenient use—and yet examples of usage are precisely what children need.

Instead of just giving dictionary-style definitions, you can explain a new word by using words children already know and then giving several examples of usage. These examples will help children see, or hear, how the word is used, and how its meaning relates to other words around it. For example, for the word *delicate*, a dictionary is likely to offer as many as seven or eight definitions of various senses, including "requiring careful handling" and "involving matters of a deeply personal nature." This information may not be optimally useful to children. A teacher can do better with just a little effort, for example, by explaining that "something that is delicate is fragile and needs to be handled carefully"; giving several examples of delicate objects (like china and glass) and asking children to name others; and then giving several sample sentences using the word, e.g., "The old newspaper was so delicate it fell apart in my hands."

Research tells us that a single exposure to a word is usually not enough for children to learn the word. One study found that young readers learn only 5–10% of unknown words from a single exposure: in other words, no better than 1 word in 10, and possibly as few as 1 in 20. Another study found that 12 encounters with a word reliably improved comprehension, whereas 4 did not. Both studies point to the same conclusion: vocabulary acquisition depends on multiple exposures to the word.

How can you achieve multiple exposures to words in your classroom? Obviously, frequent reading and reading aloud can help. Some words may appear more than once in a piece of writing. For example, the word *camel* may appear a dozen or more times in the story "How the Camel Got His Hump." You can also achieve repeated exposure by rereading some stories. During the first reading, children may get a general idea of what various words mean; during a second reading, they may be able to develop a more exact idea. A good discussion of a story can also result in several additional uses of the word, and may encourage the children to use some of the words themselves. Children are more likely to remember words they have used themselves.

You can also increase the chances of a child being exposed to certain words if you linger on a particular topic for several days or for a few weeks. For example, if you read a series of stories about farms and farm animals, you increase the chance that children will get multiple exposures to words like *cow*, *pig*, *rooster*, and *barn*.

You can also do formal vocabulary work. Although many words are learned indirectly, that does not mean that formal vocabulary work is useless. In fact, it can be very useful, as well as enjoyable. After describing what a word means and giving examples, you can use other tactics to get children actively involved in using the word and give them multiple exposures. Children can be asked to

- relate the new word to words they already know, e.g., given the word *ruby*, relate it to other precious objects like *diamonds* and *gold.*
- make up and discuss sentences using the word.
- discuss shades of meaning of the word when used in slightly different contexts, e.g., the difference between "the refrigerator stopped *running* when the power went out," and "the boy went *running* in a race."
- distinguish correct and incorrect examples of usage, e.g., "the army *courageously* charged towards the enemy" versus "the army *courageously* ran away." When children can distinguish sentences that use a word properly like the first sentence from nonsense sentences like the second sentence, they have a functional sense of a word's meaning.
- identify synonyms and/or antonyms for the word; in order to identify a similar or opposite word, children must have some sense of the word's meaning.
- match the word to a picture.
- discuss and define the word along with other words from the same domain, e.g., when defining *rooster*, refer to *chickens, chicks*, and *hens.*
- learn the word in conjunction with morphologically related words, e.g., with *elf,* learn *elfin;* with *Europe, European*; with *farm, farmer.*
- make word maps or "word webs" that show relationships between related words.
- discuss meaningful prefixes and suffixes within the word. Twenty prefixes account for 97% of the prefixed words in written English. Teaching key prefixes like *un-*, *re-*, *dis-* and *-in/-im/-il/-ir* can help children make sense of scores of words. (Note: the *Sequence* urges the teaching of specific prefixes and suffixes beginning in Grade 3, but instruction can begin earlier as opportunities arise.)

An excellent and brief (50-page) summary of vocabulary acquisition and instruction can be found in Steven A. Stahl, *Vocabulary Development* (Brookline Books, 1999), from which some of the insights and suggestions above are drawn.

Another excellent guide to classroom instruction is *Bringing Words to Life: Robust Vocabulary Instruction* by Isabel L. Beck, Margaret G. McKeown, and Linda Kucan (The Guilford Press, 2002).

Two outstanding collections of cognitive research on vocabulary acquisition and instruction are *Vocabulary Instruction: Research to Practice,* edited by James F. Baumann and Edward J. Kame'enui (The Guilford Press, 2004) and *The Nature of Vocabulary Acquisition,* edited by Margaret G. McKeown and Mary E. Curtis (Lawrence Erlbaum Associates, 1987).

II. Poetry

The Big Idea

Listening to and reading poetry helps children develop an appreciation of the music in the words and learn new vocabulary.

Text Resources

- (1) *Bed in Summer*
- (1) *Bee! I'm expecting you!*
- (2) *Buffalo Dusk*
- (3) *Caterpillars*
- (4) *Discovery*
- (5) *Harriet Tubman*
- (5) *Hurt No Living Thing*
- (6) *Lincoln*
- (7) *The Night Before Christmas*
- (7) *Rudolph Is Tired of the City*
- (8) ~~*Seashell*~~*
- (9) *Smart*
- (10) *Something Told the Wild Geese*
- (11) *Who Has Seen the Wind?*
- (12) *Windy Nights*
- (13) *There Was an Old Man with a Beard*
- (14) *There Is a Young Lady, Whose Nose*
- (14) *There Was an Old Man with a Nose*
- (15) *There Was an Old Man on a Hill*
- (15) *There Was a Young Lady Whose Bonnet*
- (16) *There Was an Old Lady of Chertsey*
- (16) *There Was a Young Lady Whose Chin*

*Unable to renew permissions for this particular version of *Seashell,* by Frederico Garcia Lorca; translated by K. F. Pearson. The poem will be removed from *Core Knowledge Text Resources for Grade 2.* You may locate the text for this poem on the Internet to share with your students.

What Students Should Already Know

Students in Core Knowledge schools should already be familiar with Mother Goose nursery rhymes, traditional poems, and modern favorites they have heard at home or in their Kindergarten and Grade 1 classes. They should have been exposed to rhyme, rhythm, alliteration, repetition, and personification.

What Students Need to Learn

- **The poems for this grade, including the ideas they express and some of the memorable words and phrases they contain**
- **Some poems may**
  - **use words or phrases that appeal to the senses of sight, sound, taste, smell, or touch.**
  - **include similes or metaphors that compare two or more things.**
  - **contain the same vowel sounds or consonant sounds within words.**
  - **contain rhyme that is not exact.**
- **A limerick**
  - **is a humorous poem with five lines.**
  - **has an AABBA rhyme scheme: (beard)A, (feared)A, (hen)B, (wren)B, (beard) A.**
  - **repeats the same rhythm in lines 1, 2, and 5, and in lines 3 and 4.**
- **Narrative poems have characters, settings, plot, and dialogue.**
- **Lyric poems are short, musical, and express the ideas and feelings of one speaker.**

What Students Will Learn in Future Grades

In future grades, students will review and extend their learning about poetry. They will be introduced to grade-appropriate poems at each level. Also, they will increase their knowledge of poetic terms, including *stanza* and *line* in Grade 4 and *onomatopoeia* and *alliteration* in Grade 5.

Vocabulary

Student/Teacher Vocabulary

alliteration: the repetition of initial consonants (T)

anaphora: the repetition of an initial sound, word, or phrase in successive lines (the word *by* in "Windy Nights") (T)

assonance: the repetition of vowel sounds within words (T)

consonance: the repetition of consonant sounds within and at the ends of words (T)

imagery: words or phrases that appeal to the senses of sight, hearing, touch, taste, and smell and help create mental images (T)

internal rhyme: rhyme that occurs within a line or verse (T)

limerick: a humorous five-line poem in which lines 1, 2, and 5 rhyme and have the same rhythm, and lines 3 and 4 rhyme and have the same rhythm (S)

lyric poem: a short poem that expresses the thoughts and feelings of a single speaker (S)

metaphor: a figure of speech in which a word or a phrase is used to describe a different thing; a resemblance is implied (T)

narrative poem: a poem that tells a story and often contains characters, dialogue, settings, and plot (T)

personification: a figure of speech in which an animal, object, or idea is given human characteristics (T)

quatrain: a four-line stanza or poem (T)

repetition: the repeating of a sound, word, phrase, or line (T)

rhyme: two or more words that end with the same or similar sounds (T)

rhyme scheme: the pattern of rhymes used in a poem, usually described by using letters of the alphabet to represent each rhyme, e.g. ABBA (T)

rhythm: a pattern of sound created by the arrangement of stressed and unstressed syllables in words (T)

simile: a figure of speech that directly compares two or more unlike things by using the words *like* or *as* (T)

slant rhyme: slant rhyme, or off rhyme, is rhyme that is not exact (T)

speaker: the person or object whose voice is heard in the poem; the speaker of a poem is not necessarily the poet (T)

Domain Vocabulary

Poetry and associated words:
description, descriptive, detail, sensory details, sight, sound, taste, touch, smell, poem, poet, poetry, poetic, conflict, mood, verse, musical, lyric, lyrical, emotions, imagination, content, form, free verse, figure of speech, symbol, symbolic, pattern, sound device, onomatopoeia, meter, beat, stress, accent, stressed, unstressed, vowel, consonant, measure, sound, meaning, sense, connotation, image, rhythmic, off rhyme, end rhyme, structure, line, stanza, couplet, theme, tone, punctuation, capitalization, dialect, slang, elision, allusion, *plus many words from the poems themselves, including Vocabulary in the selections below*

Materials

Instructional Masters 2a–3
Elements of Poetry, p. 61
Loony Limericks, p. 67

overhead projector, p. 61

chart paper, p. 61

an assortment of natural objects, such as stones, feathers, and shells, p. 61

picture of Abraham Lincoln, five-dollar bill, p. 66

a conch shell, p. 67

pennies, nickels, dimes, quarters, p. 68

copies of the poems from this section, p. 68

pointer, p. 68

mural paper, p. 69

colored pencils and markers, p. 69

Cross-curricular Connections

History and Geography

American: Westward Expansion

Native Americans

American: The Civil War

- Harriet Tubman
- President Abraham Lincoln

Music

Songs

- "Follow the Drinking Gourd"

Mathematics

Money

- Recognize relative values of a penny, nickel, dime, quarter, and dollar

Science

Cycles in Nature

Insects

- Distinguishing characteristics
- Life cycles: metamorphosis
- Social insects

At a Glance

The most important ideas for you are:

- Listening to poetry should be a delightful experience, but it can also be a learning experience as it introduces children to many words and phrases they might not otherwise encounter.
- Reading poetry can deepen vocabulary and improve children's ability to understand what they read.
- The speaker is the person or object whose voice you "hear" when you read a poem.
- Poetry often employs such literary devices as rhyme, rhythm, alliteration, and imagery.

What Teachers Need to Know

Background: Why Study Poetry?

This section offers a selection of poems by favorite 19th- and 20th-century writers. The purpose of this section is to help children appreciate the genre of poetry, build vocabulary, delight in the play of language, and perhaps become familiar with literary devices, such as alliteration, rhyme, rhythm, and imagery. As you teach this section, you may want to read with your class many more grade-appropriate poems by the same poets or by different poets.

Although some second graders may be able to read these poems on their own, we encourage you to read these poems aloud. Listening to poetry helps children develop an awareness of language that will help them become better writers and readers. By listening closely, by repeating certain lines or phrases

Teaching Idea

Before you begin teaching poetry, check that children in your class are able to differentiate between poetry and other forms of literature they may know. Ask them to name their favorite poems and poets. Invite volunteers to recite any poems or passages from poems they might know by heart.

in a poem, or by reciting poems by heart, children continue to build phonemic awareness, to learn new vocabulary words, and to develop an understanding of literary techniques used in poetry and other genres.

Children should experience the poems in print as well as oral form. You may wish to project the poem on a screen using an overhead projector, pass out copies, or use the Listen My Children *poetry anthology for this grade, so that children can follow along as you read aloud and consult the poem after the first reading.*

To encourage second graders to develop an appreciation for poetry, be sure to give them opportunities to write their own poems.

Teaching Idea

Children should have many opportunities to write poetry during the year, and the poems in this section provide a great resource to show the variety of kinds of poems. You may use the poetry in this section to model a pattern for the children to follow in writing a poem.

Reading Poetry Aloud

When you read poems to second graders, read them aloud several times. Speak slowly and clearly, pausing slightly for punctuation marks. Use your voice to emphasize the musical nature of the words, the poem's rhymes or rhyme scheme, and the rhythm. For purposes of highlighting rhythm, read those poems that have a regular pattern of accented and unaccented syllables in a singsong manner. To make characters in narrative poems come alive, try using different voices when you read lines of dialogue (e.g., in "Lincoln," and "The Night Before Christmas").

Teaching Idea

Give the children Instructional Masters 2a and 2b, Elements of Poetry, before you begin covering any poems. This graphic organizer lists key elements of a poem that you will discuss with your class (i.e., title, author, characters, setting, and subject). After the discussion of each poem, you can fill out Master 2b as a class to help provide continuity to the teaching of poems throughout the year. Please note that the graphic organizer is a tool that can be customized for use throughout the curriculum.

Focusing on Meaning

After you read a poem, discuss it. Ask questions such as these:

- Who or what is the poem about?
- What happens?
- Where do events take place?
- When do events take place?
- Why do certain events happen?

If necessary, provide additional information that will help children grasp the meaning of the poem, including definitions of difficult words, unfamiliar cultural references, or historical allusions. Then help children paraphrase the events in the poem in their own words.

After discussion, read the poem at least one more time, inviting children to join in by repeating certain words, phrases, or lines they recall. Or read the poem line by line, or sentence by sentence, inviting children to echo the lines back to you one at a time.

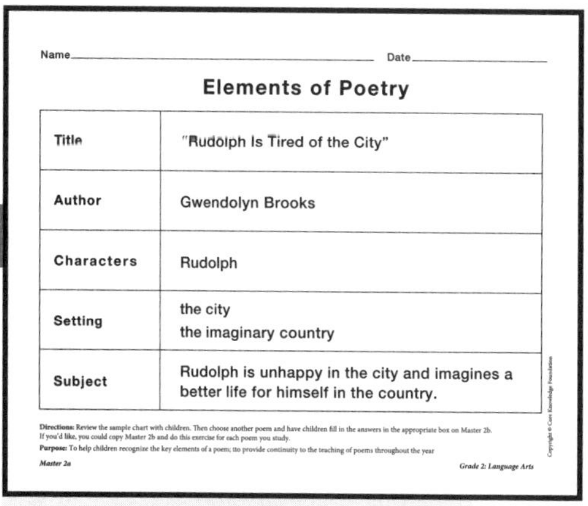

Name________________ Date________

Elements of Poetry

Title	"Rudolph Is Tired of the City"
Author	Gwendolyn Brooks
Characters	Rudolph
Setting	the city the imaginary country
Subject	Rudolph is unhappy in the city and imagines a better life for himself in the country.

Directions: Review the sample chart with children. Then choose another poem and have children fill in the answers in the appropriate box on Master 2b. If you'd like, you could copy Master 2b and do this exercise for each poem you study.

Purpose: To help children recognize the key elements of a poem; tto provide continuity to the teaching of poems throughout the year

Master 2a *Grade 2: Language Arts*

Copyright © Core Knowledge Foundation

Use Instructional Masters 2a and 2b.

Focusing on Literary Elements and Devices

One of the pleasures of reading poetry is being able to recognize different literary devices that a poet uses. Some devices—such as alliteration, assonance, consonance, and rhyme—highlight the music of the words. Other devices, such as imagery and metaphor, help convey meaning. In the following chart, you will see some literary devices commonly found in poetry.

II. Poetry

Teaching Idea

You do not need to introduce these literary terms to your class. However, you can call attention to these devices as you read. For example, to help children become aware of assonance, ask questions such as, "Which two words have the same o sound?" or to help them recognize imagery, ask "Which words or phrases appeal to your sense of smell?"

Literary Device	Definition	Example
alliteration	the repetition of initial consonants	The firelight flickered on his face
anaphora	the repetition of an initial sound, word, or phrase in successive lines	By at the gallop goes he / By at the gallop he goes
assonance	the repetition of vowel sounds with words	A crisping leaf, and kindled them
consonance	the repetition of consonant sounds within and at the end of words	Nor harmless worms that creep
elision	the omission of an unstressed syllable to achieve a pattern of rhythm	She was mighty sad to leave 'em
imagery	words or phrases that appeal to the senses of sight, hearing, touch, taste, and smell and help create mental images	All the sagging orchards / Steamed with amber spice
internal rhyme	rhyme that occurs within a line or verse	Nor dancing gnat, nor beetle fat
metaphor	a figure of speech in which a word or a phrase is used to describe a different thing; a resemblance is implied	"More rapid than coursers they came" compares flying reindeer to eagles.
personification	a figure of speech in which an animal, object, or idea is given human characteristics	Whenever the trees are crying aloud
quatrain	a four-line stanza or poem	Bee! I'm expecting you! / Was saying yesterday / To Somebody you know / That you were due
repetition	the repeating of a sound, word, phrase, or line	Nothing much but chew and chew
rhyme	two or more words that end with the same or similar sounds	night, candle-light
rhyme scheme	the pattern of rhymes used in a poem, usually described by using letters of the alphabet to represent each rhyme (ABBA)	In winter I get up by night / And dress by yellow candle-light (AA)
rhythm	a pattern of sound created by the arrangement of stressed and unstressed syllables in words	There WAS an OLD MAN with a BEARD
simile	a figure of speech that directly compares two or more unlike things by using the words *like* or *as*	And he looked like a peddlar
slant rhyme	slant rhyme, or off rhyme, is rhyme that is not exact	week, work

Introducing Seasonal and Weather-Related Poems

When reading the following poems, you may use some or all of the information provided to help children understand what the poem is about, what literary devices it contains, and who wrote it. Suggested teaching strategies and activities are also provided.

Bed in Summer

Author Information: Robert Louis Stevenson (1850–1894) was a British novelist and poet. Although best known for his adventure novels *Kidnapped* and *Treasure Island,* he also wrote poems for children. This poem is from Stevenson's beloved classic collection of poetry, *A Child's Garden of Verses* (1885).

Summary of Content: The speaker of this lyric poem is a child who objects to going to bed during daylight in the summer. Explain to the class that this poem was written before wires brought electricity into people's homes. The first two lines in "Bed in Summer" refer to the fact that families in the 19th century lit oil lamps and candles for light.

Literary Elements and Devices: rhyme scheme (AA BB CC DD EE BB), imagery (yellow candle-light, the sound of the grown-up people's feet), consonance (In, winter) (1)

> **Teaching Idea**
> You may wish to teach "Bed in Summer" and some other poems in this section in conjunction with Section I, "Cycles in Nature," in Science. Be sure children understand why it is that days are longer in summer and shorter in winter. Children may also enjoy writing "imitation" poems, e.g., "Bed in Spring" or "Bed in Fall."

Bee! I'm expecting you!

Author Information: Emily Dickinson (1830–1886) spent nearly all of her life in the small New England town of Amherst, Massachusetts. During her lifetime, 11 of her poems were published. After Dickinson's death, her sister Lavinia found and rescued more than a thousand of Dickinson's poems hidden in a box. Dickinson is now widely considered one of the greatest American poets.

Summary of Content: In this poem, the speaker is a fly. The fly writes a letter to the bee, asking when the bee will arrive.

Vocabulary: expecting: looking forward to; **due:** scheduled to arrive; **clover:** a plant with three leaves and small white flowers

Literary Elements and Devices: personification (the fly writes the bee a letter), rhyme (you, due; by, Reply, Fly), slant rhyme (Week, work; back, thick), punctuation (dashes highlight important words and break up the rhythm), alliteration (Birds, back), imagery (Clover warm and thick), speaker (a fly), quatrains (four-line stanzas) (1)

> **Teaching Idea**
> After reading "Bee! I'm expecting you!" ask children if they can guess what time of year it is in the poem. Read the poem a second time, inviting children to listen for clues. It appears to be spring, when birds and bugs return after the winter and the clover thickens. You might ask which month children think is meant by "the Seventeenth." You may also wish to invite children to write poems of their own using this poem's "letter to an animal" format as a template, e.g., "Spider, I'm expecting you" or "Fly, I'm detesting you."

Who Has Seen the Wind?

Author Information: Christina Rossetti (1830–1894) was born in London, England. Like her older brother, the Pre-Raphaelite painter Dante Gabriel Rossetti, she wrote lyric poetry and ballads. Her first book of poems, *Goblin Market,* was published in 1862.

Summary of Content: This lyric poem focuses on what happens to a few leaves when the wind passes by. Although the wind is invisible, one can clearly see its presence by watching the actions of the leaves.

Vocabulary: trembling: shaking; **bow:** bend down

Literary Elements and Devices: repetition (Who has seen the wind), rhyme (you, through; I, by), personification (the leaves bow down their heads), alliteration (neither, nor), consonance (when, bow, down), assonance (wind, is, passing) (11)

> **Teaching Idea**
> After reading "Who Has Seen the Wind?" invite children to write a poem about something that's invisible or hard to see, e.g., air, gravity, heat.

> **Teaching Idea**
> **After reading "Windy Nights," invite children to imagine why the man in the poem keeps riding by in the night. Have them write a few sentences on the subject and draw a picture of the man. Post the poem on the wall, surrounded by student interpretations.**

Windy Nights

Author Information: Robert Louis Stevenson also wrote this poem.

Summary of Content: This lyric poem contains an extended metaphor in which the sound of the wind is compared to a horseback rider passing back and forth on a highway.

Vocabulary: set: fixed in position; **gallop:** ride at a fast pace

Literary Elements and Devices: repetition (gallop), anaphora (the repetition of *by* at the beginning of lines in the last stanza), alliteration (low, loud), personification (the trees are crying aloud), rhyme scheme (ABABCC DEDGDGG), metaphor (the poem compares the sound of the wind to the sound of a rider galloping back and forth), imagery (all night long in the dark and wet), assonance (in, night, fires), consonance (highway, low) (12)

Poems About Animals

> **Cross-curricular Teaching Idea**
> **Read "Buffalo Dusk" during the second-grade history lesson on Native Americans from the Westward Expansion section to underscore the effect of the near extermination of the buffalo on Native Americans.**

Buffalo Dusk

Author Information: Poet, historian, journalist, and folklorist Carl Sandburg (1878–1967) was born in Galesburg, Illinois. One of the most popular poets of his time, he wrote poems to celebrate the United States and its people. He won the Pulitzer Prize in 1940 for the biographical work *Abraham Lincoln: The War Years* and in 1951 for *Complete Poems.*

Background: Buffalo were once plentiful on the Great Plains of the Midwest. In the late 1800s, they were nearly hunted to extinction. Tourists shot buffalo for sport, and hunters killed them for meat and hides they could sell. This wanton slaughter most affected Native American tribes that depended on the buffalo for food, shelter, and clothing. However, the buffalo has recently been making a comeback.

Summary of Content: The speaker of this poem laments the disappearance of the buffalo from the prairie.

Vocabulary: dusk: twilight; **buffalo:** ox-like mammals also known as bison; **pawed:** scraped with a foot; **prairie:** a large area of flat, rolling grassland; **sod:** grass-covered soil held together by matted roots (common on the Great Plains); **pageant:** a grand public display or show

Literary Elements and Devices: repetition (the buffalo are gone), alliteration (pawed, prairie; pawing, pageant), consonance (down, pawing), assonance (great, heads, pageant) (2)

Caterpillars

Author Information: Aileen Fisher (1906–2002) was born in Iron River, Michigan. She received the National Council of Teachers of English Award for Excellence in Poetry for Children in 1978. In books such as *In the Woods, In the Meadow, In the Sky* (1965) and *Sing of the Earth and Sky: Poems About Our Planet and the Wonders Beyond* (2001) she often deals with the unique way a child observes the world of nature.

Summary of Content: This poem conveys the limited activities and capabilities of a caterpillar but also celebrates the remarkable transformation that the caterpillar will soon undergo.

> **Teaching Idea**
> **After reading "Caterpillars," have children write a poem pretending to be a butterfly emerging from a cocoon.**

Vocabulary: caterpillar: the wormlike, wingless larvae of butterflies

Literary Elements and Devices: rhythm (NOthing MUCH but CHEW and CHEW), rhyme scheme (AA BB CC AA), repetition (chew, by), alliteration (be, butterfly), consonance (just, eat, what) (3)

Discovery

Author Information: Harry Behn (1898–1973) graduated from Harvard University. A professor and Hollywood film writer, he also wrote and illustrated children's stories and poems. Among his books for children are *The Little Hill* (1949) and *The House Beyond the Meadow* (1955).

Summary of Content: The speaker of this narrative poem tells about his adventures with his friend Joe during a spring outing.

Vocabulary: tadpole: the larva of a frog or toad that lives in water and has a tail and gills; **musty:** wet and moldy; **lichens:** crusty, fungus-like plants that grow on rock and wood; **fiddleheads**: the coiled fronds of ferns; **uncoiling:** unwinding; **Jack-in-the-pulpits:** spring wildflowers; **spotted salamanders:** lizard-like creatures with black and yellow bodies and two rows of yellow spots on their backs

Literary Elements and Devices: rhyme (Joe, grow; row, below; show, go; Joe, know), alliteration (left, last; found, fiddleheads, ferns), imagery (musty log; ferns uncoiling out of the moss), consonance (froggy, legs, beginning, grow), characters (the speaker, Joe) (4)

Hurt No Living Thing

Author Information: Christina Rossetti (author of "Who Has Seen the Wind?") also wrote this poem.

Summary of Content: This one-sentence poem is a plea to the reader to be mindful of even the smallest of creatures.

Vocabulary: ladybird: a ladybug, or a small, brightly colored beetle; **gnat:** a small, biting two-winged fly

Literary Elements and Devices: rhyme (thing, wing; leap, creep), alliteration (chirping cheerily; light of leap), rhythm (Nor MOTH with DUSTy WING), imagery (dusty wing, cricket chirping), anaphora (the repetition of *Nor* at the beginning of lines), consonance (Nor harmless worms), assonance (gnat, fat), internal rhyme (gnat, fat) (5)

Something Told the Wild Geese

Author Information: Born in New York, Rachel Field (1894–1942) was a poet, novelist, and playwright. She won the Newbery Medal in 1930 for *Hitty: Her First Hundred Years*. In 1945, she won the Caldecott Medal for *Prayer for a Child*.

Summary of Content: This lyric poem describes the instinctual behavior of wild geese to migrate in fall. The green leaves, glossy berries, and summer sun all belie the inevitable approach of cold weather and the necessity of migration to warmer climates.

Vocabulary: luster-glossed: shiny; **sagging orchards:** hanging with the weight of the ripe fruit; **amber:** brownish yellow; **spice:** sweet-smelling scent; **stiffened:** tensed

Literary Elements and Devices: rhyme (go, snow; glossed, frost; spice, ice); repetition (something told the wild geese), alliteration (steamed, spice; summer,

Teaching Idea

You may wish to teach "Discovery" in conjunction with Section I, "Cycles in Nature," in Science, which includes an examination of the life cycle of a frog. The poem celebrates the spirit of science: "how much more there is to know!"

Cross-curricular Teaching Idea

You may wish to teach "Bee! I'm expecting you!" (p. 63), as well as "Caterpillars" (p. 64), and "Hurt No Living Thing" during the second-grade science lesson on insects. Point out bees, flies, butterflies, caterpillars, crickets, grasshoppers, and other insects mentioned in these poems. Discuss how they help or harm people, what they look like, and what life cycles they go through.

Teaching Idea

Tell children that "Discovery" is a narrative poem. Remind them that a narrative poem tells a story and often contains characters, dialogue, setting, and plot. Encourage volunteers to identify the characters (Joe and the speaker), the setting of the poem (the woods in spring), and the plot (two boys explore, looking in a puddle, under a log, and under a rock to find wonders of nature).

Teaching Idea

Invite children to write their own "Hurt No Living Thing" poem by using their knowledge of animals to fill in the blanks in a form like this: "Hurt no living thing; [A], nor [B], nor [C], nor [D], etc." Ambitious children can try to make their lines rhyme.

sun), imagery (fields lay golden, leaves were green and strong, warm feathers, amber spice), consonance (told, wild), assonance (summer, sun) (10)

Poems About People

Harriet Tubman

Author Information: Award-winning author Eloise Greenfield (born 1929) has published 38 children's books, including novels, poetry, and biographies. Much of her writing is about African-American family life.

Background: Harriet Tubman was an African-American woman who was born a slave in Maryland in 1820 or 1821. In 1849, she escaped to Philadelphia and worked to free other slaves. She became a conductor on the Underground Railroad, which was a secret network of people who hid and protected slaves and gave them food and clothing as they ran away from plantations. "Conductors" like Tubman helped slaves get from one "station" (safe house) to the next. Tubman is believed to have made 19 trips back to the South and helped 300 slaves, including her parents, travel to states where they could escape slavery.

Summary of Content: The speaker of this narrative poem celebrates Harriet Tubman's character, her courage, and her determination to be free.

Vocabulary: take stuff: slang for putting up with disrespectful talk or actions; **mighty:** very; **slave catchers:** men who found and returned escaped slaves for money

Literary Elements and Devices: rhyme (neither, either; others, brothers), rhythm (She RAN for her FREEdom NINEteen TIMES), alliteration (nothing, neither; mean, men), repetition (Harriet Tubman didn't take no stuff; and didn't stay one either), dialect (didn't take no, wasn't scared of nothing neither), elision (dropping of the *th* in *them*) (5)

Lincoln

Author Information: Nancy Byrd Turner (1880–1971) was born in Virginia. She was an editor at the *Atlantic Monthly* and other magazines and published many children's poems, novels, and song lyrics.

Summary of Content: This narrative poem explores the childhood of Abraham Lincoln, the 16th president of the United States. The speaker of the poem celebrates Lincoln's strong will, especially his determination to get an education despite the obstacle of poverty. The speaker reflects on the way Lincoln met his challenges and why we still regard him as a heroic figure today.

Vocabulary: earnest: serious and determined; **trudged:** walked in a heavy-footed way, plodded; **weary:** tired; **woodmen's ways:** knowledge about living or working in the woods; **seasoned:** dried or cured; **bough:** branch; **crisping:** becoming brittle; **kindled:** burned; **ruddy:** reddish; **etched:** clearly marked; **gloom:** dark; **humble:** modest

Literary Elements and Devices: rhyme (get, set; stem, them; face, place), alliteration (wise, woodmen's, ways), imagery (ruddy blaze, firelight flickered on his face), rhythm (He GATHered SEAsoned BOUGH and STEM), assonance (met, them, when), consonance (And then no candle) (6)

Cross-curricular Teaching Idea

When teaching the section on seasonal cycles in second-grade Science, read "Something Told the Wild Geese" to your class during the lesson on the fall season to highlight the processes of ripening and migration.

Teaching Idea

After reading "Something Told the Wild Geese," invite children to write a "something told" poem about another animal. The poem should describe something a particular animal knows by instinct, e.g., "Something told the groundhog it was time to wake up," or "Something told the mouse that danger was near."

Cross-curricular Teaching Idea

Read "Lincoln" and "Harriet Tubman" when your children study the Civil War and Harriet Tubman. Also, have children read or sing the words to the song "Follow the Drinking Gourd" (found in the Text Resources), which slaves sang about the Underground Railroad.

Teaching Idea

While teaching "Lincoln," show children a picture of Lincoln's face, for example, from the five-dollar bill.

Teaching Idea

After reading "Lincoln," invite children to write a poem about another historical figure they have learned about in history, music, or science.

Rudolph Is Tired of the City

Author Information: Gwendolyn Brooks (1917–2000) won the Pulitzer Prize for *Annie Allen.* She was the first African-American poet to win this award. Her poems often focus on the experiences of urban African Americans.

Summary of Content: This poem captures a child's yearning to escape the towering buildings of the city and to enjoy the open space of the country.

Vocabulary: spread: stretch, extend, open out; **tend:** look after

Literary Elements and Devices: rhyme (away, day; too, do; chores, doors), alliteration (ch̲ickens, ch̲ores), repetition (spread), rhythm (these BUILDings ARE too CLOSE to ME), capitalization for emphasis (PUSH, A-SPREADING), consonance (all, left), assonance (spread, breath) (7)

There Was an Old Man with a Beard

Author Information: When he was a teenager, British poet Edward Lear (1812–1888) worked as an illustrator, drawing detailed pictures of animals. He published *Book of Nonsense* (1846), his first volume of humorous poems, for the Earl of Derby's children.

Summary of Content: This poem is a limerick about a man whose beard becomes home to two owls, a hen, four larks, and a wren.

Vocabulary: larks: songbirds; **wren:** a small, brownish bird

Literary Elements and Devices: rhyme scheme (AABBA), repetition (beard), alliteration (b̲uilt, b̲eard), rhythm (TWO OWLS and a HEN / FOUR LARKS and a WREN) (13)

Other Poems

Smart

Author Information: Shel Silverstein (1932–1999) was born in Chicago. A well-known children's poet, he was also an accomplished cartoonist, singer, and songwriter. His popular books of poetry include *Where the Sidewalk Ends* (1974), *A Light in the Attic* (1981), and *Falling Up* (1996).

Summary of Content: In this humorous narrative poem, the speaker tells how he parlays a dollar bill into different amounts of coins—from two quarters to five pennies. Throughout the poem, the speaker mistakenly believes he has made advantageous trades. Even at the end, when he shows his father what he has done with the dollar, he ironically misjudges his father's stunned reaction.

Vocabulary: swapped: traded; **seed-feed store:** a store that sells food for animals and seeds for planting

Literary Elements and Devices: rhyme (son, one; see, three), alliteration (s̲martest, s̲on), consonance (along, old, blind), rhythm (and TRADed THEM to LOU), imagery (two shiny quarters, got red in the cheeks), elision (dropping of the *be* in *because*), slang (he don't know), characters (the speaker, his father, Lou, Bates, Hiram Coombs), assonance (seed, feed) (9)

Teaching Idea

After reading "Rudolph Is Tired of the City," discuss the pros and cons of living in the city versus living in the country. Have children share their own experiences of city life or country life. Children may also enjoy hearing the well-known story of "The Town Mouse and the Country Mouse."

Teaching Idea

Connect "There Was an Old Man with a Beard" to the term *limerick*. Offer children one or two more examples of limericks (many can be found online). Then use Instructional Master 3, *Loony Limericks.*

Name__________ Date__________

Loony Limericks

Read Edward Lear's limerick. Then use a word from the box to complete each line in the limerick below.

There Was an Old Man with a Beard

There was an Old Man with a beard,
Who said, "It is just as I feared!—
Two Owls and a Hen,
Four Larks and a Wren,
Have all built their nests in my beard!"

— Edward Lear

rule	long	fool	song	school

There was a new student in school,
Who thought he would break every rule.
He talked all day long,
And sang a loud song.
So now he just seems like a fool!

Make Up a Limerick Clap the beat, or rhythm, as you read each limerick again. Look at the pattern of the rhyming words. Then work with a partner to make up a new limerick.

Purpose: To introduce the term *limerick* and a limerick's rhyme scheme by reading, completing, and then creating limericks

Master 3 *Grade 2: Language Arts*

Copyright ©Core Knowledge Foundation

Use Instructional Master 3.

Cross-curricular Teaching Idea

Teach "Smart" after children have studied money as part of the math curriculum. Divide children into groups and have them perform the actions of the poem with real coins to give them a better understanding of the speaker's errors. Ask children to explain why each trade the speaker makes is a bad trade. Have them calculate the amount of money (number of cents) the speaker has after each trade. Invite children to make a "bad trade" poem of their own.

Teaching Idea

Before teaching "The Night Before Christmas," lead a discussion on the many different holidays that people celebrate. Remind children that not everyone celebrates the same holidays. During the month of December, introduce this poem and "A Christmas Carol" by Charles Dickens (p. 76) prior to the holiday vacation. You may wish to find poems written about other holidays as well.

The Night Before Christmas

Author Information: Clement C. Moore (1779–1863) was a well-known scholar and professor of classics. According to legend, he wrote this poem for his children in 1822. A family friend sent the poem to the *Troy Sentinel*, where it was published anonymously in 1823. Moore did not acknowledge that he wrote the poem until 22 years later.

Summary of Content: This classic narrative poem describes the arrival of St. Nicholas in his sleigh, which is pulled by a team of reindeer. On Christmas Eve, St. Nicholas comes down the chimney to deliver presents.

Vocabulary: 'Twas: It was; **stirring:** moving or waking; **nestled:** settled snugly and comfortably; **sugar-plums:** small balls of candy; **luster:** brilliance or radiance; **coursers:** swift horses; **dash:** move quickly; **twinkling:** brief span of time; **bound:** leap or bounce; **tarnished:** discolored; **pedlar:** (British variant of *peddler*) a person who travels about to sell goods for a living; **droll:** comical; **encircled:** surrounded; **clatter:** loud noise; **flash:** a sudden display of light; **mid-day:** noon; **house-top:** roof; **dread:** fear; **the down of a thistle:** the silky, feathery down from a kind of prickly plant; **'ere:** before

Literary Elements and Devices: rhyme scheme (ABBCCDDEEFF, and so on), alliteration (kerchief, cap), consonance (Away, window, flew), assonance (chubby, plump), rhythm (the MOON on the BREAST of the NEW FALLen SNOW), metaphor (compares the swift flying reindeer to eagles), simile (his cheeks were like roses, the beard on his chin was as white as the snow), imagery (The moon on the breast of the new fallen snow; I heard on the roof / The prancing and pawing of each little hoof), characters (Mama, Papa, St. Nicholas), dialogue ("Now, Dasher! Now, Dancer! Now, Prancer and Vixen!") (7)

Review

Below are some ideas for ongoing assessment and review activities. These are not meant to constitute a comprehensive list.

- Discuss with the class their favorite poems from this section. Have children explain what makes a poem their favorite and why. Then, provide children with an individual copy of their favorite poem, and have them illustrate the poem. Post these in the classroom.
- When possible, have children read the poems aloud. You may have the poems posted on a chart tablet and, during the day, give children the opportunity to come to the front with a pointer and read the poems.
- Prepare a reader's theater script of one or more of the poems. Have children practice the script and present it to another class.
- As a reinforcing activity for this section, have children create a four seasons mural based on the poems from this section that they heard or read. Using mural paper and colored markers or pencils, have them draw one panel for each season. Encourage them to incorporate quotations and images from poems they heard to illustrate the four seasons. For example, children might draw geese migrating ("Something Told the Wild Geese") for fall or St. Nicholas riding on his sleigh ("The Night Before Christmas") for winter.

Teaching Idea

We've included some additional poems not in the *Sequence* in the Text Resources packet. If you wish to extend your teaching of poetry, you may wish to add poems 14–16 in the Text Resources.

• While reading a poem such as "Buffalo Dusk" that describes the plight of the Native Americans, have children respond to the poem in a journal. How do they think that the Native Americans felt to see that the buffalo had practically disappeared? How does the poem make the children feel about the Native Americans? Ask children to think about and then reflect on the feelings of the characters.

• "The Night Before Christmas" is a poem that uses wonderful descriptive words. Use this poem to highlight the use of adjectives. Read the poem to the class, and then have them illustrate a picture of St. Nick to go with the poem. They should try to closely illustrate what the author describes. You may want to post the lines from the poem that describe St. Nick for children to use as they draw.

• You may also want to teach children how to write poems in the shape of the object they are describing. For example, children could write the poem "Caterpillars" in the shape of a Caterpillar. Have children first lightly draw a pattern on their paper of the shape that they want to use for their poem. Then, have them write the poem over the lines of the shape. When they are done, erase the pencil lines and the poem will take the shape of the object.

The Big Idea in Review

Listening to and reading poetry helps children develop an appreciation of the music in the words and learn new vocabulary.

More Resources

The titles listed below are offered as a representative sample of materials and not a complete list of everything that is available.

For children —

These books are generally intended to be read aloud, though some children may be able to read parts or all of the simpler texts.

• *Listen My Children: Poems for Second Graders* (Core Knowledge Foundation, 2001). Includes all the poems listed in the *Sequence* for Grade 2.

• *A Child's Garden of Verses*, by Robert Louis Stevenson and illustrated by Tasha Tudor (Simon & Schuster, 1999). Hardcover, 72 pages, ISBN 0689823827.

• *Favorite Poems Old and New*, selected by Helen Ferris (Doubleday Books for Young Readers, 1957). A treasury of over 700 poems, including many old favorites. Hardcover, 598 pages, ISBN 0385076967.

• *The Kingfisher Book of Family Poems*, selected by Belinda Hollyer (Kingfisher, 2003). ISBN 0753455579.

• *The Night Before Christmas*, by Clement Clark Moore and illustrated by Douglas Gorsline (Random House, 1975). Paperback, 32 pages, ISBN 0394830199.

For teachers —

• *Rose, Where Did You Get That Red? Teaching Great Poetry to Children*, by Kenneth Koch (Vintage Books, 1990). Kenneth Koch has inspired even children who "hate" poetry. Here is a teaching method that may inspire you as well. Paperback, 416 pages, ISBN 0679724710.

• *The Word in Play: Language, Music, and Movement in the Classroom* (Paul H. Brookes Publishing Company, 2004). The author offers practical, yet creative suggestions for exploring and creating poetry with children. ISBN 1557666164.

• Every Poet.com, www.everypoet.com, contains many links to classic poetry, as does the Poetry Lover's Page, www.poetryloverspage.com.

• Poetry Alive, www.poetryalive.com/products.html. Poetry Alive sells recording and teacher materials to help you bring poetry to life in the classroom.

• Poetry Teachers.com, www.poetryteachers.com, has suggestions for poetry theater, how to teach poetry, and poetry activities.

III. Fiction

A. Stories

Text Resources

17 *Beauty and the Beast*
18 *The Blind Men and the Elephant*
19 *A Christmas Carol*
20 *Before Breakfast*
21 *The Emperor's New Clothes*
22 *The Fisherman and His Wife*
23 *How the Camel Got His Hump*
24 *How Iktomi Lost His Eyes*
25 *How the Spider Symbol Came to the People*
26 *The Rabbit Dance*
27 *The Magic Paintbrush*
28 *El Pajaro Cu*
29 *How Wendy Met Peter Pan*
30 *Talk*
31 *The Tiger, the Brahman, and the Jackal*
32 *The Tongue-Cut Sparrow*

The Big Idea

Listening to and reading stories helps children develop an understanding of the elements of a story, build vocabulary, and understand cultural references.

What Students Should Already Know

Students should already be familiar with classic stories and folktales—including fables, myths, trickster tales, and fairy tales—from picture books and from their read-aloud experiences in Kindergarten and Grade 1.

What Students Need to Learn

- **The plots, major characters, outcomes, and lessons of the stories for this grade**
- **Fiction is a narrative that comes from a writer's imagination.**
- **Stories are a kind of fiction.**
- **Some stories are folktales.**
- **Some stories**
  - **describe magical people and events that could never happen.**
  - **describe realistic people and events that could happen.**
- **Fables are short, simple stories that teach a lesson about human behavior.**
- **Trickster tales are stories about a character who outsmarts larger, stronger characters.**

What Students Will Learn in Future Grades

In future grades, students will continue to learn about different kinds of stories.

Vocabulary

Student/Teacher Vocabulary

characters: the people or animals that take part in the action of a story (S)

dialogue: the words spoken by characters in a story (T)

fable: a short, simple story that conveys a moral about human behavior (S)

fairy tale: a story that often features members of a royal family, characters with supernatural powers, and magical transformations (S)

fantasy: a story that features characters with magical powers and/or impossible events (S)

folktale: an anonymous, traditional story; kinds of folktales include trickster tales, fairy tales, myths, legends, and tall tales (T)

legend: a traditional story about the past that may or may not be based on an actual event (S)

narration: the telling of a sequence of events (T)

plot: the chain of related events in a story (T)

pourquoi tale: a type of folktale that explains how or why something has come to be; the word *pourquoi* means "why" in French (T)

setting: the time and place of the action of a story (T)

trickster tale: a story about a character, often a small, skittish animal, such as a spider or a rabbit, who outsmarts larger, stronger characters (S)

Domain Vocabulary

Stories and associated words:
narrator, narrative, prose, fiction, short story, story, title, draw conclusions, make generalizations, compare, contrast, analyze, predict, prediction, clues, context clues, real, realistic, magical, story line, author's purpose, audience, detail, introduction, conclusion, chronological order, sequence, sequential, paragraph, trickster, Br'er Rabbit, Iktomi, Anansi, Coyote, moral, tale, novel, mood, time, place, conflict, internal, external, description, descriptive, beginning, middle, ending, event, sequence of events, theme, author, writer, characterization, dialect, oral, oral tradition, *plus words found in the stories themselves, including Vocabulary in the selections below*

Cross-curricular Connections

History and Geography

World: Geography
- The seven continents

World: Early Civilizations: Asia

India

China

World: Modern Civilization and Culture: Japan

American: Westward Expansion

Native Americans

Materials

Instructional Masters 1a–1b, 4, 5a–5b, 51–52

The S.T.O.R.Y. Method, p. 73

Elements of Stories, p. 73

T-Chart, p. 74

The Blind Men and the Elephant, p. 75

Venn Diagram, p. 79

cardboard box, p. 72

monster mask, p. 72

paintbrush, p. 72

colored markers or pencils, p. 73

world map or globe, p. 75

yam, p. 76

bundle of cloth, p. 76

a stool, p. 76

baby bottle, p. 77

index cards, p. 79

Note: D. Literary Terms is not an independent subsection in this handbook. The literary terms are covered within Language Arts in the following sections: *myth* (in Section B. Mythology of Ancient Greece); *tall tale* (in Section C. American Folk Heroes and Tall Tales); and *limerick* (in II. Poetry).

At a Glance

The most important ideas for you are:

- Listening to stories helps children understand the elements of stories, builds print awareness, and increases vocabulary, cultural literacy, and reading comprehension abilities.
- Fiction can include stories, folktales, fairy tales, legends, trickster tales, and myths.
- Folktales were first passed down orally before being written down.
- Stories include characters, dialogue, narration, plot, and setting.

What Teachers Need to Know

A. Stories

Background: Why Study Folktales and Other Stories?

Second graders will enjoy listening to stories with memorable characters and magical situations like those found in fairy tales, legends, and other kinds of folktales. They can easily understand the timeless lessons and values conveyed in the stories. They can often relate to problems faced by characters. For example, children can identify with Fern's attempt to save the runt's life in the excerpt from Charlotte's Web, *Beauty's desire to help her father in "Beauty and the Beast," and Wendy's temptation to follow Peter in the excerpt from* Peter Pan. *Since most of these stories are short, involve simple plots, and feature stock characters, second graders are able to follow what happens and to recall details.*

By listening carefully to classic folktales and other stories in this section, children will develop an awareness of language and increase their vocabulary, which will later help them become both better writers and readers. In addition, these stories will help children develop an appreciation for different types of fiction from different cultures and time periods. The selections come from Asia, Africa, Europe, and the Americas, yet reflect universal themes and experiences. Although these stories are meant to be read aloud, have children read silently some fiction designed for beginning readers to give them a sense of accomplishment. The suggested activities are for listening and speaking; children are not required to read the stories listed on their own. Although only a few chapters of the longer works are given in the Text Resources, you are strongly encouraged to read the whole book to children if time allows.

As second graders continue to build on their knowledge of stories, they will develop a strong foundation for the understanding and enjoyment of fiction. In addition to the selections listed above, be sure to expose children to other worthwhile picture books and read-aloud books, as well as to nonfiction such as biographies and books about science, history, music, and art. Remember that every book on a new subject introduces new vocabulary words and helps children become stronger readers.

Teaching Idea

As you progress through the selections in this section, have groups of children choose stories to act out for the class. First, review elements of drama from the first-grade sequence. Then have children find or create props such as a cardboard box (*Charlotte's Web*), a monster mask ("Beauty and the Beast"), or a paintbrush ("The Magic Paintbrush") to bring the story to life. You may wish to search online for reader's theater scripts.

Reading Stories Aloud

Make sure to read the story through to yourself before you read it aloud to children. Here are some ideas to consider when reading a story to your second-grade class.

- Speak clearly and slowly.
- Mimic actions described in the story.
- Pause and point to any pictures that help illustrate the text; when there are no pictures, suggest that children listen carefully to the narrative to create "pictures in their heads."
- Use your voice to emphasize the use of dialogue and the voices of different characters.
- For longer selections, pause occasionally and ask children questions about the characters and plot. What do they think will happen next?
- Read a story more than once to make certain your children understand it.
- If there are vocabulary words that children need to know for the story to make sense, you may wish to pre-teach them; other words can be discussed and explained after the first reading.

Focusing on Characters and Plot

After you read each story, thoroughly discuss the characters and plot with children. Ask the class the following types of "W" questions:

- *What* happens? *What* might happen next?
- *Who* is involved?
- *Where* do events take place?
- *When* do events take place?
- *Why* do certain events happen?

Help children paraphrase the events in the story in their own words.

Focusing on Literary Elements

Folktales share many literary elements common to all types of fiction: characters, dialogue, narration, plot, and setting. Some of these stories also feature literary devices described in the poetry section, including personification, metaphor and simile, and repetition of words, phrases, sentences, or events. For example, "How Iktomi Lost His Eyes" has speaking animals, and "Talk" is a cumulative tale in which story events are repeated in a predictable pattern.

When you read the stories in this section, you do not have to use the terms for literary elements. Instead, ask questions that will lead children to appreciate these elements. To help children identify personification, for example, ask, "In what ways is the sparrow in 'The Tongue-Cut Sparrow,' like a person?" To help children recognize sequence of events in the plot, ask,"What happens first? What happens next? What happens last?"

Teaching Idea

Drawing pictures to accompany a story is always helpful to increase understanding. Have children choose a favorite story event or character and then illustrate it. Display children's work on a bulletin board in your classroom throughout the year. Instructional Master 4, titled *The S.T.O.R.Y. Method,* is useful as you read and discuss stories with the class.

The S.T.O.R.Y. Method

S: *Start with the cover and/or the title:* If the story has a cover illustration, share it with students and invite them to make predictions about the story; if there is no cover illustration, read the title, pointing to each word, and ask if children have any predictions based on the title. Mention the author and illustrator.

T: *Tell the story:* Speak clearly and slowly but read the text with animation. When appropriate, use your voice to impersonate the voices and tones of different characters. You may also wish to mimic selected actions in the story.

O: *Offer information:* If necessary clarify story language. For hard vocabulary words, give a simple definition, or repeat the sentence using another word or phrase; if possible, relate the word to children's experience; if the vocabulary word is depicted in an illustration, point to the illustration; if it is unclear who or what a pronoun (e.g., he, she, it) refers to, reread the sentence to determine the reference. Address other difficult passages as needed.

R: *Review and analyze* Ask questions to review what happens in the story. Ask questions based on the "5 Ws": *Who* is involved? *What* happens? *Where* do the events take place? *When* do they take place? *Why* do certain events happen? Then ask students to go beyond the basic details of the story and make inferences. For example, ask them to infer emotions: "How do you think this character feels?" Ask them to relate story events to their own experiences: "Have you ever done what little Red Riding Hood does?" Ask hypothetical questions: "What might have happened if...?"

Y: *Your turn:* Invite students to retell or paraphrase the story in their own words. Don't worry if they change certain details of the story: that is in the best tradition of storytelling.

Directions: Here is a method you can use when you read aloud to children. It is called the S.T.O.R.Y method, and it will work for trade books, as well as the selections in the Text Resources.

Copyright ©Core Knowledge Foundation

Master 4 *Grade 2: Language Arts*

Use Instructional Master 4.

Name________________________ Date________

Elements of Stories

Title	"The Emperor's New Clothes"
Author	Hans Christian Anderson
Setting	the emperor's kingdom
Characters	the emperor, the dishonest weavers, the emperor's advisors, the townsfolk
Themes	It is important to be honest; do not let pride get the best of you.
Opening	"There once was an emperor..."
Ending	"...the emperor...wass blushing from head to toe, as everyone could plainly see."

Directions: Review the sample chart with children. Then choose another story and have children fill in the answers in the appropriate box on Master 5b. If you'd like, you could copy Master 5b and do this exercise for each story you study.

Purpose: To help children recognize the key elements of a story; to provide continuity to the teaching of stories throughout the year

Copyright ©Core Knowledge Foundation

Master 5a *Grade 2: Language Arts*

Use Instructional Masters 5a and 5b.

Teaching the Stories

The following information and suggested activities will help you teach each story in this section. Ask the children the Before Reading questions. In some cases, you may also wish to pre-teach a word that appears in the story, or pre-teach a concept that is important to understanding the story. After reading the story, be sure children understand the plot and characters by asking them the After Reading questions.

Fairy Tales

Beauty and the Beast

Before Reading: What do you think matters most—a person's looks or the way a person acts toward others? Why?

Vocabulary: merchant: a person who sells goods; **fortune:** great wealth; **blazing:** shining brightly; **pluck:** pick; **startled:** surprised; **shuddering:** trembling, shivering; **deceived:** fooled; **refuse:** say no to, decline; **faint:** weak; **gasped:** breathed deeply

After Reading: Why is the merchant poor? What happens after he picks a rose in the Beast's garden? How does Beauty feel about the Beast at first? Why do her feelings change? Do you think Beauty makes the right decision at the end of the story? Why or why not? (17)

Teaching Idea

Connect "Beauty and the Beast" to the saying "Don't judge a book by its cover" (p. 101).

The Emperor's New Clothes

Author Information: Hans Christian Andersen (1805–1875) was a Danish writer best known for his original fairy tales. The child of a poor shoemaker and a washerwoman, he failed at several careers before he turned to writing.

Before Reading: Have you ever pretended to know something because you didn't want to appear stupid?

Vocabulary: loom: a device for making thread or yarn by weaving strands together; **chief advisor:** an important person in the kingdom who gives advice; **dishonest:** untruthful, lying; **tricky:** clever; **hush:** a silence

After Reading: Why does the emperor give the two weavers a lot of money? Why does the emperor ask his chief advisor to visit the weavers? What happens when the emperor himself visits the weavers? How do the weavers trick the emperor and the rest of the kingdom? Who finally tells the truth at the end of the story? Why do you think it is a child who tells the truth in the end? What lesson do we learn from this story? (21)

Teaching Idea

Use a T-chart, found in the Instructional Masters, to compare the actions of the adults in the "The Emperor's New Clothes" to the actions of the boy in the poem "Smart" (p. 67). Compare and contrast the characters' displays of intelligence.

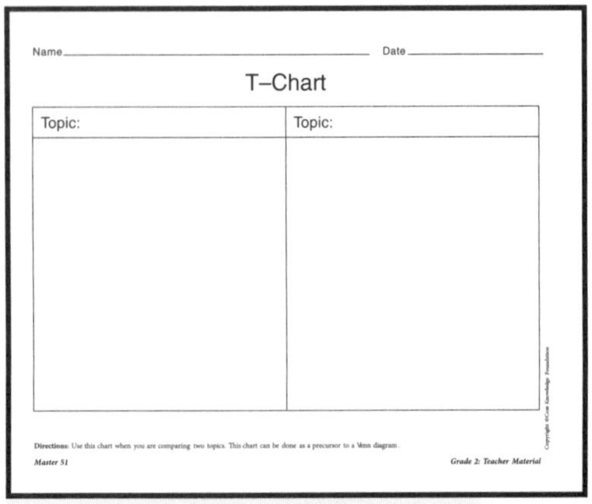
Name ______ Date ______

T–Chart

Topic:	Topic:

Directions: Use this chart when you are comparing two topics. This chart can be done as a precursor to a Venn diagram.

Master 51 *Grade 2: Teacher Material*

Use Instructional Master 51.

The Fisherman and His Wife

Author Information: Jacob Grimm (1785–1863) and his brother Wilhelm (1786–1859) began collecting German folktales in the early 1800s. The Brothers Grimm published more than two hundred tales as *Children's and Household Stories.*

Background: This is a repetitive tale in which events and sentences are repeated three times. It has these characteristics of a fairy tale: a universal setting, three wishes, a talking fish, and magic. As you read, invite children to repeat the fisherman's plea: "Hear me, please, oh magic fish, / My wife has sent me with a wish."

Before Reading: If you could wish for anything, what would you wish for?

Vocabulary: tug: a pull; **flopped:** fell heavily and noisily, plopped; **enchanted:** under a spell, bewitched; **demanded:** asked forcefully; **throne:** a ceremonial chair for kings and queens

After Reading: What does the fisherman discover in the sea? Why does he go back to the sea the first time? the second time? the third time? What kind of person is the fisherman's wife? What happens as a result of her greed? What is the moral of the story? (22)

Stories from Other Countries

The Blind Men and the Elephant

Background: This is a fable from India. Remind children that a fable is a short, simple story that conveys an important lesson, or moral, about human behavior.

Before Reading: What does an elephant look like?

Vocabulary: tusk: a large pointed tooth; **spear:** a sharply pointed weapon; **contradict:** state the opposite of; **startled:** surprised; **shudder:** shiver; **bothered:** took the time, troubled; **put their heads together:** think about

After Reading: What do each of the six blind men believe an elephant looks like? Why do they think so? What lesson do you think this fable teaches? (18)

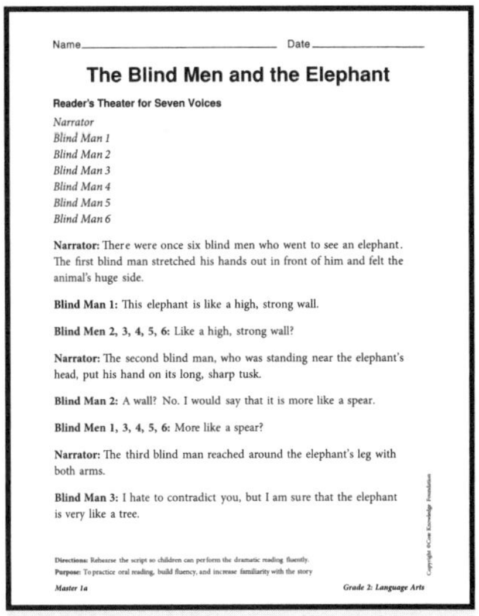

Name________________ Date________

The Blind Men and the Elephant

Reader's Theater for Seven Voices

Narrator
Blind Man 1
Blind Man 2
Blind Man 3
Blind Man 4
Blind Man 5
Blind Man 6

Narrator: There were once six blind men who went to see an elephant. The first blind man stretched his hands out in front of him and felt the animal's huge side.

Blind Man 1: This elephant is like a high, strong wall.

Blind Men 2, 3, 4, 5, 6: Like a high, strong wall?

Narrator: The second blind man, who was standing near the elephant's head, put his hand on its long, sharp tusk.

Blind Man 2: A wall? No. I would say that it is more like a spear.

Blind Men 1, 3, 4, 5, 6: More like a spear?

Narrator: The third blind man reached around the elephant's leg with both arms.

Blind Man 3: I hate to contradict you, but I am sure that the elephant is very like a tree.

Directions: Rehearse the script so children can perform the dramatic reading fluently.
Purpose: To practice oral reading, build fluency, and increase familiarity with the story

Master 1a *Grade 2: Language Arts*

Copyright ©Core Knowledge Foundation

Use Instructional Masters 1a and 1b.

Teaching Idea

"The Blind Men and the Elephant" reminds us that each of us sees things from our own point of view. Sometimes it is necessary to try to think about how things might look from somebody else's point of view. Encourage children to play with the idea of other peoples' perspective by asking them to rewrite a story from another character's point of view.

The Magic Paintbrush

Background: This is a Chinese folktale. It is also known as "Tye May and the Magic Brush" and "Liang [or Ma Liang] and the Magic Brush."

Before Reading: Have you ever painted a picture? If so, what did you paint? If not, what kind of picture would you like to paint?

Vocabulary: orphan: a child whose parents are dead; **lifelike:** something that looks real; **coat:** an animal's fur; **commanded:** ordered; **scowl:** frown; **slimy:** covered with slippery, sticky slime; **barked:** spoke sharply, snapped

After Reading: What does Ma Liang want to do? How does the teacher treat him? What does Ma Liang get from the old man? How do you know Ma Liang's paintbrush is magic? What does the emperor want Ma Liang to do? How does Ma Liang fool the emperor? Are there any lessons to be learned from the story? (27)

Cross-curricular Teaching Idea

When teaching the world history lesson about India, introduce "The Blind Men and the Elephant" and "The Tiger, the Brahman, and the Jackal" (p. 78). Before you read, help children locate India on a map. You may also want to locate countries and continents from which "The Magic Paintbrush" (China, Asia), "Talk" (Ghana, Africa), "The Tongue-Cut Sparrow" (Japan, Asia), and other tales come.

Talk

Background: This is a cumulative tale from West Africa in which certain actions, phrases, and events are repeated in a predictable pattern. The story comes from the Ashanti people who live in what is now Ghana. Many Ashanti are farmers, and their major crops include yams. According to Ashanti tradition, most men and women own a carved wooden stool that represents the owner's spirit.

Before Reading: Imagine that objects or animals suddenly started talking to you. How would you react?

Vocabulary: cud: something held in the mouth and chewed; **yam:** a sweet potato; **weaver:** a person who weaves cloth; **ford:** a shallow place in a stream, river,

Cross-curricular Teaching Idea

Help children locate the setting of "Talk"—West Africa, the country of Ghana, the Gulf of Guinea, and the city of Accra—on a map or globe. Then have groups of five children dramatize the story using simple props, such as a yam, a bundle of cloth, and a stool.

Cross-curricular Teaching Idea

You may wish to teach "The Tongue-Cut Sparrow" in connection with the History and Geography section on Japan. Alternatively, it can be taught with "The Fisherman and His Wife." A greedy wife and a magic animal are central to both tales in which kindness is rewarded, whereas excessive greed leads to disaster.

Teaching Idea

Ask children to compare "The Tongue-Cut Sparrow" with "The Fisherman and His Wife" (p. 74). Direct them to think about how the settings, characters, and theme or messages are alike and different.

Teaching Idea

You may wish to take children to a local performance of *A Christmas Carol.*

etc.; **wheezed:** breathed hoarsely; **recite:** tell; **hoarsely:** with a rough, husky voice; **scowling:** frowning

After Reading: Why does the farmer become upset? What happens when he meets the fisherman? What happens when the two men meet the weaver? What happens when the three men meet the bather? What happens when the group of four men goes to the chief? (30)

The Tongue-Cut Sparrow

Background: This is a folktale from Japan.

Before Reading: Can you think of a greedy character in a story you have heard or read? What happens to him or her?

Vocabulary: cross: annoyed; **starch:** a substance used to stiffen cloth; **pecked:** grasped and picked up with the beak; **shrieked:** screamed; **fluttering:** flapping; **peek:** look; **slithered:** glided and slid

After Reading: How does the man feel about the sparrow? How does the wife feel about the bird? Why does the wife get angry with the bird? What does she do? What happens when the man and the bird are finally reunited? Why does the wife become angry with the man? What happens when the wife takes the big basket from the sparrow? What lesson does the woman learn? (Greed leads to unhappiness.) (32)

Classic Stories

A Christmas Carol

Author Information: This story is based on Charles Dickens's classic tale, which was published in 1843. Dickens (1812–1870) was born in Portsmouth, England. A newspaper reporter, he became an overnight success with the publication of *The Pickwick Papers* in 1836. Some of his other works include the novels *A Tale of Two Cities, David Copperfield, Oliver Twist,* and *Great Expectations.*

Before Reading: How would you describe the Christmas spirit? Why is it important to keep this spirit alive all year long?

Vocabulary: carol: a song of praise or joy; **tight-fisted:** not easily giving or spending money; **grasping:** greedy; **clerk:** a person who files, keep records, and does similar business tasks; **meekly:** humbly; **bah, humbug:** words that express a person's disgust; **vanished:** disappeared; **forged:** created; **neglected:** ignored; **recalled:** remembered; **dim:** unclear; **jolly:** merry, happy; **meager:** not enough in quantity; **frail:** weak, delicate; **spared:** saved from harm; **phantom:** a ghost; **onward:** forward; **choked:** filled; **clutched:** held tightly; **prize:** worthy, first-class

After Reading: What kind of man is Ebenezer Scrooge? What is Jacob Marley's warning? What does the first spirit show Scrooge? What does the second spirit show him? What does the third spirit reveal? How does Scrooge change? Why does he change? What does it mean to call someone "Scrooge"? What lessons do we learn from the story? Why do you think the story is called "A Christmas Carol"? (19)

Before Breakfast (from *Charlotte's Web*)

Author Information: E. B. White (1899–1985) was born in Mount Vernon, New York. A poet, essayist, and children's author, he worked on the staff of *The New*

Yorker magazine for 50 years. After moving to a farm in Maine, White was inspired to write *Charlotte's Web* (1952). His other children's books are *Stuart Little* (1945) and *Trumpet of the Swan* (1970).

Background: This selection is the first chapter from the beloved classic *Charlotte's Web*. The novel tells the story of Fern, her pig Wilbur, and Wilbur's friend, a wise spider named Charlotte.

Before Reading: What do you know about pigs? Would you like to have a pig for a pet?

Vocabulary: runt: the smallest animal of a litter; **sopping:** very wet; **injustice:** unfairness; **queer:** odd; **carton:** a box; **wobbled:** moved unsteadily; **untimely:** at the wrong time; **armed:** equipped with weapons; **specimen:** an example; **blissful:** full of joy

After Reading: What does Mr. Arable plan to do with the runt? How does Fern save the runt? Do you agree or disagree with her actions? How does Fern feed the pig? What does Fern name the pig? (20)

Teaching Idea

Have groups of children act out the story of *Charlotte's Web* with simple props, such as a cardboard box and a baby bottle.

How Wendy Met Peter Pan (from *Peter Pan*)

Author Information: James M. Barrie (1860–1937) was a Scottish novelist and playwright. He wrote a successful play called *Peter Pan*, which was first produced on the London stage in 1904. The play was later turned into a popular Broadway musical, an animated movie by Walt Disney, and the classic novel *Peter Pan and Wendy* (1911).

Before Reading: Are you familiar with the story of Peter Pan? What kind of character is he? Where does he live? What qualities does he have?

Vocabulary: ragged: uneven, jagged; **silvery:** having a clear sound; **snapped:** spoke sharply; **fetched:** got; **crowed:** loudly boasted; **conceited:** stuck-up, overly impressed with one's abilities; **jangling:** harshly metallic; **wriggle:** turn and twist

After Reading: What kind of character is Peter Pan? Who is Tinker Bell? Why do Peter and Tinker Bell visit the Darlings? What does Peter want Wendy to do? What does he teach Wendy and her brothers? (29)

Pourquoi Tales

How the Camel Got His Hump

Author Information: Rudyard Kipling (1865–1936) was born in Bombay, India. He spent most of his childhood in England but returned to India when he was 16 years old to work as a newspaper reporter. His stories and novels include *The Jungle Book* (1894), *Kim* (1900), and *Just So Stories* (1902), from which this story is taken.

Background: This is a pourquoi tale that was published in *Just So Stories*. It provides an explanation for the odd physiognomy of camels, for their notoriously bad tempers, and for their remarkable ability to go without food and water for long periods.

Before Reading: What does a camel look like? How do you think the camel got his hump?

Vocabulary: tamarisks: shrubs with scalelike leaves and white, pink, or red flowers; **prickles:** thorns or spines; **'scrutiating:** excrutiatingly, or extremely;

Teaching Idea

If children enjoy "How the Camel Got His Hump," consider reading them additional *Just So Stories* from Kipling's book of the same name. (See More Resources.) Children may also enjoy the poem "The Hump,"which goes with "How the Camel Got His Hump." It begins: "The Camel's hump is an ugly lump, / Which well you may see at the Zoo; / But uglier yet is the hump we get / From having too little to do."

idle: lazy; **bit:** the metal mouthpiece of a horse's bridle; **trot:** move faster than a walk; **fetch:** go after and bring back; **yoke:** a device used to connect a draft animal to a plow or wagon; **double-time:** twice the regular amount; **palaver** and **powwow:** synonyms that mean a meeting or a coming together; **took a bearing:** chose a direction; **lolloping:** moving with a bobbing motion

After Reading: What kind of character is the Camel? Why do the Horse, the Dog, and the Ox complain to the Man and to the Djinn? How does the Djinn punish the Camel? (23)

Teaching Idea

Pair the teaching of "How the Camel Got His Hump" with another pourquoi tale, "El Pajaro Cu." Put children in groups of three, and have each group write a pourquoi tale.

El Pajaro Cu

Background: This is a folktale from Mexico. It is a pourquoi tale that explains why owls hunt at night and have a unique call, and why roadrunners move as they do.

Before Reading: What different kinds of birds do you know about? What sound does an owl make? How does a roadrunner behave?

Vocabulary: feathered: covered with feathers; **pity:** sympathy; **splendid:** very good; **strutting:** walking in a self-important way; **disgrace:** shame; **vanity:** extreme pride; **glistening:** shining; **spiraled:** circled down; **streaks:** rushes

After Reading: Why does Pajaro Cu have no feathers? How do the other birds offer to help him? What happens when Pajaro Cu gets his feathers? Why does the Roadrunner run from place to place? Why does the Owl call "Cu, Cu, Cu"? (28)

Cross-curricular Teaching Idea

You may wish to teach Iktomi stories in conjunction with your study of the Plains Native Americans in American History.

Trickster Tales

How Iktomi Lost His Eyes

Background: This is a trickster tale from the Assiniboine, a Native American tribe in Canada. It features Iktomi, a popular trickster character in the folklore of the Plains Native Americans. Unlike some trickster characters, Iktomi is not clever but is foolish and greedy.

Before Reading: Remind children that they heard about trickster characters like Anansi the spider and Bre'r Rabbit in Grade 1. What trickster tales do you know? What qualities do trickster characters often have?

Vocabulary: fluttered: flew lightly; **gasped:** breathed deeply; **pleaded:** begged; **stumbled:** walked unsteadily; **vain:** extremely proud

After Reading: What trick does the bird teach Iktomi? What happens when Iktomi ignores the bird's warning? Which animals help Iktomi? What promise does Iktomi make to the bird? What happens at the end of the story? (24)

Teaching Idea

Connect the lesson taught by "How Iktomi Lost His Eyes" to the lessons taught by the Greek myths "Pandora Brings Woe" (p. 84) and "Arachne the Weaver" (p. 86). If you wish to extend your teaching of Iktomi stories, we've added Text Resources 25 and 26, which are not listed in the *Sequence*.

The Tiger, the Brahman, and the Jackal

Background: This is a trickster tale from India. It is also a repetitive tale in which certain events and actions are repeated three times. A Brahman is a member of the highest of four Hindu social classes who studies and teaches the Vedas and officiates at religious rites.

Before Reading: What do you know about India? What kinds of animals and plants are found there? What beliefs and customs do people follow? Tell the class you are going to read a story that is set in India.

Teaching Idea

Introduce "The Tiger, the Brahman, and the Jackal." Use this story to review the concept of personification. Ask children to identify ways in which the tiger and the jackal act like animals and ways in which they act like human beings. Also, have children compare and contrast this trickster tale with "How Iktomi Lost His Eyes." Have them discuss similarities and differences between the jackal and Iktomi. Use a Venn diagram found in the Instructional Masters to compare and contrast the two stories.

Vocabulary: in vain: without success; **pious:** religious; **Nay:** no; **oaths:** curses; **consented:** agreed; **cooped up:** confined, caged; **pleaded:** begged; **pipal tree:** a fig tree in India that is believed to be sacred by Buddhists; **afield:** away from home; **fared:** got along; **gratitude:** thankfulness; **refuse:** garbage; **fodder:** food for animals; **trample:** beat down with the feet; **jackal:** a dog-like animal; **recital:** a detailed account; **whirl:** spin, in a state of mental confusion; **dexterously:** skillfully

After Reading: Why does the Brahman let the tiger out? What happens after he does so? What three things does the Brahman ask about the tiger's actions? How does each reply? How does the jackal fool the tiger? What happens to the tiger at the end of the story? Is there any lesson to be learned from the story? (31)

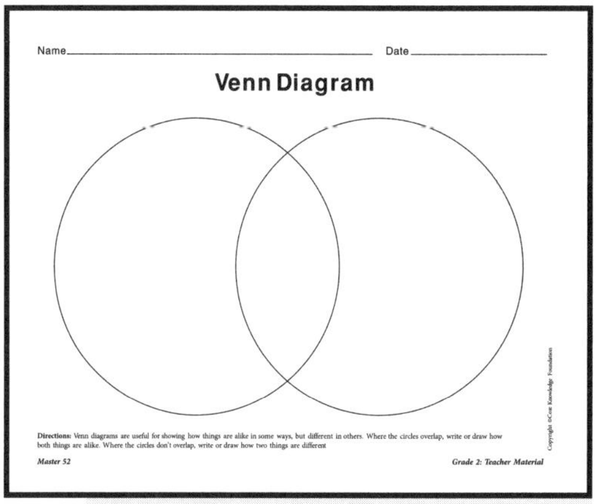

Use Instructional Master 52.

Review

Below are some ideas for ongoing assessment and review activities. These are not meant to constitute a comprehensive list.

- As a reinforcing idea for this section, give children an opportunity to write their own stories. They may model their stories after the ones that they read in this section. Remind children to include characters, a setting, dialogue, and a sequence of events. Have children share their stories with the class.
- Using the stories from the activity above and throughout the year, give children opportunities to publish their work. You may choose to put the class stories together in one big book, or you may have individual children design covers and bind their books. Ask the media specialist if you can display these books in the library, and provide opportunities for children to share their books aloud with younger children.
- You may use some of the stories from this section to reinforce reading comprehension and response skills with children. Select a story from this section, and prepare some comprehension questions on index cards for the class. Before reading the story, have children read their questions aloud from their cards. During the story, search for the answers and the details to support them. After reading the story, have children read their questions again and provide the answer from the story. If there is difficulty, go back to the text of the story, and help each child find the answer.
- In addition to having children act out some of the stories using props, you can simply have them react to the stories as you read them. Read a story to the class. After reading, designate children to play parts of the characters in the story, and have them stand in front of the class. Read the story again. When you read a part of the story containing that character, have a child pantomime what the character must have been doing while saying that line. Discuss as a class how that character must have reacted to the news in the story. You may extend this activity by having children write about the characters and how they feel about them.
- Play a concentration matching game with the class after reading a story. Make index cards that describe each character in the story. Use text from the story to describe that person. Then put the name of the character on another index card. Place all of these cards in a sentence strip holder so that children have to match the characters with the cards that describe them. Number each of the cards on the back so that children can choose two cards by the number. Each child gets a chance to turn over two cards in the chart to see if they match. If they do match, the child gets to keep the cards.

The Big Idea in Review

Listening to and reading stories helps children develop an understanding of the elements of a story, build vocabulary, and understand cultural references.

More Resources

The titles listed below are offered as a representative sample of materials and not a complete list of everything that is available.

For children —

These books are generally intended to be read aloud, though some children may be able to read parts or all of the simpler texts.

- *Beauty and the Beast*, by Jan Brett (Clarion, 1990). Paperback, 32 pages, ISBN 039555702X.
- *The Blind Men and the Elephant (Hello Reader, Level 3),* retold by Karen Backstein (Scholastic, 1992). Paperback, 48 pages, ISBN 0590458132.
- *Charlotte's Web*, by E. B. White and illustrated by Garth Williams (HarperFestival, 2003). Paperback, 192 pages, ISBN 006052779X.
- *A Christmas Carol*, by Charles Dickens and abridged by Vivian French (Candlewick Press, 1993). Library binding, 43 pages, ISBN 1564022048.
- *A Christmas Carol and Other Favorites*, an audio recording by Jim Weiss (Greathall Productions, www.greathall.com, 1-800-477-6234). Contains a retelling of Dickens's famous story.
- *The Emperor's New Clothes: A Tale Set in China*, by Demi (Margaret K. Elderry Books, 2000). Hardcover, 42 pages, ISBN 0689830688.
- *The Just So Stories*, by Rudyard Kipling and illustrated by Barry Moser (HarperCollins, 1996). Hardcover, 148 pages, ISBN 0688139574.

The Big Idea

A myth is a story created hundreds or even thousands of years ago to try to explain mysteries of nature and humanity.

What Students Should Already Know

Students may already be familiar with some myths through their listening experiences in Kindergarten and Grade 1.

What Students Need to Learn

- **Myths**
  - **try to explain some part of the worldview of a people, or explain a practice, belief, or natural phenomenon.**
  - **were created hundreds or even thousands of years ago.**
  - **include supernatural beings or events.**
  - **come from cultures around the world.**
  - **were passed down orally.**
- **Greek myths for this grade, including the ideas they express and some of the memorable characters they contain.**
- **Greek myths**
  - **tell about gods and goddesses that ancient Greeks believed in.**
  - **feature 12 powerful ruling gods called the Olympians.**
  - **include minor gods and mythical creatures.**

What Students Will Learn in Future Grades

In Grades 3 and 6, students will continue to learn about myths from ancient Greece. In Grade 3, they will also learn about Norse myths and myths from ancient Rome.

Text Resources

- (33) *Zeus (Jupiter)*
- (33) *Hera (Juno)*
- (33) *Apollo (Apollo)*
- (33) *Artemis (Diana)*
- (33) *Poseidon (Neptune)*
- (33) *Aphrodite (Venus)*
- (33) *Eros (Cupid)*
- (34) *Demeter (Ceres)*
- (34) *Ares (Mars)*
- (34) *Hermes (Mercury)*
- (34) *Hephaestus (Vulcan)*
- (35) *Athena (Minerva)*
- (35) *Hades (Pluto)*
- (35) *Dionysus (Dionysus)*
- (35) *Atlas*
- (36) *Centaur*
- (36) *Cerberus*
- (36) *Pegasus*
- (36) *Pan*
- (37) *Zeus and Io*
- (38) *Bellerophon and Pegasus*
- (39) *Prometheus Brings Fire, Pandora Brings Woe*
- (40) *Oedipus and the Sphinx*
- (41) *Theseus and the Minotaur*
- (42) *Daedalus and Icarus*
- (43) *Arachne the Weaver*
- (44) *Swift-Footed Atalanta*
- (45) *Demeter and Persephone*
- (46) *The Labors of Hercules*

Materials

Instructional Masters 14a–14b
The Greek Gods, p. 83

world map or globe, p. 84

pictures of Greek gods and goddesses, p. 84

photo of Egyptian Sphinx, p. 85

copies of mazes, p. 85

artwork depicting the Icarus myth, p. 86

class T-chart on chart paper, p. 87

chart paper, p. 87

colored markers and pencils, p. 87

various resources about Greece, p. 87

chart with three columns labeled *beginning, middle,* and *end*, p. 88

sentence strips, p. 88

Vocabulary

Student/Teacher Vocabulary

myth: a traditional story that tries to explain some part of the worldview of a people, or explain a practice, belief, or natural phenomenon (S)

Olympian: one of the twelve major Greek gods or goddesses who were said to reside on Mount Olympus (T)

Domain Vocabulary

Mythology of ancient Greece and associated words:
theme, Greece, Greek, Rome, Roman, Mount Olympus, Titan, Homer, Hesiod, mythical, mythological, supernatural, magical, god, goddess, oral, oral tradition, Zeus, Hera, Pandora, Prometheus, Oedipus, Sphinx, centaur, Minotaur, Arachne, Athena, Demeter, Persephone, Aphrodite, Hercules, *plus words from the stories themselves, including Vocabulary in the selections below*

Cross-curricular Connections

History and Geography

World: Ancient Greece

Visual Arts

Sculpture

- *The Discobolus (Discus Thrower)*

Architecture

- The Parthenon

Science

Cycles in Nature

Seasonal cycles

At a Glance

The most important ideas for you are:

- Myths try to explain some part of the worldview of a people, or explain a practice, belief, or natural phenomenon.
- Myths include these elements of fiction: characters, plot, narration, dialogue, and supernatural beings and events.
- Listening to myths helps children gain insight into the beliefs and values of a particular culture and helps them recognize references in printed matter.
- Greek myths originated in ancient Greece and were passed down orally for many generations before they were written down.

What Teachers Need to Know

B. Mythology of Ancient Greece

Background: What Are Myths?

Why do crops grow? Why do the seasons change? Why do bad things happen to people? To answer these questions and many others, ancient cultures created traditional stories called myths. Myths, like other kinds of folktales, were passed down orally from generation to generation. The purpose of myths was to explain events in nature (such as birth and death), to teach religious beliefs, and to present guidelines for behavior.

Myths, like those from ancient Greece, tell of supernatural incidents and beings who control the forces of nature. According to folklorist William Bascomb, myths share five characteristics:

- *They were originally considered to be factual.*
- *They are set in the remote past.*
- *They take place in another world or in an earlier world.*
- *They include sacred characters, such as gods and goddesses.*
- *They include nonhuman creatures.*

Greek Myths

All cultures have myths, but classical Greek mythology has had the greatest influence on Western culture and literature. The ancient Romans adopted Greek mythology as their own, simply changing the characters' names. (You can find the Roman equivalent for each Greek name, in parentheses, in the *Core Knowledge Sequence.*) Greek mythology lives today in retellings of the ancient stories; in literary allusions; in the names of planets, months, and days of the week; in common words and expressions, such as *herculean;* and in the names of companies and products, such as Atlas Van Lines, Ajax, and Nike.

Greek myths are stories about Greek gods and goddesses and other supernatural beings. Many of the Greek myths that survive today came into being in classical Greek art between 700 BCE and 500 BCE. They were passed down orally, and many of them were later recorded by the Greek poets Homer (*Iliad* and *Odyssey*) and Hesiod (*Theogony*), and much later by the Roman poet Ovid (*Metamorphoses*) in the 1st century CE.

The pantheon of Greek gods and goddesses includes the Titans, the Olympians, and lesser gods. According to the myths, only Chaos, a swirling vapor without form or shape, existed at the time of Earth's creation. Slowly, Gaia, the Earth, formed from Chaos. Gaia and Uranus, the sky, had many children, including the twelve Titans. Once Uranus lost his powers, the Titan Cronus ruled the world. Cronus and his wife, Rhea, were the parents of Zeus, the first of the Olympians. After the Titans were overthrown, the Olympians ruled.

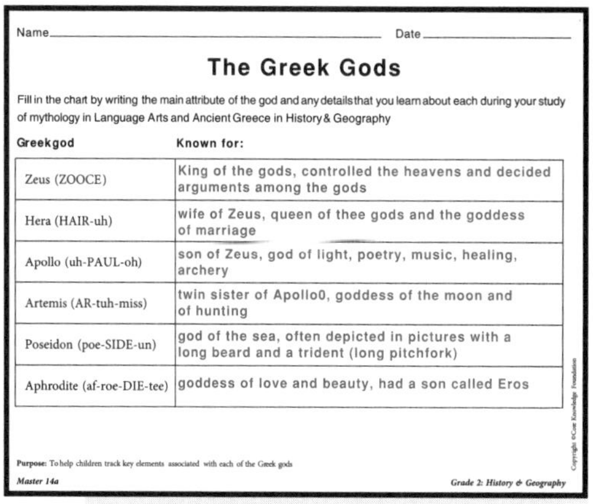

Name______________________ Date__________

The Greek Gods

Fill in the chart by writing the main attribute of the god and any details that you learn about each during your study of mythology in Language Arts and Ancient Greece in History & Geography

Greekgod	Known for:
Zeus (ZOOCE)	King of the gods, controlled the heavens and decided arguments among the gods
Hera (HAIR-uh)	wife of Zeus, queen of thee gods and the goddess of marriage
Apollo (uh-PAUL-oh)	son of Zeus, god of light, poetry, music, healing, archery
Artemis (AR-tuh-miss)	twin sister of Apollo0, goddess of the moon and of hunting
Poseidon (poe-SIDE-un)	god of the sea, often depicted in pictures with a long beard and a trident (long pitchfork)
Aphrodite (af-roe-DIE-tee)	goddess of love and beauty, had a son called Eros

Purpose: To help children track key elements associated with each of the Greek gods

Master 14a

Grade 2: History & Geography

Copyright ©Core Knowledge Foundation

Use Instructional Masters 14a and 14b.

The Olympians lived on Mount Olympus, the highest mountain in Greece. The 12 Olympians included Zeus, his wife Hera, their child Ares, Zeus's brother Poseidon, and Apollo, Artemis, Athena, and Aphrodite. In a palace hidden behind clouds, the Olympians dined on nectar and ambrosia, watched over human beings, and used their magical powers to help or punish others. Greek gods were immortal but not flawless—they meddled in the lives of humans and in each other's lives. They also exhibited human traits and emotions, such as jealousy and stubbornness.

The myths in this section feature the Olympians, lesser gods, mythical creatures (such as the Minotaur), or mythical heroes (such as Hercules). By listening carefully to these stories, children will learn the elements of myths. Reading Greek myths to second graders may also stimulate class discussion of values, ethics, and behavior. (33) (34) (35) (36)

Teaching Idea

When introducing the Greek gods, look for one or more pictures of each god and goddess in books or on the Internet. Share the pictures along with the read alouds in the Text Resources.

Teaching Idea

Have children illustrate one of the Greek myths. Display their illustrations on a bulletin board in the classroom.

Teaching Idea

If you wish to extend your teaching of Greek myths, we've added Text Resources 37 and 38, which are not listed in the *Sequence*.

Teaching Greek Myths

Before you read the Greek myths, introduce children to the Greek gods, goddesses, and mythological creatures that appear in the myths. Brief descriptions of the gods and goddesses are included in the Text Resources.

Have children keep these sheets as reinforcement as you move through the section. Using a world map or globe, point out the country of Greece and Mount Olympus. Tell children that the myths you are about to read come from ancient Greece. You might want to teach this section at the same time you teach Greece in World History and Geography.

Ask children whether they know any myths from ancient Greece. Have volunteers paraphrase myths in their own words. Read each myth. As you read, use your voice to emphasize certain key words or to differentiate between characters. Read slowly and clearly. You may wish to pause before you finish to ask children to predict what will happen next.

After you read each myth, thoroughly discuss it with your class. Make sure children understand the characters and the situation in the myth, as well as any challenging vocabulary words. Ask children questions to help them recall details. Read the myth again, encouraging children to ask any questions they may still have about meaning or vocabulary.

Then invite children to retell the myth in their own words. Retelling myths helps reinforce comprehension, build vocabulary, and intensify children's appreciation for different genres of literature.

There are many versions of Greek myths. The versions printed in the Text Resources and described below are taken from *What Your Second Grader Needs to Know.*

Prometheus Brings Fire

Summary: Long ago, only the Greek gods had fire. In this story, a giant named Prometheus [pruh-MEE-thee-us] steals fire from the gods and takes it to humans on Earth. Zeus punishes Prometheus by having him chained to a rock. Every day, an eagle comes and tears at the body of the poor giant.

Before Reading: Why is having fire important? What would the world be like if there were no fire?

Vocabulary: mankind: the human race; **furious:** very angry; **fierce:** violent

After Reading: What does Prometheus bring to humans on Earth? How does Zeus punish him? What event in nature does this myth tell you about? (39)

Pandora Brings Woe

Summary: Zeus lets humans keep fire but decides to punish them. He orders Hephaestus [hih-FES-tus], the god of the forge, to craft a woman called Pandora.

Zeus sends Pandora to Earth with a mysterious box that he tells her not to open. When Pandora disobeys Zeus and opens the box, she releases pain, disease, disaster, and other troubles into the world. She also releases hope, which allows people to keep going even in the face of bad things.

Before Reading: What bad things on Earth can you name?

Vocabulary: miserable: unhappy; **peek:** look

After Reading: Who creates Pandora? What happens when Pandora comes to Earth? According to the myth, how does sadness and trouble come into the world? Do you know of any other myths or stories that explain how bad things came into the world? (The story of Adam and Eve and the forbidden fruit is a similar story.) (39)

Teaching Idea

Tell children that the expression "Pandora's box" comes from the myth about Pandora. Explain that the phrase means "a source of unexpected troubles."

Oedipus and the Sphinx

Summary: Oedipus [ED-ih-pus] is traveling to Thebes [theebs], a Greek city. On the way, he meets a mythological creature called the Sphinx [sfinks]. If a person cannot answer a riddle posed by the Sphinx, the creature eats him or her. Luckily, Oedipus wisely solves the Sphinx's riddle.

Before Reading: Can you solve this riddle: What creature goes on four feet in the morning, on two feet at noon, and on three feet in the evening?

Vocabulary: swoop: descend upon, like a bird from the sky; **riddle:** a puzzling question that requires thought to answer; **tasty:** delicious; **doom:** a terrible fate; **grateful:** thankful, appreciative

After Reading: What kind of creature is the Sphinx? What riddle does the Sphinx ask Oedipus? What is the solution to the riddle? What happens when Oedipus solves the riddle? (40)

Teaching Idea

While studying the myth of "Oedipus and the Sphinx," pose other riddles to the class. To extend this activity, invite children to try to compose a riddle of their own.

Cross-curricular Teaching Idea

Show the class photograhs of the statue of the Sphinx built in about 2500 BCE near the pyramids in Egypt.

Theseus and the Minotaur

Summary: King Aegeus [EE-joos] of Athens must send seven girls and seven boys to King Minos [MY-noce] of Crete every nine years. The youths are put in a complicated labyrinth and eaten by a creature called the Minotaur [MIN-oh-tar]. Aegeus's son, Theseus [THEE-see-us], promises to kill the Minotaur and return home with the latest group of boys and girls. Once Theseus arrives in Crete, Ariadne [ar-ee-ADD-nee], the daughter of Minos, falls in love with him. To save his life, she finds out how Theseus can escape. After Theseus kills the Minotaur, he escapes from the labyrinth and sails home. Tragically, Aegeus falls into the sea and drowns before his son returns.

Before Reading: Have you ever walked in a maze or labyrinth? Were you able to get out on your own? What plan would you come up with if your life depended on escaping?

Vocabulary: maidens: unmarried girls; **labyrinth:** a confusing network of winding passages that are connected; **victims:** people who are harmed or killed; **bear:** stand, endure; **savage:** wild

After Reading: Why does King Aegeus have to send girls and boys to King Minos in Crete? What happens to the youths? How does Ariadne feel about Theseus? How does she help Theseus? Who helps Ariadne? How does Theseus defeat the Minotaur? How does Theseus get out of the labyrinth? (41)

Teaching Idea

Before teaching "Theseus and the Minotaur," bring in copies of mazes for children to guide their pencils through. Explain that the labyrinth is like one of these mazes.

Daedalus and Icarus

Summary: King Minos punishes the inventor Daedalus [DED-ah-lus] for revealing how Theseus might get out of the labyrinth. Daedalus and his son, Icarus

[IK-er-us], are put in the labyrinth. To escape, Daedalus makes two pairs of wings and shows his son how to fly with them. The two fly away from Crete, but Icarus ignores his father's warning about going too close to the sun. Icarus flies near the sun, the wax on his wings melts, and he plunges into the sea.

Before Reading: Why is it important to listen to older people, especially your parents?

Vocabulary: fastened: attached, joined; **puff:** a short, sudden gust of wind

After Reading: Why does King Minos punish Daedalus? How does he punish the inventor? How does Daedalus plan to save himself and his son? Does his plan work? Why or why not? (42)

> **Teaching Idea**
>
> **Many Greek myths have been illustrated by painters and artists. Children may enjoy looking at artistic versions of the Icarus myth as well as others. Versions of the Icarus myth include Brueghel's *Landscape with the Fall of Icarus* and Matisse's *Icarus*. A web search—e.g., for "mythology," "painting," or "sculpture," and the names of the characters in the myth—can often turn up multiple artistic versions of a myth.**

Arachne the Weaver

Summary: Arachne [uh-RAK-nee] is a fine weaver. When she boasts that her weaving is equal to that of the goddess Athena, Athena challenges her to a contest. Whoever loses the contest must agree to never weave again. Athena wins but takes pity on Arachne. Because Arachne loves to spin, Athena turns Arachne into a spider that spins webs.

Before Reading: How is cloth made? What qualities does a beautiful piece of cloth have?

Vocabulary: boast: brag; **snapped:** spoke sharply; **loom:** a device for making thread or yarn; **silken:** as fine and glossy as silk; **ripple:** rise and fall gently; **dazzling:** amazing, overpowering; **immortal:** not having to die

After Reading: What happens when Arachne brags about her weaving? Who wins the weaving contest, Arachne or Athena? Into what form does Athena change Arachne? What creature in nature does this myth tell about? (43)

> **Cross-curricular Teaching Idea**
>
> **Read "Arachne the Weaver" when you teach the science lesson on insects. Emphasize that spiders are not really insects but belong to a special class of animals called arachnids.**

> **Teaching Idea**
>
> **In connection with the Arachne myth, you may wish to teach children a little about weaving.**

Swift-Footed Atalanta

Summary: Atalanta [at-uh-LAN-tuh] agrees to marry the man who can beat her in a race. Different men take the challenge but fail, even though Atalanta gives them a head start. With the help of Aphrodite, Hippomenes [hip-POM-eh-neez] succeeds and marries Atalanta.

Before Reading: How fast can you run? Have you ever won a race? What qualities does a good runner have? Who are some of the fastest runners today?

Vocabulary: outrun: to run faster than; **attend to:** take care of; **head start:** a start in a race before other runners; **doom:** a terrible fate; **glittering:** sparkling; **nudge:** a gentle push; **dashed:** raced

After Reading: What happens to the men who race Atalanta? How does Aphrodite help Hippomenes? What does Hippomenes do when he races Atalanta? Who wins the race? What happens after the race? (44)

Demeter and Persephone

Summary: Demeter [dih-MEE-ter] is the goddess of grain and the harvest. After Hades takes her daughter, Persephone [per-SEF-uh-nee], to the underworld, Demeter refuses to let anything grow on the earth. Zeus sends Hermes to get Persephone, but she is not supposed to leave Hades because she has broken a law. However, Zeus compromises. He agrees to allow Persephone to spend part of the year in the underworld with Hades and the other part with Demeter.

Before Reading: What are the four seasons? What happens during each one? You are about to hear a myth that the ancient Greeks used to explain the seasons.

> **Cross-curricular Teaching Idea**
>
> **Read "Demeter and Persephone" when you teach the science lesson on seasonal cycles in nature.**

Vocabulary: chariot: an ancient two-wheeled vehicle that was pulled by horses; **snatched:** seized, grabbed; **pomegranate:** a type of fruit with many seeds

After Reading: What happens to Persephone? How does Demeter react? What "law" of the gods does Persephone break? What does Zeus do to please Demeter and Hades? What event in nature does this myth tell about? (45)

The Labors of Hercules

Summary: Hercules, the strongest man on Earth, accidentally kills someone. To make up for his mistake, Apollo tells him to do whatever King Eurystheus [yur-ISS-thoos] asks. The king asks Hercules to accomplish twelve difficult tasks, four of them were as follows: kill a dangerous lion, kill a nine-headed monster, clean the filthy stables of King Augeas [aw-GEE-us], and find golden apples guarded by three magical women. After Hercules successfully completes each task, he is allowed to travel wherever he wants.

Before Reading: What are four of the most difficult jobs you can think of?

Vocabulary: labor: job, a task; **blow:** sudden hit; **hide:** an animal skin; **pierce:** cut; **ditch:** a long narrow trench dug in the ground; **chuckled:** laughed; **load:** a heavy weight

After Reading: What is the first task King Eurystheus asks Hercules to do? What is the second task? What is the third task? What is the final task? How does Hercules accomplish each of these tasks? (46)

Teaching Idea

When reading "Hercules," connect Hercules with two folk heroes in tall tales, Paul Bunyan (p. 91) and John Henry (p. 92). Also, explain that the adjective *herculean* means "of unusual size, power, or (when describing a task) difficulty."

Teaching Idea

As a reinforcing activity for Greek myths, have pairs of children act as TV news reporters in ancient Greece. Have them summarize events in one of these myths by reporting to the class what happens to the human or mythical characters.

Review

Below are some ideas for ongoing assessment and review activities. These are not meant to constitute a comprehensive list.

- After studying all the myths in this section, ask children which mythological character they would want to have around to do various things, e.g., to carry a message across town rapidly (Atalanta), to solve a difficult problem (Daedalus), to lift a heavy weight (Atlas), etc.
- Discuss with children the differences between myths and stories that they read in the previous sections. How are the types of literature alike and different? Create a class T-chart on chart paper with the descriptions of each kind of story and feedback from children about each type of story.
- Have children create a class alphabet book of ancient Greece. On chart paper, write each letter of the alphabet. Provide resources about Greece, such as books of Greek myths. As a class, have children identify words, including names of the Greek gods and goddesses, that might be included in an alphabet book to represent each letter. Then, at the bottom of the page, have each child write a sentence to complete the page using that word. For example, children might choose Athena for "A" and write "Athens, the capital of Greece, is named after the goddess Athena." Then, have children illustrate the pages of their book with markers and crayons. Check for understanding by making sure the picture and sentence make sense.
- After reading the Greek myths, have children imagine what might happen if the gods and goddesses lived today. What would they be able to do with their powers, and how would other people treat them? Have children write about one god or goddess

The Big Idea in Review

A myth is a story created hundreds or even thousands of years ago to try to explain mysteries of nature and humanity.

in their journals and how they would survive in today's world. Have children make a connection between their world and the ancient worlds from the stories.

- Discuss the characters of the Greek myths, and ask children to write a letter to their favorite character. In the letter, have children ask the character any questions that they would like answered from the stories. Encourage children to use details from the myths in their letters to enrich their writing and to go back to the text as a reference.
- While reading the Greek myths, have children identify the events from the beginning, middle, and end of the story. Make a simple chart with three columns labeled *beginning, middle,* and *end* for children to use as a graphic organizer. Then, have them write a couple of sentences for each column. Share these with the class, and have other children give input about events from the story.
- Use the Greek myths to have children practice sequencing story events. Write different sentences from a myth on sentence strips, and then pass them out to the class. Have children read the sentence from the strip and then come to the front of the room. Children in the front must arrange themselves in the correct order. The rest of the class may help children arrange themselves correctly. Then select one child from the class to read the sentences in order.
- Use pictures based on Greek mythology as a review. Show a picture of a myth, and ask children if they can guess which of the myths is depicted. If they have trouble, talk them through the picture, asking questions such as "What is happening here?"

More Resources

The titles listed below are offered as a representative sample of materials and not a complete list of everything that is available.

For children —

These books are generally intended to be read aloud, though some children may be able to read parts or all of the simpler texts.

- *D'Aulaire's Book of Greek Myths,* by Ingri D'Aulaire and Edgar Parin D'Aulaire (Doubleday, 1962). A highly acclaimed book of myths. Hardcover, 196 pages, ISBN 0385015836.
- *Greek Myths,* retold by Geraldine McCaughrean (Margaret McElderry, 1993). Hardcover, 96 pages, ISBN 0689505833.
- *Greek Myths,* an audio recording by Jim Weiss (Greathall Productions, www.greathall.com, 1-800-477-6234). Tells the stories of Arachne and Hercules. *She and He: Adventures in Mythology* includes the myth of Atalanta. *Heroes in Mythology* includes the stories of Prometheus, and Theseus and the Minotaur.
- *Greek Myths for Young Children,* edited by Heather Amery and illustrated by Linda Edwards (Usborne, 2000). Includes the myths of Persephone, Pygmalion, Ulysses, and others. Hardcover, 128 pages, ISBN 0746037252.

For teachers —

- *Classic Myths to Read Aloud,* compiled and edited by William F. Russell (Three Rivers Press, 1992). Paperback, 272 pages, ISBN 0517588374.
- *Mythology: Timeless Tales of Gods and Heroes,* by Edith Hamilton (Warner, 1999). Paperback, 352 pages, ISBN 0446607258.
- *Till We Have Faces: A Myth Retold,* by C. S. Lewis (Harvest Books, 1980). A captivating retelling of the myth of Psyche by the author of *The Chronicles of Narnia* and *The Screwtape Letters.* Paperback, 324 pages, ISBN 0156904365.
- Bulfinch's Mythology can be read online at www.bulfinch.org.
- MythWeb, www.mythweb.com, is a site on Greek mythology geared for a younger audience.

III. Fiction

C. American Folk Heroes and Tall Tales

The Big Idea

Tall tales are stories about American folk heroes who are larger than life.

Text Resources

47 *Paul Bunyan*
48 *Johnny Appleseed*
49 *John Henry*
50 *Pecos Bill*
51 *Casey Jones*

What Students Should Already Know

In Kindergarten, students should have heard tall tales about Johnny Appleseed and Casey Jones. They may be familiar with stories about Paul Bunyan, Pecos Bill, and other American folk heroes through their exposure to stories, cartoons, television programs, and videotapes.

What Students Need to Learn

- **The tall tales for this grade, including the ideas they express**
  - **Paul Bunyan**
  - **Johnny Appleseed**
  - **John Henry**
  - **Pecos Bill**
  - **Casey Jones**
- **A tall tale is a funny story about a larger-than-life character.**

III. Fiction

C. American Folk Heroes and Tall Tales

Materials

Instructional Master 6
Real or Tall Tale? *p. 93*

map of the United States, **p. 91**

colored markers or pencils, **p. 93**

chart paper, **p. 94**

children's journals, **p. 94**

Vocabulary

Student/Teacher Vocabulary

ballad: a folk song that tells a story (T)

dialect: the form of language, including different pronunciations, grammar, and expressions, used by people from a particular region (T)

exaggeration: to say that something is greater than it actually is (S)

hyperbole: an exaggerated statement (T)

tall tale: a humorous story that may be based on fact, but exaggerates the truth (S)

Domain Vocabulary

American folk heroes and tall tales and associated words:
tall tale, legend, legendary, hero, exaggeration, oral, oral tradition, folklore, folktale, folk hero, Johnny Appleseed, Paul Bunyan, Casey Jones, Pecos Bill, John Henry, comic, comical, humor, humorous, fact, fiction, fictional, *plus words from the stories themselves including Vocabulary in the selections below*

Cross-curricular Connections

History and Geography

American: Westward Expansion

American: Geography of the Americas

North America

Music

Songs

- "Casey Jones"
- "John Henry"

At a Glance

The most important ideas for you are:

- A tall tale is a story about a larger-than-life character.
- A tall tale is a humorous story that uses hyperbole, or exaggeration.
- A tall tale uses everyday language, especially dialect.
- Tall tales are often linked to 19th-century folk heroes of the American frontier.
- A tall tale stretches the truth.
- Some tall tales are based on the lives of real people.
- Johnny Appleseed, John Henry, and Casey Jones were real people.

What Teachers Need to Know

C. American Folk Heroes and Tall Tales

Background: What Are Tall Tales?

Tall tales are stories from the oral tradition. They are usually about the lives of real-life heroes who lived on the American frontier in the 1800s. For example, John Henry was believed to be a real person who worked for the Chesapeake and Ohio Railroad in the late 1800s. His deeds inspired people to tell tall tales.

Tall tales are humorous. One source of humor in a tall tale comes from the narrator's use of language. To make characters seem believable, the narrator of a tall tale uses common, everyday language—especially dialect—in a matter-of-fact way. For example, the narrator of "Pecos Bill" says, "Bill took out an extra long lariat, gave it a good hard toss, and bingo!"; and the narrator of "Paul Bunyan" says, "when Babe kicked over a huge bucket of water to fill the canal, well, that there became the Mississippi River."

The exaggeration of details serves as another source of humor in tall tales. The main character in a tall tale has larger-than-life qualities and abilities. For example, Pecos Bill could supposedly lasso a cyclone, and Paul Bunyan could supposedly cause an earthquake when he hiccupped!

Who Is Paul Bunyan?

Paul Bunyan is a fictional folk hero who was probably created by lumberjacks in logging camps in the early 1900s. In 1906 and 1910, James McGillivray, a former logger, published in the *Detroit News Tribune* some Paul Bunyan tales that he recalled from his youth. In 1914, another former logger named William B. Laughhead used the character of Paul Bunyan in advertising brochures for the Red River Lumber Company. Tall tales about Paul Bunyan have inspired books; poems by Robert Frost, Carl Sandburg, and Richard Wilbur; and an operetta by W. H. Auden with music by Benjamin Britten.

Teaching "Paul Bunyan"

Before Reading: Explain to the class that Paul Bunyan is a fictional character. Make sure children understand the vocabulary words listed below. What does a logger do? What kinds of tools does a logger use today? What kinds would a logger have used 100 years ago? What qualities or abilities should a successful logger have?

Vocabulary: mighty: very; **logger:** a person who cuts down trees and brings them to a lumber mill; **match:** equal; **ditch:** a long narrow trench dug in the ground; **telescope:** an instrument used to look at faraway objects; **hauled:** dragged; **dump:** dropped in large amounts; **mounds:** piles

After Reading: Read the tale at least once, possibly twice. Then discuss different aspects of a tall tale that children hear. For example, tell them one feature of tall tales is exaggeration. When Paul Bunyan sneezes, he supposedly blows the

Teaching Idea

Select a tall tale to read aloud. Stop reading at a point in the story, and ask children to write about what they think will happen next. Have children share their writing before you complete the read aloud.

Cross-curricular Teaching Idea

Have children use a map of the United States to locate geographic places and features mentioned in this tall tale. For example, have children find the Grand Canyon, the Rocky Mountains, the Mississippi River, and the Appalachians. Help them trace Paul Bunyan's journey from Maine to Oregon.

birds from Maine to California. He carries a tree-sized ax and can cut a hundred trees down at once. What is one quality or ability Paul Bunyan has? What are two things he supposedly created? What animal does he rescue during the Winter of the Blue Snow? What is one thing in the story that probably could happen? What is one thing that probably could not happen in real life? (47)

Who Was Johnny Appleseed?

Folk hero John Chapman was born September 26, 1774, in Leominster, Massachusetts. In 1797, Chapman began traveling alone from western Pennsylvania to the territories of Ohio, Michigan, Illinois, and Indiana on the western frontier. A humble man, he often went without shoes and wore his tin cooking pot on his head. Chapman earned the nickname "Johnny Appleseed" because he planted apple seeds he had bought from cider mills in Pennsylvania. To encourage the growth of apple trees, he also gave free apple seeds to pioneers who were headed west. Chapman died on March 10, 1845.

Teaching "Johnny Appleseed"

Before Reading: Explain to the class that Johnny Appleseed was a real person, not a fictional figure. Have you ever seen an apple tree? If you wanted to grow an apple tree, what would you do? How do the apples get from the trees to your house?

Vocabulary: awestruck: surprised; **twig:** a small branch; **lugging:** carrying a heavy object; **tike:** a small child; **handy:** convenient; **tramping:** walking heavily; **pouch:** a small bag

After Reading: Read this tall tale at least once, possibly twice. Then discuss different aspects of a tall tale that children hear. For example, tell them that heroes of tall tales were often real people. What is one thing that Johnny does that shows you he is a real person? Do you think Johnny Appleseed was a hero? Why or why not? (48)

Who Was John Henry?

John Henry is believed to have been an African-American railroad worker who helped lay tracks for the Chesapeake and Ohio line in the 1870s. He used a heavy hammer to drive steel spikes or to force sharp, pointed tools called drills into rock. After the invention of the steam drill, John Henry agreed to take part in a legendary drilling contest pitting man against machine. The contest was held in West Virginia in the Big Bend Tunnel. Henry won, but after the contest he died.

Teaching "John Henry"

Before Reading: Explain to the class that John Henry may have been a real person. Review what children know about working on a railroad, and introduce some of the work involved in laying a railroad track. Tell children that this selection is a ballad, or a folk song that tells a story. Invite children to join in by repeating the last line of every stanza.

Vocabulary: captain: the head of the work crew; **steam drill:** a drill powered by steam; **whop:** strike with a heavy blow; **mighty:** very; **strikin' fire:** making sparks

Teaching Idea

Most of the tall tales in this section exist in numerous versions. Children may enjoy hearing a slightly different version of the story. For example, after hearing a prose version of the Johnny Appleseed story, they might like to hear a poetic version, such as "Johnny Appleseed," by Stephen Vincent Benét.

Teaching Idea

Before you read "John Henry," review elements of poetry, such as rhyme, repetition, and rhythm (Section II, pages 61–62), with the class. Also, point out examples of dialect, such as "a man ain't nothin' but a man" or "every locomotive comes a-roarin' by." Tell the class that tall tales often contain words and expressions used by people in particular areas of the country.

Teaching Idea

One theme in "John Henry" that you could build on is the man-versus-machine theme. Humans are always inventing machines to do things formerly done by humans, and this often causes problems, as when workers are replaced by machines. Discuss with children some cases in which machines do what humans do and compete with them, e.g., computers versus chess champions, etc.

Teaching Idea

Julius Lester's *John Henry*, illustrated by Jerry Pinkney (see More Resources), includes some anecdotes about John Henry's early life and has a very different mood than this ballad. Children might enjoy comparing the poem and the ballad.

After Reading: Read the story at least once, possibly twice. What quality or ability did John Henry have? What is one thing in the song that probably did happen? What is one thing that probably did not happen? Do you think John Henry was a hero? Why or why not? (49)

Who Is Pecos Bill?

Pecos Bill is a fictional folk hero who may have been invented by cowboys in the West in the late 1800s. In 1923, journalist Edward O'Reilly first published stories about Bill's exploits in *Century* magazine. Bill's name comes from the Pecos River in Texas, the area where he is said to have grown up.

Teaching "Pecos Bill"

Before Reading: Explain to the class that Pecos Bill is a fictional character. Make sure children understand the vocabulary words listed below. Where do cowboys live? What skills and abilities do cowboys have?

Vocabulary: fussing: becoming upset; **hollering:** yelling; **keeping his eyes peeled:** looking carefully; **coyote:** a small, wolflike animal; **den:** a wild animal's home; **roam:** wander; **steer clear:** avoid; **bucked:** leaped up; **shrivel:** dry up; **funnel cloud:** a cloud shaped like a funnel, with a wide top and a narrow bottom; **cyclone:** a violent, rotating windstorm

After Reading: Read the story at least once, possibly twice. Then discuss different aspects of a tall tale that children hear. For example, the characters in tall tales often have unusual childhoods. Point out that Pecos Bill was raised in the West. What is one quality or ability Pecos Bill has? How does he feel about Widow-Maker? What does he do to help people in Texas? What is one thing in the story that probably could happen? What is one thing that probably could not happen? (50)

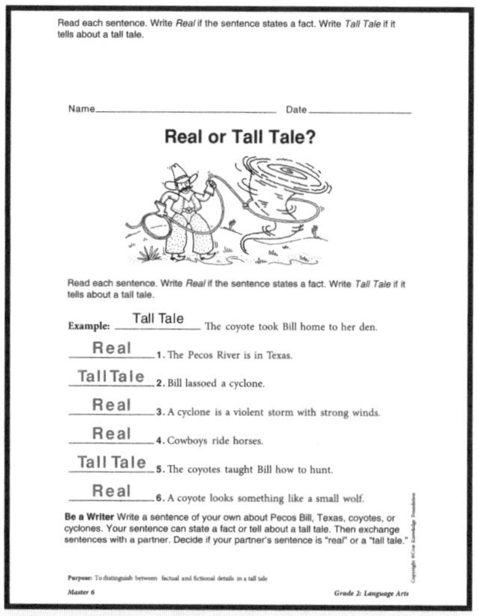
Read each sentence. Write *Real* if the sentence states a fact. Write *Tall Tale* if it tells about a tall tale.

Name__________ Date__________

Real or Tall Tale?

Read each sentence. Write *Real* if the sentence states a fact. Write *Tall Tale* if it tells about a tall tale.

Example: Tall Tale The coyote took Bill home to her den.

Real **1.** The Pecos River is in Texas.

Tall Tale **2.** Bill lassoed a cyclone.

Real **3.** A cyclone is a violent storm with strong winds.

Real **4.** Cowboys ride horses.

Tall Tale **5.** The coyotes taught Bill how to hunt.

Real **6.** A coyote looks something like a small wolf.

Be a Writer Write a sentence of your own about Pecos Bill, Texas, coyotes, or cyclones. Your sentence can state a fact or tell about a tall tale. Then exchange sentences with a partner. Decide if your partner's sentence is "real" or a "tall tale."

Purpose: To distinguish between factual and fictional details in a tall tale

Master 6 *Grade 2: Language Arts*

Use Instructional Master 6.

Who Was Casey Jones?

John Luther Jones was born in Missouri in 1863. He grew up in Cayce, Kentucky, the source of his nickname, "Casey." Known for his signature six-tone calliope whistle, Jones worked as an engineer for the Illinois Central Railroad. On April 30, 1900, Jones replaced a sick engineer on the southbound run of the Cannonball Express from Memphis, Tennessee, to Canton, Mississippi. At Vaughan, Mississippi, two freight trains blocked the main track. Jones could not stop in time to avoid an accident. He stayed on the train and slammed on the brakes, but his engine smashed into the back of the two freight trains. Jones's bravery probably saved many passengers' lives. Casey Jones was the only person killed in the wreck.

Teaching "Casey Jones"

Before Reading: If children learned about Casey Jones in Kindergarten, have them tell you what they already know. Explain to the class that Casey Jones was a real person. Make sure children understand the vocabulary words listed below.

Vocabulary: whizzing: rushing past; **coyote:** a wolf-like animal; **lonesome:** feeling alone; **dog tired:** very tired; **stoking:** feeding a fire; **mounted:** climbed; **squealed:** made a loud, shrill cry; **post:** position

Teaching Idea

After your children have studied these tall tales, have them create a comic strip version of one of them.

After Reading: Read the story at least once, possibly twice. What is one quality or ability Casey Jones had? What are some of the things that happened to animals as Casey's train came down the track? Do you think those things really happened? How do you think Casey's family felt after the wreck? Do you think Casey Jones was a hero? Why or why not? (51)

The Big Idea in Review

Tall tales are stories about American folk heroes who are larger than life.

Review

Below are some ideas for ongoing assessment and review activities. These are not meant to constitute a comprehensive list.

- Use some of the tall tales to practice cause and effect with children. Select an event from a tale, and then describe it to the class. Have children tell you what caused that event. You may also list events from a tale on chart paper, and then have children write about the causes of events in the tale. Extend this discussion by talking about how the main character changed the course of events. What would have happened if the characters had not acted the way they did in the tale?
- Draw a T-chart on chart paper with two columns labeled *before* and *after*. Write sentences from the text in the column labeled *before*, and have children tell you what happened *after*. This is another variation of practicing cause and effect. You may also make individual charts for children to complete and share with the class.
- As a journal activity, have children write about their favorite tall tale hero. Why was this character their favorite? Have children support their opinions with details from the text. Children can also be asked to pen a sequel: "The Further Adventures of Paul Bunyan," or "Paul Bunyan in the Modern World." The idea is for children to create new adventures for the character that are, generally speaking, consistent with the character's attributes and skills.
- Have children select another character from one of the tall tales and then tell the story from that character's perspective. Have children write their alternative tall tales and then read these aloud to the class.
- Invite children to write a tall tale of their own. Encourage them to focus on one skill—e.g., on a person who can run super fast, or jump very, very high, or scream extremely loud—and then think of a funny name for the character (possibly a name that suggests the character's skill, e.g., Shane Shrieklouder). Finally, have children think up one or more adventures in which the person's distinguishing skill can be put to good use.

More Resources

The titles listed below are offered as a representative sample of materials and not a complete list of everything that is available.

For children —

These books are generally intended to be read aloud, though some children may be able to read parts or all of the simpler texts.

- *American Tall Tales,* an audio recording by Jim Weiss (Greathall Productions, www.greathall.com, 1-800-477-6234). Tells the stories of Paul Bunyan, Pecos Bill, and Johnny Appleseed.
- *Casey Jones,* by Allan Drummond (Farrar, Straus & Giroux, 2001). Whimsical pictures in pen-and-ink and watercolor. Rhyming text creates a train-like rhythm. Hardcover, 32 pages, ISBN 0374311757.
- *John Henry,* by Julius Lester (Puffin, 1999). Paperback, 40 pages, ISBN 0140566228.
- *Johnny Appleseed,* by Reeve Lindbergh and illustrated by Kathy Jakobsen (Little, Brown & Co., 1993). Illustrated in an engaging folk-art style, this original poem tells the story of the determined and generous John Chapman. Paperback, 32 pages, ISBN 0316526347.
- *Johnny Appleseed (Rookie Biographies),* by Christin Ditchfield (Children's Press, 2003). An easy reader that is well told and nicely illustrated. Library binding, 24 pages, ISBN 0516228536.
- *Paul Bunyan,* by Steven Kellogg (William Morrow, 1985). Paperback, 48 pages, ISBN 0688058000.
- *Paul Bunyan Swings His Axe,* by Dell J. McCormick (Caxton Press, 1936). "Seventeen of the most interesting and authentic stories of the mighty logger are here presented in such a way that children can understand and enjoy them. The author collected these yarns firsthand during several years in the logging camps of Washington and Idaho; and he has arranged them so that they tell the complete story of Paul Bunyan's amazing adventures in the North Woods." Hardcover, 111 pages, ISBN 0870040936.
- *Pecos Bill,* retold and illustrated by Steven Kellogg (HarperTrophy, 1992). Paperback, 48 pages, ISBN 0688099246.

For teachers —

- John Henry: The Steel Driving Man, www.ibiblio.org/john_henry. A rich website for adults and children to enjoy. Contains discussions on the legend of John Henry as well as 17 musical interpretations of the famous African-American legend. Teachers are advised to review the songs and lyrics.
- Water Valley Casey Jones Railroad Museum, www.watervalley.net/users/caseyjones/casey.htm#cj, offers a historical account of what happened to Casey Jones and his train on the night of August 29, 1900, a link to the official wreck report, photographs, newspaper accounts, and more.

IV. Sayings and Phrases

The Big Idea

Sayings and Phrases are important to study because they are widely used in everyday language and writing—and their meanings are not always immediately clear.

What Students Should Already Know

Students may have heard sayings and phrases used in conversation at home, in school, on television or radio programs, or in cartoons, films, and videotapes. Children in Core Knowledge schools should also have studied sayings and phrases in Kindergarten and Grade 1.

What Students Need to Learn

- **The meanings and appropriate uses of the sayings and phrases for this grade**
- **Proverbs**
  - **are brief statements that express a general truth or observation about life.**
  - **may have a literal meaning and a figurative meaning.**
  - **have been passed down orally from one generation to the next.**
- **An idiom is an expression whose meaning differs from the literal meaning of its individual words.**
- **Proverbs and idioms are commonly used in spoken and written English.**

What Students Will Learn in Future Grades

In future grades, students will review and extend their learning about different sayings and phrases and will study their literal and figurative meanings.

Vocabulary

Student/Teacher Vocabulary

figurative: a meaning beyond the literal level (T)

idiom: an expression whose meaning differs from the literal meaning of its individual words (S)

literal: the exact meaning of a word or series of words (T)

proverb: a short, popular saying of unknown authorship (S)

Domain Vocabulary

Sayings and phrases and associated words:
saying, wisdom, wise, proverbial, expression, figure of speech, connotation, denotation, exaggeration, idiomatic, oral, oral tradition, allusion, contrast, compare, comparison, inference, infer, generalization, generalize, write, poem, birthday, late, never, diving, cold, spill, milk, bee, book, judge, easy, hard, hopeless, food, pig, heaps, too much, taste, pills, hot, cold, warm, cool, five, cross, right, wrong, good, bad, trick, fetch, sit up, old, young, *plus words from the sayings themselves, e.g.,* spill, preach, *and* will, *and words relevant to the sayings, e.g.,* grumpy *and* grouch *in "Get up on the wrong side of the bed" and* pointless *in "Don't cry over spilled milk"*

Materials

Instructional Master 7
Sayings and Phrases Fill-In, p. 105

large white easel paper, p. 99

poster board, p. 99

colored pencils and markers, p. 99

chart paper, p. 105

At a Glance

The most important ideas for you are:

- Proverbs are short, popular folk sayings by an unknown author that express general observations and truths about life.
- An idiom is an expression whose meaning goes beyond the meaning of its individual words.
- Proverbs and idioms often have a literal meaning as well as a figurative meaning.
- Proverbs and idioms employ such literary devices as repetition, alliteration, and metaphor.
- Because proverbs are used frequently in speech and writing, a child who can recognize and understand common proverbs will be better able to understand what he or she reads and hears.

What Teachers Need to Know

Background: The Origins of Proverbs and Idioms

The English language is peppered with familiar sayings and phrases. One kind of familiar expression is called a proverb. Proverbs are short, traditional folk sayings that have been passed along orally from generation to generation or quoted in works of literature and other printed materials. Proverbs usually express general truths based on the experiences and observations of everyday life.

Another kind of familiar saying is an idiom. An idiom is a phrase, or a group of words read or spoken as a unit. Idioms have their own meaning apart from the dictionary definitions of the words in the expression. Like proverbs, idioms have also been passed down orally or quoted in literature and other printed text.

Many proverbs and idioms reveal the concerns, interests, and folk beliefs of different peoples in the past. Some proverbs and idioms address commonplace topics such as the weather, medicine, animals, and codes of behavior. Made up by ordinary people long ago, these sayings often reflect the wisdom of those who earned their living from the soil or the sea, or who practiced different trades and crafts.

While your second graders will primarily study proverbs that originated in the English language, proverbs and idioms exist in most languages, cultures, and countries around the world. In many instances, proverbs and idioms from different cultures express similar ideas. Even though proverbs and idioms may express ideas that derived from a particular craft, belief, or practice that is now obsolete, the sayings are still meaningful and relevant today.

Teaching Idea

Introduce one of the proverbs or idioms from this section. Then ask children to recall other proverbs or idioms that they have heard. Encourage volunteers to share with the class any proverbs or idioms they may know.

Teaching Proverbs and Idioms

Because proverbs and idioms are widely used in the English language, second graders should be introduced to some common ones. Encouraging children to identify familiar proverbs and idioms and learn their meanings will help them better understand and communicate ideas. Children who are learning English as a second language will especially benefit from learning proverbs and idioms, since their meaning often does not derive from the dictionary definitions of the words.

Some proverbial sayings do have literal meanings; that is, they mean exactly what they say. But most proverbs and all idioms have a richer meaning beyond the literal level. To teach proverbs and idioms, you must help children understand the difference between the literal meanings of the words and their implied or figurative meanings. If you do not want to use the terms "literal" and "figurative," you can speak of "surface" meaning and "deeper" meaning.

Focusing on Meaning

As you introduce each of these proverbs and idioms to your children, first read it aloud several times. Then have children repeat it. Discuss what the proverb or idiom means. Provide clear examples to illustrate the meaning of the saying and to show in which situations it would be appropriate to use it. (In *What Your Second Grader Needs to Know,* there are additional examples of real-life situations in which it might be appropriate to use a particular proverb or idiom.)

Reinforcing Understanding

To reinforce children's understanding of the meaning of the sayings in this section, watch for opportunities to use them in applicable classroom situations or in connection with any aspects of the curriculum where using them makes sense. For example, in discussing a story about hypocrisy, you might use the saying "Practice what you preach"; or when grouping children into pairs for work, you might remind them that "Two heads are better than one." Throughout the school year, encourage children to pay attention to the use of proverbs and idioms in conversation at home or in school. Ask them to think about situations when they might use the sayings they have learned. Encourage children to bring in other proverbs they hear outside of class; you can write these on slips of paper and pin them to a bulletin board set aside for proverbs.

Teaching Idea

Before you begin, use colored markers to write out each proverb or idiom you will be discussing that day on a sheet of white easel paper. After you study each saying or phrase, have children illustrate it to show what it means. Then have the class create a series of proverb and idiom posters. Display these posters in the classroom to foster print awareness and to remind children of the sayings they have learned.

Recognizing Literary Elements and Devices

Many proverbs and idioms have common stylistic features. As you read the sayings and phrases, you may want to point out examples of the literary devices as shown in the chart below.

Literary Device	Definition	Example
alliteration	the repetition of initial consonants	Practice what you preach.
antithesis	words that have contrasting meaning	You can't teach an old dog new tricks.
ellipsis	the omission of words that are not necessary for understanding the meaning of a sentence	[It is] easier said than [it is] done.
hyperbole	exaggeration for emphasis	Eaten out of house and home
metaphor	a figure of speech in which a word or phrase is used to describe a different thing; a resemblance is implied	"An old dog" is an older person who is set in his or her ways.
parallelism	the use of words, phrases, or sentences that have a similiar grammatical structure	Where there's a will there's a way.
repetition	the repeating of a sound, word, phrase, or line	Where there's a will there's a way.

Helping children to notice the use of literary devices in proverbs and idioms opens a door to their understanding and appreciation of literature. Although you do not need to teach technical terms, you can call attention to the devices that make these expressions vivid and easy to remember as you discuss them.

IV. Sayings and Phrases

Introducing Sayings and Phrases

When you teach the following expressions, guide children to understand what they mean. You may also want to use the information about literary devices and origins to enrich children's understanding.

Teaching Idea

Before discussing "Back to the drawing board," explain to children that a drawing board is a large, rectangular board used by architects, engineers, graphic designers, and others for drawing up plans.

Back to the drawing board

Meaning: This idiom means that a person will have to start over again because his or her initial effort has failed.

Example: "When I grow up, I want to be a fashion designer," Jared told his teacher. "Just look at this sweater I made for my stuffed animal."

Miss Song picked up the sweater. "It's very nice, Jared, but you forgot to leave a neck hole."

Jared wrinkled his nose in frustration. "I guess it's back to the drawing board for me."

Literary Elements and Devices: alliteration (back, board), metaphor (the drawing board, which can be wiped clean, represents starting over again) Ask children, "Which two words begin with the same sound?"

Origin and History: This saying has been around for several centuries but was popularized during World War II by cartoonist Peter Arno. Arno used this idiom in a caption for a cartoon he published in *The New Yorker* magazine. The cartoon showed a plane exploding on takeoff and the plane's creator scratching his head and inspecting a huge roll of drawings. A related idiom is "Back to square one."

Teaching Idea

Invite children to compare the Kindergarten proverb "The early bird gets the worm" with "Better late than never." Are they contradictory?

Better late than never

Meaning: It is better to do something late than not to do it at all.

Example: Sylvie rushed into the library, out of breath. "I'm so sorry I'm late! I was so involved gathering the materials for our group project that I forgot all about the time. I hope you're not mad at me."

"Well, I'm not mad as long as you brought the materials," Pedro replied. "Now let's get down to work—better late than never."

Literary Elements and Devices: ellipsis ([It is] better [to be] late than never [to do something at all]), antithesis (late, never)

Origin and History: This proverb was recorded as early as the 1st century CE by the Roman historian Livy and was used in America by Puritan John Winthrop in about 1630.

Teaching Idea

After discussing "Cold feet," have children discuss other physical reactions people may have when they are afraid, such as clammy hands, rapid breathing, a lump in the throat, a knot in the stomach, and so on.

Cold feet

Meaning: A person is said to have cold feet if he or she becomes afraid to do something.

Example: "I'm trying out for the school play," Bill told Tony. "Why don't you come, too?"

"Oh, I'm no good at auditioning," Tony replied. "Every time my name is called, I get cold feet and run the other way."

Literary Elements and Devices : metaphor (cold feet represent the difficulty a person has in taking steps to do something)

Origin and History: This saying dates back to the 19th century. Some scholars believe it derives from the experience of soldiers with frozen feet who had to give up and retreat during long winter marches. This happened to Napoleon's troops on their way to Russia in the 1800s, and it happened to Hitler's troops on a similar march toward Moscow in the 20th century. It may also come from a common physiological response to stress: a person who is anxious or nervous may get cold hands and feet.

Don't cry over spilled milk.

Meaning: This proverb means that once something is done or lost you should not keep regretting or worrying about it.

Example: "I know I hadn't worn my green dress in more than a year," Keiko admitted, "but I wish Mom hadn't donated it to charity."

"There's no use crying over spilled milk," replied her sister. "The dress is gone now, and nothing can be done about it."

Literary Elements and Devices: metaphor (spilled milk implies something that is irrecoverable)

Origin and History: This saying is sometimes associated with Aesop's fable "The Maid and the Milk Pail" (Grade 1). An English proverb, it dates back to about 1659 and has since been used by such celebrated writers and thinkers as Jonathan Swift (1738), Theodore Roosevelt (1918), and H. G. Wells (1942).

Don't judge a book by its cover.

Meaning: This proverb means that one should not decide the value or worth of something or someone based solely on its appearance.

Example: Mr. Rivera placed the family's dinner on the table. "Dig in, everyone!"

"Blech!" spat Carmen. "What *is* that? It looks disgusting."

"Don't judge a book by its cover," warned her father. "I know it doesn't look like much, but this is an old family recipe that I love. Try a bite, and then decide if you like it."

Literary Elements and Devices: metaphor (the book represents a person or an object, and the cover represents the appearance of that person or object)

Origin and History: The use of this proverb dates back to about 1929 in the United States and to about 1954 in Britain.

Easier said than done

Meaning: It is easier to say what should be done than it is to actually do it.

Example: Arthur was disappointed about the grade he received on his spelling test. "I will travel back in time and study harder so I can get a better grade," he said.

"Easier said than done," Adrian replied. "Just how do you think you're going to do that? There's no such thing as a time machine."

Literary Elements and Devices: ellipsis ([It is] easier said [than it is] done), parallelism (Easier said than done), antithesis (said, done) Ask children, "Which two words could you add before *easier*? Which three words could you add after *said*?"

Origin and History: This proverb probably came from ancient Rome and was used by Miguel de Cervantes (1605–1615) in his novel *Don Quixote*.

Teaching Idea

Ask volunteers to create original variations of the proverb "Don't cry over spilled milk" to help them recognize its figurative meaning. For example, they might suggest "Don't cry over a broken crayon" or "Don't cry over ripped jeans."

Teaching Idea

After discussing "Don't judge a book by its cover," refer children to the story "Beauty and the Beast" (p. 74). Beauty finally recognizes the Beast's positive qualities despite his horrible appearance and agrees to marry him; her action illustrates the figurative meaning of this proverb.

Teaching Idea

The concept of "Easier said than done" is memorably illustrated in Aesop's fable known as "Belling the Cat," in which a bunch of mice propose to put a bell around the cat's neck so they will know when the cat is coming. Great idea—but who is willing to go and attach the bell? Children might enjoy hearing the story, which is available online and in editions of Aesop's fables.

Teaching Idea

To make sure your children understand the proverb "Easier said than done," read aloud both the elliptical version and the full sentence from which it is derived. Then have volunteers share experiences in which they talked about doing something and then realized how much more difficult the task was once they undertook it.

IV. Sayings and Phrases

Eaten out of house and home

Meaning: Such a huge amount of food has been eaten that the host is ruined.

Example: "Mom, can I have a snack?" Tara asked.

Mrs. Broussard opened the kitchen cabinet and sighed. "I don't have much left to offer you; your brother's soccer team was just here celebrating their win, and they nearly ate us out of house and home."

Literary Elements and Devices: alliteration (house, home), hyperbole (out of house and home)

Origin and History: This idiom can be traced back to about 40 CE. It appears in *Henry IV* by William Shakespeare (1564–1616).

Teaching Idea

Connect "Get a taste of your own medicine" to the lessons Ebenezer Scrooge learns from the spirits who visit him in "A Christmas Carol" (p. 76).

Get a taste of your own medicine

Meaning: This idiom means "to receive the same unpleasant treatment one has given to others."

Example: Ben handed Nathan the list of classmates he was inviting to join in a kickball game.

"I see that Irina is not on this list," observed Nathan.

"No," replied Ben. "I got so sick of being left out of the games she organizes that I decided to give her a taste of her own medicine."

Literary Elements and Devices: metaphor (the medicine represents something unpleasant) Ask children, "What do you think the medicine in this idiom stands for?"

Origin and History: This expression, which dates back to about 1896, derives from the fact that medicine often has a bad taste.

Teaching Idea

When discussing "Get up on the wrong side of the bed," share with children the superstition about the right and wrong sides of the bed. You can use it as a jumping off point for a discussion of other superstitions, e.g., broken mirror, black cat, step on crack, etc.

Get up on the wrong side of the bed

Meaning: This idiom means that someone is in a bad mood because he or she started the day wrong after waking up.

Example: "Lana, I need to ask you something," confided James. "Are you mad at me for some reason? You were acting very unfriendly yesterday."

"I'm sorry," Lana apologized. "You did nothing wrong and I shouldn't have been rude to you. I was in a terrible mood yesterday; I guess I just got up on the wrong side of the bed."

Origin and History: This saying derives from the superstition that there is a "wrong" side of a bed; it was generally believed that the wrong side was the left side. According to ancient custom, it is unlucky to put your left foot on the ground first or to put your left shoe on before your right; otherwise, you will have gotten off on the "wrong foot" for the day. These ideas can be traced back at least to ancient Rome. The Roman Emperor Caesar Augustus (1st century CE), whom children will study in third grade, not only avoided getting out of bed on the left side but was careful to always put his right shoe on first.

In hot water

Meaning: This idiom means "in bad trouble."

Example: "Mrs. Vidal reminded us 10 times to practice memorizing our poems for the school assembly today. I can't believe I forgot. Boy, am I going to be in hot water when it's my turn to recite and I don't know the words to my poem!"

Literary Elements and Devices: metaphor (hot water represents pain and suffering)

Origin and History: This saying appears in writing as early as 1537. Some scholars believe that hot water is associated with big trouble because boiling water was used as a weapon during the Middle Ages. Soldiers trying to scale the walls of a fortress or storm its gates were often repelled by boiling oil or water, which was poured down on them. Also, the Spanish Inquisition used water or oil as an instrument of torture when they wanted someone to confess.

Keep your fingers crossed.

Meaning: This idiom means "to hope that nothing bad will happen" or "to help make a wish come true."

Example: "I feel very nervous about letting Rosalin take the train alone to visit Auntie Ana," Mrs. Flores told her husband.

"She's in good hands—the conductor and the train porters know to keep an eye on her—and the ride is only 15 minutes," Mr. Flores replied. "But if it makes you feel better, we can keep our fingers crossed."

Origin and History: This idiom has been in use since the 1920s. It derives from the superstition that making the sign of the cross—the Christian symbol of salvation—could protect someone from harm.

Practice what you preach.

Meaning: Act the way you tell others to act.

Example: "I asked the boys three times to pick up their dirty clothes off the floor, and they still haven't done it," Mr. Cohen griped to his wife.

"That may be true," Mrs. Cohen replied, "but you've also left *your* laundry lying around. Maybe if you practiced what you preach, they'd be more likely to do what you say."

Literary Elements and Devices: alliteration (practice, preach), antithesis (practice, preach), parallelism (practice, preach), ellipsis ([You should] practice what you preach)

Origin and History: This saying has been traced back to ancient Rome and China. It is one of the wise sayings of Confucius collected in the *Analects*. It was later used by the Irish scholar Columba in the 6th century, by the English poet Geoffrey Chaucer in the 14th century, and by the Spanish novelist Miguel de Cervantes in the 17th century. It has been in use in the United States since at least 1702.

Turn over a new leaf.

Meaning: This idiom means "to make an important change in the way you act" or "to make a fresh start."

Example: "Wow!" Mom exclaimed. "What happened here? You used to be such a slob, but now your bedroom is so neat and tidy."

"I'm turning over a new leaf," Yoshi replied. "Before, all my toys were getting lost and broken. Now I know that if I keep everything organized, I can keep my things nice."

Literary Elements and Devices: metaphor (a leaf represents a place to begin anew)

Origin and History: The word *leaf* in this idiom refers to a blank sheet of paper that has been folded into two or more pages in a book. The idiom derives from the idea that one turns over a leaf to begin writing on a fresh page. This expression originated sometime in the 16th century, after the advent of the bound book in the 1400s.

Teaching Idea

When discussing the proverb "Two heads are better than one," invite volunteers to describe a difficult problem they solved or a task they completed with the help of another person.

Two heads are better than one.

Meaning: When one person has a problem to solve or a job to do, a second person can often help out.

Example: Kenneth called his friend Jen on the phone. "I can't understand the directions for the new game I got for my birthday. Will you come over and help me? Two heads are better than one, and I know that by working together we can figure this out. Then, we can play the new game!"

Literary Elements and Devices: antithesis (two, one), ellipsis (Two heads are better than one [head]), metaphor (heads represents thoughts and ideas)

Origin and History: This proverb is found in *Heywood's Collection* (1546), a volume of proverbs by John Heywood. Different versions of it date back to ancient Greece where it appears in the writings of Homer, Plato, and Aristotle. Aristotle's version, from the *Politics*, is "Two good men are better than one." The corollary is, of course, that two bad men are worse than one.

Cross-curricular Teaching Idea

The proverb "Where there's a will, there's a way," which was also taught in Kindergarten, is illustrated by the poems "Harriet Tubman" (p. 66) and "Lincoln" (p. 66). Remind children that Harriet Tubman and Abraham Lincoln were determined to achieve their goals despite the obstacles they faced. Tubman had to overcome fear and danger to help free slaves, and Lincoln had to overcome poverty in order to get an education.

Where there's a will, there's a way.

Meaning: If you want to do something badly enough, you will find a way to do it.

Example: "Mom, can I have a new bike?" Franny asked. "My old bike is too small for me."

"Bicycles are very expensive," her mother replied. "But if you are willing to save up your allowance and babysitting money to pay for one-half of the cost, I will pay for the other half."

"Aw, but that's impossible!" Franny complained.

"It will be hard," her mother admitted, "but not impossible. Where there's a will, there's a way. Just think of how proud you will be when you are able to walk into the store and buy the bike with your own money."

Literary Elements and Devices: alliteration (where, will, way), parallelism (there's a will, there's a way), repetition (there's) Ask children, "Which word is repeated in this proverb?"

Origin and History: This proverb is found in George Herbert's 1640 collection, *Outlandish Proverbs*, in slightly different form: "To him that will, ways are not wanting." There are similar versions in many other languages: in French ("Vouloir c'est pouvoir"), in Italian ("A chi vuole, non mancano modi"), in Spanish ("Donde hay gana, hay mana"), and in German ("Wer will, dermag"). It was first noted in the United States in 1838.

Teaching Idea

Encourage the class to discuss whether they feel the proverb "You can't teach an old dog new tricks" is true. To get them thinking critically, ask children to provide examples of well-known older people who have broken records, accepted new challenges, or learned new skills. Children might cite examples from real-life or fictional stories they have heard that contradict the wisdom of this proverb.

You can't teach an old dog new tricks.

Meaning: This proverb means that people become more set in their ways as they grow older. Someone who is accustomed to doing something in a certain way finds it difficult to learn another way to do it.

Example: Susan and James were trying to get their mother interested in the music they liked. They played song after song for her, but still she didn't like it.

Finally, Susan decided it was never going to work. She sighed and said, "You can't teach an old dog new tricks."

Literary Elements and Devices: antithesis (old, new), metaphor (the dog represents people who are set in their ways, and the tricks represent skills), parallelism (old dog, new tricks) Ask children, "Which two words have the opposite meaning?"

Origin and History: A version of this proverb was used by English poet Geoffrey Chaucer in the 14th century, and it appears in the writing of British authors Laurence Sterne (1713–1768), Sir Walter Scott (1771–1832), and Anthony Trollope (1815–1882).

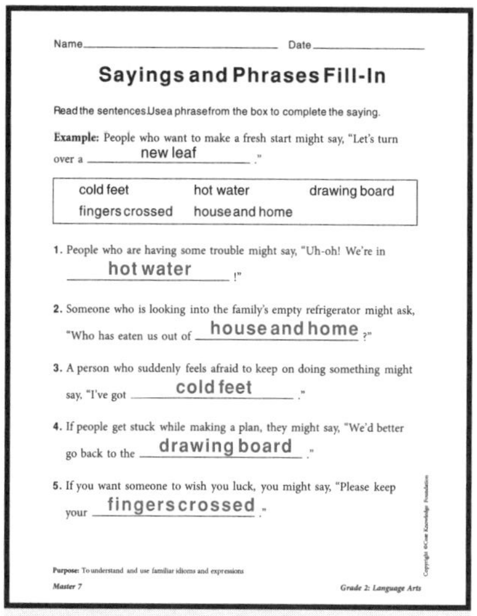
Name________________ Date________

Sayings and Phrases Fill-In

Read the sentences. Use a phrase from the box to complete the saying.

Example: People who want to make a fresh start might say, "Let's turn over a ___new leaf___."

cold feet	hot water	drawing board
fingers crossed	house and home	

1. People who are having some trouble might say, "Uh-oh! We're in ___hot water___!"
2. Someone who is looking into the family's empty refrigerator might ask, "Who has eaten us out of ___house and home___?"
3. A person who suddenly feels afraid to keep on doing something might say, "I've got ___cold feet___."
4. If people get stuck while making a plan, they might say, "We'd better go back to the ___drawing board___."
5. If you want someone to wish you luck, you might say, "Please keep your ___fingers crossed___."

Purpose: To understand and use familiar idioms and expressions

Master 7 — Grade 2: Language Arts

Use Instructional Master 7.

Review

Below are some ideas for ongoing assessment and review activities. These are not meant to constitute a comprehensive list.

- Use Instructional Master 7, *Sayings and Phrase Fill-In*, to help children recall and understand the meaning of each idiom. Invite volunteers to give examples of how to use each one.
- Use the sayings and phrases from this section as part of a morning message to your class. Post a saying or phrase on the board or chart paper, and then have children identify grammatical concepts as a review. You may also then review the definition of the saying or phrase.
- Look at the group of sayings and phrases, and then have children think of the stories they have read in this section. Select the sayings and phrases that best match the story's lesson. This will be an interesting way to review the stories and their main ideas.
- Ask the class to illustrate the sayings and phrases and then collect them into a class book. You can refer to the book when teaching a particular saying and phrase.
- As a class book-buddy activity in which children from different grades are paired together, have each pair of children share sayings and phrases from their grade levels. Then, have them compare the sayings and phrases and their meanings. Illustrate both on one sheet of paper.

The Big Idea in Review

Sayings and Phrases are important to study because they are widely used in everyday language and writing—and their meanings are not always immediately clear.

More Resources

The titles listed below are offered as a representative sample of materials and not a complete list of everything that is available.

For children —

These books are generally intended to be read aloud, though some children may be able to read parts or all of the simpler texts.

• *There's a Frog in My Throat: 440 Animal Sayings a Little Bird Told Me*, by Loreen Leedy and illustrated by Pat Street (Holiday House, 2003). Hardcover, 48 pages, ISBN 0823417743.

For teachers —

• *Clichés: Over 1500 Phrases Explored and Explained*, by Betty Kirkpatrick (Griffin, 1999). Paperback, 224 pages, ISBN 0312198442.

• *Concise Dictionary of Phrase and Fable*, edited by Elizabeth Knowles (Oxford, 2003). Paperback, 608 pages, ISBN 0192801252.

• *Dictionary of Phrase and Fable*, by E. Cobham Brewer (HarperResource, 2000). Hardcover, 1,326 pages, ISBN 006019653X.

• *Dictionary of Word and Phrase Origins*, by William and Mary Morris (HarperResource, 1988). Hardcover, 688 pages, ISBN 006015862X.

• *Familiar Quotations: A Collection of Passages, Phrases and Proverbs Traced to their Sources in Ancient and Modern Literature (17th edition)*, by John Bartlett and edited by Justin Kaplan (Little, Brown & Company, 2002). Hardcover, 1,472 pages, ISBN 0316084603.

• *Random House Dictionary of Popular Proverbs and Sayings (Second Edition)*, by Gregory Y. Titelman (Random House, 2000). Paperback, 480 pages, ISBN 0375705848.

• *Scholastic Dictionary of Idioms and Phrases*, by Marvin Terban (Scholastic, 1996). More than 600 phrases and expressions. Includes a keyword index. Paperback, 245 pages, ISBN 0590381571.

History and Geography

Percentages beside major topics provide a rough guide for allocating time for History and Geography during the year.

History and Geography in Second Grade

WORLD HISTORY AND GEOGRAPHY

Grade 2 begins with a review and extension of the basic geography concepts of place, region, human and physical characteristics, and relative location, which were introduced in Kindergarten and expanded upon in Grade 1. Children review that maps have symbols, keys to decipher those symbols, and that maps also show direction, though only the cardinal directions are taught at this level. Children review the continents and identify all four oceans along with Canada, the United States, Mexico, and Central America on the North American continent. Their exploration of the globe continues through identification and location of the Equator and the Northern and Southern Hemispheres, as well as a review of the location of the North and South Poles. New concepts and vocabulary dealing with physical features are also introduced.

Section II on Early Civilizations of Asia continues the exploration of world history studies begun in Grade 1. In discussing the various civilizations with children, review the basic elements of civilization—the development of permanent settlements; the evolution of some settlements into cities, often with monumental buildings; the division of labor; the establishment of political organization and a social class structure; and, often, the development of writing. Religion accompanied these innovations as people strove to make sense of their environment. It should be noted that civilization is not a value judgment but simply the determination that a certain group of people had developed these characteristics.

Children begin their study of civilizations in ancient Asia by focusing on the geography of China, India, and Japan. They then learn about the first civilization in India along the Indus River Valley. The concept of settling near a river to farm should be familiar to children, having studied in Grade 1 the ancient civilizations that sprang up along the Tigris and Euphrates Rivers and the Nile.

Discussion of the Ganges River can be a good segue into the topic of Hinduism, because the river is sacred to Hindus. Children will learn about the basic tenets of Hinduism and its three most important deities, Brahma, Vishnu, and Shiva, as well as the Vedas, Hinduism's holy books. Buddhism, although no longer a dominant religion in India, began in this region. Children will learn about Buddha, what he taught, and how Buddhism spread to other lands. They will also learn about King Asoka, the ancient king who put Buddha's teachings into practice.

The discussion of ancient China also begins with a discussion of two of China's most important rivers, the Yellow (Huang He) River and the Yangtze (Chang Jiang or Ch'ang) River. Children will then learn about the teachings of Confucius and several achievements of the ancient Chinese—the Great Wall of China, the invention of paper, and the importance of silk culture in the economic development of China. The contemporary theme of holidays is introduced with an explanation of the rituals of the Chinese New Year.

In teaching about Hinduism and Buddhism, the emphasis should be on conveying some of the most important beliefs of each religion, as well as a sense of each religion's historical importance—not on teaching which religious ideas are true or false. The goal is not to train children to believe or disbelieve in the validity of a religion but to enable them to understand religious ideas that are important to millions of people around the world. Confucianism is a philosophy rather than a religion. Confucianism, with its emphasis on duties and proper treatment of elders, has had a tremendous impact on the development of all aspects of Chinese life. Although they have sometimes been attacked by critics, Confucian ideas remain influential today, not only in China but also in Japan, South Korea, Vietnam, and Singapore.

The section on Japan focuses not so much on its ancient history but on its contemporary culture. The section begins with the location of Japan in relation to the Asian mainland. Children will also learn about Japan's modern cities and about some of its traditions—the art of origami and the kimono, the traditional clothing of Japanese men and women.

Ancient Greece is the topic of the final section in the World History strand. The section begins with locating Greece and moves on to a discussion of the city-states of Sparta and Athens, with emphasis on the development of Athenian democracy. Several stories are told to show the heroism of the early Greeks, and profiles are presented for the philosophers Socrates, Plato, and Aristotle, and the empire-builder, Alexander the Great.

Note: *Traditionally, the abbreviations AD or BC have been written alongside dates to indicate whether the events in question took place before or after the birth of Jesus. BC means "Before Christ." AD comes from a Latin phrase, "Anno Domini," meaning "Year of the Lord." AD 1000 means one thousand years after the birth of Jesus; 1000 BC means one thousand years before the birth of Jesus. However, scholars increasingly prefer to write 1000 BCE (Before the Common Era) instead of 1000 BC, and 1000 CE (Common Era) instead of AD 1000. Therefore, BCE and CE are used in this book.*

I. Geography

The Big Idea

Maps and globes are convenient ways to show the location and some of the human and physical characteristics of our planet.

Remember that each subject you study with children expands their vocabulary and introduces new terms, thus making them better listeners and readers. As you study geography, use map work, read alouds, and discussions to build children's vocabularies.

What Students Should Already Know

Students in Core Knowledge schools should be familiar with

Kindergarten and Grade 1

- what maps and globes represent and how to use them
- what rivers, lakes, and mountains are and how they are represented on maps and globes
- the location of the Atlantic and Pacific Oceans, the North and South Poles, and the seven continents
- the name and location of their continent, country, state, and community
- the use of map keys, symbols, and directions (north, south, east, west) on a map
- the location of the Indian and Arctic Oceans; Mexico and Central America; the countries of North America (Canada and the United States); the Equator; the Northern and Southern Hemispheres
- the meaning of *peninsula, harbor, bay,* and *island*

What Students Need to Learn

- **The map and globe skills listed in the *Sequence***
- **The terms *coast, valley, prairie, desert,* and *oasis***

What Students Will Learn in Future Grades

In future grades, students will review and extend their learning about geographic concepts and vocabulary.

Grade 3

- the use of bar scales, an atlas, and online resources
- the terms *boundary, channel, delta, isthmus, plateau, reservoir,* and *strait*

Grade 4

- the use of map scale; latitude, longitude, coordinates, and degrees
- Prime Meridian (0° Longitude); Greenwich, England; 180° Line (International Date Line)
- how to read relief maps: elevations and depressions

Grade 5

- the Tropics of Cancer and Capricorn
- how to read climate and time zone maps, and different map projections

Vocabulary

Student/Teacher Vocabulary

bay: a section of the ocean that is partially surrounded by land (S)

coast: the land that runs along an ocean or gulf (S)

desert: dry land that gets little moisture (S)

Equator: an imaginary line around the center of the world that divides the globe into the Northern and Southern Hemispheres (S)

harbor: an area of water that is protected by land; an inlet along a coast (S)

hemisphere: half of a sphere; in geography, it refers to half of Earth (S)

island: land completely surrounded by water (S)

isthmus: a narrow strip of land connecting two larger landmasses (S)

landmass: a large area of land (S)

locate: to find the place where something is (S)

location: the place where something is (S)

North Pole: the northern point at which Earth rotates on its axis (S)

oasis: an area of green in a desert (S)

peninsula: a piece of land surrounded by water on three sides (S)

prairie: a large area of level or gently rolling grasslands (S)

South Pole: the southern point at which Earth rotates on its axis (S)

valley: a long expanse of lowland lying between hills or mountains (S)

Domain Vocabulary

States and associated words:
North America, continent, landmass, United States, country, boundary, border, 50 states, Hawaii, islands, Alaska, state, locate, community, city, town, township, village, suburb, rural, urban, *plus the names of specific cities, states, and countries*

Maps, globes, and associated words:
Earth, sphere, place, symbol, stand for, pictures, forest, desert, mountain, water, ocean, river, lake, park, city, dot, capital, star, road, house, building, country, border, key, legend, direction, way to go, east, west, north, south, northeast, northwest, southeast, southwest, up, down, top, bottom, right, left, near, close to, far, next to, beside, distance, mile, direction finder, compass rose

Oceans and associated words:
four, most of Earth, water, deep, waves, tides, Pacific, largest, deepest, island, Japan, Asia, Hawaii, United States, North America, South America, Atlantic, second-largest, Europe, Africa, Indian, third-largest, monsoon, wind, rain, rainy season, Asia, Australia, Arctic, smallest, ice-covered, Pacific, coast, coastal, beach, shore, coastline, warm, cold, saltwater, fresh

Continents and associated words:
seven, landmass, largest bodies of land, islands

Asia and associated words:
largest, Eurasia, share, Europe, Northern Hemisphere, highest, Himalayas, Mount Everest, cold, rugged, steep, rocky, cliff, slope, climb, Indian Ocean, Pacific Ocean, wind, monsoon, rainy season, panda, farming, rice, desert, oil, oil well, Middle East, Israel, Israelis, ancient, Palestine

Materials

Instructional Masters 8–9, 50

K-W-L Chart, p. 114

The United States of America, p. 116

Treasure Hunt, p. 117

wall map of the world and a globe, p. 113

encyclopedias, p. 116

construction paper, p. 118

paints or markers, p. 118

a variety of maps of different regions and places, p. 118

pictures from magazines of people dressed for different climates, p. 119

children's journals, p. 119

index cards, p. 119

As a general rule of thumb, when choosing projects to do with your children, they should be well-thought-out and relate directly to the unit objectives and time allotments outlined in the beginning of each section. Projects have an important place, especially in the early grades when they help reinforce vocabulary and content and don't serve purely as time fillers. Throughout this subject, we have added teaching ideas with fun and purposeful extensions to further children's understanding. Keep in mind that a useful way to engage young children in History and Geography topics can be through the use of structured simulations (acting out events).

Vocabulary continued

Domain Vocabulary

Africa and associated words:
second-largest, Equator, Northern Hemisphere, Southern Hemisphere, North Africa, desert, Sahara, sand, camel, Nile River, longest, Egypt, Egyptians, pyramid, hot, tropical, rainforest, desert, grassland, savanna, mountains, Mount Kilimanjaro, high, tall, cold, ice, snowcapped, Atlantic, Pacific, Indian, Mediterranean Sea

North America and associated words:
third-largest, Northern Hemisphere, Canada, United States, Mexico, Central America, seven, Belize, Costa Rica, El Salvador, Guatemala, Honduras, Nicaragua, Panama, Native Americans, Spanish, Native American languages, Atlantic, Pacific, Western Hemisphere

South America and associated words:
fourth-largest, Equator, Northern Hemisphere, Southern Hemisphere, Equator, hot, rainy, rainforest, Amazon River, Brazil, Andes Mountains, Pacific, Atlantic

Antarctica and associated words:
fifth-largest, Equator, Southern Hemisphere, ice-covered, snow-covered, very cold, seal, penguin, whale, scientist, Pacific, Atlantic

Europe and associated words:
sixth-largest, Eurasia, share, Asia, Northern Hemisphere, north, North Pole, cold, dark, winter, long nights, reindeer, snow, south, warm, sunny, orchard, olives, fishing, beach, Atlantic, Arctic, Mediterranean Sea

Australia and associated words:
smallest, Equator, Southern Hemisphere, "the land down under," kangaroo, koala bear, warm, sunny, little snow, desert, seasons, winter, summer

Globe and associated words:
halfway down, around, very hot, year-round, hemisphere, Northern, top, Southern, bottom, Equator, divides, separates, poles, North, South, cold, thick ice, little snow

Geographical terms and associated words:
coast, coastline, shore, shoreline, sandy, rugged, rocky, waves, surf, bird, valley, gentle, sloping, river, stream, mountains, hill, elevation, altitude, prairie, flat, plains, grass, grasslands, savanna, tundra, desert, sand, arid, dry, hot, sun, temperature, oasis, cactus, camel, Sahara

Cross-curricular Connections

Language Arts

Fiction

Stories

- "The Blind Men and the Elephant" (India)
- "A Christmas Carol" (England)
- "Before Breakfast," from *Charlotte's Web*" (United States)
- "The Magic Paintbrush" (China)
- "Talk" (West Africa)
- "The Tongue-Cut Sparrow" (Japan)

At a Glance

The most important ideas for you are:

- Children should be able to locate on a map the state in which they live and the approximate location of their community within that state.
- Maps have keys, or legends, to explain the symbols that represent the human and physical characteristics of a place.
- Unless otherwise indicated, most maps are oriented with the North Pole at the top.
- Children should be able to locate on a map or globe the seven continents and four oceans; Canada, the United States, Mexico, and Central America; and the North and South Poles.
- The Equator is an imaginary line around the center of the world that divides the globe into the Northern and Southern Hemispheres.
- All continents are in at least two hemispheres at once—Northern or Southern, and Eastern or Western.
- Children understand the meaning of and can use the terms *coast, valley, prairie, desert,* and *oasis.*
- Children should have frequent opportunities to work with maps and globes, not only as part of their geography study, but also while studying topics in world and American history.

What Teachers Need to Know

A. Spatial Sense

Background

This section provides children with opportunities to work with maps, globes, and other geographic tools in order to foster their geographic awareness. Throughout the year, have children regularly locate where they are on maps and globes in relation to the places they are studying. Also, have them locate the continents of origin of the songs, music, and paintings they are studying.

Teaching Idea

Begin the discussion of geography by reviewing with children the definitions of maps and globes and their uses. Ask what they remember about the seven continents as a way to reintroduce the North American continent and the locations of the United States, their state, and their community. Use a wall map of the world and a globe to locate the continents and the oceans.

The Continents

Places and regions have certain characteristics that distinguish them from other places and regions. These characteristics are both physical (landforms, climate, and vegetation) and human (population, settlement, and culture, including a form of government, economic activity, and other aspects of a people's way of life). No two places have the same physical and human characteristics. The North and South Poles and the four oceans—Pacific, Atlantic, Indian, and Arctic—are human categories for natural phenomena. These classifications, or categories, are ways that people make sense of what they see. "Continents" is a similar category.

I. Geography

Teaching Idea

Use Instructional Master 50, *K-W-L Chart*, to activate children's prior knowledge about the seven continents.

Name________________ Date________

K—W—L Chart

What students KNOW about a topic	What students WANT to know about a topic	What students LEARNED about a topic

Directions: Use this chart to activate a child's prior knowledge about a topic. Fill in the last column as you conduct the unit of study.

Master 50 *Grade 2: Teacher Material*

Copyright ©Core Knowledge Foundation

Use Instructional Master 50.

There are seven continents, or large landmasses: Asia, Africa, North America, South America, Antarctica, Europe, and Australia. People live on all the continents, as do plants and animals. While people are not native to Antarctica, a number of countries keep research camps on the continent today. There are few plants and animals that are native to this continent.

Asia

Asia is the largest continent of the seven. The Arabian Peninsula and the eastern shore of the Mediterranean, as well as Iran and Iraq, are called the Middle East. India, Pakistan, and Bangladesh are known as South Asia; China, Korea, and Japan as East Asia. The peninsula that includes Thailand, Vietnam, Laos, and Cambodia, and the island countries of Indonesia and the Philippines are called Southeast Asia.

Africa

Africa is the second-largest continent. Africa, more than any other continent, illustrates the latitudinal banding of climates and ecosystems. Temperate conditions prevail in the south and northwest, while the northern and southern interior experience hot, dry desert conditions. Hot, wet tropical conditions occur in the equatorial latitudes. Between the desert and the rainforest, a region periodically wet and dry, tropical conditions support savanna grasslands, which are home to Africa's big-game animals.

North America

North America is the third-largest continent. Children should associate it with the location of the United States. While Mexico and the countries of Central America are often referred to as being part of Latin America, geographically they are part of the North American continent. It is their Spanish-speaking culture that ties them to Latin America.

South America

South America is the fourth-largest continent. The Andes Mountains range from north to south on the far western side of South America. The equatorial portion of the continent, including much of Brazil, is covered by tropical rainforest.

Antarctica

Antarctica is the fifth-largest continent and is ice- and snow-covered yearround. People did not live on Antarctica until the middle of the 20th century, when several countries set up more than 40 research camps for scientists. It would be incorrect to say that no plants live on Antarctica, but the lichens, mosses, and fungi that do survive on the continent will be unfamiliar to children. More familiar animals, such as seals, penguins, and whales, live on the coasts and in the offshore waters of the continent.

Europe

Europe is the sixth-largest continent. It shares part of the same landmass as Asia, but the two are considered separate continents, separated by the Ural Mountains. That part of Europe that is near the North Pole is cool to cold much of the year. As one moves south, the climate becomes warm and sunny much of the year.

Teaching Idea

Help children review certain characteristics associated with each of the continents they may have learned about in previous grades:

Asia: rice, panda, oil well
Europe: olive, Eiffel Tower, Tower Bridge
Africa: lion, peanut, Great Pyramid of Giza, Nile River
North America: Statue of Liberty, ear of corn
South America: horse, rainforest
Antarctica: penguin, whale, seal
Australia: kangaroo, koala bear, eucalyptus tree

As children continue to learn about different regions and countries of the world, encourage them to discuss animals, plants, and places that they have learned about.

Australia

Australia is the smallest of the seven continents and is often referred to as "the land down under." Children learned this term when they first studied hemispheres in Grade 1. Much of the western portion of the continent, along with the central region, is hot and dry, while the eastern side is milder and wetter. It is in this area along the higher mountains in the Great Dividing Range that snow falls. About 90% of the people of Australia live near the coasts, most in a narrow ribbon along the eastern and southeastern coasts. Less populous areas that are located in the middle of the continent and are far from large cities are known as the "outback."

The Oceans

The world's four oceans are the Pacific, Atlantic, Indian, and Arctic.

Pacific Ocean

The Pacific is the largest and deepest of the four oceans, extending over about a third of Earth's surface. The Pacific reaches from the Arctic to Antarctica and separates North and South America from Asia and Australia. Thousands of islands dot the ocean's surface from the Bering Strait to the South China Sea and beyond to the southeast. These include the islands of Oceania, such as Guam and the Marshalls, as well as Japan, the Philippines, Hawaii, and New Zealand. The Ring of Fire is a series of volcanoes that ring the ocean.

Atlantic Ocean

The Atlantic Ocean is the second-largest of the world's four oceans. It separates North and South America from Europe and Africa and reaches from the Arctic to Antarctica. A major feature of the ocean is the Gulf Stream, a warm ocean current. The current begins in the Gulf of Mexico, where the water temperature is 80°F. As the current flows northeast into the Atlantic, it becomes the North Atlantic Drift. Although the water temperature decreases as it flows across the Atlantic, it is still responsible for the year-round moderate climate of Western Europe.

Indian Ocean

The Indian Ocean is the world's third-largest ocean. It stretches from Antarctica in the south to southern Africa in the west to Australia and Indonesia in the east. The Arabian Sea, Persian Gulf, Gulf of Aden, Red Sea, Bay of Bengal, and Andaman Sea are its major arms. An important climate feature in south Asia to which the ocean contributes is the monsoon. This wind system reverses direction with the seasons, bringing cool, dry weather in winter and very wet, hot weather in summer.

Arctic Ocean

The Arctic Ocean is the smallest of the four oceans. It is ice-covered yearround except along the edges. It is bordered by Greenland, Canada, Alaska, Russia, and Norway. Its access to the Pacific Ocean is through the Bering Sea, and to the Atlantic Ocean through the Greenland Sea.

Teaching Idea

Children should also know about their own state and community. You can learn about states from encyclopedias. To learn about your local community, visit your local public library or historical society.

Teaching Idea

Have children locate and color their state on Instructional Master 8, *The United States of America.* Have children find the approximate location of their community and put a dot there. The dot should be larger than their pencil point but not by much. Explain that a dot is the map symbol for cities. Then have children locate the state that is either east or west of their state and label it with its abbreviation.

You may extend this activity by explaining that a star is the conventional map symbol for a state or national capital. Have children locate the approximate location of their state capital and draw a star there.

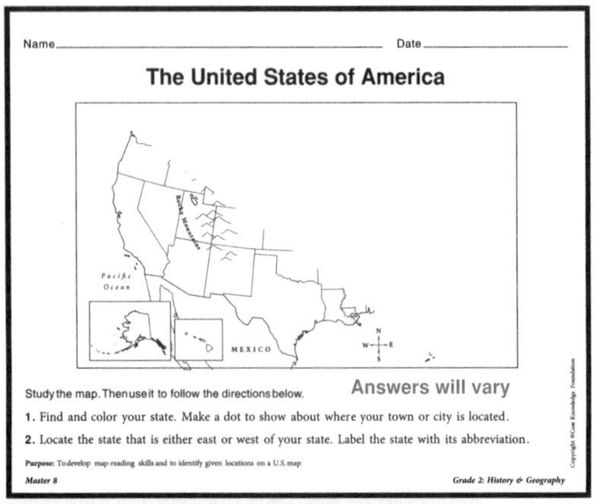

Name __________ Date __________

The United States of America

Study the map. Then use it to follow the directions below. Answers will vary

1. Find and color your state. Make a dot to show about where your town or city is located.
2. Locate the state that is either east or west of your state. Label the state with its abbreviation.

Purpose: To develop map-reading skills and to identify given locations on a U.S. map

Master 8 *Grade 2: History & Geography*

Copyright ©Core Knowledge Foundation

Use Instructional Master 8.

North America and Its Countries

North America is the third-largest continent and is part of both the Northern Hemisphere and the Western Hemisphere. The continent stretches from the Isthmus of Panama to beyond the Arctic Circle, and includes Canada, the United States (including Alaska), Mexico, the Caribbean islands, Greenland, and the Central American countries of Belize, Guatemala, El Salvador, Honduras, Nicaragua, Costa Rica, and Panama. North America is bordered by the Arctic Ocean to the north, the Atlantic Ocean to the east, and the Pacific Ocean and Bering Sea to the west. The continent of South America is to the south.

The United States is the oldest independent country on the North American continent. Its founding predates modern Mexico, Canada, and the countries of Central America. The Latin American countries did not gain their independence from European countries until the early 1800s, whereas the United States declared its independence in 1776 and defeated its British overlords in 1781. Canada, which was also once a British colony, is today a member of the British Commonwealth of Nations, with an elected prime minister and parliament. (Greenland is part of the kingdom of Denmark and is not an independent country.)

State and Community

The original 13 of the United States' 50 states joined the Union between 1787 and 1790. By 1800, Vermont, Kentucky, and Tennessee had been admitted to statehood. In 1912, when New Mexico and Arizona joined the Union, the United States consisted of the 48 contiguous states. The remaining two states, Alaska and Hawaii, were admitted to statehood in 1959. Alaska had been purchased from Russia in 1867, and Hawaii had been annexed by the United States in 1898.

Map Symbols and Keys

A map is a representation of a place. Different kinds of maps show different things—countries, states, cities, and towns. Maps also show rivers, lakes, mountains, and oceans. A map of a town or city will show streets and important places, such as municipal buildings, schools, churches, mosques, synagogues, and shopping centers. A town or city map may also show the location of houses and apartment buildings.

A map is not the same as a picture of a place. It does not show the actual places or things in an area, but uses symbols to represent them, such as a thin line for a street and a thicker line for a highway. Map symbols may be lines, colors, shapes, or pictures. So people can understand the symbols, maps have keys, or legends, which show each symbol with an explanation next to it. Symbols represent human and physical characteristics.

Direction

People use maps and globes to find places and locations. A basic convention is that most maps are oriented with the North Pole at the top of a map, unless otherwise indicated. North, south, east, and west are the cardinal directions; the intermediate directions are northeast, southeast, southwest, and northwest. A compass rose indicates the directions on a map.

The Equator, Poles, and Hemispheres

Earth rotates on its axis as it revolves around the sun. The North and South Poles are the points through which the axis passes; they are the northernmost and southernmost points on Earth. These points are called Earth's poles. Many maps are drawn with north at the top and south at the bottom.

Because Earth is round, it cannot be seen completely at any one time. Even an astronaut looking down from space can see only half the world at once. Half the world is called a *hemisphere,* meaning half of a sphere, or ball. The northern part of Earth is called the Northern Hemisphere and the southern part of the globe is called the Southern Hemisphere. But the world can also be looked at as having a Western Hemisphere and an Eastern Hemisphere. Any continent occupies portions of at least two hemispheres. For example, North America is in the Northern Hemisphere and also in the Western Hemisphere. Europe falls within three hemispheres (Northern, Eastern, and Western), and Africa falls within all four.

Around the center of Earth is an imaginary line called the Equator. It is 0° latitude and is located halfway between the North and South Poles. The Equator divides Earth into the Northern and Southern Hemispheres. The dividing lines for the Eastern and Western Hemispheres are the Prime Meridian (also called the Greenwich Meridian) and the 180th Meridian. The Prime Meridian refers to 0° longitude, an imaginary line that runs from the North Pole to the South Pole and goes through the Royal Observatory in Greenwich [GREN-ich], a suburb of London, England. The International Date Line also runs from the North Pole to the South Pole, generally following the 180th Meridian (it deviates in a few places to avoid dividing Siberia and again to include the Aleutian Islands with Alaska). The Prime Meridian (0° longitude) and the 180th Meridian are on opposite sides of Earth, and together divide the globe into Eastern (0° to 180° east of the Prime Meridian) and Western (0° to 180° west of the Prime Meridian) Hemispheres.

B. Geographical Terms and Features

In Grade 1, children learned the following physical geographical terms:

A peninsula is a body of land that is almost surrounded by water. Florida and Baja California are both peninsulas that jut out into water. The word *peninsula* comes from Latin: *paene* (almost) + *insula* (island). This etymology neatly captures the meaning of the term: a peninsula is "almost an island."

A harbor is an area of water that is protected by land. It is an inlet along a coast. While there are natural harbors, today the term usually applies to an area in which ships can anchor or dock and that has facilities to load and unload passengers and cargo.

A bay is a small area of an ocean or a lake that creates an opening in the land. It is an indentation, like a dimple. Some bays, such as San Francisco Bay and Galveston Bay, are large and deep enough to be used as ship harbors.

An island is land completely surrounded by water. It is smaller than a continent, however, so Australia is not considered an island.

Teaching Idea

To practice using directions, refer children to the compass rose on a map. Ask them directionality questions about states and oceans in relation to their state and community, e.g., "What state/town is north of ours? South?"

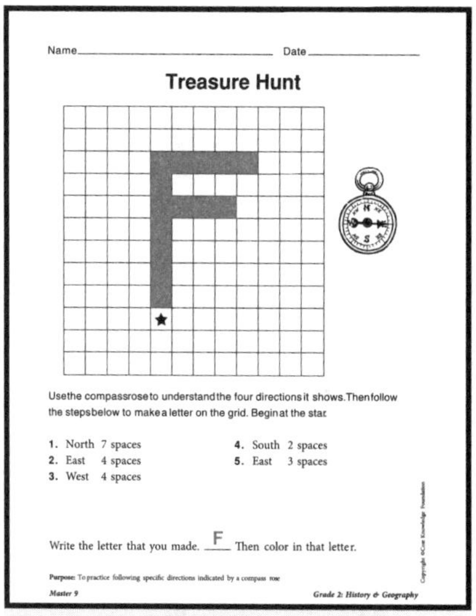

Name______________ Date______________

Treasure Hunt

Usethe compassroseto understandthe four directionsit shows.Thenfollow the stepsbelow to makea letter on the grid. Beginat the star.

1. North 7 spaces
2. East 4 spaces
3. West 4 spaces
4. South 2 spaces
5. East 3 spaces

Write the letter that you made. F Then color in that letter.

Purpose: To practice following specific directions indicated by a compass rose

Master 9 — Grade 2: History & Geography

Use Instructional Master 9.

Teaching Idea

Divide children into groups. Assign a continent to each group. Encourage children to find islands, peninsulas, deserts, etc., on each continent on a map and to write down the names of these features.

Teaching Idea

Make sure to include map-related tasks when teaching children geography concepts. Children need to practice and review map skills frequently. You may wish to reference *Helping Your Child with Maps and Globes,* by Frazee and Guardia for some excellent teaching tips and activities about direction, scale, distance, location, and symbols. (See More Resources.)

Teaching Idea

To build knowledge of deserts, play "I'm thinking of a desert" with children. In this game, you describe a desert using map terms children know, and they move their fingers on the map: "I'm thinking of a desert . . . it's in Africa . . . it's in the northern part of Africa . . . the name of this desert starts with an 'S,'" etc. Once children get close enough, they may be able to read the name from the map, or, possibly, guess the name. Once children have located and identified the desert, share a fun fact about this particular desert.

Teaching Idea

Divide the class into five small groups, and provide each child with construction paper and paints or markers. Assign a geographic term to each group (*coast, valley, desert, prairie, oasis*), and have children paint a picture representing their geographic feature. Encourage children to add details to their pictures, such as palm trees to their oasis, and boats to their coastline.

The Big Idea in Review

Maps and globes are convenient ways to show the location and some of the human and physical characteristics of our planet.

As you review these terms, have children trace the coastline of some part of the world on a wall map. As they trace, have them describe the curves along the coast, "Here it's smooth, and here it sticks out like a finger." Encourage them to think of vocabulary terms they know as they see bays, peninsulas, cities, and islands and to name these features.

As they study world and American history topics in Grade 2, children will come in contact with a number of terms that represent geographical features. Be sure to focus on the following terms in this grade:

The coast is the land that runs along an ocean, bay, or gulf. It is also called the coastline and the shore. Continents have coasts, as do islands and peninsulas. America's original 13 colonies were mostly settled along the eastern coastline.

A valley is a long expanse of lowland lying between hills or mountains. Some valleys have rivers or streams flowing along the length of the valley floor. The Tennessee River flows through a long valley.

A prairie is a large area of level or gently rolling grasslands. The Canadian plains are prairie, as are the Great Plains in the United States.

Desert is dry land that gets little moisture. Most deserts are rock- and stone-covered. Very few of the world's deserts consist of sand. The Sahara in Africa is the world's largest desert. The Mojave Desert in Southern California is home to Death Valley.

An oasis is an area of green in a desert. An oasis may be very small or thousands of square miles in area. Underground springs or streams flowing into a desert from a moister region provide water for the trees and grasses that grow and also water for humans and animals. Today, some countries are creating oases in the desert to claim land for habitation and cultivation. One example is Israel, which has built oases in the Negev Desert.

Review

Below are some ideas for ongoing assessment and review activities. These are not meant to constitute a comprehensive list.

- As you teach the sections on world and American history, use the geography topics and terms to highlight your study. For example, while studying the geography of China, provide children with a map of the country. Have them trace the coast and the river valleys for the Yangtze and Yellow Rivers and locate the Gobi Desert.
- Assign a scavenger hunt for geographic terms, and have children find as many features as they can on maps of countries. You can often find interesting maps of different areas in the travel section of bookstores or map stores.
- Invite children to look for a map of a place they have gone on vacation or where a relative lives, or even where they would like to go someday. Ask them to explore different aspects of the map. For example, have them describe the area, locate the bodies of water, and identify the countries or states. Then, have them present their place of choice to the class.

• Provide groups of children with a picture cut out of a magazine that show a person dressed for a particular climate. For example, you may give one group a picture of a person in a bathing suit, and another group a picture of a person in a heavy jacket. Then, have children write about where they think that person lives and why. There will obviously be several options from which children may choose. They must choose a continent and country and then explain their answers in writing. Share these aloud with the class.

• As a journal topic, have children choose a continent that they would like to visit and explain why they would like to visit that place.

• Using index cards, make a deck of cards that lists a variety of names of countries, continents, states, and cities that children have studied. Then, have them identify each name as a continent, country, state, or city. Make sure that you include names of local places, but you may also include areas that you have studied in the *Core Knowledge Sequence.* Challenge children by having them find each place on a map or globe.

• You may also ask the following questions at the end of this section:

1. Why are symbols used on maps?
   There is not enough space on a map to show the real things.
2. How can you tell what map symbols mean?
   Maps have keys (legends) that tell you what the symbols mean.
3. How can you tell the direction on a map?
   You can use the compass rose to tell the direction on a map. North is usually at the top, and then east, south, and west are arranged like the face of a clock.
4. What is the Equator? Have children locate it on the globe.
   The Equator is an imaginary line around the center of the world that divides the world into the Northern and Southern Hemispheres.
5. What is a hemisphere?
   A hemisphere is half of the world (or a globe or sphere).
6. What are the hemispheres called? Have children locate them.
   The four hemispheres are called the Northern, Southern, Eastern, and Western Hemispheres.
7. Where might you find valleys in the United States?
   You might find valleys in the Rocky and Appalachian Mountains, among many other places.
8. Where do trees grow in a desert?
   Trees grow in oases in a desert.

More Resources

The titles listed below are offered as a representative sample of materials and not a complete list of everything that is available.

For children —

These books are generally intended to be read aloud, though some children may be able to read parts or all of the simpler texts.

- *The Antarctic Ocean,* by Anne Ylvisaker (Bridgestone, 2003). One of a series of books on the five oceans. Each follows the same basic template and covers location, depth, climate, plants, and animals, with a hands-on activity at the end. Hardcover, 24 pages, ISBN 0736814205.
- *Geography from A to Z : A Picture Glossary,* by Jack Knowlton and Harriet Barton (HarperTrophy, 1997). Paperback, 48 pages, ISBN 0064460991.
- *Greetings Asia! (Our Amazing Continents),* by April Pulley Sayre (Millbrook Press, 2003). Paperback, 32 pages, ISBN 0761319913. See also *G'day Australia* in this same series.
- *How to Make an Apple Pie and See the World,* by Marjorie Priceman (Random House, 1996). A whimsical, yet educational tour. Paperback, 40 pages, ISBN 0679880836.
- *Living in a Desert (Rookie Read-About Geography),* by Allan Fowler (Children's Book Press, 2000). Great pictures and straightforward text. Paperback, 32 pages, ISBN 0516270494. Just a few of the many titles in this series that cover rainforests, mountains, and seas.
- *MacMillan First Atlas,* by Nicola Wright and others (Atheneum, 1992). Includes a special 8-page section on the U.S.A. with state flags. Hardcover, 40 pages, ISBN 0027749207.
- *Map Scales (Rookie Read-About Geography),* by Mary Dodson Wade (Children's Book Press, 2003). Paperback, 32 pages, ISBN 0516277677. See also in this series: *Looking at Maps and Globes*; *We Need Directions*; *Map Keys*; *Latitude and Longitude*; and *Types of Maps.*
- *Maps and Globes,* by Jack Knowlton and illustrated by Harriet Barton (HarperTrophy, 1986). Written for 7 to 10-year-olds, but may need to be read aloud and explained. Paperback, 48 pages, ISBN 0064460495.
- *Paddle-to-the-Sea,* by Holling C. Holling (Houghton Mifflin, 1941). The classic tale of the voyage of a little boy's miniature canoe from a Canadian river's source to the Atlantic Ocean. Teaches basic geography in a story form. Library binding, 64 pages, ISBN 0395150825. See also *Minn of the Mississippi* by the same author.

For teachers —

- *Goode's World Atlas, 20th Edition,* edited by John C. Hudson (Rand McNally & Company, 1999). Long a standard reference in classroom libraries. "Overall, Goode's is the best deal available in an atlas today and the first choice for a basic reference atlas for any elementary school library or children's room" (*School Library Journal* on the 19th edition). Hardcover, 384 pages, ISBN 0528843362.
- *Helping Your Child with Maps and Globes,* by Bruce Frazee and William Guardia (Goodyear Publishing Company, 1995). "Fun-to-do games and activities that help young children learn about direction, scale, distance, location, and symbols" (from the publisher). Paperback, 216 pages, ISBN 0673361314.
- *Janice VanCleave's Geography for Every Kid: Easy Activities that Make Learning Geography Fun,* by Janice VanCleave (John Wiley & Sons, 1993). A teacher-directed activity book geared for 9 to 12-year-olds. Paperback, 224 pages, ISBN 0471598429.
- The National Geographic Society, www.nationalgeographic.com/education. This multifeatured website includes a map machine, printable maps, and online adventures, to name a few.
- Nystrom, www.nystromnet.com or 1-800-621-8086, and Rand McNally, www.k12online.com or 1-800-678-7263, both offer a variety of maps and other geography teaching aids.
- The United States Geological Survey, www.usgs.gov. From the home page, click on the link for "Students and Teachers" to view a wide range of resources. There is also a comprehensive glossary of terms on this site. To reach it from the "Students and Teachers" page, scroll to the bottom of the column labeled "Explorers," and click on the picture labeled "Glossary" (or, type in the address http://interactive2.usgs.gov/learningweb/explorer/geoglossary.htm).

II. Early Civilizations: Asia

The Big Idea

Two major world religions and an important system of philosophy developed among ancient Asian cultures.

Remember that each subject you study with children expands their vocabulary and introduces new terms, thus making them better listeners and readers. As you study historical people and events, use read alouds and discussions to build children's vocabularies.

The items in bold relate to content in Grade 2. In discussions with children, use terminology such as "long, long ago" to set this information in time.

3500–1800 BCE	Sumerian civilization, first civilization in Mesopotamia (Grade 1)
2700–2200 BCE	Old Kingdom in Egypt (Grade 1)
2050–1750 BCE	Middle Kingdom in Egypt (Grade 1)
2500–1500 BCE	**Indus Valley Civilization**
1766–1122 BCE	Shang in northeastern China
1500 BCE	**Invasion of Aryans into Indus Valley**
1550–1050 BCE	New Kingdom in Egypt (Grade 1)
1540–1482 BCE	Hatshepsut, pharaoh (Grade 1)
1361–1352 BCE	Tutankhamen, pharaoh (Grade 1)
1000 BCE	**Chinese silk culture**
563–483 BCE	**Buddha**
200s BCE	**Asoka, emperor of Mauryan dynasty Great Wall of China begun**
105 CE	**Chinese invent paper**

What Students Should Already Know

Students in Core Knowledge schools should be familiar with

Grade 1

- Judaism
- Christianity
- Islam

What Students Need to Learn

- **Geography of Asia**
  - **The largest continent, with the most populous countries in the world**
  - **Location of China, India, and Japan**
- **India**
  - **The importance of the Indus and Ganges Rivers**
  - **Hinduism: Brahma, Vishnu, and Shiva; the holy books, including the Rig Veda**
  - **Buddhism: Buddha, spread of Buddhism, King Asoka**
- **China**
  - **The importance of the Yellow (Huang He) and Yangtze (Chang Jiang or Ch'ang) Rivers**
  - **Teachings of Confucius (for example, "Honor your ancestors")**
  - **Great Wall of China**
  - **Invention of paper and importance of silk**
  - **Chinese New Year**

What Students Will Learn in Future Grades

In future grades, students will review and extend their learning about China.

Grade 4

- Dynasties and Conquerors
  - Qin Shihuangdi
  - Han dynasty
  - Tang and Song dynasties
  - Mongol invasions and rule
  - Ming dynasty

II. Early Civilizations: Asia

Text Resources

(52) *Rama and Sita: A Tale from the Ramayana*

(53) *Buddha: The Enlightened One*

(54) *Teachings of Confucius*

Materials

Instructional Master 10
Asia, p. 125

overhead projector, p. 125

chart paper, p. 129

sample of Chinese Characters, p. 131

paper and the shape of a person for a cutout, p. 131

scissors, p. 131

a copy of the *Analects of Confucius*, p. 132

plastic tub, p. 132

shredded paper, p. 132

a screen, p. 132

magazines, p. 133

maps and globes, p. 134

Chinese New Year decorations, p. 134

Chinese robes for the children, p. 134

Vocabulary

Student/Teacher Vocabulary

archipelago: an island chain or group (T)

Asoka: the greatest of the Mauryan emperors, who embraced Buddhism (S)

Brahma, Vishnu, Shiva: the three most important Hindu gods (S)

Buddha: meaning "Enlightened One," the founder of Buddhism (S)

Buddhism: a religion based on the teachings of Buddha (S)

Chinese New Year: a holiday celebrated in late January or February; the first day is a religious celebration, and the next 14 days are highlighted by parades, fireworks, and gift-giving (S)

Ganges River: a river in India that is sacred to Hindus, for they believe it to be a reincarnation of the female deity Ganga (S)

Great Wall of China: a network of walls built to keep out invaders; it stretches 2,150 miles across North China (S)

Hinduism: a religion based on the belief that everything that exists is Brahman, an absolute or ultimate spiritual force (S)

Indian Subcontinent: a mix of mountains, plateaus, and plains. The Himalaya Mountains, the highest mountain range in the world, form most of the northern border of the subcontinent. The Hindu Kush Mountains in the north, and several smaller ranges bordering India on both the west and east, form the rest of the subcontinent. (T)

Indus River: the river upon which the first civilization on the Indian Subcontinent was located (S)

Mauryan dynasty: the dynasty under which Buddhism hit its peak (T)

right action: good behavior toward another person (T)

Vedas: the earliest holy writings of Hinduism (S)

Yangtze (Chang Jiang or Ch'ang) River: a river that flows through the northeastern portion of China (S)

Yellow (Huang He) River: a river that was the location of the first Chinese civilization (S)

Domain Vocabulary

Geography of Asia and associated words:
largest continent, most populous, Indian Subcontinent, India, Pakistan, Bangladesh, Brahmaputra River, mountains, plateaus, tablelands, plains, Deccan Plain, Gangetic Plain, Himalayas, Hindu Kush, climate, desert, dry, tropical, hot, wet, rainy, humid, temperate, mild, cool, warm, monsoon, wind system, dry and cold, floods, flooding, China, natural borders, Gobi Desert, Himalaya Mountains, China Sea, fertile, good soil, North China Plain, flat, desert, arid, sandy, hills, valley, river, Korean Peninsula, Huang He, Ch'ang, swollen river, death, destruction, irrigation, fertile soil, Japan, archipelago, island system, Hokkaido, Honshu, Shikoku, Kyushu

India and associated words:
floods, flooding, fertile soil, irrigation, farming, Indus Valley civilization, cities, crowded, dense, population, large, well-planned, streets, grid pattern, street plan, houses, one-story, two-story, courtyards, shops, craftworkers, artisans, crafts, goods, merchants, trade, trade goods, trading network, business, sacred, holy, holy cities, pilgrims, pilgrimages, reincarnation, new life, cycle of life and death, rebirth, moksha, Ganga, female deity, goddess, religion, Hindu, follower, believer, worshiper, Brahman, spiritual force, all-powerful, unchanging, Absolute Reality, Ultimate Reality, the creator, universe, balancer,

Vocabulary continued

the preserver, the protector, goodness, mercy, the destroyer, good and evil, creation and destruction, destroyer and giver of new life, fertility and asceticism, lack of worldly desire, caste system, station in life, social class, rank, position, social standing, Aryans, invaders, language family, Rig Veda, oral tradition, spoken word, handed down, Upanishads, basis for Hinduism

Buddhism and associated words:
Siddhartha Gautama, enlightenment, understanding, "enlightened one," Four Noble Truths, Eightfold Path, suffering, nirvana, lack of desire, Asoka, Ashoka, Zen, meditation

China and associated words:
farmland, Shang dynasty, city-states, social classes, noble warriors, peasant farmers, ideographic writing, ideogram, symbol, sound, representation, idea or thing, Confucius, philosopher, Confucianism, philosophy, *Analects of Confucius,* management of society, social structure, hierarchy, jen, human-heartedness, sympathy, sensibility, basic relationship, right action, virtue, filial piety, respect, ancestor worship, Great Wall of China, Qin dynasty, Ming dynasty, emperor, North China, defense, fortification, invasions, invaders, attack, silk culture, silkworm, silk making, Silk Road, Chinese New Year, dragon, celebration, religious, secular, population, city, crowded

Cross-curricular Connections

Language Arts

Fiction

Stories

- "The Blind Men and the Elephant" (fable from India)
- "The Magic Paintbrush" (Chinese folktale)
- "The Tiger, the Brahman, and the Jackal" (folktale from India)

Visual Arts

Sculpture

- *Flying Horse, One Leg Resting on a Swallow* (China)

Architecture

- Great Stupa
- Himeji Castle

At a Glance

The most important ideas for you are:

- Children should be able to locate China, India, and Japan on a map or globe.
- The first civilization on the Indian Subcontinent was along the Indus River.
- The Ganges River has religious significance for Hindus.
- Hinduism has many holy writings collected as the Vedas and many deities of which Brahma, Vishnu, and Shiva are the most important.
- Buddhism is based on the teachings of Buddha and spread across Asia from India.

At a Glance continued

- King Asoka is an example of someone who put Buddha's teachings into practice.
- The first historical dynasty in China, the Shang, developed along the Yellow (Huang He) River.
- Confucius developed a philosophy based on right relationships and right action.
- Among important Chinese achievements are the Great Wall of China, the development of papermaking, and the silk culture.

What Teachers Need to Know

Background: Setting the Stage

The following is a general description of how civilizations developed. Any specific region may have had variations.

The earliest cultures were based on hunting wild animals and gathering wild plants. At different times on different continents, humans learned to domesticate edible plants and animals; that is, they learned to plant, cultivate, and harvest wild plants and to breed wild animals for food and as beasts of burden. Some of these societies continued a seminomadic existence, but others settled in one place. With a predictable food base, populations in these settled communities grew. In time, these permanent communities gave rise to cities and, in turn, to what is known as civilization.

The term civilization *is not intended to be a value judgment but the designation of a culture displaying certain characteristics. In anthropological terms, the components of a civilization are the rise of cities, often with monumental architecture (large buildings); division of labor; the establishment of political organization and of social class structure; and, usually, the development of some form of writing.*

To some scholars, the presence of cities is the crucial element in the development of a civilization. A city needs a political structure by which it can be governed. The first cities were the seats of power and organization for outlying areas and, later, kingdoms and empires.

Because people in cities did not farm, they had to make their living in other ways. Crafts and commerce developed and with them the concept of division of labor. While some people made their living by becoming potters, bricklayers, and weavers, others became merchants. Inevitably, some groups made more money than others, or were more respected than others, and so social classes developed.

Although each ancient society had its distinctive aspects, most were organized into broadly similar classes. At the top of the social pyramid was the ruler, who was often considered divine. Then came the high priests who served the deities of the society's religion. Next came the nobles, often military leaders because these early cities waged war to gain territory and wealth. Then came merchants, artisans, and scribes. At the bottom of the social structure were slaves, who were often captives taken in battle.

The development of writing was an important element of many civilizations. With a large number of people in proximity to one another, there could be a rapid dissemination of ideas. This exchange fostered creative and intellectual development. Writing enabled people to document these ideas and create a record of their thoughts and creative works. Writing also enabled governments to organize more efficiently and to spread their authority more effectively and over larger areas. Laws could be written down and sent to distant parts of an empire with the expectation that they would be obeyed. The development of written symbols for numbers also allowed records, such as tax payments, treaties, and business contracts, to be written down for reference and enforcement. Until about 300 years ago, only a small group of people within any civilization could read and write, but this small group had a great impact on the society as a whole.

Because religion has been such a central force in shaping the development of civilizations, the Core Knowledge Sequence *introduces children in the early grades to major world religions for the purpose of providing a basic vocabulary for understanding many events and ideas in history. The goal is to familiarize children with major ideas in world history; it is not to proselytize. The tone should be one of respect and balance. Should questions about truth and rightness come up in discussion, an appropriate answer is that "People of different faiths believe different things to be true. The best people to guide you right now are your parents or caregivers at home."*

A. Geography of Asia

Asia is the largest continent in the world and houses six of the most populous countries in the world: China, India, Indonesia, Pakistan, Bangladesh, and Japan. Until 1947, Bangladesh and Pakistan were part of India.

China's estimated population of approximately 1.3 billion people is about 20% of the world's total population. India has over 1 billion people. By comparison, the United States, the world's third-most-populous country, has over 275 million people, roughly a quarter of India's population and about 1 billion fewer people than China.

India

The subject of this section is ancient India, which at one time encompassed a larger area than the modern country. India was a British colony for many years prior to gaining its independence in 1947. In that same year, the northwestern and eastern sections were split off as West Pakistan and East Pakistan. Religion was a major factor in the split: both of the breakaway areas were predominantly Muslim, whereas the remaining portion of India was (and is) predominantly Hindu. In 1971, East Pakistan declared its independence and became Bangladesh.

The Indian Subcontinent, so named because it is cut off from the rest of Asia by high mountains, is a mix of mountains, plateaus, and plains. The Himalaya

Teaching Idea

Create an overhead from Instructional Master 10, *Asia*, and use it to orient children to the three Asian countries that they will be studying in Grade 2: India, China, and Japan. You can then have children complete this worksheet as you teach the material.

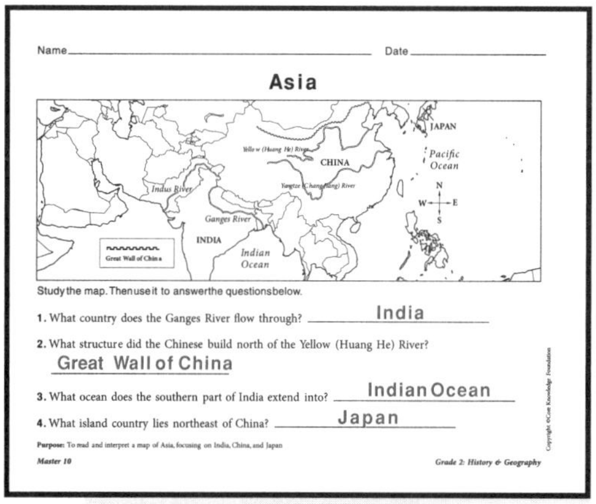
Name________ Date________

Asia

Study the map. Then use it to answer the questions below.

1. What country does the Ganges River flow through? India
2. What structure did the Chinese build north of the Yellow (Huang He) River? Great Wall of China
3. What ocean does the southern part of India extend into? Indian Ocean
4. What island country lies northeast of China? Japan

Purpose: To read and interpret a map of Asia, focusing on India, China, and Japan

Master 10 *Grade 2: History & Geography*

Copyright ©Core Knowledge Foundation

Use Instructional Master 10.

Teaching Idea

The statistics about Asia's population are not important for children to know. What is important is an understanding that the populations of these countries are huge in comparison with that of the United States. To help make this point visually, create a bar graph to show children the difference in population between the United States and China. You could also have 3 children stand together to represent the United States, 10 children to represent India, and 13 children to represent China. An extension of this last suggestion could be to tie in the areas of the respective countries. Have the groups of children representing the United States and China stand in about the same area. Have the group of children representing India stand in one-third of the area of China or the United States. You could then explain how India is more densely populated than the United States, because there are more people per square mile.

Mountains, the highest mountain range in the world, form most of the northern border of the subcontinent. The Hindu Kush Mountains in the north, and several smaller ranges bordering India on both the west and east, form the rest of its northern border.

The major rivers of the subcontinent are the Indus, Brahmaputra, and Ganges. The Indus and Ganges were important in the early development of India. Like the Nile River in Africa, which children in Core Knowledge schools should have studied in Grade 1, these rivers flooded, leaving fertile soil as the floodwaters receded.

The climate of the subcontinent can be divided into desert, tropical, and temperate. The area around the Indus River is very dry. The climate along the west coast is tropical and supports rainforest vegetation. With minor exceptions, the rest of the subcontinent is temperate. The major weather system is the monsoon. This wind system reverses direction with the seasons, bringing a cool, dry climate in winter and very wet, hot weather in summer. The resulting rains can be devastating, causing flooding and deaths, but the monsoons also provide the moisture needed for agriculture.

China

The climate of China varies greatly between its northern and southern borders, but winters are generally cool and dry while summers are hot and wet. China is at the other end of the monsoon pattern. There, too, the summer monsoon rains can bring devastation, but they also bring life-giving rainfall for farming.

China is ringed by natural borders: the China Sea to the east and southeast, the Himalaya Mountains to the south and southwest, the Tien Shan Mountains and Taklimakan Desert to the west, and the Gobi Desert and several mountain ranges to the north. Northern China is mostly fertile plains, whereas the west is a mix of desert and plateaus, and the south is hills and valleys. Jutting out from the northeastern corner of China is the Korean Peninsula. To the east of it is the Japanese archipelago.

The major river systems in China are the Yellow (Huang He) and Yangtze (Chang Jiang or Ch'ang) Rivers. The latter is the longest river in Asia. Like other major rivers, the Huang He has flooded, bringing death and destruction, but also leaving fertile soil across the North China Plain.

Japan

The Japanese archipelago, or island chain or group, contains around 3,000 islands, but the majority of the population lives on the four largest islands: Hokkaido, Honshu, Shikoku, and Kyushu. Japan is one of the most densely populated nations on Earth. It has one of the largest populations packed into a small amount of land. The population density of Japan is about 336 persons per square kilometer. By comparison, the population density of the United States is about 29 persons per square kilometer, and the population density of Canada is about 3.2 persons per square kilometer. Japan is discussed in detail in World History and Geography, Section III (pp. 136–142).

B. India

The Indus and Ganges Rivers

The earliest civilization on the Indian Subcontinent began in the northwest along the Indus River, in much of what is today Pakistan. The Indus River Valley was ideally suited to the development of population centers. Like the Nile in Egypt, the Indus flooded on a regular basis, leaving fertile soil as it receded and providing a large area for agriculture. Most people in the Indus Valley were farmers. Among their crops were wheat, barley, and bananas. Indian farmers harnessed the waters of the Indus with irrigation canals.

This agricultural base supported the development of large, well-planned cities with streets running in a regular grid pattern of east-west and north-south. Houses were one and two stories in height and built around interior courtyards. Craftworkers and merchants mingled with priests and government officials in the streets and shops of the cities. Craftworkers created objects in gold, silver, copper, and bronze, which found their way into the trading network that developed among the Indus Valley cities and beyond. By 2000 BCE, Indus Valley ships were carrying trade goods as far away as Mesopotamia. The Indus Valley peoples also had a written language. Unfortunately, no experts have been able to decipher this writing, so little is known about these people. The Indus Valley civilization flourished from around 2500 BCE to 1500 BCE, when Aryans from Central Asia invaded the region and conquered it.

The Ganges River is considered sacred to Hindus. They believe that it is the reincarnation (rebirth of the soul) of the female deity Ganga. Several Hindu holy cities are built along its banks, and bathing in the Ganges is a part of Hindu ritual. The river is also a major source of water for irrigation in Bangladesh and India.

> **Teaching Idea**
>
> **Ask children why rivers are important and why so many civilizations develop along the banks of a river. Make a chart of other civilizations and key rivers (e.g., the Nile in Egypt, the Tigris and Euphrates in Mesopotamia) children have studied. Add to this chart as new civilizations are studied.**

Hinduism

Hinduism is the religion of most people in India. Hindu influence can be found in Asian countries such as Vietnam, Cambodia, and Bali. Hindus also live in the United States and in European and African countries.

Hinduism is a religion that is hard for many Westerners to understand. Indeed, some scholars would argue that it is not a single religion at all but a cluster of related religious ideas. Both of these factors can make it hard to talk about Hinduism with second graders. Nevertheless, it should be possible to convey at least some of what follows.

The basic Hindu belief is that everything that exists is Brahman, an absolute, ultimate spiritual force. No statue or picture exists that can capture the Absolute. However, in an effort to put form to idea, Hindus worship a variety of deities—male and female—who each represent some aspect of Brahman, which represents the oneness of ultimate reality.

Among the major Hindu deities are Brahma, the creator; Vishnu, the preserver; and Shiva, the destroyer. Brahma created the universe and represents the Absolute. He is the balance between Vishnu and Shiva. Brahma is portrayed with four arms and four faces.

Vishnu is the preserver and protector, the model of goodness and mercy. Vishnu, too, is represented as having four hands. Each hand holds one of the following: a conch shell, a discus, a mace (a symbol of authority), or a lotus flower.

Shiva represents good and evil, creation and destruction, and fertility and asceticism.

Hindus believe in reincarnation, or rebirth. That is, they believe that the body of a person may die but the soul will live many lives and may return in a future life as a person, or even an animal. Until a soul reaches *moksha*, or union with Brahman, it must live, die, and be born again through successive lives. The purpose of this cycle is to allow the soul to work toward moksha, which will be achieved when the soul is able to let go of worldly desires.

Reincarnation gave rise to the caste system, a system that has played a very important role in Indian history. According to the caste sytem, one's progress along the road to union with Brahman is indicated by one's station in life. A member of one of the higher castes would be seen as closer to moksha than a member of the lower castes.

At the top of the caste system were *Brahmins* or priests believed to have sprung from the mouth of a primeval male. (Note that *Brahmin* is spelled differently than *Brahman.*) Beneath Brahmins were rulers and warriors or *kshatriyas* (literally, "empowered ones"), who had sprung from the arms. Further down the scale stood merchants and farmers or *vaishyas,* who had sprung from the thighs, and at the base were menial workers or *sudras,* generally "dasas" or indigenous peoples. These were also known as "untouchables." Little more than slaves, "fit to be beaten," they could be "slain at will." Within each of these major divisions, thousands of castes existed (each with its own rules).

It is not important that children understand the details of the caste system, but it will be useful for them to have a general sense of caste as a kind of social ranking system. Such systems have existed in different forms in many societies—e.g., the relation between master and slave.

The Aryans who conquered the Indus Valley centers were a major influence on the development of Hinduism. They were Brahmins, or members of the highest class. Much of what is known about the Aryans comes from their writings, known collectively as the Vedas. The Rig Veda, composed between 1400 BCE and 900 BCE, consists of a little over 1,000 hymns organized in ritual cycles.

Together with other works, like the Upanishads, these writings contain the prayers, hymns, and religious teachings that provide much of the basis for Hinduism. The terms *writings* or *books* are often used to describe them, but, for many centuries, the Vedas were part of Aryan oral tradition, memorized and passed down from one generation of Aryan priests to the next.

Hinduism includes several ideas that may seem mysterious to many Westerners, but they are key to the Hindu understanding of the union with the divine, or becoming "one with the one." The first, already mentioned above, is reincarnation, or the rebirth of souls. This is the notion that life is an ongoing cycle of death and rebirth for each creature, and that one's deeds in an earlier life influence one's station and form in the next. The soul is granted as many lives as necessary to attain spiritual perfection. One could be born as a mosquito or a manual laborer, and by fulfilling one's duties and living a good life (karma), attain betterment and be reborn in a higher station in the next life. Reincarnation offers possibilities for downward mobility as well. Failure to perform one's duties or live nobly could result in rebirth into a lower caste, or life as a worm.

The physical and spiritual discipline of yoga, with its techniques of meditation, aids Hindus with clarity and understanding in their spiritual struggle. Those who meditate often repeat over and over the Sanskrit word *om.* Indeed, the Sanskrit character for *om,* the mantra used in meditation, came to be regarded as the symbol of Hinduism. (52)

Diwali

Diwali is the Hindu festival of lights, which is celebrated in October or November. It honors Rama, one of the nine incarnations of Vishnu, and Lakshmi, the deity of wealth and good luck. Lamps made of small clay containers with oil and a wick are lit. Families buy new clothes and shoes for all of the members of the family and exchange food dishes with neighbors, relatives, and friends. Traditional dishes vary by region. In northern India, popular dishes include *pakora* and *lassi.* Pakora are small pieces of vegetable fried in oil with lentil batter. Lassi is a drink that can be made from yogurt, applesauce, apple juice, nutmeg, and cinnamon.

Buddhism

Unlike Hinduism, whose beginnings are unknown, Buddhism originated with the thinking of Siddhartha Gautama in the late 6th century BCE. A son of a wealthy Hindu family, he lived in luxury behind palace walls, shielded from poverty and human suffering. One day while out riding, Gautama came across a sick man, a poor man, and a dead man. For the first time, he saw what it meant to be human. He gave up his life of privilege and began six years of wandering while he looked for an answer to life. After sitting under a tree meditating for 48 days, he said that he suddenly received "enlightenment," that is, he understood the answer.

Taking the name Buddha, meaning "Enlightened One," he began to teach others the Four Noble Truths and the Eightfold Path. The Four Noble Truths are as follows:

1. Pain, suffering, and sorrow are natural components of life.
2. Desire is the cause of suffering.
3. Overcoming desire—achieving nirvana—is the only way to end suffering.
4. Achieving nirvana is possible by following the Eightfold Path.

The Eightfold Path to nirvana means living a life that embraces these steps:

1. Right views
2. Right aspirations
3. Right speech
4. Right conduct
5. Right livelihood
6. Right effort
7. Right mindfulness
8. Right contemplation

Teaching Idea

Consider having children discuss brief quotations that are important to Hindus, such as "Truth (God) is one; and wise people call it by different names" (from the Rig Veda) or "Lead us from falsehood to truth; lead us from darkness to light; and lead us from death to life" (Upanishads).

Teaching Idea

If you have an Indian restaurant in your town, consider taking children on a field trip to have lunch and taste traditional dishes. If there are any Hindu families in your community, ask if a volunteer will bring dishes to your class for everyone to taste. (Be sure to check your school's policy on foods and for any children who might have food allergies.)

Teaching Idea

During your study of the Buddha, you may wish to introduce children to a few "Jataka Tales." Buddhists believe that the Buddha lived on Earth many times, as various forms of animals and men, before his life as the Buddha. The Jataka Tales are stories about his adventures in previous lives. They often teach virtues like generosity and kindness.

Teaching Idea

Use a chart to connect what children are learning about Hinduism and Buddhism to what they have already learned about Judaism, Christianity, and Islam. You can add rows for each religion and columns for god(s) worshipped, place of origin, important human beings associated with each religion, etc. Add to the chart as new religions are introduced.

Teaching Idea

In first grade, children in Core Knowledge schools should have learned about Hammurabi and the Code of Hammurabi, the world's first-known, written code of laws. Hammurabi had the laws written down and sent throughout his empire, so people would know what the laws were. Asoka had the laws of his empire carved on tall stone pillars.

Have children discuss why it is important to have laws and rules and why Hammurabi and Asoka posted the rules. Why would it be important to post rules? Write these reasons on chart paper for the class. Then, as a class, brainstorm reasonable rules for the classroom and post them for reference. This would be a good way to review and practice brainstorming to use for writing in Language Arts. After this activity, have children write about their discussion of laws and rules. Ask the question, "Why are laws and rules important?"

Cross-Curricular Teaching Idea

You may wish to teach about the architectural site the Great Stupa of Sanchi (see Art Resources) in connection with Asoka.

Teaching Idea

As you teach children about the civilization that grew up along the Chinese rivers, remind children of their previous study of civilizations emerging along flooding rivers (Egypt from the Nile, Mesopotamia from the Tigris and Euphrates, and India from the Indus and Ganges).

Buddha's followers spread his teachings throughout India and to what are now the countries of China, Tibet, Korea, Japan, Sri Lanka, and countries in Southeast Asia, except for Indonesia, Malaysia, and the Philippines. Buddhism reached its greatest heights in India under the Mauryan dynasty from 322 BCE to 185 BCE, and then its importance declined as a result of competition from Hinduism. Please note that Zen refers to Zen Buddhism and also means meditation (not to be confused with the principle of jen, central to Confucianism). Zen Buddhism is a Chinese and Japanese school of Mahayana Buddhism that seeks enlightenment by meditation, self-contemplation, and intuition rather than by the scriptures.

The greatest of the Mauryan emperors was Asoka (also spelled Ashoka) who ruled in the 3rd century BCE. He greatly expanded the empire by waging bloody warfare against any group that resisted.

After the last great battle, Asoka ruled a vast empire. He was a very powerful king—fabulously wealthy, the ruler of millions. And yet Asoka was not happy. He began to feel remorse for all the suffering his wars had caused. Asoka realized the pain, suffering, and deaths that he had caused with his wars. He became a Buddhist and devoted the rest of his life to serving his people. Asoka established irrigation projects for farmers, built hospitals for the sick, and built roads for travelers and traders.

He published laws to keep peace and order, and he had his edicts (laws) and Buddhist teachings carved onto gigantic stone pillars and placed along the roads so people would see them as they traveled. Some of the stone pillars also recorded Asoka's achievements and his love for the people. One pillar reported that Asoka looked on all men as his children and wished to see all men happy. Another boasted that Asoka had given orders that trees be planted along the roads to provide shade for travelers, and that wells and resting spots be set up to provide refreshment for men and animals alike.

Asoka also built dome-shaped Buddhist shrines called *stupas*, including one on the hill of Sanchi. (Children will study the famous Great Stupa at Sanchi as part of the art curriculum for this grade.) Asoka also sent missionaries to other lands to spread the teachings of Buddhism. The peoples of China, Japan, Thailand, Vietnam, and other parts of southeast Asia would be profoundly influenced by these emissaries for the Buddhist faith. (53)

C. China

Yellow and Yangtze Rivers

The Yellow (Huang He) and the Yangtze (Chang Jiang or Ch'ang) Rivers flow through the eastern portion of China and water some of the richest farmland in the country. The word *huang* means "yellow" and refers to the sediments that the river carries to the ocean. The name Yangtze comes from the ancient fiefdom called Yang and has been applied to the river mainly by Europeans. In China, the Yangtze River is called Chang Jiang, meaning "Long River," or simply Ch'ang, meaning "The River." Chinese civilization emerged along these rivers at approximately the same time as civilizations in Mesopotamia, Egypt, and India, though apparently independently. Rice was one of the most important crops grown along the Yangtze River.

For much of its history, China was governed by a series of dynasties, or ruling families. The Shang dynasty is the earliest dynasty for which there are historical records. It developed first along the Huang He and then spread outward, eventually reaching the area of the Yangtze River. The Shang ruled from around 1766 BCE to 1122 BCE.

According to current theory, the Shang were probably organized into individual city-states ruled by a king. Society was divided into classes—noble warriors, then merchants and craftworkers, and then peasant farmers. Most members of the Shang civilization were peasant farmers who lived in villages outside the city centers. By the time of the Shang, the Chinese had developed ideographic writing. This is writing in which pictures or symbols represent ideas rather than letters representing sounds.

Teaching Idea

As you discuss Chinese writing, remind children of other early forms of writing, e.g., hieroglyphics and cuneiform. Discuss the basic differences between English and Chinese writing: the Chinese use thousands of different symbols, not an alphabet of 26 letters. Show children some Chinese characters. Let them spend five minutes trying to copy some of the characters.

The Teachings of Confucius

Whereas Judaism, Christianity, Islam, Buddism, and Hinduism are religions, the teachings of Confucius are a philosophical system for the management of society. Confucius lived in China from 551 BCE to 479 BCE. A teacher, he had a wide following of students. After his death, his sayings and activities were collected as the *Analects of Confucius.*

The principle tenet of Confucianism is *jen*, which can be translated as "human-heartedness" or "sympathy." Human-heartedness is a sensibility that relates every person to every other person. Human-heartedness sets up certain relationships in society and requires that people treat others as they would wish to be treated themselves.

According to Confucius, there are five basic relationships:

- Father to son
- Elder brother to younger brother
- Husband to wife
- Ruler to subject
- Friend to friend

Except for the relationship between friends, these relationships are unequal. In the first four relationships, the father, the elder brother, the husband, and the ruler are superior and are owed allegiance and obedience by the lower person. In turn, the superior person owes protection to the lower. These duties and responsibilities set up a system of right action that governs relationships.

Confucius saw the family as the basic unit of society, and government as an extension of the family. It was within the family that a person learned right action. Filial piety, respect for one's parents, was the most important virtue. (It was built on a much older Chinese tradition of ancestor worship.) A person who practiced right action in the family—honoring his elders, obeying them, and taking care of them—would transfer this sense of correct behavior to relationships outside the family. (54)

The students of Confucius called him "Master" and came to study with him to hear the wise things he said. The *Analects* record some of the advice he gave his students:

Teaching Idea

To help children understand the focus on families in Confucian teaching, have them write statements about why families are important. Trace the shape of a person on a piece of paper, draw writing lines, and make one copy for each child. Have children print their statements on the sheets and then cut out the shape of the person. Place the cutouts on the bulletin board so that they are connected by their "hands." This will help to reiterate the teaching of Confucius that all people are connected through human-heartedness.

You might wish instead to focus on the concept of right action, or good behavior toward another person. Substitute that idea for the focus on families, and the rest of the activity can remain the same.

Teaching Idea

Get a copy of the *Analects of Confucius* from a local library, and select a few of the simpler and clearer episodes to share with children. The *Analects* contains many stories about what Confucius said to his disciples and information on how one ought to behave in life. By listening to excerpts from the *Analects*, children will also get a sense of Confucius as a "master," who was consulted, followed, and emulated by his admiring students.

IV.18 The Master said, "In serving his parents, a son may remonstrate with them, but gently; when he sees that they do not incline to follow his advice, he shows an increased degree of reverence, but does not abandon his purpose; and should they punish him, he does not allow himself to murmur."

XV.23 Tsze-kung asked, saying, "Is there one word which may serve as a rule of practice for all one's life?" The Master said, "Is not RECIPROCITY such a word? What you do not want done to yourself, do not do to others."

XIII.6 The Master said, "When a prince's personal conduct is correct, his government is effective without the issuing of orders. If his personal conduct is not correct, he may issue orders, but they will not be followed."

XV.20 The Master said, "What the superior man seeks, is in himself. What the mean man seeks, is in others."

XVII.2 The Master said, "By nature, men are nearly alike; by practice, they get to be wide apart."

After Confucius died, schools were established to teach Confucianism. During some of the later dynasties Confucian ideas became even more important in China. The emperors decided that people who had studied Confucius would make the most honest and reliable government officials, so they required aspiring officials to pass an exam on the Analects and other key Confucian texts.

While Confucianism had a tremendous impact on the development of all aspects of Chinese life for 2,000 years—familial, societal, political, and economic—it was attacked by Chinese reformers after the downfall of the last emperor in the early 1900s. Confucianism was seen as a conservative force in Chinese life that kept China from modernizing. Today, Confucius is again venerated as a great teacher in China. Confucian teachings remain quite influential today in other Asian societies, most notably in Japan, South Korea, Vietnam, and Singapore.

The Great Wall of China

The Great Wall of China

The Great Wall was begun during the Qin dynasty in the 3rd century BCE, and additions were made during subsequent dynasties. The last work was completed during the Ming dynasty (1368–1644 CE). The wall, which was built to keep out invaders, stretches 2,500 miles across North China. Made of earth, stones, and brick, the wall is an average of about 25 feet high and 20 feet wide. It is the world's longest fortification. People can still walk along the top of the Great Wall today, and it is a major tourist attraction.

Teaching Idea

Have children make paper themselves. As a base, use shredded newspaper mixed with water in a tub. Have each child create a sheet of paper on a screen to dry. When the paper is dry (and, assuming it is intact), have children use it to write a book explaining what they have learned about China. Each child should write and/or draw on his or her page.

Invention of Paper and the Importance of Silk Culture

The Chinese invented paper in 105 CE, although knowledge of papermaking from plant fibers, such as bamboo and tree bark, or pulped rags did not make its way to Europe until several centuries later. Until the invention of paper, those few people who could write used papyrus, the stem of a Mediterranean plant cut into thin strips, as the Egyptians did, or used parchment, which was goatskin or sheepskin specially treated for writing.

While the production of paper combined with the invention of the printing press would have far-reaching importance for humankind, silk culture had a more immediate impact on the Chinese. By 1000 BCE, the Chinese were making silk thread from the cocoons spun by silkworms. The silkworms were raised on the leaves of mulberry trees that were grown for this purpose. Women workers first made silk thread from the cocoons and then spun the thread into cloth, which was dyed and made into robes.

Silk became such an important export that the trade route along which silk merchants traveled became known as the Silk Road. It stretched from eastern China to the Mediterranean, and in the 6th century CE to Constantinople (modern-day Istanbul). Caravans of camels carried silk and other valuable goods west along the road. It was along this route that the knowledge of papermaking reached the West, but the Chinese kept the secret of silk making for themselves for many centuries.

Teaching Idea

Children might be interested in a Chinese legend about the discovery of silk. An emperor was said to be troubled at the blight suffered by a grove of his mulberry trees. He asked his wife to find out what was damaging his trees. Strolling in the garden, she discovered strange, hungry worms feeding on the trees, and she pulled a cocoon from one of the trees. The empress is said to have accidentally dropped the cocoon into her teacup, whereupon it released a shiny white strand. Intrigued by the possibility that the glistening thread might be woven into cloth, the empress asked her husband for a grove of mulberry trees to cultivate the silkworms. This Chinese legend is charmingly retold for children in Lily Toy Hong's picture book *The Empress and the Silk Worm* (Albert Whitman, 1995).

Chinese New Year

The Chinese celebrate their New Year in late January or February—anywhere from January 21 to February 19. The celebration lasts for 15 days. The first day is a religious celebration, and the next 14 days are highlighted by parades, fireworks, and gift-giving.

The gifts are money enclosed in red envelopes; red symbolizes good fortune and happiness. The purpose of the New Year's celebration is to give thanks for the good luck and happiness of the past year and to wish for another year with similar good fortune.

The dancing dragon is a prominent figure in the parade of lanterns on the last night of the New Year celebration. One dancer holds the head aloft on a pole and a number of dancers provide the body and feet. The dragon winds it way down streets from side to side, roaring as it goes. According to legend, the evil dragon comes out only once a year and can be frightened away by the color red, fire, and loud noises. This is why many Chinese people celebrate the New Year by carrying red lanterns, setting off fireworks, and playing loud music.

Review

Below are some ideas for ongoing assessment and review activities. These are not meant to constitute a comprehensive list. Teachers may also refer to the *Pearson Learning/Core Knowledge History & Geography* series for additional information and teaching ideas.

- As you are studying the civilizations in this section, prepare two displays on chart paper, one for India and one for China. Have children talk about what they have learned and write facts on the chart paper. Also, have them search magazines for pictures that would illustrate what they have learned. When finished with a section, invite another second-grade class to visit, and have children present what they have learned, using the display in their presentations.
- The rivers in India and China were vital to the civilizations that lived near them. Ask children why rivers are important, and have them locate the Indus and Ganges Rivers (India) and Yellow and Yangtze Rivers (China) on a map or globe. Ask children to write about how rivers support civilizations, and have them illustrate their writing.
- Introduce vocabulary from the study of India through reading the story "The Tiger, the Brahman, and the Jackal" from the Language Arts section (see pp. 78).

The Big Idea in Review

Two major world religions and an important system of philosophy developed among ancient Asian cultures.

Before reading the story, list unfamiliar words from the text on a piece of chart paper. You may choose some words, but also ask the class to choose words that are unfamiliar to them. Ask the class to predict the meanings of the words. List these predictions and then read the story once without interruption. Research shows that stopping to explain vocabulary is more effective after one uninterrupted reading. During the second reading, each time you come to a part of the story that discusses one of the words, stop and carefully read the passage again. Ask children to read carefully to see if they can define the word. Then, post a correct definition. As a way to check for understanding, ask children to write about what they learned from the story using at least three words from the posted list.

- Make connections between the teachings of Confucius and the sayings and phrases from the Language Arts section. Have children think about what is important in their lives and what they would like to teach others about behavior. Then, have them write their sayings down in sentences and write an explanation of their teaching. Try to have children make their sentences short and to summarize how they want to teach others to act.

- As a culminating activity for this section, celebrate the Chinese New Year in your classroom with decorations and special activites. You can have children dress in Chinese robes for presentations and write about what they have learned. Have class presentations for children to share their writings.

- You may also ask the following questions at the end of this section:

1. Where did people first develop a civilization in India?
   People first developed a civilization along the Indus River.
2. What are two important religions that come from India?
   Two important religions that come from India are Buddhism and Hinduism.
3. Name the three most important deities that Hindus worship.
   The three most important deities that Hindus worship are Brahma, Vishnu, and Shiva.
4. Why did Buddha give up his wealth to become a teacher?
   Buddha wanted to help people who were suffering, and he believed he had found the way to help people.
5. How did King Asoka show he was a believer in Buddhism?
   King Asoka gave up war and practiced what Buddhism taught.
6. Where did the Chinese develop their first civilization?
   The Chinese developed their first civilization along the Huang He River.
7. Who was Confucius and what are some of the things he taught?
   Confucius was a philosopher. He taught respect for elders and proper behavior.
8. What are three great achievements of the ancient Chinese?
   Three great achievements of the ancient Chinese are the Great Wall of China, papermaking, and the way to make silk thread and cloth.

More Resources

The titles listed below are offered as a representative sample of materials and not a complete list of everything that is available.

For children —

These books are generally intended to be read aloud, though some children may be able to read parts or all of the simpler texts.

- *Ancient China,* edited by E. D. Hirsch, Jr. (Pearson Learning, 2002), and *Ancient India,* edited by E. D. Hirsch, Jr. (Pearson Learning, 2002). Two units in the official *Pearson Learning/Core Knowledge History & Geography* series. Each includes a small picture book for children and a teacher's guide with read alouds. To order, call 1-800-321-3106.
- *Ancient China* (Schlessinger Media, 1998). This videotape or CD-ROM will require some explanations at points. Distributed by Schlessinger Media, a division of Library Video.com, www.libraryvideo.com or 1-800-843-3620.
- *Ancient Civilizations: China,* by Tami Deedrick (Raintree/Steck-Vaughn, 2001). Good general overview. Note its simplistic definition of communism. Hardcover, 48 pages, ISBN 0739835807. See also *India,* by Julie Nelson, in this same series.
- *China,* by Anne Heinrichs (Children's Press, 1997). Paperback, 48 pages, ISBN 0516261657. See also *India,* by Elaine Landau, in this same series.
- *The Empress and the Silk Worm,* by Lily Toy Hong (Albert Whitman, 1995). Library binding, 32 pages, ISBN 0807520098.
- *Greetings, Asia! (Our Amazing Continents),* by April Pulley Sayre (Millbrook Press, 2003). Library binding, ISBN 0761321241. See also *Asia,* by Mike Graf (Bridgestone Books, 2003). Hardcover, 24 pages, ISBN 0736814167.
- *The Jatakas: Tales of India,* retold by Ellen C. Babbitt (Century Company, 1912). May be read online through The Baldwin Project at www.mainlesson.com.
- *The Land of China,* by Lynn M. Stone (Rourke, 2001). Scenic photographs complement an easy-to-read text. Hardcover, 24 pages, ISBN 1559163186.

For teachers —

- *Ancient China (Eyewitness Books),* by Arthur Cotterell (Dorling Kindersley, 2000). Hardcover, 64 pages, ISBN 0789458667.
- *Confucius: The Golden Rule,* by Russell Freedman and illustrated by Frederic Clement (Arthur A. Levine Books, 2002). Hardcover, 48 pages, ISBN 0439139570.
- *An Illustrated Atlas of Asia (Continents in Close-Up),* by Malcolm Porter and Keith Lye (Raintree/Steck-Vaughn, 2001). Library binding, 48 pages, ISBN 0739832425.
- *Life in Ancient China (The Way People Live),* by Amy Allison (Lucent, 2001). Hardcover, 112 pages, ISBN 1560066946. See also *Ancient Chinese Dynasties (World History Series),* by Eleanor J. Hall (Lucent, 2000). Hardcover, 128 pages, ISBN 1560066245.
- *The Story of the World (Volume 1): Ancient History for the Classical Child,* by Susan Wise Bauer (Peace Hill Press, 2002). Read-aloud stories from around the world for children ages 5–11. The first volume of this planned four-volume set has five chapters (15 stories) devoted to India and China. Available in hardcover (ISBN 0971412960) or paperback (ISBN 0971412901) through any bookstore, or in a spiral-bound edition directly through Peace Hill Press, www.peacehillpress.com or 1-888-329-3869.
- *World Religions: Eastern Traditions,* by Willard G. Oxtoby (Oxford University Press, 2001). This is a helpful resource for teaching concise presentations on Hinduism, since it bears the marks of a practicing Hindu. Contains lots of pictures. Paperback, 518 pages, ISBN 0195415213.
- Asia for Educators, http://afe.easia.columbia.edu. Includes background information and lesson plans on China.

III. Modern Civilization and Culture: Japan

The Big Idea

Modern Japan is a major industrial country that is also firmly rooted in tradition.

Remember that each subject you study with children expands their vocabulary and introduces new terms, thus making them better listeners and readers. As you study historical people and events, use read alouds and discussions to build children's vocabularies.

What Students Should Already Know

Students in Core Knowledge schools should be familiar with

- location of Asia and the Pacific Ocean in relation to Japan

What Students Need to Learn

- **The location of Japan relative to continental Asia, including its position in relation to the Pacific Ocean and the Sea of Japan**
- **Japan: "land of the rising sun"**
- **Japan as an island nation; four major islands; Mount Fuji; Tokyo; Japanese flag**
- **Modern cities as sites of industry and business**
- **Example of a traditional craft: origami**
- **Example of traditional clothing: the kimono**

What Students Will Learn in Future Grades

In future grades, students will review and extend their learning about Japan.

Grade 5

- History and culture including
  - The roles of the emperor and the shogun
  - Samurai and the code of Bushido
  - The class system of feudal Japanese society
  - The closing of Japan to outsiders
  - Buddhism and Shintoism
- Geography
  - The location of Japan; Tokyo
  - The four main islands: Hokkaido, Honshu, Shikoku, Kyushu
  - Typhoons and earthquakes; the Pacific Rim

Vocabulary

Student/Teacher Vocabulary

dormant volcano: a volcano that has not erupted in a long time (T)

haiku: a traditional form of Japanese poetry (S)

kimono: a long narrow robe with wide sleeves, worn as an outer garment (S)

Mount Fuji: the highest mountain in Japan (S)

obi: the sash that is worn with a kimono (T)

origami: the Japanese traditional art of folding paper into figures (S)

Sea of Japan: a body of water that separates Japan from the Asian continent (S)

Tokyo: the capital of Japan and its largest city (S)

Domain Vocabulary

Geography and associated words:
archipelago, island chain, island system, Pacific Ocean, Hokkaido, Honshu, Shikoku, Kyushu, mountaintops, barren, rocky, infertile, uninhabited, forested, rice cultivation, rice paddies, terraced mountains, eruption, lava, ash, molten, snowcapped, Tokyo, Edo, capital, largest city, Yokohama, Osaka, Nagoya, Sapporo, Kyoto, modern, skyscrapers, business, offices, industry, factories, cars, subways, population, crowded, density

Culture and associated words:
flag, national symbol, sun, paper art, folding paper, traditional craft, crane, peace symbol, traditional clothing, narrow robe, wide sleeves, obi, sash

Materials

Instructional Masters 10–12

Asia, p. 139

Origami Hat, p. 140

Land of the Rising Sun, p. 140

pictures of Tokyo, p. 139

photographs and pictures of Mount Fuji, p. 139

examples of origami and folding paper, p. 140

4 x 6 index cards, p. 140

pictures of Japanese and American flags, p. 140

Cross-curricular Connections

Language Arts

Fiction

Stories

- "The Tongue-Cut Sparrow" (Japanese folktale)

Visual Arts

Elements of Art

- Katsusika Hokusai, *The Great Wave at Kanagawa*

Architecture

- Himeji Castle

At a Glance

The most important ideas for you are:

- Japan is made up of about 3,000 islands, many of which are small, rocky, and uninhabited.
- Mount Fuji, once an active volcano, has long inspired Japanese poets and artists.
- Tokyo is Japan's capital and largest city.
- A number of Japanese cities are centers of industry and commerce.
- Origami, the art of paper folding, is an ancient tradition.
- Kimonos are the traditional clothing of Japanese men and women.

What Teachers Need to Know

A. Geography

Japan: A Nation of Islands

Japan is east of the Asian continent, separated from it by the Sea of Japan, and is bordered by the Pacific Ocean to its east.

Japan is an archipelago, that is, a chain of about 3,000 islands. The islands are the crests of mountaintops that rise above sea level. No island is more than 200 miles wide. Most of the islands are barren and rocky with no inhabitants.

From northeast to southwest, the four largest islands are Hokkaido, Honshu, Shikoku, and Kyushu. Honshu is the largest, comprising 60% of the land area of Japan. The majority of Japanese people live on Honshu along its southern coastal plain. This is an area of heavy industrial development. Tokyo, the country's capital, is located on Honshu.

Hokkaido is the second-largest island, but it is sparsely inhabited because of its mountainous terrain, great stands of forests, and harsh winter climate.

Kyushu, like Honshu, is heavily populated. The island has coal deposits, which helped it become an early center for industry. People on Shikoku, the smallest of the large islands, live mostly along the northern coast in industrial areas.

Less than 20% of Japan is suited to agriculture because it is so mountainous and heavily forested. As a result, the ancient Japanese learned to farm rice, their staple crop, in small paddies on the sides of terraced mountains. Beginning in the late 1800s, wealthy Japanese, with the help of the government, began a program to industrialize the country. Though World War II destroyed much of the country's industry and infrastructure, Japan was rebuilt and is today a leading exporter of electronics, automobiles, and many other manufactured goods.

Teaching Idea

In conjunction with this section you may wish to have children write poems in a traditional Japanese form, the haiku. First, explain the haiku and its syllable count—5 in the first line, then 7, then 5 again. Show children how to count syllables (e.g., by placing a hand on their chin and feeling how it dips and lifts). Share several examples of haiku. Then invite children to write their own haiku. Have them illustrate the poems and hang them on the wall.

Mount Fuji

Mount Fuji, also known as Fujiyama, is the highest mountain in Japan. At about 12,500 feet above sea level, it is twice as tall as most other mountains in Japan. Mount Fuji is a dormant volcano, like many of Japan's mountains, and has not erupted since 1707. It is also one of the most-climbed mountains in the world.

Mount Fuji is considered sacred by many Japanese. Over the centuries, its snowcapped peak has been the subject of numerous Japanese paintings and poems.

Teaching Idea

Share images of Mount Fuji—both photographic and painted—with children. Also share pictures of the skyscrapers and crowded streets of Tokyo.

Tokyo

Originally known as Edo, Tokyo was established in the 1100s CE. In 1868, it was renamed Tokyo and became the official capital of Japan. Devastated by earthquakes and by its bombardment during World War II, the city has been rebuilt several times, making it very modern in appearance. Tokyo is one of the world's largest cities. About 10% of Japan's population lives in its metropolitan area. Tokyo is also a center of commerce, industry, finance, and education. There are over 100 colleges and universities in the city. High-speed bullet trains, which can travel over 150 miles an hour, link Tokyo with other cities on the island of Honshu.

Teaching Idea

Use Instructional Master 10, *Asia*, to review the location of Japan. Talk about Japan's location in relation to the Asian continent. Ask, "In what direction does Japan lie in relation to China? In relation to India? Where is Japan in relation to the Pacific Ocean? From what country does the Sea of Japan separate Japan?" and so on.

B. Culture

The Japanese Flag

The Japanese flag is a red circle on a white background. The circle represents the rising sun. Japan is often called the "land of the rising sun," because the sun rises in the east, and, for Westerners, Japan is in the Far East. The Japanese call their own country "Nippon," which means "source of the sun." The rising sun flag was adopted in 1854 at the beginning of a period of rapid modernization and industrialization. For centuries, Japan had been closed to Westerners, but, in 1853, Commodore Matthew Perry of the U.S. Navy sailed into Edo Bay and demanded trading rights. Within 20 years, the Japanese had ousted the shoguns, who had wielded the real power in the Japanese empire; moved the emperor to Tokyo; written a constitution modeled on the German one; and adopted a national flag.

Modern Japanese Cities

Modern Japanese cities are centers of industry, finance, and education. In addition to Tokyo, there are several other cities with populations of 1.5 million people: Yokohama, Osaka, Nagoya, and Sapporo. Japan's industrial centers manufacture and export electrical and electronic equipment, automobiles, machinery, chemicals, and steel. Children will probably be familiar with some Japanese companies, e.g., Toyota, Honda, Mitsubishi, Fujifilm, etc. Because of its industrial development, Japan has one of the highest per capita incomes of any country in the world.

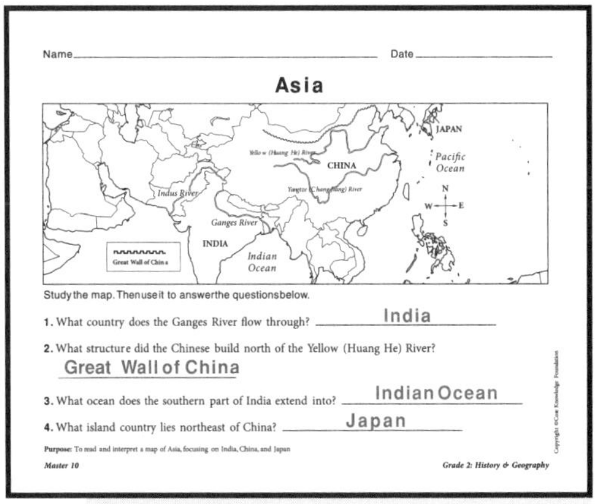

Name________ Date________

Asia

Study the map. Then use it to answer the questions below.

1. What country does the Ganges River flow through? India
2. What structure did the Chinese build north of the Yellow (Huang He) River? Great Wall of China
3. What ocean does the southern part of India extend into? Indian Ocean
4. What island country lies northeast of China? Japan

Purpose: To read and interpret a map of Asia, focusing on India, China, and Japan

Master 10 — Grade 2: History & Geography

Use Instructional Master 10.

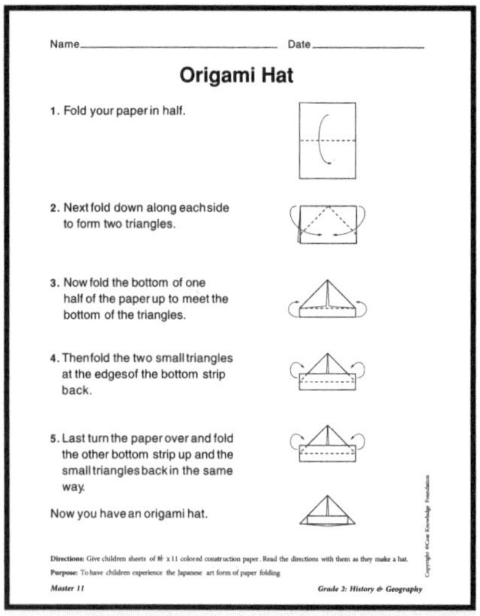

Name______________________ Date__________

Origami Hat

1. Fold your paper in half.
2. Next fold down along each side to form two triangles.
3. Now fold the bottom of one half of the paper up to meet the bottom of the triangles.
4. Then fold the two small triangles at the edges of the bottom strip back.
5. Last turn the paper over and fold the other bottom strip up and the small triangles back in the same way.

Now you have an origami hat.

Directions: Give children sheets of 8½ x 11 colored construction paper. Read the directions with them as they make a hat.
Purpose: To have children experience the Japanese art form of paper folding

Master 11 *Grade 2: History & Geography*

Copyright ©Core Knowledge Foundation

Use Instructional Master 11.

Origami: A Traditional Craft

Origami originated in Japan in the 900s CE. It is the traditional art of folding paper to make figures, such as birds and animals. Scissors and other tools are used only occasionally during the process.

Often, the first figure that is taught is the crane, which is the symbol of peace.

Kimono: Traditional Clothing

For centuries the Japanese wore kimonos. These are long narrow robes with wide sleeves that are worn as outer garments. Kimonos for girls and young women are of bright colors enhanced with embroidery. Kimonos for men are fairly plain and are made in dark colors. The obi, the sash that is worn with a kimono, is wide and often made of rich material for women. When tied, it forms a flat bow in the back of the kimono.

Today, kimonos are worn mainly for special occasions, such as weddings. Ordinarily, contemporary Japanese wear Western-style dress.

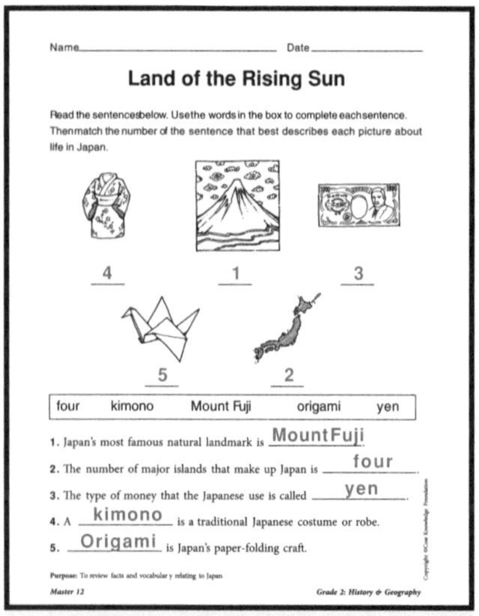

Name______________________ Date__________

Land of the Rising Sun

Read the sentences below. Use the words in the box to complete each sentence. Then match the number of the sentence that best describes each picture about life in Japan.

4 1 3

5 2

four	kimono	Mount Fuji	origami	yen

1. Japan's most famous natural landmark is Mount Fuji.
2. The number of major islands that make up Japan is four.
3. The type of money that the Japanese use is called yen.
4. A kimono is a traditional Japanese costume or robe.
5. Origami is Japan's paper-folding craft.

Purpose: To review facts and vocabulary relating to Japan

Master 12 *Grade 2: History & Geography*

Copyright ©Core Knowledge Foundation

Use Instructional Master 12.

Review

Below are some ideas for ongoing assessment and review activities. These are not meant to constitute a comprehensive list. Teachers may also refer to the *Pearson Learning/ Core Knowledge History & Geography* series for additional information and teaching ideas.

- Using resources and websites that explain how to teach origami, have children create a simple origami figure. After children have had an opportunity to fold some simple figures, have them write about the process and whether they enjoyed it. You may also partner up with a "buddy class" so that one child has an opportunity to teach another child how to use origami.
- Read "The Tongue-Cut Sparrow" with the class in conjunction with Language Arts. (See the Grade 2 Text Resources for Language Arts.) Review with children what they know about Japan, and have them describe the setting of the story. After reading the story, provide paper to make a book that summarizes the beginning, middle, and end of the story. Have children illustrate each part using details they have learned about Japan. What might the characters be wearing? What would the home look like? What would the surroundings look like? Check each paper for children's understanding of Japan.
- Have children design postcards of Japan on 4 x 6 index cards. On the front of the card, have children illustrate some aspect of Japan that they found interesting. On the back of the card, children should write a short note to someone describing their picture and what they learned about Japan.
- Show children pictures or small replicas of the Japanese and American flags. Discuss the saying "land of the rising sun" and how it relates to the flag of Japan. Then, review or discuss the symbolism of the American flag (see p. 236). Have children design another flag for Japan, using symbols to show what they have learned about the country. Have children draw the flag on white paper and then write on the back why they chose specific symbols for their flags.

The Big Idea in Review

Modern Japan is a major industrial country that is also firmly rooted in tradition.

• Display pictures of Tokyo to help children understand the aspects of a big city. What do they see when they look at each picture? Have them describe what it would be like to live in a large city.

• You may also ask the following questions at the end of this section:

1. Where is the island nation of Japan?
   Japan is located northeast of China and in the Pacific Ocean.
2. Why is Japan called an island nation?
   Japan is called an island nation, because it is made up of 3,000 islands. The islands are the tops of mountains that stick up out of the ocean.
3. What is Japan's tallest mountain?
   Japan's tallest mountain is Mount Fuji.
4. What is the capital and largest city of Japan?
   Tokyo is the capital and largest city of Japan.
5. What does Japan's flag look like?
   The Japanese flag is white with a red circle representing the sun.
6. What is origami?
   Origami is the art of folding paper to make it look like birds or other shapes.
7. What is a kimono?
   A kimono is the traditional robe that Japanese men and women used to wear all the time and now wear for special occasions.

More Resources

The titles listed below are offered as a representative sample of materials and not a complete list of everything that is available.

For children —

These books are generally intended to be read aloud, though some children may be able to read parts or all of the simpler texts.

• *Japan Today,* edited by E. D. Hirsch, Jr. (Pearson Learning, 2002). A unit in the official *Pearson Learning/Core Knowledge History & Geography* series. It includes a small picture book for children and a teacher's guide with read alouds. To order, call 1-800-321-3106.

• *Count Your Way Through Japan,* by Jim Haskins and illustrated by Martin Skoro (Carolrhoda, 1988). Paperback, 24 pages, ISBN 0876144857.

• *How My Parents Learned to Eat,* by Ina R. Friedman and illustrated by Allen Say (Houghton Mifflin, 1987). Paperback, 32 pages, ISBN 0395442354.

• *I Live in Tokyo: A Japanese Calendar,* by Mari Takabayashi (Houghton Mifflin, 2001). Hardcover, 32 pages, ISBN 0618077022.

• *Japan (Rookie Read-About Geography),* by David Marx (Children's Press, 2000). Paperback, 32 pages, ISBN 0516267930.

• *Let's Learn Japanese Picture Dictionary,* illustrated by Marlene Goodman (NTC/Contemporary Publishing, 1992). Hardcover, ISBN 0844284947.

• *The Way We Do It in Japan,* by Geneva Cobb Iijima and illustrated by Paige Billin-Frye (Albert Whitman, 2002). Library binding, 32 pages, ISBN 0807578223.

For teachers —

• *Japan: A Global Studies Handbook,* by Lucien Ellington (ABC-CLIO, 2002). An introduction to Japan's history, culture, economics, and society. Written by one of the expert reviewers for the Core Knowledge curriculum, this book draws on the author's experience in leading teacher institutes on Japan in more than 20 states. Contains an extensive resource section. Hardcover, 307 pages, ISBN 1576072711.

More Resources continued

• *Japan Video Encyclopedia* (NHK International, 1996). Features six-minute segments on topics including homes, food, clothing, and daily life for children in Japan. Available for free-loan from Japanese Consulate offices. Though the series is not intended for young children, there are some segments that will offer a nice visual addition to your curriculum. Consulates also offer a variety of other materials for loan. To find the nearest Japanese Consulate, go to www.japanatlanta.org/cgofj.html, or phone the Japanese Embassy in Washington, D.C., at 202-238-6700.

• *Shipwrecked! The True Adventures of a Japanese Boy,* by Rhoda Blumberg (HarperTrophy, 2003). Follow the story of 14-year-old Manjiro, whose adventures brought him to a place of influence in Japan's reacceptance of foreign trade. Paperback, 80 pages, ISBN 068817485X. See also *Commodore Perry in the Land of the Shogun* by the same author. Both titles may offer some opportunities for reading aloud.

• Asia for Educators, at http://afe.easia.columbia.edu, provides much background information in their online unit "Contemporary Japan: Culture and Society." Features videotaped clips of two Harvard professors covering topics such as urban and rural life, the Japanese family, and education and work in Japan.

• Student Activity: The Making of a Class Carp Streamer. Lesson plan available online from SPICE (Stanford Program on International and Cross-Cultural Education), at http://spice.stanford.edu/lp/carp/index.html.

IV. Ancient Greece

The Big Idea

The Greeks developed a rich and varied civilization, many aspects of which have been passed down to subsequent generations.

Remember that each subject you study with children expands their vocabulary and introduces new terms, thus making them better listeners and readers. As you study historical people and events, use read alouds and discussions to build children's vocabularies.

The items below relate to the content in Grade 2. In discussing ancient Greece, use terminology such as "long, long ago" to place it in time. All dates are BCE.

2500	Settling of Athens
1750–1500	Minoan civilization
776	First Olympics
600–500	Founding of Sparta
594	Solon as leader in Athens
490	Battle of Marathon
480	Battle of Thermopylae
469–399	Socrates
461–429	Age of Pericles in Athens
427–347	Plato
384–322	Aristotle
356–323	Alexander the Great

What Students Need to Learn

- **Geography: Mediterranean Sea, Aegean Sea, Crete**
- **Sparta**
- **Athens as city-state: the beginnings of democracy**
- **Persian Wars: Marathon and Thermopylae**
- **Olympic Games**
- **Worship of gods and goddesses**
- **Great thinkers: Socrates, Plato, and Aristotle**
- **Alexander the Great**

What Students Will Learn in Future Grades

In future grades, students will study Rome, which inherited many ideas and traditions from Greece, and review and extend their learning about Greece.

Grade 3

- Ancient Rome

Grade 6

- Ancient Greece
  - The Greek polis (city-state) and patriotism
  - Beginnings of democratic government
    - Roots of modern American democratic government
    - The Assembly
    - Suffrage, majority vote
  - The "classical" ideal of human life and works
    - The ideal of the well-rounded citizen
    - Pericles and the "Golden Age"
    - Architecture: the Parthenon
    - Games: The Olympics
  - Greek wars: victory and hubris
  - Socrates and Plato
  - Plato and Aristotle
  - Alexander the Great and the spread of Greek culture
- Ancient Rome

IV. Ancient Greece

Text Resources

(55) *Taming of Bucephalus*

(56) *Training of Spartan Girls*

Materials

Instructional Masters 13–15

Ancient Greece, p. 146

The Greek Gods, p. 151

Alexander the Great's Empire, p. 154

overhead projector, p. 146

pictures or news clippings about a marathon, p. 149

knotted string, p. 155

chart paper, p. 156

index cards, p. 156

pictures of various aspects of Greek history, p. 156

pictures of ancient Olympic events, p. 156

pictures of current Olympic athletes, p. 156

Vocabulary

Student/Teacher Vocabulary

Aegean Sea: the sea to the east of Greece (S)

Alexander the Great: a ruler who created the largest empire of his time and tried to mix the cultures within his empire to create new cultures (S)

Aristotle: a famous Greek philosopher and a student of Plato (S)

Athens: a Greek city-state; the birthplace of democracy (S)

city-state: a state consisting of a ruling city and the surrounding territory (S)

Crete: a Greek island that was once home to the Minoan civilization (S)

cultural blending: mixing cultures together to create new ones (T)

democracy: a form of government in which citizens help create the laws and govern themselves (S)

Hellenism: the name given to the merging of Greek and Middle Eastern cultures (T)

Marathon: a battle site of the Persian Wars (S)

Mediterranean Sea: one of the seas surrounding Greece (S)

Olympic Games: athletic competitions begun in the Greek city-states (S)

Plato: a famous Greek philosopher and a student of Socrates (S)

representative democracy: a form of democracy in which citizens elect representatives to speak for them in government (T)

Socrates: a famous Greek philosopher (S)

Sparta: an ancient Greek city-state that developed into a fierce military state (S)

Thermopylae: a battle site of the Persian Wars, where the Spartans fought to the last man (S)

Domain Vocabulary

Geography and associated words:
Balkan Peninsula, Ionian Sea, islands, mountainous, Peloponnesus, fertile lowlands, seafarers, trading network, colonies, colonization, Sicily, Asia Minor, Southwest Asia, European Turkey, small, independent, competitive, rivals, rivalry, Crete, Minoan civilization, Minos, Knossos, crossroads

Sparta and associated words:
ideal of war, soldier, citizen, noncitizen, helot, slave, spartan, laconic, Council of Elders, advisors, Persian Wars, Persia, Darius, Battle of Marathon, Pheidippides, runner, messenger, heroic, Olympic race, marathon, Xerxes, Leonidas, pass, defend, defense, last stand, heroic, resist, to the death

Athens and associated words:
evolution, archons, officials, oversee, manage, Assembly of Citizens, Solon, Cleisthenes, Athenian Assembly, Council of Five Hundred, direct democracy, debate, discuss, vote, limited democracy, restrictions, representative democracy, Pericles, jury

Culture and associated words:
Zeus, supreme god, honor, Olympia Valley, Mount Olympus, competition, competitive, sports, races, religion, worship, honor, shrine, temple, deity, deities, god, goddess, family, guardians, Hera, women, Athena, wisdom, agriculture, crafts, Poseidon, sea, oracle, priest, male and female, soothsayer, petition, petitioner, Delphi, Apollo, Parthenon, Athens, philosophers, great thinkers, Socratic method, ask questions, questioning, objective truth, "Know thyself," self-knowledge, correct behavior, hemlock, academy, dialogues, ideals, higher world, by reason, republic, ideal government, real world, moderation, balance, moral behavior, self-control, self-reliance, Lyceum

Vocabulary continued

Alexander the Great and associated words:
Philip II, Macedonia, Persian Empire, rival, threat, warfare, Darius, Battle of Issus, Phoenicia, Egypt, Mesopotamia, Indus River, Hellenistic, merging of cultures, cross cultural, Gordian Knot, Gordium, Asia Minor, legend, sword, cut, slice, clever, Alexandria

In the Text Resources for this section, words are bolded that should be included as part of Domain Vocabulary.

Cross-curricular Connections

Language Arts

Fiction

Mythology of Ancient Greece

- Gods of ancient Greece
- Mount Olympus
- Mythological creatures and characters
- Greek myths

Visual Arts

Sculpture

- *The Discobolus (Discus Thrower)*

Architecture

- Parthenon

At a Glance

The most important ideas for you are:

- Because of Greece's terrain and location, Greek city-states developed differently than other ancient civilizations.
- Crete was the location of an ancient seafaring civilization.
- Sparta developed as a military state.
- Athens developed as a direct democracy, though its definition of citizenship was limited.
- The battles at Marathon and Thermopylae provided models of heroic behavior.
- The Olympic Games were started in honor of Zeus, the chief deity of the ancient Greeks.
- The ancient Greeks had a pantheon of 12 major male and female deities, whom they honored.
- Socrates, Plato, and Aristotle developed different philosophical insights into ethical behavior.
- Alexander the Great created the largest empire in the then-known world.

What Teachers Need to Know

Background: The Geographic Setting of Greece

Greece is situated on the Balkan Peninsula, which juts into the Mediterranean Sea. To the east is the Aegean Sea and to the west, the Ionian Sea. About one-fifth of Greece is made up of islands. Crete, which marks the southern end of the Aegean Sea, is the largest Greek island. About 75% of Greece—mainland and islands—is mountainous.

The terrain greatly affected how ancient Greece developed. Greece has no flooding rivers, like the Nile or the Tigris and Euphrates (which children should have learned about in Grade 1), or the Ganges, Indus, Huang He, and Yangtze. Nor does it have fertile valleys or broad plains to farm. Only an area known as the Peloponnesus on the mainland's southern tip has some fertile lowlands, and some of the larger islands also have small fertile valleys.

Some early Greeks did farm, but many others took to the sea to earn their living. The position of Greece in the Mediterranean, Aegean, and Ionian Seas led to the development of a large and profitable trading network for the Greeks. The early Greeks established colonies around the coasts of the Aegean, Ionian, Black, and Mediterranean Seas. Especially important were the Greek colonies in southern Italy, on the island of Sicily, and in Asia Minor. (Asia Minor is the historical name for the peninsula jutting out from Southwest Asia between the Mediterranean and the Black Seas; it is the area known today as the Anatolian Peninsula, or what forms the greater part of Turkey.)

Unlike the Egyptians, Sumerians, and others who developed civilizations around rivers in flat regions, the ancient Greeks did not build vast empires. The mountains, valleys, and water surrounding Greece cut off groups of people from one another. Instead, the Greeks developed a series of small, independent city-states that were highly competitive. In fact, the intense rivalry often led to war. The two most famous city-states were Athens, famous for its democracy and culture, and Sparta, famous for its conservatism and military might.

Teaching Idea

Make an overhead of Instructional Master 13, *Ancient Greece*, to orient children to the Greek mainland and islands.

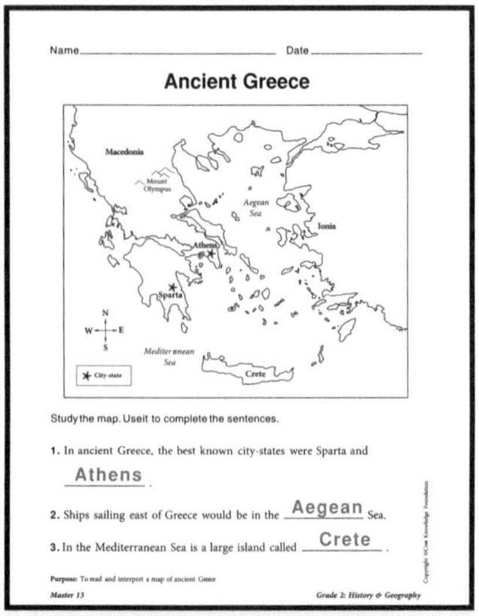

Name________ Date________

Ancient Greece

Study the map. Use it to complete the sentences.

1. In ancient Greece, the best known city-states were Sparta and Athens.
2. Ships sailing east of Greece would be in the Aegean Sea.
3. In the Mediterranean Sea is a large island called Crete.

Purpose: To read and interpret a map of ancient Greece

Master 13 *Grade 2: History & Geography*

Copyright © Core Knowledge Foundation

Use Instructional Master 13.

Crete

Today, Crete is an agricultural center and popular tourist site. The main cash crops are grapes, olives, and oranges. By 1600 BCE, Crete was the seat of the Minoan civilization, named after its legendary king, Minos.

The island was at the crossroads of a trading network that joined ancient Egypt in North Africa with Mesopotamia in the Middle East. In addition to its warm, sunny climate, one of the reasons that tourists visit Crete today is the palace at Knossos, the one-time capital of Minoan civilization. The palace is famed for its frescoes, watercolor murals painted on wet plaster. The paintings chronicle Minoan life, their religious practices, and their clothes, hairstyles, and activities, and indicate the place that the sea held in the lives of the Minoans.

By around 1400 BCE, Minoan civilization had disappeared. An earthquake or a volcanic eruption on a nearby island could have destroyed it, or invaders could have conquered the island.

Sparta

One of the fiercest of the Greek city-states was Sparta, founded on the ideal of war. Between 600 BCE and 500 BCE, the Dorians from the north had moved into the Peloponnesus and conquered the inhabitants, whom they enslaved and called helots. In order to maintain their power, the Spartans turned their city-state into a military machine. The only occupation a full-fledged citizen could have was that of soldier. All other jobs were done by helots and other noncitizens. The Spartans kept the helots under strict control and crushed all helot uprisings ruthlessly.

Spartan education was designed to raise fearless, obedient soldiers. Boys were cared for by their mothers until age seven and then were taken from their homes to become part of a military company. The military training they received was intense and brutal. It included marching, fighting, and gymnastics. The young soldiers were fed too little in an effort to force them to steal food and thus learn craftiness, a useful skill in times of war. If caught stealing, they were beaten, which they were expected to accept without complaint, or risk disgrace.

Spartan mothers urged their sons to return from wars "with your shield or upon it," in other words, "victorious in combat or dead." Spartan boys learned Homer's *Iliad* by ear and songs of war as well, but reading and writing were not considered important parts of their education. The qualities prized in Spartan men are those we still associate with the phrase "spartan virtue"—stoic endurance of hardship, disdain for luxury, and toughness of mind and body.

Spartan boys were also taught to be succinct and direct in their speech. According to one story, students who gave answers that were too long were bitten on their fingers by their teachers! Our modern word *laconic,* meaning "terse" or "of few words," derives from the speech habits of Spartans.

Soldiers were allowed to marry when they turned 20. However, military control was so strict that soldiers had to live in the barracks until they were 30. Even then, to maintain discipline, soldiers had to take their meals in the barracks until they were 60.

This training, brutal though it was, had the desired effect. Sparta's dominion and military strength were so indisputable that the city itself had no surrounding defensive walls for years. Legend has it that the Spartan lawgiver Lycurgus once boasted that Sparta did not need walls of stone because it had "walls of men."

Spartan girls were given different training. They were expected to exercise and remain in good physical condition. Reading and writing were seen as having little value, although dancing was considered important because it was good exercise. (56)

Sparta was ruled by kings and by a council of elders. The council of elders was a group of 28 men over the age of 60 who acted as advisers to the king as a law court. In addition, the council was responsible for inspecting all new babies. Those whom the council deemed too sickly were left to die on a mountain.

Cross-curricular Teaching Idea

The stories of "Theseus and the Minotaur" and "Daedalus and Icarus" both take place on the island of Crete. (See Language Arts, Mythology of Ancient Greece, p. 85.) You may wish to introduce them in conjunction with this history content.

Teaching Idea

Relate archaeologists' study of frescoes in the palace at Knossos to how archaeologists a thousand years from now would use photographs to determine what life in your community was like—what people wore, what they ate, how they got from one place to another, what they did for recreation, how they made their living, and so on.

Have children decide what things in your community would help archeologists answer these questions. Then have small groups create illustrations.

Spartan Soldiers

Sparta was a closed society. Spartans could not travel outside Spartan territory, except in case of war; nor could foreigners travel within Spartan territory. This was because the Spartan leaders believed their way of life was best and did not want this way of life corrupted by foreign ideas.

> **Teaching Idea**
>
> **Help children see the difference between the democratic government of ancient Greece and the kinds of government they have encountered previously, e.g., government by pharoahs or emperors. Extend the discussion to include how these governments formed the root of our present system of government.**

Athens: The Beginnings of Democracy

Athens was the other well-known ancient Greek city-state, and it was about as different from Sparta as it could be. While Sparta was ruled by a few, Athens was the birthplace of democracy. While Sparta kept its people at home, Athenians traveled and traded all around the world. While Sparta emphasized military training at the expense of all other forms of education, Athens aimed to develop well-rounded citizens. While Spartan children were taught to speak only a few words, Athenian writers and philosophers wrote plays, poems, and philosophical works that are still read today.

Athens is located on the eastern side of the Greek mainland toward the center of the peninsula. The government of Athens slowly evolved over time from one ruled by a king to one governed by its citizens. The first people settled in this area before 3000 BCE.

> **Teaching Idea**
>
> **Tell the class that they are members of an ancient Greek city-state that is in the initial stages of development. Have the children discuss whether they want a monarch to rule them; whether they want to decide every law, tax, and appointment of a public official themselves; or whether they want to elect some people whose job it is to represent them. Ask what the advantages and disadvantages of each system of government would be. Point out that the founders of the United States chose the last form of government—a representative democracy.**

Originally, the Athenian government seems to have consisted of a king and nobles who owned much of the land. The nobles eventually displaced the king and dominated the government, choosing the three archons, or officials, who oversaw the government. Although there was a general assembly made up of all adult male citizens, the only power was in the hands of the landowning nobles.

Poor harvests created hard economic times that increased the feelings of powerlessness among ordinary people. Independent farmers lost their lands and became tenant farmers on estates of the wealthy nobles. Some farmers even sold themselves into slavery to pay off their debts. The economic problems added to the political discontent. Merchants clamored for their rights, and foreign craftworkers—those from other Greek city-states—resented their lack of citizenship.

In 594 BCE, Solon was appointed as the chief officer. A wise and thoughtful leader, he made many reforms that not only eased problems in Athens, but also began its evolution to democracy. Solon outlawed debt slavery and freed those who were already enslaved for debt. The status of citizen was granted to some foreign craftworkers. Rather than have birth be the criterion for political participation, Solon made wealth the deciding factor. He then divided the assembly into four levels based on four levels of wealth. The general assembly was given the right to approve government decisions.

After Solon, leaders with varying degrees of interest in maintaining and expanding the rights of Athenian citizens came to power. Some attempted to restrict those rights, and others like Cleisthenes furthered democracy. Under Cleisthenes, the people of Athens were divided into 10 tribes, which were based on location of residence, replacing the four tribes based on aristocratic descent. The Athenian assembly became the legislative, or lawmaking, branch of the government. All citizens, whether property owners or not, were eligible to attend and debate. A council of 500 proposed laws for the general assembly. Any citizen over 30 was eligible to serve on the council, whose members were drawn by lottery.

The council of 500 proved to be too large and unwieldy to function effectively as an administrative branch, so it was divided into 10 committees of 50 men each, which were further divided into smaller units representing towns. The Athenians referred to each of the latter as a *deme*, from the Greek word for "people." This is the root of the English word *democracy*. The word *democracy* is a Greek word meaning "rule by the demos, or people."

Unlike the representative democracy of the United States, in which citizens elect representatives to speak for them in government, Athenian democracy was direct democracy. Citizens discussed, debated, and voted on laws themselves. In order to decide on issues, at least 6,000 citizens had to be present in the assembly, which met several times a month.

Although Athens pioneered democratic government, their insitutions differed in some key ways from modern American democracy. Citizenship did not extend to women, slaves, and most non-native residents. This was true even during the greatest age of Athenian democracy, which occurred under the rule of Pericles from 461 BCE to 429 BCE. Pericles extended the ability of poor men to serve in public office by paying a small salary to public officeholders. He also saw to it that jurors were paid for the time they spent in jury duty.

Besides democracy, Athens was also famous for its culture. It was the birthplace of both comedy and tragedy in theatre, and was also the home of the great philosophers Socrates, Plato, and Aristotle.

The Persian Wars: Marathon and Thermopylae

While Greek city-states warred with one another, the threat of war from outside the peninsula could unite them. In 499 BCE, Athens had aided fellow Greek city-states in Ionia, the Greek area of Asia Minor, when they rebelled against rule by the Persians and their king, Darius. Persia is the historical name given to the high plateau area of what is today Iran.

Marathon

In 490 BCE, Darius launched an attack against Athens in retaliation for its earlier support of the Ionian Greeks. Few of the other Greek city-states answered Athens's call for help. As a result, the Athenian force of 11,000 soldiers was greatly outnumbered as it faced 15,000 Persian invaders on the battlefield at Marathon. Through fierce hand-to-hand combat, the Athenian soldiers ousted the Persians.

The battle at Marathon is known as much, however, for the story of Pheidippides as it is for the Athenian victory. The leader of the Athenian forces, Miltiades, sent the runner Pheidippides to Athens to announce the victory. Pheidippides ran so fast and so hard over the 26 miles that, after he gave his message, he collapsed and died on the spot. The Olympic marathon, roughly 26 miles long, honors Pheidippides's feat.

Teaching Idea

A marathon is 26 miles, 385 yards. Ask children if they know anyone who has ever run a marathon and if that person ever talked about what it was like to run that far. If you are a marathoner, you might bring in your number from a race and any pictures or news clippings and talk about how long you had to train for the race, any special foods you needed to eat, and how you felt while running and when you finished.

Or, if you know someone who has run a marathon, invite that person as a special guest. If your class has read the Greek myth about Atalanta, you can discuss her race with Hippomenes.

Thermopylae

When Darius's son Xerxes attacked Greece in 480 BCE, Sparta and other city-states joined Athens to fight the Persians. The Persian army landed above a narrow pass called Thermopylae, which at the time controlled the only road between northern and central Greece. On one side of the pass are mountains and on the other side,

> **Teaching Idea**
> **C. P. Cavafy wrote a poem titled "Thermopylae" in 1901. Discuss with children what the following lines might mean:**
> **Honor to those who in the life they lead define and guard a Thermopylae.**
> **Never betraying what is right,**
> **consistent and just in all they do**
> **but showing pity also, and**
> **compassion; . . .**
> **generous in small ways, still helping as much as they can;**
> **always speaking the truth . . .**

cliffs and the sea. Before the battle, Xerxes sent a message to the Spartan commander, Leonidas, telling the Spartans to lay down their weapons. As noted earlier, the Spartans were famous for sending short, "laconic" answers. Leonidas's reply was "come and take them."

The early stages of the battle were described by the Greek historian Herodotus in his work *The Persian Wars:*

> The pass's defenders [the Greeks] are deployed around the rocks and as the Persians attempt to move through the pass, they are speared. Many of the wounded fall into the sea.
>
> After some fighting Xerxes learned from a Greek traitor that there was a back way that would enable him to outflank the Greeks. Xerxes ordered his soldiers to take the mountain path and attack the Greeks from the rear. On the third and final day of the battle, the pass was defended by 300 Spartans and 400 Thebans, soldiers from the city-state of Thebes, all commanded by Leonidas, the king of Sparta. These brave men faced thousands of Persian soldiers. They knew that they would almost certainly die, but they were willing to sacrifice their lives in order to slow down the Persian advance and allow the remainder of the Greek army to retreat to safety. In the end, all of them were killed defending the pass.

The Spartans' refusal to surrender and willingness to die for their city-state has come to symbolize heroic resistance. The last stand at Thermopylae has been immortalized in a short epitaph:

> Go and tell the Spartans, stranger passing by,
> That here, obedient to their laws, we lie.

After mowing down the brave Spartans and Thebans, the triumphant Persians headed for Athens. The people of the city had been evacuated, and the Persians entered an empty city. They burned Athens and would probably have achieved complete victory, had it not been for the cunning of the Athenian commander, Themistocles. Themistocles tricked the Persians into bringing their entire fleet into a narrow channel along the Bay of Salamis, from which Greek fighting ships called triremes emerged to ram and attack. The Persians lost over 200 ships and this naval victory proved to be the turning point of the war. In 479 BCE, the Greeks took the war to Persian territory and defeated them.

The cultural significance of the Persian Wars was enormous. The great Battles of Marathon, Thermopylae, and Salamis acquired almost mythic status and were retold in drama, poetry, sculpture, and wall paintings for years to come. These battles were indicators of the greatness of Greece and the bravery of the Greek people.

Olympic Games

> **Teaching Idea**
> **Allow children to research an ancient (or modern) Olympic sport and write or tell about what they find. You may also wish to work with physical education instructors to set up a school olympics.**

The earliest recorded Olympic Game occurred in 776 BCE. It was a footrace held to honor Zeus, the supreme god of Greek mythology. The original location for the games was Olympia Valley in the shadow of Mount Olympus.

The games were held every four years and were one of the few times that the Greek city-states came together—but still as competitors. During the games, a truce was declared and there was no fighting allowed between the city-states. The games included such sports as boxing, wrestling, footraces, chariot racing, discus throwing, and the broad jump.

Emperor Theodosius of the Eastern Roman Empire stopped the Olympic Games in 393 CE. Cheating among the athletes and the use of professional athletes rather than amateurs had become problems. In addition, the dedication of the games to Greek deities came into conflict with the newly adopted Christianity of the Roman Empire. Christians insisted that there was only one God, and they objected to games held in honor of Zeus and other pagan gods. The modern Olympic Games were reinstated in 1896, and now take place every four years. The games were suspended in 1916 during World War I, and in 1940 and 1944 during World War II. After the 1992 games, the summer and winter games were split so that instead of taking place during the same year, the two sets of games occur in two-year intervals. The next winter games were held in 1994 and the next summer games in 1996. In 2004, the Olympic Games returned to Athens for the first time since 1896.

Worship of Gods and Goddesses

The Greeks believed in a family of deities, and the 12 most powerful gods lived on Mount Olympus. The most important of the Greek gods are listed below:

Zeus: the ruler of all gods; he was notorious for throwing his lightning bolt and chasing after young girls. This last pastime did not endear him to his wife, Hera.

Hera: the goddess of marriage, guardian of women, jealous wife of Zeus

Apollo: the god of music and poetry

Artemis: the goddess of hunting, sister of Apollo

Poseidon: the god of the seas and earthquakes. He carried a trident, a three-pronged staff, that he used to stir up the oceans.

Aphrodite: the goddess of love, unfaithful wife of Hephaestus. She was said to have been born from the foam of the sea.

Demeter: the goddess of grain and the harvest

Ares: the god of war

Hermes: the speedy messenger of the gods, who wore winged sandals

Hephaestus: the crippled blacksmith of the gods

Athena: the goddess of wisdom and war. She was said to have sprung, full-grown, from the head of Zeus. She was the patron goddess of Athens and the goddess to whom the Parthenon was dedicated.

Dionysus: the god of wine and theater

These 12, with their great virtues and huge defects, were believed to dwell in splendor on the craggy peaks of Mount Olympus in northern Greece. There they feasted, drank ambrosia, quarreled, fell in love, protected their mortal allies, hatched plans against enemies, plotted revenge, and sometimes outwitted each other. Many delightful stories are told about these gods and goddesses. Some of these are listed in the Language Arts curriculum for this grade. Others may be found in the works of Homer and Hesiod, and in modern collections of Greek mythological stories.

Teaching Idea

You may wish to teach the sculpture *The Discobolus (Discus Thrower)* in conjunction with your study of the Olympics, since the discus was one of the Olympic sports.

Cross-curricular Teaching Idea

Relate the section on Greek deities to the stories and myths children are learning in Language Arts (p. 84). Help children to see the connection between literature (and all art) and the time and place in which it was created.

Teaching Idea

Have children fill in the graphic organizer in Instructional Masters 14a and 14b, *The Greek Gods,* which lists the name of the god or goddess in the *Sequence*. Have children list the main "attribute" that he or she is known for, and any details they have read about the god or goddess in their study of mythology in Language Arts and Ancient Greece in History and Geography.

Name ______________________ Date ____________

The Greek Gods

Fill in the chart by writing the main attribute of the god and any details that you learn about each during your study of mythology in Language Arts and Ancient Greece in History & Geography

Greekgod	Known for:
Zeus (ZOOCE)	King of the gods, controlled the heavens and decided arguments among the gods
Hera (HAIR-uh)	wife of Zeus, queen of thee gods and the goddess of marriage
Apollo (uh-PAUL-oh)	son of Zeus, god of light, poetry, music, healing, archery
Artemis (AR-tuh-miss)	twin sister of Apollo0, goddess of the moon and of hunting
Poseidon (poe-SIDE-un)	god of the sea, often depicted in pictures with a long beard and a trident (long pitchfork)
Aphrodite (af-roe-DIE-tee)	goddess of love and beauty, had a son called Eros

Purpose: To help children track key elements associated with each of the Greek gods

Master 14a

Grade 2: History & Geography

Copyright ©Core Knowledge Foundation

Use Instructional Masters 14a and 14b.

The Temple at Delphi

City-states set aside certain days every year for festivals to honor their patron deities. City-states also established shrines and temples in their honor. Some of the shrines were noted for their oracles, male and female priests through whom the deities spoke. A petitioner could ask a god a question about the future and the god would answer through the oracle. The oracle at Delphi, a shrine to Apollo, was famous throughout Greece.

Some of the finest sculpture and architecture of the Greeks was created to serve and honor the deities. The Parthenon in Athens, for example, was built to honor Athena.

Great Thinkers

Socrates, Plato, and Aristotle were three Athenian philosophers whose lives were connected. Plato was a student of Socrates, and Aristotle was a student of Plato. These three great philosophers attempted to use reason to discover truth and an ethical system of behavior. Prior to their work, Greek philosophers had focused on trying to understand what the universe was made of. With Socrates, Plato, and Aristotle, the focus was more on human behavior.

Socrates (469–399 BCE)

Socrates developed what is known as the Socratic method. Through a series of questions, he attempted to prod his students into seeing the inconsistencies and contradictions in their thinking about fundamental questions like "How should we live? What is goodness? What is justice?" He believed that there was an objective truth and that people could discover this truth for themselves by looking inside themselves. "Know thyself," he taught his students. This ultimate truth would, hopefully, lead people to adopt a course of correct behavior.

Socrates had a distinctive way of teaching, which involved asking questions—"How do you know? What do you mean?"—and then using these questions to guide his hearers toward his point of view. Through reasoned dialogue, he helped make abstract concepts, such as "courage," "justice," and "beauty," specific and meaningful. His questioning method is still used in many colleges and universities today. The following brief example of the Socratic method is taken from a dialogue called the *Meno*, written by Plato in 380 BCE:

> Meno. If you want to have one definition of [all virtue], I know not what to say, but that virtue is the power of governing humankind.
>
> Socrates. And does this definition of virtue include all virtue? Is virtue the same in a child and in a slave, Meno? Can the child govern his father, or the slave his master; and would he who governed be any longer a slave?
>
> Meno. I think not, Socrates.
>
> Socrates. No, indeed; there would be small reason in that. Yet once more, fair friend; according to you, virtue is "the power of governing"; but do you not add "justly and not unjustly"?
>
> Meno. Yes, Socrates; I agree there; for justice is virtue.

Fellow Athenians were suspicious of Socrates and the way he questioned everything. They came to see him as a troublemaker. He was accused of blaspheming the deities and corrupting the youth of Athens with his teaching. Socrates was tried, found guilty, and sentenced to death by an Athenian court. He was given numerous opportunities to escape. But Socrates refused to flee Athens. Each city-state, he taught, was governed by time-tested laws and constitutions. No citizen had the right to stand above the rule of law. Socrates accepted his fate as a good citizen of Athens. He agreed to drink a cup of a poison called hemlock. The trial and last days of Socrates are described in a series of short and very readable dialogues by Plato, *The Apology, Crito,* and *Phaedo.*

Plato (427–347 BCE)

Socrates left no writings, but his student Plato wrote a series of dialogues that show Socrates' influence as a questioner. Plato's later dialogues present his own views. Plato also taught his ideas in a school he founded, called the Academy.

Plato believed that there is an objective, or ultimate, set of universal truths called Ideals, such as Truth and Beauty. However, people will never be able to discover these universal truths solely through observation because what they see around them is ever changing. Ideals can only be grasped through reason.

One of Plato's most famous dialogues is *The Republic.* In this work, Plato explores the idea of an ideal government based on a true understanding of justice. This government would be very different from the actual government of Athens. (Plato did not like Athenian democracy, which he blamed for the death of his mentor, Socrates.) In Plato's Republic there would be no democracy, but also no slaves. There would be only three social classes: workers, soldiers, and philosophers (or philosopher-kings). The first group would produce the essentials of life, the second would protect the state, and the third would govern through just and humane laws. All property would be held in common. Plato's *The Republic* is still widely read and is available in many translations.

Aristotle (384–322 BCE)

Aristotle was a student in Plato's Academy in Athens; however, he disagreed with Plato about some things, including the essence of the ideal. Aristotle believed that the ideals were inherent in the real world, not separated off in a higher world of their own. Aristotle was not willing to confine himself to the realm of ideas, to the theory of knowledge. He was acutely interested in the physical world. In general, Aristotle focused much more on the world as it really exists, whereas Plato focused more on an "ideal" world that he thought should be brought into existence. The distinction between the two philosophers is memorably captured in Raphael's famous painting *The School of Athens,* in which Plato is shown pointing to the heavens, the location of the abstract ideals, while Aristotle holds his arm parallel to the earth.

Aristotle adopted a philosophy of moderation. He believed that humans must find a balance between the extremes of good and evil. This balance would result in moral behavior. Among the highest virtues, according to Aristotle, were self-control and self-reliance. A phrase commonly associated with Aristotle is "the golden mean." An example of the golden mean comes from Aristotle's *Nicomachean Ethics,* books 2 and 3, in which Aristotle explains that a shortage of courage is cowardice, but an excess of courage is recklessness. True courage is the "golden mean" between these two extremes. In other words, it is possible to have too much of a good thing: if one has too much courage it ceases to be a virtue. In the same way, Aristotle held that temperance was the golden mean between indifference and boundless desire.

Teaching Idea

While the explanations of the philosophies of Socrates, Plato, and Aristotle given here are simplified, the themes can be explored with children to focus on the importance of good behavior.

Talk about how sometimes we know that we are doing something that is not right—a little voice tells us—but we ignore it and do the thing anyway. Apply this to "Know thyself."

Try a similar approach with the Aristotelean concept of balance. Too much of a good thing is too much—too much running, too much candy, staying up too late, and so on. Ask children for the negative effects of each action to make the point.

Aristotle was a multifaceted genius who wrote on many different subjects. For example, he wrote a book on politics in which he examined different kinds of government, including the governments of city-states, like Athens and Sparta. He wrote a book on poetry and theater that describes how we feel when we see a hero suffering in a Greek tragedy. He also wrote on various scientific subjects. Aristotle's scientific ideas were extremely important during the Middle Ages. During the Renaissance and the Enlightenment, some of his central ideas were challenged, but some of his works are still widely read.

For a time, Aristotle tutored Alexander, the son of the king of Macedonia. This young lad would grow up to be Alexander the Great, conqueror of much of the known world. After Alexander rose to power, he gave his former tutor a gift that Aristotle used to establish his own school, the Lyceum.

Alexander the Great

Teaching Idea

Make an overhead of Instructional Master 15, *Alexander the Great's Empire.* It is not important that children learn the particulars of Alexander's conquest, only the extent of his empire north, south, east, and west.

Using the map overhead also provides another context for children to learn the location and names of certain geographical features. You can also use the map of Alexander's conquests to review civilizations studied earlier, many of which Alexander conquered or invaded, e.g., Egypt, Mesopotamia, India.

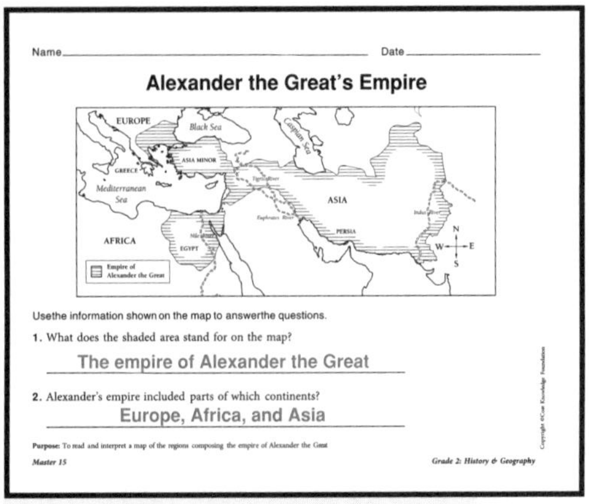
Name________ Date________

Alexander the Great's Empire

Usethe information shown on the map to answerthe questions.

1. What does the shaded area stand for on the map?
The empire of Alexander the Great

2. Alexander's empire included parts of which continents?
Europe, Africa, and Asia

Purpose: To read and interpret a map of the regions composing the empire of Alexander the Great

Master 15 — Grade 2: History & Geography

Copyright ©Core Knowledge Foundation

Use Instructional Master 15.

Phillip II was king of Macedonia, a region north of Greece. At the time he was king, from 359 BCE to 336 BCE, the Persian Empire was still a major threat to the Greek city-states. Phillip was determined to conquer the Greek city-states and combine their forces with his Macedonians. He believed he would then be strong enough to defeat the Persians. Before Phillip could fully realize his plan, he was assassinated. His son, the 20-year-old Alexander, ascended the throne.

This was the same Alexander who had been tutored by Aristotle. The young man had never learned to pursue Aristotle's golden mean. He did everything to the extreme. But his studies with Aristotle did affect him in at least one important way. Under Aristotle's tutelage he had studied Homer's epic poem *The Iliad*, with its great warrior-hero Achilles. Alexander carried a copy of *The Iliad* with him for the rest of his life, and the poem seems to have inspired him to become a great warrior-hero in his own right.

Phillip had succeeded in conquering the Greeks. Now his son Alexander packed his copy of *The Iliad* and led his joint Macedonian and Greek army into Asia Minor. Alexander soon proved himself a brilliant warrior and stunning tactician. Leading from the front lines of any battle, he took the greatest risks himself and galvanized his troops. His forces defeated the Persians in Asia Minor, and then moved farther into Persian territory. At Issus, they defeated Darius, the Persian emperor. Alexander then turned his attention west to Phoenicia and Egypt, seizing power by force. Once these areas were subdued, Alexander moved back through the former Persian Empire fighting more battles and seizing more territory, including Mesopotamia, until his forces reached the Indus River in India.

As Alexander won battles, his ego grew and grew. He named many cities after himself. (Alexandria in Egypt would become the most important.) He also began to adopt the Persian customs of kingship. Forcing his men to treat him as Persian subjects treated their kings, Alexander made supplicants lie prostrate on the ground before him. Greeks did not believe in these sorts of customs for men, believing that it was too subservient. Alexander's troops were not pleased, and he was obliged to discontinue the practice.

Alexander continued his wars in the east until, during the monsoon season, with his troops poorly supplied, he and his men encountered the horror of war elephants expertly trained in India. The Greeks did not lose, but Alexander's men did lose heart. They would fight no more. It was said that when Alexander realized he must turn back, he broke down in tears, sobbing that for him there were no more worlds to conquer. Nevertheless, Alexander turned westward. On his return through Babylon in 323 BCE, the great conqueror became ill after an extended period of particularly heavy drinking. Alexander died at age 33, having gone well beyond his father's dream, conquering much of the known world.

Aristotle's influence was apparent in Alexander's attitude toward the people he conquered. He did more than fight wars and seize territory. Alexander was also very interested in spreading Greek culture among the peoples he ruled, and blending Greek, Persian, Indian, and Egyptian customs and institutions. Greek scholars, artists, government officials, and merchants followed Alexander's army. In Egypt, he founded the city of Alexandria, which became a center of Hellenistic learning. *Hellenism* is the name given to the merging of Greek and Middle Eastern cultures.

Bucephalus and the Gordian Knot

Two stories are commonly told about Alexander the Great, both of which emphasize his cleverness and ability to solve problems that baffled others.

The first story is the story of Alexander's horse, Bucephalus. This horse was so wild that nobody could ride it. Dozens tried, and dozens got tossed to the ground. As a young man, Alexander watched the horse's behavior and quickly realized that the animal was scared by his own shadow. Alexander took the horse and turned his face toward the sun so that he couldn't see his shadow, and thus Alexander succeeded where so many others had failed. Bucephalus became Alexander's faithful horse for many years to come. When the animal was killed during the Indian campaign, Alexander set up a town and named it after his horse. (55)

The other famous story is the story of the Gordian knot. In Gordium, one of the cities in Asia Minor that Alexander conquered, there was supposedly a knot that was so complex that no one had been able to untie it. An ancient prophecy maintained that whoever succeeded in untying the Gordian knot would go on to rule Asia. When presented with the Gordian knot, Alexander did not attempt to untie it; he simply thought a moment, then drew his sword and sliced it in two. Presto! No more knot. Within the next nine years, Alexander had succeeded in conquering the largest empire the world had yet seen, thus fulfilling the ancient prophecy. Even today, people will speak of "cutting a Gordian knot" when someone comes up with a surprising and unexpected solution to a problem that has puzzled others.

Teaching Idea

Present the story of the Gordian knot to children, but do not tell them Alexander's solution. Ask them how they might attempt to "untie the knot." Give each child a knotted string, and three minutes to think about how to undo it. After they have tried, tell children how Alexander solved the puzzle, and ask them what his solution tells us about Alexander.

The Big Idea in Review

The Greeks developed a rich and varied civilization, many aspects of which have been passed down to subsequent generations.

Review

Below are some ideas for ongoing assessment and review activities. These are not meant to constitute a comprehensive list. Teachers may also refer to the *Pearson Learning/Core Knowledge History & Geography* series for additional information and teaching ideas.

- The Greek myths from the Language Arts section (pp. 81–88) provide an opportunity to learn more about the Greek gods and goddesses described in this section. Read a myth to children, and then create a family tree of the gods and goddesses for the class on chart paper so that children are able to see the connections between each character in the myth. Have children do a character study on those who were involved. What were their talents? What were their powers?
- Provide pictures of different elements of Greek history on index cards. For example, have pictures of the gods and goddesses, landmarks in Athens, or events from the ancient Olympic Games. Then, shuffle the deck and pass out a card to each child. Have children write about the picture on their card for 5–10 minutes, including all of the important facts they know. Have children share the picture and their writing with the class when they are finished.
- Collect pictures and illustrations of athletes and events from the ancient and modern Olympic Games. Provide a copy of *The Discobolus (Discus Thrower)* in the Grade 2 Art Resources, which children study in Visual Arts this year. Post these pictures and have children compare and contrast the ancient games and the modern games. Illustrate these similarities and differences on a class Venn diagram.
- When learning about Alexander the Great, read *Taming of Bucephalus* (in the Grade 2 Text Resources) aloud from the Language Arts section. Ask children what they learned about Alexander from the story. What kind of person was Alexander? Ask children to write a character sketch of Alexander, and then have them go back to the story to support their details.
- Make Greek myth riddle cards on index cards for children to answer as a way to review the gods and goddesses. For example, write on one card, "Who is the king of gods and threw lightening bolts?" On the back of the card, write "Zeus." You can design the cards to have as much detail as needed to help children remember the gods and goddesses.
- Organize a simple Olympic Games day for your class. You can organize the activities with the physical education teacher and then have children participate in the events.
- When reviewing the great thinkers Plato, Socrates, and Aristotle, ask children to describe the characteristics of a good teacher. You may incorporate the relationship between Socrates and Plato. Then discuss why it is important to think carefully and observe the world around you.
- You may also ask the following questions at the end of this section:

1. Where are Greece and Crete located?

   Greece is situated on the Balkan Peninsula and juts out into the Mediterranean Sea; Crete is located in the Aegean Sea and is the largest Greek island.

2. What was life like for a soldier in Sparta?

   Life was hard. Boys had to live in a barracks from the age of seven and train to be a soldier. Even when they got married, they had to live in the barracks for 10 years and eat with other soldiers until they were 60. They were trained to fight with weapons and to wrestle and run.

3. What happened after the battle at Marathon?
   A runner ran from the battlefield back to Athens to announce the victory against the Persians. The runner ran so fast and so hard that he delivered his message and then immediately died.
4. Why do people remember the battle at Thermopylae?
   People remember the battle at Thermopylae because a small force of Spartans and other Greek soldiers fought to the death to defend the pass.
5. Why was Athens called a democracy?
   Athens was called a democracy because all citizens were able to debate and vote on the laws that governed the city.
6. Whom did the Olympic Games honor?
   The Olympic Games honored Zeus, the chief Greek god.
7. What are two reasons that Alexander the Great is remembered?
   Alexander the Great created the largest empire in the world up to his time. He also wanted to have cultures mix together and form new cultures.
8. How many of the Greek gods and goddesses can you name?
   Answers will vary.
9. What do Socrates, Plato, and Aristotle have in common?
   All three were Greek philosophers and teachers.

More Resources

The titles listed below are offered as a representative sample of materials and not a complete list of everything that is available.

For children —

These books are generally intended to be read aloud, though some children may be able to read parts or all of the simpler texts.

- *Ancient Greece,* edited by E. D. Hirsch, Jr. (Pearson Learning, 2002). A unit in the official *Pearson Learning/Core Knowledge History & Geography* series. It includes a small picture book for children and a teacher's guide with read alouds. To order, call 1-800-321-3106.

For teachers —

- *Ancient Greece,* by Andrew Solway (Oxford University Press, 2001). Hardcover, 220 pages, ISBN 0199108102.
- *The Oxford Illustrated History of Greece and the Hellenistic World,* edited by John Boardman, Jasper Griffin, and Oswyn Murray (Oxford, 2001). Paperback, 454 pages, ISBN 0192854380.
- *The Parthenon: How It Was Built and How It Was Used (Great Buildings),* by Peter Chrisp (Raintree/Steck-Vaughn, 1997). Intended for older children, but provides useful background information. Library binding, 48 pages, ISBN 0817249176.
- *The Story of the World (Volume 1): Ancient History for the Classical Child,* by Susan Wise Bauer (Peace Hill Press, 2002). Read-aloud stories from around the world for children ages 5–11. The first volume of this planned four-volume set has six chapters on the Greeks. Available in hardcover (ISBN 0971412960) or paperback (ISBN 0971412901), through any bookstore, or in a spiral-bound edition directly through Peace Hill Press, www.peacehillpress.com or 1-888-329-3869.
- Ancient Greece, www.ancientgreece.com.
- The Greeks, www.pbs.org/empires/thegreeks, has information, images, and an interactive map of Athens. You can also hear what scholars believe to be close approximations of the spoken language.
- The Olympics, www.olympic.org, is the official site of the Olympic movement. On the home page, click "Olympic Games." From here you can view images and/or videos of the modern games (1896–present), and much more.

History and Geography in Second Grade

AMERICAN HISTORY AND GEOGRAPHY

The purpose of the American History and Geography sections in Kindergarten through Grade 2 is to provide a brief overview of major events in U.S. history from the earliest days to recent times, leaving in-depth study to Grades 3 through 5. The Grade 2 *Sequence* begins where Grade 1 ends—with the writing of the U.S. Constitution—and progresses through the War of 1812, Westward Expansion before and after the Civil War, the Civil War itself, and late 19th-century immigration. The *Sequence* then deals with thematic topics—citizenship, civil rights, the geography of the Americas, and U.S. symbols.

The discussions of the Constitution (Section I), citizenship (Section V), and civil rights (Section VI) provide opportunities for cross-referencing topics. The Constitution defines citizenship and underlies our civil rights. The pioneers discussed in Section VI worked to ensure the spread of civil rights to various denied groups—Susan B. Anthony and the suffrage of women; Eleanor Roosevelt and the extension of civil and human rights to all people; Mary McLeod Bethune and the right to an education for African-American youth; Jackie Robinson and the end to segregation in professional sports; Rosa Parks and Martin Luther King, Jr., and the end to African-American segregation in all aspects of public life; and Cesar Chávez and the rights of Hispanic migrant workers to a living wage and decent working and living conditions.

The War of 1812 (Section II) is significant in that although the new United States did not win the war, it did not lose it either. The United States fought Great Britain, the most powerful country in the world at that time, to a draw and ensured its continuation as an independent country. The discussion of westward expansion in Section III explores the reasons why settlers went west, how they got there, and the effect of this westward migration on Native Americans.

The discussion of the Civil War in Section IV focuses on the controversy over slavery and how the compromises over slavery's extension into new territories ultimately broke down, resulting in the Civil War. The profile on Harriet Tubman helps to humanize the topic. Abraham Lincoln's decision to issue the Emancipation Proclamation and its importance to the war effort are explored.

The final section continues children's exploration of U.S. symbols and icons, which they began in Kindergarten. They should return to the discussion of the American flag and the Statue of Liberty with a greater understanding of what it means to be American and what these symbols have meant to people over time. They will also learn about the Lincoln Memorial and how the ancient Greek temple of the Parthenon influenced the design of this monument to the 16th president.

Note: *Traditionally, the abbreviations* AD *or* BC *have been written alongside dates to indicate whether the events in question took place before or after the birth of Jesus.* BC *means "Before Christ."* AD *comes from a Latin phrase, "Anno Domini," meaning "Year of the Lord."* AD *1000 means one thousand years after the birth of Jesus; 1000* BC *means one thousand years before the birth of Jesus. However, scholars increasingly prefer to write 1000* BCE *(Before the Common Era) instead of 1000* BC, *and 1000* CE *(Common Era) instead of* AD *1000. Therefore,* BCE *and* CE *are used in this book.*

I. American Government: The Constitution

The Big Idea

The United States is founded on the principle of consent of the governed as stated in the opening phrase of the Constitution, "We the people."

What Students Need to Learn

- **The government of the United States is based on the U.S. Constitution, the highest law of our land.**
- **James Madison is known as the "Father of the Constitution."**
- **Government by the consent of the governed: "We the people"**

What Students Will Learn in Future Grades

In future grades, students will review and extend their learning about the U.S. Constitution.

Grade 4

- from the Declaration of Independence to the Constitution: making a new government
- Constitution of the United States: Preamble, separation and sharing of powers, limitations, Bill of Rights
- national, state, and local levels and functions of government

Remember that each subject you study with children expands their vocabulary and introduces new terms, thus making them better listeners and readers. As you study historical people and events, use read alouds and discussions to build children's vocabularies.

The items in bold relate to the content in Grade 2. In discussions with children, use terminology such as "long, long ago" to set this information in time.

1776	Declaration of Independence
1777	Adoption of Articles of Confederation by Congress
1781	End of Revolutionary War
1781–1789	Government under the Articles of Confederation
1787	**Constitutional Convention**
1787–1789	Ratification of the Constitution by the 13 original states
1789	Swearing in of new U.S. government under the Constitution
1789	Writing of the Bill of Rights
1791	Ratification of the Bill of Rights by the states

I. American Government: The Constitution

Text Resources

(57) *Preamble to the Constitution*

Materials

Instructional Masters 16, 52

Venn Diagram, p. 163

Preamble to the Constitution, p. 164

overhead projector, p. 164

chart paper, p. 164

As a general rule of thumb, when choosing projects to do with your children, they should be well-thought-out and relate directly to the objectives and time allotments outlined in the beginning of each section. Projects have an important place, especially in the early grades when they help reinforce vocabulary and content and don't serve purely as time fillers. Throughout this subject, we have added teaching ideas with fun and purposeful extensions to further children's understanding. Keep in mind that a useful way to engage young children in History and Geography topics can be through the use of structured simulations (acting out events).

Vocabulary

Student/Teacher Vocabulary

amendments: additions to legal documents (T)

consent: agreement or acceptance as to an opinion or course of action (S)

Constitutional Convention: a meeting held in 1787, at which delegates from many of the states met to discuss what would later become the Constitution of the United States (T)

government: the control and organization of a country (S)

preamble: the introduction or first section of a document (S)

U.S. Constitution: the highest law of the United States, it outlines the rights and laws of the country (S)

Domain Vocabulary

Constitution and associated words:
highest law of the land, constitutional government, limits on government, Supreme Court, U.S. federal courts of appeal, judicial review, decision, uphold, strike down, unconstitutional, constitutional, landmark cases, adaptability, flexibility, amendment process, six principles, federalism, division of powers, national, federal, central, states, separation of powers, branches, executive, legislative, judicial, checks and balances, among, between, three branches, limited government, assignment of powers, enumeration of powers, necessary and proper clause, elastic clause, rights, due process, separation of church and state, Bill of Rights, guarantees, individual rights, First Amendment, freedoms, James Madison, John Jay, Alexander Hamilton, Federalist Papers, arguments, debate, persuade, sway opinion, ratify, approve, ratification, Preamble, "We the people," popular sovereignty

In the Text Resources for this section, words are bolded that should be included as part of Domain Vocabulary.

At a Glance

The most important ideas for you are:

- The government of the United States is based on the Constitution.
- Because the Constitution is the highest law of the land, no action of the executive or legislative branches may contradict the Constitution. The judicial branch has the power to decide if the Constitution has been contradicted.
- James Madison was instrumental in the development of the Constitution and the Bill of Rights.
- The opening words of the Constitution, "We the people," indicate that the government of the United States is based on the principle of consent of the governed.

Cross-curricular Connections

Music

Songs

- "The Star-Spangled Banner"

What Teachers Need to Know

Background

Only basic questions about our government need to be addressed at Grade 2, such as: What is government? Why do we need government? What are some basic functions of our government? What is a constitution? In Grade 4, children will examine in more detail specific issues and institutions of the U.S. government, including separation of powers and the relationship between the state and federal governments.

What Is a Constitution?

Many countries and organizations—states, associations, and clubs, for example—have a constitution. The constitution is the basic law that tells how that country (or organization) should be governed: what officers there should be, how they should be chosen, and what their responsibilities are. It may include other things as well. Almost all constitutions have a few things in common:

1. They are written.
2. They are approved by the people of the country (or the members of the organization); usually they are written by delegates representing the people.
3. They can only be changed by the people.
4. They include a list of things that the officers of the government or organization must do (for example, defend the country, issue money, or settle legal disputes) and specify how to choose these officers.
5. They contain a list of things that the government or organization may not do (for example, violate citizens' rights).

Constitutions, as defined above, were actually an American invention. The idea of a written constitution approved by the people was developed by American colonists during the difficult years of their struggle for independence from Britain. The reason that leading Americans wanted independence from Britain was that they were convinced the British government was doing things it had no rightful power to do—most famously, collecting tax money from them without letting them be represented in the debate over taxes, but also taking Americans to Britain for trial by British juries, and refusing to agree to the decisions of colonial American legislatures. But the colonists could not prove that Britain was exceeding its rightful powers, because Britain had no written constitution. American colonial leaders came to believe that a written constitution would serve as a safeguard against a government abusing its power, as the British government had done to them.

The first reason for creating written constitutions, then, was negative: to spell out the limits on governmental power. As each of the Thirteen Colonies broke off its relationship with Britain, its representatives wrote a constitution. Many of these constitutions began with a statement of citizens' rights against the government (a "Bill of Rights"), and carefully went on to define what the government was not allowed to do.

Teaching Idea

Use analogies to familiar settings, such as the family, the school, and the community, to discuss basic questions about what government is and what government does (make and enforce laws, settle disputes, protect rights and liberties, and so on). Ask children for some examples that show government in action (Congress in session, police officers, courts, fire department, soldiers, and so on).

But a second reason for constitutions was to create a new kind of government, based on the will of the people. Americans were aware that they were doing something no people in history had done before: they were creating their own government, based not on tradition but on reason.

The U.S. Constitution: The Highest Law of the Land

During the Revolutionary War, the Second Continental Congress wrote and adopted the Articles of Confederation as the framework of government for the new country as it waged war against Great Britain. The Articles of Confederation were not exactly a constitution. They were more like an agreement or treaty between the various states. The states agreed to defend each other if attacked and to consult each other before making significant decisions, such as signing treaties or declaring war.

When peace was won, the new United States continued to operate under this document. However, the Articles of Confederation had a number of shortcomings. For instance, there was no executive department to coordinate the actions of the states or to act for the country as a whole, for example, in dealing with foreign affairs. Also, in Massachusetts in the winter of 1786, there was an uprising (Shays's Rebellion) against the state government by farmers who lacked money to pay their debts. It was put down, but it raised the possibility of a larger, more general revolt. If one came, would the government have the resources to deal with it? And what if the British decided to attack again and reclaim their lost colonies? Could the states defend themselves?

When it became clear that the central government under the Articles of Confederation was not working, a convention was called to revise the Articles. Important men like George Washington and Benjamin Franklin attended the Constitutional Convention as delegates, or representatives, of their states. Instead of revising the Articles, these delegates wrote the constitution under which we live today.

The U.S. Constitution is a document that is the result of heated debate among men with differing viewpoints representing different parts of the country with sometimes competing interests. However, as Benjamin Franklin said in signing it, "I am not sure it is not the best." As a result of the work of these delegates, the United States has a constitutional government, that is, one in which the law limits what government can do. The Constitution is the highest law in the land. No actions of either the legislative or executive branches may violate the Constitution. The judicial branch determines the constitutionality of their actions—laws, executive orders, regulations, and so on.

The United States is the oldest constitutional government in the world. One of the reasons for its success is its adaptability. The delegates built an amendment process into the document. Yet only 27 amendments have been added since ratification, and the Constitution remains remarkably similar to what it was in 1789.

There are six basic principles on which the Constitution rests: popular sovereignty, the will of the people; federalism, the division of power among national and state governments; separation of powers between executive, legislative, and judicial branches; checks and balances among the three branches of government; judicial review of executive and legislative actions; and limited government, the delineation of the powers between federal and state government.

James Madison

The delegates to the Constitutional Convention voted to keep the proceedings secret, but James Madison, who represented Virginia, kept notes, which were not published until 1840. Because of his notes, we have a full record of the proposals and the debates over the wording of the Constitution.

Madison was not a large man—he stood only five foot four—but he was one of the most intelligent and well-read men in America. He had read what the ancient and modern philosophers had to say about government and had served in Congress during the war. He had also served on the committee that wrote the state constitution for Virginia. He came to believe that a democratic government could be set up for the whole United States, and that it was needed to prevent a British takeover. He was persistent and hardworking in promoting this view before, during, and after the Constitutional Convention.

James Madison

Madison was an active participant in the Constitutional Convention. He proposed a new plan of government, called the "Virginia Plan." This plan was debated and ultimately modified in various ways, but much of the framework of the Constitution we have today is based on Madison's Virginia Plan. Key elements of the plan include the need for a strong central government, the basing of representation on population (the formula for the distribution of seats by state in the House of Representatives), a bicameral legislature of two houses, and the federal system itself.

Once the Constitution was passed, Madison joined Alexander Hamilton and John Jay in writing the Federalist Papers, a set of newspaper articles that set out arguments explaining why the states should ratify the Constitution. After the Constitution was ratified and the new government took office, Madison, as a member of the first Congress, submitted a proposal for a Bill of Rights, which Congress then debated, revised, and sent to the states for ratification. Among the rights that these first 10 amendments to the Constitution guarantee are freedom of religion, freedom of the press, freedom of assembly, the right to a fair and speedy trial, and the right to a trial by jury. The document is framed in such a way that it is a "living constitution," favoring a broad interpretation of the document, and helping to prepare the way for amendments over time. Children will study constitutional amendments in greater detail in later grades.

Because Madison worked hard to bring about the Constitutional Convention, proposed the plan that became the Constitution, took careful notes on the debates during the convention, and helped write the Federalist Papers, he is often referred to as the "Father of the Constitution." (James Madison is discussed in greater detail in Section II of American History and Geography in Grade 4, "Making a Constitutional Government.")

Teaching Idea

If children have already studied ancient Greece, invite them to compare and contrast Greek democracy and American democracy. Use Instructional Master 52, *Venn Diagram*, to show similarities and differences.

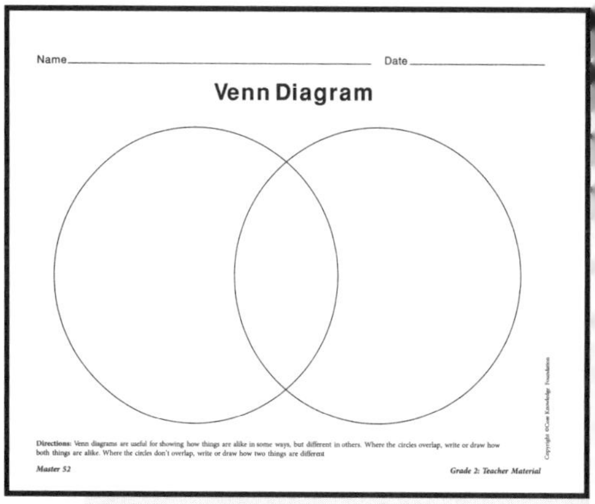

Name____________ Date________

Venn Diagram

Directions: Venn diagrams are useful for showing how things are alike in some ways, but different in others. Where the circles overlap, write or draw how both things are alike. Where the circles don't overlap, write or draw how two things are different

Master 52 *Grade 2: Teacher Material*

Copyright ©Core Knowledge Foundation

Use Instructional Master 52.

Government by Consent of the Governed

The Constitution begins with a Preamble, or introduction, that explains the purpose of the document and establishes it on the principle of the consent (or agreement) of the governed:

Teaching Idea

Use the overhead of Instructional Master 16, *Preamble to the Constitution,* to introduce children to the concept of consent of the governed. Read aloud the Preamble and, depending on your class, discuss each phrase or focus only on the phrase "We the people."

Among the ideas that the Preamble sets out are cooperation among the states (more perfect union), equal justice, peace within the country (domestic tranquility), a national military force (common defense), a good life for everyone (general welfare), and liberty in the present and for future generations (posterity).

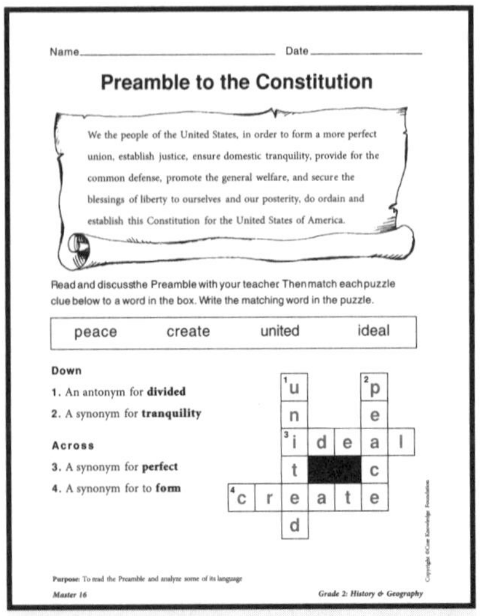

Name__________ Date__________

Preamble to the Constitution

We the people of the United States, in order to form a more perfect union, establish justice, ensure domestic tranquility, provide for the common defense, promote the general welfare, and secure the blessings of liberty to ourselves and our posterity, do ordain and establish this Constitution for the United States of America.

Read and discussthe Preamble with your teacher Thenmatch eachpuzzle clue below to a word in the box. Write the matching word in the puzzle.

peace create united ideal

Down

1. An antonym for **divided**
2. A synonym for **tranquility**

Across

3. A synonym for **perfect**
4. A synonym for to **fom**

Purpose: To read the Preamble and analyze some of its language

Master 16 Grade 2: History & Geography

Copyright ©Core Knowledge Foundation

Use Instructional Master 16.

The Big Idea in Review

The United States is founded on the principle of consent of the governed as stated in the opening phrase of the Constitution, "We the people."

> We the people of the United States, in order to form a more perfect union, establish justice, insure domestic tranquility, provide for the common defence, promote the general welfare, and secure the blessings of liberty to ourselves and our posterity, do ordain and establish this Constitution for the United States of America.

The Preamble explains that this government is not forced upon the people by a king or emperor, but is created with the consent, or agreement, of the governed. Indeed, the Constitution announces itself as a creation of "We the people." These words signaled the fundamental change that the people, not the states, entered into the compact to establish "a more perfect union." This was a major change. The people themselves establish the laws and agree to live under them; this principle is also known as "popular sovereignty." (57)

Subsequent articles of the Constitution describe the branches of government in more detail. Children will learn more about the Constitution in Grade 4.

Review

Below are some ideas for ongoing assessment and review activities. These are not meant to constitute a comprehensive list. Teachers may also refer to the *Pearson Learning/Core Knowledge History & Geography* series for additional information and teaching ideas.

- After reading the Preamble and reviewing the vocabulary, have children brainstorm what a class constitution might look like. What words would you want to include to show how the class should behave? Using chart paper, have children draft a classroom constitution. Be sure that all the children have a say in its development to reflect "consent of the governed." Have all children sign a copy of the class constitution, and display the final copy in your classroom. Then, follow up with a writing activity in which children write about why the U.S. Constitution and the class constitution are important.
- Ask children to think about what would happen if we did not have a Constitution. What would our country be like? Have them write a reflection on our county without a Constitution and then discuss why it is important to have a law of the land.
- How did James Madison contribute to the writing of the Constitution? Have children perform a simple role play about how James Madison might have acted while helping with the Constitution. You may have some children speak as if they were James Madison. What would he say to the group about the Constitution?
- You may also ask the following questions at the end of this section:

1. What is the Constitution?

   The Constitution is the highest/most important law in the United States; our government is based on it.

2. What does government do for people?

   Some possible answers might be: The government makes laws, sees that people obey the laws, protects people from criminals, and helps people by fighting fires.

3. What does it mean that the Constitution is the highest law in the land?
This means that no law can be passed that is different from what the Constitution says.

4. Why do we remember James Madison?
We remember James Madison because he helped write the Constitution; his ideas were used in the Constitution.

5. What does "We the people" at the beginning of the Constitution mean?
"We the people" means that citizens/people are agreeing to live according to what the Constitution says, and under the government that it sets up.

More Resources

The titles listed below are offered as a representative sample of materials and not a complete list of everything that is available.

For children —

These books are generally intended to be read aloud, though some children may be able to read parts or all of the simpler texts.

- *Making the Constitution*, edited by E. D. Hirsch, Jr. (Pearson Learning, 2002). A unit in the official *Pearson Learning/Core Knowledge History & Geography* series. It includes a small picture book for children and a teacher's guide with read alouds. To order, call 1-800-321-3106.
- *A More Perfect Union: The Story of Our Constitution*, by Betsy and Giulio Maestro (HarperTrophy, 1990). Describes the convention, the delegates, the ideas, and some of the arguments. Makes a good read aloud with an adult to answer questions. Paperback, 48 pages, ISBN 0688101925.
- *America Rock (Schoolhouse Rock)*, by various artists (Rhino Records, 1997). Contains a rock version of the Preamble to the Constitution. Audio CD, ASIN B0000033XR.
- *The Constitution*, by Warren Colman (Children's Book Press, 1999). Conveys in clear and direct language how the Constitution was conceived, drafted, and ratified. Library binding, ISBN 0516012312.
- *If You Were There When They Signed the Constitution*, by Elizabeth Levy and illustrated by Richard Rosenblum (Scholastic, 1992). A read aloud. Paperback, ISBN 0590405195.
- *We the Kids: The Preamble to the Constitution of the United States*, illustrations and foreward by David Catrow (Dial Books for Young Readers, 2002). Hardcover, ISBN 0803725531.

For teachers —

- *Decision in Philadelphia: The Constitutional Convention of 1787*, by Christopher Collier and James Lincoln Collier (Ballantine Books, 1987). Paperback, 448 pages, ISBN 0345346521.
- *The Dictionary of the U.S. Constitution*, by Barbara Silberdick Feinberg (Watts, 1999). Hardcover, 224 pages, ISBN 0531115704.
- *Founding Fathers: Brief Lives of the Framers of the United States Constitution (Second, Revised Edition)*, by M. E. Bradford (University Press of Kansas). Paperback, 244 pages, ISBN 0700606572
- *From Colonies to Country: 1735–1791*, by Joy Hakim (Oxford University Press, 2002). Book 3 in the highly acclaimed series *A History of Us*. Paperback, 160 pages, ISBN 0195153243.
- *Miracle at Philadelphia*, by Catherine Drinker Bowen (Amereon Limited, 2001). Hardcover, ISBN 0848825659.
- Ben's Guide to U.S. Government for Kids, http://bensguide.gpo.gov, has content organized by grade level.
- Congress for Kids, www.congressforkids.net, has a tutorial on the Constitution. Once you've entered the site, look for the "Tour of Federal Government" link. Mouse over that link and click on "Constitution." Click on the "Learn About the U.S. Constitution" link beside a red star.
- The Constitution Society, www.constitution.org, has links to several resources, including the Federalist and Anti-Federalist papers.
- The Founders Almanac, www.heritage.org/research/features/almanac, features notable events, leading founders, useful quotations, primary documents, and resources. An online version of the book edited by Matthew Spalding (Heritage Foundation, 2002).

II. The War of 1812

Remember that each subject you study with children expands their vocabulary and introduces new terms, thus making them better listeners and readers. As you study historical people and events, use read alouds and discussions to build children's vocabularies.

The items in bold relate to the content in Grade 2. In discussions with children, use terminology such as "long, long ago" to set this information in time.

1775–1783	**American Revolution**
1787–1789	Ratification of the Constitution by the 13 original states
1789	Swearing in of new U.S. government under the Constitution
1790s–early 1800s	Capture of U.S. trading vessels by French and British warships in violation of American neutrality
1792–1812	**Impressment of American sailors by the British**
1811	Battle of Tippecanoe
1812	**United States declaration of war against Great Britain**
1814	**Burning of Washington, D.C., by the British Dolley Madison saves the Washington portrait; Battle for Fort McHenry; "The Star-Spangled Banner" written by Francis Scott Key**
1814	Treaty of Ghent signed, ending the War of 1812
1815	**Battle of New Orleans**
1830	**Rescue of "Old Ironsides"**

The Big Idea

The new United States faced its first foreign conflict in the War of 1812 against Great Britain.

What Students Should Already Know

Students in Core Knowledge schools haven't studied the War of 1812 in previous grades; however, they have received the crucial background needed as a point of departure for new learning in this section. Students in Grade 1 should have learned about the Colonial and Independence eras. Students with this background will understand that the War of 1812 came after the American Revolution and will be able to view the war as the culmination of a long period of conflict between Great Britain and the United States.

What Students Need to Learn

- **British impressment of American sailors**
- **President James Madison and Dolley Madison**
- **British burning of the White House**
- **Fort McHenry, Francis Scott Key, and "The Star-Spangled Banner"**
- **Battle of New Orleans, Andrew Jackson**
- **"Old Ironsides"**

What Students Will Learn in Future Grades

In future grades, students will review and extend their learning about the War of 1812.

Grade 4

- early presidents and politics
- James Madison and the War of 1812

Vocabulary

Student/Teacher Vocabulary

Battle of New Orleans: the final battle in the War of 1812 (S)

Fort McHenry: the site of a major battle between the Americans and the British in the War of 1812. This battle was the inspiration for "The Star-Spangled Banner." (S)

impressment: forcing a person to work in public service (S)

"Old Ironsides": a nickname for the USS *Constitution*, an American ship (S)

"The Star-Spangled Banner": the national anthem of the United States (S)

Domain Vocabulary

The Madisons and associated words:
President James Madison, Dolley Madison, heroic, evacuate, White House, George Washington portrait, Gilbert Stuart, save, rescue, safekeeping, British, capture, seize, burn

Impressment and associated words:
navy, ship, sailor, deserter, capture, seize, kidnap, neutrality, combatants

USS Constitution *and associated words:*
warship, cannonball, huge, well-built, war duty, saved, rescued, tourist attraction

"The Star-Spangled Banner" and associated words:
Baltimore, battle, fight for, siege, defend, cannon fire, barrage, shells, rockets, missiles, noise, hissing sound, explode, burst, light up, glare, British, lose, not able to defeat, ramparts, bursting, perilous, gleaming, retreat, Francis Scott Key, national anthem, patriotic, patriot, patriotism

Battle of New Orleans and associated words:
communications problem, importance, significant, British relinquish, toehold, Andrew Jackson, image, popular imagination, enhance

In the Text Resources for this section, words are bolded that should be included as part of Domain Vocabulary.

Text Resources
(58) *Dolley Madison*

Materials

Instructional Master 17
The Star-Spangled Banner, p. 171

overhead projector, p. 170

colored paper for a book cover, p. 170

stapler, p. 170

pictures of Old Ironsides, p. 172

cutouts of Old Ironsides from lined paper for writing, p. 172

chart paper, p. 172

index cards, p. 172

sentence strips, p. 173

Cross-curricular Connections

Music

Songs

- "The Star-Spangled Banner"

At a Glance

The most important ideas for you are:

- The War of 1812 was a significant challenge for the United States at a time when the nation was young and not as firmly established as it is today.
- British impressment of American sailors showed a disregard for U.S. sovereignty.
- Dolley Madison showed remarkable courage in her effort to save a national treasure.
- The fight for Fort McHenry inspired Francis Scott Key to write "The Star-Spangled Banner."
- The Battle of New Orleans was fought after the peace treaty was signed to end the War of 1812.
- The poem "Old Ironsides," written about the USS *Constitution,* is an example of a symbol in the making.

What Teachers Need to Know

Background: Setting the Stage

The War of 1812 began in the year that is part of its name, making the date easy to remember; but like the Mexican War, Spanish-American War, and Korean War, it has long been one of our "forgotten conflicts." Historians usually regard the war as a draw, but it was important nonetheless, for the United States emerged from the war with a new confidence that their nation would survive and prosper.

British Impressment of American Sailors

In 1793, European countries were involved in a great war. Fearful of the spread of the ideas of the French Revolution to their countries, the rulers of countries such as Great Britain, Spain, Austria, and the Netherlands waged war against France. The United States, recently independent and still struggling to establish itself as a country, declared its neutrality and pledged not to sell guns and other war supplies to any combatant. The British, however, began capturing American ships in the Caribbean Sea that were trading with the French colonies there. In seizing the ships, the British also seized sailors suspected of being deserters from the British navy. In some cases, there may have been real British deserters on the American ships, but in other cases the "deserter" argument was just a handy excuse for captains who needed more sailors. The Royal Navy had a chronic manpower shortage. While it was the best and largest navy in the world, conditions on its warships were harsh, and punishment of the sailors was arbitrary and brutal. For these reasons, many British sailors jumped ship. British captains tried to make up for runaway sailors by seizing American ships and forcing American sailors into the British navy. This practice was known as impressment.

The impressment of sailors as well as other violations of American neutrality almost led to war with Great Britain in the 1790s. However, negotiations with Great Britain resulted in Jay's Treaty, named after Chief Justice John Jay who worked out the agreement with the British. The United States was allowed to trade with British colonies in the Caribbean, and a committee would determine a solution to the impressment problem. Unfortunately, this never occurred and impressment continued.

President Thomas Jefferson tried to put an end to impressment by passing the Embargo Act of 1807. Under this act, U.S. ports were closed to foreign ships and U.S. ships were confined to coastal waters. The thinking was that Great Britain would agree to end the seizure of U.S. ships and impressment in return for the resumption of trade. But the embargo was very unpopular. American markets suffered greatly under the embargo, whereas the lack of American trade goods barely affected European countries like Great Britain. In the end, the U.S. government had to abandon the law.

It is estimated that the British impressed 6,000 or more American sailors. British impressment humiliated Americans. American leaders were embarrassed that they could not protect their own men at sea. Impressment was one of the factors that led to the War of 1812.

War Hawks

While the problem of impressment grew worse, the states along the western U.S. frontier were agitating for war against the British for a different reason. They believed that the British were using their Canadian outposts to aid Native Americans who were attacking American frontier settlements. In Congress, these advocates for war were known as "War Hawks." The War Hawks were mostly younger congressmen from the western and southern states. The term, later shortened to "hawks," came to mean those who advocate an aggressive foreign policy and a strong military with war as an option in diplomacy. In addition to the satisfaction of beating the British, the War Hawks saw Canada as a vast territory that should be added to the United States.

The Battle of Tippecanoe, between the United States and Native Americans in Indiana Territory in 1812, tipped the scale to war. The commanding general of the U.S. forces, General William Henry Harrison, allegedly found British weapons in the Native American camp. This seemed to prove what the War Hawks had been saying—that the British were arming the Native Americans. On hearing this, Congress passed a war resolution, and the War of 1812 began.

President James Madison and Dolley Madison

The War of 1812 began during the presidency of James Madison. (Children should be familiar with Madison from their study of the Constitution.) In August 1814, the British easily routed the American army defending Washington, D.C., and set fire to much of the city, including the White House. President Madison was away at the time, and his wife, Dolley, was waiting for his return when the British took the city.

Dolley had been a young widow with two children in 1794 when she married James Madison, who was then a member of the House of Representatives. She had

Teaching Idea

Talk with children about how brave Dolley Madison was to stay in the White House. Discuss also the importance that the painting of George Washington must have held for her and probably for other Americans. Note that there was no easy way to make copies of images at that time—no photocopiers, no cameras, no scanners on computers. (Washington had died in 1799, so there was no way for another painting to be made from life.)

become an influential hostess—first in Philadelphia and later in Washington, D.C.—and she acted with an acute sense of political interest. When the widower Thomas Jefferson became president, she acted as his unofficial First Lady. By then, her husband had been appointed secretary of state. In 1808, after Jefferson announced that he would not seek a third term, James Madison was elected president.

When word reached her of the British victory, Dolley Madison prepared to evacuate. However, she bravely risked capture by refusing to leave Washington until her husband's most important papers and other items, including a portrait of former President George Washington, had been secured. (The portrait was by Gilbert Stuart, and it is considered to be among his most famous works.) She wrote the following to her sister:

> At this late hour, a wagon has been procured; and I have had it filled with the plate [silverware] and the most valuable portable articles belonging to the house. . . . Our kind friend, Mr. Carroll, has come to hasten my departure, and is in a very bad humor with me because I insist on waiting until the large picture of Gen. Washington is secured, and it requires to be unscrewed from the wall. This process was found too tedious for these perilous moments; I have ordered the frame to be broken, and the canvas taken out; it is done,—and the precious portrait placed in the hands of two gentlemen of New York, for safe keeping. And now, dear sister, I must leave this house, or the retreating army will make me a prisoner in it, by filling up the road I am directed to take. . . .

Dolley Madison finally left Washington just ahead of the British. The British entered the White House and ransacked it before setting it on fire. (58)

Teaching Idea

Use the overhead made from Instructional Masters 17a–17b, *The Star-Spangled Banner,* and follow directions on the Masters to focus children's attention. Read the anthem aloud once through. Then read pairs of lines and talk with children about the meaning of the lines and words. Help them to create mental images of the fighting and that night.

Have children work with partners to think about and draw pictures of an image from the song. Each child should draw his or her own version of their shared idea, while providing suggestions to each other. Have them write the lines or phrases from the anthem that their pictures illustrate.

Combine the sheets into a Big Book of "The Star-Spangled Banner."

The Star-Spangled Banner

After the British burned Washington, D.C., they moved toward Baltimore and attacked Fort McHenry, which guarded the city. Francis Scott Key, a U.S. civilian, was on one of the British warships in the harbor. He had gone aboard to try to gain the release of a friend who had been taken prisoner by the British during the capture of Washington. Key watched anxiously during the 25-hour siege as the British fired 1,800 shells at the fort. During the night, in the glare of bursting shells, Key was able to catch occasional glimpses of the U.S. flag flying atop Fort McHenry, but it was not until daylight that he knew that the flag was still flying and the Americans still held the fort. The British retreated and Key and his companions were freed.

On September 14, 1814, Key wrote a poem about what he had experienced the night of September 13–14. It began with a question:

O say, can you see, by the dawn's early light,
What so proudly we hail'd at the twilight's last gleaming?
Whose broad stripes and bright stars, thro' the perilous fight,
O'er the ramparts we watch'd, were so gallantly streaming?
And the rockets' red glare, the bombs bursting in air,
Gave proof thro' the night that our flag was still there.
O say, does that star-spangled banner yet wave
O'er the land of the free and the home of the brave?

In later verses, Key answered his own question: yes, the flag was still flying. Within a day, his poem was printed and distributed in Baltimore. Within a month, it had been set to music and performed for the first time.

Throughout the 19th century, "The Star-Spangled Banner" was a popular patriotic song. Beginning in 1895, it was the official song played when the flag was lowered on army installations. Nine years later, the navy adopted it for the raising and lowering of the flag. In 1931, Congress made "The Star-Spangled Banner" the national anthem. Although there are four verses, typically only the first verse, printed above, is sung.

The Battle of New Orleans and Andrew Jackson

The Battle of New Orleans actually took place two weeks after Great Britain and the United States had agreed to end the War of 1812. The commissioners signed the draft peace treaty in Europe on Christmas Eve 1814, but communications across the ocean were slow. Word did not reach either Andrew Jackson, who commanded the American forces, nor the British forces under Major General Sir Edward Pakenham until after the battle on January 8, 1815.

Even though the war had officially ended, if the British had won the battle, they might not have willingly surrendered New Orleans. Great Britain maintained that Napoleon had no claim to the Louisiana Territory and, therefore, could not sell it to the United States. The British intended to use the War of 1812 to establish a toehold in the Louisiana Territory, but at the Battle of New Orleans they came up against Andrew Jackson. Jackson commanded a ragtag force of frontiersmen from Kentucky, Creoles and African Americans from New Orleans, and even a few Gulf Coast pirates. The Americans erected defenses on the Mississippi River below the city. When English soldiers and Scottish highlanders charged across an open field, they faced cannon fire and the rifles of some of the best marksmen in the world. They never reached the Americans. In a valiant attempt to rally his army after repeated charges, General Pakenham personally led the final attack, and died on the field with 288 of his men. The number of injured men on the British force totalled to more than 2,000. "Old Hickory" (Jackson) was as tough as the wood for which he was named. He lost less than 50 men. It was a brilliant victory, one of the most one-sided in American history, and a stunning defeat for Britain. It reinforced the treaty that had already been signed. And, in just over a dozen years, it put Jackson in the White House.

Although the Battle of New Orleans was a great victory, the War of 1812 as a whole was not an outright victory for either side. Native American resistance to westward expansion had been stopped, but the war did not change the boundaries between the United States and British territories in North America. Canada was not annexed to the United States, as the War Hawks had hoped, and the British had burned Washington, D.C. On the other hand, impressment was no longer a problem. The most important effect of the war, however, was to boost the confidence of Americans. They had fought the most powerful country in the world to a standstill and in the process had acquired new symbols (e.g., Old Ironsides), new slogans (e.g., "Don't give up the ship!"), and new heroes (e.g., Jackson). The War of 1812 seemed to prove that the United States of America could hold its own against the great powers of Europe.

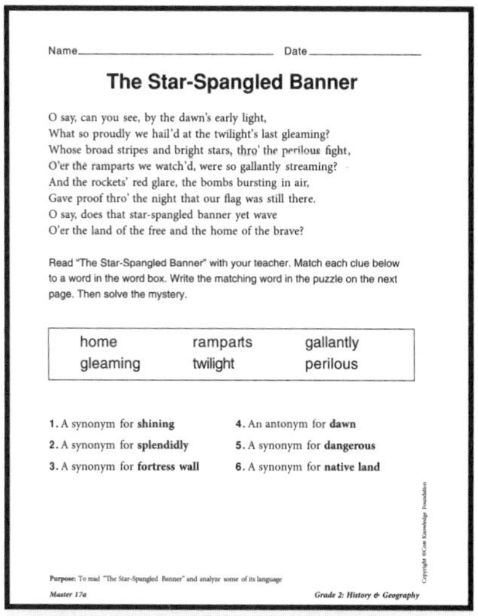

Name__________ Date__________

The Star-Spangled Banner

O say, can you see, by the dawn's early light,
What so proudly we hail'd at the twilight's last gleaming?
Whose broad stripes and bright stars, thro' the perilous fight,
O'er the ramparts we watch'd, were so gallantly streaming?
And the rockets' red glare, the bombs bursting in air,
Gave proof thro' the night that our flag was still there.
O say, does that star-spangled banner yet wave
O'er the land of the free and the home of the brave?

Read "The Star-Spangled Banner" with your teacher. Match each clue below to a word in the word box. Write the matching word in the puzzle on the next page. Then solve the mystery.

home	ramparts	gallantly
gleaming	twilight	perilous

1. A synonym for **shining**
2. A synonym for **splendidly**
3. A synonym for **fortress wall**
4. An antonym for **dawn**
5. A synonym for **dangerous**
6. A synonym for **native land**

Copyright ©Core Knowledge Foundation

Purpose: To read "The Star-Spangled Banner" and analyze some of its language

Master 17a *Grade 2: History & Geography*

Use Instructional Masters 17a and 17b.

Teaching Idea

Teach children the fun song "The Battle of New Orleans," which begins "In 1814 we took a little trip / Along with Colonel Jackson down the mighty Mississip." The lyrics can be found by searching the Internet, and children will be prepared to understand them after studying this section. (See suggested websites in More Resources.)

Teaching Idea

"Old Ironsides" was to Oliver Wendell Holmes and other Americans of his era a symbol of the courage of Americans at that time: sturdy, tough, and not easily defeated. Talk with children about what courage means to them. The conversation need not deal with large acts but may focus on small day-to-day ones, like standing up to a bully or doing something when one is fearful such as swinging high on a swing.

"Old Ironsides"

One of the ships that fought in the War of 1812 was the USS *Constitution,* nicknamed "Old Ironsides." The ship was built of huge timbers similar to those used in British ships-of-the-line, the largest warships of the time. A sailor once saw an enemy cannonball bounce off the ship's side and yelled to his friends, "Her sides are made of iron!" (Ships are often referred to in the feminine gender.)

In 1828, there was talk of breaking up the ship. A furor arose and Oliver Wendell Holmes, a well-known author, wrote the poem "Old Ironsides" in 1830 to help build public interest in saving the ship. Holmes urged his fellow citizens not to tear down the ship's "tattered ensign," or flag:

Long has it waved on high,
And many an eye has danced to see
That banner in the sky;
Beneath it rung the battle shout,
And burst the cannon's roar—

The ship was rescued. It was used by the U.S. Navy as a squadron flagship or training vessel until 1897. Repaired and restored several times, and still a commissioned (in service) ship of the U.S. Navy, today the ship is docked in Boston Harbor, where it had been originally launched in 1797.

Review

The Big Idea in Review

The new United States faced its first foreign conflict in the War of 1812 against Great Britain.

Below are some ideas for ongoing assessment and review activities. These are not meant to constitute a comprehensive list. Teachers may also refer to the *Pearson Learning/Core Knowledge History & Geography* series for additional information and teaching ideas.

- Show children pictures of Old Ironsides and discuss how important it was to save and preserve the ship. Provide children with cutout shapes of Old Ironsides on white, lined paper. On the paper, have children write a few sentences about the ship and what its purpose was during the War of 1812. Post them around the room.
- Make a chart on chart paper with the class to describe James and Dolley Madison. Brainstorm adjectives to describe each of them. Review his role in the writing of the Constitution, and then discuss their roles during the War of 1812. Have children write about the traits that defined James and Dolley Madison and their service to the country. You could also have children compare themselves to James and Dolley Madison. For example, have children include a sentence in their writing that starts, "James Madison was smart because he helped write the Constitution. I am smart, too. I can ________." Or have children write, "Dolley Madison was brave because she saved so many things in the White House. I am brave, too. I can ________."
- When studying "The Star-Spangled Banner," make a set of vocabulary cards with words from the song. Put the words you would like to study from the text on index cards, and put the definitions on separate cards. As children enter the room, give each child a card from the deck. The children then have to find the person with the card that matches their definition or word. When

they find the matching card, both children sit on the floor. Then, as you reread "The Star-Spangled Banner," have pairs read their words and definitions to the group; if there are mismatches, work with children to match the correct word and definition.

- Make a set of sentence strips with the lines of "The Star-Spangled Banner" on each strip. Then, have the children sequence the lines from the song. As they sequence the lines, have them explain what each line means.
- Have children discuss what happened when the troops in New Orleans did not receive word that the War of 1812 was over. What was the result of the Battle of New Orleans? Have children write about the impact of slow communication. Pick another historical event from this section, and have children describe another outcome if the events had happened differently.
- You may also ask the following questions at the end of this section:

1. What does the word *impressment* mean?

   Impressment ***means to force someone to work for the navy. (Technically, this term would apply to any public service, but in the context, the narrow definition should be accepted).***

2. Why was impressment wrong?

   Impressment forced American sailors to work for Britain instead of the United States.

3. Who was president during the War of 1812?

   James Madison was president during the War of 1812.

4. Why did Dolley Madison have George Washington's picture taken from its frame?

   The British had defeated the soldiers guarding Washington, D.C., and were marching on the city. Dolley Madison was told to leave the city, but she was afraid that the British would damage the White House. She wanted to save Washington's picture because he was the first president and the painting was an important reminder of him.

5. Why did Francis Scott Key write the words to "The Star-Spangled Banner"?

   Francis Scott Key was a witness to the fight for Fort McHenry and tried all night during the shelling of the fort to see whether the Americans still held it. The song describes what he saw and felt during that night and early the next morning.

6. Who led the American troops at the Battle of New Orleans?

   Andrew Jackson led the troops at the Battle of New Orleans.

7. The War of 1812 was already over during the Battle of New Orleans, so why was the battle important?

   It was an important battle because the Americans won. If the British had won, they might not have surrendered New Orleans. They wanted to gain more territory in North America.

8. What was "Old Ironsides"?

   It was a U.S. Navy ship that was hard to sink.

More Resources

The titles listed below are offered as a representative sample of materials and not a complete list of everything that is available.

For children —

These books are generally intended to be read aloud, though some children may be able to read parts or all of the simpler texts.

- *The War of 1812,* edited by E. D. Hirsch, Jr. (Pearson Learning, 2002). A unit in the official *Pearson Learning/Core Knowledge History & Geography* series. It includes a small picture book for children and a teacher's guide with read alouds. To order, call 1-800-321-3106.
- *An American Army of Two*, by Janet Greeson and illustrated by Patricia Rose Mulvihill (Carolrhoda, 1992). Twenty-year-old Rebecca Bates and her younger sister, Abigail, figure out how to trick the British into believing that American troops are coming to their town's rescue. This easy-to-read story with large print is based on a true incident in the War of 1812. Library binding, 56 pages, ISBN 0876146647.
- *By the Dawn's Early Light: The Story of the Star-Spangled Banner*, by Steven Kroll (Scholastic, 2000). Paperback, 40 pages, ISBN 0590450557.
- *Cornstalks and Cannonballs*, by Barbara Mitchell and illustrated by Karen Ritz (Carolrhoda, 1980). How the small town of Lewes, Delaware, defeated the British navy during the War of 1812. Based on a true story. Hardcover, 46 pages, ISBN 0876141211.
- *The National Anthem (True Book),* by Patricia Ryon Quiri (Children's Press, 1998). Gives good background on the War of 1812 and the writing of Key's poem. Library binding, 48 pages, ISBN 0516206257.
- *The Star-Spangled Banner,* illustrated by Peter Spier (Yearling Books, 1992). Beautifully illustrated text of our national anthem. Spier's artwork will captivate readers of all ages. Paperback, 56 pages, ISBN 0440406978.

For teachers —

- *The Battle of New Orleans*, by Robert V. Remini (Penguin, 2001). Paperback, 226 pages, ISBN 0141001798.
- *The Burning of Washington: The British Invasion of 1814,* by Anthony S. Pitch (Naval Institute Press, 2000). Paperback, 336 pages, ISBN 1557504253.
- *Dolley Madison: Her Life, Letters, and Legacy*, by Holly C. Shulman and David B. Mattern (PowerPlus Books, 2003). Library binding, 112 pages, ISBN 0823957497. The authors also created The Dolley Madison Project website, http://moderntimes.vcdh.virginia.edu/madison.
- *Founding Mothers: The Women Who Raised Our Nation*, by Cokie Roberts (Perennial, 2005). Paperback, 400 pages, ISBN 006009026X.
- *The Jeffersonian Republicans: The Louisiana Purchase and the War of 1812, 1800–1823 (The Drama of American History)*, by Christopher Collier and James Lincoln Collier (Benchmark, 1998). Library binding, 96 pages, ISBN 0761407782.
- *The Naval War of 1812*, by Theodore Roosevelt (Modern Library, 1999). The future president would make history, but was also an accomplished historian. His account is dated, but still exciting reading. Paperback, 308 pages, ISBN 0375754199.
- *The New Nation: 1789–1850*, by Joy Hakim (Oxford University Press, 2002). Book 4 in the highly acclaimed series *A History of Us.* Paperback, 160 pages, ISBN 019515326X.
- *The War of 1812*, by Henry Adams (Cooper Square Press, 1999). "President Madison submitted to Napoleon in order to resist England; the New England Federalists preferred submitting to England in order to resist Napoleon; but not one American expected the United States to uphold their national rights against the world" (Henry Adams). Extracted from Henry Adams's multi-volumed *History of the United States,* originally published from 1889–1891. Perhaps the best history of this often over-looked war. Paperback, 394 pages, ISBN 0815410131.
- *The War of 1812*, by Harry L. Coles (University of Chicago Press, 1965). A brief but comprehensive and well-written survey. Paperback, 298 pages, ISBN 0226113507.
- The General Society of the War of 1812, www.societyofthewarof1812.org, offers a time line as well as a wealth of links to other websites on the war.
- The War of 1812 website by Galafilm, www.galafilm.com/1812/e/index.html, has an interesting presentation on the war's people, events, forts, songs, and much more.

III. Westward Expansion

Items in bold relate specifically to the content in Grade 2. In discussions, use milestones in U.S. history as points of reference, that is, something happened before or after the Civil War.

1600s	Coastal plain as the first frontier
mid-1700s	Frontier at the Appalachian Mountains
1775–1783	American Revolution
1803	Louisiana Purchase
1804–1806	Lewis and Clark
1807	**Fulton's steamship sails up the Hudson River**
1812–1814	War of 1812
1817–1825	**Erie Canal built**
1821	**Sequoyah devises the Cherokee alphabet**
1825–1850s	**Canal Era**
1830	Frontier beyond the Rockies
1835–1850	**First railroads built in Northeast and Southeast**
1838	**Trail of Tears**
1840s–1860s	**Oregon Trail**
1840s–1850s	Frontier moves to Southwest and Far West
1846–1848	Mexican War
1860	**Pony Express**
1861–1865	Civil War
1869	**Transcontinental railroad**
1890	Massacre at Wounded Knee, end of Native American fighting Frontier officially closed

The Big Idea

The development of major transportation systems accelerated westward expansion and contributed to the demise of Native American ways of life.

What Students Should Already Know

Students in Core Knowledge schools should be familiar with

Kindergarten

- Native American Peoples, Past and Present

Grade 1

- the location of the Appalachian and Rocky Mountains, and the Mississippi River
- the colonial exploration and settlement of the 13 English colonies
- the early exploration of the American West
  - Daniel Boone and the Wilderness Road
  - the Louisiana Purchase and its exploration by Lewis and Clark, Sacajawea

What Students Need to Learn

- **Pioneers Head West**
  - **New means of travel: Robert Fulton, invention of the steamboat; Erie Canal; transcontinental railroad**
  - **Routes west: wagon trains on the Oregon Trail**
  - **The Pony Express**
- **Native Americans**
  - **Sequoyah and the Cherokee alphabet**
  - **Forced removal to reservations: the "Trail of Tears"**
  - **Some Native Americans displaced from their homes and ways of life by railroads (the "iron horse")**
  - **Effects of near extermination of the buffalo on the Plains Native Americans**

What Students Will Learn in Future Grades

In future grades, students will review and extend their learning about westward expansion.

Grade 5

- the geography of the shifting Western frontier
- the exploration of the West in the early 1800s and the trails west
- the increase in westward migration after the Civil War
- Native American resistance from the 1790s to 1890

III. Westward Expansion

Text Resources

(59) *The Oregon Trail*

(60) *Trail of Tears*

Materials

Instructional Masters 18–20, 51

T-Chart, p. 178

Expanding the West, p. 179

Pioneers Head West, p. 182

Going West, p. 184

overhead projector, p. 179

rulers, p. 181

masking tape, p. 181

brown butcher paper, p. 185

pieces of white 8½" x 11" paper, p. 185

chart paper, p. 186

Vocabulary

Student/Teacher Vocabulary

Canal Era: a time period in which a network of canals was built, especially in the Northeast (S)

frontier: an imaginary line between settled and unsettled land (S)

"iron horse": a nickname for the first trains (S)

transcontinental railroad: a railway that ran across the entire continental United States (S)

Domain Vocabulary

Travel and associated words:
the West, wilderness, shifting line, mountains, river valleys, forests, passengers, freight, downstream, canoes, rafts, flatbed boats, wet, rocky, shallows, rapids, dangerous, overland, walk, trudge, wagons, bounce, jounce, pack animals, dirt roads, mountain trails, paths, muddy, dry, dusty, quagmires, treacherous, ruts, rutted, James Watt, steam engine, Robert Fulton, steamboat, *Clermont,* Hudson River, New York City, Albany, Mississippi River, navigate, steam, upstream, downstream, comfortable, DeWitt Clinton, Great Lakes, Erie Canal, Atlantic Ocean, Lake Erie, faster, reliable, dependable, cheaper, less dangerous, railroads, iron rails, laying track, railroad network, rail system, convenient, comfortable, cheap, Baltimore and Ohio Railroad, Omaha, Nebraska, San Francisco, Union Pacific, Irish immigrants, rolling plains, Rocky Mountains, Central Pacific, Chinese immigrants, rugged, gorges, desert, Promontory Point, Utah, regional railroads, prairie schooner, small, four-wheeled, canvas top, wooden body, light, compact, sturdy, home on wheels, all families' belongings, oxen, strong, hardy, St. Joseph, Missouri, Council Bluffs, Iowa, Oregon Territory, California, Independence, Oregon Trail, California Trail, Humboldt River, Santa Fe Trail, Independence, Missouri, Santa Fe, Spanish, plains, wagon train, walk, trudge, alternate ride, ford rivers, rafts, climb, stumble, broken wheels, broken axles, hard, hard work, cook, gather firewood, clean up, shoot dinner, Native Americans, friendly, helpful, paid, Pony Express, speed, mail delivery, St. Joseph, Missouri, Sacramento, station, fresh horse, change horses, leather saddlebags, slung, saddle, hurry, breathless, hustle

Native Americans and associated words:
Sequoyah, Cherokee, oral language, word of mouth, hand down, syllabary, representations, signs, written characters, syllables, alphabet, 85, Trail of Tears, Five Civilized Tribes (nations), Choctaw, Chickasaw, Creek, Seminole, European-American ways, Southeast, North Carolina, South Carolina, Georgia, Alabama, Mississippi, Florida, Andrew Jackson, president, Indian Removal Act, Indian Territory, Oklahoma, lawsuits, courts, appeals, Supreme Court, upheld, ignored, trek, journey, heartbreaking, heartless, cruel, inhumane, torturous, freezing cold, snowy, dying, deaths, decimated, buffalo, hide, American bison, almost extinct, killed, hunting, gun, shoot, Homestead Act of 1862, Plains Native Americans, northern Plains, southern Plains, way of life, food, clothing, shelter, Indian Appropriation Act of 1871, nonrecognition, sovereign nations, separate nations, treaty, honor, false promise, hollow promise, reservations, isolate, Bureau of Indian Affairs, farmers, allotments of food and clothing, sustain, survive, survival, corruption, steal, greed, resell, Dawes Act of 1887, breakup, give, land parcels, assimilate, adapt, pioneer, settler, horse, rider, telegraph, stage, rail, station, immigrant

In the Text Resources for this section, words are bolded that should be included as part of Domain Vocabulary.

Cross-curricular Connections

Language Arts

Fiction

American Tall Tales

- "Paul Bunyan"
- "Johnny Appleseed"
- "John Henry"
- "Casey Jones"
- "Pecos Bill"

Visual Arts

Kinds of Pictures: Landscapes

- Thomas Cole, *View from Mount Holyoke, Northampton, Massachusetts, after a Thunderstorm—The Oxbow* (depiction of the "New World")

Music

Songs

- "Casey Jones"
- "The Erie Canal"
- "Good-Bye, Old Paint"
- "John Henry"
- "Buffalo Gals"
- "Clementine"
- "Home on the Range"
- "I've Been Working on the Railroad"

At a Glance

The most important ideas for you are:

- The frontier shifted west and southwest as the country grew.
- Population pressure and ambition sent people west.
- The invention and application of a practical steam engine to power the steamboat began the transportation revolution.
- The Canal Era was short-lived but created an important interstate transportation network, especially in the Northeast.
- Railroads replaced canals and eventually linked many parts of the country.
- People went west by wagon train, using many routes including the Oregon Trail.
- Thousands of Cherokee died on the "Trail of Tears."
- The transcontinental railroad, the influx of settlers onto the plains, and the resulting near extermination of buffalo displaced Plains Native Americans.

Teaching Idea

Using Instructional Master 51, *T-Chart,* talk with children about how people travel today and compare these modes of transportation with how people traveled before there were planes, trains, and cars. Children will probably talk about boats, wagons, horses, and walking. Discuss the pros and cons of each mode.

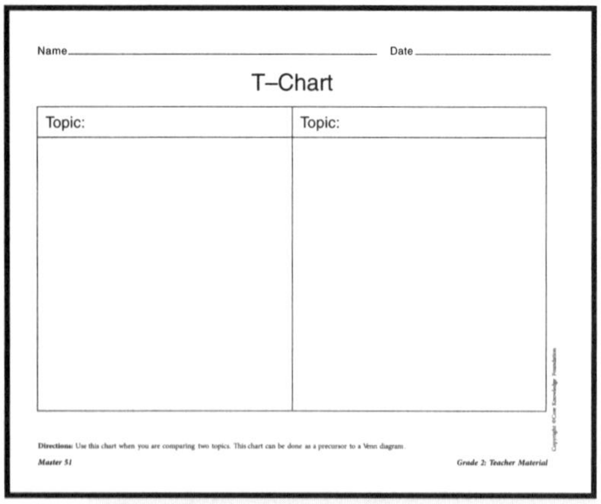
Name ______ Date ______

T–Chart

Topic:	Topic:

Directions: Use this chart when you are comparing two topics. This chart can be done as a precursor to a Venn diagram.

Master 51 *Grade 2: Teacher Material*

Copyright ©Core Knowledge Foundation

Use Instructional Master 51.

Teaching Idea

As a way of introducing this section, you may wish to review what children should have learned about Daniel Boone and Lewis and Clark in Grade 1.

What Teachers Need to Know

Background: Setting the Stage

The frontier shifted as the country moved west and southwest, but it was not a steady progression across the country. The Far West was settled before the middle of the country, because people mistakenly considered the interior of the country to be the Great American Desert.

The Louisiana Purchase opened up an area west of the Mississippi River, as far as the British territory of Oregon in the Northwest and the Spanish lands in the Far West. The United States acquired the Oregon Territory (Oregon and Washington) as a result of a treaty with the British in 1846. It was not until the Mexican War (1846–1848) that the Spanish lands in the West became U.S. territories and then states. The former Spanish-held area of Texas also joined the Union.

What prompted people to leave settled areas to live in the wilderness? Both native-born Americans and immigrants, who came in greater numbers after 1820, wanted to better themselves. The coastal plain was becoming crowded, and there was little land left to buy and few jobs. To own land and to make a living, people were forced to move to less-settled areas.

The settlement of the Great Plains—the area between the Mississippi River and the Rocky Mountains—did not take place to any great degree until after the Civil War, when the Homestead Act encouraged people to settle there and the railroads provided easy, cheap transportation. The government gave 160 acres of land to any citizen or immigrant who was willing to farm it for five years. Before then, people bypassed the Great Plains in favor of the fertile Northwest or were lured to California by the get-rich-quick tales of the Gold Rush.

In 1890, the U.S. census declared the frontier closed. All areas were either states or organized as territories on their way to statehood. Between 1864 and 1912, 13 states were admitted to the Union, making the contiguous United States complete.

A. Pioneers Head West

New Means of Travel

The first white settlers to move into the land beyond the mountains traveled either down the rivers or overland through the valleys and gaps between mountains. Going downstream on the rivers was the easiest way to travel, and people used canoes, rafts, and flatbed boats to carry passengers and freight. Going upstream against the current was another matter: it could be done, but it was difficult and slow. A crew of men used long poles to push against the riverbed and propel the boat upstream. Overland, people used wagons and pack animals on dirt roads and mountain trails, both of which were little more than tracks that became muddy quagmires in the rainy season and treacherous ruts in the winter.

The transportation revolution of the early 1800s soon changed these means of travel and greatly spurred the movement of people inland.

Steamboats

In the 1760s, James Watt of Scotland had invented the first practical steam engine. In 1807, Robert Fulton used Watt's steam engine to power his boat, the *Clermont,* up the Hudson River from New York to Albany, making the trip in 32 hours. (It would have taken a sailing boat about four days, depending on winds and tides.) Soon, Fulton ran the first commercially successful steamboat company. By 1811, the steamboat *New Orleans* was plying up and down the Mississippi, carrying passengers and freight. Not only were steamboats fast and large, so they could carry many passengers and much cargo, but also they could easily navigate upstream against the current.

Erie Canal

The steamboat began the transportation revolution, but without canals, the network of inland waterways would have been incomplete. Canals were built to connect two bodies of water, e.g., a river and a lake, or two rivers. Often canals were named for the bodies of water they were meant to connect. For example, the Chesapeake and Ohio Canal in the Mid-Atlantic region was intended to connect the Chesapeake Bay with the Ohio River. The Canal Era lasted from about 1825 to the 1850s, when the boom in railroad building began and interest in canals began to decline.

The most famous canal built during the canal age was the Erie Canal in New York. In 1817, when DeWitt Clinton (governor of New York) proposed a canal linking the Hudson River near Albany with the Great Lakes, a natural route to the West, his critics mocked him and called the canal itself "Clinton's big ditch." But Clinton believed in the project. Work began in 1817 and was not completed until 1825. Irish immigrants fleeing a potato famine in their own country did much of the hard work.

The Erie Canal was, in fact, a big ditch—a ditch that streched 363 miles. The original canal was about four feet deep and forty feet wide. Flat-bottomed boats carrying 30 tons of cargo could be towed down the canal by mules and horses, who walked on a tow path on the embankment beside the canal. Sometimes the canal passed under low bridges and the people on the boats had to duck down, or even lie down, to get under the bridges.

The canal also included more than 80 locks. A lock is a device for moving a boat up or down, to deal with an increase or decrease in elevation. (See illustration to the right.) Imagine a flatboat being towed upstream. With the upstream gate closed, the horses and mules would tow the boat into the lock through the downstream gate. Then the tow ropes would be disconnected and the downstream gate would be closed. Sluice gates would be opened in the upstream gate to allow water from upstream to flow into the lock. The boat would rise as the water flowed in. When the water in the canal had raised the boat to the proper level and "topped off," the sluice gates would be closed, and the upstream gate opened. Then the tow rope would be reconnected and the mules would be given a nudge. The boat would glide off along the canal—now at a slightly higher elevation.

When the Erie Canal opened in 1825, it joined the Hudson River to Lake Erie. (Governor Clinton marked the opening by pouring a bucket of water from the Great Lakes into the Hudson River.) The canal meant that products and people could be

Teaching Idea

Make an overhead from Instructional Master 18, *Expanding the West,* and use it to help children understand how the Erie Canal, the Oregon Trail, and the transcontinental railroad helped to connect different parts of the country. Explain that these innovations took place over a long span of time (1817–1869).

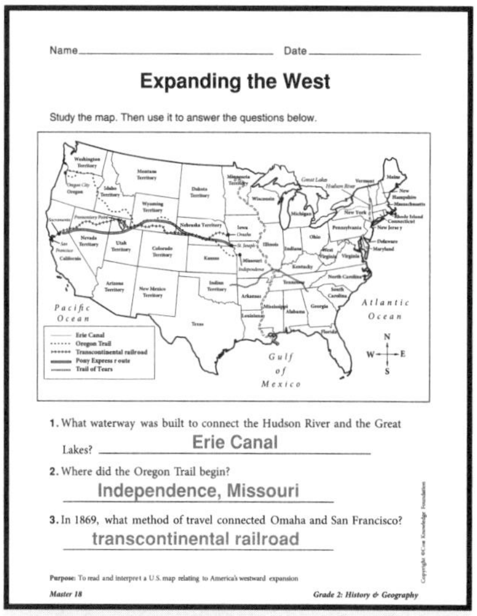

Name________________ Date________

Expanding the West

Study the map. Then use it to answer the questions below.

1. What waterway was built to connect the Hudson River and the Great Lakes? Erie Canal
2. Where did the Oregon Trail begin? Independence, Missouri
3. In 1869, what method of travel connected Omaha and San Francisco? transcontinental railroad

Purpose: To read and interpret a U.S. map relating to America's westward expansion

Master 18 *Grade 2: History & Geography*

Copyright ©Core Knowledge Foundation

Use Instructional Master 18.

Erie Canal (showing a series of locks)

moved from the Atlantic Ocean, up the Hudson River, across the Erie Canal, to Lake Erie, into the Great Lakes region, and beyond. Besides speeding people and goods west, the canal helped New York City dominate other eastern seaboard ports, such as Philadelphia, Baltimore, and Boston, which lacked direct links to the West. The canal also dramatically cut the cost of goods, for example, from $100 a ton to $10 a ton between New York City and Buffalo. Governor Clinton had proved to be correct.

Other cities and states soon imitated the Erie Canal but never equaled its success. Canals crisscrossed Pennsylvania, New York, Massachusetts, Connecticut, Rhode Island, Virginia, Maryland, the District of Columbia, Ohio, and Indiana.

The canals, especially in the northeastern section of the United States, served as an early interstate transportation system. Until they were overtaken by the railroads, the canals were the best form of transportation available, especially for heavy, bulky cargoes, such as coal, timber, and stone. Passengers also found travel by canal boat smoother, less tiring, and less dangerous than land travel.

Railroads

Railroads had several advantages over roads, rivers, and canals. Railroads were dependable, cheap, convenient, and comfortable. The first railroads were built in European coal mines, but, in 1831, the Mohawk and Hudson line was inaugurated between Albany and Schenectady, New York. When the Baltimore and Ohio Railroad reached Wheeling, West Virginia, in 1852, it achieved with iron rails what the Erie Canal had done years earlier: it had joined east and west. A rail network spread quickly across the Northeast and the Upper Midwest in the 1840s. The 1850s were the great railroad building era in the Southeast.

By 1861, some 300,000 miles of railroad track had been laid in the United States. The Midwest was the focus of much of this track laying. As a result, it was easier for people to travel to the Midwest from the East, and land became more expensive as more and more settlers arrived. Fast, cheap transportation for foodstuffs meant such goods could be shipped to the Northeast for sale, and manufactured items from the Northeast could, in turn, be shipped to consumers in the Midwest. Over time, larger, faster, and more powerful engines pulling heavier cars required stronger iron, and eventually steel rails. Bigger and stronger railroad bridges were also needed, because even the strongest wooden bridge would not support a heavy train across a wide river. The demands of the emerging railroad business were an enormous stimulus for the U.S. iron, steel, and coal mining industries after the Civil War. (Coal powered the steam engines.)

The Transcontinental Railroad

Before the Civil War, Congress could not agree on a route for the first transcontinental railroad; some members wanted it built along a southern route, and others wanted a more central route. Work began in 1863 and took the route from Omaha, Nebraska, on the Missouri River to Sacramento, California. The Union Pacific Railroad built west from Omaha, and the Central Pacific Railroad built east from California. Irish immigrants did much of the work on the eastern section, which was largely flat and gently rolling plains until it reached the Rocky Mountains. Chinese immigrants did most of the labor on the western portion of the railroad, facing rugged, dangerous work over and through mountains and across gorges and desert.

Cross-curricular Teaching Idea

Introduce to children the song "The Erie Canal," from the *Sequence.* It begins "I've got a mule-Her name is Sal-Fifteen years on the Erie Canal." The song describes a trip along the Erie Canal.

Teaching Idea

Read *The Amazing Impossible Erie Canal* to children. (See More Resources.) Have them make a sequence book by drawing pictures of a journey along the canal. Alternatively, you could have each child take a scene along the canal and make a mural of the journey.

Cross-curricular Teaching Idea

This is a good opportunity to introduce the songs about railroads from the *Sequence:* "Casey Jones," "I've Been Working on the Railroad," and "John Henry."

Teaching Idea

Work with children to build a time line for westward expansion. As you discuss new inventions and events, add them to your time line.

The United States paid the two companies for each mile of track laid, including higher payments for work in the mountains. The two competing railroads continued building east and west past each other, until the government made them join their tracks in 1869 at Promontory Point, Utah, near the Great Salt Lake. By the 1890s, four more transcontinental railroads had been built joining East and West across more northern and southern routes.

Routes West: The Oregon Trail

Before the transcontinental railroads and regional lines were built linking all parts of the country, people went west by wagon. The wagons, known as prairie schooners, were small, four-wheeled vehicles with canvas tops and wooden bodies, and were light enough so that they would not sink easily into the soft prairie sod. The wagons were often pulled by teams of oxen rather than by horses. Horses were faster but not as strong or hardy. Most pioneers, including most of the children, walked west across the Great Plains. People only rode in the wagons with the supplies when they were too sick or tired to walk, or when the weather was very bad.

Between 1840 and 1860, some 250,000 people went west from places like St. Joseph and Independence, Missouri, and Council Bluffs, Iowa. Most settlers went to the Oregon Territory, but some went to California. One trail used by early travelers was the Santa Fe Trail, which went from Independence, Missouri, to the former Spanish capital of Santa Fe, New Mexico. It was a relatively short distance—800 miles—on open plains across Kansas and then up the Arkansas River or across the desert.

The most famous route was the Oregon Trail, which began in Independence and crossed 2,000 miles of plains, mountains, and rivers. In southern Idaho, the trail diverged, and those wanting to go to California followed the California Trail along the Humboldt River through northern Nevada into California and the Sacramento Valley. The ruts cut by thousands of wagon wheels can still be seen today along parts of the Oregon Trail.

Wagon Trains on the Oregon Trail

Travelers on the trails, "overlanders" as they were known, often started with too many belongings, including cast-iron stoves, heavy furniture from the homes they left behind, and huge supplies of food. The first 50 miles or so after the jumping-off points became littered with abandoned goods. Jumping-off points were often the western end of a railroad or steamboat line and marked the end of white settlements.

Some pioneers went west alone, including individual women. Others traveled in small groups, either on foot or on horseback. The most common arrangement was for groups of families to organize into a wagon train under the command of an experienced leader, or an elected head assisted by guides.

Many people have a picture in their minds of wagon trains fighting off almost continuous assaults by Native Americans. In fact, recent evidence indicates that, although there were some attacks, Native Americans helped overlanders far more than they warred against them, especially before government policies after the Civil War radically changed the lives of Plains Native Americans. The Native

Cross-curricular Teaching Idea

Ask if anyone has ever ridden on a train and whether that child will describe the trip. Explain that the first railroads were really carriages pulled by horses along tracks. The first steam engines were nicknamed "iron horses" for that reason.

Teaching Idea

Have children draw a picture putting themselves in a scene with a wagon going west. Have them write a caption explaining what they are doing or what is happening in the scene.

Cross-curricular Teaching Idea

To help children understand the size of a typical wagon used on the Oregon Trail, help them measure the outline of a prairie schooner (about 10–12 feet long and 4 feet wide), using masking tape to tape off the dimensions of the wagon on the floor. If you do this activity close to a wall, you could also mark the typical height of a wagon, which was 10 feet. Have children make a list of items their family could take in the wagon, and give them an idea of how much would fit by placing objects inside the wagon outline.

Teaching Idea

Read *They're Off!: The Story of the Pony Express* to children. (See More Resources.) Have the class discuss what the Pony Express rider would have seen, done, and thought about along the way. Point out that the rider would only ride for a day and then turn over the mail to the next rider. If children envision an attack by Native Americans, remind them that many of the stories of Native American attacks are not true.

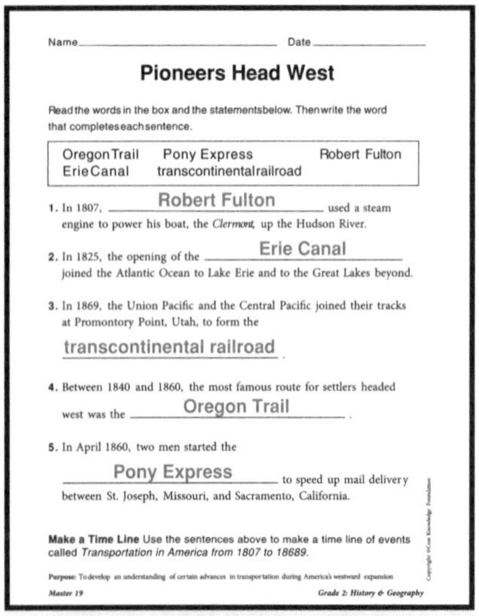

Name______________ Date__________

Pioneers Head West

Read the words in the box and the statements below. Then write the word that completes each sentence.

Oregon Trail	Pony Express	Robert Fulton
Erie Canal	transcontinental railroad	

1. In 1807, Robert Fulton used a steam engine to power his boat, the *Clermont*, up the Hudson River.
2. In 1825, the opening of the Erie Canal joined the Atlantic Ocean to Lake Erie and to the Great Lakes beyond.
3. In 1869, the Union Pacific and the Central Pacific joined their tracks at Promontory Point, Utah, to form the transcontinental railroad.
4. Between 1840 and 1860, the most famous route for settlers headed west was the Oregon Trail.
5. In April 1860, two men started the Pony Express to speed up mail delivery between St. Joseph, Missouri, and Sacramento, California.

Make a Time Line Use the sentences above to make a time line of events called *Transportation in America from 1807 to 18689.*

Purpose: To develop an understanding of certain advances in transportation during America's westward expansion

Master 19 *Grade 2: History & Geography*

Use Instructional Master 19.

Americans often asked for payment for collecting firewood, driving cattle, hunting game, or piloting a wagon across a river. Some charged a fee for crossing their land. In 1851, the Cayuse built a toll road in the Grande Ronde Valley south of Portland, Orgeon. A pioneer was more likely to die from accidental gunshot, drowning, being kicked by a horse, or even starvation, than from an attack by Native Americans. (59)

Pony Express

Because of the Gold Rush in 1848, California had attracted many men and some women seeking their fortune. Few found gold, but many stayed because of the climate and availability of land. If they wanted to communicate with their families and friends in the East, or if someone wanted to write to the new Californians, it could take as long as a month for a letter to reach its destination.

In April 1860, two men started the Pony Express to speed mail delivery. The 1,800-mile route went from St. Joseph, Missouri, to Sacramento, California. Every 10 to 15 miles, there was a station that provided a fresh horse to the Pony Express rider, who carried the mail in saddlebags slung over his saddle. Although called the Pony Express, the riders rode horses, not ponies. The route took 10 days to complete.

The company's ads recruited young, wiry, single men, preferably orphans, who were excellent riders and willing to risk their lives to carry the mail. There were many volunteers. Pony Express riders included many colorful characters such as young William "Buffalo Bill" Cody, who would later go on to form a famous Wild West show.

The Pony Express lasted only a year and a half, from April 1860 to October 1861. By then, a transcontinental telegraph line had been built. Since the telegraph could send a message in seconds, the Pony Express went out of business.

B. Native Americans

The days of peaceful coexistence between the Pilgrims and the Wampanoag that resulted in the first Thanksgiving celebration were short-lived. By the 1630s, New England was afire with warfare between Native Americans and colonists. The colonists wanted Native American lands, and the Native Americans resisted. This became the predominant pattern for Native American–colonial relations throughout the 17th and 18th centuries and for relations between Native Americans and the United States from the late 18th century through the 19th century.

The Trail of Tears

One of the saddest chapters in U.S.–Native American relations is the government's poor treatment of the so-called Five Civilized Tribes. The nations of the southeastern United States—the Cherokee, Creek, Choctaw, Chickasaw, and Seminole—had adopted European-American ways, becoming farmers and converting to Christianity. However, as the frontier moved south and west, their lands in the Carolinas, Georgia, Alabama, Mississippi, and Florida were coveted by Americans.

Andrew Jackson, a landowner in Tennessee as well as a politician and military man, was no friend to the Native Americans. He had a long record of fighting the

Native Americans of the Southeast. For example, at the Battle of Horseshoe Bend, Jackson's forces defeated the Creeks, who were forced to cede 23 million acres to the United States. In the First Seminole War, Jackson invaded Spanish Florida in an effort to end Seminole raids into the United States. Weakened by war and in need of money, Spain sold Florida to the United States, and the Seminole were forced south to live in the Everglades, an area of swamps.

According to estimates, Jackson acquired for the United States and white settlement "nearly three-fourths of Alabama and Florida, a third of Tennessee, and a fifth of Georgia and Mississippi."

In 1830, Congress passed the Indian Removal Act, which gave Jackson the power to force the Native Americans of the Southeast to move to what was then known as the Indian Territory, now part of the state of Oklahoma. The first to leave were the Choctaw in 1831, then the Creek in 1836, and the Chickasaw in 1837. The last to leave were the Seminole after the Second Seminole War, which lasted from 1835 to 1842.

The Cherokee chose legal means rather than warfare to resist removal. In two lawsuits, one in 1831 and one in 1832 that went all the way to the Supreme Court, Cherokee rights to their lands were upheld, but President Jackson and the state of Georgia ignored both decisions. By 1835, some 2,000 Cherokee, seeing the inevitable, agreed to move. But by 1838, some 14,000 still remained in the Southeast. Jackson was no longer president, but his successor, Martin Van Buren, decided to enforce the law. The forced march to the Indian Territory became known as the "Trail of Tears." The four-month trek took place in winter, and some 4,000 Native American men, women, and children died on the way. There was not enough food for the Cherokee, and the troops escorting them refused to stop the march to allow the Cherokee who were sick or tired to rest. The cost of the removal was subtracted from the money to be paid to the Cherokee for their lands, so they were left with only $3 million.

The Cherokee and the other nations removed to Indian Territory were promised that this land would remain theirs forever. "Forever" lasted a generation. First, they lost part of their land to other Native American peoples whom the federal government resettled in the Territory in 1866. As the West filled up, there was pressure on the government to open Native American lands to settlers. In 1889, the Creek and the Seminole sold 50,000 acres to the United States for European-American settlement. By 1907, there were more non–Native Americans than Native Americans in the Territory, and in that year, it was made part of the new state of Oklahoma. (60)

Sequoyah and the Cherokee Alphabet

Before Europeans came to the Americas, Native American peoples did not have written languages. They relied on storytelling, folktales, and even dance to express themselves and to hand down their laws, rituals, histories, and traditions from generation to generation.

Each group of Native Americans had to develop its own kind of writing. In 1821, Sequoyah, a Cherokee silversmith, developed a way of writing the Cherokee language.

Teaching Idea

Talk with children about the importance of Sequoyah's invention and connect it with their own studies in reading and writing. Ask what having a written language might enable a person to do (take notes, write a letter, read a book, write out a shopping list so as not to forget anything, and so on). In Grade 1, children learned about the cuneiform writing of the Sumerians and the hieroglyphics of the Egyptians. Draw out what children remember about these two innovations and make comparisons to the Cherokee language.

Have children create headlines for the front page of a newspaper announcing Sequoyah's invention.

Painted Buffalo Hide

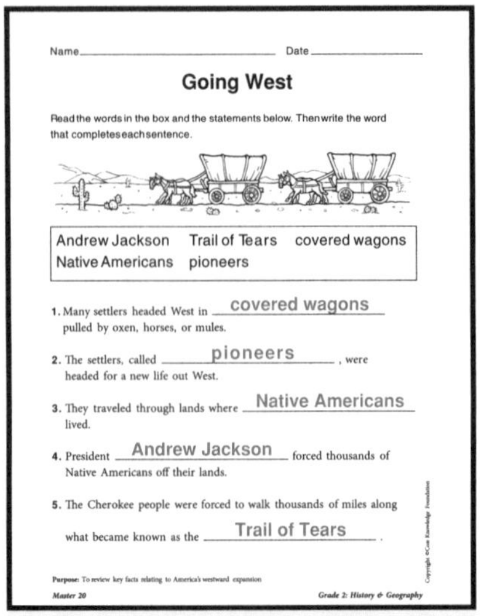

Name________ Date________

Going West

Read the words in the box and the statements below. Then write the word that completes each sentence.

Andrew Jackson	Trail of Tears	covered wagons
Native Americans	pioneers	

1. Many settlers headed West in covered wagons pulled by oxen, horses, or mules.
2. The settlers, called pioneers, were headed for a new life out West.
3. They traveled through lands where Native Americans lived.
4. President Andrew Jackson forced thousands of Native Americans off their lands.
5. The Cherokee people were forced to walk thousands of miles along what became known as the Trail of Tears.

Purpose: To review key facts relating to America's westward expansion

Master 20 — Grade 2: History & Geography

Use Instructional Master 20.

Sequoyah was the son of a European father (a fur trader) and a Cherokee mother. He was born in the 1770s near the Tennessee River. He was abandoned by his father and raised by his mother. Sequoyah and other Cherokee enlisted on the side of the United States under General Andrew Jackson to fight the British troops and the Creek Native Americans in the War of 1812. During the war (and perhaps earlier as well) Sequoyah saw European Americans communicating using writing and sheets of paper, which some Native Americans called "talking leaves." Although Sequoyah never learned English or the English alphabet, he began working on a way of writing down the Cherokee language.

Sequoyah developed something like an alphabet. Actually, it was a syllabary. Sequoyah noticed that all Cherokee words were composed of a set of syllables, and he developed 86 written signs, or characters, to represent syllables in the Cherokee language. He taught his daughter, Ayoka, to use the symbols and went with her to a tribal council to demonstrate his system. At first the members of the tribal council did not believe he could do what he claimed. Sequoyah told the council to take his daughter to the far end of the village. While she was away, he wrote down some things the council members said and explained that his daughter would be able to read what he had written down. When Ayoka returned, Sequoyah gave her the sheet he had written on, and she was able to repeat what Sequoyah had written. Finally, the tribal elders were convinced.

The Cherokee adopted Sequoyah's writing system. It was the first written Native American language in North America. The Cherokee people used Sequoyah's alphabet to write their own constitution and, beginning in 1828, to publish a newspaper, *The Phoenix.*

Plains Native Americans: The Railroad and the Buffalo

The coming of the railroad and the influx of Easterners and European immigrants onto the plains changed the way of life of Plains Native Americans forever. Up until the 1860s, the northern and southern plains had few European-American settlers. But the Homestead Act of 1862 encouraged settlement by giving 160 acres of land to any citizen or immigrant willing to live on and farm it for five years. Unfortunately, this land was home to Plains Native Americans who lived by hunting buffalo.

By the turn of the 20th century, the buffalo were gone in many places. One count indicated that there were only 34 left on the northern plains. It is estimated that as many as 15 million buffalo were killed during the 1800s. When Native Americans killed buffalo, they used every part of the animal. They ate the meat for food and turned the skins into teepees, clothing, and storage vessels. White hunters killed buffalo to feed the construction crews that built the railroads, but they also shot the animals for sport and to supply hides to tanneries to be made into leather goods. Those who killed for sport and for the hides left the meat on the carcasses to rot.

In an effort to deter Native Americans from fighting for their right to roam the plains and hunt buffalo, the federal government in 1871 passed the Indian Appropriation Act. Under the provisions of the law, the U.S. government withdrew recognition of separate Native American peoples as sovereign nations and stated that it would no longer enter into treaties with any Native American group. Treaties that were in force would be honored. That, however, proved to be a hollow promise whenever gold or silver was found on Native American lands or American settlers wanted more land. (Native Americans were not granted U.S. citizenship until 1924.) Like the Five Civilized Tribes, Plains Native Americans were herded onto reservations.

Unlike the Five Civilized Tribes, who had been farmers before they were moved to Oklahoma, Plains Native Americans were hunters. However, the federal government tried to turn them into farmers. Not only did they not know how to farm, but the lands they were forced to live on were not particularly suited to farming. The Bureau of Indian Affairs was supposed to oversee the reservations and provide food, clothing, and other necessities to the Native Americans. However, greed and corruption often guided the actions of government agents in the bureau, and the Native Americans saw little of the aid that was meant to sustain them in their new lives.

The corruption became so rampant that the protests of Native Americans and their white supporters could no longer be ignored. In 1887, Congress passed the Dawes Act, which broke up the reservations. The land was divided into parcels of 160 acres, and each head of a household received a parcel. Any land that was not disposed of in this way could be sold to settlers. Native American families had to hold the land for 25 years, at which time they could sell it. Many did sell their land, and then had nothing to live on when the money was gone. By 1932, 96 million acres of the 138 million acres set aside for Native Americans in 1887 had passed out of Native American control.

Teaching Idea

Native Americans used buffalo hides not only for the sides of their teepees and for their clothing but also to record their history. They painted the story of their deeds on buffalo robes and rugs.

Have children talk about what it must have been like to hunt buffalo on horseback—how big the buffalo were, how fast the horses might have run, how much dust they might kick up.

Then have children draw a story about hunting buffalo on horseback. To simulate the idea of buffalo hide, have children draw their work on brown butcher paper. You may wish to read *Dancing Teepees: Poems of American Indian Youth,* by Virginia Driving Hawk Sneve to accompany this activity. (See More Resources.)

Review

Below are some ideas for ongoing assessment and review activities. These are not meant to constitute a comprehensive list. Teachers may also refer to the *Pearson Learning/Core Knowledge History & Geography* series for additional information and teaching ideas.

- Discuss with children how different it is to travel west today. Compare and contrast modes of travel today with the ones during westward expansion. Discuss the steamboat and the railroad and compare them to trains and airplanes today. How would you rather travel? Have children fold a piece of white 8½″ x 11″ paper in half. On one side have them draw a picture of what it was like to travel west in the 1800s. On the other side, have them draw a picture of traveling west today. Then have children write sentences describing the journey.
- After learning about the importance of the buffalo to the Native Americans, have children write a story from the perspective of the Native Americans explaining why the buffalo is so important to the tribe. Ask children to try to persuade the readers to think carefully about why the extermination of the buffalo would be so devastating to the tribe.
- Have children fold a piece of white 8½″ x 11″ paper into three parts, creating three panels on the page. In each panel, have children draw a picture. In the first panel, have them depict the life of a Native American tribe before being moved from their homes. In the second panel, have them draw a picture of the reaction of the

The Big Idea in Review

The development of major transportation systems accelerated westward expansion and contributed to the demise of Native American ways of life.

tribe when they have to move. In the third panel, have them show life on a reservation and how it was different from the first panel on the page. Have children write sentences under each picture to tell what was happening to the Native American tribe.

- Have children describe how the experience of the pioneers moving west was different from the Native American experience. Create a Venn diagram on chart paper with the pioneers on one side and the Native Americans on the other. Discuss the experiences of each group. Then, use the Venn diagram as a resource for writing paragraphs describing experiences.

- You may also ask the following questions at the end of this section:

1. Who built the first American steamboat?
   Robert Fulton built the first American steamboat.
2. Why was the steamboat an important invention?
   Steamboats were fast and large, could carry many people and much cargo, and could easily navigate upstream against the current.
3. Where is the Erie Canal located?
   It is in New York State.
4. Why was the Erie Canal important?
   The Erie Canal linked the Atlantic Ocean to the Great Lakes so that people and goods could move west more quickly and cheaply; it helped the expansion of the country westward.
5. Why was the transcontinental railroad important?
   It connected the East Coast with the West Coast.
6. Imagine that you are going to set up the Pony Express to speed mail delivery from the East Coast to the West Coast and back. What resources will you need to set up and run your business?
   I will need money, horses, riders, and stations to take care of the horses and riders.
7. Who developed a system that enabled the Cherokee people to read and write?
   Sequoyah developed a syllable-based writing system for the Cherokee.
8. Why was the removal of the Cherokee to the Indian Territory called the "Trail of Tears"?
   The removal of the Cherokee to the Indian Territory was called the "Trail of Tears" because the Cherokee did not want to leave their homes in the East and go to the Indian Territory. When they were forced to leave, it was winter, the conditions were difficult, and 4,000 Cherokee died on the way.
9. How did Plains Native Americans get their food before settlers and miners came to the plains?
   The Plains Native Americans hunted buffalo.
10. Why did Plains Native Americans have to give up hunting buffalo and move to reservations?
    Plains Native Americans had to give up hunting buffalo because settlers and miners wanted their lands to farm and to mine gold and silver. There were also fewer buffalo because they had been killed by hunters to feed railroad construction crews, for sport, and to provide hides for tanneries to make leather goods.

More Resources

The titles listed below are offered as a representative sample of materials and not a complete list of everything that is available.

For children —

These books are generally intended to be read aloud, though some children may be able to read parts or all of the simpler texts.

- *Americans Move West*, edited by E. D. Hirsch, Jr. (Pearson Learning, 2002). A unit in the official *Pearson Learning/Core Knowledge History & Geography* series. It includes a small picture book for children and a teacher's guide with read alouds. To order, call 1-800-321-3106.
- *The Amazing Impossible Erie Canal*, by Cheryl Harness (Aladdin Library, 1999). A very informative (and challenging) read aloud. Paperback, 32 pages, ISBN 0689825846.
- *Araminta's Paint Box*, by Karen Ackerman (Aladdin Books, 1998). In this work of historical fiction, Araminta loses her paint box on her journey from Boston to California in 1847. The box exchanges hands many times before Araminta gets it back. Includes a map detailing the routes of Araminta's family and the paint box. Paperback, 32 pages, ISBN 0689820917.
- *Dancing Teepees: Poems of American Indian Youth*, by Virginia Driving Hawk Sneve (Holiday House, 1989). Library binding, 32 pages, ISBN 0823407241.
- *Following the Great Herds: The Plains Indians and the American Buffalo (Library of the Westward Expansion)*, by Ryan P. Randolph (PowerKids Press, 2003). Lots of photos and illustrations. Library binding, 24 pages, ISBN 0823962962. Other titles in this series include *The Oregon Trail, Frontier Women Who Helped Shape the American West, Lewis and Clark's Voyage of Discovery, The Quest for California's Gold, The Santa Fe Trail,* and *The Transcontinental Railroad.*
- *Food and Recipes of the Westward Expansion (Cooking Throughout American History)*, by George Erdosh (PowerKids Press, 2001). Library binding, 24 pages, ISBN 0823951154.
- *Going West*, by Jean Van Leeuwen and illustrated by Thomas B. Allen (Puffin, 1997). A family's journey west is told from seven-year-old Hannah's point of view. Paperback, 48 pages, ISBN 0140560963.
- *Mailing May*, by Michael Tunnell (HarperTrophy, 2000). Paperback, 32 pages, ISBN 0064437248.
- *A Picture Book of Davy Crockett*, by David Adler and illustrated by John and Alexandra Wallner (Holiday House, 1998). Paperback, ISBN 0823413438. See also *A Picture Book of Lewis and Clark* by the same author.
- *They're Off!: The Story of the Pony Express*, by Cheryl Harness (Aladdin, 2002). Paperback, 32 pages, ISBN 0689851219.
- *Trail of Tears*, by Joseph Bruchac and illustrated by Diana Magnuson (Random House, 1999). Paperback, 48 pages, ISBN 0679890521.
- *Warm as Wool*, by Scott Russell Sanders and illustrated by Helen Cogancherry (Simon & Schuster, Inc., 1992). Set on the Ohio frontier in 1803 and based on a true story. Library binding, 32 pages, ISBN 0027781399. See also *Aurora Means Dawn* and *The Floating House* by the same author.

For teachers —

- *The American West: An Illustrated History*, by Liz Sonnenborn (Fair Street, 2002). Hardcover, 144 pages, ISBN 0439219701.
- *Andrew Jackson's America: 1824–1850*, by Christopher Collier and James Lincoln Collier (Benchmark Books, 1999). Library binding, 96 pages, ISBN 0761407790.
- *Daily Life in a Covered Wagon*, by Paul Erickson (Scott Foresman, 1997). Paperback, 48 pages, ISBN 0140562125.
- *Frontier Living: An Illustrated Guide to Pioneer Life in America*, by Edwin Tunis (Lyons Press, 2000). Paperback, 168 pages, ISBN 158574137X.
- *Indian Chiefs*, by Russell Freedman (Holiday House, 1992). Paperback, ISBN 0823409716.
- "Lewis and Clark: The Language of Discovery," in *Smithsonian in Your Classroom*, Fall 2003. Available online at http://smithsonianeducation.org.
- *Lewis & Clark: Voyage of Discovery*, by Stephen E. Ambrose with the photography of Sam Abell (National Geographic, 1998). Hardcover, 256 pages, ISBN 0792270843.

More Resources continued

- *The New Nation: 1789–1850*, by Joy Hakim (Oxford University Press, 2002). Book 4 in the highly acclaimed series *A History of Us*. Paperback, 160 pages, ISBN 019515326X. See also *Liberty for All?: 1820–1860*, book 5 in the same series.
- *The Oregon Trail*, by Francis Parkman (National Geographic Society, 2002). Paperback, 287 pages, ISBN 0792266404.
- *Stout-Hearted Seven*, by Neta Lohnes Frazier (Harcourt, 1973). A well-researched account of the Sagers, a family of seven orphaned children who traveled along the Oregon Trail after the death of their parents. Corrects many errors in the movie *Seven Alone*. A possibility as a read aloud. Hardcover, 174 pages, ISBN 0152814507.
- The American West, www.americanwest.com. Click on "Expansion" to find a number of good links.
- *The Letters of Narcissa Whitman, 1836–1847* and related letters may be found online at http://www.pbs.org/weta/thewest/resources/archives/two/whitman1.htm. Narcissa Whitman and Eliza Spalding were the first two white women to cross the Rocky Mountains, leading to the opening of the Oregon Trail.
- Lewis and Clark's Historic Trail, www.lewisclark.net. Includes maps, a time line, journals, and more.
- Oregon Trail Interpretive Center, http://oregontrail.blm.gov. Includes a "Just for Kids" section with coloring book pages, a teacher's resource section, and historical tidbits.
- The Orphan Trains (PBS), www.pbs.org/wgbh/amex/orphan. Includes a teacher's guide.

IV. The Civil War

Remember that each subject you study with children expands their vocabulary and introduces new terms, thus making them better listeners and readers. As you study historical people and events, use read alouds and discussions to build children's vocabularies.

The items in bold relate to the content in Grade 2.

1776	Omission in the Declaration of Independence of King George's place in the slave trade
1787	Adoption of the three-fifths clause in the Constitution
1820	Missouri Compromise
1820	**Birth of Harriet Tubman**
1830–1861	**Underground Railroad**
1850	Compromise of 1850
1854	Kansas-Nebraska Act
1860	**Lincoln elected president**
1860	**Secession of South Carolina**
1861	**Confederate States of America formed**
1861	**Clara Barton as nurse for the Union**
1861–1865	**Civil War**
1862	**First victories for the Union under Grant**
1863	**Emancipation Proclamation**
1864	**Grant made general of all Union armies**
1865	**Surrender of Confederate army by Lee** **Ratification of the 13th Amendment, abolishing slavery**
1881	**Founding of American Red Cross**

The Big Idea

The controversy between the North and the South over slavery resulted in the Civil War.

What Students Should Already Know

Students in Core Knowledge schools should be familiar with

Kindergarten and Grade 1

- Early Exploration and Settlement
  - Slavery in early America
  - Plantations in Southern colonies

What Students Need to Learn

- **Controversy over slavery**
- **Harriet Tubman, the Underground Railroad**
- **Northern versus Southern states: Yankees and Rebels**
- **Ulysses S. Grant and Robert E. Lee**
- **Clara Barton: the "Angel of the Battlefield" and founder of the American Red Cross**
- **President Abraham Lincoln: keeping the Union together**
- **Emancipation Proclamation and the end of slavery**

What Students Will Learn in Future Grades

In future grades, students will review and extend their learning about the Civil War.

Grade 5

- slavery in the Southern colonies
- toward the Civil War, including abolition, the Missouri Compromise, the Dred Scott decision, *Uncle Tom's Cabin*, John Brown's raid, the Lincoln-Douglas debates
- the Civil War:the leaders, important battles, the Emancipation Proclamation, the reelection and assassination of Lincoln
- Reconstruction: the Radical Republicans, the Freedmen's Bureau, the Reconstruction Amendments to the Constitution, the Black Codes, and the Compromise of 1877 to end Reconstruction

IV. The Civil War

Text Resources

(61) *Reminiscences of Levi Coffin*

Materials

Instructional Masters 21–23

The Civil War, p. 194

Major Civil War Battles, p. 195

Civil War Matchup, p. 197

overhead projector, p. 194

articles about the current work of the American Red Cross cut out from newspapers and magazines, or articles from its website, p. 195

dress-up clothes for historical figures, p. 196

chart paper, p. 197

lined pages for class ABC book, p. 198

Vocabulary

Student/Teacher Vocabulary

abolitionist: a person who worked to end slavery (T)

conductor: a person who helped slaves escape on the Underground Railroad (T)

Confederacy: the Southern states that seceded from the Union at the onset of the Civil War (S)

controversy: a disagreement over a topic (T)

Emancipation Proclamation: the document issued by Abraham Lincoln that freed all slaves in the Confederate states (S)

secede: to withdraw formally from membership in a group (S)

slavery: a system based on the ownership and enforced work of other people (S)

Underground Railroad: a network of people who helped slaves escape to the North or to Canada (S)

Union: the Northern states that remained in the United States at the onset of the Civil War (S)

Domain Vocabulary

Pre–Civil War and associated words:
controversy, economic system, way of life, ideal, romanticized, social, political, economic, moral, cotton, "King Cotton," tobacco, labor-intensive agriculture, plantation, big house, planter, slave owner, slaveholder, slave, enslaved African American, field hand, house slave, slave quarters, overseer, slave auction, buy, sell "downriver," Deep South, Upper South, Lower South, sell families apart, break up families, abolition, do away with, compromise, Declaration of Independence, U.S. Constitution, three-fifths clause, Missouri Compromise (Compromise of 1820), free state, slave state, balance, Compromise of 1850, Fugitive Slave Act, slaver, bounty, Kansas-Nebraska Act, popular sovereignty, Frederick Douglass, North Star, William Lloyd Garrison, Liberator, Harriet Beecher Stowe, *Uncle Tom's Cabin,* Quakers, Northeast, Midwest, north to freedom, conductors, stations, stops, safe houses, Harriet Tubman, scout, spy

Civil War and associated words:
1860 election, Abraham Lincoln, Republican, South Carolina, heated, angry, extension of slavery, free states, slave states, balance of power, secession, slaveholding states, Confederate States of America, constitution, General Robert E. Lee, successful career, gentlemanly, principled, United States of America, General Ulysses S. Grant, undistinguished, mediocre career, Civil War, Northern States versus Southern States, War Between the States, border states, loyal, advantages, disadvantages, industrial, agricultural, economic, financial centers, natural resources, railroads, rail system, navy, private ships, army, soldiers, officers, better-equipped

Clara Barton and associated words:
"Angel of the Battlefield," assertive, courageous, organized, competent, practical, efficient, American Red Cross, influential

Emancipation Proclamation and associated words:
Abraham Lincoln, preserve Union, abolish slavery, end, goal, aim, purpose, restate, shift, change, issue, declare, decree, free, abolish, under control, practical, actual, effect, outcome, result, affect, symbolic, Thirteenth Amendment, passage, ratify, free, freedom

In the Text Resources for this section, words are bolded that should be included as part of Domain Vocabulary.

Cross-curricular Connections

Language Arts	Music
Poetry	**Songs**
• "Harriet Tubman"	• "Follow the Drinking Gourd"
• "Lincoln"	• "When Johnny Comes Marching Home"
	• "Dixie"
	• "Swing Low, Sweet Chariot"

At a Glance

The most important ideas for you are:

- The controversy between the North and the South over slavery went back to at least the late 18th century.
- Nineteenth-century compromises never settled the issue of slavery.
- People like Harriet Tubman helped slaves escape through the Underground Railroad.
- Ulysses S. Grant and Robert E. Lee, the generals on either side of the war, had contrasting careers.
- Clara Barton was a pioneering battlefield nurse who also lobbied for the founding of the American Red Cross.
- Abraham Lincoln's major objective was to preserve the Union.
- The Emancipation Proclamation freed slaves in rebellious states.

What Teachers Need to Know

Background

Children will study the Civil War in greater depth and detail in Grade 5. The task in Grade 2 is to provide a simple introduction to the topic, as a foundation for later study.

The Controversy Over Slavery

The Civil War, or the War Between the States as it was known in the South, arose out of social, political, and economic differences between the Northern and Southern states. In the Northern states, slavery had gradually been abandoned. In the Southern states, slavery had become both an economic system and a way of life.

There were about 1,800 large plantations in the South and hundreds of thousands of small farms. The large plantations had 100 or more slaves and raised rice, tobacco, or cotton, depending on whether the plantation was located in Virginia, Kentucky, Tennessee, North Carolina, along the coast, or in the Deep South, where cotton was king. Small farmers owned no slaves and raised their own food and a

Teaching Idea

If you teach in a Core Knowledge school, consider using "buddy classes." You can buddy up with a class that is studying the same topic in a different grade level. Pair off children from each class, and give them a common topic to discuss. Both the older and younger children will enjoy having an audience and hearing from a different source. When children return to their class, have them write about what they discussed so you can clear up any incorrect information. In this section, you can pair up second-grade and fifth-grade children who are learning about the Civil War.

Teaching Idea

Check for prior knowledge by asking children to define slavery. Remind them that there were slaves in other countries for centuries, not just in the United States. Talk with them about how not everyone understood that it was wrong to make another person a slave. Depending on the maturity level of your class, talk about the economic reasons for slavery. The Southern climate was suited to the growing of tobacco and cotton, which were both labor-intensive crops. The demand for cotton was increasing as the North and Great Britain turned to large-scale textile mills to manufacture cotton cloth. Slaves were a cheap source of labor. They did not require wages or very much in the way of clothing, food, or housing. Children as well as the aged could be made to work.

small cash crop like tobacco or cotton. There were few rich Southerners. However, the rich planter with a large plantation worked by hundreds of slaves became the ideal to which many poor Southern whites aspired. This ideal took hold in their imaginations and helps explain why so many poor Southerners were willing to fight for a cause in which they did not participate.

Southern intellectuals developed certain arguments to justify the continued use of human beings as slaves. One argument said that slavery was essential to the Southern economy, which was based on the cultivation of cotton, a very labor-intensive crop. These same white Southerners pointed to the abuse of workers in Northern mills and factories and extolled the virtues of slavery, which ensured that slaves had food, clothing, and shelter, regardless of whether they were healthy and able to work or too ill or too old to work. Southerners also pointed to precedents for slavery in the Bible and in ancient Greece and Rome.

Compromises

Beginning with the Declaration of Independence, when the delegates to the Second Continental Congress removed references to King George's part in the slave trade in order to mollify Southern slaveholders, the United States made compromises over slavery. These compromises did not solve the controversy over slavery—they only prolonged it and raised the stakes each time a new compromise was reached.

Among the compromises were the following:

- In 1787, the Constitutional Convention compromised and agreed to count every five enslaved Africans and African Americans as three free men for purposes of determining representation in the House of Representatives. This is the three-fifths clause. The new Constitution did mandate an end to the importation of slaves by 1808, but it did not abolish slavery nor end the internal slave trade.
- The Fugitive Slave Act of 1793 declared it illegal for slaves to run away. Hence, the federal government endorsed the hunting of slaves.
- In 1820, the Missouri Compromise enabled Missouri to enter the Union as a slave state, as long as Maine entered as a free state and any new states created from the Louisiana Purchase above the 36th parallel would be free. The Compromise kept the balance between free and slave states but set up future conflicts over the entrance of new states into the Union.
- The Compromise of 1850 kept the balance of slave and free states by allowing California to enter the Union as a free state and the Utah and New Mexico Territories to decide for themselves if they would enter as free or slave states. Congress also abolished the slave trade in the District of Columbia and tightened the Fugitive Slave Act, requiring the return of escaped slaves to their owners and rewarding those who assisted in the catching of slaves.
- The Kansas-Nebraska Act of 1854 took up the issue of slavery in lands above the 36th parallel and overturned the Compromise of 1850. The new law allowed voters in the territories of Nebraska and Kansas to determine for themselves whether the states should be free or slave states. Nebraskans voted to become a free state, whereas bloody fighting broke out in Kansas as proslavery and antislavery factions fought each other for power and the outcome of the vote.

Abolitionists

During this course of unfolding political events, ordinary people, many of them slaves or former slaves, actively opposed slavery, giving voice to what became known as the abolitionist movement. Among the most notable abolitionists was Frederick Douglass, an escaped slave, who wrote an autobiography describing his life as a slave in Maryland and later published the abolitionist newspaper, *North Star.*

Influential white abolitionists included William Lloyd Garrison, who published the *Liberator,* another abolitionist newspaper, and Harriet Beecher Stowe, who wrote *Uncle Tom's Cabin,* which sold over 300,000 copies in its first year. The novel describes the life of the gentle slave Tom who eventually dies at the brutal hands of the overseer.

The Underground Railroad

The idea of the Underground Railroad possibly dates back to as early as the late 1700s, when Quakers in Philadelphia and New Jersey began to aid the escape of enslaved Africans and African Americans. We do not know who came up with the metaphor of the "railroad," according to which the houses where runaway slaves rested along the way are called "stations" or "stops," and the leader of the escaping slaves is called the "conductor;" but we do know that by the early 1800s, there were "stops" on the "railroad" across a large section of the Northeast and Midwest. The most active time for the railroad was from the 1830s to 1861, when the Civil War began.

The Underground Railroad operated mainly in the Midwest and Northeast, although there are authenticated stations in Virginia, West Virginia, Florida, and Colorado. The Underground Railroad was a network of houses, farmsteads, churches, and Quaker meetinghouses, or "stations," where escaping slaves would be safe. The conductor, the person who helped move the escaped slaves, might be an African-American blacksmith in one town and a white merchant in another. In the beginning, most escaping slaves were single men, but later women and children also took the train north. They walked under cover of night and rode in the false bottoms of farm wagons and in closed carriages. Slave-catchers sometimes pursued them with hunting dogs.

Estimates of the number of slaves who escaped through the Underground Railroad vary considerably. Because of the need for secrecy, few records were kept, so it is difficult to know with certainty. (61)

Harriet Tubman

Harriet Tubman was born in 1820 on the eastern shore of Maryland to Harriet and Benjamin Ross, who were field hands and slaves. Her grandparents had been born in Africa and carried to the Americas in chains. At 13, when Tubman tried to save another slave from punishment, her owner hit her so hard with a rock that he fractured her skull. As a result of this injury, she had blackouts for the rest of her life.

At 22, she was married by order of her owner to a freed slave named John Tubman. When she learned that she and several of her family of 11 were to be sold "downriver," meaning into the Deep South, she escaped to Philadelphia and went

Teaching Idea

Introduce the abolitionists by talking about why slavery is wrong. Point out that some people—in the North and in the South, white and African American, male and female—worked to end slavery. They spoke out against it, wrote against it, and even helped slaves escape to freedom in the North and in Canada. Talk about how these people risked imprisonment, and sometimes their lives, if they lived in the South. Point out that they were breaking the law for the sake of their beliefs.

Cross-curricular Teaching Idea

You may wish to teach the poem "Harriet Tubman" in connection with this unit.

to work in a hotel. But she was concerned about her family and began making trips on the Underground Railroad to bring them north to freedom. It is believed that Tubman made 19 trips on the railroad and brought some 750 men, women, and children to freedom, including her parents. Because she did not keep written records (it would have been too dangerous if they had ever been found) we will never really know the exact numbers.

Tubman was a strict "conductor." As Eloise Greenfield says in her poem "Harriet Tubman," which is listed in the *Sequence* for this grade, Tubman "didn't take no stuff." She carried a gun and threatened to shoot any slave who talked too much, or was tired and ready to give up. Southern whites offered a massive reward for her capture, but Tubman swore that she would not be taken alive. In fact, she never got caught. When the Civil War began, Tubman became a scout and a spy for the Union.

Teaching Idea

Make an overhead from Instructional Master 21, *The Civil War*, to orient children to the states that made up the Confederate States of America. Ask whether your state was part of the Union or the Confederacy or was not yet a state during the Civil War.

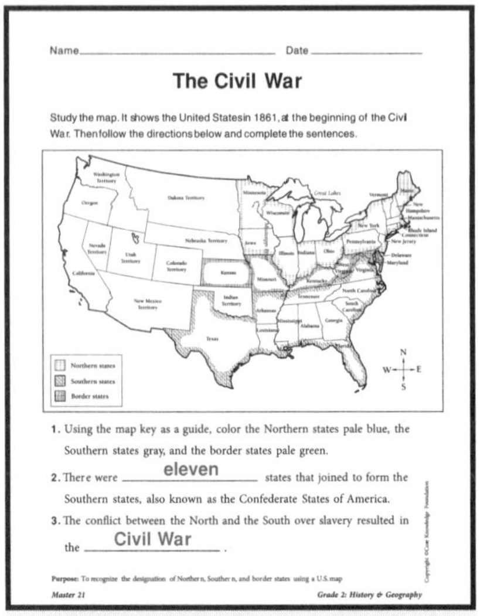
Name______ Date______

The Civil War

Study the map. It shows the United States in 1861, at the beginning of the Civil War. Then follow the directions below and complete the sentences.

1. Using the map key as a guide, color the Northern states pale blue, the Southern states gray, and the border states pale green.
2. There were eleven states that joined to form the Southern states, also known as the Confederate States of America.
3. The conflict between the North and the South over slavery resulted in the Civil War.

Purpose: To recognize the designation of Northern, Southern, and border states using a U.S. map

Master 21 — Grade 2: History & Geography

Copyright ©Core Knowledge Foundation

Use Instructional Master 21.

Northern Versus Southern States

The issue of slavery divided the country in the election of 1860. Abraham Lincoln, the candidate of the new Republican Party, which pledged to stop the spread of slavery, won against three opponents. The Democratic Party had split into Northern and Southern factions and supported two different candidates. A fourth party, the Constitutional Party, campaigned on a platform to uphold the Union and the Constitution.

South Carolina had threatened to secede if Lincoln was elected. In December 1860, South Carolina made good on its word and passed an ordinance of secession. By spring 1861, 11 states had joined to form the Confederate States of America. (The western part of Virginia refused to follow the rest of the state out of the Union and, in 1863, it joined the Union as the state of West Virginia.) The 11 states of the Confederacy in order of secession were the following: South Carolina, Mississippi, Florida, Alabama, Georgia, Louisiana, Texas, Virginia, Arkansas, Tennessee, and North Carolina. The Union included the states of the Northeast and Midwest and the western territories: Connecticut, Illinois, Indiana, Iowa, Kansas, Maine, Massachusetts, Minnesota, New Hampshire, New Jersey, New York, Ohio, Pennsylvania, Rhode Island, Vermont, and Wisconsin; the Indian Territory, and the Colorado, Dakota, Nebraska, New Mexico, Nevada, Utah, and Washington Territories.

Delaware, Kentucky, Maryland, Missouri, and West Virginia were known as border states. They remained loyal to the Union even though they were slave-holding states.

The Union had many advantages over the Confederacy, including an industrial economy, as opposed to the Confederacy's economic dependency on agriculture. The Union had most of the natural resources, such as coal, iron, and gold, and also had a well-developed rail system. Most of the financial centers were in the North, which made borrowing money to fight the war difficult for the South. The Union had a small navy, but the Confederacy had to resort to using private ships because it had no naval vessels. While the South had better officers, the North had twice as many soldiers.

Northern soldiers wore blue uniforms and were called "Yankees," or "Yanks." Confederate soldiers wore grey uniforms and were known to Northerners as

"Rebels." Yankees and Rebels clashed at great battles like Antietam (1862), Gettysburg (1863), and Chancellorsville (1863). More than 600,000 Americans died in the war. The number killed equaled our total dead from all other American wars, until the final toll from the Vietnam War raised the cumulative body count above the Civil War losses.

Grant **Lee**

Ulysses S. Grant and Robert E. Lee

Although the Union had the advantage because of the size of its army, its generals were far less capable than those of the Confederacy. At first, the war went badly for the Union armies, both on the western front along the Mississippi, and in the East. The first victories for the Union came in 1862 under General Ulysses S. Grant. His subsequent victories in Tennessee gave the Union control of the Mississippi River, split the Confederacy, and effectively ended the war in the west. Union control of the Mississippi River cut off the flow of much-needed supplies and reinforcements from Texas and Arkansas to the rest of the Confederacy.

In 1864, Lincoln consolidated command of all the Union armies under Grant. Grant moved to the eastern front and soon began to wear Lee down. By 1865, Grant had defeated the Confederate Army of Northern Virginia under Robert E. Lee. Lee surrendered to Grant at Appomattox Court House on April 9, 1865. Grant went on to become the 18th president of the United States in 1869.

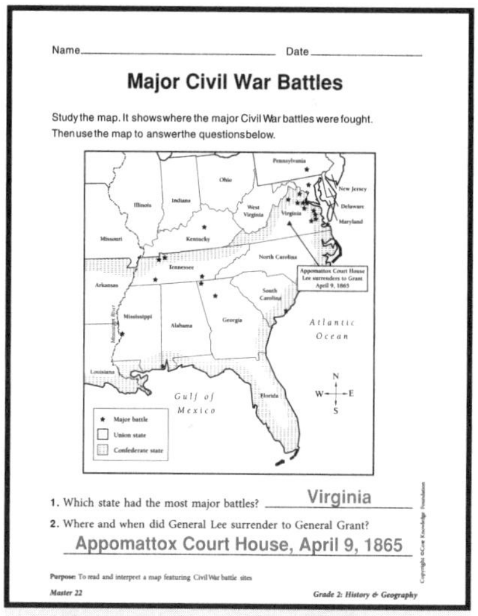

Name________________ Date________________

Major Civil War Battles

Study the map. It shows where the major Civil War battles were fought. Then use the map to answer the questions below.

1. Which state had the most major battles? Virginia

2. Where and when did General Lee surrender to General Grant? Appomattox Court House, April 9, 1865

Purpose: To read and interpret a map featuring Civil War battle sites

Master 22 *Grade 2: History & Geography*

Copyright ©Core Knowledge Foundation

Use Instructional Master 22.

Grant and Lee are frequently compared and contrasted. Grant was born on a small Ohio farm, whereas Robert E. Lee was born on a large plantation in northern Virginia. Grant was a mediocre student at the U.S. Military Academy at West Point and had an undistinguished military career as well as several other failed careers before the Civil War. Lee also graduated from West Point but had a highly successful military career. He served with distinction in the Mexican War and was superintendent of West Point for a period in the 1850s.

When the Civil War broke out, Lincoln asked Lee to assume command of the Union forces, but Lee refused out of loyalty to Virginia. He instead accepted a command in the Confederate army, even though he was against slavery. Lee scored a number of important victories in the early months of the war, but, faced with dwindling resources, his army was unable to withstand the larger, better-equipped Union army.

Clara Barton and the American Red Cross

At the beginning of the Civil War, Clara Barton was working in Washington, D.C., for the federal government. At the First Battle of Bull Run in 1861, she organized efforts to get medicine and supplies to the wounded. Ordinarily, female nurses were not allowed on battlefields. Concerned that wounded soldiers were not getting the treatment that they needed quickly enough, which resulted in an abundance of unnecessary deaths, Barton asked that female nurses be allowed to attend to the wounded on the battlefield. Ultimately, her request was granted and she worked with the Union army in Virginia. She was present at the horrific battle of Antietam in Pennsylvania, the most deadly one-day battle of the Civil War. Barton tended to the wounded as bullets flew around her. A male surgeon present at the battle compared Clara Barton favorably to then Union Commander-in-Chief, George McClellan: "In my feeble estimation, General McClellan, with all his

Teaching Idea

Point out that the American Red Cross is still active today. Use clippings you can find in newspapers and magazines or information from the American Red Cross's website to suggest some things that the Red Cross has done recently.

Compare Clara Barton to the abolitionists who worked to make a difference and to make life better for others.

laurels, sinks into insignificance beside the true heroine of the age, the angel of the battlefield." Barton was appointed superintendent of Union nurses in 1864. She was widely admired for her service in gathering and distributing medical supplies and nursing the wounded.

After the war, Barton traveled to Europe to rest and became involved with the International Red Cross, which had been founded to help victims of the Franco-Prussian War. Barton brought the idea back to the United States and lobbied Congress to establish a branch in the United States. In 1881, the American Red Cross was founded, and Barton was named its first president, a post she held until 1904. She was very influential in the International Red Cross, and it was through her efforts that the Red Cross broadened its scope to include relief work during natural disasters and national emergencies.

Lincoln

Abraham Lincoln

Abraham Lincoln was born in poverty on the frontier in Kentucky. As a child, Lincoln moved with his family to Indiana, where they lived in a log cabin that his father had built. There was no mandatory public education at the time, and children were expected to work in the family business, whether it was a farm or a store. However, as a boy Lincoln taught himself to read and write by firelight at the end of his long workdays on the farm. While plowing the fields, Lincoln kept a book in his back pocket to read during breaks. One of his favorite books was Parson Weems's biography of George Washington. The Bible and Shakespeare's plays were two more favorites.

As a young boy, Lincoln worked various jobs and educated himself by reading widely. At age 22, he moved to New Salem, Illinois. There, he taught himself the law while supporting himself by working in a store, as a surveyor, and as postmaster. In time, Lincoln became a much-respected attorney in the state.

Lincoln was first elected to public office in 1834 when his district sent him to the state legislature. He served there until 1841. Lincoln ran successfully for the U.S. House of Representatives in 1846, but was turned out of office in the next election because of his opposition to the Mexican War. He gained national attention in 1858, when he ran for the Senate and held a series of debates with Stephen A. Douglas. With no competition from modern forms of entertainment, and without electronic media to report what was said, tens of thousands of Illinois residents listened to the two men argue about slavery, race, the Union, and the principles of American democracy, from one end of the state to the other. Lincoln lost the election, but the debates made him famous.

In 1860, Lincoln ran for president of the United States on the platform of the new Republican Party, which pledged to stop the spread of slavery into any new states admitted to the Union. Neither the party nor Lincoln himself promised to abolish slavery.

When the Southern states seceded in 1861, Lincoln declared their act unconstitutional. He threatened to use force if necessary to protect U.S. property, enforce U.S. laws, and return the Southern states to the Union. Preservation of the Union continued to be his public stance until he issued the Emancipation Proclamation in September 1862. (Children should have some familiarity with Abraham Lincoln, since he is discussed in detail in Kindergarten, Section IV, "Presidents, Past and Present.")

Teaching Idea

Have children do simple biographical research and give oral reports on various figures of the Civil War, such as Abraham Lincoln, Clara Barton, Harriet Tubman, Robert E. Lee, Ulysses S. Grant, etc. Children may also dress up as their subject. As an extension, consider creating a "wax museum" event at your school. Older children can dress up as their research subjects and act as "wax figures" by standing still in front of signs that say "play." Younger children touring the museum can press "play" to hear the older children give a short talk, speaking as the subject. This extension is a good way to match up second graders with fifth graders who are also learning about the Civil War.

The Emancipation Proclamation

The Emancipation Proclamation was a step that Lincoln took reluctantly because he feared it would harm the Union. Emancipating, or freeing, the slaves was opposed by many Northern workers who feared competition from newly freed—and jobless—slaves. Lincoln was also concerned that the border states would leave the Union if their slave owners were deprived of their slaves. On the plus side, however, Lincoln believed that an Emancipation Proclamation would win over Europeans who had already abolished slavery, especially the British. It was important to the North that the British not trade with the South. By selling cotton to British textile mills, the South gained access to credit and supplies.

Abolitionists had lobbied for the end of slavery since the early 1800s and, as the war continued, more Northerners began to see the need for emancipation. In addition to humanitarian concerns, they were moved either by a desire to punish the South for secession or by the idea that once guaranteed their freedom, slaves would rise up in revolt and the war would end more quickly.

Finally, in September 1862, Lincoln issued the Emancipation Proclamation, which was to go into effect on January 1, 1863. There is often confusion about what the Emancipation Proclamation actually did. The document did not free all slaves. It promised to free all slaves in those states or parts of states still under the control of the Confederacy on January 1, 1863. Since the Union had no force of law in the Confederacy, there was no practical effect on the lives of slaves in those states. The document did not affect slaves in border states or in states or areas of states under the control of the Union army. They were still enslaved. Therefore, the Emancipation Proclamation actually set no one free.

The importance of the Emancipation Proclamation was symbolic. It broadened the purpose of the Civil War from merely preserving the Union to preserving the Union and freeing the slaves.

Enslaved African Americans were finally freed through passage and ratification of the Thirteenth Amendment in 1865.

Teaching Idea

After a discussion about the intent of the Emancipation Proclamation—to free slaves—focus the discussion on how Abraham Lincoln wanted to change something, to correct an injustice. Ask children what they would like to see changed or abolished—in school, in the local community, in the country, or in the world. Have each child write his/her idea in sentence form on a sheet of paper and put a border around it to look like an official document. Hang the "documents" around the room.

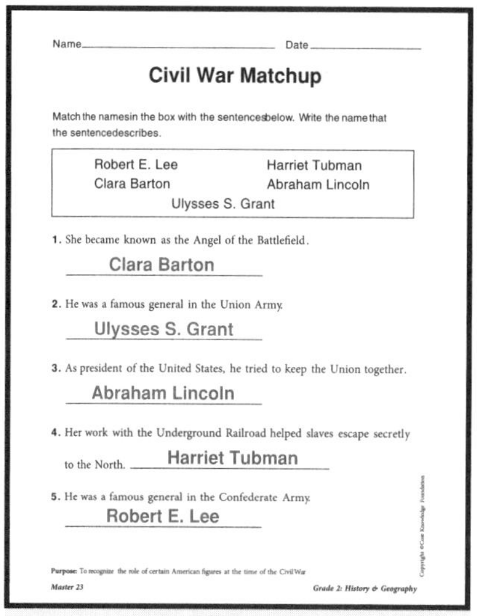
Name________ Date________

Civil War Matchup

Match the namesin the box with the sentencesbelow. Write the name that the sentencedescribes.

Robert E. Lee	Harriet Tubman
Clara Barton	Abraham Lincoln
Ulysses S. Grant	

1. She became known as the Angel of the Battlefield.
Clara Barton

2. He was a famous general in the Union Army.
Ulysses S. Grant

3. As president of the United States, he tried to keep the Union together.
Abraham Lincoln

4. Her work with the Underground Railroad helped slaves escape secretly to the North. Harriet Tubman

5. He was a famous general in the Confederate Army.
Robert E. Lee

Purpose: To recognize the role of certain American figures at the time of the Civil War

Master 23 — Grade 2: History & Geography

Copyright ©Core Knowledge Foundation

Use Instructional Master 23.

Review

Below are some ideas for ongoing assessment and review activities. These are not meant to constitute a comprehensive list. Teachers may also refer to the *Pearson Learning/Core Knowledge History & Geography* series for additional information and teaching ideas.

- Sing the songs "Follow the Drinking Gourd" and "Swing Low, Sweet Chariot" with the class. Provide a piece of chart paper with the lyrics written for the class to sing. Ask the class if they can identify the words that the slaves would listen for in their quest for freedom. Have children write a song that could be sung to alert the slaves how to escape. Remind children to use symbols in their songs so that the plantation owners do not get suspicious when they hear the songs. You may challenge children to actually sing their songs to the class.
- Have children write about Abraham Lincoln and how he must have experienced his job as president. You may compare Lincoln to James Madison from your earlier

The Big Idea in Review

The controversy between the North and the South over slavery resulted in the Civil War.

study of the War of 1812. How were their jobs alike and different? What kinds of problems did they face?

- Team up with a fifth-grade class to write an ABC book of the Civil War. Have each second grader pair up with a fifth grader to create a page for each letter. On the pages, have children write about famous people and places of the Civil War. Assign each pair with a word that you want reviewed from the section.
- You may also ask the following questions at the end of this section:

1. Why was slavery a problem between the Northern states and the Southern states?
   Slavery was a problem because Northern states no longer had any slaves and many people thought that slavery was wrong. Wealthy Southern plantation owners depended on slavery to farm their crops and did not want to free their slaves.
2. What was the Underground Railroad?
   The Underground Railroad was not really a railroad, but a network of people in different places who helped slaves escape to freedom in the North or in Canada. These people were called conductors and hid slaves, gave them food to eat, and helped them get to the next station/house on the railroad.
3. What did the Southern states do when Abraham Lincoln was elected?
   The Southern states seceded/left the Union and started the Confederate States of America.
4. Which side was called "Rebels"? Which side was called "Yankees"?
   The Southerners were called Rebels, and the Northerners were called Yankees.
5. Which side ultimately won the war?
   The North won.
6. Who was the most famous Confederate general?
   Robert E. Lee was the most famous Confederate general.
7. Who took command of the Union army and ultimately defeated the Confederate forces?
   Ulysses S. Grant took command of the Union army and defeated Lee's army.
8. Why was Clara Barton called the "Angel of the Battlefield"?
   Clara Barton was called the "Angel of the Battlefield" because she took care of wounded soldiers on the battlefield. Up until then, women were not allowed on a battlefield.
9. What was President Abraham Lincoln's goal when the Civil War began?
   Abraham Lincoln wanted to keep the Union together. He wanted to bring the Confederate states back into the Union.
10. How did the Emancipation Proclamation change Lincoln's goals?
    The Emancipation Proclamation said that slaves should be free. Freeing/emancipating slaves became an additional reason for fighting the war.

More Resources

The titles listed below are offered as a representative sample of materials and not a complete list of everything that is available.

For children —

These books are generally intended to be read aloud, though some children may be able to read parts or all of the simpler texts.

- *The Civil War,* edited by E. D. Hirsch, Jr. (Pearson Learning, 2002). A unit in the official *Pearson Learning/Core Knowledge History & Geography* series. It includes a small picture book for children and a teacher's guide with read alouds. To order, call 1-800-321-3106.

- *50 American Heroes Every Kid Should Meet,* by Dennis Denenberg and Lorraine Roscoe (The Millbrook Press, 2002). Contains profiles of Robert E. Lee, Abraham Lincoln, and Harriet Tubman. Paperback, 128 pages, ISBN 0761316450.

- *The Blue and the Gray,* by Eve Bunting (Scholastic, 2001). Paperback, 32 pages, ISBN 0590602004.

- *Clara Barton,* by Kathleen W. Deady (Bridgestone, 2003). Hardcover, 24 pages, ISBN 0736816046.

- *Escape North: The Story of Harriet Tubman (Step into Reading, Step 3),* by Monica Kulling (Random House, 2000). Paperback, 48 pages, ISBN 0375801545.

- *Follow the Drinking Gourd,* by Jeanette Winter (Knopf, 1992). The story of the Underground Railroad, along which slaves were able to reach freedom by following the Big Dipper, known as the "Drinking Gourd." Includes words and music. Paperback, 48 pages, ISBN 0679819975. See also *The Big Dipper (Let's-Read-and-Find-Out Science, Stage 1),* by Franklyn M. Branley (HarperCollins, 1991). Paperback, 32 pages, ISBN 0064451003.

- *Food and Recipes of the Civil War,* by George Erdosh (PowerKids Press, 2001). Library binding, 24 pages, ISBN 082395112X.

- *Harriet and the Promised Land,* by Jacob Lawrence (Aladdin Library, 1997). A simply told story in pictures and poetry. Paperback, 40 pages, ISBN 0689809654.

- *Just a Few Words, Mr. Lincoln: The Story of the Gettysburg Address,* by Jean Fritz and illustrated by Charles Robison (Grosset & Dunlap, 1993). Includes full text of the speech. Paperback, 48 pages, ISBN 0448401703.

- *Nettie's Trip South,* by Ann Turner and illustrated by Ronald Himler (Aladdin Library, 1995). Young Nettie takes a trip from Albany to Richmond and gets her first glimpse of slavery. Paperback, 32 pages, ISBN 0689801173.

- *A Picture Book of Abraham Lincoln,* by David Adler (Holiday House, 1990). Paperback, 26 pages, ISBN 0823408019. See also Adler's other *Picture Book* biographies on Harriet Tubman, Harriet Beecher Stowe, Frederick Douglass, and Robert E. Lee.

For teachers —

- *American Voices from the Civil War,* by Susan Provost Beller (Benchmark Books, 2003). Uses primary source material. Hardcover, 104 pages, ISBN 0761412042.

- *The Civil War,* by Bruce Catton (Houghton Mifflin, 1988). Paperback, 382 pages, ISBN 0828103054.

- *Growing Up in the Civil War (Our America),* by Duane Damon (Lerner, 2003). Library binding, 64 pages, ISBN 0822506564.

- *Harriet Tubman: The Road to Freedom,* by Catherine Clinton (Little, Brown and Company, 2004). Hardcover, 272 pages, ISBN 0316144924. See also *Harriet Tubman: The Life and the Life Stories,* by Jean McMahon Humez (University of Wisconsin Press, 2004). Hardcover, 464 pages, ISBN 0299191206.

- *Lee,* by Douglas Southall Freeman (Scribner, 1997). An abridgment of the four-volume Pulitzer Prize–winning biography. Paperback, 656 pages, ISBN 0684829533.

- *Lincoln,* by David Herbert Donald (Simon & Schuster, Inc., 1996). Paperback, 720 pages, ISBN 068482535X.

- *The National Museum of Civil War Medicine,* www.civilwarmed.org. Wartime medicine during the mid-19th century was tough for those practicing as well as for those being "practiced upon."

- *The Valley of the Shadow: Two Communities in the American Civil War,* www.iath.virginia.edu/vshadow2. Filled with primary source documentation comparing two counties—Augusta County in Virginia, and Franklin County in Pennsylvania—before, during, and after the Civil War.

- *War, Terrible War: 1855–1865,* by Joy Hakim (Oxford University Press, 2002). Book 6 in the highly acclaimed series *A History of Us.* Paperback, 160 pages, ISBN 0195153308. See also *Reconstructing America: 1865–1890,* book 7 in the series (ISBN 0195153324).

V. Immigration and Citizenship

Remember that each subject you study with children expands their vocabulary and introduces new terms, thus making them better listeners and readers. As you study historical people and events, use read alouds and discussions to build children's vocabularies.

The items in bold relate to the content in Grade 2. In discussing the immigration of the late 19th century, refer to it as having occurred after the Civil War.

1776	2 million people in the 13 British colonies
1782	***E pluribus unum* adopted as national motto**
1790–1815	Immigration of 250,000 Europeans
1820–1860	4.6 million European immigrants
1861–1865	Civil War
1868	**Ratification of the Fourteenth Amendment defining U.S. citizenship**
1870	**Ratification of the Fifteenth Amendment, giving African-American men the right to vote**
1880–1920	**Peak of immigration with 23 million new arrivals**
1892–1954	**Ellis Island as port of entry for European immigrants**
1910–1940	**Angel Island as port of entry for immigrants to the West Coast**
1920	**Ratification of the Nineteenth Amendment, giving women the right to vote**

The Big Idea

The United States is a country of immigrants who came to its shores for a variety of reasons.

What Students Should Already Know

Students in Core Knowledge schools should be familiar with

Kindergarten

- the Statue of Liberty

What Students Need to Learn

- **America was perceived as a "land of opportunity."**
- **The meaning of *e pluribus unum* (a national motto you can see on the back of coins)**
- **Ellis Island and the significance of the Statue of Liberty**
- **Millions of newcomers to America**
- **Large populations of immigrants settle in major cities (such as New York, Chicago, Philadelphia, Detroit, Cleveland, Boston, and San Francisco).**
- **The idea of citizenship**
  - **What it means to be a citizen of a country**
  - **American citizens have certain rights and responsibilities (for example, voting, eligibility to hold public office, and paying taxes).**
  - **Becoming an American citizen (by birth, naturalization)**

What Students Will Learn in Future Grades

In future grades, students will review and extend their learning about immigration and citizenship.

Grade 3

- how all colonists were immigrants

Grade 4

- the Great Seal of the United States

Grade 6

- Immigration
  - Waves of new immigrants from about 1830 onward
    - Great migrations from Ireland (potato famine) and Germany
    - From about 1880 on, many immigrants arrive from southern and eastern Europe.
    - Immigrants from Asian countries, especially China
    - Large populations of immigrants settle in major cities.
- The tension between ideals and realities
  - The metaphor of America as a "melting pot"
  - America perceived as a "land of opportunity" versus resistance, discrimination, and "nativism"
  - Resistance to Catholics and Jews and the Chinese Exclusion Act

Vocabulary

Student/Teacher Vocabulary

Angel Island: an immigrant processing center on the West Coast (S)

citizen: a member of a state or country (S)

***e pluribus unum*:** the national motto of the United States, it means "out of many, one" (S)

Ellis Island: an immigrant processing center on the East Coast (S)

ethnic group: a group of people of the same culture (T)

immigrant: someone who has left his or her home country to settle elsewhere (S)

naturalize: to be granted citizenship in a foreign country (S)

newcomers: people who are new to a place or an organization (S)

opportunity: a chance, a possibility (S)

pull factors: the conditions in the United States that attract people to settle there (T)

push factors: the factors that drive people to leave their native country (T)

rights and responsibilities: the privileges and obligations that a government expects its citizens to understand and abide by (S)

Domain Vocabulary

Immigration and associated words:
land of immigrants, land of opportunity, better one's self, emigrant, emigrate, immigrate, waves, old immigrants, new immigrants, reasons to leave, reasons to come, economic problems, famine, drought, political persecution, oppression, religious persecution, *plus names of immigrants' former countries, e.g.,* Ireland, Irish, Germany, German, *etc.*

E pluribus unum *and associated words:*
one from many, one nation, motto, saying, slogan, Great Seal of the United States

Ellis Island and associated words:
New York Harbor, Europe, Statue of Liberty, immigration center, processed, evaluated, allowed in, deported, forced to leave, San Francisco Bay, Asia

Newcomers and associated words:
immigrant centers, cities, urban areas, factory jobs, construction jobs, shops, businesses, hire, employ, labor for, work for, Europeans, East Coast, Midwest, Asians, Chinese, Japanese, West Coast, Boston, New York, Philadelphia, Chicago, Detroit, Cleveland, San Francisco, neighborhoods, group, cluster, support, help, aid, assist, Little Italy, Chinatown

Citizenship and associated words:
state, province, nation, country, loyalty, native-born, naturalization, resident, Immigration and Naturalization Service, duties, balance, Bill of Rights, U.S. Constitution, vote, taxes, obey laws, law-abiding, respect, serve on a jury, juror, analyze, judge, evaluate, decide, guilt, innocence, free, convict, oath

Cross-curricular Connections

Music

Songs

- "This Land Is Your Land"
- "The Star-Spangled Banner"

Text Resources

(62) *Quotes from Immigrants Who Came Through Ellis Island*

Materials

Instructional Masters 24, 50

K-W-L Chart, p. 204

Freedom Fill-In, p. 206

world map or globe, p. 203

map of United States, p. 203

dollar bill, coins, p. 204

white construction paper, p. 204

magazines with pictures that show various facets of life in the United States today, p. 204

scissors, p. 204

crayons and markers, p. 204

paste, p. 204

children's journals, p. 205

a suitcase or bag, p. 206

chart paper, p. 207

V. Immigration and Citizenship

At a Glance

The most important ideas for you are:

- From the first colonists of what would be the United States to the most recent immigrant, this land has represented opportunity.
- The motto *e pluribus unum* is very appropriate for a country crafted by immigrants.
- Seeing the Statue of Liberty and landing at Ellis Island were the first experiences in the United States for several generations of immigrants, from the late 1880s to the 1950s.
- Because of the opportunities for work and support that cities offered immigrants, many cities developed large ethnic neighborhoods.
- Citizenship involves the exercise of responsibilities as well as the enjoyment of rights.
- There are two ways to become an American citizen: by birth or by naturalization.

What Teachers Need to Know

Background

In Grade 2, introduce children to the concept of immigration by using stories, biographies, and autobiographies of immigrants as a basis for discussing why people have come and continue to come to the United States, what hardships and opportunities immigrants have found or find, and what it must be like to be a newcomer to the United States. It is possible that some children in your class or their parents may be immigrants. Some of these parents may be willing to come to class to talk about their original culture, why they came to the United States, and the experience of being an immigrant.

America: The Land of Opportunity

From the first Spanish colonists who founded St. Augustine, Florida, in 1565, to the latest immigrants to arrive at John F. Kennedy Airport in New York City, America has been a land of immigrants. The first permanent English settlement was established at Jamestown, Virginia, in 1607. By the time of the American Revolution, the eastern seaboard from Maine to Georgia had a population of 2 million—many of them immigrants from England, Ireland, and Germany.

Between 1790 and 1815, another 250,000 Europeans immigrated to the United States, and between 1820 and 1860, some 4.6 million more arrived, most of them after 1840 and many of them from Ireland. The first half of the 19th century saw 2 million Irish emigrate, pushed out of Ireland by the potato famine and oppressive British rule. These newcomers joined earlier immigrants, such as the English, Irish, and Germans, as well as the Dutch, French, and Swedish, in building the United States. Until the African slave trade was suppressed in 1807, tens of thousands of Africans entered the country in chains.

The greatest period of immigration to America occurred between 1880 and 1920, when approximately 23 million immigrants arrived. Immigration records were not kept well during that time, and it is impossible to know the exact number of immigrants who entered the country. By 1914 and the onset of World War I in Europe, one-third of all Americans were either an immigrant themselves or had at least one parent who was an immigrant. However, the latest immigrants came from different parts of Europe than the earlier immigrants. The "old immigrants," as historians call those who moved to the colonies or emigrated in the early days of the United States (roughly before the Civil War), originated mainly in northern and western Europe. They came from countries like England, Scotland, Ireland, and Germany. The new immigrants who came after the Civil War were primarily from southern and eastern Europe, including Russia, Italy, Poland, and Austria-Hungary. Between 1890 and 1917, about 75% of immigrants to the United States came from these countries. A very small number of immigrants were allowed into the United States from Asia at this time because of racial prejudice against Asians on the part of native-born Americans.

Teaching Idea

Use a world map to review where American immigrants came from. Use a map of the United States to point out cities where many immigrants settled.

Why did (and do) immigrants come to the United States? Historians have isolated a number of what they term "push and pull factors" at work in immigration. The push factors drive people to leave their native countries. The exact factors depend on the immigrants' country of origin. The pull factors are conditions in the United States that attract people to settle here, such as economic opportunity, political freedom, and religious freedom.

In the period after the Civil War, economic problems, political oppression, and religious persecution caused people to emigrate. In Austria-Hungary, Bulgaria, Romania, and Poland, large landholdings were broken up and leased to tenant farmers, many of whom found it nearly impossible to earn a living by farming such small parcels of land. In Italy, farmers were faced with declining prices for their fruit and wine. In the wars of the 19th century, Poland had been carved up by victors and no longer existed. Poles, especially Polish Catholics, were persecuted as the new rulers tried to eradicate all traces of Polish customs and traditions. Russian Jews were also persecuted on account of their religion.

To all these people, the United States offered a place of refuge, the promise of religious freedom and political freedom, and an opportunity for a better life. Earlier immigrants wrote home, urging their families and friends to come to America. One immigrant wrote home the following:

> I am getting along well, very well. I have worked in a factory and I am now working in a hotel. I receive 18 (in our money 32) dollars a month, and that is very good. . . . We eat here every day what we get only for Easter in our country.

Midwestern states and steamship companies published pamphlets extolling the possibilities of life in the United States. Minnesota published the following advertisement:

> To Laboring Men, who earn a livelihood by honest toil; to Landless Men, who aspire to the dignity and independence which comes from possession in God's free earth; to All Men of moderate means, and men of wealth. . . . It is well to exchange the tyrannies and thankless toil of the old world for the freedom and independence of the new.

The letters and advertisements turned out to be far from truthful for most immigrants. Those who settled in cities had a hard time making a living in the factories and sweatshops. Farm families found life on the plains far from the nearest neighbor lonely and at times dangerous when blizzards, floods, illness, or serious accidents struck. Still, to many of these immigrants, their new life seemed better than life back home, trying to scratch out a living on a poor, postage-stamp plot of land or living in fear because of their politics or religion.

E Pluribus Unum

The motto *e pluribus unum* is Latin for "out of many, one". The word *plural* comes from the same root as *pluribus.* The phrase appears on the front of the Great Seal of the United States, which was adopted in 1782. The phrase also appears on the reverse of the dollar bill and on coins.

E pluribus unum is a good motto for a country crafted by immigrants. Each year, several hundred thousand new immigrants come to the United States looking for opportunities and a better life. As these immigrants assimilate and become American, they become part of one nation.

Ellis Island and the Statue of Liberty

After 1886, one of the first things that immigrants would have seen as their ships sailed into New York Harbor was the Statue of Liberty. Its torch held high was a beacon of hope for those millions of new arrivals. The Jewish-American poet Emma Lazarus wrote a famous poem called "The New Colossus" about the Statue of Liberty, in which she imagines Lady Liberty speaking to the nations of Europe and asking them to send immigrants:

Give me your tired, your poor,
Your huddled masses yearning to breathe free,
The wretched refuse of your teeming shore;
Send these, the homeless, tempest-tost to me,
I lift my lamp beside the golden door!

The whole poem is now inscribed at the base of the statue. For more information on the Statue of Liberty, see the section on Symbols and Figures (pp. 238–239). Beginning in 1892, immigrants to the East Coast came through Ellis Island in New York Harbor. Ships docked there and passengers were processed in a great hall on the island before being allowed to enter the United States. The new arrivals were first examined by doctors and then questioned by immigration officials about how they planned to earn their living. Their names were recorded and sometimes simplified, e.g., the last name "Kantorowitz" might be shortened and recorded as "Cantor." Most immigrants were allowed to enter the United States, but about 1% of those examined and interviewed were turned back, mainly because they had a contagious disease or improper papers. As many as 20 million people may have entered the United States through Ellis Island between 1892 and its closing in 1954. Nearly 40% of Americans have at least one ancestor who was processed there. (62)

On the West Coast, Angel Island served the same purpose as Ellis Island, only here the immigrants were Asians, mainly Chinese and Japanese, rather than Europeans. The center operated from 1910 to 1940.

Teaching Idea

Show children a dollar bill and coins that show the expression *e pluribus unum.*

Teaching Idea

Have children work in pairs to create advertisements to promote immigration now and/or in the historical context being taught. Have them begin their ads with the line "Look What the U.S. Has for You." Have magazines, scissors, crayons, markers, and paste available.

Teaching Idea

Use Instructional Master 50, *K-W-L Chart,* to check for prior knowledge about the Statue of Liberty. The topic also appears in Section VIII on p. 236.

Children may also be familiar with Ellis Island if their grandparents or great-grandparents entered the country through this portal. Encourage them to ask their parents or caretakers about their family background: do they know how or when their family came to this country?

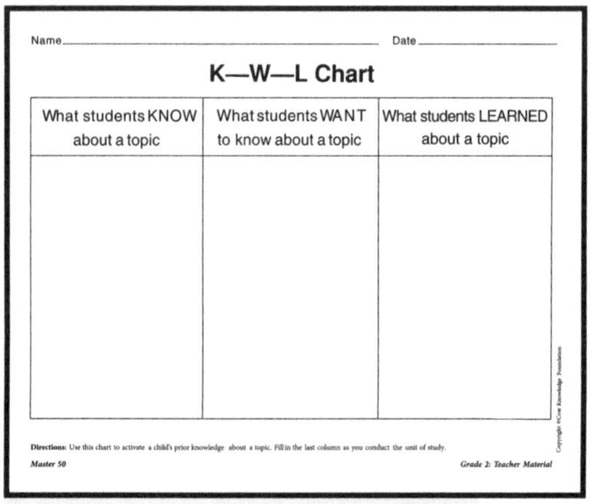
Name________________ Date________

K—W—L Chart

What students KNOW about a topic	What students WANT to know about a topic	What students LEARNED about a topic

Directions: Use this chart to activate a child's prior knowledge about a topic. Fill in the last column as you conduct the unit of study.

Master 50 *Grade 2: Teacher Material*

Copyright ©Core Knowledge Foundation

Use Instructional Master 50.

Newcomers to U.S. Cities

Cities in late 19th-century America were busy centers of commerce and offered many jobs in factories and growing businesses. While many immigrants who were farmers in Europe and Asia sought out farmland to settle on, many more immigrants settled in cities, especially Irish and Italians who had had little luck with farming in their native countries. Some Europeans went no farther than the cities of the East Coast, while others moved to the Midwest.

The small number of Japanese and Chinese immigrants who came to America settled mainly on the West Coast. Many became farmers and farmworkers, although San Francisco had a large number of both Japanese and Chinese residents.

In cities like Boston, New York, Philadelphia, Chicago, Detroit, Cleveland, and San Francisco, neighborhoods of immigrants from the same countries—even the same villages—developed, with names like Little Italy and Chinatown. Ethnic groups tended to concentrate in neighborhoods for support. Immigrants who had been in the United States for a while, even a few months, could help newcomers learn to navigate the ways of their new home: where to live, where to get a job, how to act toward the boss, where to buy food, how to speak English—all the things of daily life that were foreign to newcomers.

Hostility to Immigrants

Although many immigrants saw America as a land of opportunity, and a place to escape from prejudice, not all Americans welcomed immigrants. In many places, native-born Americans looked down on immigrants. In Boston, for example, many old immigrants looked down on the Irish. Some politicians called for laws restricting immigration. Unions representing skilled craftworkers were worried that immigrants would do the same work for a lower wage; they wanted to keep wages up by keeping immigrants out, or by minimizing their numbers. Various strands of pseudoscientific racism were also widely accepted. Advocates of these theories argued that the "new immigrants" were inferior to the old northern Europeans and would "degrade" American society. Even people characterized as reformers and "progressives" often favored restrictive legislation, arguing that America could not assimilate so many people so quickly.

The Idea of Citizenship

To be a citizen means to be a member of a state or country who owes loyalty to that country and has certain rights and responsibilities under that government. According to the Fourteenth Amendment to the U.S. Constitution, a person is a citizen of the United States because she or he was born in the United States or became a naturalized citizen. A person who is born outside the country may also be a U.S. citizen if at least one parent is a U.S. citizen and has lived in the United States for a period of time. In recent years, some 250,000 people annually have become naturalized citizens.

To be considered for citizenship, a person must

1. be eighteen years of age or older.
2. have lived in the United States continuously for at least five years from the time of admission for permanent residency.
3. be of good moral character.

Teaching Idea

Have children interview parents or caregivers on their own ancestry and discuss their findings in class. Although teachers must be careful about assigning this to children who are adopted, those children can still learn about the ancestry of their adoptive parents. As an extension activity, have children choose one country of origin and do a simple report on that country.

Teaching Idea

Talk with children about what it must have been like to move to another country and to know that you would never go back to your home country again. This is very different from many immigrant families today who regularly go back "home."

Have children imagine what it must have been like to be a newcomer in a place where the language was new, the way they earned their living was new (for example, a farmer turned factory worker), the kind of place they lived in was strange (an apartment building rather than in a house), and so on. Have children write a journal entry describing this newness.

Teaching Idea

In addition to talking about immigration as a general phenomenon, try to look at some specific examples. If parents, caretakers, or other people in your community are immigrants or naturalized citizens, invite some of them to visit your class and talk about their experiences in moving to America and/or becoming a citizen. If not, search for "immigrant stories" on the web. Many are available online through museums and other organizations.

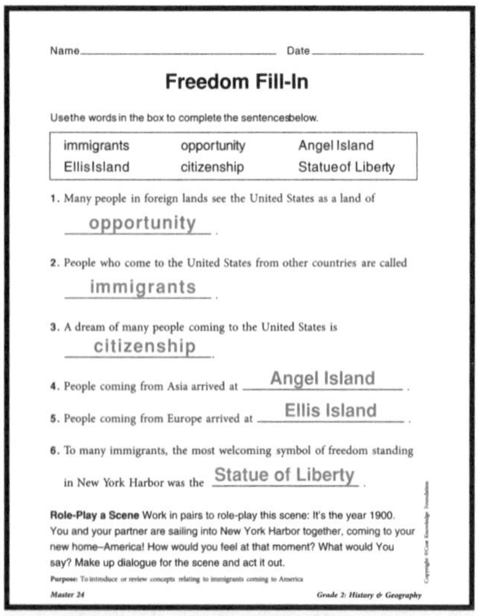

Name__________ Date__________

Freedom Fill-In

Usethe words in the box to complete the sentencesbelow.

immigrants	opportunity	Angel Island
EllisIsland	citizenship	Statueof Liberty

1. Many people in foreign lands see the United States as a land of opportunity.
2. People who come to the United States from other countries are called immigrants.
3. A dream of many people coming to the United States is citizenship.
4. People coming from Asia arrived at Angel Island.
5. People coming from Europe arrived at Ellis Island.
6. To many immigrants, the most welcoming symbol of freedom standing in New York Harbor was the Statue of Liberty.

Role-Play a Scene Work in pairs to role-play this scene: It's the year 1900. You and your partner are sailing into New York Harbor together, coming to your new home–America! How would you feel at that moment? What would You say? Make up dialogue for the scene and act it out.

Purpose: To introduce or review concepts relating to immigrants coming to America

Master 24 *Grade 2: History & Geography*

Use Instructional Master 24.

The Big Idea in Review

The United States is a country of immigrants who came to its shores for a variety of reasons.

4. demonstrate the ability to read, write, and speak the English language.
5. demonstrate a knowledge and an understanding of the fundamentals of U.S. history and the principles and form of government of the United States.

The last two items are demonstrated through an interview before an officer of the Immigration and Naturalization Service. Once the requirements have been met, the applicant is allowed to become a citizen. Naturalization ceremonies are held from time to time all around the country.

The role of citizen comes with certain rights and responsibilities. In the United States, the Bill of Rights (the first 10 amendments to the Constitution) guarantee the rights of citizens. Among them are freedom of religion, speech, press, assembly, and petition; protection against unlawful search and seizure; the right to due process in criminal proceedings; the right to a speedy and fair trial; and freedom from cruel and unusual punishment for crimes.

The Fifteenth Amendment passed after the Civil War guaranteed the right to vote to all male citizens regardless of "race, color, or previous condition of servitude." This amendment made it possible for African-American males to vote, although many places in Southern states ignored the amendment until the 1960s. Women were not allowed to vote until ratification of the Nineteenth Amendment in 1920.

The rights of citizens go hand in hand with responsibilities. Exercising one's right to vote entails the responsibility to learn about the candidates and issues in order to cast one's vote intelligently. Enjoying the benefits of living in the United States requires that people pay taxes to ensure the continuation of those benefits. Other responsibilities of citizenship include obeying the laws of the country and its individual states and serving on juries.

Review

Below are some ideas for ongoing assessment and review activities. These are not meant to constitute a comprehensive list. Teachers may also refer to the *Pearson Learning/Core Knowledge History & Geography* series for additional information and teaching ideas.

- Have children observe a map and discuss the various countries that immigrants have traveled from. Then, have children pick a country to travel from and select one of the big cities where immigrants have settled (New York, Chicago, Philadelphia, Detroit, Cleveland, Boston, and San Francisico). Have children write about why they chose to travel to that city and describe how their lives will be different. Have them explain why they decided to move their families. Then, read the writing aloud to the class.
- Have children design a simple role play on seeing the Statue of Liberty for the first time from a ship. You may even have them stand closely together as if on the deck of a ship, or sit very closely together. Before you have them role play, review some of the stories on immigration and how immigrants felt when arriving in this country. Role-play the scene of seeing the Statue of Liberty, and then have children talk about why they reacted a certain way.
- Provide children with a suitcase or a bag to be used as a prop. Have them think about what they would bring on a long trip to America, and remind them that they would not have a lot of space. What would they put in their bag to bring to America

from their country? Have them draw pictures of those items and write sentences describing what they would bring and why.

• Make connections between being a citizen of a country and being a student in the classroom. What privileges do the children enjoy? What kinds of rules and regulations do they have to follow? What kinds of rights and responsibilities do they have as students in the room? Then brainstorm as a class how their experience is like being a citizen of a country. What kinds of freedom do they enjoy in America? Record their responses on a class chart.

• Have children pair up and pretend that they are interviewing someone who has just arrived in America. Before the interviews, have each child write two or three questions to ask the newly arrived immigrant. You may have children ask questions about the trip and how the person felt when they arrived. Children can trade parts so they each have a chance to play both roles.

• Have an "immigration ceremony" in which each child memorizes a different sentence about where they're from and why they came to America: "I'm [name] from [country]. I came to America because [reason]." After reciting the statement, each child can join the others in an area that designates America.

• You may also ask the following questions at the end of this section:

1. Why was America the "land of opportunity" to immigrants?
   Immigrants were looking for a better land, and they thought the United States offered it. They wanted a place where they had a better chance to earn a living, would be free to practice their religion, and have other freedoms like the right to vote.

2. What does the national motto *e pluribus unum* mean?
   E pluribus unum *means "out of many, one." It means that the United States is made up of many different people from many different places and yet is one country.*

3. Why is Ellis Island important?
   Ellis Island is important because immigrants from Europe entered the United States through Ellis Island in New York Harbor for 62 years.

4. Why is Angel Island important?
   Angel Island is important because immigrants from Asia entered the United States through Angel Island for 30 years.

5. Why did many immigrants settle in cities?
   Immigrants settled in cities because that is where many jobs were and because their families and friends who had come before them had already settled there. These earlier immigrants helped newcomers find jobs and places to live and taught them how to live in the cities.

6. What does it mean to be a citizen of the United States?
   A citizen of the United States has certain rights or privileges, as well as certain responsibilities toward the United States.

7. How does a person become a citizen of the United States?
   A person is a citizen if he or she is born in the United States or becomes a citizen through naturalization.

8. What are some rights of U.S. citizens? Some responsibilities?
   Some rights are the right to vote, freedom of religion, and freedom of the press. Some responsibilities are paying taxes and serving on juries.

More Resources

The titles listed below are offered as a representative sample of materials and not a complete list of everything that is available.

For children —

These books are generally intended to be read aloud, though some children may be able to read parts or all of the simpler texts.

- *Immigration and Citizenship,* edited by E. D. Hirsch, Jr. (Pearson Learning, 2002). A unit in the official *Pearson Learning/Core Knowledge History & Geography* series. It includes a small picture book for children and a teacher's guide with read alouds. To order, call 1-800-321-3106.
- *A Very Important Day,* by Maggie Rugg Herold and illustrated by Catherine Stock (Morrow Junior Books, 1995). Characters are fictional, but the experience is based on important facts about what it means to become a citizen of the United States. Hardcover, 40 pages, ISBN 0688130658.
- *Coming to America: The Story of Immigration,* by Betsy Maestro and illustrated by Susannah Ryan (Scholastic, 1996). Very thorough overview. Children will need some further explanations as well as a world map to better understand this read aloud. Library binding, 40 pages, ISBN 0590441515.
- *Ellis Island: New Hope in a New Land,* by William Jay Jacobs (Atheneum, 1990). Library binding, 40 pages, ISBN 0684191717. See also *If Your Name Was Changed at Ellis Island,* by Ellen Levine (Scholastic, 1994). Paperback, ISBN 0590438298.
- *Molly's Pilgrim,* by Barbara Cohen (HarperTrophy, 1998). "[I]t takes all kinds of Pilgrims to make a Thanksgiving" (from the book). Based on the true story of a Russian immigrant. Paperback, 32 pages, ISBN 0688162800.
- *The Story of the Statue of Liberty,* by Betsy Maestro and illustrated by Giulio Maestro (HarperTrophy, 1989). The fascinating story of how the Statue of Liberty was designed, built in Paris, taken apart, and shipped to America to become one of our most important national symbols. Paperback, 48 pages, ISBN 0688087469.
- *Wagon Wheels,* by Barbara Brenner and illustrated by Don Bolognese (Scott Foresman, 1993). An African-American family who moves to Kansas in the 1870s faces a bitter winter, a prairie fire, and other hardships and adventures. Based on a true story. Paperback, 64 pages, ISBN 0064440524. Also published as a book and audiocassette package, ISBN 0694700010.

For teachers —

- *An Age of Extremes: 1880–1917,* by Joy Hakim (Oxford University Press, 2002). Book 8 in the highly acclaimed series *A History of Us.* Paperback, 160 pages, ISBN 0195153340. See also *War, Peace, and all that Jazz: 1918–1945,* book 9 in the same series.
- *American Mosaic: The Immigrant Experience in the Words of Those Who Lived It,* edited by Joan Morrison and Charlotte Fox Zabusky (University of Pittsburgh Press, 1993). Paperback, ISBN 0822954885.
- *Immigrant Kids,* by Russell Freedman (Scott Foresman, 1995). Focuses on immigrant children at home, school, work, and play in New York City during the late 1800s and early 1900s. Photographs and a child's perspective may make this a good read aloud. Paperback, 72 pages, ISBN 0140375945.
- *Immigrants,* by Martin W. Sandler (HarperTrophy, 2000). Paperback, 96 pages, ISBN 0064467449.
- *Immigration: From the Founding of Virginia to the Closing of Ellis Island,* by Dennis Wepman (Facts on File, 2002). Diary entries, letters, speeches, newspaper articles, official documents, maps, and more help tell the story of immigration in this volume of the *Eyewitness History* series. Hardcover, 430 pages, ISBN 0816039992.
- The Statue of Liberty–Ellis Island Foundation, Inc., www.ellisisland.org. Click on the link "Immigrant Experience" to read the stories of six American immigrant families searching for their relatives, and explore an interactive time line of immigration history.
- Statue of Liberty National Monument and Ellis Island (National Park Service), www.nps.gov/stli/serv02.htm. Contains a history, children's activities, museum exhibits, and more.

VI. Civil Rights

The items in bold relate to the content in Grade 2.

1861–1865	Civil War
1869	**National Suffrage Association cofounded by Susan B. Anthony**
1914–1918	World War I
1920	**Ratification of the Nineteenth Amendment**
1923	**Bethune-Cookman College founded by Mary McLeod Bethune**
1933	**White House Conference on the Emergency Needs of Women**
1936	**Appointment of Mary McLeod Bethune to head Division of Negro Affairs**
1939	**Resignation of Eleanor Roosevelt from Daughters of the American Revolution in protest of treatment of Marian Anderson**
1939–1945	**World War II**
1945	**Appointment of Eleanor Roosevelt to UN**
1947	**Jackie Robinson plays in major-league baseball**
1948	Adoption of UN's Universal Declaration of Human Rights
1955	**Montgomery bus -boycott begun by Rosa Parks's act**
1963	**March on Washington led by Dr. Martin Luther King, Jr.**
1965–1970	**First major strike by Cesar Chávez and National Farm Workers Association**

The Big Idea

When faced with injustice, ordinary people can make extraordinary changes for good.

What Students Need to Learn

- **Susan B. Anthony and the right to vote**
- **Eleanor Roosevelt and civil and human rights**
- **Mary McLeod Bethune and educational opportunity**
- **Jackie Robinson and the integration of major-league baseball**
- **Rosa Parks and the bus boycott in Montgomery, Alabama**
- **Martin Luther King, Jr., and the dream of equal rights for all**
- **Cesar Chávez and the rights of migrant workers**

What Students Will Learn in Future Grades

In future grades, students will review and extend their learning about civil rights.

Grade 4

- Women's rights
  - Seneca Falls convention
  - Elizabeth Cady Stanton
  - Lucretia Mott
  - Amelia Bloomer
  - Sojourner Truth

Grade 6

- Reform
  - Populism
  - The Progressive Era
  - Reform for African Americans
    - Ida B. Wells
    - Booker T. Washington
    - W. E. B. DuBois
  - Women's suffrage
    - Susan B. Anthony
  - The Socialist critique of America: Eugene V. Debs

VI. Civil Rights

Text Resources

(65) *Martin Luther King, Jr.: "I Have a Dream"*

Materials

Instructional Masters 25, 51

T-Chart, p. 212

Who Am I?, p. 219

Susan B. Anthony silver dollar or a picture of one, p. 213

index cards, p. 219

slips of paper for voting ballots, p. 219

7 brown paper grocery bags or lunch bags, p. 219

chart paper, p. 220

Vocabulary

Student/Teacher Vocabulary

boycott: to refuse to do something as a form of protest (S)

civil disobedience: nonviolent protest (T)

civil rights: the obligations that government has to protect its citizens from discrimination and to guarantee equal citizenship (S)

equal rights: all citizens sharing the same rights without discrimination (S)

human rights: a broad term that in Western society generally refers to equality, a focus on the rights of the individual, and the passage of fair laws that protect the individual's rights (S)

migrant worker: someone who moves from place to place to find work (S)

nonviolence: a form of protest that does not involve violence (S)

organize: to work together for united action, as in a union (T)

suffrage: the right to vote (T)

union: a group of workers who band together for a common cause (T)

union contract: an agreement between a union and an employer (T)

Domain Vocabulary

Civil rights and associated words:
obligation, duty, responsibility, government, protect, safeguard, guard, guarantee, citizens, discrimination, equality, individual, fair laws, shield

Women's suffrage and associated words:
Susan B. Anthony, women's rights, movement, Elizabeth Cady Stanton, Lucretia Mott, Seneca Falls, New York, limited, restricted, discrimination, work, property ownership, National Suffrage Association, organization, franchise, vote, voting, constitution, amendment, Fifteenth Amendment, African-American men, vote

Eleanor Roosevelt and associated words:
First Lady, social activist, tireless, hardworking, dedicated, devoted, lobby, ask for, access, pipeline, conduit, Great Depression, social causes, public well-being, public welfare, relief, unofficial, informal, African-American viewpoint, Marian Anderson, Lincoln Memorial, discrimination, United Nations, Commission on Human Rights, Universal Declaration of Human Rights

Mary McLeod Bethune and associated words:
teacher, Division of Negro Affairs, National Youth Administration, segregation, discrimination, education, separate, "separate but equal" principle, Daytona Normal and Industrial Institute for Negro Girls, Cookman Institute for Men, Bethune-Cookman College, National Council for Negro Women, National Association for the Advancement of Colored People, United Nations, observer, advisor

Jackie Robinson and associated words:
major-league baseball, hitter, home run, professional sports, segregation, segregated, integration, racism, National Negro League, white leagues, color bar, Baseball Hall of Fame

Rosa Parks and associated words:
National Association for the Advancement of Colored People, Montgomery, Alabama, bus, seat, colored section, segregated, tired, hardworking, refusal, get up, give up seat, boycott, arrested, don't use, walk, carpool, Montgomery Improvement Association, Martin Luther King, Jr., U.S. Supreme Court, overturned, declared unconstitutional, negated

Vocabulary continued

Martin Luther King, Jr., and associated words:
young, youthful, fearless, forceful, eloquent, dedicated, pastor, Dexter Avenue Baptist Church, family, generations, African Americans, Mahatma Gandhi, India, nonviolence, civil disobedience, principles, adopted, acceptance, central figure, organizer, initiate, support, influence, influential, March on Washington (1963), Lincoln Memorial, "I Have a Dream" speech, Civil Rights Acts of 1964 and 1965, pressure, lobby for, demand, Nobel Peace Prize, racial equality, assassinated, murdered, segregationist, *plus words from his speeches*

Cesar Chávez and associated words:
Mexican American, hispanic, activist, Community Service Organization, San Jose, California, migrate, migrant workers, farmworkers, itinerant, immigrant, citizens, noncitizens, unionize, organize a union, join, membership, united action, force of numbers, National Farm Workers Association, strike, marches, demonstrations, fasts, days without food, countrywide boycott, national boycott, refusal to buy grapes, AFL-CIO, United Farm Workers, bargain collectively, order, mandate, require

Cross-curricular Connections

Language Arts

Poetry

- "Harriet Tubman"

Music

Songs

- "Follow the Drinking Gourd"
- "This Land Is Your Land"
- "Swing Low, Sweet Chariot"

At a Glance

The most important ideas for you are:

- Susan B. Anthony and independent-minded women like her fought to remove societal barriers to what was legal and considered proper for women of good character to do in the 19th century.
- Eleanor Roosevelt spent her adult life working to enlarge the number of people who enjoyed the full benefits of civil and human rights.
- Mary McLeod Bethune worked to broaden educational opportunities for African-American youth in a society that provided few resources to segregated schools.
- Jackie Robinson broke the color barrier and led the way into major-league professional sports for members of minority groups.
- Rosa Parks's refusal to give up her bus seat to a white man sparked the Montgomery bus boycott and the nonviolent resistance movement that forever changed the United States.
- Martin Luther King, Jr., emerged from the Montgomery bus boycott as a leader in the civil rights movement.
- Cesar Chávez was the first person to gain a voice for migrant workers.

Teaching Idea

Before starting this section, brainstorm with children the names of important historical figures that they have learned about in prior months or grades. Talk about what makes these ordinary people extraordinary. Chart this information on Instructional Master 51, *T-Chart*. Then tell children you are going to talk about some more extraordinary people who made a difference in the world. Continue to list their names and accomplishments on your T-chart. Don't forget to include people from your local school community.

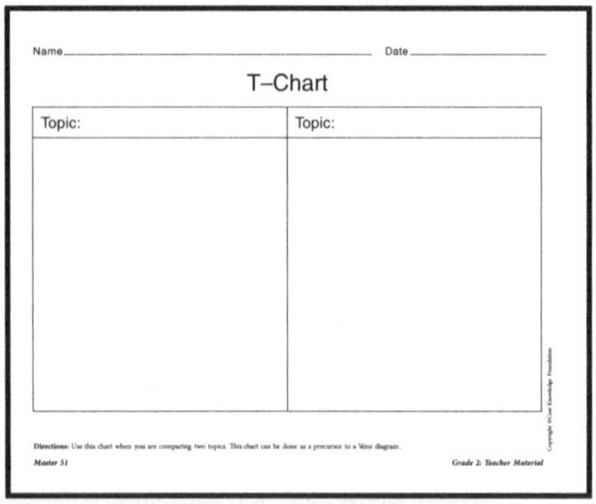
Name________________ Date________

T–Chart

Topic:	Topic:

Directions: Use this chart when you are comparing two topics. This chart can be done as a precursor to a Venn diagram.

Master 51 *Grade 2: Teacher Material*

Copyright ©Core Knowledge Foundation

Use Instructional Master 51.

What Teachers Need to Know

Background

The goal of this section is to use narrative, biography, and autobiography to introduce children to the idea that, while the United States is founded on the proposition that "all men [and, by extension, women] are created equal," equality has not always been granted to all Americans. Many people have dedicated themselves to the struggle to extend equal rights to all Americans.

Note that there is a difference between civil liberties and civil rights. Civil liberties is a term that includes all the protections, or safeguards, that citizens enjoy against the abusive power of government. For example, the rights guaranteed under the Bill of Rights are civil liberties.

Civil rights include the right of citizens to protection from discrimination and the right to equal citizenship, rights long denied certain groups in our society. That is the fight that women and African Americans fought in the 19th century and continued to wage in the 20th century joined by other minority groups such as Hispanics, Native Americans, and Asians.

Human rights is a broad term that in Western society generally refers to equality, a focus on the rights of the individual, and the passage of fair laws that protect the individual's rights. Specific rights revolve around political, economic, and religious concerns.

Susan B. Anthony

The struggle for women's rights began earlier than 1869, when Susan B. Anthony and Elizabeth Cady Stanton founded the National Suffrage Association (NSA). In 1848, Stanton and Lucretia Mott organized the first women's rights convention at Seneca Falls, New York, after they had been denied official recognition at an international antislavery convention in London. At that time, women had very limited public roles. They usually could attend meetings, but were not allowed to speak in public.

Women were, for the most part, not allowed to enter professions such as medicine and law. Few girls were educated past eighth grade because education was not considered important for girls. People were concerned that education would weaken women's minds. Married women could not own property. If they had property in their names before they were married, they had to turn it over to their husbands after marriage. Women could not vote or hold public office.

Women like Anthony, Stanton, and Mott, who were educated and not intimidated by the strictures of society, set out to do something about their circumstances. During the 1850s, many women supported the abolition of slavery. Once the Civil War was over and slavery was abolished, they expected abolitionists to support their cause.

However, few male abolitionists returned the favor. In 1869, when the Fifteenth Amendment, which gave African-American males the vote, was proposed, Anthony and Stanton founded the NSA to protest the amendment because it did not include women. The amendment was ratified nonetheless.

Anthony continued to be one of the prominent leaders of the women's rights movement until her death in 1906. Although she did not live to see the passage and ratification of the Nineteenth Amendment in 1920, which gave women the vote, she was instrumental in gaining support for the law. Throughout the last part of the 19th century, Anthony crisscrossed the country speaking for women's suffrage and helped women gain the vote in state and local elections in California, Michigan, and Colorado. In 1892, she became president of the National American Women Suffrage Association, an organization that combined the NSA and a rival group. She held this post until 1900.

One of the most notable episodes in the long, busy life of Susan B. Anthony began on November 1, 1872, when Anthony and several other women marched into a New York barbershop where voters were registered, and demanded to be added to the registration lists. When the registrars tried to stop the women from registering, Anthony read them the Fourteenth Amendment:

> All persons born or naturalized in the United States, and subject to the jurisdiction thereof, are citizens of the United States and of the State wherein they reside. No State shall make or enforce any law which shall abridge the privileges or immunities of citizens of the United States; nor shall any State . . . deny to any person within its jurisdiction the equal protection of the laws.

Anthony reasoned that "privileges" must include voting, and pointed out that the amendment did not state that the privileges were restricted to men. Still, the registrars hesitated. Anthony threatened to bring charges against them. At last, they grudgingly allowed the women to register, and on November 5, Anthony and seven other women cast their ballots. (Anthony voted for former Civil War general Ulysses S. Grant, among others.)

Some time later, Anthony was arrested and indicted. This created a national uproar. Anthony spent the months leading up to her trial speaking in one local town after another. Her topic was "Is It a Crime for a Citizen of the United States to Vote?" During the speeches, she spoke for women's suffrage and urged potential jury members to acquit her.

The judge in the trial was opposed to women's suffrage and seems to have written his opinion against Anthony before the trial even started. He refused to let Anthony testify and ordered the jury to find her guilty. Before sentencing, the judge asked if Anthony had anything to say. Her words stunned the many observers in the court:

> Yes, your honor, I have many things to say; for in your ordered verdict of guilty, you have trampled under foot every vital principle of our government. My natural rights, my civil rights, my political rights, my judicial rights, are all alike ignored. Robbed of the fundamental privilege of citizenship, I am degraded from the status of a citizen to that of a subject; and not only myself individually, but all of my sex, are, by your honor's verdict, doomed to political subjection under this, so-called, form of government.

The judge tried several times to silence Anthony, but she continued to speak in protest. Finally, he got her to sit down and sentenced her to pay a fine of $100. Anthony declared she would never pay:

Teaching Idea

Bring in a Susan B. Anthony silver dollar or a picture of one to show children. This silver dollar, which was coined in 1979, was the first U.S. coin to bear the picture of a woman.

Children in Core Knowledge schools should have learned in first grade that Sacajawea, the Shoshone interpreter and guide on the Lewis and Clark expedition, also has a silver dollar cast in her honor.

May it please your honor, I shall never pay a dollar of your unjust penalty. All the stock in trade I possess is a $10,000 debt, incurred by publishing my paper . . . the sole object of which was to educate all women to do precisely as I have done, rebel against your manmade, unjust, unconstitutional forms of law, that tax, fine, imprison and hang women, while they deny them the right of representation in the government; and I shall work on with might and main to pay every dollar of that honest debt, but not a penny shall go to this unjust claim. And I shall earnestly and persistently continue to urge all women to the practical recognition of the old revolutionary maxim, that "Resistance to tyranny is obedience to God."

Anthony went to her grave with the fine unpaid.

Eleanor Roosevelt

Eleanor Roosevelt Talking With Handicapped

In the 20th century, Eleanor Roosevelt was a tireless worker for civil and human rights. Biographies of her refer to her as a diplomat, writer, humanitarian, and First Lady. As the wife of President Franklin Roosevelt, she had the opportunity to publicize the problems of African Americans, women, and young people during the Great Depression and to lobby her husband and his administration to provide work programs for these groups. But even before she became First Lady in 1933, Eleanor Roosevelt had been interested in and actively engaged in working for social causes as a member of the Women's Trade Union League and the Democratic Party.

As a result of her interest in social justice, Eleanor Roosevelt introduced her husband to African-American leaders and pushed him to establish the informal Black Cabinet to advise him on policies for African Americans. Often the laws passed to aid the victims of the Depression, providing work programs and relief, were not applied fairly to African Americans or to women—both groups were often passed over in favor of married white men. African Americans could be refused acceptance into certain kinds of skilled jobs. They could also be paid at a lower rate than white men working at the same type of job. Eleanor Roosevelt brought these and other issues to her husband's attention and pushed him to make changes. She championed the establishment of the National Youth Administration and the Division of Negro Affairs within it.

To aid women, Eleanor Roosevelt called a White House Conference on the Emergency Needs of Women in 1933. Because of the Great Depression, some 400,000 women needed relief help. Each state was mandated by the federal government to set up a Women's Division and to begin relief projects to employ women.

In 1939, Eleanor Roosevelt resigned from the Daughters of the American Revolution when it refused to allow Marian Anderson to sing in their hall in Washington, D.C. Anderson was a world-famous African-American opera singer. Eleanor Roosevelt obtained permission for Anderson to sing at the Lincoln Memorial.

After her husband's death in 1945, Eleanor Roosevelt continued to play a prominent role in social activism—this time on a world stage. In 1945, she was named a delegate to the new United Nations, an organization for world peace that grew out

Teaching Idea

One of Mary McLeod Bethune's jobs was to ensure that African-American high schools and colleges received the federal money set aside for them. Schools were segregated at that time, so there were schools for whites and schools for African Americans. Bethune said, "I cannot rest while there is a single . . . boy or girl lacking a chance to prove his [or her] worth."

Talk to children about how education is important in helping a person be and do the best that he or she can. Ask what kinds of knowledge people learn in school and how this knowledge can help them outside of school. You can extend this activity by reading a book with a related message, *Amazing Grace*, by Mary Hoffman. (See More Resources.)

of World War II. The following year, she became chair of the UN's Commission on Human Rights and coauthored the UN's Universal Declaration of Human Rights. She served at the world organization until 1952 and again in 1962.

Mary McLeod Bethune

One of the people who worked with Eleanor Roosevelt when she was First Lady was Mary McLeod Bethune (1875–1955). A Southerner by birth and a teacher by profession, Bethune brought vast experience to her post as head of the Division of Negro Affairs in the National Youth Administration (NYA) under Franklin Roosevelt. Bethune was part of a group of African-American presidential advisors known as the "Black Cabinet."

Bethune was born in South Carolina, the 15th child of freed slaves. Against all odds, she managed to get an education and promptly dedicated herself to teaching others. Bethune began her teaching career in small Southern schools for African Americans. At that time, education across the South was segregated, and African Americans had few educational opportunities. In 1904, she moved to the east coast of Florida and began her own school, Daytona Normal and Industrial Institute for Negro Girls. (*Normal* was the designation given to colleges that taught students to become teachers.) The school had just six pupils when it first opened. Bethune didn't have enough money to buy furniture or supplies, so children used crates as desks and wrote with small pieces of charcoal. To keep the school afloat, Bethune acted as the teacher, principal, and custodian. Bethune and her students also baked and sold pies to raise money for the school.

The Daytona school grew over the years. In 1923, Bethune merged the high school with the Cookman Institute for Men, and the joint college became Bethune-Cookman College in 1931. Bethune was president until 1936, when she took the position in the NYA.

Bethune was also active in the women's suffrage movement, like Susan B. Anthony before her. Bethune encouraged African-American men and women in Daytona Beach to vote, and helped them overcome the obstacles white Southerners had put into place to keep them from voting. Before African Americans could vote, they had to pass a literacy test and pay a poll tax. Bethune taught special classes to help African Americans pass the literacy test. She also went door to door to raise money to pay the poll tax. When the local branch of the Ku Klux Klan heard about her efforts, they threatened to burn down her school if she didn't stop. Bethune stood guard all night, ready to defend her institution, but the Klansmen never came. When election day arrived, Bethune proudly led dozens of African Americans to the polls to vote.

Her continuing interest in the rights of African-American women had led her to found the National Council for Negro Women in 1935. Bethune was also active in the National Association for the Advancement of Colored People (NAACP), serving as vice president of the organization from 1940 to 1955. She accompanied Eleanor Roosevelt as an official observer to the first session of the United Nations in 1945.

Teaching Idea

It may be difficult for children to understand that formerly—and not that long ago—women were not allowed to vote, to hold public office, and to own property by law. By custom, women were not supposed to go to college, to become doctors and lawyers, to work outside the home, or to speak in public. The stricture about work, of course, did not apply to lower-class women who were often forced to work outside the home to feed their families.

You can simulate this type of inequality in your classroom. Divide the class into groups (possibly boys and girls) and give privileges to one group and restrictions to another. For example, the "disadvantaged group" will have to ask for permission before getting out of their seats, while the privileged group can freely move about the classroom. Continue this long enough for one group to feel "persecuted" and start to protest about the unfairness. Talk about the situation, and then relate it to the idea of women not being allowed to do the same things as men.

Depending on your local and state representation, have children write letters to one or more female political officeholders for your area and ask how they became interested in politics, how they got elected or appointed, what they do in their jobs, and whether they feel what they do makes a difference. You can extend this activity by having children write to local female lawyers, doctors, company executives, etc.

Jackie Robinson

On April 15, 1947, Jackie Robinson put on a Brooklyn Dodgers uniform, walked to the plate in Ebetts Field, struck the batter's pose, and waited for the pitch. These simple actions broke the color barrier in major-league baseball. Robinson was African-American, and up until then baseball had been segregated. Any African American who wanted to play professional baseball had to play in separate "negro leagues."

Raised in California, Robinson was a standout athlete at Pasadena Junior College and UCLA. He was on the football, basketball, baseball, and track teams in college. Robinson served as an officer in the army during World War II. After the war, he began playing professional baseball in the negro leagues, where Branch Rickey, the president and general manager of the Brooklyn Dodgers, discovered him.

Rickey thought Robinson's skills and temperament might allow him to break the color barrier in major-league baseball. Before allowing him to play for the Dodgers, Rickey had deliberately tested Robinson's nerves by shouting insults at him. Rickey wanted to see if Robinson could hear the kind of insults and taunts he was sure to receive from bigoted fans without losing his cool. In October 1945, Rickey offered Robinson a contract to play on a Dodgers farm team, the Montreal Royals of the International League.

Robinson played well for the Montreal Royals and had the best batting average in 1946. In 1947, he earned a spot playing for the Dodgers in the major league. Robinson faced tremendous abuse during his first months. Fans yelled insults and threw bottles when he played. Some even called in death threats. Players on other teams deliberately threw balls at his head and spiked him with their cleats when they slid into bases. Some of his own teammates were supportive and friendly, but others complained about having to play with an African American. Because of Jim Crow laws, Robinson was not allowed to stay in the same hotel or eat in the same restaurant with his teammates. Despite all of these hardships, Robinson kept his cool. He later said, "Plenty of times I wanted to haul off when somebody insulted me for the color of my skin, but I had to hold to myself. I knew I was kind of an experiment. The whole thing was bigger than me."

But Robinson not only endured, he ultimately prevailed. It helped that he was an excellent player. He led the National League in stolen bases during his rookie season and was chosen Rookie of the Year. In 1949, he hit a league-leading .342 and was selected as the league's Most Valuable Player (MVP). He went on to lead Brooklyn to six league championships and a World Series triumph. In 1962, Jackie Robinson became the first African American named to the Baseball Hall of Fame. Major-league baseball retired his number (42) in 1997, the 50th anniversary of his debut.

Later athletes who benefited from Robinson breaking the color barrier were not only African Americans but also Hispanics and Asians—none of whom could have played before Robinson stepped up for that first at bat.

Rosa Parks

Rosa Parks was born and raised in Alabama. She joined the National Association for the Advancement of Colored People (NAACP) in 1943 after she moved to Montgomery, Alabama. As secretary of the Montgomery chapter, she was actively involved in its work.

On her way home from her job on the night of December 1, 1955, she took a seat in the first row of the colored section of a Montgomery bus. Buses, trains, restaurants, and movie theaters—all public places and means of transportation—were segregated in the South. As the bus became crowded, the driver ordered Parks to give up her seat to a white man. She refused and was arrested and later fined $10.

Local leaders of the NAACP and others within the African-American community laid out a plan to boycott Montgomery buses. An organization called the Montgomery Improvement Association was set up, and a young clergyman, Dr. Martin Luther King, Jr., was elected to lead it. Some 75% of the city's bus ridership was African-American, and even though most did not own cars, they observed the boycott—for 382 days. The U.S. Supreme Court handed down a ruling in late 1956 that segregation on Alabama buses was unconstitutional. The Montgomery bus companies began rolling again without "colored" sections.

The civil rights movement would continue through the '50s and '60s, but many people feel that it got its start when Rosa Parks refused to move to the back of the bus. For her simple refusal to comply with a law that she viewed as unjust, Rosa Parks has become a hero to millions.

Martin Luther King, Jr.

One of the people who came to national prominence as a result of the Montgomery bus boycott was Dr. Martin Luther King, Jr. He was the young pastor of the Dexter Avenue Baptist Church in Montgomery, Alabama. Both his father and his grandfather were ministers, and both had worked for equal rights for African Americans.

King supported Rosa Parks and the Montgomery bus boycott, and continued to do so even though his home was dynamited and his family threatened. When desegregation of the buses was achieved, it was a victory not only for the African-American community, but also for the young pastor.

Following Montgomery, the movement for civil rights soon engulfed the South. A forceful and eloquent speaker, King became the central figure in the civil rights movement that took shape in the mid-1950s after the bus boycott. With nearly 100 other religious leaders, King founded the Southern Christian Leadership Conference (SCLC) in 1957. Influenced by the writings and model of Mahatma Gandhi's movement in India, King and the SCLC dedicated themselves to change through civil disobedience and nonviolence. They were never to lash out at their attackers but to accept violence—even beatings—without hitting back.

King and his followers demonstrated their belief in this philosophy on many occasions. One of the most egregious shows of force by segregationists occurred in Birmingham, Alabama, in 1963, when white policemen unleashed attack dogs and pointed fire hoses at nonviolent civil rights demonstrators. King was thrown in jail along with many demonstrators including several hundred schoolchildren. The events were widely televised and tipped many who had previously hesitated toward support for the civil rights movement. While in jail, King wrote his famous "Letter from the Birmingham Jail," in which he explained his goals and also argued that, while just laws must be obeyed, unjust laws, including segregation laws, need not be obeyed. The letter, available in many books and on numerous websites, is considered one of King's most powerful works.

In August 1963, King led over 200,000 people in the March on Washington to pressure the government into passing the Civil Rights Act of 1964. In front of the Lincoln Memorial, King delivered his famous "I Have a Dream" speech, in which he looked forward hopefully to a world without segregation, a world in which people would be judged not by the color of their skin, "but by the content of their character." The last few lines are among the most famous lines in American oratory:

> When we let freedom ring, when we let it ring from every village and every hamlet, from every state and every city, we will be able to speed up that day when all of God's children, black men and white men, Jews and Gentiles, Protestants and Catholics, will be able to join hands and sing in the words of the old Negro spiritual, 'Free at last! free at last! thank God Almighty, we are free at last!'

The momentum that this march started also resulted in the passage of the Voting Rights Act of 1965. In 1964, King was awarded the prestigious Nobel Peace Prize for his work toward racial equality. He was assassinated in 1968 by a segregationist.

In 1983, the U.S. Congress designated the third Monday in January as a federal holiday in King's honor. (65)

Teaching Idea

One of the lessons of this section should be that ordinary people do extraordinary things. Jackie Robinson was an unusual athlete. Susan B. Anthony was trained as a teacher, one of the few occupations open to unmarried, middle-class women. Mary McLeod Bethune was also a teacher, Rosa Parks was a seamstress, Martin Luther King, Jr., was a minister, and Cesar Chávez was a migrant worker. But when faced with a challenge to help others win their rights, they responded.

Ask children to think of something that they could do to make a difference—in their classroom, in the school, or at home. It does not need to be a huge thing, but something helpful (keep the room clean, say "thank you"). Challenge children to practice this for a week.

Cesar Chávez

Cesar Chávez (1927–1993) saw that the goals and tactics of the civil rights movement need not be limited to African Americans. Growing up in Arizona and California, he worked in the fields and saw firsthand the miserable conditions in which migrant farm laborers lived. After starting a career as a union organizer, in 1962 he devoted himself full-time to organizing a union for farm laborers.

A Mexican American, Cesar Chávez began his activism as a volunteer with the Community Service Organization (CSO) in San Jose, California, registering migrant workers like himself to vote. When he was fired from his job picking apricots for urging his fellow workers to unionize, he went to work for the CSO.

Chávez left the CSO when its members refused to back a unionization effort. Chávez was convinced that the only way working and living conditions would get better for migrant workers would be through the force of numbers and united action that comes with a union. In 1962, Chávez established the National Farm Workers Association (NFWA) to organize migrant workers.

Teaching Idea

Play "Civil Rights Jeopardy." After the class has studied all the leaders described in this section, play "Jeopardy" by giving children a statement about one of the leaders and having them respond with "Who is ___?" Rather than having children try to beat one another in calling out a question, go around the room in order or call on children to respond.

In 1965, Chávez called a strike against grape growers. Even with a series of strikes, marches, fasts, and a countrywide boycott that brought national attention to the union and its cause, it took five years to gain a union in the vineyards and a resulting work contract. Chávez and the union went on to win recognition and contracts from other large-scale growers and farmers, but each time it was a struggle.

In 1972, the NFWA joined the AFL-CIO and changed its name to the United Farm Workers. In 1975, the California legislature passed a law mandating that farmers bargain collectively with their farmworkers' union. Chávez died in 1993, a national figure and hero to many Americans.

Chávez's thinking was influenced by the ideas of Mahatma Gandhi and also by the speeches and writings of Martin Luther King, Jr. Chávez pursued his goals through nonviolence, much as Gandhi and King had done. Chávez also followed Gandhi's example by going on hunger strikes, protesting by refusing to eat for long periods of time. In 1968, he fasted for 25 days to show support for the UFW (United Farm Workers) commitment to nonviolence.

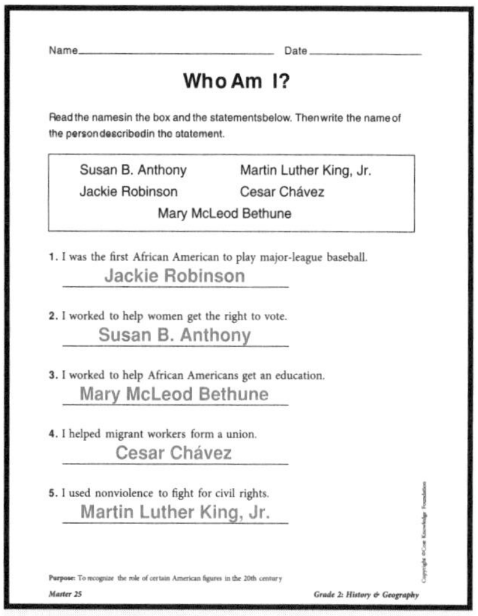
Name ______ Date ______

Who Am I?

Read the names in the box and the statements below. Then write the name of the person described in the statement.

Susan B. Anthony
Martin Luther King, Jr.
Jackie Robinson
Cesar Chávez
Mary McLeod Bethune

1. I was the first African American to play major-league baseball.
Jackie Robinson

2. I worked to help women get the right to vote.
Susan B. Anthony

3. I worked to help African Americans get an education.
Mary McLeod Bethune

4. I helped migrant workers form a union.
Cesar Chávez

5. I used nonviolence to fight for civil rights.
Martin Luther King, Jr.

Purpose: To recognize the role of certain American figures in the 20th century

Master 25 *Grade 2: History & Geography*

Copyright ©Core Knowledge Foundation

Use Instructional Master 25.

Review

Below are some ideas for ongoing assessment and review activities. These are not meant to constitute a comprehensive list. Teachers may also refer to the *Pearson Learning/Core Knowledge History & Geography* series for additional information and teaching ideas.

- Have children think of questions that they would like to ask one of the extraordinary people discussed in this section. Then, have children write the questions on index cards and read them aloud to the class. What does the class think that the answer might be? If possible, use some of the resources from the school and local libraries to answer questions.
- As a way to introduce Susan B. Anthony, role-play a situation on voting rights. Have the class think about what they would like to do for a reward that week, such as extra recess, reading time, or other activities. As you list the possibilities on the board, pass out slips of paper only to the boys in the room and instruct them to vote. The girls will not be able to vote. After this, talk with the class about that situation and how it made them feel. Have them write about the activity and share their feelings. Then, make a connection to Susan B. Anthony and the fight for women's suffrage.
- Have children pair up and pretend that they are interviewing one of the people discussed in this section. You may create questions for the interviewer to use, or you may have children create their own questions. Have them write questions based on what you have learned about each person's life, and then ask the child posing as each historical figure to respond as the person would.
- Bring enough brown grocery or lunch bags to class to represent each person from this section. Divide children into groups, and have them draw pictures of items that they want to include in their bag that represent the person they have studied. For example, for Susan B. Anthony, they might want to create a ballot to put in their bag to represent her work with voting rights. Then, have the group present their bags to the class and see if children can guess who the bags represent.
- Ask children to select one of the people they admire from this section. Then have children write a letter to that person describing our world today and how this person helped change it. After writing the letter, have children trade letters and write a response. Ask children to write the response as if they were that historical figure. You could share the responses in class.

The Big Idea in Review

When faced with injustice, ordinary people can make extraordinary changes for good.

• Work with children to develop a map showing similarities between the seven civil rights figures. First, have them remember the names of the seven. Write these names on chart paper in a configuration that allows you to draw lines from any name to any other name. Then ask children to think of similarities, e.g., both Susan B. Anthony and Mary McLeod Bethune fought for suffrage; Eleanor Roosevelt and Bethune worked together; Martin Luther King, Jr., and Cesar Chávez were influenced by Gandhi; Rosa Parks and King were involved in the Montgomery bus boycott; etc. You can extend this activity by having children do a basic research report, inviting them to learn more about one of the figures that interested them the most. Have them share their findings with the class.

• You may also ask the following questions at the end of this section:

1. What did Susan B. Anthony work for?
   Susan B. Anthony worked to get women the right to vote.

2. Why is Eleanor Roosevelt's work important?
   Eleanor Roosevelt made her husband, President Franklin Roosevelt, aware of the problems that African Americans, young people, and women were having in getting help during the Great Depression. After World War II, she served in the United Nations for the United States and helped to write the United Nations' Universal Declaration on Human Rights.

3. What goal did Mary McLeod Bethune work for?
   Mary McLeod Bethune worked to make sure that African-American children got a good education and to better the rights of African-American women.

4. Besides being a great baseball player, why is Jackie Robinson remembered?
   Jackie Robinson was the first African American to play major-league baseball.

5. What did Rosa Parks do that started the Montgomery bus boycott?
   She refused to give up her seat in "the colored" section to a white man once there were no more seats in the "white section" of the bus.

6. What did Martin Luther King, Jr., believe about violence?
   Martin Luther King, Jr., believed that you should not meet violence with violence. He believed that if people hit marchers, they should not hit back. Other people like the government would see how evil the violent people were and stop them.

7. What did Cesar Chávez do for migrant workers?
   Cesar Chávez helped migrant workers join a union and get better wages and working conditions from big farmers.

More Resources

The titles listed below are offered as a representative sample of materials and not a complete list of everything that is available.

For children —

These books are generally intended to be read aloud, though some children may be able to read parts or all of the simpler texts.

- *Civil Rights Leaders,* edited by E. D. Hirsch, Jr. (Pearson Learning, 2002). A unit in the official *Pearson Learning/Core Knowledge History & Geography series.* It includes a small picture book for children and a teacher's guide with read alouds. To order, call 1-800-321-3106.
- *50 American Heroes Every Kid Should Meet,* by Dennis Denenberg and Lorraine Roscoe (The Millbrook Press, 2002). Contains profiles of all seven figures studied in this section. Paperback, 128 pages, ISBN 0761316450.
- *Amazing Grace,* by Mary Hoffman (Dial, 1991). Hardcover, ISBN 0803710402.
- *Cesar Chávez: A Photo-Illustrated Biography,* by Lucile Davis (Bridgestone Books, 1998). Library binding, 24 pages, ISBN 1560655690.
- *Harvesting Hope, The Story of Cesar Chávez,* by Kathleen Krull and Yuyi Morales (Harcourt Children's Books, 2003). Paperback, 48 pages, ISBN 0152014373.
- *Martin's Big Words: The Life of Dr. Martin Luther King, Jr.,* by Doreen Rappaport and illustrated by Bryan Collier (Jump at the Sun, 2001). A Caldecott Honor Award book. Hardcover, 40 pages, ISBN 0786807148.
- *A Picture Book of Martin Luther King,* by David Adler (Holiday House, 1991). Paperback, 30 pages, ISBN 0823408477. Other titles in this series tell the stories of Rosa Parks, Jackie Robinson, and Eleanor Roosevelt.
- *The Story of Ruby Bridges,* by Robert Coles and illustrated by George Ford (Scholastic, 1995). Library binding, ISBN 0590572814.
- *Susan B. Anthony,* by Martha E. H. Rustad (Pebble Books, 2001). Library binding, 24 pages, ISBN 0736809988.
- *Teammates,* by Peter Golenbock (Voyager, 1992). Pee Wee Reese befriends African-American sports pioneer Jackie Robinson as he breaks the color line. Paperback, 32 pages, ISBN 0152842861.
- *When Marian Sang,* by Pam Muñoz Ryan and illustrated by Brian Selznick (Scholastic, 2002). The story of Marian Anderson. Winner of several awards. Hardcover, ISBN 0439269679.

For teachers —

- *All the People: 1945–2001,* by Joy Hakim (Oxford University Press, 2002). Book 10 in the series *A History of Us.* Paperback, 160 pages, ISBN 0195153383.
- *Eyes on the Prize: America's Civil Rights Years, 1954–1965,* by Juan Williams (Penguin, 1988). Paperback, 320 pages, ISBN 0140096531.
- *My Lord, What a Morning: An Autobiography,* by Marian Anderson (University of Illinois Press, 2002). In chapter 17, she recalls the emotions and thoughts surrounding her appearance at the Lincoln Memorial, which is also described in the children's book *When Marian Sang.* Paperback, 352 pages, ISBN 0252070534. For a videotape of the event at the Lincoln Memorial, go to www.library.upenn.edu/exhibits/rbm/anderson/lincoln.html.
- *Not for Ourselves Alone: The Story of Elizabeth Cady Stanton and Susan B. Anthony, An Illustrated History,* by Geoffrey C. Ward (Knopf, 2001). Paperback, 256 pages, ISBN 037570969X.
- *Parting the Waters: America in the King Years, 1954–63,* by Taylor Branch (Simon & Schuster, Inc., 1989). Winner of the Pulitzer Prize. Paperback, 1,088 pages, ISBN 0671687425.
- *Promises to Keep: How Jackie Robinson Changed America,* by Sharon Robinson (Scholastic, 2004). For older children, but a good resource. Written by Jackie Robinson's daughter. Hardcover, 64 pages, ISBN 0439425921.
- *Through My Eyes,* by Ruby Bridges and edited by Margo Lundell (Scholastic, 1999). Hardcover, 64 pages, ISBN 0590189239.
- *Unshakable Faith,* by John Perry (Multnomah, 1999). A dual biography of George Washington Carver and Booker T. Washington. Hardcover, 400 pages, ISBN 1576734935.
- *Why We Can't Wait,* by Martin Luther King, Jr. (Signet Classics, 2000). First published in 1964, this is King's thoughtful and eloquent examination of the history of the civil rights struggle and the choices that faced future generations. Paperback, 176 pages, ISBN 0451527534.
- Martin Luther King, Jr., Papers Project of Stanford University, www.stanford.edu/group/King.

VII. Geography of the Americas

The Big Idea

People have adapted to the diverse landscape of North and South America.

Remember that each subject you study with children expands their vocabulary and introduces new terms, thus making them better listeners and readers. As you study about historical people and events, use read alouds, and discussions to build children's vocabularies.

What Students Should Already Know

Students in Core Knowledge schools should be familiar with

Kindergarten and Grade 1

- location of North America, the United States, Alaska, and Hawaii on a map or globe
- location of South America on a map or globe

What Students Need to Learn

- **Location of Canada, the United States, Mexico, and Central America on the North American continent**
- **Familiarity with the 50 states of the United States, its territories, the Mississippi River, the Appalachian and Rocky Mountains, and the Great Lakes on a map**
- **Location of the Atlantic and Pacific Oceans, Gulf of Mexico, Caribbean Sea, and West Indies**
- **Location of Brazil, the Amazon River, Peru, Chile, the Andes Mountains, Venezuela, Colombia, Ecuador, Bolivia, Argentina, and the pampas on the South American continent**
- **Main languages of South America: Spanish and Portuguese**

What Students Will Learn in Future Grades

In future grades, students will review and extend their learning about the geography of the Americas.

Grade 3

- location of Canada, United States, Mexico, and Central America

Grade 5

- location of the Western Hemisphere, North America, the Caribbean Sea, and the Gulf of Mexico
- the Gulf Stream and climate
- the eight regions of the United States; the 50 states and their capitals

Grade 6

- Latin American Independence Movements
  - Haitian and Mexican revolutions
  - Liberators (Bolivar, San Martín, O'Higgins)
  - New nations in Central America: Costa Rica, El Salvador, Guatemala, Honduras, Nicaragua
  - Brazilian independence from Portugal

Vocabulary

Student/Teacher Vocabulary

Amazon River: the second-longest river in the world; supports several rainforests in South America (S)

Appalachian Mountains: the oldest mountain chain in North America; stretches from Newfoundland to central Alabama (S)

Argentina: one of the southernmost countries of South America (S)

Bolivia: a South American country bordered by Peru and Chile to the west and Brazil to the east (S)

Brazil: the largest country in South America (S)

Canada: the largest country in North America; located north of the United States (S)

Central America: the name given to the narrow land bridge that connects North and South America, and is home to seven independent countries (S)

Chile: a country located on the southwestern coast of South America, bordered by the Pacific Ocean and the Andes Mountains (S)

Colombia: a South American country bordered by Ecuador, Peru, Venezuela, and the Pacific Ocean (S)

contiguous: shares a boundary (T)

Ecuador: a South American country located between Peru and Colombia, and bordered by the Pacific Ocean (S)

gaucho: an Argentinian cowboy (T)

Great Lakes: freshwater lakes that form a chain from western New York State to northern Minnesota (S)

mestizos: people of mixed European and Indian descent (T)

Mexico: the third-largest country on the North American continent; located south of the United States (S)

Mississippi River: an important river in the United States; begins in Minnesota and empties into the Gulf of Mexico below New Orleans (S)

navigable: able to be traveled by ship or boat (T)

pampas: the grasslands of Argentina and Uruguay (S)

Peru: a country located on the northwestern coast of South America, bordered by Ecuador, Colombia, Brazil, Bolivia, and Chile (S)

rainforest: a thick forest found in areas that receive heavy rainfall, in both tropical and temperate zones (S)

Rocky Mountains: a mountain range that extends for more than 3,000 miles from Alaska to New Mexico (S)

subsistence farmer: a farmer who grows enough to eat but no surplus to sell (T)

tributary: a stream or small river that feeds into a larger body of water (T)

Venezuela: one of the northernmost countries of South America, bordered by Colombia, Brazil, Guyana, and the Caribbean Sea (S)

Materials

Instructional Masters 26–27

North America, p. 229

South America, p. 230

pictures of flags to color, p. 225

puzzle of the United States, p. 227

overhead projector, p. 230

colored markers or crayons, p. 230

flash cards of states and their capitals, p. 231

a class library on books about North and South America, p. 231

index cards, p. 231

chart paper, p. 231

pictures of various animals from these geographic regions, p. 231

4 x 6 index cards, p. 232

sheets of paper with the outline of a body, p. 232

Vocabulary continued

Domain Vocabulary

Geography and associated words:
North America, United States, land bridge, isthmus, South America, varied, rugged, mountainous, rocky, plains, flat, gently rolling, grasslands, agriculture, coastal plains, sandy beaches, scrub forest, erosion, Iroquois-Huron word, vast area, sparsely populated, few people, per square mile, Pacific Ocean, Arctic Ocean, Atlantic Ocean, borders, natural boundary, St. Lawrence River, St. Lawrence Seaway, New England, plains, provinces, Commonwealth of Nations, Ottawa, capital, Rio Grande, shallow river, narrow, natural boundary, Gulf of Mexico, Gulf of California, Pacific Ocean, Belize, Guatemala, plateau, tableland, top of mountain, Sierra Madre Occidental, Sierra Madre Oriental, land bridge, connects, joins, independent, countries, Costa Rica, El Salvador, Honduras, Nicaragua, Panama, Caribbean Sea, hot, steamy, dense

United States and associated words:
Alaska, same, similar, share, Great Plains, Pacific Ocean, Atlantic Ocean, joined, touching, noncontiguous, Guam, American Samoa, Virgin Islands, territories, empty, Gulf of Mexico, New Orleans, south, below, tributaries, flow into, join, Ohio River, Missouri River, oldest, Newfoundland, Alabama, long, wide, range, barrier, obstacle, movement, settlement, highest peak, mountaintop, Mount Mitchell, Maria Mitchell, astronomer, Hudson River, Delaware River, Susquehanna River, Potomac River, Tennessee River, flow, water, Alaska, New Mexico, Mount Elbert, highest peak, barriers, formidable, harder, pass, way through, route, South Pass, Wyoming, Oregon Trail, Continental Divide, separating line, Great Lakes, freshwater, chain, system, New York State, Minnesota, Ontario, Erie, Huron, Michigan, Superior, connected, joined, waterway, rivers, canals, locks, able to sail, access through, St. Lawrence Seaway, *plus names of the 50 states*

Pacific Ocean and associated words:
largest, deepest, Arctic, Antarctica, North America, South America, Asia, Australia, islands, dot, here and there, chains, series, system, Bering Strait, South China Sea, Oceania, Guam, Marshall Islands, Japan, Philippines, New Zealand, Ring of Fire, volcanoes, active, inactive, lava, fire, molten rock

Atlantic Ocean and associated words:
second-largest, North America, South America, Europe, Africa, Arctic, Antarctica, Gulf Stream, ocean current, warm, Gulf of Mexico, flows, North Atlantic Drift, moderate, moderating influence, warming, western Europe

South America and associated words:
varied, plains, grasslands, mountains, largest, Amazon River Basin, waters, flows through, huge, hot, humid, steamy, rainy, diversity, diverse, varied, species, plants, animals, birds, insects, destruction, cutting down, bulldozing, burning, global warming, Andes Mountains, parallel ranges, two ranges, plateau, high tableland, altiplano, "high plain," Inca Empire, narrow lowlands, coastal plain, Native Americans, eat what they grow, survive, survival, barely enough, eke out, make do, nothing left over, Central Valley, fertile, rich soil, population centers, business centers, farming, agriculture, landlocked, no sea access, no ports, Lake Titicaca, Simon Bolivar, the Liberator, liberate, free, independence, freedom, self-government, fight for, Spanish Viceroyalty of New Granada, province, seat, capital, Gran Colombia, Panama, in honor of, celebrate, thank, Caribbean Sea, Guyana, Highlands, Atlantic Ocean, Pacific Ocean, Panama, lowlands, fertile valleys, Uruguay, grasslands, grassy plains, flat area, temperate climate, mild, cattle herders, cowboys, part Spanish, part Indian, large ranches

Languages and associated words:
Spanish, Portuguese, Native American languages, Latin America, roots in Latin, Latin languages

Cross-curricular Connections

Visual Arts	Music
Kinds of Pictures: Landscapes	**Songs** • "The Erie Canal" • "This Land Is Your Land"

At a Glance

The most important ideas for you are:

- Children should be able to locate the North American continent, Canada, the United States, Mexico, and Central America on a map or globe.
- Among the variety of physical features on the North American continent are mountains, rivers, and plains.
- Children should be able to locate the Appalachian, Rocky, and Andes Mountains; the Atlantic and Pacific Oceans; the Gulf of Mexico and the Caribbean Sea; and the West Indies on a map or globe.
- Among the variety of physical features on the South American continent are mountains, rivers, grasslands, and rainforests.
- Children should be able to locate Brazil, Peru, Chile, Venezuela, Colombia, Ecuador, Bolivia, and Argentina on a map or globe.
- The Amazon River and its basin support vast rainforests and are located in Brazil.
- Bolivia is named after Simon Bolivar, the Liberator of South America.

What Teachers Need to Know

A. North America

Background

Canada is the northern neighbor of the United States, and Mexico is its southern neighbor. South of Mexico is Central America, which forms a bridge between the continents of North and South America.

Teaching Idea

Allow children to color flags of Canada, Mexico, and other countries from this section.

Canada

The word *Canada* is derived from an Iroquois-Huron word. Canada is the largest country in North America and the second-largest in the world. (Russia has the largest land area in the world.) To the west, Canada is bordered by the Pacific Ocean and Alaska, to the north by the Arctic Ocean, to the east by the Atlantic Ocean, and to the south by the United States. Part of Canada's more than 5,000-mile boundary with the United States is formed by one of Canada's major rivers, the St. Lawrence. This river, along with the St. Lawrence Seaway, forms the border with the United States from New England to the Great Lakes. The Rocky Mountains run north to south along Canada's western coast, and the Appalachian Mountains stretch along the eastern side of the country. The center of the country is a great plain. Although Canada is larger than the United States, it has a smaller population and, except for a few areas close to the U.S. border, is much less densely populated.

Canada is made up of 10 provinces and three territories. Canada's capital is Ottawa and it is a member of the British Commonwealth of Nations. Canada has both a French and English heritage, as the first settlers were French, but the country later fell under British control. Today, English and French are both official languages of Canada. Over half of all Canadians speak English as their first language, but in Quebec, over three-quarters of the people speak French as their first language.

The United States

Prairie, Badlands National Park, SD

The United States is the second-largest country on the North American continent. It shares much of the same physical geography as Canada. The Rocky Mountains begin in Alaska and continue south through Canada and the United States. The Appalachian Mountains also continue south from Canada through the United States to Alabama. The Great Plains in the United States are a continuation of the plains that occupy the center of Canada. Both countries are bordered by the Pacific Ocean on the west and by the Atlantic Ocean on the east.

The United States is the oldest country on the North American continent. Its founding predates modern Mexico, Canada, and the countries of Central America. Mexico and the Central American countries did not gain their independence from European countries until the 1800s.

The original 13 of the United States' 50 states joined the Union between 1787 and 1790. In 1912, when New Mexico and Arizona joined the Union, the United States consisted of 48 contiguous states. The remaining two states, Alaska and Hawaii, were admitted to statehood in 1959. Alaska had been purchased from Russia in 1867, and the islands of Hawaii had been annexed by the United States in 1898.

The Territories and Commonwealths

The United States has a governing relationship with territories and commonwealths located outside of the 50 states. Territories, also known as possessions, are less independent than commonwealths. The three large territories that the United States oversees are Guam, American Samoa, and the U.S. Virgin Islands. These are not states, but their residents enjoy all the rights of citizens of the 50 states, except they cannot vote in federal elections. Each territory has a governor and an elected legislature. Guam and American Samoa are in the Pacific Ocean, and the U.S. Virgin Islands are in the Caribbean Sea.

As part of its effort to establish an American foothold in the Pacific in the late 1800s, the United States acquired what became American Samoa. At the end of the Spanish-American War, the United States received Guam from Spain. During World War I, the United States received what became the U.S. Virgin Islands from Denmark in order to set up strategic defenses.

Puerto Rico, a self-governing commonwealth in association with the United States, is located about 1,000 miles southeast of Florida. Puerto Ricans, like residents of the United States, territories of Guam, American Samoa, and the U.S. Virgin Islands, also have the same rights as citizens residing in the United States, except they do not have voting privileges in federal elections. Commonwealths, however, are self-governing and have more autonomy than territories.

Christopher Columbus claimed the island now called Puerto Rico for Spain in 1493, and it remained under their rule until 1898. After the Spanish-American War, Puerto Rico was seized by the United States, who hoped to use the island to develop a strong naval presence in the Caribbean Sea. Since then, the political status of Puerto Rico has been debated. Many favor an autonomous status, with Puerto Rico independent of the United States, some would like it to remain a commonwealth with more self-governing powers, while others would like to see Puerto Rico become the 51st state in the United States of America. Despite the political debate, the U.S. presence in Puerto Rico is strong, with a naval base, many manufacturers, and numerous cultural influences.

The Mississippi River

The Mississippi River has played an important part in the expansion and development of the United States. Control of the Mississippi was one reason for the Louisiana Purchase. Starting in Minnesota, the river flows 2,340 miles to empty into the Gulf of Mexico below New Orleans. Along its course, more than 250 tributaries flow into it. Its two major tributaries are the Ohio and Missouri Rivers.

The Appalachian Mountains

The Appalachian Mountains are the oldest mountain chain in North America and stretch from Newfoundland to central Alabama. They are about 1,800 miles long and range from 120 to 375 miles wide. The highest peak is Mount Mitchell in North Carolina, named for Maria Mitchell, a 19th-century astronomer. Major rivers that flow through the mountains are the Hudson, Delaware, Susquehanna, Potomac, and Tennessee Rivers. The mountains are rich in iron and coal deposits, but proved a barrier to westward movement in the early days of the new United States.

The Rocky Mountains

The Rocky Mountains extend for more than 3,000 miles from Alaska to New Mexico. The highest point is Mount Elbert in Colorado. The Rocky Mountains were more formidable barriers to travel than the Appalachians because the Rockies are, in general, twice as high as the Appalachians, around 12,000 feet in comparison to the Appalachians' 6,000 feet. The major pass through the Rockies for travelers in the 19th century was South Pass in Wyoming. The Oregon Trail took this route.

Of major topographical interest is the Continental Divide that runs north and south through the mountains. Rivers to the east of this long, high crest flow to the east toward the Arctic or Atlantic Oceans, and rivers to the west flow toward the Pacific.

Teaching Idea

The *Core Knowledge Sequence* calls for children to learn the 50 states and their capitals in Grade 5. Teachers in Grades 2 through 4 may want to introduce these incrementally to prepare for the Grade 5 requirement. One way to do this in Grade 2 may be to have children learn their own state capital and to learn the neighboring states and capitals. Additionally, putting a puzzle of the United States (with the state names on it) out in a learning center is an excellent way for children to become familiar with more states' locations over time.

The Great Lakes

The Great Lakes are freshwater lakes that form a chain from western New York State to northern Minnesota. From east to west the lakes are Ontario, Erie, Huron, Michigan, and Superior. The lakes are connected by a series of rivers, canals, and locks and provide a navigable waterway from Minnesota to the Atlantic Ocean, via the St. Lawrence Seaway at the head of Lake Ontario.

The Pacific Ocean

The Pacific Ocean is the largest and deepest of the world's four oceans, extending over about a third of the surface of the earth. The Pacific reaches from the Arctic to Antarctica, and separates North and South America from Asia and Australia. Thousands of islands dot the ocean's surface from the Bering Strait to the South China Sea and beyond to the southeast. These include the islands of Oceania, such as Guam and the Marshalls, as well as Japan, the Philippines, and New Zealand. The Ring of Fire is a series of volcanoes that ring the ocean in a horseshoe shape. It runs from New Zealand in the south, north to Japan, forms the Aleutian Islands in Alaska, and then follows the coast of North and South America.

The Atlantic Ocean

The Atlantic Ocean is the second-largest of the world's four oceans. It separates North and South America from Europe and Africa and reaches from the Arctic to Antarctica. A major feature of the ocean is the Gulf Stream, a warm ocean current. The current begins in the Gulf of Mexico, where the water temperature is 80°F. As the current flows northeast into the Atlantic, it becomes the North Atlantic Drift. Although the water temperature decreases, it is still responsible for the year-round moderate climate of western Europe. Thus, when it is 20°F in New England in January, it is 40°F in London.

Gulf of Mexico, Caribbean Sea, and West Indies

The Gulf of Mexico borders the southeastern United States and the east coast of Mexico. The Straits of Florida allow access to the Atlantic Ocean, and the Strait of Yucatán provides access to the Caribbean Sea. The Mississippi and Rio Grande Rivers empty into the Gulf.

The Caribbean Sea lies between the West Indies to the north and east, Central America to the west, and South America to the south. The Caribbean is actually an arm of the Atlantic Ocean.

The Greater and Lesser Antilles are island groups in the Gulf of Mexico and Caribbean Sea that together are often called the West Indies. These islands were explored by Columbus on his first voyage. Columbus called them the Indies because he falsely believed he had sailed all the way around the world to Asia and arrived in the East Indies. The West Indies span the area from the Florida peninsula to Venezuela on the northern coast of South America.

Mexico and Central America

The Rio Grande River, known in Mexico as the Rio Bravo, forms much of the border between the United States and Mexico. Mexico is the third-largest country on the North American continent and the third-largest country in Latin America. On the east, Mexico is bordered by the Gulf of Mexico, and on the west by the Gulf of California and the Pacific Ocean. To the south are the Central American countries of Guatemala and Belize. About 75% of Mexico is a wide plateau that stretches between the Sierra Madre Occidental on the west and the Sierra Madre Oriental on the east. Central America is the name given to the narrow land bridge that connects North and South America. The region includes seven independent countries: Belize, Guatemala, El Salvador, Honduras, Nicaragua, Costa Rica, and Panama. Central America is bordered on the east by the Caribbean Sea and on the west by the Pacific Ocean. Much of the region is hot, steamy rainforest.

Children in Core Knowledge schools should have some familiarity with Mexico from their study of Mexico, the Maya, and the Aztec in Grade 1.

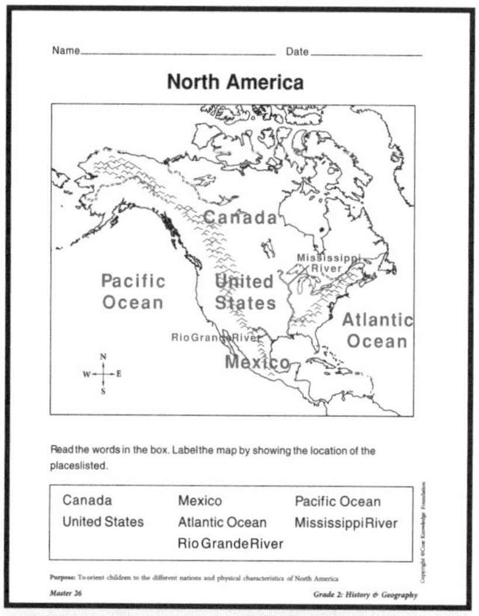

Use Instructional Master 26.

B. South America

Brazil

Brazil is the largest country in South America, containing more than half the people and land area of the continent. All the countries of South America, except Ecuador and Chile, share its borders. Brazil is home to the Amazon River, the second-largest river in the world, and its basin, which holds a rainforest that covers more than half of the country. The rainforest, with its hot and humid climate, supports a huge diversity of plant and animal life, much of which lives nowhere else in the world. Destruction of the rainforest to harvest its resources adds to the problem of global warming. The clearing and burning of trees causes carbon monoxide to be released into the atmosphere. This gas creates a greenhouse effect, causing temperatures on Earth to warm. As a result, the impact of rainforest deforestation has global consequences.

Teaching Idea

To make the countries more memorable for children, discuss crops children probably know about that are grown in various parts of South America, e.g., coffee, bananas.

Peru and Chile: The Andes Mountains

The Andes Mountains are the longest mountain range in the Western Hemisphere, running north to south down the western side of South America. In Peru and Bolivia, the mountains break into parallel ranges creating a wide plateau known as the altiplano. This area was the seat of the Inca Empire, which children learned about in Grade 1.

From 50% to 60% of Peru's people live in the highland plateau. About a third of the country's population lives in the narrow lowlands between the Andes and the Pacific Ocean. To the east of the Andes are low mountains and rainforest, which is part of the Amazon River basin. Almost half of all Peruvians are native Americans, most of whom farm the land and eke out an existence as subsistence farmers.

The Andes run north to south along the entire coast of Chile. As a result, most of the population lives in the Central Valley between the Andes and the coastal mountains. The Central Valley, a fertile area, is home to large cities, manufacturing centers, and agriculture.

VII. Geography of the Americas

Venezuela, Colombia, and Ecuador

Venezuela is bordered on the north by the Caribbean Sea, on the south by Brazil, on the east by Guyana, and on the west by Colombia. The Andes Mountains, called the Highlands in Venezuela, are the area of greatest population.

Colombia is bordered by both the Atlantic and Pacific Oceans. Its northern neighbors are Panama and Venezuela, and to the south, Colombia borders Ecuador, Peru, and Brazil. Three ranges of the Andes Mountains extend through Colombia, and most of Colombia's population lives in the Andean highlands. To the east of the Andes lie lowlands, a part of which is an extension of the Amazon River basin.

Ecuador is bordered by the Pacific Ocean on the west, Colombia on the north, and Peru on the east and south. The Andes Mountains are the dominant physical feature of the country, and most of the population lives in fertile valleys within the mountains. To the east of the Andes is a large area of the Amazon River basin.

Teaching Idea

To help children understand the importance of Simon Bolivar to many people in South America, explain that he is like George Washington in the United States—the man who led the fight for independence.

Bolivia

Bolivia is a landlocked, mountainous country. Because it has no ports, Bolivia has no easy way of transporting goods by water, although Lake Titicaca, high in the Andes between Peru and Bolivia, provides some water transportation. Like many Peruvians, most Bolivians are of native American descent and make their living by subsistence farming.

Simon Bolivar

Bolivia is named after Simon Bolivar, who is known as the Liberator. Bolivar began the liberation of Spanish South America from Spain in the early 1800s by defeating a large Spanish force and seizing the capital of the Spanish Viceroyalty of New Granada. This province became the seat of the new republic of Gran Colombia, which through years of fighting with the Spanish came to include what one day would be the modern countries of Colombia, Ecuador, Panama, and Venezuela. Bolivar waged the final battle against the Spanish in 1824, liberating Upper Peru, which was renamed Bolivia in his honor.

Teaching Idea

Use the overhead made from Instructional Master 27, *South America,* to orient children to the countries and physical features of South America. To review the use of map legends, have children color the mountainous areas brown, the rainforest green, the pampas orange, and the oceans blue, then have them mark their map keys accordingly. They could color the rest of the countries any colors but those four.

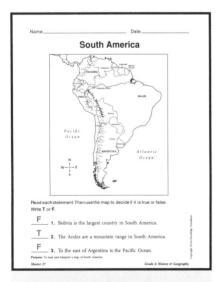

Name________________ Date__________

South America

Read each statement. Then use the map to decide if it is true or false. Write **T** or **F**.

F 1. Bolivia is the largest country in South America.

T 2. The Andes are a mountain range in South America.

F 3. To the east of Argentina is the Pacific Ocean.

Purpose: To read and interpret a map of South America

Master 27 *Grade 2: History & Geography*

Copyright ©Core Knowledge Foundation

Use Instructional Master 27.

Argentina and Uruguay

A major physical feature of Argentina and Uruguay is the pampas, grassy plains with a temperate climate, which extend from central and northern Argentina into Uruguay. Today, the eastern regions of the pampas, which have some rainfall, produce wheat and corn. In the drier western area, raising livestock is an important livelihood.

At one time gauchos, Argentinian cowboys, herded cattle on the pampas. Gauchos were mestizos who, beginning in the 17th century, earned their living working on the large ranches of the pampas. The gauchos' livelihood was destroyed by the coming of the railroad, fenced-in ranges, and settlers in the 19th century.

The Main Languages of South America

Two major European groups colonized South America: the Spanish and the Portuguese. In 1494, Spain and Portugal carved up the Americas through the Treaty of Tordesillas, deciding which country would settle which part. The Spanish received everything west of a certain degree of longitude and the Portuguese everything east. As a result, the main language of most South American countries, except Brazil, is Spanish, and the language of Brazil is Portuguese.

Review

Below are some ideas for ongoing assessment and review activities. These are not meant to constitute a comprehensive list. Teachers may also refer to the *Pearson Learning/Core Knowledge History & Geography* series for additional information and teaching ideas.

- Ask children to describe the direction in which they would travel to go from one specific place to another. For example, if going from Chile to Argentina, you would go east across the Andes Mountains. Use this activity throughout the year to reinforce the location of places discussed in other topics.
- The places discussed in this section can be connected with many other topics in the curriculum for this grade, e.g., Mexico with Cesar Chávez, Canada as a destination for runaway slaves, and Mexico and South America as sources of much current immigration to the United States.
- Although children will not be expected to know the 50 states and their capitals until fifth grade, you can start laying the foundation now. Set up a center with flash cards of the states and their capitals. As you familiarize children with the different states, they can also start learning the capitals.
- Use literature to reinforce each of the geography sections on North and South America. During one class period on geography, provide the class with a selection of books on North and South American geography and culture from the school library or a local library. Give each child an index card, and tell them that they will have a set amount of time to browse through the books. They should write two facts that they learn about North or South America while reading and looking at the pictures. At the end of the time, have the class gather and read what they have learned. Make a class list on chart paper of facts about North and South American geography and culture.
- As you are studying the various types of environments on each continent, include some of the animals that would live in those areas. This will provide a connection between science and the geography of the regions. The rainforests of Brazil are home to many exotic animals that children can discover. As you progress in the study of these areas, children can make animal flash cards with the geographic name on the back. For example, a card with a sloth on the front of the card would have Brazil on the back of the card.

The Big Idea in Review

People have adapted to the diverse landscape of North and South America.

• Assign each child a region or country that you have studied from this section. Then, give children 4 x 6 index cards to use as postcards. Have children decorate the front of the card with a map indicating the place from which they are writing. Then, on the back have them write a message describing that geographic point.

• Provide the class with individual copies of an outline of a body. Tell children that they need to pick one of the regions that they have studied in North or South America and draw the clothes that they would need to take to that region. For example, if traveling to the Rocky Mountains, the child might need a parka for the snow and cold temperatures in the winter. If traveling near the Equator, the child might need shorts and a T-shirt, or a bathing suit. Have the class write sentences to tell where the person would be traveling and why they would need that clothing.

• You may also ask the following questions at the end of this section:

1. What are the three largest countries on the North American continent? Have children locate them on the classroom or overhead map.
   The three largest countries on the North American continent are Canada, the United States, and Mexico.
2. Where are the Rocky Mountains? The Appalachian Mountains? Have children locate them on the classroom or overhead map.
   The Rocky Mountains run north to south along the western side of Alaska, Canada, and the continental United States. The Appalachian Mountains run north and south from eastern Canada through the eastern United States to central Alabama.
3. Where are the Gulf of Mexico and the Caribbean Sea? Have children locate them on the classroom or overhead map.
   The Gulf of Mexico borders the southeastern United States and the west coast of Florida. The Caribbean Sea lies between the West Indies to the north and east, Central America to the west, and South America to the south.
4. How did the West Indies get their name?
   The West Indies got their name when Columbus landed in the islands and thought that he had arrived in India by going west. He thought the islands were west of India, so he named them the "West Indies."
5. Where are the Andes Mountains? Have children locate them on the classroom or overhead map.
   The Andes Mountains run from Venezuela through Colombia, Ecuador, Peru, and Bolivia to Chile and Argentina.
6. What are the grasslands in Argentina and Uruguay called?
   The grasslands in Argentina and Uruguay are called pampas.
7. How did Bolivia get its name?
   Bolivia was named after Simon Bolivar, who freed most of Spanish South America from the Spanish Empire.

More Resources

The titles listed below are offered as a representative sample of materials and not a complete list of everything that is available.

For children —

These books are generally intended to be read aloud, though some children may be able to read parts or all of the simpler texts.

- *Geography of the Americas,* edited by E. D. Hirsch, Jr. (Pearson Learning, 2002). A unit in the official *Pearson Learning/Core Knowledge History & Geography series.* It includes a small picture book for children and a teacher's guide with read alouds. To order, call 1-800-321-3106.
- *A Child's Alaska,* by Claire Rudolf Murphy with photographs by Charles Mason (Alaska Northwest Books, 1994). Hardcover, 47 pages, ISBN 0882404571.
- *Amazing Rain Forest (Discovery Library of Rain Forests),* by Lynn Stone (Rourke Publishing, 1994). Hardcover, 24 pages, ISBN 0865933928.
- *Hill of Fire,* by Thomas Lewis and illustrated by Joan Sandin (HarperTrophy, 1983). The story of the man who discovered a volcano in his cornfield. A true story (except for the hot-dog stand, according to one reviewer). Paperback, 64 pages, ISBN 0064440400.
- *The Scrambled States of America,* by Laurie Keller (Henry Holt, 2002). Paperback, 40 pages, ISBN 0805068317.

For teachers —

- *Across This Land: A Regional Geography of the United States and Canada,* by John C. Hudson (Johns Hopkins University Press, 2002). Clearly organized and well written. A good reference. Paperback, 504 pages, ISBN 0801865670.
- *The Central Americans (The Peoples of North America),* by Faren Maree Bachelis (Chelsea House, 1990). Library binding, 110 pages, ISBN 0877548684.
- Visual Geography Series, www.vgsbooks.com, by Lerner Books features downloadable photos and maps, plus reviewed web links for Mexico, Brazil, Argentina, Guatemala, Peru, and the island of Puerto Rico. Learn about a family with seven children who perform as street clowns in Mexico City, listen to the roar of a jaguar in the Amazon rainforest, and look at stunning photographs of Argentina's Patagonia Wilderness. Check the website for additions to their selections.

VIII. Symbols and Figures

The Big Idea

People use symbols as shorthand for larger ideas and values. Symbols of America include the flag, the Statue of Liberty, and the Lincoln Memorial.

Remember that each subject you study with children expands their vocabulary and introduces new terms, thus making them better listeners and readers. As you study about historical people and events, use read alouds and discussions to build children's vocabularies.

What Students Should Already Know

Students in Core Knowledge schools should be familiar with

Kindergarten

- American flag
- Statue of Liberty
- Mount Rushmore
- The White House

Grade 1

- Liberty Bell
- Current U.S. president
- American flag; legend of Betsy Ross
- Eagle

What Students Need to Learn

- **The U.S. flag, current and earlier versions**
- **Statue of Liberty**
- **Lincoln Memorial**

What Students Will Learn in Future Grades

In future grades, students will review and extend their learning about American symbols and figures.

Grade 4

- Recognize and become familiar with the significance of
  - *Spirit of '76* (painting)
  - White House and Capitol Building
  - Great Seal of the United States

Vocabulary

Student/Teacher Vocabulary

ally: a country that gives support to another one for the achievement of a common cause (S)

Executive Order: a regulation issued by the president, based on Constitutional or statutory authority; has the force of law (T)

Lincoln Memorial: a memorial honoring the 16th president of the United States (S)

Statue of Liberty: a major symbol of freedom in the United States (S)

Domain Vocabulary

American flag and associated words:
stars and stripes, "The Star-Spangled Banner," "Stars and Stripes Forever," "Old Glory," 13 stars, blue field, background, 13 stripes, red, white, alternate, Continental Congress, Flag Day, June 14, unwieldy, too many, revert, go back, original, 13 colonies, stars, change, increase, 50 stars, 50 states, Fourth of July, July 4, Independence Day, Hawaii, 50th state

Statue of Liberty and associated words:
"Lady Liberty," symbol, country, freedom, better life, torch, crown, tablet, New York Harbor, Liberty Island, watches, guards, welcomes, immigrants, poem, Emma Lazarus, coming home, France, ally, gift, friendship, copper, metal

Lincoln Memorial and associated words:
Abraham Lincoln, Civil War, president, honor, celebrate, remember, memorialize, marble, white, clean lines, box-like, horizontal, huge, Greek columns, Doric columns, Parthenon, Daniel Chester French, sculptor, sculpture, seated figure, brooding, thoughtful, Lincoln penny, reverse, back of, excerpts, parts of, inscriptions, inscribed, chiseled, "Gettysburg Address," "Second Inaugural Address," speeches, equality, freedom, emancipation, affirm, rededicate, Marian Anderson, March on Washington (1963), Martin Luther King, Jr.

In the Text Resources for this section, words are bolded that should be included as part of Domain Vocabulary.

Text Resources

(63) *Abraham Lincoln: The Gettysburg Address*

(64) *The Pledge of Allegiance*

(66) *The New Colossus*

Materials

copies of the Gettysburg Address and the Second Inaugural Address, p. 237

a penny for each child, p. 237

postcards from Washington, D.C., and New York City, p. 238

chart paper, p. 238

Cross-curricular Connections

Language Arts	Visual Arts	Music
Poetry	**Architecture**	**Songs**
• "Lincoln"	• Parthenon	• "The Star-Spangled Banner"

At a Glance

The most important ideas for you are:

- The United States has various symbols that over time have come to represent the country and/or what its people generally value.
- As the United States has evolved over time, so has the flag evolved to represent the union of 50 states built on a foundation of the original 13 states.
- The Statue of Liberty is as much a symbol of freedom to today's immigrants as it was when it was erected in 1886.
- The Lincoln Memorial, by honoring Abraham Lincoln, the Great Emancipator, represents the concepts of democracy and freedom.

Teaching Idea

This is the third year in which children will study the American flag. Ask children what they already know about the history of the flag—what it represents, why the new United States would need a flag, what seeing the flag must have meant to Francis Scott Key standing on the ship, and so on. Then ask what the flag means to them. Talk about why the flag is a symbol and what it represents.

What Teachers Need to Know

The U.S. Flag: Current and Earlier Versions

The U.S. flag has evolved over time, not only in terms of the number of stars but also in the number of stripes and the proportions of the elements on the flag. The original flag had 13 stars in a circle on a blue field and 13 alternating red and white stripes, established by a law passed by the Continental Congress on June 14, 1777. This date is now commemorated as Flag Day.

Children may be familiar with the legend of Betsy Ross and the American flag based on their studies in Grade 1. According to legend, General George Washington, Robert Morris (who helped to finance the war), and Colonel George Ross visited the upholstery shop of Betsy Ross, who was the widow of Colonel Ross's nephew John. The three men asked her to design and sew the first flag. The story did not come to light until 1870, when a grandson of Ross, William J. Canby, first told it. There is no documentation to prove the account. Historians do not even know if Betsy Ross actually lived in the house in Philadelphia that is considered "the birthplace of the American flag." Nevertheless, the story has been told and retold and has entered American cultural literacy; it can be taught to children as a legend.

As more states entered the Union, more stripes as well as stars were added until the flag became unwieldy. By 1795, there were 15 stripes and 15 stars. In 1818, Congress passed another law stating that the number of stripes would revert to 13 to represent the original 13 states and that the number of stars would reflect the total number of states. The change in the number and pattern of stars would take place on the Fourth of July of the year after a new state was admitted to the Union.

In 1912, when two more states were added—New Mexico, the 47th state, and Arizona, the 48th—President William Howard Taft issued an Executive Order once more changing the look of the flag. For the first time, the proportions of the flag were established and also the arrangement of the stars, six horizontal rows of eight stars. Up until this time, there was no official arrangement of stars, and flagmakers made whatever pattern they wished. As a result, there was no consistent design among 19th-century flags other than the number of stripes and stars. The latest change to the flag occurred in 1959 with the admission to statehood of first Alaska and then Hawaii, the 49th and 50th states. Some nicknames for the flag include the "Stars and Stripes" and "Old Glory." (64)

The Statue of Liberty

The Statue of Liberty, a present from the French people to the United States, stands on Liberty Island in New York Harbor. The statue, designed by sculptor Frederic Bartholdi, is 152 feet tall. Its outer covering is copper. Its interior framework was designed by Alexandre Eiffel, the engineer who designed the Eiffel Tower in Paris.

The Statue of Liberty was given to the United States by France in honor of the country's independence and to celebrate the friendship between France and the

United States that dates back to the Revolutionary War. France was the first and main European ally of the new United States.

The gift was originally meant to be presented in 1876 in commemoration of American independence, but lack of funding delayed the project. It was not dedicated until 1886. To celebrate the statue's own 100th anniversary, it was closed for two years for a cleaning and general restoration and was reopened on July 4, 1986, during a four-day celebration.

The lines of poetry on the statue's base are from the poem "The New Colossus" by Emma Lazarus. For the best-known lines of the poem, reference the information on Ellis Island and the Statue of Liberty in the Immigration and Citizenship section (p. 204). 66

The Lincoln Memorial

The Lincoln Memorial in Washington, D.C., was dedicated in 1922 in honor of the 16th president, Abraham Lincoln. The design of the memorial is based on the Parthenon in Athens. The memorial's 36 Doric columns represent the number of states during Lincoln's presidency. The central feature of the memorial is a huge seated figure of Abraham Lincoln, created by the noted American sculptor Daniel Chester French, who also sculpted *The Minute Man,* a statue at North Bridge in Concord, Massachusetts. The memorial is reproduced on the reverse of the penny.

On the walls of the memorial are inscribed Lincoln's most famous speeches, the Gettysburg Address and his Second Inaugural Address. Other inscriptions are excerpts from Lincoln's speeches about equality, freedom and emancipation, and the Union itself. 63

The Lincoln Memorial has been a gathering place for affirming the country's belief in democracy, while striving to ensure that democracy is for all its people. In 1939, the soprano Marian Anderson gave a stirring performance in front of the memorial after she had been barred from singing at Constitutional Hall in Washington because she was African-American. Eleanor Roosevelt, an ardent advocate for social justice, invited her to sing in front of the memorial. In 1963, during the March on Washington, several hundred thousand people assembled in front of the memorial to hear Dr. Martin Luther King, Jr., and others speak against racial discrimination and for a civil rights legislation that was then before Congress. The bill was ultimately approved.

Teaching Idea

While you may need to paraphrase some of Emma Lazarus's poem "The New Colossus" for children, read it aloud and discuss what the imagery means. Point out that in Europe at the end of the 19th century, many people were very, very poor. Compared to life at home, the streets of America were "paved with gold," or so immigrants wrote in letters home that urged their families and friends to make the long journey by ship to America.

Teaching Idea

Both the Gettysburg Address and the Second Inaugural Address are very short and very moving. Both are widely available in books and online. Consider sharing one or both with your class.

Teaching Idea

The Lincoln Memorial is considered to be a symbol of American democracy. Work with children to determine why. Show children the Lincoln Memorial on the back of a penny. (Its design is based on the Parthenon. The ancient Greeks were the first to practice democracy, even in a limited form. The memorial honors Abraham Lincoln and his efforts to save the Union and to extend the country's freedoms to African Americans.) Remind children that Lincoln is called the Great Emancipator.

The Big Idea in Review

People use symbols as shorthand for larger ideas and values. Symbols of America include the flag, the Statue of Liberty, and the Lincoln Memorial.

Review

Below are some ideas for ongoing assessment and review activities. These are not meant to constitute a comprehensive list. Teachers may also refer to the *Pearson Learning/Core Knowledge History & Geography* series for additional information and ideas.

- One effective way to study these symbols and figures is to incorporate them into the historical studies from this section. There are activities that review the Statue of Liberty in earlier sections, particularly when studying immigration and citizenship. Children also review the American flag in this section. You may want to discuss the Lincoln Memorial during the study of the Civil War to highlight how this country memorialized Lincoln.
- Gather postcards from Washington, D.C., and New York City to display pictures of the Statue of Liberty and the Lincoln Memorial from different perspectives. Have children write about how they feel when they look at these memorials. Why do they feel this way?
- You may also ask children if any of them have visited these two memorials. Have those children give a description of visiting these sites.
- Discuss the meanings of symbols with the class. What do these memorials represent? Have children design their own statue on a piece of paper. If they were going to be remembered by a statue or memorial, what would they have built to symbolize them? Have them design and draw the memorial, and then write a description. Post these around the room, and see if children can guess who designed each picture.
- Make a list of the symbols from this section on chart paper, and then have the class brainstorm adjectives that describe each symbol. Use those adjectives in a writing assignment to describe each symbol.
- You may also ask the following questions at the end of this section:

1. How many stars are in our current flag?
   There are 50 stars in our current flag.
2. What do the stars represent?
   The stars represent the 50 states.
3. Has the flag always had 50 stars?
   No, the United States had only 13 states in the beginning and the flag had only 13 stars. Each time a state was added, a star was added.
4. What did the Statue of Liberty mean to immigrants?
   Seeing the Statue of Liberty meant that they were entering a land of freedom/liberty. It was one of the first things that immigrants saw when they arrived in New York from Europe.

More Resources

The titles listed below are offered as a representative sample of materials and not a complete list of everything that is available.

For children —

These books are generally intended to be read aloud, though some children may be able to read parts or all of the simpler texts.

- *The Flag We Love,* by Pam Munoz Ryan (Charlesbridge, 2000). Paperback, 32 pages, ISBN 0881068446.
- *The Lincoln Memorial (National Landmarks),* by Kathleen Deady (Bridgestone Books, 2002). Library binding, 24 pages, ISBN 0736811141.
- *The Lincoln Memorial (Symbols of Freedom),* by Tristan Boyer Binns (Heinemann, 2001). Paperback, 32 pages, ISBN 1588104044. Series also includes titles on the American Flag and the Pledge of Allegiance.
- *The Pledge of Allegiance* (Scholastic, 2001). Paperback, 32 pages, ISBN 0439241847. See also *I Pledge Allegiance,* by Bill Martin, Jr., and Michael Sampson, and illustrated by Chris Raschka (Candlewick Press, 2002). Hardcover, ISBN 0763616486.
- *Red, White, and Blue: The Story of the American Flag (All Aboard Reading, Level 2),* by John Herman and illustrated by Robin Roraback (Grosset & Dunlap, 1998). Paperback, 48 pages, ISBN 0448412705.
- *Stars and Stripes: The Story of the American Flag,* by Sarah L. Thomson (HarperCollins, 2003). A clear history that will make a good read aloud. Has an endnote that challenges the familiar Betsy Ross story. Hardcover, 32 pages, ISBN 0060504161.
- *The Star-Spangled Banner,* by Francis Scott Key and illustrated by Peter Spier (Yearling Books, 1992). The text of the national anthem accompanied by Caldecott medalist Peter Spier's wonderfully detailed, full-color drawings. Includes a facsimile of Key's original manuscript. Paperback, 56 pages, ISBN 0440406978.
- *The Statue of Liberty (Step into Reading, Step 1),* by Lucille Recht Penner and illustrated by Jada Rowland (Random House, 1995). Simple text and good illustrations. Paperback, 32 pages, ISBN 067986928X.
- *The Story of the Statue of Liberty,* by Betsy Maestro and illustrated by Giulio Maestro (HarperTrophy, 1989). Paperback, 48 pages, ISBN 0688087469.

For teachers —

- *Capital,* by Lynn Curlee (Atheneum Books for Young Readers, 2003). Hardcover, 44 pages, ISBN 0689849478.
- *The Stars and the Stripes: The American Flag as Art and History from the Birth of the Republic to the Present,* by Boleslaw Mastai and Marie-Louise d'Otrange Mastai (William S. Konecky Associates, 2002). Flags from the amazing Mastai Collection, the result of decades of work and devotion. 255 color plates. Hardcover, 248 pages, ISBN 1568523823.
- Corbis, www.corbis.com, has hundreds of images available on the Statue of Liberty and the Lincoln Memorial, including the head of the statue on display in Paris in 1883, the torch at the Philadelphia Centennial Exposition in 1876, and Martin Luther King, Jr., delivering his "I Have a Dream" speech at the Lincoln Memorial on August 28, 1963.
- The Great Buildings Collection, www.greatbuildings.com. Search for "Statue of Liberty."
- The Statue of Liberty–Ellis Island Foundation, Inc., www.ellisisland.org. Click on the item "Immigrant Experience" to read the stories of six American immigrant families searching for their relatives, and explore an interactive time line of immigration history.
- Lincoln Memorial (National Park Service), www.nps.gov/linc. Much information, very few pictures.
- Statue of Liberty National Monument and Ellis Island (National Park Service), www.nps.gov/stli. Contains a history, children's activities, museum exhibits, and more. Scroll down this page to see all that is offered here.
- The Statue of Liberty Photo Tour, www.nyctourist.com/liberty1.htm. Tourist-oriented trip to the Statue of Liberty.

Visual Arts

Percentages beside major topics provide a rough guide for allocating time for Visual Arts during the year.

Visual Arts in Second Grade

Second graders should arrive with some understanding and appreciation of the visual arts from their experiences in earlier grades. Children in Core Knowledge schools should be familiar with specific pieces of art by famous artists. In Grade 2, their knowledge, skills, and understanding will be increased by looking at a variety of artworks.

Many children will already have acquired some knowledge about the elements of art. They will review and extend their learning about how artists use lines. Line is a vital element in art. It can define both the inside and outside of objects, and it can establish a sense of mood. A composition filled with only straight, hard-edged lines will have a different feeling than one full of sinuous lines. Likewise, artists can use lines to direct our eyes along particular pathways when viewing their work. While studying line, children will look at works by such artists as Pablo Picasso and Katsusika Hokusai.

Real and implied lines also exist in three-dimensional works, such as sculpture. They can serve the same function, establishing a mood, sense of direction, and/or degree of movement. In sculpture, however, we can walk around the lines (and forms) themselves, changing our point of view, as compared to a two-dimensional work that can be examined only from a single perspective. Second graders will learn about such famous pieces of sculpture as *The Discobolus (Discus Thrower), Flying Horse, One Leg Resting on a Swallow,* and *The Thinker.*

Within art, landscapes are an important subject (or genre). Although most people think of landscapes as paintings that depict a rural environment, they can also depict an urban scene. Seascapes, too, are a subgenre of landscapes.

When working abstractly, some artists continue to link their images more or less loosely to the recognizable world. Others depart completely, creating what are known as "nonobjective" compositions. Children will have an opportunity to learn about abstract art that uses familiar animals, such as Paul Klee's *Cat and Bird.*

Architecture, on the other hand, remains tightly bound to the human sphere. This might be because it is virtually the only art form humans can experience inside and outside! As three-dimensional entities, buildings can contain an enormous variety of lines, forms, and textures. Architecture can visually convey its purpose, such as the sweeping scale or ornate decoration of a sacred temple or the fortified walls and tall towers of a castle. Visible to nearly everyone, architecture has been one of the most "public" forms of art from the earliest of times until the present. Children will be introduced to several of the world's most famous buildings, including the Parthenon and the Great Stupa of Sanchi. Several of these buildings are connected with cultures studied in the History and Geography curriculum for this grade.

In this grade, children are building a framework of skills that will help them in future grades to learn more about and appreciate both classic and contemporary works of art.

I. Elements of Art

The Big Idea

Deeper investigation of the element of line will increase children's appreciation of works of art.

What Students Should Already Know

Students in Core Knowledge schools should be familiar with

Kindergarten and Grade 1

- Color
  - Warm and cool
  - Primary and secondary
- Line
  - Identify and use different lines: straight, zigzag, curved, wavy, thick, thin
  - Observe different kinds of lines in specific artworks
- Shape
  - Recognize basic geometric shapes in nature, objects, and artworks
- Texture
  - Describe qualities such as rough, smooth, bumpy, scratchy, slippery, etc.

What Students Need to Learn

- **Recognize lines as horizontal, vertical, or diagonal**
- **Observe the use of line in**
  - **Pablo Picasso, *Mother and Child***
  - **Katsusika Hokusai, *The Great Wave at Kanagawa* from *Thirty-Six Views of Mt. Fuji***

What Students Will Learn in Future Grades

In Grade 3, students will explore three new elements of art.

- Light
- Space in artworks
- Design: how the elements of art work together

I. Elements of Art

Materials

Art Resources

Pablo Picasso, *Mother and Child*

Katsusika Hokusai, *The Great Wave at Kanagawa* from *Thirty-Six Views of Mt. Fuji*

Instructional Masters 28–29b

Between the Lines, p. 246

Talking to Children About Works of Art, p. 247

ruler, p. 247

drawing materials, pp. 248–249

surface for the children to carry and write on (clipboards), p. 248

paintings with prominent lines, p. 248

chart paper, p. 249

different kinds of paper, p. 249

index cards, p. 249

Vocabulary

Student/Teacher Vocabulary

implied lines: lines that are suggested by a series of separate points or edges of shapes that the viewer tends to see as connected (S)

implied movement: in art, lines and/or shapes that convey or suggest motion (T)

line: a continuous mark with length and direction (S)

Domain Vocabulary

Elements of art (line) and associated words:
sketch, pencil, ink, pen, charcoal, pigment, brush, chalk, pastel, horizontal, vertical, print, woodblock, reproduction, diagonal, outline, linear, curve, zigzag, swirl, clockwise, circular, jagged, spiral, slant, droop, loop, visible, composition, organize, movement, two-dimensional, realistic, lifelike, natural, recognizable, space, abstract, patterned, subject matter, united, foreground, background, *plus words that describe things in paintings, e.g.,* forest, tower, bull, horns, hare, goat, gaze, maternal, nestled, wave, *etc.*

Cross-curricular Connections

History and Geography

World: Geography

- Locate Asia and Europe on maps and/or globes

World: Modern Civilization and Culture: Japan

Mathematics

Geometry

- Identify lines as horizontal, vertical, perpendicular, and parallel

At a Glance

The most important ideas for you are:

- Single, straight lines can be horizontal, vertical, or diagonal.
- Other lines can zigzag, curve, spiral, swirl, wave, and so forth.
- Artists use implied lines, as well as those that are clearly visible, to help organize compositions and focus the viewer's gaze.
- Lines in art can suggest movement.
- Children should have opportunities to practice using lines in art projects.

What Teachers Need to Know

Background

It is vital to engage children in art during the second-grade year. Drawing, painting, cutting, tearing, modeling, and pasting help develop small-motor and coordination skills. Likewise, talking about art develops their verbal and visual abilities through identifying (colors, lines, objects, actions), sorting (warm colors from cool colors), and communicating ideas (the children are playing a game). Children develop visual literacy by looking at pictures, and they build language skills by describing what is happening in a specific artwork.

Remember, too, that children need practice exploring and creating art. Children need plenty of opportunities to draw, squeeze clay, cut and paste paper, and paint. Be sure to supplement art viewing with activities that allow children to create art. Creativity is not limited to a few people with a special talent; we all have the capacity to be creative.

Note: The descriptions and activities in the main text below are intended to help you become familiar with the artworks before presenting them to children; however, some of the activities might be adapted for classroom use. Activities intended specifically for children can be found in the Teaching Idea sidebars. The Looking Questions given below are also printed on the reverse side of the *Art Resources* and have been written with children in mind so that they might be used as a rough plan for class discussion. You should feel free to use these questions or develop questions of your own. Be sure children have time to look at the reproductions carefully before asking the Looking Questions.

Straight Lines

Draw a tic-tac-toe grid. Mark the three different types of lines you can use to win the game: horizontal, vertical, and diagonal lines. What do these lines have in common? Each one is straight. However, their various orientations differ, which makes them distinct in art.

First, let's recall where we see these single, straight lines in the world around us. You'll find straight lines in fences, wall corners, sidewalks, building outlines, windows, plaid designs—even in the lines the fuel makes after rockets take off.

Straight lines appear mostly in human-made elements. It's challenging to think of examples that occur organically in nature. Most lines, in fact, are not perfectly straight—in real life or in art. They dip, curve, zigzag, wave, swirl, wobble, and so forth. Examine the included reproduction of Pablo Picasso's *Mother and Child.* How many perfectly straight lines can you detect? There are far more curving, arching, and bending lines. What adjectives would you use for these lines—perhaps soft, gentle, or calm? Consider how different the portrait would appear if Picasso had only used straight lines. Everything would be much more angular. Picasso's lines convey the physicality of the two figures and also their relationship—which seems warm and close. It might be helpful to show children a reproduction of a Picasso analytic Cubist portrait, in which he uses mostly straight lines, to provide an example of contrasting styles. (See discussion in the Looking Section on p. 247.)

Teaching Idea

Help children review various types of lines in the world around them. Begin with the three basic single, straight lines, having them use Instructional Master 28, *Between the Lines*. Remind children that life-like drawing is not important for this activity, but rather their ability to identify the kinds of objects in which they can find particular lines.

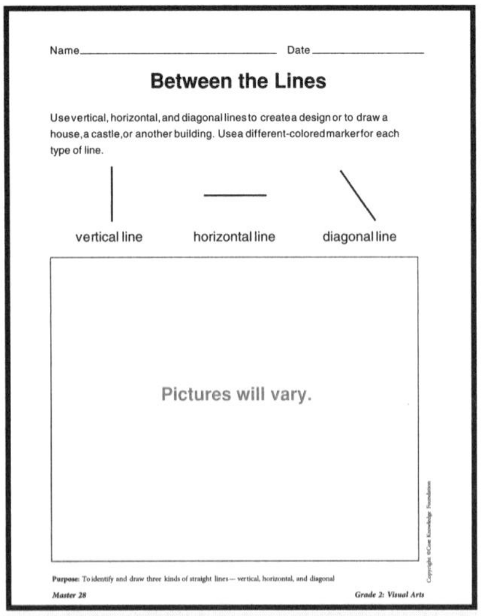
Name________________ Date__________

Between the Lines

Use vertical, horizontal, and diagonal lines to create a design or to draw a house, a castle, or another building. Use a different-colored marker for each type of line.

vertical line | horizontal line | diagonal line

Pictures will vary.

Purpose: To identify and draw three kinds of straight lines — vertical, horizontal, and diagonal

Master 28 *Grade 2: Visual Arts*

Copyright ©Core Knowledge Foundation

Use Instructional Master 28.

Teaching Idea

Review what children learned about different types of lines in Kindergarten and Grade 1. Then have them help you create a master list on the board of as many lines as possible. Examples may include horizontal, diagonal, vertical, jagged, spiraling, curved, bent, zigzag, wavy, loopy, swirling, bouncing, and drooping lines.

Implied Lines—In Life and Art

When is a line there, but sort of "not there"? When it's an implied line. On scrap paper, draw three dots in a straight row. You have created an implied line—one that is suggested, but not actually drawn. The place where a book edge meets a tabletop is an implied line, as are the corners where two walls converge.

Implied lines don't have to be straight. The space between your lips when you press them together is an implied line, which you can form into a downward curved frown or upward curved smile. Artists frequently use implied lines in their compositions.

Guiding Lines

Many viewers have noticed that the figures in Picasso's *Mother and Child* seem to be arranged along an implied diagonal line, sloping from upper left to lower right. This line leads our eye from the mother's face to the child's face, then downward toward her hand and knee. Some viewers see this line as part of a larger triangular arrangement in the painting. The eye looks first at the mother, then moves diagonally to the child, the mother's hand and knee, and then across to the left again before sweeping right back up to her face.

Artists can use both visible and implied lines to guide our gaze from one area of the composition to another. Typically, this is so subtle that viewers might not even notice the artist intentionally doing this. Observe how Katsusika Hokusai [HOE-coo-sye] steers our eye in a circle in *The Great Wave at Kanagawa.* We follow the wave from the bottom of the trough, up the side of the wave, to the crest, and we imagine what it will be like when the crest crashes down on the water beneath it. His curving lines emphasize the wave's force while simultaneously keeping our eye moving from one area to another within the print. (See discussion in the Looking Section on p. 247.)

Linear Movement—Implied Movement

By guiding our vision, real and implied lines also evoke an intuitive sense of movement. Obviously, the lines in a two-dimensional artwork don't actually move, so it is implied movement.

Compare Hokusai's implied movement to that in Picasso's portrait. Which is more static? Picasso's implied linear triangle conveys a sense of stillness, not swelling, energetic motion.

If two-dimensional art is inherently inert, why would artists want to establish a sense of motion? In Picasso's painting, the stillness seems to augment the subjects' mood and message; we feel that the mother and child are comfortable as they are, comfortable with each other, and not about to rearrange themselves. The motion in Hokusai's more energetic print implies a sense of time. The print appears to capture a split second—encouraging us to view it as part of a continuum with scenes that happened just before and right after the one we're looking at. For example, the image allows, perhaps even encourages, us to ask, "What will happen to the boats in the next few seconds?" In this way, a work's implied motion can seem to defy its inherently static nature.

Looking at Line

art resource 1

Pablo Picasso, *Mother and Child* (1922)

In his very early career, Picasso drew realistically, capturing the lifelike details of his models. When Pablo Picasso (1881–1973) painted his first wife, Olga, and their young son, Paulo, he had long since explored different abstract styles. Despite the painting's recognizable subject, Picasso included abstract elements, such as the minimally patterned leaves on the right side that hang in an indiscernible space.

Use a straight edge (ruler or book edge) to connect the crown of the mother's head to just inside her left knee. What does this implied diagonal line (moving from the upper-left side of the picture to the lower-right side) intersect? The suggested diagonal line unites the mother and son. Picasso further enhances their relationship with two additional implied lines. Locate the vertical line from the woman's head down to her hips; and also the horizontal line from the woman's right hip to her left kneecap. What shape do these three lines form? It is a right triangle, which subtly conveys a sense of stability. Picasso uses the triangle to ground his family unit visually, thereby increasing its emotional message. (See discussion in sections above.)

Looking questions

- **Tell me what you see in this picture.** ***Answers will vary, but children should see a woman, child, and leaves.***
- **With your finger, draw a line from the top of the mother's head, along the edge of the child, to the mother's knee. What kind of line did you make?** ***Children should make a diagonal line.***
- **Where else do you see diagonal lines?** ***There are diagonal lines in the child's arms and legs and in the leaves.***
- **Where do you see horizontal lines?** ***There are horizontal lines in the eyebrows, mouths, fingers, and clothes.***
- **Can you see any areas where Picasso left out details?** ***The leaves in the background aren't attached to a vine. Shoelaces haven't been drawn either.***
- **How does the artist show the warm, loving feeling between mother and child?** ***The mother's gaze, her hand around her son's waist, the boy calmly nestled, the peaceful expressions, the quiet/still composition, and the closeness of the figures all indicate warm, loving feelings.***

art resource 2

Katsusika Hokusai, *The Great Wave at Kanagawa* from *Thirty-Six Views of Mt. Fuji* (1823–1829)

The Japanese artist Katsusika Hokusai (1760–1849) was passionate about depicting the natural world around him. He is perhaps best known for his woodblock print series *Thirty-Six Views of Mt. Fuji* (1831), which he completed approximately between the ages of 64 and 74 years old. Each print in the series describes a different landscape of his homeland, in which he included Mount Fuji.

Hokusai worked steadily well into his 80s, leaving behind literally thousands of artworks as a legacy. When he died at 89, Hokusai was reported to have said

Teaching Idea

After carefully reviewing implied lines with children, help them hone their identification skills with the following activity. Pair up children and ask them to list on a sheet of paper all the places on their partner's face and hands that they can find implied lines. Thus, an eyelash or eyebrow doesn't count, but the line between their lips or their fingers when pressed together would be correct. The lines where their cuticles and nails meet is an additional example.

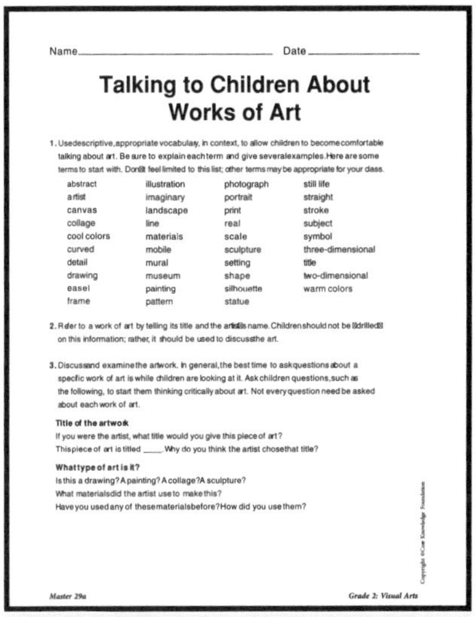
Name ____________ Date ____________

Talking to Children About Works of Art

1. Use descriptive, appropriate vocabulary, in context, to allow children to become comfortable talking about art. Be sure to explain each term and give several examples. Here are some terms to start with. Don't feel limited to this list; other terms may be appropriate for your class.

abstract	illustration	photograph	still life
artist	imaginary	portrait	straight
canvas	landscape	print	stroke
collage	line	real	subject
cool colors	materials	scale	symbol
curved	mobile	sculpture	three-dimensional
detail	mural	setting	title
drawing	museum	shape	two-dimensional
easel	painting	silhouette	warm colors
frame	pattern	statue	

2. Refer to a work of art by telling its title and the artist's name. Children should not be "drilled" on this information; rather, it should be used to discuss the art.

3. Discuss and examine the artwork. In general, the best time to ask questions about a specific work of art is while children are looking at it. Ask children questions, such as the following, to start them thinking critically about art. Not every question need be asked about each work of art.

Title of the artwork
If you were the artist, what title would you give this piece of art?
This piece of art is titled ____. Why do you think the artist chose that title?

What type of art is it?
Is this a drawing? A painting? A collage? A sculpture?
What materials did the artist use to make this?
Have you used any of these materials before? How did you use them?

Copyright © Core Knowledge Foundation

Master 29a — Grade 2: Visual Arts

Use Instructional Masters 29a and 29b.

Teaching Idea

Have children draw lines to visually depict the movements of waves, streams, and waterfalls. Then have children study how nature creates these natural water movements.

that if heaven had only given him another ten, or even five, years, he would then have been sure "to become a true artist."

Look again at the included reproduction of Katsusika Hokusai's *The Great Wave at Kanagawa.* No matter where you start—the boat in the foreground, the surging wave, or the distant mountain—Hokusai keeps our eyes moving in a circular, clockwise motion. As our eye travels around his print, Hokusai helps us translate the rolling waves into an internalized, physical sensation. The circular motion reinforces his subject matter—boats caught in turbulent waters. Hokusai's implied swift movement places us within the sea vessels for an adventure—of fun or terror—depending on your point of view. (See further discussion in section above.)

Looking questions

Note: Cover up the title on the front of the print before showing to children.

- **What do you see in this picture?** ***Answers will vary, but children should see giant waves, sea foam, one or more boats, a mountain, and writing.***
- **Do you see any people?** ***Yes, they look very small in a long, narrow boat.***
- **What do you think is about to happen to the people? Would you like to be them? Why or why not?** ***A wave is about to crash down on the boat. Children may say that the scene looks exciting or dangerous.***
- **There is a snowy mountain in the distance. What do you notice about the lines of the mountain and the lines of the waves?** ***They are similar, almost vertical, as though the waves are mountains.***
- **Are there any signs that this is a Japanese picture?** ***Yes, there are printed letters in Japanese in the upper left-hand corner.***

The Big Idea in Review

Deeper investigation of the element of line will increase children's appreciation of works of art.

Review

Below are some ideas for ongoing assessment and review activities. These are not meant to constitute a comprehensive list.

- Review types of lines by taking the children on a line scavenger hunt around the building and school grounds. Ask them to take a piece of paper, a pencil, and a hard surface for writing (for example, a clipboard). Have children look for different types of lines and then record on a piece of paper where they are seeing them. When you return to the classroom, have children read their lists of places and types of lines they identified.
- Place the art prints of Pablo Picasso's and Katsusika Hokusai's paintings next to each other. Based on your discussion of line in the pictures, have children write a paragraph describing the picture and the use of line in the picture. Without identifying the picture they are describing, have children read their paragraphs aloud, and then their classmates can try to guess which picture they are describing.
- To deepen children's understanding of line, choose other paintings with prominent lines for them to inspect.
- Give each child a set of one to three simple lines drawn on a sheet of paper, and ask them to draw a picture of something shaped more or less like these lines.

For example, two vertical lines might be turned into a tall building, two diagonal lines sloping down into a waterfall, a semicircle into a bridge or a cupped hand, etc. Give the same set of lines to several different children so their use of line can be compared. Have children show their pictures and invite others to guess what the original pattern was. You may wish to give out the line patterns a day or two before you ask children to draw, so they can have time to look for things in their world that are shaped like the lines.

- Use a Venn diagram on chart paper to compare and contrast the two works of art from this section. What are the similarities and differences? Ask the class to talk about which piece is their favorite and why.

- Post the two pictures on the wall and designate a child as teacher for the day. When a visitor comes into the room, have the teacher for the day stand and give a short talk about the use of line in either of the pictures.

- Give children an opportunity to draw their own pictures using a variety of lines on different kinds of paper. They may want to refer to the bank of vocabulary that describes lines and then create different pictures. Have children write a description of their use of line in their pictures, and then print those descriptions on an index card. Post the pictures and the index cards in a class gallery.

- In general, the best time to ask questions about a specific painting is while children are looking at it. However, by the end of the section, children should be able to answer the general questions on line. You may also ask the following questions at the end of this section:

1. What are three basic kinds of straight lines?
   Three basic kinds of straight lines are vertical, horizontal, and diagonal.
2. What is an implied line?
   An implied line is one that is suggested, but not actually drawn.

More Resources

The titles listed below are offered as a representative sample of materials and not a complete list of everything that is available.

For children —

These books are generally intended to be read aloud, though some children may be able to read parts or all of the simpler texts.

• *Come Look with Me: Enjoying Art with Children,* by Gladys S. Blizzard (Lickle Publishing, 1996). A great discussion starter. Includes two paintings by Pablo Picasso. Hardcover, 32 pages, ISBN 0934738769. Also in this same series is *The Artist at Work,* which has examples of Japanese (Suzuki Harunobu) and Japanese-inspired (James McNeil Whistler) paintings. Available through Lickle Publishing, www.licklepublishing.com or 1-866-454-2553.

• *Draw Write Now, Book 6: Animals & Habitats,* by Marie Hablitzel and Kim Stitzer (Barker Creek Publishing, 1999). A drawing and handwriting course for young children. Good cross-curricular connections. Paperback, 64 pages, ISBN 0963930761. Other titles in the multiple-volume series include *Animals of the World, Part II (Savannas, Grasslands, Mountains and Deserts); The Polar Regions, The Arctic, the Antarctic;* and *The United States, From Sea to Sea, Moving Forward.*

• *Hokusai: The Man Who Painted a Mountain,* by Deborah Kogan Ray (Frances Foster Books, 2001). Hardcover, 40 pages, ISBN 0374332630.

For teachers —

• *Drawing with Children,* by Mona Brookes (J. P. Tarcher, 1996). Teaches the basics of realistic drawing—the five "elements of shape"—to children as young as four or five. Useful for any age level. Paperback, 272 pages, ISBN 0874778271.

• *How to Teach Art to Children,* by Joy Evans and Tanya Skelton (Evan-Moor Corporation, 2001). An excellent companion to *Drawing with Children.* Covers color, patterns, designs, textures, and more. Paperback, 160 pages, ISBN 1557998116.

• Art Print Resources (209 Riverdale Avenue, Yonkers, NY 10705, www.artprintresources.com, or 1-800-501-4278) sells a set of 10 posters of artworks in the *Sequence* for this grade.

• Art Sense (www.artsense.net) provides an art program using videotapes and trade books.

• Art to the Core (Davis Publications, www.davis-art.com or 1-800-533-2847). A kit of materials that includes slides of artworks, lesson plans, assessment masters, and vocabulary masters, all keyed to the *Core Knowledge Sequence* for this grade.

• Crizmac (www.crizmac.com) sells a wide range of art education materials.

• Usborne (www.edcpub.com) has a wide range of art books, coloring books, and workbooks for the early grades.

II. Sculpture

The Big Idea

Children's appreciation of sculpture can be enhanced by exploring line, form, and mass.

What Students Should Already Know

Students in Core Knowledge schools should be familiar with

Kindergarten

- Recognize and discuss the following as sculptures:
  - Northwest Coast Native American totem pole
  - Statue of Liberty
  - Mobiles: Alexander Calder's *Lobster Trap and Fish Tail*

Grade 1

- Art from Long Ago
  - Art of Ancient Egypt: Bust of Queen Nefertiti

What Students Need to Learn

- **Observe shape, mass, and line in sculptures, including**
  - **Myron of Athens, *The Discobolus (Discus Thrower)***
  - ***Flying Horse, One Leg Resting on a Swallow* (from Wu-Wei, China)**
  - **Auguste Rodin, *The Thinker***

What Students Will Learn in Future Grades

In future grades, students will review and extend their learning about sculpture.

Grade 3

- Elements of Art
  - space in artworks

Grade 4

- The Art of Africa
  - Yoruba sculptures
  - bronze sculptures of Benin

Grade 5

- Art of the Renaissance
  - Donatello, *Saint George*
  - Michelangelo, *David*
- Art of Japan
  - the Great Buddha

II. Sculpture

Materials

Art Resources

Myron of Athens, *The Discobolus (Discus Thrower)*

Flying Horse, One Leg Resting on a Swallow

Auguste Rodin, *The Thinker*

Instructional Master 30

Looking at Sculpture, p. 255

decorative object, p. 254

supplemental art prints, p. 254

frisbee, p. 256

number line, p. 258

paper for sculpture, p. 258

modeling clay, p. 258

styrofoam, p. 258

a cup of water for each child, p. 258

sports magazines, p. 259

pipe cleaners, p. 259

Vocabulary

Student/Teacher Vocabulary

form: an element of design that is three-dimensional and encloses volume (S)

mass: the quantity of matter an object contains (S)

negative space: the space defined by the positive elements (shapes in two-dimensional art, forms in three-dimensional art); sometimes referred to as "empty space" (T)

patina: a green film resulting from oxidation that is typically found on copper or bronze (T)

sculpture: a three-dimensional work of art (that may be carved, modeled, or assembled (S)

shape: a two-dimensional enclosed area (S)

Domain Vocabulary

Sculpture and associated words:
carve, balance, position, pose, in the round, high relief, low relief, proportion, form, volume, organic, perspective, gravity, tension, motion, expression, representation, illusion, sculptor, enclosed area, three-dimensional versus two-dimensional, 360 degrees, height, width, depth, relationship, statue, public art, media, metal, balance, freestanding sculpture, function, spiritual, ritual, decorated, represent, subject matter, pole, lifelike, form, chisel, mallet, hammer, marble, stone, wood, clay, metal, wax, plaster, cast, bronze, *plus words that describe the sculptures, e.g.,* discus, competition, galloping, gaze, *etc.*

Cross-curricular Connections

Language Arts

Fiction

Mythology of Ancient Greece

- Gods of ancient Greece (and Rome)
- Greek myths

History and Geography

World: Geography

- Locate Asia and Europe on maps and/or globes

World: Early Civilization: Asia

Geography of Asia

- Locate China

World: Ancient Greece

- Geography
- Olympic Games

Mathematics

Measurement

- Mass and volume

Geometry

- Identify solid figures—sphere, cube, pyramid, cone, cylinder

At a Glance

The most important ideas for you are:

- Sculptures can have real and implied lines.
- Three-dimensional elements in sculpture are called forms.
- Sculpture typically can be viewed from 360 degrees.
- Sculptures have mass.
- Sculptures can suggest movement or motion.
- More than one version of a sculpture can exist.
- Sculptures reveal information about the cultures in which they were made.

What Teachers Need to Know

Background

Discuss with children three types of sculpture—sculpture in the round, in high relief, and in low relief. Although all sculptures are three-dimensional, not all can be walked around. We can walk around freestanding sculpture, but our viewing options are more limited with relief sculpture. We divide relief sculpture into two categories: high relief and low relief. High relief sculpture can be seen in carved scenes along the tops of buildings. The images on U.S. coins, however, are in very low, or bas-relief [bah-reeleef], barely coming forward from the metal surface.

Note: The descriptions and activities in the main text below are intended to help you become familiar with the artworks before presenting them to children; however, some of the activities might be adapted for classroom use. Activities intended specifically for children can be found in the Teaching Idea sidebars. The Looking Questions given below are also printed on the reverse side of the *Art Resources* and have been written with children in mind so that they might be used as a rough plan for class discussion. You should feel free to use these questions or develop questions of your own. Be sure children have time to look at the reproductions carefully before asking the Looking Questions.

Lines in Three Dimensions

Close your eyes and imagine a line. People usually think of a line as a mark between two points on a flat surface—such as a line drawn on paper. But examine the included reproduction of the ancient Greek sculptor Myron's *The Discobolus (Discus Thrower)*. What lines can you discover? The man's arms, legs, and even his torso are lines—three-dimensional lines. These lines have length, height, and width.

Cross-curricular Teaching Idea

You may wish to teach *The Discobolus (Discus Thrower)* in conjunction with your discussion of the ancient Greeks and the Olympics, and *Flying Horse, One Leg Resting on a Swallow* in conjunction with the section on China. Have children write about the use of art in these ancient civilizations and how it reflects what they have learned about the people of these civilizations. Share these with the class.

Teaching Idea

When teaching sculpture, remind children that they are looking at two-dimensional ("flat") pictures of three-dimensional objects. Before looking at prints, you may wish to bring in a decorative item that children can look at from various angles—ideally an object that looks significantly different from various angles. You can even take a picture of the object and have children talk about the difference between the two-dimensional and three-dimensional objects. While teaching the works listed here, you may wish to look for supplemental art prints that show the same object from slightly different angles.

Cross-curricular Teaching Idea

Have children hunt in school for examples of various geometric forms that can be found in sculpture. Then, ask children to repeat the exercise at home. Examples of forms found at home might include the following:

Cylinder—canned goods, paper towel or toilet paper rolls
Sphere—apples, oranges, balls, marbles
Disk—wall clock, CD, pancake
Cube—sugar cube, box of tissues

Teaching Idea

Help children detect lines, shapes, and forms in sculpture by leading them through the investigation for both real and implied lines relating to *The Discobolus (Discus Thrower)* as described in the text for Instructional Master 30, *Looking at Sculpture.*

There's another strong line in *The Discobolus (Discus Thrower),* although it's implied (suggested) rather than physically tangible. Look for a diagonal line oriented from the upper-left down toward the lower-right. (Hint: it starts at the athlete's head.)

The man's gaze thrusts the implied diagonal line back across his muscled torso down to his hip. Myron's powerful implied line underscores the athlete's wound-up, twisting action. (More information about the artwork appears in the Looking Section on p. 256.)

Sculptural Elements

Taking Form

What's the shape of a tennis ball or an orange? Actually, neither a tennis ball nor an orange has the artistic element of shape—they have form. Form is the element of art that is three-dimensional and encloses volume. The form of a tennis ball or an orange is a sphere. A circle, which is flat, would be an example of a shape.

Search for some forms in the included reproduction of *The Discobolus (Discus Thrower).* The discus itself is a disk form. The man's head is an egg form, and the tree trunk is a cylinder form. These are fairly geometric forms. Sculptors also use organic forms, as Myron did in the articulation of the man's muscles in his chest and legs.

Forms are "positive" in that they consist of matter. In art, we refer to the empty areas between the forms as "negative space." The most obvious example in *The Discobolus (Discus Thrower)* is the triangular "empty" form created by the athlete's curving torso, left arm, and right thigh. Even though negative space is essentially empty, it plays an important role in a sculpture's overall composition. We often don't notice these negative areas because our eyes tend to rest on the positive, physical forms of the work itself.

Multiple Views

Look at any of the reproductions of sculpture for this section. What could you do in real life that you can't with the reproduction? The reproductions can only show you one view—but if you were in front of the actual sculptures, you could see them from virtually endless perspectives. Ordinarily, people just walk around them, but theoretically you could peer up from far below, stand above and look down, and so forth.

Sculpture literally moves into our space. Unlike a painting, it punctures the space in which we stand. This three-dimensional, physical quality can evoke an immediate, visceral response within us.

Mass in Sculpture

Which has more mass, a mouse or a giraffe? Mass is the quantity of matter in an object. Although two-dimensional art has mass, it's fairly negligible when compared to most sculpture.

Compare the included reproductions of *Flying Horse, One Leg Resting on a Swallow* and Rodin's *The Thinker*. Both pieces obviously have mass. But the way a sculptor arranges the mass can affect the way we perceive the actual three-dimensional forms. In *Flying Horse, One Leg Resting on a Swallow,* the animal's splayed legs, flying tail, and energized head suggest a lean creature that seems to defy its bulk. The horse seems barely to be touching the ground. Conversely, the inwardly turned, densely packed pose of *The Thinker* emphasizes the man's mass—and, by extension, the "massiveness" of the worldly issues he seems to shoulder.

Sculptural Motion

Unless it's a mobile, sculpture doesn't move. In fact, its mass makes it inert. Look again at the reproduction of Myron's *The Discobolus (Discus Thrower).* Myron's careful study of real athletes and human anatomy guided his choice of pose. Try twisting your body into this stance and you will actually feel the tension and energy of the windup before the uncurling motion in which you would toss the heavy discus as far as possible. The pose in *Flying Horse, One Leg Resting on a Swallow* likewise lends a sense of dynamic movement. Caught in midaction, the creature appears to defy gravity and be gliding through the air.

Once and Again

Sometimes in sculpture, one is not enough. Unlike paintings, numerous exact versions of a sculpture can exist. These are not copies, but versions—all cast from the same mold. For instance, look again at the reproduction of *Flying Horse, One Leg Resting on a Swallow.* Sometime around the 2nd century CE, an artist carved an initial version (out of wax, clay, or some other malleable material). A reusable mold was formed around the sculpted steed and then used to make multiple versions.

The Discobolus (Discus Thrower) is also one of numerous versions. In the mid-5th century BCE, Myron sculpted the initial version, a mold was made, and his final piece was cast in bronze. As often happened, subsequent ancient Roman artists carved marble versions of Myron's athlete. The best copy today is in Rome, Italy.

It is only in fairly modern times that the idea of uniqueness in art—as in only one, singular version—has gained value. Today, it would be fairly unusual for an artist to paint two exact versions of the same work. The prevailing sentiment is that the importance of the two would be less if they were exactly alike. This was not the case in earlier times, and sculptors and painters alike frequently made multiple versions of their work.

In fact, ancient Roman versions of sculptures are an essential window into ancient Greek sculpture. Few certifiable bronze works remain by any of the great ancient Greek sculptors. Many were melted down or otherwise destroyed. Therefore, the Roman marble versions are the surviving examples of this vital period of Greek sculpture.

No Art Stands Alone

Art of any sort is always a product of the culture in which it is created. Whether consciously or unconsciously, artists are spokespeople for the time and context in which they work. This is particularly apparent in the ancient Chinese *Flying Horse, One Leg Resting on a Swallow* and classical Greek *The Discobolus (Discus Thrower).*

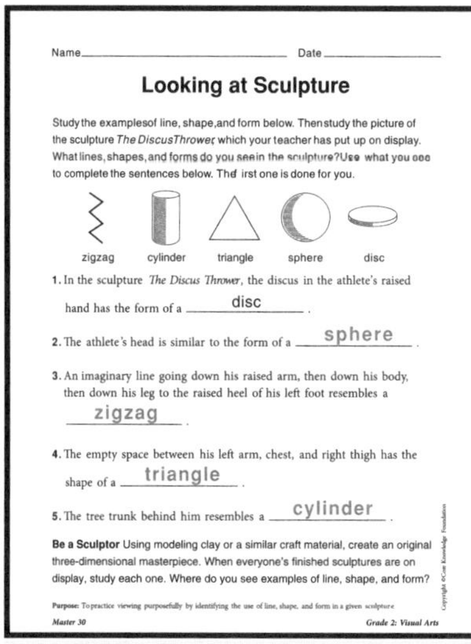

Name__________ Date__________

Looking at Sculpture

Study the examples of line, shape, and form below. Then study the picture of the sculpture *The Discus Thrower,* which your teacher has put up on display. What lines, shapes, and forms do you see in the sculpture? Use what you see to complete the sentences below. The first one is done for you.

zigzag cylinder triangle sphere disc

1. In the sculpture *The Discus Thrower,* the discus in the athlete's raised hand has the form of a disc.
2. The athlete's head is similar to the form of a sphere.
3. An imaginary line going down his raised arm, then down his body, then down his leg to the raised heel of his left foot resembles a zigzag.
4. The empty space between his left arm, chest, and right thigh has the shape of a triangle.
5. The tree trunk behind him resembles a cylinder.

Be a Sculptor Using modeling clay or a similar craft material, create an original three-dimensional masterpiece. When everyone's finished sculptures are on display, study each one. Where do you see examples of line, shape, and form?

Purpose: To practice viewing purposefully by identifying the use of line, shape, and form in a given sculpture

Master 30 *Grade 2: Visual Arts*

Copyright ©Core Knowledge Foundation

Use Instructional Master 30.

Teaching Idea

Invite children to try to exactly imitate the pose in either *The Discobolus (Discus Thrower)* or *The Thinker.* One or more children can serve as a model while the others critique and improve the pose.

Flying Horse, One Leg Resting on a Swallow is steeped in Chinese history. In the 2nd century CE, the famous Chinese emperor Wu-ti waged an enormous campaign with 60,000 soldiers to obtain the mighty "Celestial" or "Heavenly Horses" from Southeast Asia. He was determined to bring home these legendary horses of Ferghana (Turkistan). Unlike the Chinese indigenous breeds, these horses had the height, muscle, and stamina Wu-ti needed to enhance his army's military strength. These horses were particularly unusual because they sweated blood, most likely due to a parasite. Once in China, these esteemed "celestial horses" became status symbols for rich men and officials—as reflected in their appearance in art. *Flying Horse, One Leg Resting on a Swallow* is just one of many "celestial horse" sculptures found in a 2nd-century CE tomb that were meant to follow a general into his next life.

Myron's *The Discobolus (Discus Thrower)* likewise reveals aspects of classical Greece. Sports were central to Greek society and even played a large role in religious festivals. Men exercised and swam at public facilities. Women weren't allowed to go to these facilities, but they did attend religious festivals, which included wrestling, boxing, foot and chariot races, jumping, and javelin throwing. The most famous of these festivals, the Olympic Games (which originated in the 8th century BCE), brought together factions from throughout the Greek world. Wars were even suspended during the games. So Myron's sculpture does not merely attest to the esteem in which the ancient Greeks held the human form, but also denotes the prestige of athletics in Greek social, religious, and military life.

Looking at Sculpture in Included Reproductions

art resource 3

Myron, *The Discobolus (Discus Thrower)* (c. 450 BCE)

After observing many young athletes in action, Myron chose to depict the young man in full backswing—the discus flat against his upper arm and hand, and his fingers curling around the rim. In the next instant, he will complete a full turn to gain speed and power and then hurl the discus at the end of another half turn. The man's head is an egg form, and the tree trunk is a cylinder form. There is a triangular "empty" form created by the athlete's curving torso, left arm, and right thigh.

Myron's careful study of real athletes and human anatomy guided his choice of pose. For all its accuracy in the details of the anatomy and pose, Myron's figure is more ideal than real. There is no hint of strain in his expression. *The Discobolus (Discus Thrower)* is not a portrait, but rather immortalizes the essence and spirit of the Olympic Games and everything that they connote. (For a deeper discussion of the Olympic Games, see Section IV of World History and Geography.)

Looking questions

- **What do you see?** ***Answers will vary. Explain that this is a statue more than 2,000 years old from Greece.***
- **What is this figure doing?** ***He is trying to throw a discus. Explain what a discus is and how it is thrown.***
- **Do you think he will throw the discus far? Why?** ***Answers will vary, but the athlete's taut muscles and powerful twist suggest that he is about to put all his strength behind the throw.***

Teaching Idea

The discus is not a frisbee! Originally constructed out of stone or metal, it took tremendous precision and effort to toss the round plate as far as possible. The ancient Greeks featured the discus throw, one of the oldest sports, in their Olympic Games. The winner of this event was considered the greatest athlete. The discus throw is still an Olympic sport. Using a frisbee, have children take the pose of a discus thrower. If possible, do this activity out of doors, so they can actually toss the frisbee.

- **When you throw something heavy, does your face look like this?** ***Explain that the Greeks preferred to make human beings look calm and thoughtful. This was part of their idea of beauty.***
- **What would your body look like if you were throwing a ball or a flying disc?** ***Answers will vary.***
- **Are there any details that might suggest this is a sculpture from ancient Greece?** ***Children who have studied Greek history may connect the statue with the Olympic Games, where athletes competed in the nude.***
- **Remind children that this a flat print showing a three-dimensional sculpture. Ask them what they might see if they walked behind the figure.** ***Answers will vary.***

art resource 4

Flying Horse, One Leg Resting on a Swallow (c. 2nd century CE, sculptor unknown)

Imagine uncovering an entire army of these magnificent creatures. They were discovered in 1969, inside a general's tomb from the 2nd century CE, near Wu-wei (Gansu province). The mighty bronze steed barely touches the ground as it gallops forward, and its hoof rests on the back of a flying swallow. Sculptures such as this example, one of the finest of the period, revere the great Ferghana horses that Chinese emperor Wu-ti had brought back from Central Asia to enhance his army's military power. (See previous text for more information.)

Notice the sculptor's great skill in balancing the entire animal on a single hoof, increasing the illusion that it is "flying," and, hence, reflecting the reference to the real horses as "celestial" or "heavenly"—or barely of this world. Caught in midaction, the creature appears to defy gravity and be gliding through the air. The animal's splayed legs, flying tail, and energized head suggest a lean creature that seems to defy its bulk.

Looking questions

Note: Cover up the title on the front of the piece before showing to children.

- **What do you see?** ***Answers will vary, but most children will recognize the figure as a horse.***
- **Does the horse look like it's going fast or slow? How can you tell?** ***Children may notice from the horse's stride and tail that it is traveling fast.***
- **What do you think the horse's leg is resting on?** ***Explain the title, then point to the swallow. Ask if knowing the title changes what they see.***
- **How did the artist make the horse look alive and full of action?** ***The galloping leg position, open mouth, and flying tail make the horse look alive and full of action.***
- **How did the sculptor make the animal appear strong?** ***A solid body, forcefully moving forward, makes the animal appear strong.***
- **How would it feel to ride on the back of this horse?** ***Answers will vary.***
- **If the work is called *Flying Horse*, why do you think one foot is touching the bottom?** ***It's for balance; the sculptor needed a way to make this heavy piece stand up.***

Teaching Idea

As an extension, when studying *Flying Horse, One Leg Resting on a Swallow*, share the 8th-century poem below by Tu Fu. Make a Venn diagram on the board, having children fill it in by comparing and contrasting Fu's evocative words and the *Flying Horse, One Leg Resting on a Swallow* sculpture. Next, ask them to describe why either the literary form or the visual art form best captures the spirit of the legendary horses. Have them use specific references to support their opinions.

The Ferghana horse is gamed among nomad breeds.
Lean in build, like the point of a lance;
Two ears sharp as bamboo spikes;
Four hoofs light as though born of the wind.
Heading away across the endless spaces,
Truly, you may entrust him with your life. . . .

Tu Fu, Chinese poet (8th century)

Teaching Idea

Create a number line across the board, and have children plot the time when the three sculptures you examined in this section were created. This activity will help children deepen their math and history skills as well as gain a sense of when each artwork was made.

art resource 5

Auguste Rodin, *The Thinker* (1880)

Late 19th-century French sculptor Auguste Rodin [oh-GOOST roh-DAN] (1840–1917) imbued *The Thinker* with both psychological and physical weight and stillness. Yet, the visible marks of Rodin's fingerprints, made when he pushed and prodded the original wax, plaster, or clay of the initial sculpture, give the cast bronze version a sense of immediacy. The light plays off the uneven surfaces, making it seem that Rodin (although long dead) just recently formed the muscle-bound figure. The inwardly turned, densely packed pose of *The Thinker* emphasizes the man's mass—and, by extension, the "massiveness" of the worldly issues he seems to shoulder.

Unlike his contemporaries, the post-Impressionist painters, Rodin wished to emphasize the sculptural process, providing evidence of the artist's touch. He was less interested in capturing the Impressionists' elusive optical effects and scenes of bourgeois life. Rodin depicted universal, historic, psychological, often romantic themes. Rodin made endless versions and variations of his sculptural figures, and countless hands, fingers, and other body parts littered his Paris studio.

Looking questions

Note: Cover up the title on the front of the print before showing to children.

- **What do you see?** ***Answers will vary.***
- **What is this figure doing?** ***Answers will vary.***
- **Tell children the title and ask: What is he thinking about?** ***Answers will vary.***
- **How does Rodin tell you what the man is doing?** ***The seated position; the hand-to-chin position; and the downward, inward gaze make the figure look like he's thinking.***
- **How did Rodin make his figure look very still?** ***The seated pose—its mass densely packed together—increases a sense of heavy stillness.***
- **What might this sculpture look like from different angles?** ***Answers will vary.***

The Big Idea in Review

Children's appreciation of sculpture can be enhanced by exploring line, form, and mass.

Review

Below are some ideas for ongoing assessment and review activities. These are not meant to constitute a comprehensive list.

- Have children walk around the school building and identify pieces of sculpture. If the school does not have any pieces of sculpture, ask children to identify anything that reminds them of sculpture—such as any three-dimensional items. Have children explain their sculpture discoveries.
- Have children explore making sculptures with a variety of materials. Provide different materials for them to try and use, such as paper, modeling clay, or styrofoam. Invite children to sculpt animals, as in *Flying Horse, One Leg Resting on a Swallow*, or humans engaged in sports or other activities, as in *The Thinker* and *The Discobolus (Discus Thrower)*. Also, provide each child with a cup of water, and have

a discussion about making sculpture from water. Is it possible? What would have to happen to the water for it to be used for sculpture? This activity can provide time to review the states of matter because the water would have to turn to ice for it to be used for sculpture.

• Have children find images in sports magazines of figures involved in the same sports as those of the original Olympics: wrestling, boxing, racing, jumping, javelin throwing, discus throwing, and so forth. Have them make quick line sketches of the athletes in action, trying to catch the action of the figure in each sport. Help children translate these poses into three-dimensional sculptures made out of pipe cleaners. Have children closely observe the lines in the pictures and in their sculptures for form and movement.

• If you know a local sculptor, a craftworker who carves wood, or even a potter, invite that person to class to show his or her work and discuss how it is done.

• In general, the best time to ask questions about a specific sculpture is while children are looking at it. However, by the end of the section, children should be able to answer the general questions on line, form, and mass. You may also ask the following questions at the end of this section:

1. What two types of lines can you find in sculpture?
   The two types of lines you can find in sculpture are real and implied.
2. Which has more mass, an 8' x 8' drawing or an 8' x 8' x 8' sculpture?
   The sculpture has more mass.
3. Do all sculptures appear stationary/still?
   Only mobiles actually move, but many sculptures suggest motion.

More Resources

The titles listed below are offered as a representative sample of materials and not a complete list of everything that is available.

For teachers —

• Art Print Resources (209 Riverdale Avenue, Yonkers, NY 10705, www.artprintresources.com, or 1-800-501-4278) sells a set of 10 posters of artworks in the *Sequence* for this grade.

• Art Sense (www.artsense.net) provides an art program using videotapes and trade books.

• Art to the Core (Davis Publications, www.davis-art.com or 1-800-533-2847). A kit of materials that includes slides of artworks, lesson plans, assessment masters, and vocabulary masters, all keyed to the *Core Knowledge Sequence* for this grade.

• Crizmac (www.crizmac.com) sells a wide range of art education materials.

• Silk Road Foundation, www.silk-road.com, has an article on Emperor Wu-Ti and the Ferghana horses. From the home page, search on Wu-Ti and/or Ferghana.

• Usborne (www.edcpub.com) has a wide range of art books, coloring books, and workbooks for the early grades.

III. Kinds of Pictures: Landscapes

The Big Idea

Like the portrait and the still life, the landscape is another important genre of art.

What Students Should Already Know

Students in Core Knowledge schools should be familiar with

Grade 1

- portraits and still lifes

What Students Need to Learn

- **Recognize as landscapes and discuss**
  - **Thomas Cole, *View from Mount Holyoke, Northampton, Massachusetts, after a Thunderstorm—The Oxbow***
  - **El Greco, *View of Toledo* (also known as *Toledo in a Storm*)**
  - **Henri Rousseau, *Virgin Forest at Sunset***
  - **Vincent van Gogh, *The Starry Night***

Vocabulary

Student/Teacher Vocabulary

anthropomorphize: to give human qualities to something nonhuman (T)

genre: a category of art (landscape, portraiture, still life, etc.) (T)

genre painting: a composition that depicts everyday life (T)

kimono: a loose Japanese robe with a wide sash, worn as an outer garment (T)

landscape: an image depicting a land scene (S)

oxbow: a U-shaped collar placed around an ox's neck when it is hitched to a plow; also applied to bends in a river that curve back on themselves to form a large loop (S)

pastoral: a rural scene (T)

patron: in the visual arts, one who commissions and/or supports an artist's work. Traditionally, patrons came from the wealthy and elite classes of royalty, aristocracy, and Catholic church officials. (T)

scape: a view of scenery of any kind (S)

seascape: an image of a body of water (can include ships or boats) (S)

urbanscape: an image of the urban environment (T)

Domain Vocabulary

Landscapes and associated words:
pen-and-ink, silk, scroll, sketch, canvas, pigment, brush, view, environment, rural, urban, visible, visual, atmosphere, arrangement, frontier, wilderness, vista, romantic, modern, contemporary, photographic, realism, reality, portray, texture, water, trees, grass, sky, rivers, leaves, houses, people, stars, moon, night, plus words that describe things in paintings, e.g., river, hill, grandeur, vista, rustic, perspective, jaguar, fanciful, etc.

Cross-curricular Connections

Language Arts

Reading and Writing

Writing

Poetry

- "Who Has Seen the Wind?"
- "Windy Nights"

History and Geography

World: Geography

- Locate Europe on maps and/or globes

World: Early Civilizations: Asia

China

World: Modern Civilization and Culture: Japan

Science

Cycles in Nature

Seasonal Cycles

- Spring

At a Glance

The most important ideas for you are:

- Genres are categories of art. Portraits, still lifes, and landscapes are important art genres.
- Landscapes are images that describe the outdoors.
- Landscapes can include rural or urban images.
- Seascapes are a subgenre of landscape painting.
- Artists produce landscapes in a variety of styles.
- Landscape painting in the West has roots in ancient times and artists still practice it today.
- Chinese and Japanese artists have painted pen-and-ink landscapes on silk and paper for centuries.
- Landscapes can reflect information about the physical environment, as well as the times in which the artists painted them.

Materials

Art Resources

Thomas Cole, *The Oxbow*

El Greco, *View of Toledo*

Henri Rousseau, *Virgin Forest at Sunset*

Vincent van Gogh, *The Starry Night*

copies of visual arts magazines and journals, pp. 264–265, p. 267

drawing materials, p. 267

local landscape, p. 267

index cards, p. 267

examples of different music and songs, p. 268

What Teachers Need to Know

Background

Look out the window and imagine taking a snapshot. What would be the genre of your resulting photograph? If you're peering out onto nature, you would likely say "landscape." The term refers to a scene describing the land. But what if the "land" is full of buildings or other signs of industry? Well, it's still a landscape. Some people would use the term "urbanscape" or "cityscape"—which is a subcategory of landscape.

Now, what if you were looking out onto a large body of water? How could you possibly call this a landscape if there really isn't much, if any, land? These sorts of scenes, too, are a subcategory of landscapes—called "seascapes."

In Grade 1, children discovered that pictures of people (and animals) are called "portraits." Look at the figures in the reproductions of Henri Rousseau's Virgin Forest at Sunset *and Thomas Cole's* View from Mount Holyoke,

Teaching Idea

Give teams of children visual arts magazines and journals. Review the definitions of the three genres they'll be searching for—portraits, still lifes, and landscapes. Give the groups five minutes to search through their magazines, tearing out and stacking in three separate piles as many examples as possible for each genre. The team with the most correctly placed examples in any given genre wins for that category.

Northampton, Massachusetts, after a Thunderstorm—The Oxbow. *Rousseau's man and jaguar are center stage in* Virgin Forest at Sunset, *but notice their size. Cole's figure in* The Oxbow *is even smaller. On the bottom, to the right of center, is an artist—actually Cole himself. So, why aren't these paintings called portraits—or self-portraits? Here, and also in the included reproduction of El Greco's* View of Toledo, *the land dominates the images, and so it is the subject itself; hence, they are considered landscape paintings.*

Review what children learned about genre and genre painting in earlier grades (portraiture and still lifes). Show them a number of reproductions of landscape paintings (without using the term), and ask them what word or term they think applies to this genre of painting.

Note: The descriptions and activities in the main text below are intended to help you become familiar with the artworks before presenting them to children; however, some of the activities might be adapted for classroom use. Activities intended specifically for children can be found in the Teaching Idea sidebars. The Looking Questions given below are also printed on the reverse side of the *Art Resources* and have been written with children in mind so that they might be used as a rough plan for class discussion. You should feel free to use these questions or develop questions of your own. Be sure children have time to look at the reproductions carefully before asking the Looking Questions.

Landscape Painting History

Landscapes have never simply documented the visible world. Like all art, landscapes also reveal information about the artists who made them and the times in which they lived.

In the Western world, wealthy ancient Romans were among the earliest patrons to commission landscapes. Artists were hired to create "illusional real estate" by painting landscapes on the garden walls of villas. The art was intended to decorate the patron's home, while increasing the patron's social and economic status by showing the beauty and scale of his estate.

For many centuries, though, landscapes were neither a serious nor primary subject matter. During the medieval and Renaissance periods, artists added landscapes as backdrops in historical and religious scenes. When they included landscapes in portraits, the land typically represented the particular holdings of the sitters.

After the Reformation, landscape itself became an important subject. For example, Albrecht Altdorfer (German, c. 1480–1538) was an accomplished painter of the Danube River Valley. Seventeenth-century Dutch artists also depicted the land alone. The newly wealthy middle class hungered for the small, affordable painted images of their nation, which had just won its independence from the Hapsburg Empire. Seascapes thrived as well, because much of the growing nation's wealth came from its prosperous sea trade.

Landscape on Its Own

Pure landscapes began to take hold in the 19th century in the United States. Although artists tended to realistically render the observable world, they did not necessarily make objective recordings. Many painted the land with a personality or temperament of its own. Through arrangements of color, light, and composition, artists explored concepts about God, nature, and the beauty and/or dangers of the wilderness that reflected the beliefs of the societies in which the artists lived.

Thomas Cole was a leader among artists of the American Hudson River School (c. 1835–1870). These artists painted romantic views of the wilderness in the Hudson River Valley in New York State (some also ventured into the Rockies and to South America). Their typically vast vistas captured the light in mists, sunsets, and other memorable idyllic moments. These painters explored nature artistically at the same time that explorers were exploring it geographically.

For the Impressionists in the second half of the 19th century (e.g., Monet), nature served as the basis for their artistic explorations of color and light. At the same time, the locales were the very ones in which these bourgeois artists spent time—with family, friends, and like-minded artists.

Late 19th-century post-Impressionists sometimes anthropomorphized nature. In *The Starry Night,* Vincent van Gogh transformed nature's divine energy into brushstrokes that dance across the sky and embolden the cypress trees, which reach heavenward. Knowledge of both van Gogh's deep spiritual feelings and inner turmoil imbue the nighttime landscape with even more impact.

The land itself sometimes becomes nothing more than a mere suggestion in modern and contemporary abstract paintings. Artists might simply render atmospheric elements of a view or distort the forms so that it's difficult or even impossible to distinguish components within the scene. Today, other artists extend the realistic tradition. Sometimes they explore what humans have done to the natural world. In other instances, they capture the quickly disappearing areas of natural beauty in the world in which we live.

Traditional Chinese Landscape Painting

Many centuries ago, Chinese artists started painting images of mountains, rivers, waterfalls, trees, and misty forests on paper or silk. Viewers were meant to feel as though they were traveling through these scrolls—just like the tiny painted figures making their way through the scenes. These visual journeys calmed viewers' minds, providing rest and escape from the daily world.

Traditionally, Chinese landscape painters did not employ Western perspective techniques. Instead, the size of objects relative to one another indicated their relationship in space. To Western-trained eyes, Chinese landscapes might look "flat" or two-dimensional. But the viewers' imaginary walk through the land adds its own dimension—the one of time passing by. (The art of China is discussed in detail in Grade 4.)

Cross-curricular Teaching Idea

Like the Chinese, Japanese artists painted landscapes on scrolls for centuries. (Consider the work of Katsusika Hokusai, described in Section I.) However, Japanese artists also painted scenes on an early type of short-sleeved kimono (called a *kosode*). These kosodes were like "walking landscapes." Have children design their own nature scenes that could be drawn on a kosode.

Looking at Landscapes in Artworks

art resource 6

Thomas Cole, *View from Mount Holyoke, Northampton, Massachusetts, after a Thunderstorm—The Oxbow (1836)*

Ironically, British-born artist Thomas Cole (1801–1848) is perhaps best known for his romantic views of the American land. For him, the young country's rustic, rugged beauty epitomized the United States. Cole came to Ohio with his family from England in 1818. He studied both in the United States and Europe, but was ultimately drawn to America, where he painted vistas of a wilderness that would soon vanish as the mainstream population and industry encroached upon the virgin land.

Look at the included reproduction of *The Oxbow*. What's the weather like in this view? Cole detailed the sunlight on the lingering mist after a thunderstorm. Although realist artists like Cole appear to work in a nearly photographic style, they often change certain elements in their scenes. They might move, eliminate, enlarge, decrease, and/or add items in their compositions.

Cole divided the painting into two. The left half represents the powerful, uncontrollable, yet sublime aspect of nature, symbolized by the broken tree trunk and dark clouds. On the right, Cole painted a quiet, sunny view, "civilized" by humans, who have cultivated nature into bucolic, prosperous farms. Cole's painting reflects a debate among Americans during his day: Would civilization wipe out the wilderness or could the two coexist?

Looking questions

- **What do you see?** ***Answers will vary, but children should see a river, trees, a landscape, an umbrella, and perhaps a person.***
- **What are some of the colors you see?** ***Children will mention shades of blues and greens seen in nature.***
- **Do you see any people in the painting?** ***If children say no, point out the painter at the bottom, in the middle, turned toward the viewer.***
- **Can you tell what the person is doing?** ***Answers will vary. The figure is very small. He is painting the scene.***
- **Why do you think Cole made his self-portrait so small? (Hint: How does his size affect the way you see the rest of the scene?)** ***The small figure greatly enhances the grandeur and enormity of the vista.***
- **Compare the left half and the right half of the landscape. How are they different?** ***The left side is rustic, wild, and dark; the right side is quiet, sunny, and has cultivated fields.***
- **Which half of the painting would you rather visit?** ***Answers will vary.***
- **This painting is called *The Oxbow*. Why do you think the painter chose this title?** ***Children may identify the bow shape. Explain that the river makes the shape of an oxbow, a curved harness that is put over the necks of oxen.***

Teaching Idea

Thomas Cole painted himself working in *The Oxbow*—he is in the bottom front, very small in relation to the overall scene. In fact, Cole typically sketched out of doors and worked on his final canvases in the studio. Take children out into the local urban or rural environment and have them make quick sketches for a scene that they then may expand into a final drawing or painting upon their return to the classroom. Afterward, ask them to describe the challenges and advantages in working outdoors and indoors.

art resource 7 El Greco (Domenikos Theotokopoulos), *View of Toledo* (c. 1597)

Born in what is now Crete, Domenikos Theotokopoulos (1541–1614) was called El Greco [el GREHK-oh] (the Greek) by the Spanish. The artist worked primarily in Spain, painting elegant, elongated, distorted images with dramatic, flickering white highlights that enhance the scene's underlying emotional content.

Turn to the reproduction of El Greco's *View of Toledo.* Would you say the artist was concerned with strict realism? Although each individual element remains identifiable, El Greco was less concerned with visible details than with the overall sensation his view evokes. His amplified colors and shapes shift toward abstraction, thereby emphasizing the landscape's underlying agitation.

El Greco lived in Toledo, Spain's cultural center, for nearly 40 years. His view of the city is his only surviving independent landscape. El Greco also painted his portraits and religious compositions in the same ardent style so that they, too, resonate with life.

Did El Greco describe a night sky with the moon shining through on the top portion of *View of Toledo*—or did he depict a turbulent, daytime storm? El Greco's brooding colors increase the intense, mysterious atmosphere.

Looking questions

Note: Cover up the title on the front of the print before showing to children.

- **What do you see?** ***Children may see a landscape, sky, and a city in the distance.***
- **What does the artist show in this landscape?** ***The artist shows a city in the hills, a turbulent sky, a bridge, and trees.***
- **Does this painting look up toward the city, or down on it? How can you tell?** ***You can introduce the term* perspective: *the artist's perspective or viewpoint is from a high place.***
- **Have you ever seen a sky like this one?** ***Children might have seen such a sky during a thunderstorm.***
- **What words would you use to describe this painting?** ***Answers will vary.***
- **What title would you give it?** ***Answers will vary. Tell them the title. Explain that Toledo is in Spain.***

Teaching Idea

Review with children El Greco's spirited use of color and shape to describe Toledo, Spain's 16th-century cultural center. Then, ask children to draw a picture about their own school, focusing on color and shape to convey their emotions. (Realism isn't important.) Have children share the colors and shapes they chose, explain why they chose them, and describe the emotion they want to convey about school in their drawings.

Modern Toledo

art resource 8 Henri Rousseau, *Virgin Forest at Sunset* (1910)

French painter Henri Rousseau [roo-SOH] (1844–1910) didn't pursue art full-time until after he retired at age 40 from his job as a toll collector, gathering taxes on goods coming into Paris. The job had allowed Rousseau to support his family and draw during free time at his post.

Rousseau built his landscapes with fastidious renderings of exotic plants he studied in the Paris botanical gardens and scientific books. But by greatly enlarging and combining these items together, Rousseau built purely imaginative landscapes stemming from some sort of dreamworld.

Henri Rousseau's *Virgin Forest at Sunset* is a realistic-abstract paradox. On the one hand, Rousseau detailed each leaf, stem, and petal with scientific rigor, but taken all together, his painting doesn't look like any identifiable earthly location. In fact, Rousseau never visited a jungle at all. He carefully studied animals at the zoo. His resulting landscape is like a dream—a fantasy of the artist's and, by extension, of our own imagination.

Although he was a self-taught artist, Rousseau showed his paintings in exhibitions alongside trained artists of the day. Avant-garde artists admired his work, but it wasn't until after his death as a poor man that Rousseau gained wider recognition.

Looking questions

Note: Cover up the title on the front of the print before showing to children.

- **What does the painting show?** ***It shows the sky and sun, and a man and jaguar wrestling in a jungle.***
- **Which does Rousseau make more important—the figures or the landscape?** ***The landscape dominates; the figures are barely noticeable at first.***
- **What would you call this painting?** ***Tell children the title. Explain that a virgin forest is a forest where no trees have been cut down.***
- **Does this scene look like a real or imaginary place?** ***The details of the plants look real, but they are enlarged and put together in a fanciful way.***

art resource 9

Vincent van Gogh, *The Starry Night* (1889)

Despite his mental instability, Dutch painter Vincent van Gogh [van GOH] (1853–1890) produced all of his work in about 10 years. He died at age 37.

The included reproduction of Vincent van Gogh's famous *The Starry Night* edges even further toward abstraction. Van Gogh suggests the essence of what he felt about death with thick, swirling patterns of paint that take our eyes on a roller-coaster ride across the canvas.

Van Gogh's landscapes exude their own personality—rich and deeply spiritual. His richly applied paint stands up on the flat surface of the canvas, giving it a rough, physical, and easily visible texture. (Although texture and brushstrokes can be hard to see on a two-dimensional print, van Gogh's textures were so dramatic that they are often partially visible, even on a flat print.) Van Gogh lets us see nature's vibrant energy, portraying it with a strong palette and bold, moving lines that form small areas of lively pattern. He animated nature—the sky, hills, and cypress trees—far more than the town, which he nestled amid the more active landscape.

Looking questions

Note: Cover up the title on the front of the print before showing to children.

- **What do you see in this painting?** ***Children should see the town, the church, the swirls of paint, and the shape on the left.***
- **Does the sky in the painting look like the sky you see at night? How is it different?** ***The swirling lines in the sky are unusual.***
- **What might the blue swirls in the sky show?** ***Answers will vary. Help children see that these could show swirling wind.***

- **What might the yellow circles in the sky be?** ***Answers will vary. Tell children that the title might be a clue:*** **The Starry Night.**
- **Is there anything unusual about the stars? Do they look like the stars you see in the sky at night?** ***The stars in this painting are larger and less focused than actual stars. Some people think they look like they are exploding!***
- **What might the black shape rising up from the ground on the left side of the painting be?** ***Answers will vary. Most people believe it is a tree.***
- **Do you think van Gogh used a lot of paint or very little paint to create this picture?** ***The paint is laid on very thickly.***
- **Could this painting be called *The Peaceful Night* instead of *The Starry Night?* Why or why not?** ***Answers will vary, but most people think it is a very lively, turbulent night.***

Review

The Big Idea in Review

Like the portrait and the still life, the landscape is another important genre of art.

Below are some ideas for ongoing assessment and review activities. These are not meant to constitute a comprehensive list.

- If possible, supplement this selection of landscapes with a landscape of a place near where you live, or one that is similar to the landscape where you live. A local artist or museum may have a landscape.
- Have children draw landscape pictures of where they live. Then have them create a landscape picture that reflects the "opposite" of where they live, based on the detail they have put into their pictures. For example, if children have already drawn a picture of the countryside, have them draw a picture of the city. What did they draw differently?
- Meld the study of landscape pictures into the History and Geography curriculum by having children study images of the lands you are studying, such as China, India, and Japan. What did the topography look like? What do paintings, photographs, or artwork describing the era and locations indicate about how humans interacted with the environment? Have children draw landscape pictures of the different civilizations and then explain why they chose certain elements for their pictures. What did they study about a civilization that appeared in their pictures?
- Use one of the landscape pictures from this section to identify lines and colors. Have children examine one of the pictures closely and then identify various different kinds of lines. Consider having children write about how lines give us a sense of the landscape.
- Post the four pictures from this section in the classroom and have children write a description of each picture on a separate index card. Each child will have four index cards. Then, invite other classes to visit the room, and have the children in your class read their cards to describe the pictures. You may also post the index cards by the pictures for visitors to read when they enter the room.

• Introduce the elements of music while studying the art from this section. Ask the class to identify songs or music that they think would match each picture. For example, a more serene landscape might represent a calm, quiet song, and a more hectic landscape picture might represent a fast song. Bring in examples of different music, and use the songs from Section III in Music to select songs that are good companions for the pictures. Then, have children write about why they chose different music. You may play the music while visitors study the different landscape pictures.

More Resources

The titles listed below are offered as a representative sample of materials and not a complete list of everything that is available.

For children —

These books are generally intended to be read aloud, though some children may be able to read parts or all of the simpler texts.

• *Come Look with Me: Exploring Landscape Art with Children,* by Gladys Blizzard (Lickle Publishing, 1992). Children are encouraged to think about such different works as Vincent van Gogh's *The Starry Night,* and George Inness's *Lackawanna Valley.* Twelve reproductions in all. Hardcover, 32 pages, ISBN 0934738955. Available through Lickle Publishing, www.licklepublishing.com or 1-866-454-2553.

• *A Picture for Harold's Room,* by Crockett Johnson (HarperCollins Juvenile Books, 1981). Young artist Harold wields his purple crayon through an unusual series of adventures and a humorous lesson in perspective (specifically, foreground/background in landscapes). Paperback, 64 pages, ISBN 0934738955.

For teachers —

• *Van Gogh (Getting to Know the World's Greatest Artists),* by Mike Venezia (Children's Book Press, 2002). Many reproductions of van Gogh's works. Deals directly with his emotional instability and suicide. Paperback, 32 pages, ISBN 0516269984.

• *Visiting Vincent van Gogh (Adventures in Art),* by Caroline Breunesse (Prestel USA, 1997). Hardcover, 30 pages, ISBN 3791318764.

• Art Print Resources (209 Riverdale Avenue, Yonkers, NY 10705, www.artprintresources.com, or 1-800-501-4278) sells a set of 10 posters of artworks in the *Sequence* for this grade.

• Art Sense (www.artsense.net) provides an art program using videotapes and trade books.

• Art to the Core (Davis Publications, www.davis-art.com or 1-800-533-2847). A kit of materials that includes slides of artworks, lesson plans, assessment masters, and vocabulary masters, all keyed to the *Core Knowledge Sequence* for this grade.

• Crizmac (www.crizmac.com) sells a wide range of art education materials.

• Integrating the Art Disciplines: Looking to the Sky for Color is a lesson plan for young children that focuses on the landscape portraits of Vincent van Gogh. Children apply their skills in mixing colors using the primary hues and black-and-white tempera paints to create landscapes that prominently feature the sky. Available online at the Getty ArtsEdNet, www.getty.edu/artsednet/resources/Aeia/disc-lp.html.

• National Gallery of Art, www.nga.gov, has a number of images and lesson plans.

• Thomas Cole Online, www.artcyclopedia.com/artists/cole_thomas.html. A number of valuable links to Thomas Cole's works, organized by their current location. His *View from Mt. Holyoke, Northampton, Massachusetts, after a Thunderstorm—The Oxbow* is located at the Metropolitan Museum of Art, New York.

• Usborne (www.edcpub.com) has a wide range of art books, coloring books, and workbooks for the early grades.

• Van Gogh Museum, www.vangoghmuseum.nl. The official website of the Van Gogh Museum in Amsterdam. Includes a three-dimensional virtual tour of the museum.

IV. Abstract Art

The Big Idea

Exploring various aspects of abstract art, art that does not (if at all) strongly represent the actual object, will help children understand this type of art.

What Students Should Already Know

Students in Core Knowledge schools should be familiar with some examples of abstract art, including

Kindergarten

- Looking at and Talking About Works of Art
  - Helen Frankenthaler, *Blue Atmosphere*
  - Joan Miró, *People and Dog in the Sun*

What Students Need to Learn

- **Compare lifelike and abstract animals, including**
  - **Paintings of birds by John James Audubon**
  - **Albrecht Dürer, *Hare***
  - **Paul Klee, *Cat and Bird***
  - **Pablo Picasso, *Bull's Head* (made from bicycle seat and handlebars)**
  - **Elaine Marie de Kooning, *Baseball Players***
  - **Henri Matisse, *The Snail* (also known as *Chromatic Composition*)**
- **Observe and discuss examples of abstract painting and sculpture, including**
  - **Marc Chagall, *I and the Village***
  - **Constantin Brancusi, *Bird in Space***

IV. Abstract Art

Materials

Art Resources

Albrecht Dürer, *Hare*

Paul Klee, *Cat and Bird*

Pablo Picasso, *Bull's Head*

Elaine Marie de Kooning, *Baseball Players*

Henri Matisse, *The Snail*

John James Audubon, *Passenger Pigeon*

Marc Chagall, *I and the Village*

Constantin Brancusi, *Bird in Space*

Instructional Masters 31, 51–52,

Real or Abstract?, p. 274

Venn Diagram, p. 274

T-Chart, p. 277

coins (preferably quarters), p. 271

magazines and newspapers, p. 271

scissors, p. 271

overhead projector, p. 273

leaves, stones, flower petals, p. 275

drawing materials, p. 275, p. 279

"found" materials for three-dimensional animals, such as aluminum foil, bubble wrap, plastic food containers, pipe cleaners, crushed cans, buttons, yarn, tape, glue, p. 276

books or Internet printouts to study the artists from this section, p. 276, p. 279

abstract and realistic images of animals and/or objects, p. 278

drawing paper, p. 278

crayons and colored markers, p. 278

Joan Miro's *People and Dog in the Sun*, p. 278

chart paper, p. 278

Vocabulary

Student/Teacher Vocabulary

abstract: art that does not (if at all) strongly represent the actual object; stresses the formal elements of art, such as line, color, shape, form, and so forth (S)

nonobjective: completely abstract art that has no reference to recognizable objects (*nonobjective,* literally art that represents "no object") (T)

realistic: art that depicts images as true to life (S)

representational: art that describes a recognizable object; it can be semiabstract or completely realistic (S)

semiabstract: art that makes reference to recognizable objects from the world, but does not adhere to strict realism. Aspects of objects may be eliminated or distorted for effect. (S)

Domain Vocabulary

Abstract art and associated words:
nonrepresentational, organic, geometric, symbolize, reference, reduced, resemble, detail, quality, pigment, watercolor, gouache, woodcut, engraving, print, oil paint, interpretation, inspiration, assemble, scissors, cut-paper, composition, observation, flat, *plus words that describe things in paintings, e.g.,* windmill, hare, baselines, spiral, extinct, milkmaid, *etc.*

Cross-curricular Connections

Language Arts

Reading and Writing

Writing

Poetry

- "Caterpillars"
- "Something Told the Wild Geese"

Music

Elements of Music

- Camille Saint-Saëns, *Carnival of the Animals*

At a Glance

The most important ideas for you are:

- Art can be realistic or abstract.
- There are degrees of abstraction, from semiabstract to completely nonrepresentational.
- Semiabstract art remains linked to recognizable elements of the visible world.
- Artists create abstract art in both two and three dimensions.
- Artists can use completely nonrepresentational abstract art to explore the visual elements of art and/or to suggest particular ideas and emotions.
- Abstraction has been an aspect of Western art from Neolithic times to the present.

What Teachers Need to Know

Background

It is vital to engage children in art during the second-grade year. Drawing, painting, cutting, tearing, modeling, and pasting help develop small-motor and coordination skills. Likewise, talking about art develops their verbal and visual abilities through identifying (colors, lines, objects, actions), sorting (warm colors from cool colors), and communicating ideas (the children are playing a game). Children develop visual literacy by looking at pictures, and they build language skills by describing what is happening in a specific artwork.

Remember, too, that children need practice in exploring and creating art. Children need plenty of opportunities to draw, squeeze clay, cut and paste paper, and paint. Be sure to supplement art viewing with activities that allow children to create art. Creativity is not limited to a few people with a special talent; we all have the capacity to be creative.

In this section, we have included Baseball Players, *a painting by Elaine Marie de Kooning, a notable female artist of the 20th century. This art resource is an addition to the artworks listed in the* Sequence *for this grade.*

Note: The descriptions and activities in the main text below are intended to help you become familiar with the artworks before presenting them to children; however, some of the activities might be adapted for classroom use. Activities intended specifically for children can be found in the Teaching Idea sidebars. The Looking Questions given below are also printed on the reverse side of the *Art Resources* and have been written with children in mind so that they might be used as a rough plan for class discussion. You should feel free to use these questions or develop questions of your own. Be sure children have time to look at the reproductions carefully before asking the Looking Questions.

Artistic Styles: Realism and Abstraction

In the simplest terms, visual images are created in one of two basic styles: realism or abstraction. Take a moment to explore both styles.

First, create a coin rubbing. (A quarter is preferable because it's big.) After placing a sheet of plain paper over the coin and rubbing its surface with the side of a lead pencil, look at the image. It's easily identifiable as a coin, and, if you pressed down correctly, you can likely make out many of the exact details on the actual coin itself. The rubbing is a realistic image—the item looks true to life.

Place the coin on top of your paper, and trace its outline. Remove the coin and consider the image. You have a perfect circle. When you look at it, the circle is an abstract depiction or symbol of the coin. In abstraction, objects can still relate to the observable world, but do not detail them exactly. Sometimes, abstract images don't look much like the original object. This type of art is referred to as *nonobjective* because there are no recognizable "objects" in the composition.

Teaching Idea

Distribute images from magazines or newspapers of fairly simple scenes or objects (for instance, a teapot, a close-up portrait, a pair of sneakers, etc.). Point out that these images are realistic. Review the definition of realism—images that are true to life. Then, have children carefully cut their images into four different sections and rearrange them on their desk. The resulting recombined images are abstract. Their resulting compositions no longer describe the object as it would appear in the observable world. Then, have children select one shape and one color to represent their object. This, too, can be a form of abstract art.

A Matter of Degrees: Realism to Abstraction

You can think of the artistic styles of realism, semiabstraction, and pure abstraction as forming a continuum.

Let's begin with the easiest style to identify: realism. Look at any photograph in a newspaper or magazine. Does the image appear "real"—that is, pretty much as you might see the image in actual life? These images and, indeed, any art that closely imitates life, are defined as realistic. Examine the reproduction of Albrecht Dürer's *Hare*. Dürer's exacting, realistic style makes the furry creature seem as alive today as when Dürer painted it 500 years ago. Dürer's style is so realistic in this painting that you get the sense that you can almost reach out and stroke the hare's fur.

Now, look at the reproduction of Paul Klee's *Cat and Bird*. This painting doesn't look very lifelike. Klee reduced the feline to just a few simple shapes and lines. We can still tell what it is—a cat's face—but it is highly stylized, and, therefore, semiabstract.

In full abstraction, artists don't even necessarily make any reference to the known world. Particularly in modern times, artists have become interested in exploring how the elements of art, such as color, shape, line, form, space, and so forth, work together to form visually arresting images. They are often interested in these elements of art for their own sake, not because they look like something else.

There are also artists like Henri Matisse who have used these basic elements to create abstract compositions that don't particularly resemble elements of the real world, but do refer to them, albeit in a distant way. At first glance, Matisse's *The Snail* seems to be just an interplay of assorted color shapes. Each sits majestically on the surface of his work. However, if you move from the central green shape to the black shape, and then outward, you'll notice that Matisse created a spiral. Thus, loosely, or abstractly, he is referring to the creature of his title—a snail. Matisse's abstract work doesn't show you exactly what a snail looks like, but rather refers to the spiral quality of its shell. (See discussion in the Looking Section below on pp. 275–276.)

Abstract art can be either two- or three-dimensional. Look at the included reproduction of Pablo Picasso's *Bull's Head* sculpture. This is a two-dimensional image of a three-dimensional work of art. Picasso didn't render a bull in precise detail. In fact, he used just two found objects—a discarded bicycle seat and handlebars—and rearranged them into the mighty creature's horned head. Even though Picasso's art and a real bull are both three-dimensional, his sculpture is no more realistic than a two-dimensional painting. Indeed, it is much more abstract than many paintings.

Cross-curricular Teaching Idea

Use selections related to animals from your poetry readings in Language Arts, such as "Caterpillars" or "Something Told the Wild Geese," to discuss how poems are also like abstract art. Poems use word-pictures to create images and sensations, just like abstract art does. Have children create poems to describe any of the abstract works in the included reproductions.

Abstract History

As early as Neolithic times, artists used abstract images, carving them in stone. (Cave paintings of stick-like animals are an example.) Although realism virtually dominated Western art from ancient civilization until the late 19th century, abstraction always had its place. Abstract images often were an important decorative component in art—appearing in design on textiles as well as in paintings.

By the late 19th century, particularly in Western Europe, artists began to explore abstraction for its own sake, and eventually as the sole subject matter of art. In the 20th century, artists invented an abundant variety of abstract styles—from purely nonobjective art to semiabstract modes.

In non-Western and many indigenous cultures, including Oceanian, Latin American, Middle Eastern, and African societies, abstraction was always the norm. In Islam, adherence to abstraction stems from the traditional religious edict that no figurative (considered graven) images ever be made. This is why pages of the Qur'an are illustrated with geometric patterns but not with pictures of people.

Today, abstract styles are as varied as the artists who practice them. Some are rooted in ancient traditions, while others are inspired by the contemporary, highly technical digitized and computerized world.

Real and Abstract Art

art resource 10

Albrecht Dürer, *Hare* (1502)

German artist Albrecht Dürer [DUR-uhr] (1471–1528) strove to describe every nuance of his subjects, whether working on secular themes—such as animals that he loved, portraits, and self-portraits—or painting religious altarpieces. His precise observation and realism typified the Northern Renaissance style. Dürer used line and color to capture great detail, indicating every hair in *Hare* rather than simply painting the creature's coat as a single mass.

Dürer was versatile: he used oil paints, watercolor, gouache (an opaque watercolor, like poster paint, with a chalky look), woodcuts, and copper engravings to produce a large array of art. Dürer created works like *Hare* either as studies for oil paintings or prints, or for his own pleasure.

Dürer valued all his art, whether they were studies on paper or substantive paintings. He wished to raise the status of art, which until this time had been considered a craft. Thus, he included his monogram and a date to his work—a rare act for the time.

Looking questions

- **What do you see?** ***It's a painting of a hare or a rabbit.***
- **Do you see any lines in the painting?** ***There are lines that describe the fur, the whiskers, the ears, the toes, etc.***
- **What different textures do you see?** ***Children will identify a smooth nose, soft fur, stiff whiskers, and hard claws.***
- **Would you describe this painting as realistic or abstract?** ***It is very realistic.***
- **Can you tell when the painting was created?** ***It is dated 1502. Explain to children that this was a few years after Columbus sailed to America.***
- **The artist's name was Albrecht Dürer. Can you see where he put his initials on the painting?** ***A large A stands above a smaller D at the bottom of the painting.***

Teaching Idea

Have children complete the following "blind contour drawing" for a fun abstract portrait drawing activity. Ask children to place a sheet of paper on top of a notebook. Then have children work in pairs to make portraits of one another, drawing the partner without ever lifting the pencil from their paper. Children should draw very slowly and look only at their partner while drawing. When the drawings are complete, have children show the works to one another. The results will be abstract faces. Another fun experiment would be to darken the room and have a child's profile projected on the screen. Children can try to draw the profile as another abstract activity.

Teaching Idea

After studying Albrecht Dürer's *Hare*, introduce the class to the occupation of scientific illustrator. If possible, have a scientific illustrator who works for a natural history magazine, local zoo, or natural history museum come to speak to the class about their job. Finally, discuss how Dürer's art and that of a scientific illustrator are similar and different. (One difference has to do with intent. Dürer depicted the hare for artistic reasons; it wasn't meant for scientific use or study.)

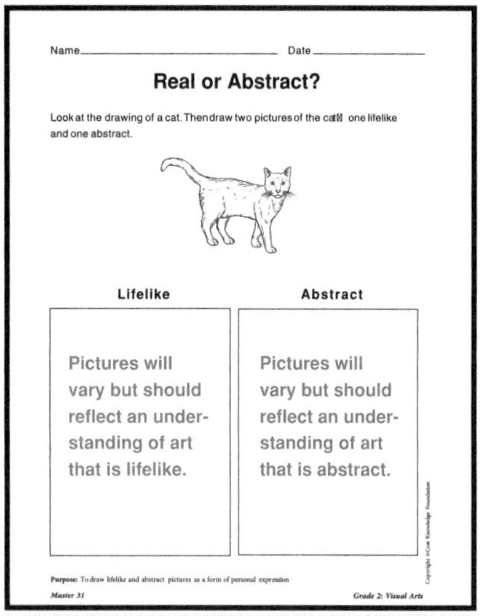
Name______ Date______

Real or Abstract?

Look at the drawing of a cat. Then draw two pictures of the cat: one lifelike and one abstract.

Lifelike	Abstract
Pictures will vary but should reflect an understanding of art that is lifelike.	Pictures will vary but should reflect an understanding of art that is abstract.

Purpose: To draw lifelike and abstract pictures as a form of personal expression

Master 31 Grade 2: Visual Arts

Copyright ©Core Knowledge Foundation

Use Instructional Master 31.

Teaching Idea

Use Instructional Master 52, Venn Diagram, with children to compare Albrecht Dürer's *Hare* and Paul Klee's *Cat and Bird.*

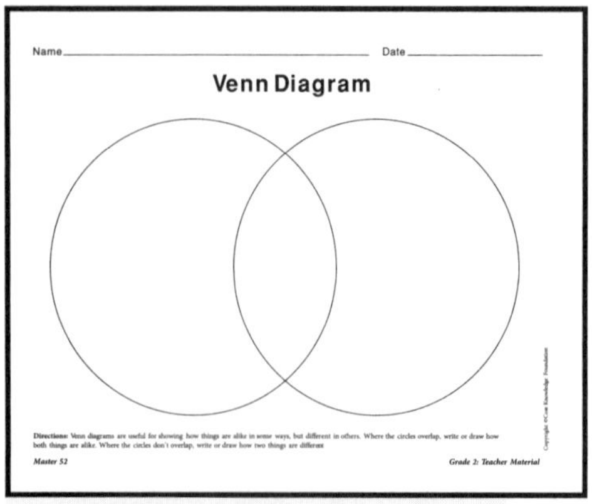
Name______ Date______

Venn Diagram

Directions: Venn diagrams are useful for showing how things are alike in some ways, but different in others. Where the circles overlap, write or draw how both things are alike. Where the circles don't overlap, write or draw how two things are different

Master 52 Grade 2: Teacher Material

Copyright ©Core Knowledge Foundation

Use Instructional Master 52.

(art resource 11) Paul Klee, *Cat and Bird* (1928)

German artist Paul Klee [CLAY] (1879–1940) was born and died in Switzerland, but spent most of his life in Germany. Klee created many mirthful artworks that tickle our funny bone. Here, his cat (made sweet by the tiny, heart-shaped nose) contemplates its prey—and possibly dinner. Klee deliberately used an abstract style that had a childlike quality—further reinforcing the mood of his jovial artwork.

Klee became, in his own words, "possessed by color" in 1914, and for the next 20 years he developed a mastery of delicate hues that transformed his disarmingly simple drawings into skilled compositions of shape, line, and color.

Looking questions

Note: Cover up the title on the front of the print before showing to children.

- **What do you see?** ***Children should see the cat. If necessary, help them see the bird.***
- **Why might Klee have shown the bird on the cat's forehead?** ***Answers will vary; perhaps the bird is sitting on the cat, or perhaps the cat is thinking of a bird and the bird is "in the cat's head."***
- **What are some colors Klee used?** ***He used pink, green, blue, orange, and red.***
- **Is this painting realistic or abstract?** ***It's somewhat abstract.***
- **Let's compare this abstract painting to Dürer's very realistic *Hare*. Which do you like more? Why?** ***Answers will vary.***

(art resource 12) Pablo Picasso, *Bull's Head* (1943)

Pablo Picasso (1881–1973) "assembled" his famous *Bull's Head* in February and March of 1943. This type of constructed art is called assemblage. Picasso used an abandoned seat and handlebars from a bicycle to form the creature, which was later cast in bronze.

Throughout his career, Picasso mastered and frequently invented numerous styles, ranging from realism to many forms of abstraction. Picasso also explored numerous artistic avenues, creating endless drawings, paintings, and prints; constructing metal, clay, and found-object sculptures; working in ceramics; and designing theatrical costumes and stage sets.

Looking questions

Note: Cover up the title on the front of the print before showing to children.

- **What do you see?** ***Answers will vary. If children see bicycle parts, go over which parts are shown (handlebars and seat). Then ask: Do the handlebars and seat look like anything else? Do they look like an animal? If children see a bull right away, ask: Where are the horns? Where is the nose? Then ask them what this bull is made of.***
- **How is this sculpture different from other sculptures you have seen?** ***It is not made of typical sculpture materials, e.g., stone. It's simpler and more abstract.***

- **Would you describe this work as realistic or abstract?** ***Help children see that it is abstract.***

- **How do you think Picasso might have come up with the idea of putting the handlebars and seat together to make a bull?** ***Answers will vary.***

- **Do you like this sculpture? Why or why not?** ***Answers will vary.***

art resource 13

Elaine Marie de Kooning, *Baseball Players* (1953)

Elaine Marie de Kooning (1918–1989) was an Abstract Expressionist painter who took the art world by storm in the late 1940s and 1950s. Like the other artists of this abstract mode, de Kooning worked in a large, physical style with clearly visible, aggressive brushwork. Her free-looking strokes show the energy and speed with which she worked.

De Kooning captured the active motion of a baseball game in her painting *Baseball Players.* She used lines that slash in many directions. The rush of visible brushstrokes creates a sense of immediacy, as though she had just laid down the paint and brush moments ago. De Kooning's bright accents of orange and red also add to the sense of movement in the composition, which is a tribute to baseball, the epitome of American sports.

Note: This work, although not in the *Sequence,* has been added to give children another example of abstract art.

Looking questions

- **What things in this painting tell you that it is about baseball?** ***Children might recognize the players, uniforms, baselines, or the base.***

- **How does the artist show you the action of the game?** ***The artist shows strong movement of the figures. Also, children might notice the quick, broad brushstrokes.***

- **What sounds does this painting make you think of?** ***Children might think of the roar of a crowd, other sounds of a ballpark, or the announcer.***

- **How is this painting different from a photograph of a baseball game?** ***Answers will vary, but comments should show understanding that a photograph is realistic and detailed, whereas the painting is abstract, showing simplified forms and few details.***

- **What does this style of painting tell you about baseball that a photograph might not?** ***It captures the energy, excitement, and motion of a game.***

art resource 14

Henri Matisse, *The Snail* (1953)

Henri Matisse (1869–1954) became bedridden at the end of his long and active career. But this didn't stop him from producing art. No longer able to stand at an easel to paint, Matisse "painted" with scissors or "sculpted" with paper—as others might say.

Matisse's lifelong fascination with color came to its fullest fruition in his late cut-paper works. *The Snail* is perhaps his most abstract work—with Matisse intentionally omitting any immediately recognizable description of the creature. Instead, Matisse created a joyous spiral of color and light, echoing the snail's spiral shell.

Teaching Idea

Henri Matisse made drawings of mollusks while holding them in the palm of his hand—attempting to create an image that was an abstract sign or symbol for the creature. Have children also study items from nature in their hands (leaves, stones, flower petals, and so forth) and then translate the patterns they detect on the items into abstract compositions. This looking activity should help sharpen their scientific observation and also their drawing skills.

Teaching Idea

Have children use "found" materials (such as aluminum foil, bubble wrap, plastic food containers, pipe cleaners, crushed cans, buttons, yarn, tape, glue, etc.) to construct their own menagerie, or collection, of animals, inspired by either the included reproductions from this section or animals they've studied in science.

Teaching Idea

Editions of John James Audubon's work are available in many libraries, as are coffee-table books collecting the works of great abstract artists like Pablo Picasso, Marc Chagall, Henri Matisse, Joan Miró, and Wassily Kandinsky. You can use books like these to supplement your study of realistic and abstract art.

Looking questions

Note: Cover up the title on the front of the print before showing to children.

- **What do you see?** ***Answers will vary.***
- **What colors and shapes do you see?** ***There are rectangular shapes in blue, green, red, yellow, and black.***
- **How did Matisse create a spiral in this piece?** ***He started from the central green shape, moved up to the black one, and then spiraled counter-clockwise in an outward direction.***
- **What animal has a spiral?** ***A snail's shell is a spiral. The title of the work is*** **The Snail.**
- **Is this a realistic or abstract piece of art?** ***It is very abstract.***

art resource 15

John James Audubon, *Passenger Pigeon*

Born in Santo Domingo (now Haiti) and raised in France, John James Audubon (1785–1851) was 18 when he moved to the United States. Always fascinated by birds, Audubon began to draw the local species as a pastime. In 1819, after the business he owned failed, Audubon made the decision to pursue his hobby in earnest. For nearly 20 years, Audubon traveled the length and breadth of America recording its vast variety of birds and their habitats. The result was a collection of 435 life-sized prints depicting 1,065 individual birds, which was published in four volumes and called *Birds of America.*

The remarkable accuracy and detail of Audubon's work have provided an unsurpassed benchmark in ornithological illustration. *Passenger Pigeon* is a particularly important example of his work. It records for posterity an eastern North American bird that once numbered in the billions and is now extinct. In his notes about the bird, Audubon comments about how they darkened the sky with their incredible numbers and created great noise as the huge flocks took off for flight.

Looking questions

- **What things tell you that the artist worked hard to make these birds look realistic?** ***Children might mention the amount of detail, the accurate color, or the lifelike poses.***
- **Audubon used several long, curving lines in the arrangement of this scene. Can you find them?** ***Children may find the branches that curve in opposite directions or the line made by the outer right edge of the birds. The birds' wings are another example of a curved line.***
- **The artist shows one bird with its wings down, and the other with its wings up. Why?** ***The artist wanted to show the feathers on the underside of the bird. He included as much detail as he could.***
- **Would you be able to recognize real birds by using paintings like these?** ***Children will probably say yes because the birds are painted so accurately. In fact, Audubon meant to help with bird identification.***
- **Why is it important that we have this very true-to-life image of a bird that no longer exists?** ***Answers will vary.***

Marc Chagall, *I and the Village* (1911)

art resource 16

Born into a Jewish family in Vitebsk, Russia, Marc Chagall (1887–1985) studied art in St. Petersburg. During World War II, he fled to the United States, and after the war he settled permanently in France. Chagall often used Russian village life as a subject for his paintings. These works are fantastic visions that interweave figures, scenes, and symbols from his memories.

Chagall spent a brief period (1910–1914) in Paris and painted *I and the Village* during that time. The fractured space of the work is clearly influenced by the Cubist work he was seeing in Paris. The simplified forms and vivid colors assimilated from the Fauvists combine to make it an abstract vision created from the artist's imagination. Rather than causing a person to feel discomfort, Chagall's poetic works are endearing and enchanting.

Looking questions

Note: Cover up the title on the front of the print before showing to children.

- **What are some of the things you see?** ***Children might recognize people, buildings, a cow and a milkmaid, and the faces of a cow and a man.***
- **Is this painting realistic or abstract?** ***Encourage children to point out ways in which the painting is abstract and ways in which it is realistic.***
- **What are some colors you see?** ***The colors are mainly green, red, blue, gray, and black.***
- **What is on the left of the painting? What is on the right? What does this tell you about the relationship of people and animals in the village?** ***The animal on the left seems to be a lamb or calf. On the right is a person—a farmer, maybe. By the way they are looking at each other, the artist suggests that animals and people understand each other in the village.***
- **What would you call this painting?** ***Tell children the title.***
- **This is a painting in which the artist remembers the village where he grew up. Do you think he has fond memories of it?** ***Answers will vary, but the painting suggests memories of harmony, security, and gentleness.***

Teaching Idea

After studying both John James Audubon's *Passenger Pigeon* and Constantin Brancusi's *Bird in Space*, use Instructional Master 51, *T-Chart*, to draw comparisons between abstract and realistic art.

Constantin Brancusi, *Bird in Space* (1928)

art resource 17

Constantin Brancusi (1876–1957) was fascinated with birds and flight, but from a very different perspective than John James Audubon (see *Passenger Pigeon*). As one of the leading sculptors of the modernist movement, Brancusi focused on distilling form to its essence. The Romanian sculptor created several series related to birds. There are 16 examples in the *Bird in Space* group.

Unlike Audubon, whose mission was to render the most accurate representations possible, Brancusi eliminated all connections to realism and created nonrepresentational forms. *Bird in Space* is intended to communicate the idea of flying and a sense of soaring. The pure, smooth abstraction accomplishes this goal with its simple arched form.

Looking questions

Note: Cover up the title on the front of the print before showing to children.

- **What do you see?** ***Answers will vary.***

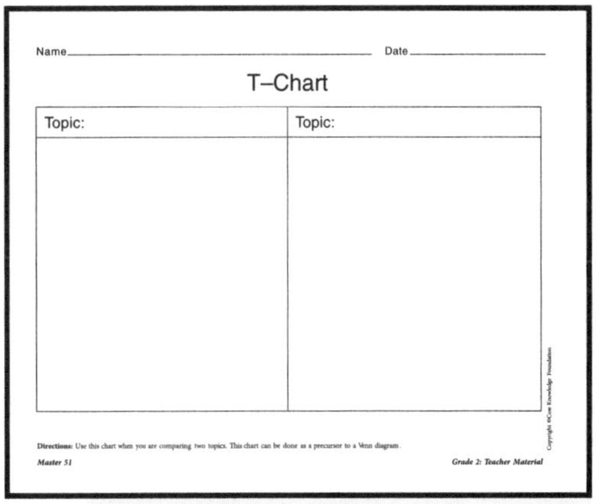
Name ______ Date ______

T–Chart

Topic:	Topic:

Directions: Use this chart when you are comparing two topics. This chart can be done as a precursor to a Venn diagram.

Master 51 *Grade 2: Teacher Material*

Copyright ©Core Knowledge Foundation

Use Instructional Master 51.

- **The title of this piece is *Bird in Space*. What makes it look like a bird?** ***It seems to be rising gracefully. All the energy goes straight up. The highly polished metal suggests sunlight, too. Children will have additional impressions.***
- **How did Brancusi design *Bird in Space* so that it looks very simple?** ***It is a single, continuous form; it is one color; it has a smooth, untextured surface; and it has a basic form for the base.***
- **Why do you think Brancusi made his idea of a bird so simple and abstract?** *Answers will vary.*

The Big Idea in Review

Exploring various aspects of abstract art, art that does not (if at all) strongly represent the actual object, will help children understand this type of art.

Review

Below are some ideas for ongoing assessment and review activities. These are not meant to constitute a comprehensive list.

- Search the Internet for abstract images of animals and/or objects to print out, e.g., search for "abstract," "painting," and the name of the object or animal you are looking for. Then pair the abstract images you find with realistic images of the same things. Use the pairs to solidify children's understanding of the differences between abstract and realistic images.
- Give children opportunities to create abstract art while studying this section. They may want to create a culminating piece of abstract art from materials that you provide for the teaching ideas within this section. Then, have children write about their piece and how they were inspired to create it. Have them also describe how their piece illustrates the components of abstract art. Organize a class art show and invite other classes to view the pieces.
- To give children a sense of how abstract art can be created by individual children, give each child a piece of paper and different-colored crayons or markers. Then, give a set of drawing directions to the class. You can make up the directions and have as many steps as you like. For example, direct children to draw a circle on the paper. Then, have them draw three triangles. Have them draw a square, and then a line through the square. After you have finished the directions, have them finish the picture any way they would like, coloring it or adding other shapes. When the class is finished, have them share their pictures. Have the class observe the common elements in the pictures from the set of directions, but then have them note the different artistic license of each child—where they placed their shapes and what colors they used. Discuss this process.
- Bring the piece by Joan Miró entitled *People and Dog in the Sun* to class. Review this piece, which children studied in Kindergarten, and ask them to observe the Miró piece and the other abstract art from this section. Have the class write reviews of the abstract art. What are their opinions of abstract art compared to the lifelike pieces? Do they prefer one kind of art over the other? Have them explain why or why not.
- Create a Venn diagram on chart paper for the class. Have the class compare and contrast the pieces of lifelike and abstract animals from this section. What are the similarities and the differences? Which pieces do children prefer? Why? Have

children extend this activity by writing about which kind of art they prefer and then writing the reasons to support their arguments.

• While studying the pieces in this section, provide the class with books or Internet printouts to study the different artists who created the works. Have an "artist study" in which children find other pieces that the artists created and share them with the class. Organize children into groups, have them research the artist, and then have them find two other pieces that the artist created. Share these with the class.

• If you have already studied Camille Saint-Saën's *Carnival of the Animals* in music class, then have children create realistic and abstract images of the animals represented in the piece. Children can write about the differences in their representations of the animals, and why they chose certain techniques (line, shape, color) to represent the animal in an abstract way. You can post these realistic and abstract images and writing samples in the hallway for others to enjoy.

• In general, the best time to ask questions about a specific painting is while children are looking at it. However, by the end of the section, children should be able to answer the general questions on the genres they have studied. You may also ask the following questions at the end of this section:

1. How would you describe realistic art?
   Realistic art is art that imitates the world we see.

2. What is the definition of abstract art?
   Abstract art is art that does not (if at all) strongly represent the actual object. It stresses the formal elements of art, such as line, color, shape, form, and so forth.

More Resources

The titles listed below are offered as a representative sample of materials and not a complete list of everything that is available.

For children —

These books are generally intended to be read aloud, though some children may be able to read parts or all of the simpler texts.

- *Audubon: Painter of Birds in the Wild Frontier,* by Jennifer Armstrong (Abrams, 2003). Hardcover, 40 pages, ISBN 0810942380.
- *Come Look with Me: Enjoying Art with Children,* by Gladys S. Blizzard (Lickle Publishing, 1996). A great discussion starter. Includes two paintings by Pablo Picasso. Hardcover, 32 pages, ISBN 0934738769. See also in this series *Animals in Art* (has Paul Klee's *Cat and Bird* as well as a painting by Albrecht Dürer); *The Artist at Work* (includes two masks by Picasso); *Exploring Modern Art* (with an abstract by Helen Frankenthaler); and *Art in Early America* (includes a painting by John James Audubon). All are available through Lickle Publishing, www.licklepublishing.com or 1-866-454-2553.
- *Dreaming Pictures: Paul Klee (Adventures in Art),* by Paul Klee and Juergen von Schemm (Prestel USA, 1997). Hardcover, 32 pages, ISBN 3791318756.
- *Paul Klee (Getting to Know the World's Greatest Artists),* by Mike Venezia (Children's Press, 1992). Paperback, 32 pages, ISBN 0516422944.

For teachers —

- *The Birds of America,* by the National Audubon Society (Random House, 1996). Paperback, ISBN 0517201194.
- Art Print Resources (209 Riverdale Avenue, Yonkers, NY 10705, www.artprintresources.com, or 1-800-501-4278) sells a set of 10 posters of artworks in the *Sequence* for this grade.
- Art Sense (www.artsense.net) provides an art program using videotapes and trade books.
- Art to the Core (Davis Publications, www.davis-art.com or 1-800-533-2847). A kit of materials that includes slides of artworks, lesson plans, assessment masters, and vocabulary masters, all keyed to the *Core Knowledge Sequence* for this grade.
- Crizmac (www.crizmac.com) sells a wide range of art education materials.
- Usborne (www.edcpub.com) has a wide range of art books, coloring books, and workbooks for the early grades.

V. Architecture

The Big Idea

Architecture is the art of designing buildings.

What Students Need to Learn

- **Understand architecture as the art of designing buildings**
- **Understand symmetry and a line of symmetry, and observe symmetry in the design of some buildings (such as the Parthenon)**
- **Note line, form, and special features (such as columns and domes) in**
  - **The Parthenon (Athens, Greece)**
  - **Great Stupa (Buddhist temple in Sanchi, India)**
  - **Himeji Castle (also known as "White Heron Castle," Japan)**
  - **The Solomon R. Guggenheim Museum (New York City)**

What Students Will Learn in Future Grades

In future grades, students will review and extend their learning about architecture.

Grade 4

- Art of the Middle Ages in Europe
  - Gothic architecture
- Islamic Art and Architecture
- The Art of a New Nation: The United States
  - Monticello

V. Architecture

Materials

Art Resources

Iktinus and Kallikrates, *Parthenon*

Great Stupa

Himeji Castle

Frank Lloyd Wright, *Solomon R. Guggenheim Museum*

Instructional Masters 32–33

Parts of Buildings, p. 286

Building Your Architectural Know-How, p. 287

magazines featuring environments, p. 284

photograph of the Lincoln Memorial and pictures of Elgin Marbles, p. 285

newspapers, p. 287

tape, p. 287

drawing materials, p. 287

photographs of local buildings, p. 289

Vocabulary

Student/Teacher Vocabulary

arch: a curved or pointed span over a doorway or window (S)

architecture: the art of designing buildings (S)

column: an upright (vertical) post (S)

façade: the front (or "face") of a building (S)

line of symmetry: an imaginary line running down the middle of a symmetrical image (S)

pediment: a triangular space that forms the gable of a pitched roof (T)

stupa: a dome-like mound built in memory of Buddha and the Buddhist cosmic or "World Mountain" (T)

symmetrical: having both sides exactly the same (S)

texture: in art pieces, real or implied surface quality (S)

Domain Vocabulary

Architecture and associated words:

bricks, mud, figures, light, natural and manufactured materials, private, public, carve, stadium, arena, mall, tent, canvas, hide, shelter, monument, temple, frieze, stories, skylight, exterior, interior, design, 360 degrees, inhabitants, commission, decorate, dome, Buddha, Athens, acropolis, roof, floor, spiral

Cross-curricular Connections

Language Arts

Fiction

Stories

- "The Blind Men and the Elephant" (India)
- "The Tongue-Cut Sparrow" (Japan)

Mythology of Ancient Greece

- Gods of ancient Greece and Rome

History and Geography

World: Geography

- Locate Asia and Europe on maps and/or globes

World: Ancient Greece

- Geography
- Worship of gods and goddesses

World: Early Civilizations: Asia

Geography of Asia

India

- Buddhism

World: Modern Civilization and Culture: Japan

Geography

Mathematics

Geometry

- Identify and draw basic plane figures: square, rectangle, triangle, circle
- Identify lines as horizontal, vertical, perpendicular, and parallel
- Identify a line of symmetry, and create symmetric figures
- Identify solid figures: sphere, cube, pyramid, cone, cylinder

Science

Simple Machines

- Tools to perform specific jobs

At a Glance

The most important ideas for you are:

- Viewers can physically experience and interact with architecture.
- Form, color, texture, and line are the major elements of architecture.
- Architecture can be constructed from many different natural and manufactured materials.
- Architecture has two major divisions: private and public.

What Teachers Need to Know

Background

As a child, did you ever build a tent out of a sheet draped over pillows and/ or chairs? Did you ever build a "house" to play in, using found objects at home or outside? Did you ever draw fantasy abodes while doodling on paper? Some of our earliest play focuses on being an architect.

At the most basic level, architecture is the art of designing buildings. What makes it an art? Sketch a simple house on paper. No matter how minimal your design may be, you had to consider the forms (not shapes, because they're three-dimensional) you would use. For a more sophisticated rendering, you'd also have to take line, color, and texture into account.

On the other hand, what separates architecture from most other sorts of art? Stop to reflect: What's your relationship to a painting? Basically, you can stand in front of it. And your relationship to sculpture? Well, you can walk around sculpture and view it from 360 degrees. However, unlike paintings and sculptures, you can experience both the exterior and interior of architecture.

The fact that architecture is physically experienced greatly influences decisions in its design. An architect must decide how it will look on the outside as you approach the façade. And what will it be like to enter the structure? What feelings and sensations will be evoked? Grandeur, intimacy, power, wealth, humility, artistry? Is the building designed so that you must walk through it in a particular way—or can you gain access to any area from many different avenues?

These are just some of the many issues that architects throughout the ages have had to wrestle with, whether building a simple shelter or a public monument for the masses.

Note: The descriptions and activities in the main text below are intended to help you become familiar with the artworks before presenting them to children; however, some of the activities might be adapted for classroom use. Activities intended specifically for children can be found in the Teaching Idea sidebars. The Looking Questions given below are also printed on the reverse side of the *Art Resources* and have been written with children in mind so that they might be used as a rough plan for class

discussion. You should feel free to use these questions or develop questions of your own. Be sure children have time to look at the reproductions carefully before asking the Looking Questions.

Teaching Idea

As a way to help children start thinking about architecture, ask them to write about a short walking tour through their classroom. They will practice their writing and scientific directional skills by describing exactly what happens from the moment you walk in the door until you've toured all corners of the room. As an extension, have children repeat this exercise at home and illustrate their texts, making them into "How to Visit My Home" manuals.

Why Build?

The earliest architects constructed shelters to protect people from heat, humidity, cold, snow, rain, sunshine, and so forth. The idea of "home"—a building in which we live—remains a primary physical and emotional concern for us today. We can build entire worlds of our own inside our private domains. The buildings we live in, and how we design and decorate their interiors, are direct reflections of our individuality.

But buildings also have had a long history in the public sphere as well. In cultures across the world, some of the first "public" buildings—typically the largest and most elaborate in the community—were spiritual centers. The Parthenon, a temple to the Greek goddess Athena, is a prime example of such a structure in Western history. From the 1st century CE in India, we have the Buddhist burial structure, the Great Stupa. In contemporary times, we also build "temples" of art, such as the Solomon R. Guggenheim Museum in New York City.

Architectural Materials and Locations

Who were the very first architects? They may have been people who modified existing caves and/or used local materials and the labor of animals to build shelters.

Wood, stone, and earth remain important architectural ingredients. Modern technology has broadened the availability of materials to include all sorts of metals, plastics, and plaster, among others.

Materials are important because they directly affect the function and structure of a building. You wouldn't build a small pup tent from metal, or a commercial mall with twigs. Today, we can transport materials just about anywhere in the world, so local resources are less of a concern to most architects. But, consider the human labor that had to go into locating, cutting, dragging, and then placing the impressive stones for the Parthenon in Greece, seen in the *Art Resources.*

The earliest builders used materials that were nearest at hand. As civilization advanced, and buildings became symbolic as well as functional, the issue of location became even more important. Glance at the included reproductions of the Parthenon and Himeji Castle. If you had commissioned these great buildings, where would you most likely wish to situate them? They both stand on top of large hills—making impressive silhouettes against the sky.

Teaching Idea

Have children look through magazines, such as *National Geographic,* which have reproductions of many types of environments. Have children make a list of all the different types of natural materials that would be available to build shelters in each locale. Branches, leaves, stalks, grass, straw, animal hides, mud, and stones are some examples. Connect this to the social studies curriculum if there is time, looking at the way early indigenous inhabitants in different regions used natural materials for building.

Color and Texture in Architecture

Architects select materials not only for their function, but also for their aesthetic qualities. White marble, dark wood, and gray stone have their own individual colors—and, just as importantly, produce varying textures. The appearance of a brick or stone façade would be quite different from one made with wood slats or metal siding. Seeing also relates to feeling, because the texture itself arouses an intuitive physical response. Imagine what it would feel like to run your hand along a stone fireplace versus one constructed out of pressed metal.

Architectural Lines

Most of us associate line with two-dimensional art, but, in fact, it is a major component of three-dimensional architecture. Look again at the reproductions of the Parthenon and Himeji Castle. Where can you detect the lines that dominate these buildings? The Greek temple is marked by strong vertical and horizontal lines: vertical lines from the columns support the horizontal line visible in the remains of the roof. The lines in the Japanese Himeji Castle are equally as pronounced. Notice how the roof lines sweep upward at the ends—almost like wing tips. This is part of the reason why the building is sometimes called "White Heron Castle."

There is a major, invisible line in both of these architectural structures and in a great many buildings. Imagine drawing a line straight down the exact middle of the Parthenon's façade. This line is called a line of symmetry, and the two halves of the Parthenon's façade will be exactly equal (or symmetrical) on either side, with the same number of columns. Imagine the same line in the Great Stupa of India. It, too, is symmetrical, meaning it is even on both sides of the imaginary line.

Himeji Castle

Looking at Included Reproductions of Architecture

art resource 18

Iktinus and Kallikrates, Parthenon (448–432 CE)

The architects Iktinus and Kallikrates are credited with building the Parthenon more than 2,000 years ago. Children may have learned about the importance of Athens and the Parthenon in their study of World History. The Parthenon is part of a complex of buildings called the Acropolis, which sits on a hill in Athens, Greece. (*Acropolis* means "high city" in Greek.) The Parthenon was a temple that honored the Greek goddess Athena, the patron deity of Athens. The building, made entirely of Pentelric marble, remains a classic example of the high point of ancient Greek architecture. The repetitive vertical columns create an even rhythm around the entire structure, while each column's slightly tapered form moves the eyes upward, toward the heavens—Athena's realm. At one time, a frieze [FREEZE] around the four sides of the building, above the 46 columns of the inner part, contained reproductions of a procession in Athens that honored Athena, which occurred every four years.

Above the outside columns were panels that showed scenes from Greek mythology. In the triangular entablature and pediment were brightly painted sculptures. The surviving marble statues from the frieze and pediments have been detached from the building and now reside in museums in London and Athens. For example, the so-called Elgin Marbles are on display in the British Museum.

Echoes of the Parthenon's regal columns frequently appear in government and other official public buildings throughout the United States, lending an air of ancient authority to the modern structures.

Looking questions

- **What do you see?** ***Children should see a building made of stone that has columns.***
- **What building materials were used?** ***Only stone was used.***
- **When do you think this building was built?** ***Children should say long ago. Ask them how they know. The decay of the building is a clue.***

Cross-curricular Teaching Idea

In connection with History and Geography for this grade, show children a picture of the Lincoln Memorial and explain how an ancient Greek temple, the Parthenon, influenced the design of this monument to the 16th president. Children may also enjoy seeing pictures of the Elgin Marbles.

Cross-curricular Teaching Idea

Draw a connection between architecture, civilizations, and language arts. While studying the Parthenon, read selections of mythology of ancient Greece.

- **Does anyone have an idea of where this building might be? *It is in Athens, Greece. It was built thousands of years ago in ancient times.***
- **What do you think the building might have been used for? *Answers will vary. It was a temple to the goddess Athena.***
- **What are some elements of art that you can see in this building? *It has straight lines; round, square, and rectangular shapes.***
- **Where do you see symmetry in this building? *There are four columns on either side of the center, and the columns look exactly alike.***

Great Stupa (1st century BCE)

art resource 19

Stupas, dome-like burial mounds, symbolize Buddha, the founder of Buddhism, which is a major religion in Asia. Children learn about Buddha in their study of India in World History in Grade 2.

Stupas were originally burial mounds that covered relics of the Buddha or his adherents. Stupas can be made of brick, stone, or a mixture of brick and rubble. The Great Stupa at Sanchi, restored in the second decade of the 20th century, covers an earlier version that was created from large, burnt bricks and mud.

The Great Stupa, like the Parthenon, is part of a larger architectural complex. It is the most elaborate and famous of the more than 50 Buddhist monuments on the hilltop in Sanchi that architects built between the 3rd century BCE and the 12th century CE. The original Stupa at Sanchi is said to have been built by the Emperor Ashoka, whom children study in the unit on India and Buddhism.

The Stupa is no longer a burial mound, but has become a purely symbolic object—an architectural structure of great importance to Buddhist followers. Buddhists make pilgrimages to the Great Stupa and walk around the dome along a circular, paved walkway, which has been worn smooth by the steps of many previous pilgrims.

Cross-curricular Teaching Idea

Draw a connection between architecture, civilizations, and language arts. While studying the Great Stupa, read the story "The Blind Men and the Elephant," which is also from India.

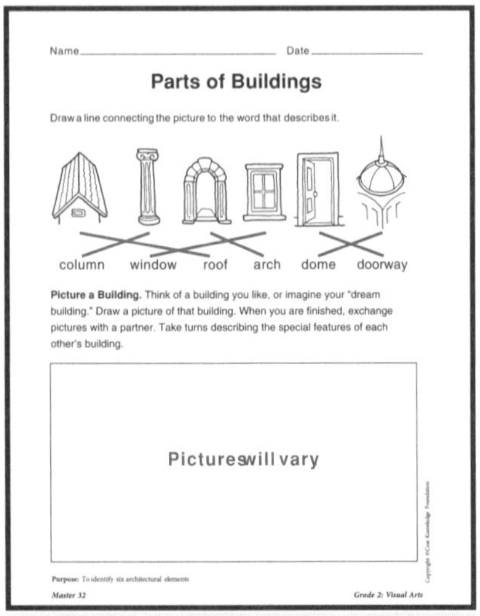
Name ______ Date ______

Parts of Buildings

Draw a line connecting the picture to the word that describes it.

Picture a Building. Think of a building you like, or imagine your "dream building." Draw a picture of that building. When you are finished, exchange pictures with a partner. Take turns describing the special features of each other's building.

Pictures will vary

Purpose: To identify six architectural elements

Master 32 *Grade 2: Visual Arts*

Copyright ©Core Knowledge Foundation

Use Instructional Master 32.

Looking questions

- **What do you see? *Most children will recognize the structure as a building.***
- **What is the biggest form you see in the Great Stupa? *The dome, or half a sphere, is the biggest form. Explain that a stupa is a dome-shaped Buddhist temple.***
- **Where else on the building can you see rounded forms like the dome? *Children might mention the terrace, the triple "parasol" on top, and the stone-paved procession path enclosed by the encircling stone balustrade (railing).***
- **What shapes did the architect use? *The architect used circles, rectangles, and ovals.***

Himeji Castle ("White Heron Castle") (early 17th century)

art resource 20

Himeji Castle has withstood wars, time, and even earthquakes for more than 400 years. White plaster covers the wooden structure, acting as both a fireproof material and also reinforcing the walls.

Cross-curricular Teaching Idea

Draw a connection between architecture, civilizations, and language arts. While studying the Himeji Castle, read the story "The Tongue-Cut Sparrow," which is also from Japan.

The main tower, with its five projecting roofs, actually includes six stories plus a basement. The stories become smaller as the building gets higher. The upward-tilted roof edges give the building an illusion of a giant bird. It was the central tower of a huge complex of more than 50 buildings built in the early 17th century.

Designed as a castle to be well fortified against intruders, it was laid out in a confusing way. Visitors today still get lost within the complex when attempting to find the central portion of the castle, despite signs pointing in the right direction.

Looking questions

- **This Japanese building is sometimes called the "White Heron Castle." Why do you think its nickname refers to the white bird?** ***It is white in color and its eaves look like flapping wings.***
- **What different kinds of line can you see on the building?** ***There are horizontal, vertical, diagonal, and curving lines.***
- **Which two shapes do you see most often?** ***Rectangles and triangles appear most often.***
- **Because this is a castle, the architect wanted to give the impression of strength, power, and privacy. How did he do this?** ***The building is tall and not welcoming. The windows are only slits, perhaps for archers to shoot arrows from. The horizontal and vertical lines make the castle look as steep and rugged as a canyon wall. The sweep of the roof makes the building look proud.***

art resource 21

Frank Lloyd Wright, Solomon R. Guggenheim Museum (1956–1959)

The American architect Frank Lloyd Wright (1867–1959) was highly concerned with the relationship between his architecture and its surroundings. Unlike his rural buildings, Wright's Solomon R. Guggenheim [GOO-guhn-hime] Museum spirals its way upward amid a crowded urban landscape. Surrounded by straight-edged, rectangular box-like buildings, the teacup-like form illustrates Wright's love of mixing straight-edged and rounded forms.

The four exterior disks fuse into a single, spiraling ramp inside the museum. From any location in the building, whether walking upward or downward, you can lean over the railing and look up through the skylight above or across to any other part of the museum. The museum houses a modern art collection.

Controversy remains over Frank Lloyd Wright's Solomon R. Guggenheim Museum. Its interior spiral ramp dictates that every exhibition must be shown and viewed in a linear manner (either walking up or down the ramp). Critics say that the building may be great, but it's poor for showing art. Other people believe it is a perfect place to show art because it is a work of art itself!

Looking questions

Note: Cover up the title on the front of the print before showing to children.

- **What do you see?** ***Answers will vary.***
- **What is unusual about this building?** ***It is round.***
- **What type of building do you think it might be? What is its purpose?** ***Answers will vary. It is a museum of modern and contemporary art.***

Teaching Idea

Have children try to re-create the Solomon R. Guggenheim Museum using newspaper and tape. Give children 20 minutes, and see which groups can create a building that has rounded forms. For an additional challenge, tell children that their building must be able to hold a dictionary on top. After children experiment, talk about the challenge of creating a building and art.

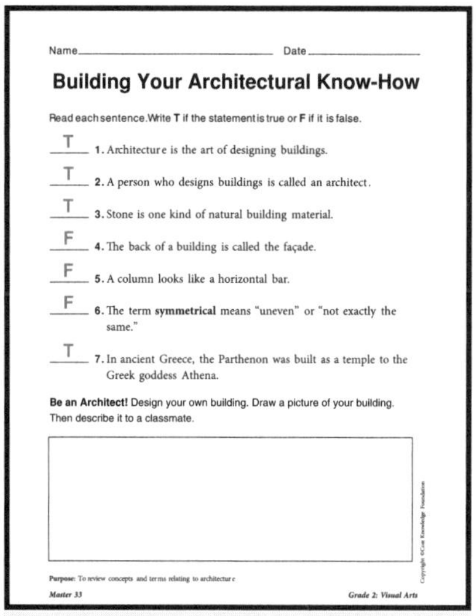
Name________ Date________

Building Your Architectural Know-How

Read each sentence. Write **T** if the statement is true or **F** if it is false.

T 1. Architecture is the art of designing buildings.
T 2. A person who designs buildings is called an architect.
T 3. Stone is one kind of natural building material.
F 4. The back of a building is called the façade.
F 5. A column looks like a horizontal bar.
F 6. The term **symmetrical** means "uneven" or "not exactly the same."
T 7. In ancient Greece, the Parthenon was built as a temple to the Greek goddess Athena.

Be an Architect! Design your own building. Draw a picture of your building. Then describe it to a classmate.

Purpose: To review concepts and terms relating to architecture

Master 33 *Grade 2: Visual Arts*

Copyright ©Core Knowledge Foundation

Use Instructional Master 33.

- **What do you think it would feel like to walk through this building? Why?** ***Answers will vary. Point out that the building spirals upward, so walking around it means walking in a circle while going up.***

- **How is this building different from the ones surrounding it? Why do you think the architect made it round?** ***Its roundness contrasts with the rectangular shapes of other city buildings; this makes it stand out because it catches your eye. The building can be seen as a work of art itself, like all the art it contains.***

Review

The Big Idea in Review

Architecture is the art of designing buildings.

Below are some ideas for ongoing assessment and review activities. These are not meant to constitute a comprehensive list.

- Give the class a list of elements in architecture from this section, and have each child design a building. After they have drawn their structure, have them write a paragraph describing the architectural elements and the purpose of their building. Share with the class.
- Make a local connection by showing the class pictures of buildings from your area and identifying the architectural elements on and within those buildings. You may also want to organize a field trip in your local area to look at buildings and identify elements of architecture.
- Arrange for an architect to come to your class and give a presentation about what is involved in being an architect. Have the presenter give details about what kind of subjects you have to study to be an architect and share some projects he or she is working on. After the visit, have your class write thank-you letters and talk about what they learned about architecture.
- Make a connection between the study of symmetry in architecture and in math. Have children practice drawing symmetrical lines and shapes, and make sure they are able to describe what makes them symmetrical. Have children design a picture of either a symmetrical set or an unsymmetrical set of objects or lines. They may color and decorate the pictures. Then, have children share their pictures with the class, and have the class guess whether the set of items is symmetrical or not symmetrical. Make sure that they can explain why or why not.
- In general, the best time to ask questions about architecture is while children are looking at it. However, by the end of the section, children should be able to answer the general questions on the genres they have studied. You may also ask the following question at the end of this section:

1. What is architecture?
   Architecture is the art of designing buildings.
2. What are some of the key elements of art in architecture?
   Key architectural elements include color, line, form, and texture.
3. What natural materials do some architects use (or have used in the past)?
   Materials architects use include wood, stone, clay, straw, leaves, and animal hides.

More Resources

The titles listed below are offered as a representative sample of materials and not a complete list of everything that is available.

For children —

These books are generally intended to be read aloud, though some children may be able to read parts or all of the simpler texts.

• *Architecture Counts,* by Michael J. Crosbie and Steve Rosenthal (John Wiley & Sons, 1993). Though intended for a younger audience, this book will introduce children to architectural features such as columns, dormers, brackets, and pinnacles. Board book, 16 pages, ISBN 0471143669. Also in this series are *Architecture Shapes, Architecture Animals,* and *Architecture Colors,* by the same authors.

• *How a House Is Built,* by Gail Gibbons (Holiday House, 1996). Paperback, ISBN 0823412326.

• *Let's Fly a Kite,* by Stuart J. Murphy (HarperCollins, 2000). A lesson in symmetry. Paperback, 32 pages, ISBN 0064467376.

• *Round Buildings, Square Buildings, and Buildings that Wriggle Like a Fish,* by Philip M. Isaacson (Knopf, 1988). A fairly thorough introduction with easily understood explanations and good photography. Hardcover, 128 pages, ISBN 0394893824.

• *William's House,* by Ginger Howard (Millbrook Press, 2001). William must modify his "Old World" house to fit "New World" conditions. Library binding, 32 pages, ISBN 0761316744.

For teachers —

• *Architecture: A Very Short Introduction,* by Andrew Ballantyne (Oxford University Press, 2002). Paperback, 152 pages, ISBN 0192801791.

• *Building Big,* by David Macaulay (Houghton Mifflin/ Walter Lorraine, 2004). A companion book to the PBS series by the same title, this is a look at the technical aspects of building bridges, dams, tunnels, domes, and skyscrapers. Paperback, 192 pages, ISBN 0618465278. See also *Unbuilding,* by the same author.

• *Guggenheim New York/Guggenheim Bilbao,* photography by Ezra Stoller and Jeff Goldberg (Princeton Architectural Press, 1999). Paperback, 80 pages, ISBN 1568981937.

• Art to the Core (Davis Publications, www.davis-art.com or 1-800-533-2847). A kit of materials that includes slides of artworks, lesson plans, assessment masters, and vocabulary masters, all keyed to the *Core Knowledge Sequence* for this grade.

• Art Sense (www.artsense.net) provides an art program using videotapes and trade books.

• Crizmac (www.crizmac.com) sells a wide range of art education materials.

• The Great Buildings Collection, www.greatbuildings.com, "documents a thousand buildings and hundreds of leading architects, with 3D models, photographic images and architectural drawings, commentaries, bibliographies, web links, and more." (from the site) Search by building name. Note also the CD-ROM version, *The Great Buildings Collection,* by Kevin Matthews (Artifice, 1999). Dual Platform for Windows and Macintosh, ASIN: 0966709845.

• Usborne (www.edcpub.com) has a wide range of art books, coloring books, and workbooks for the early grades.

Music

Percentages beside major topics provide a rough guide for allocating time for Music during the year.

There are many ways for children to enjoy music: they may listen to it, sing it, perform it, move to it, and more. In Grade 2, children will continue to explore all these forms of musical participation and, in the process, learn more of the rudiments of theory and notation. Children will also continue their study of the orchestra.

Music is made up of several basic elements, including rhythm, melody, harmony, form, dynamics, and timbre. Children will explore these elements through active participation, developing a sense of how each element is musically significant, and at the same time they will learn the terms to describe it. This year, children will also continue their study of music notation, and will learn to recognize and understand more music symbols, building on what they learned in Grade 1.

In Grade 2, children will review the different families of instruments and further study strings, percussion, and keyboards. They will also be introduced to new composers. They will become familiar with pieces by Camille Saint-Saëns, Antonio Vivaldi, Carlos Chavez, Wolfgang Amadeus Mozart, Ludwig van Beethoven, Felix Mendelssohn, and Johann Sebastian Bach.

Children will learn and sing a repertoire of traditional songs. These songs provide an accessible and fun way for children to master short musical works. Through the process of learning these songs, children will develop a valuable intuitive sense of the elements of music at work.

Music can be a source of great pleasure and satisfaction; at the same time, the observational and analytical skills used to understand music are valuable in making sense of any form of art and many other aspects of the world around us. Ideally, in Grade 2, children will enjoy the pleasures of music and in the process gain a more nuanced understanding of it.

I. Elements of Music

The Big Idea

Music is described with terms such as rhythm, melody, harmony, form, dynamics, and timbre. Musical notes have names and are organized into scales.

What Students Should Already Know

Students in Core Knowledge schools should be familiar with

Kindergarten and Grade 1

- recognize, play, and move to a steady beat
- recognize short and long sounds
- discriminate between fast and slow
- discriminate between high and low pitches
- discriminate between loud and quiet
- recognize like and unlike phrases
- sing unaccompanied, accompanied, and in unison
- recognize, sing, and play simple rhythms and melodies
- recognize that music has timbre or tone color
- notation: whole note, half note, and quarter note

What Students Need to Learn

- **Increase ability to recognize elements of music learned in previous grades**
- **Downbeat**
- **Gradual changes of tempo and dynamics**
- **Verse and refrain**
- **Names of musical notes, scales, to sing the C-major scale using "do re mi"**
- **Notation: staff, treble clef (including names of lines and spaces), whole rest, half rest, quarter rest**

What Students Will Learn in Future Grades

In future grades, students will review and extend their learning about music.

Grade 3

- harmony; singing rounds
- notation: eighth note, bar lines, measure, meter, repeat signs, dynamic markings (***p*** and ***pp***; ***f*** and ***ff***)

Grade 4

- *legato* and *staccato*
- introduction and coda
- theme and variations
- notation: tied and dotted notes, sharps and flats, *da capo* and *al fine*, dynamic markings (***mp*** and ***mf***)

I. Elements of Music

Materials

Instructional Masters 34–37

Melody Listening Guide, p. 297

Reading Rhythms, p. 299

The Sound of Silence, p. 300

Name the Notes, p. 303

recording of "The Star-Spangled Banner," p. 297

xylophone, resonator bells, or a piano, if available, p. 302

stairstep ladder, p. 302

lined index cards, p. 303

chart paper, p. 303

pieces of sheet music from various songs for children to read and observe, p. 304

overhead projector and overheads with the notes of songs written for class, p. 304

a long scarf or piece of ribbon for each child in class, p. 304

Vocabulary

Student/Teacher Vocabulary

beat: the steady pulse that can be felt underneath during a piece of music (S)

C-major scale: an important scale found on the white keys of the piano, from C to C (S)

chorus: the section of a song that is usually repeated; also called the refrain (S)

clef: a symbol placed at the beginning of each staff in written music to indicate the pitches of the notes (S)

downbeat: the first and strongest beat of every measure of music (S)

dynamics: the element of music dealing with how loudly or softly music is performed (T)

form: the element of music that deals with musical structures and patterns (T)

half rest: two beats of rest or silence (S)

harmony: the element of music that deals with the relationships between simultaneous pitches (T)

measure: units of a specific number of beats depending on the meter; the space between two barlines (T)

melody: an arrangement (order) of individual sounds (pitches); the element of music that deals with "tune"; the arrangement of individual pitches into musical "lines" (S)

meter: the specific way the beat is organized in a piece of music; number of beats per measure (T)

notation: a way of representing sound on paper (S)

note: the written symbol used in music (S)

phrase: a short section of music, usually a discrete "chunk" of the melody; something like the musical equivalent of a spoken "clause" (T)

pitch: a particular standard by which tones may be compared with respect to their relative level; how "high" or "low" a sound or tone is; specific pitches are named with letters from A to G (S)

quarter rest: a one-beat rest or silence (S)

range: the notes, from highest to lowest, that someone's voice is able to produce (T)

refrain: the section of a song that is usually repeated; also called the chorus (S)

rhythm: long and short durations of sound; the element of music that deals with the way sounds are organized through time (S)

scale: a series of notes in order (S)

scale degree: one of the seven differently named pitches that make up a scale, in terms of its position in the scale. For example, E is the third scale degree of the C-major scale (C D E F G A B). (T)

score: a piece of notated music (T)

solfège: (SOLE-fezh) the syllables "do re mi fa so la ti" that are traditionally sung to the pitches of the scale in rising order (T)

staff: the set of five parallel lines on which music notation is placed (S)

tempo: the speed of a musical performance (T)

timbre: the element of music concerned with the distinctive quality of sound or "flavor" that identifies a certain musical instrument or voice (S)

Vocabulary continued

treble clef: a symbol 𝄞 that, when placed on a staff, designates a high range known as the treble (S)

verse: a set of lyrics that tell the story of a song, changing with each repeat (S)

whole rest: four beats of rest or silence (S)

Domain Vocabulary

Elements of music and associated words:
tune, line, up, down, row, air, vibration, piece, work, movement, listen, perform, sing, dance, march, skip, jump, clap, tradition, stress, arrangement, color, tone, symbol, high, low, slow, fast, instruments, string, woodwind, brass, percussion, bow, pick, mallets, brassy, clear, sharp, tone, accent, accompaniment, suite, musician, instrumental, vocal, composer, orchestra, *plus words in song lyrics*

Cross-curricular Connections

Mathematics

Numbers and Number Sense

- Manipulating scale degrees and regular beats is comparable to number theory.

At a Glance

The most important ideas for you are:

- The elements of music include rhythm, melody, harmony, form, dynamics, and timbre.
- Pitches take letter names from A to G.
- A scale is a series of notes in order.
- The C-major scale is an important scale found on the white keys of the piano, from C to C.
- "Do re mi fa so la ti" is a way to sing the degrees of any major scale.
- The strong downbeat is the first beat of a measure.
- Verse and refrain are the two major contrasting sections of a song.

What Teachers Need to Know

Background

Though we tend to enjoy music as a whole, it is made up of several different basic elements. Rhythm, melody, harmony, form, dynamics, and timbre are the most fundamental of these elements, each contributing something unique to the music. Being able to make observations about each of these individual elements is useful for listeners and performers alike. Awareness of these elements can be a tool to help us better understand how music works, but it can also be a way to deepen our enjoyment. The better we are at identifying what it is that we are hearing, the more we are able to become involved with it and respond. In Kindergarten and Grade 1, children learned about these basic elements of music. It would be helpful to review them with children as you introduce new elements and songs.

Rhythm

In order to understand rhythm, it is important to first understand beat. The steady beat is the most basic way music is organized. This is a steady, constant pulse that can be felt underneath a whole piece of music. When we clap or tap in time to music, we are intuitively marking the steady beat. Being aware of the steady beat is central to the experience of understanding music; it is the foundation upon which all music is built.

Individual steady beats always occur at regular intervals. For example, in the line "Twinkle, twinkle, little star," there are steady beats on "TWIN," "KLE," "TWIN," "KLE," "LIT," and "TLE." These marked, steady beats reflect the meter, the specific way the beat is organized in a piece of music. This song has the most basic meter of $\frac{4}{4}$, meaning there are four beats per measure and each beat in the measure is a quarter note. When teaching children about notes and rests, it is best to use examples in this basic $\frac{4}{4}$ meter. Children will expand their knowledge of meter in Grade 3.

Twin-kle, twin-kle, lit - tle star, how I won-der what you are.

The rhythm of the song itself is found in the actual pitches of the music. Unlike the pulses of the steady beat, musical pitches do not all last the same amount of time; some are longer, and some are shorter. The exact arrangement of long and short pitches, arranged against the steady beat, makes the rhythm of the music. In the line "Twinkle, twinkle, little star," notice that the seventh pitch (on the word "STAR") is a longer sound than each of the first six pitches (the syllables "TWIN," "KLE," "TWIN," "KLE," "LIT," "TLE"). In fact, it is exactly twice as long. This particular relationship of long and short pitches or sounds is part of what defines this song, and even when we change the speed of the steady beat (known as the *tempo*), these proportions will not change. Fast and slow performances of the same song all have the same rhythms.

Downbeat

The downbeat is the first and strongest beat of every measure of music. Children have already learned that individual steady beats always occur at regular intervals, but not all beats are equal in emphasis: some are accented, and we call these downbeats. Children haven't yet learned these terms, but they have been exploring these concepts every time they interact rhythmically with music.

In "Twinkle, Twinkle, Little Star" the downbeat falls on the first quarter note of every measure.

The downbeat is distinguished by the fact that it usually feels like the most natural place to take a step in time with the music. Children should be encouraged to feel the downbeat as a natural emphasis in the beat and not worry about figuring it out by any conscious method. One's inner sense of pulse is always the most important tool in navigating the steady beat.

Melody

When we sing a song, we are singing its melody, or tune. Melody combines different pitches in a row to produce what is sometimes called a musical line. We recognize a melody from the shape of this line: the particular way it travels up and down, and where it starts and where it ends. When we say a sound is "high" or "low," we are describing its pitch. Melody is the arrangement of several pitches in a row. Sing or play a recording of "The Star-Spangled Banner" for the class. Have children listen for features of a melody. Does it start by moving up or down? When does it change direction? Does it stay on some pitches for longer than others? You may want to tie in rhythm by having children pay attention to how long each pitch is held.

Harmony

Two or more pitches can also be combined so that they are played or sung simultaneously. When a tune is supported or accompanied, we call the supporting pitches harmony. A tune will often be accompanied by a simple underlying structure of chords, and these chords constitute the harmony of the piece. Harmony can add color to a piece of music, making the music seem happy or sad, relaxed or tense. Although children need not investigate harmony in any great detail this year, they may begin to notice two or more pitches at the same time when they listen to or sing a song such as "Do-Re-Mi." (See p. 302.)

Form

Melody, harmony, and rhythm are all ways in which the individual notes of a piece of music are organized and structured, but if we stand back and look at the big picture, we might see many other kinds of structure. Just as letters make up words and words make up sentences, so individual notes combine into phrases, and, in

Teaching Idea

You may use Instructional Master 34, *Melody Listening Guide*, to help children visually connect with what they are hearing when they listen to "Twinkle, Twinkle, Little Star." Help them discriminate between differences in high and low pitches.

Name________________ Date________________

Melody Listening Guide

Directions: Sing the first four measur es of "Twinkle, Twinkle Little Star" three times. The first time, have children look at the simple lines going up and down in #1 as the melody goes up and down. The second time you sing it, have children look at #2, and see that each X represents an individual pitch in the melody. Finally, sing it one last time, and look at the actual notes in #3.

Purpose: To help children visually connect sounds that they are hearing in a song with musical notation

Copyright ©Core Knowledge Foundation

Master 34 *Grade 2: Music*

Use Instructional Master 34.

Teaching Idea

Some children may forget to attend to the rhythm when they are singing or playing melodies. Call children's attention to the fact that all melodies have rhythm by isolating the rhythms of some familiar songs, such as "Clementine" or "John Henry." Have children speak the words in rhythm before they attempt to play or sing melodies and rhythms. You can even play a guessing game in which children try to identify a tune when only its rhythm is performed.

> **Teaching Idea**
> **To help children understand the concept of form and phrasing in music, teach children the chorus of "Clementine," which is in the Text Resources. Tell them you are going to sing each verse and they are going to sing the refrain or chorus together when you lift up your arms. You can repeat this activity with other songs listed in Section III.**

turn, phrases can be arranged and combined into even larger units. The word *form* refers to all of these other levels of structure and organization.

One of the simplest ways a piece can have form is by repeating sections. In many traditional songs, such as "The Erie Canal," there is only one phrase, which repeats over and over for each new line of the text. Another simple and very common form for songs is to have two distinct sections that alternate, often called the verse and refrain (or chorus); "Clementine" is an example. "Clementine" has several different verses sung to the same tune; each verse is followed by a singing of the chorus, "Oh, my darling, Oh, my darling . . . ." (See "The Erie Canal" and "Clementine" on p. 329.) In pieces such as *Carnival of the Animals* (*see* p. 310); the form is determined by the story being told by the different instruments.

Verse and Refrain

Verse and *refrain* are terms for contrasting sections of a song. The refrain (or chorus) always has the same lyrics when it appears, while the verse varies from one appearance to another, often telling a story as the lyrics progress.

In some songs, though, the tune is the same for the verse and the refrain, and it is only the lyrics that distinguish them. For example, "Clementine" has only one melody, which functions as the refrain when it has the lyrics "Oh, my darling, Oh, my darling . . ." and as the verse for the intervening stanzas that tell the story. However, in other songs, the verse and the refrain have different melodies.

Not all songs have a verse-and-refrain structure. For example, "She'll Be Comin' Round the Mountain" has only one section in which the lyrics change partially on each repetition.

This is the children's first encounter with issues of form, which can be one of the most elusive aspects of music. Even with something as straightforward as verse and refrain, it is difficult to pin down exact definitions. There are too many exceptions and variations. It's best, then, not to spend a lot of time defining verse and refrain for the children. Simply note what constitutes the verse and the refrain in the various songs you sing as they come up. Once the song sections have been identified this way, you may call on the class to sing "just the refrain" of a particular song, etc. As the year progresses and children become familiar with hearing these terms applied to many examples, they will develop a suitable intuitive understanding of the definition. By the end of the year, you might prompt them to identify the verse and refrain in newly learned songs; they should be able to do so without difficulty.

Dynamics

Another feature of musical sound is dynamics. The dynamics of a musical sound reflect how loud or soft it is. Dynamics often change throughout a piece of music and can have dramatic effects. Try having the class begin singing a favorite song softly and then get louder, or begin loudly and get softer. Children might enjoy singing the classroom favorite, "Dixie," in this way.

> **Teaching Idea**
> **To demonstrate a change in dynamics, sing "The Star-Spangled Banner" with your class. Tell children that you want them to sing the first half of the song softly. When they get to the words "And the rockets' red glare," ask them to gradually increase their volume and to maintain the sound level through the end of the piece. Discuss with children how a change in dynamics can help express the lyrics of a song.**

Timbre

Timbre, or tone color, concerns the qualities of the musical sound itself. In particular, instruments have different timbres—the sound of a piano or the sound of a flute are clear and recognizable, though we may not always have words to describe what it is about the timbre that we recognize. The timbre of an instrument has a lot to do with how the instrument works. In string instruments, a taut string vibrates to produce the sound. In woodwind and brass instruments, air blown into the instrument produces the sound. Percussion instruments vibrate to produce sound when they are struck. (See Section II, "Listening and Understanding," on pp. 306–326 for more about the different families of instruments.)

Notation

There are many musical traditions in the world that have been passed from musician to musician without ever being written down. However, in our present-day musical culture, written music serves a very large role; nearly all the music we encounter has been transmitted from composers to performers through written scores. Musicians use a special system of symbols, or notation, to write down music. A piece of notated music, known as a score, contains many different kinds of information about the music it describes. In addition to specifying what pitches are used in a piece and in what order they appear, a score also records exactly how long each pitch lasts, how each pitch relates to the underlying beat, how loud or soft each pitch is, how fast the piece is meant to be performed, and many other details. Some of this information is conveyed with words or instructions written right into the score, but most of it is written in its own special way.

The system of notation that we use is several hundred years old and has its origins in the European classical music tradition. Today it is used all over the world. Comprehending notated music is a valuable way of improving our musical understanding, just as reading is beneficial to our understanding of language. Music can sometimes be a difficult thing to explain in words; notation is a tool for describing music clearly and precisely.

Whole Note, Half Note, and Quarter Note

As you might guess from looking at a score, each little circle represents a note of music, and they are read, like a book, in order from left to right. The duration of each note is indicated not by the spacing, as you might expect it to be, but by the way the circle, or note head, is written. It is important to notice whether a note head is solid black or just an outline, and whether or not it has a line extending from it, known as a stem. The pitch is indicated by a note's location on the staff.

Three common durations are the whole note 𝅝, half note 𝅗𝅥, and quarter note ♩. Notice that the whole note, which lasts the longest, has an open notehead and no stem. When a stem is added, it becomes a half note, which lasts exactly half as long as a whole note. When the half note is darkened, it becomes a quarter note, lasting half again as long as a half note, or one quarter as long as a whole note. Other notations that you may encounter, involving dots next to the noteheads or lines extending from the stems, will be introduced in later grades.

Teaching Idea

Listen to the musical selections from Section II, "Listening and Understanding," on pp. 306–326. Have children close their eyes and listen to the timbre of the instruments. Can they identify a certain instrument? If so, they are hearing the different timbres. Children should try to name the instruments they hear. Keep practicing this all year long with a variety of musical pieces. With practice, children will become better at identifying instruments and naming their families as well (e.g., woodwind, brass, string, percussion).

Teaching Idea

If a score to one of the listening selections is available, show it to children, and remind them that everything they hear in the music is notated in the score. Explain that the score is what the composer created when he or she first wrote the piece. Reinforce the idea that music is a universal written language; everyone follows the same "rules" so people can play the same music around the world.

Name________ Date________

Reading Rhythms

Whole note = 4 beats each	Half note = 2 beats each	Quarter note = 1 beat each
𝅝	𝅗𝅥 𝅗𝅥	♩ ♩ ♩ ♩
Clap on "1," whisper "2, 3, 4"	Clap on "1," whisper "2" and clap on "3," whisper "4"	Clap on each note "1, 2, 3, 4"

Directions: Have children clap the rhythms of the sequences. Tell the children to whisper as they are counting a note held for more than one beat.

Purpose: To help children understand rhythm and musical notation

Master 35 Grade 2: Music

Copyright ©Core Knowledge Foundation

Use Instructional Master 35.

Teaching Idea

Help the class understand that just as four quarters make up a dollar, four quarter notes last as long as a whole note. Have them clap or speak rhythms from notation. After they have practiced reading notation, you may wish to give them a simple rhythm and have them draw the notation.

Teaching Idea

Echo clapping is a game in which children repeat, or echo, the teacher's clapped rhythms. Teachers could start by clapping an easy pattern of four to establish the meter. If children are having trouble feeling the meter, you can quietly chant "1, 2, 3, 4" while children echo clap. When they are very successful at this, children can then begin leading the echo clapping in 4. For a challenge, echo-clapping rhythms can be made more difficult by the inclusion of long or unexpected rests. You can begin more difficult rhythms and then have children take turns leading. In trying to stump each other with unusual rhythms, children will hone their counting skills and awareness of rests.

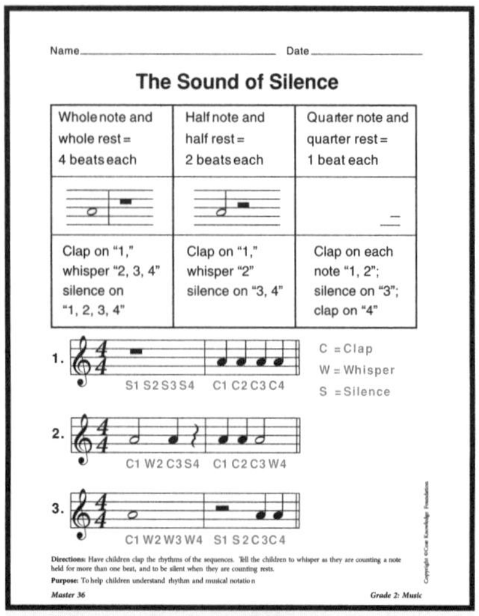

Name________________ Date________

The Sound of Silence

Whole note and whole rest = 4 beats each	Half note and half rest = 2 beats each	Quarter note and quarter rest = 1 beat each
Clap on "1," whisper "2, 3, 4" silence on "1, 2, 3, 4"	Clap on "1," whisper "2" silence on "3, 4"	Clap on each note "1, 2"; silence on "3"; clap on "4"

C = Clap
W = Whisper
S = Silence

1. S1 S2 S3 S4 C1 C2 C3 C4

2. C1 W2 C3 S4 C1 C2 C3 W4

3. C1 W2 W3 W4 S1 S2 C3 C4

Directions: Have children clap the rhythms of the sequences. Tell the children to whisper as they are counting a note held for more than one beat, and to be silent when they are counting rests.

Purpose: To help children understand rhythm and musical notation

Master 36 *Grade 2: Music*

Copyright ©Core Knowledge Foundation

Use Instructional Master 36.

Rests

A rest is a musical pause of a determined length. Rests are just as important as the notes themselves in creating music, but since they are, by definition, silent, they can sometimes go overlooked. The notational symbols for three basic rests are shown below.

The whole rest and half rest symbols can be confusingly similar. When they appear off the staff (as they occasionally do), they are almost indistinguishable. The crucial difference is, of course, that the half rest extends upward from a line, while the whole rest extends downward. When the rests are placed on the staff, they appear in the third space, either extending down or up from the adjacent line. With practice, you and the children will grow accustomed to discerning one from the other.

To remember which symbol takes which value, it may be helpful to keep this tip in mind: Think of the rest symbol as a bucket. When the bucket is only half-full, it rests on top of the line; but when it is completely full, it is so heavy that it drops below the line.

It is common for children to omit or distort rests while singing or playing melodies. Draw their attention to the importance of observing rests by singing or performing a familiar song but omitting the rests (thus distorting the rhythm—this can actually be difficult to do intentionally!) and asking them what was missing. If they have difficulty recognizing the problem, suggest that they try clapping in rhythm. Getting them to observe the fact that silence can be a necessary element of music will encourage them to handle rests more carefully in their own performance.

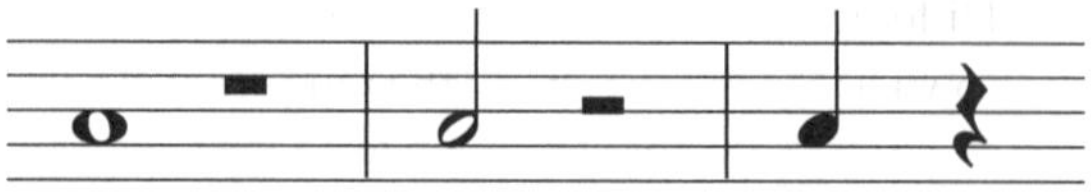

Sometimes silence is part of the music. A whole rest lasts as long as a whole note. A half rest lasts as long as a half note. A quarter rest lasts as long as a quarter note.

Note Names

Musical pitches are named with seven letters of the alphabet. The letter- names always refer to the same, unchanging pitches. This means that to sing C, for example, first you will need to find it with a pitch pipe or a tuned instrument. The seven letter-names are found in order as the white keys of the piano. You can identify them by their relationship to the groups of black keys as seen on p. 302.

The alphabet of seven letters repeats itself all the way up the piano; after every G comes A again. There are many As on the piano; some are higher or lower than others, but they all sound similar, so they take the same letter. If instruments are available, play two different notes with the same letter and let children hear how they are alike.

The Staff and the Treble Clef

The staff is the set of five parallel lines on which music notation is placed. A note printed alone on the page could be any pitch. Notes placed higher on the staff will sound higher, and any notes placed on the same line of the staff will take the same pitch. When a treble clef is present, a musician can know exactly what pitches the notes on a staff will take. In particular, whenever the treble clef appears on the staff, the lines and spaces, from bottom to top, represent the pitches shown below.

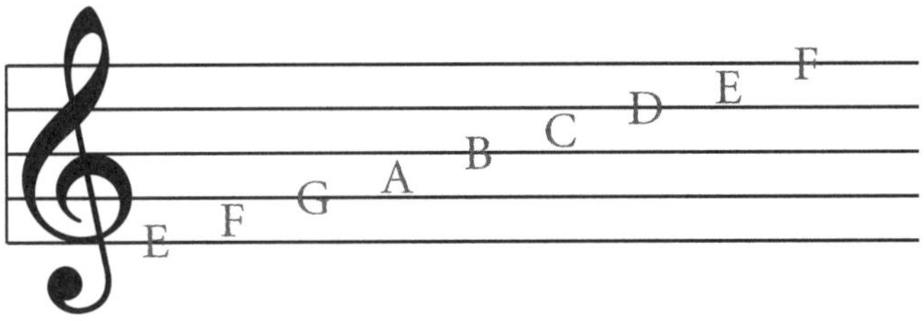

Without a clef, the staff isn't complete; a note on a staff without a clef could be any number of different notes, depending on which clef was intended. For now, we will be dealing only with the treble clef, but be sure that children understand that the identities they have learned for the spaces and lines of the staff are true only because the treble clef is present.

Music is read from left to right along the staff, just like English. Notice that the treble clef is not the only possible clef that the staff can take. Consider that there are only nine positions (lines or spaces) on a staff, but 52 white keys on a piano. To be able to present all the possible notes, the staff has to be able to "move" up or down the keyboard. Different clefs place the staff in different ranges. The treble clef designates a range known as the treble. This is the range in which children are most comfortable singing and is traditionally the range (and clef) in which most melodies are notated.

Middle C

Middle C is the C that falls just below the bottom of the treble clef. This note can be represented by a note placed exactly at the height where a C would be if the staff lines continued. Musicians then draw a horizontal line through it to suggest the imaginary extra staff line on which it would fall; this horizontal line is called a ledger line. Middle C is so-called because it is found very near the middle of a piano keyboard. It is the fourth C up from the bottom of the keyboard,

Middle C

and the fifth C down from the top. Middle C is often used as a reference point, because many instruments—whether they are pitched high or low—can reach this note, or at least near to it, as can most singing voices.

Teaching Idea

Well-known mnemonic devices, such as "Every Good Boy Does Fine," are meant to help children memorize the names for the lines of the treble clef staff in ascending order. The names of the notes in the spaces spell "FACE." It is more important that children understand that they can derive all the rest of the letters as long as they know any one of them. A child who knows that the bottommost line is an E can fill in the letters simply by working upward through the scale and filling in each line and space.

Teaching Idea

Children need to be actively involved in the sounds before they are presented with the notation. To introduce scales to children, begin by playing a C scale on a xylophone, on resonator bells, or even on a piano before showing children the notation. Another idea is to use a "stairstep ladder" on which tone bar resonator bells can be placed to create a C-major scale. By building a scale in this manner, second graders have a visual and kinesthetic experience of placing bells from low to high, which brings greater understanding of scales.

A scale is a series of notes in order. Children will be working with the C-major scale, which consists of the notes C D E F G A B. (Traditionally, when this scale is sung or played, it is completed by following the B with another C.) To play the C-major scale on the piano, first locate a C. (The black keys are grouped in sets of two and three; a C is always the first key immediately below a set of two black keys.) Then, beginning on that C, play only the white keys, moving upward along the keyboard (to the right) until you reach the next C, for a total of eight notes. Children should become familiar with the name and sound of this scale and be able to recognize it, sing along with it, and, if possible, play it on their instruments.

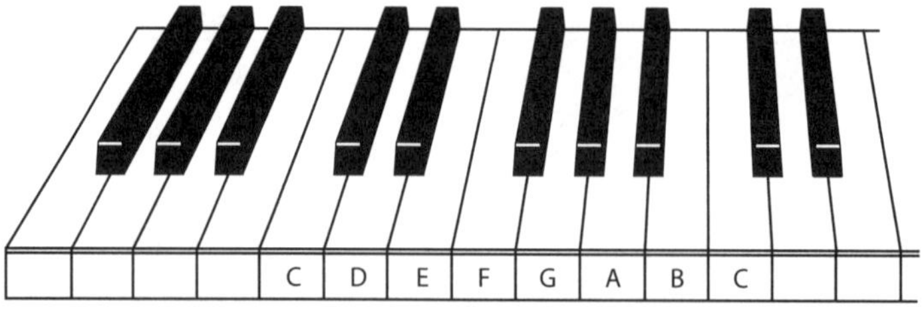

Do re mi" Syllables

The syllables "do re mi fa so la ti" are traditionally sung to the pitches of the scale in rising order. These syllables (sometimes called solfège [SOLE-fezh] syllables) are a standard way to sing any major scale. Children should use these syllables when singing the scale as a tool to help them articulate and remember the individual notes that constitute it. For this purpose, the solfège syllables are preferable to the letter-names of the notes for several reasons. First, they are simply better sounds for singing. ("F," for example, doesn't lend itself very well to singing!) Second, unlike the letter-names, these syllables have another meaning besides their musical significance and thus form a stronger association with the pitches on which they are sung.

The most important reason for using these syllables is their flexibility. While major scales can be sung beginning on any pitch, singing the letter names "C D E F G A B C" is correct only when the first pitch is a C, which for most children (and adults) will require referring to an instrument. It is much more important that the children become comfortable with the sound of the major scale in general than that they are able to sing a C. The "do re mi" syllables are correct no matter where a child begins singing a scale. Thus scale-singing (and the "Do-Re-Mi" song) may be practiced independent of any instrument or accompaniment.

The form of solfège described here is called the "movable 'do'" system, rather than the "fixed 'do'" system. "Movable 'do'" is thought to be the most effective system with young children. Mi, for example, is always the third note of a major scale, no matter what letter name that note happens to have. This third note is known as the third scale degree. "Do, re, mi," etc., then, are names for the seven degrees of the major scale.

Teaching Idea

Teach children the song "Do-Re-Mi" and connect the solfège to the names of the notes on the staff. They can also act out the music by adding movements to help them remember the words. "Do-Re-Mi" is a particularly fun song because it has a fun play-on-words (Doe—a deer, a female deer; Ray—a drop of golden sun; Me—a name I call myself; etc.).

Teaching Idea

Once children are familiar with the song "Do-Re-Mi," have eight children hold out the initial syllable of each line as it is sung so that the class can more clearly hear the scale underlying the song. If you'd like, try learning the second part of the song ("do mi mi, mi so so . . ."), which is good practice for singing the notes of the scale out of order.

do C · re D · mi E · fa F · so G · la A · ti B · do C

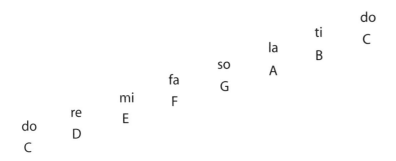

Once children are comfortable singing the scale in ascending order, "do re mi fa so la ti do," have them practice singing the scale in descending order, "do ti la so fa mi re do." Singing the scale in both directions helps children to be more aware of the identities of the individual notes, rather than just memorizing the ascending scale as a single "chunk." You may even wish to challenge children to sing the notes in other orders or sing melodies with these syllables. "Twinkle, twinkle, little star / How I wonder what you are," for instance, becomes "do do so so la la so / fa fa mi mi re re do." Active awareness of these scale degrees is an important step toward music theory that children will be learning in years to come. For now, it is most important that they are comfortable with singing them in order.

Learning by Participating

Children in second grade are not expected to memorize all the technical terms for the elements of music. However, by singing, marching, and performing, they can learn to recognize such elements as short and long sounds, phrases, and beat, as well as discriminate between high and low sounds, fast and slow pieces, loud and quiet, etc. The songs in Section III (pp. 327–333) lend themselves to this type of learning.

Review

The best time to ask questions about a musical piece is usually immediately after children have listened to it, or even in the middle of the piece. Below are some ideas for ongoing assessment and review activities. These are not meant to constitute a comprehensive list.

- Have children make a set of flash cards for notes, simple scales, or other notations from music. Use a set of lined index cards so children can practice drawing a staff using the lines and spaces on the cards, then adding the notes. In small groups, children can practice identifying and singing the notes on their cards.
- Using chart paper, write the words to the song "Bingo." The song, which most children will already know from Kindergarten, is a familiar example of a song that requires careful rest-counting. On each successive verse, another letter of the word *Bingo* is replaced with a handclap, until, on the sixth verse, the entire word is simply clapped in rhythm. Once children are comfortable with this version, try singing the song without clapping or simply remaining silent for the duration of the omitted letters. This can be tied to a visual demonstration of rest notation by writing rest notes to replace each letter as you go through each verse of the song.

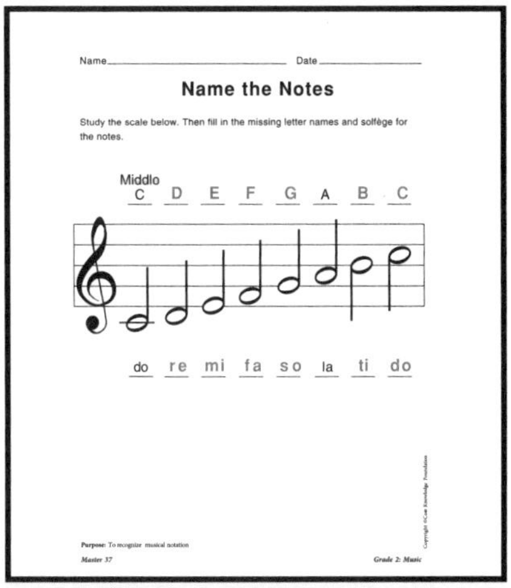

Use Instructional Master 37.

Teaching Idea

In order to teach children to recognize like and unlike phrases in pieces of music, start with "Twinkle, Twinkle, Little Star." Have children sing the song once with the words, and a second time just singing "la la" in place of the words. Next, have the children sing "Baa, Baa, Black Sheep"—the first time with the words and the second time just singing "la la" in place of the words. Finally, divide the class into two groups, and have one group sing the tune of "Twinkle, Twinkle, Little Star" while the other group sings "Baa, Baa, Black Sheep" at the same time. What do children notice about the melodies? (The melodies are the same or "like" each other.) What do children notice about the words? (The words are different or "unlike" each other.) Refer back to this exercise in the next section, "Listening and Understanding," when children are listening to music. Encourage children to find phrases (or short melodies) that sound the same (like), and ones that sound different (unlike).

I. Elements of Music

The Big Idea in Review

Music is described with terms such as rhythm, melody, harmony, form, dynamics, and timbre. Musical notes have names and are organized into scales.

- Make the sheet music from different songs available to children, and have them explore what the music looks like. Ask them to start identifying the notes and make other observations about the music. Then, as a challenge, ask children to follow along with their finger as the song is played or sung on a recording. Have each child write a short paragraph describing the piece of sheet music. What are their observations? You may then make this activity the springboard for explaining some of the elements of music in this section.
- When teaching the treble clef, use a song from the *Core Knowledge Sequence* to show how the named notes correspond with the sounds in the song. Practice reading the music with the class by writing the notes of a song on an overhead and then pointing out the names of the notes while learning the song.
- Provide each child with a long scarf or a long piece of ribbon. Play a selection of music from this section, and encourage the class to move responsively to the music, using their scarves and ribbons as they move. When the music is finished, have children talk about that experience. What was it like to hear the music, and why did they move in that way?
- You may also ask the following questions at the end of this section:

1. What are the notes, in order, in the C-major scale?
   The notes in the C-major scale are C D E F G A B C.
2. Is "do" always the same as "C"?
   No; "do" can be the start of any major scale.
3. When we see a note on the page, how do we know what pitch it takes?
   Look at where the note falls on the staff and what clef the staff is in.
4. Which lasts longer, a half note or a half rest?
   They last exactly the same amount of time.

More Resources

The titles listed below are offered as a representative sample of materials and not a complete list of everything that is available.

For children —

These books are generally intended to be read aloud, though some children may be able to read parts or all of the simpler texts.

- *The Core Knowledge Music Collection: Grades 1 and 2* (Core Knowledge Foundation). A multi-CD set that includes works listed in the *Sequence* for Grade 2, such as Beethoven's Sixth Symphony and Vivaldi's *The Four Seasons.*
- *Buzz and Ollie's Steady Beat Adventure,* by Donna Sloan Thorne and Marilyn Sloan Felts (Sloan Publishing, 2002). A rhyming story that teaches the basic concept of rhythm. Hardcover, 36 pages, ISBN 097241472X. See also *Buzz and Ollie's Loud, Soft Adventure* (on dynamics); and *Buzz and Ollie's High, Low Adventure* (on pitch). For lesson plans, flash cards, and coloring pages, go to their website at www.childrens-book.com.
- *I Can Make Music: Simple-to-Make and Fun-to-Play Musical Instruments for Young Children,* by Michael Purton (Lorenz Books, 2000). Simple musical instruments to make out of everyday objects. Paperback, 48 pages, ISBN 075480223X.
- *Max Found Two Sticks,* by Brian Pinkney (Aladdin, 1997). A young boy finds a way to make music. This story can spark discussion of homemade musical instruments and the joy of musical "invention." Paperback, 40 pages, ISBN 068981593X.

More Resources continued

- *My Family Plays Music,* by Judy Cox and illustrated by Elbrite Brown (Holiday House, 2003). "[T]his upbeat picture book explores 10 different types of music . . . from bluegrass to marching band to rock 'n' roll to church hymns" (*School Library Journal*). Winner of the Coretta Scott King/John Steptoe Award for New Talent (Illustrator). Library binding, 32 pages, ISBN 0823415910.
- *You Can Teach Yourself Recorder* (Mel Bay Publications). One of the easiest and least expensive ways to learn the basics of melody and written music. Paperback, 80 pages, ISBN 0871667428. Also comes in a book/CD or a book/DVD combination. Can be ordered through your local music store or directly from Mel Bay Publications at www.melbay.com, 1-800-863-5229.

For teachers —

- *Moving and Learning Across the Curriculum,* by Rae Pica (Delmar, 1999). Section Four of this book covers a variety of music topics (tempo, volume, pitch, mood, rhythm, staccato/legato) with several good activities and games. Paperback, 274 pages, ISBN 0827385374.
- *Usborne Music Theory for Beginners,* by Emma Danes and Gerald Wood (Usborne, 2003). A brief, but full, introduction built around short (4–5 measure) excerpts from classic scores. Paperback, 48 pages, ISBN 0794503896.
- *What Charlie Heard: The Story of Charles Ives,* by Mordicai Gerstein (Live Oak Media, 2003). Can you hear any of Charles Ives's favorite boyhood sounds in his music? An ear-opener to the sounds around us. Book and CD edition, ISBN 1591124972.
- Creating Music, www.creatingmusic.com, is an interactive website for children that teaches the basics of musical patterns. Children can write music using the mouse and hear it played back.
- Kindermusik, www.kindermusik.com or 1-800-628-5687, has several simple instruments available for young people.
- Music in Motion, www.musicmotion.com or 1-800-445-0649, offers a variety of instruments, games, software, and more.

II. Listening and Understanding

A. The Orchestra B. Keyboard Instruments

The Big Idea

Exploring string and percussion instruments helps children learn the composition of an orchestra. Keyboard instruments rarely appear in the orchestra.

What Students Should Already Know

Students in Core Knowledge schools should be familiar with

Kindergarten

- instruments: guitar, piano, trumpet, flute, violin, drum
- some orchestral music, including selections by Grieg, Herbert, Rodgers, and Saint-Saëns

Grade 1

- know that composers write music
  - Mozart as a composer of classical music
  - the first movement of *Eine kleine Nachtmusik*
- families of instruments in the orchestra: strings, brass, woodwinds, and percussion
  - know that conductors lead orchestras
  - Prokofiev, *Peter and the Wolf*

What Students Need to Learn

- **Instruments in the string family: violin, viola, cello, double bass**
  - **Listen to Saint-Saëns, *Carnival of the Animals* ("The Swan" [cello] and "The Elephant" [double bass]); Vivaldi, *The Four Seasons***
- **Instruments in the percussion family: drums (timpani, snare), xylophone, wood block, maracas, cymbals, triangle, tambourine**
  - **Listen to Chavez, *Toccata for Percussion*, third movement**
- **Keyboard instruments: piano, organ**
  - **Listen to Mozart, "Rondo alla Turca" from Piano Sonata K. 331; Beethoven, *Für Elise*; Mendelssohn, "Spring Song" from *Songs Without Words***

What Students Will Learn in Future Grades

In future grades, students will review and extend their learning about instruments and the orchestra.

Grade 3

- instruments in the brass family: trumpet, French horn, trombone, tuba
- instruments in the woodwind family: flute, piccolo, clarinet, oboe, bassoon

Grade 4

- Benjamin Britten, *The Young Person's Guide to the Orchestra*

Vocabulary

Student/Teacher Vocabulary

brass: a family of instruments that produce sound when the air inside a tube is made to vibrate by the motion of the player's lips (S)

cello: a large string instrument (S)

cymbal: an instrument in the percussion family; a large, thin metal plate that is designed to vibrate when struck (S)

double bass: the largest string instrument; it can produce the lowest sound of almost any instrument (S)

drum: the basic percussion instrument, featuring a tight, resonant surface pulled over a round frame (S)

harp: a string instrument with a triangular frame and about 47 strings; it is played by plucking the strings (T)

harpsichord: a keyboard instrument that has horizontal strings plucked by leather or quill points connected to the keys (T)

keyboard: an array of many keys, where each key controls a different note; examples are the piano, harpsichord, and organ (S)

organ: a keyboard instrument consisting of pipes that sound tones when supplied with air (S)

percussion: a family of instruments that produce sound when the surface of the instrument itself is made to vibrate, usually by striking it (S)

piano: the best-known keyboard instrument (S)

pitched percussion: percussion instruments that produce sounds with specific pitches, e.g., xylophone, timpani (T)

pizzicato: played by plucking rather than bowing the strings (T)

strings: a family of instruments that produce sound when the instruments' taut strings vibrate (S)

tambourine: an instrument in the percussion family that is built like a drum, with a tight, resonant surface pulled over a round frame—but in the rim of the frame, there are several tiny sets of cymbals, designed to make a jangling sound when the instrument vibrates (S)

timpani: an instrument in the percussion family; also known as a kettledrum. This instrument can produce a particular pitch. (S)

toccata: a piece of music with a relatively free construction, meant to sound a bit like an improvisation (T)

triangle: an instrument in the percussion family; a metal rod bent into a triangle, which the performer suspends from above and strikes with a small metal beater (S)

unpitched percussion: percussion instruments that produce sounds with no specific pitch, e.g., snare drum, cymbal (T)

viola: a string instrument that is slightly larger than the violin; it also has a slightly deeper tone (S)

violin: the smallest string instrument; it also has the highest range (S)

woodwinds: a family of instruments that produce sound when the air inside a tube is made to vibrate by blowing air into or across it (S)

xylophone: a tuned (pitched) percussion instrument that is arranged almost like a keyboard instrument (S)

Materials

Instructional Masters 38–40

Questions to Always Ask Children About Music, p. 309

Music Appreciation Ideas for Children, p. 309

Name That Instrument!, p. 314

record, CD, audiotape, or videotape of the following:

Carnival of the Animals, Saint-Saëns, *p. 310*

The Four Seasons, Vivaldi, *p. 312*

Toccata for Percussion, Chavez, *p. 314*

Piano Sonata K. 329, Mozart, *p. 315*

Für Elise, Beethoven, *p. 316*

Songs Without Words, Mendelssohn, *p. 316*

examples of musical instruments, p. 310

examples of percussion instruments, p. 313

posters of various instruments, p. 314

a piano, pp. 315, 316

of dried beans, p. 316

a jar or can with a lid for each child in class, p. 316

chart paper, p. 317

pictures of instruments from each family of instruments, p. 317

the performance schedule of a local symphony or chamber music group, p. 317

a class set of cards with pictures of the different instruments for the string family and the percussion family, p. 317

a notebook, or paper stapled together, to use as a listening journal for music, p. 317

Vocabulary continued

Domain Vocabulary

Instruments and associated words:
play, pluck, bow, notes, sheet music, music stand, chair, orchestra, keyboard, conductor, player, score, symphony, band, pound, bang, clash, family, string, note, hands, feet, fingers, head, move, rhythm, long, short, high, low, shape, wood, catgut, hard, practice

Cross-curricular Connections

Visual Arts

Abstract Art

- Abstract representation of animals in Camille Saint-Saëns's *Carnival of the Animals*

At a Glance

The most important ideas for you are:

- The violin, viola, cello, and double bass are closely related string instruments that vary in size and pitch.
- String instruments may be played either with the bow or pizzicato (plucked).
- Percussion instruments vary widely in appearance and sound; some are pitched and some are not.
- Keyboard instruments allow a single performer to play many notes at once.

What Teachers Need to Know

Background

There are many different musical instruments, each with its own unique sound, or timbre. The nature of the timbre that an instrument produces is determined by the way the instrument is constructed and the way it is performed. In fact, each musical instrument in the orchestra is generally assigned to one of four basic instrument families depending on the way it produces sound. The four families are woodwinds, brass, strings, and percussion. Learning to recognize an instrument means being able to identify its sound, its appearance, and the method by which it is played. This year, children will focus on two of the instrument families found in the orchestra: strings and percussion. Children will take a closer look at the brass and woodwind families in Grade 3. Children will also learn about keyboard instruments, a category of musical instruments that rarely appears in the orchestra.

A. The Orchestra

A traditional orchestra contains instruments from all four families: strings, brass, woodwinds, and percussion. Instruments are classified into families based on the way they produce sound. Instruments of the same family often have similarities of timbre. The combination of all the variations in timbre from all the different families gives the orchestra the ability to produce an endless variety of sounds.

The Woodwind Family

The woodwind family of instruments produces sound when the air inside a tube is made to vibrate by blowing air into or across it. The flute, clarinet, oboe, and bassoon are all woodwind instruments, though the flute, for example, is not necessarily made of wood. The timbres of woodwind instruments range from the open, airy quality of the flute to the nasal, reedy sound of the oboe, and can often be used to remind us of the voices of humans and animals, as in Sergei Prokofiev's *Peter and the Wolf.*

The Brass Family

The brass family of instruments produces sound when the air inside a tube is made to vibrate by the motion of the player's lips. Not every instrument made of brass is in the brass family: the saxophone, for example, is made of brass but works as a woodwind instrument. The trumpet, trombone, horn, and tuba are all true brass instruments. Brass instruments tend to have a very prominent, bright timbre, but they can also produce a wide range of sounds. The larger the instrument, the lower the sounds it is able to make. The tuba is famous for making very low sounds.

The String Family

The string family of instruments produces sound when taut strings vibrate. The violin, viola, cello, and double bass form an important group within the string family. They are all constructed and played similarly, and differ mostly in how large they are and the sounds they make. The difference in size has a direct relationship to the kinds of sounds that the instruments produce. The longer a string, the lower the range of sounds it can produce. Longer strings require a larger instrument.

The violin, which is the string instrument with the highest range, is also the smallest. It is held sideways, between the chin and the shoulder. Many people compare the sound of the violin to a singing voice, and it has always been one of the most popular instruments for its ability to play beautiful melodic lines. Many violins together create a sound that is even smoother and more lush than a single violin, and the "violin section" is the central core of most orchestras. The viola comes next, with a slightly darker tone color and deeper range. Violas and violins are so similar in shape that at first it may be difficult to tell them apart. Look carefully at the size, and listen for the quality of the tone—a viola is slightly larger and has a deeper sound, while the violin's sound is higher and brighter. A cello is so large, in fact, that it cannot be held under the chin, like the violin and viola. Instead, it is held upright on the ground and played from a seated position. Finally, the largest string instru-

Teaching Idea

It is important for children to have a framework for listening to music. They also need to hear pieces multiple times. Instructional Masters 38–39, *Questions to Always Ask Children About Music* and *Music Appreciation Ideas for Children*, will help with these activities.

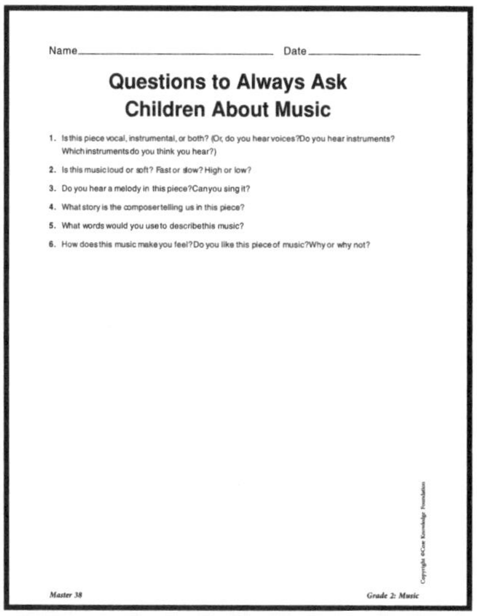

Name________ Date________

Questions to Always Ask Children About Music

1. Is this piece vocal, instrumental, or both? (Or, do you hear voices? Do you hear instruments? Which instruments do you think you hear?)
2. Is this music loud or soft? Fast or slow? High or low?
3. Do you hear a melody in this piece? Can you sing it?
4. What story is the composer telling us in this piece?
5. What words would you use to describe this music?
6. How does this music make you feel? Do you like this piece of music? Why or why not?

Master 38 *Grade 2: Music*

Copyright ©Core Knowledge Foundation

Use Instructional Master 38.

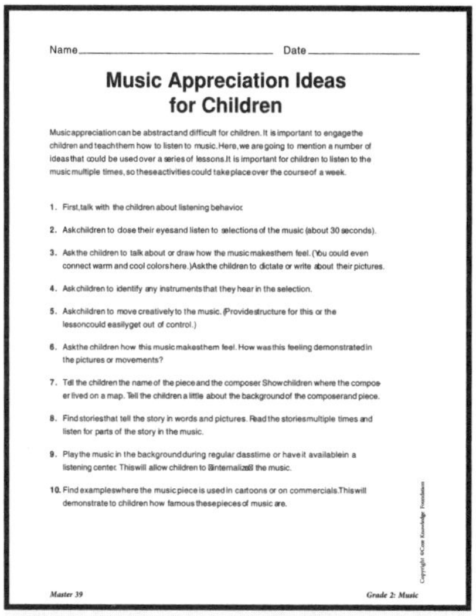

Name________ Date________

Music Appreciation Ideas for Children

Music appreciation can be abstract and difficult for children. It is important to engage the children and teach them how to listen to music. Here, we are going to mention a number of ideas that could be used over a series of lessons. It is important for children to listen to the music multiple times, so these activities could take place over the course of a week.

1. First, talk with the children about listening behavior.
2. Ask children to close their eyes and listen to selections of the music (about 30 seconds).
3. Ask the children to talk about or draw how the music makes them feel. (You could even connect warm and cool colors here.) Ask the children to dictate or write about their pictures.
4. Ask children to identify any instruments that they hear in the selection.
5. Ask children to move creatively to the music. (Provide structure for this or the lesson could easily get out of control.)
6. Ask the children how this music makes them feel. How was this feeling demonstrated in the pictures or movements?
7. Tell the children the name of the piece and the composer. Show children where the composer lived on a map. Tell the children a little about the background of the composer and piece.
8. Find stories that tell the story in words and pictures. Read the stories multiple times and listen for parts of the story in the music.
9. Play the music in the background during regular class time or have it available in a listening center. This will allow children to "internalize" the music.
10. Find examples where the music piece is used in cartoons or on commercials. This will demonstrate to children how famous these pieces of music are.

Master 39 *Grade 2: Music*

Copyright ©Core Knowledge Foundation

Use Instructional Master 39.

ment, the double bass, requires the performer to stand next to the upright instrument in order to reach the neck. A double bass can produce very low sounds, among the lowest of any instrument.

These four string instruments all work in very much the same way. The fingers of the performer's left hand press down on the strings in different places to choose the note (by changing the length of the part of the string that will vibrate), while the performer's right hand draws a bow of fine hair across the strings to produce the sound. Another way of playing these instruments is known as *pizzicato*, or plucking. To play pizzicato, a performer simply plucks the string with his or her right hand. Notes produced with the bow can be long, smooth, and expressive, like a singing voice, but pizzicato notes last only very briefly and have a light quality, sounding almost like drops of water.

Teaching Idea

Bring in samples of instruments for children to see. Perhaps local middle school or high school students can come to your class to perform and share their instruments.

Guitar

In Kindergarten, children learned that the guitar is a stringed instrument that is held in the arms and played by pressing down on the strings with one hand to choose the pitches while strumming with the other hand. Often, guitarists strum using a pick, which can allow them to strum more forcefully. The guitar is an instrument that doesn't appear in classical music very often, but is used often in folk and popular music to accompany songs.

Harp

The harp is another instrument that is usually considered part of the string family. It is made of a large triangular frame with about 47 strings of varying length. The harp is held upright and is played by plucking, instead of bowing, the strings. The use of pedals and the length of the string determines the pitch. Harps can be used for solo or group performances and provide a heavenly or ethereal musical sound.

Play the following pieces for children, and help them to recognize the various instruments in the string family as you talk about the composer and the piece.

Camille Saint-Saëns: "The Swan" and "The Elephant" from *Carnival of the Animals*

Camille Saint-Saëns [san-SAHNS] was a French composer who lived from 1835 to 1921. Although only a few of his works are still played frequently, during his lifetime he was extremely famous and widely respected. Today, *Carnival of the Animals* is probably his most famous work, which is ironic because when he composed it in 1886, it was meant only as a private joke, and he did not allow it to be published during his lifetime.

The work is a humorous collection of short pieces that illustrate various animals, using different instruments and effects to imitate the sounds and behaviors of those animals. In the movement entitled "The Swan," he uses the singing tone of the cello to produce an image of the swan's grace as it glides over the water. Listen to the rich, voice-like qualities of the sound of the second-deepest instrument of the string family.

In "The Elephant," Saint-Saëns makes a musical joke: by setting a light dance tune (borrowed from the composer Louis-Hector Berlioz) for the huge, heavy-sounding double bass, he suggests the image of the great lumbering elephant trying to dance elegantly. The double bass rarely gets a chance to play melody in more serious music; usually such deep sounds are used to provide support for melodies in the higher instruments.

In Kindergarten, in Core Knowledge schools, children learned about this piece in detail. It is presented here as a review, if needed.

The movements are:

1. **Introduction and Royal March of the Lion**

   A proud march for the lions; listen for the sound of the lion's roar made with piano and strings.

2. **Cocks and Hens**

   The strings and pianos imitate the pecks, clucks, and crows of the chickens.

3. **Wild Asses**

   This movement reflects the running speed of the creatures, portrayed by the pianos.

4. **The Tortoise**

   Borrowed melodies by the composer Jacques Offenbach (including the famous "Can-can") are played slowly on a double bass to reflect the pace of the tortoise.

5. **The Elephant**

   The tune is an elegant dance by the composer Berlioz, but here it is played by the double bass to sound low and a little clumsy, somewhat like a giant elephant attempting ballet.

6. **Kangaroos**

   The pianos mimic the sound of kangaroos hopping from place to place.

7. **Aquarium**

   Saint-Saëns uses mysterious and flowing sounds on a glockenspiel to create an impression of the underwater world.

8. **People with Long Ears**

   This joking title turns out to refer to donkeys, whose characteristic "hee-haw" can be heard in the violins.

9. **The Cuckoo in the Depths of the Woods**

   The peaceful and mysterious sounds of the woods are interrupted by the "cuckoos" of the clarinet.

10. **Birds**

    A whole flock of birds can be heard, but the flute, in particular, reminds us of birdcalls.

11. **Pianists**

    Saint-Saëns jokingly includes pianists as some of the animals in the carnival. These particular pianists can be heard practicing their scales.

12. **Fossils**

    The bones of these fossils get up and dance to the bone-like sounds of the xylophone, which plays a fragment from another Saint-Saëns skeleton dance, the *Danse Macabre.* A second layer of the joke is the suggestion that this fragment (and some other famous melodies heard in the movement, including the tune to "Twinkle, Twinkle, Little Star") is so old and familiar that they are "fossils."

13. **The Swan**

    The cello portrays the beauty of the swan's grace as it moves across the water.

14. **Finale**

    A cheerful tune celebrates the entire carnival. Listen for brief appearances by many of the animals, including the lion, the asses, the hens, the kangaroos, and at the very end, the "people with long ears."

Cross-curricular Teaching Idea

If you have already studied abstract art, have children create realistic and abstract images of the animals represented in *Carnival of the Animals*. Children can write about the differences in their representations of the animals and why they chose certain techniques (line, shape, color) to represent the animal in an abstract way. You could even have children create an abstract representation of the cello and double bass. Finally, you can post these realistic and abstract images and writing samples in a public display area or around the classroom for others to enjoy.

Teaching Idea

To build familiarity with classical musical selections, play pieces for children as background music during art periods and other projects. Be sure to tell children the name and composer of the piece to which the class is listening.

Antonio Vivaldi: *The Four Seasons*

Antonio Vivaldi's [on-TONE-ee-oh vi-VAUL-dee] *The Four Seasons* is a set of violin concertos. In this type of musical composition, strings are used in two different roles; some are used in a large group as an orchestra, but one violin is singled out to play a slightly different role in the music. Listen to the first movement of the first concerto, "Spring," and have children note the difference between the sound made by the solo violin and the sound made by the string orchestra playing together. Is one warmer than the other? More or less personal? Notice that the solo violin imitates a bird singing. Why do you think Vivaldi chose to give the sound of the bird to the solo violin and not to the whole orchestra?

Also, listen to the way the violins, violas, cellos, and basses playing together can sound like one big instrument rather than several instruments with different ranges. A talented composer like Vivaldi can make the different members of the string family cooperate in such a way that it is hard to pick out the violins from the violas, and the violas from the cellos. All we hear, and all he wants us to hear, is a string section combining the ranges of their instruments into a large, continuous range.

For more information about Vivaldi and *The Four Seasons*, see Section II C, "Composers and Their Music," on pp. 319–326.

Teaching Idea

If resources are available, introduce children to percussion performances from other musical cultures, such as African drumming and Latin American music with percussion.

The Percussion Family

Unlike the instruments of the string family, the instruments of the percussion family are very different from one another. They look different, they sound different, they're played differently, and they work differently. A percussion instrument produces sound when the instrument itself vibrates (rather than a string or a column of air inside the instrument). To create this vibration, percussion instruments must be struck—sometimes with the performer's hand, sometimes with a mallet or a stick. A percussion instrument can be identified by its distinct sound resembling something hitting something else. If you hear some kind of "smack!" or "thunk!" you know you're listening to a percussion instrument. (In fact, we often call such sounds *percussive*.) Some percussion instruments are pitched and some are not. Pitched percussive instruments produce sounds with specific pitches, e.g., xylophone and timpani. Unpitched percussive instruments produce sounds with no specific pitch, e.g., drum, cymbal, woodblock, triangle, and maracas.

Drum

The drum is the basic percussion instrument, and the name *drum* can be given to a wide variety of instruments that are constructed and played in the same way: a vibrating surface, stretched tight over a hollow cylinder, which is played by striking the surface directly, either with the hands or with sticks. There are many types of drums. Some of the most common are the snare drum, bass drum, and timpani (sometimes called a kettledrum). These are all played with sticks: hard wooden sticks for the snare drum, and mallets with padded ends for the larger bass drum and kettledrum. Drums can create many diverse sounds, from the deep thump of the bass drum to the buzzing, military sound of the snare drum (the buzzing is created by the snares, which are vibrating strips of metal on the bottom of the drum). Drums, with very few exceptions (notably the timpani, or kettledrums, heard in the symphony orchestra), produce sounds that do not have a specific pitch—they cannot play melodies or harmonies, but are simply rhythmic.

For this reason, they generally are used to provide the rhythms that are the foundation of a musical piece.

Snare drums are often associated with military bands and marching, though they're used in many other situations as well. Bass drums and timpani are both much larger and produce deep, resonant sounds. One major difference between them is that a bass drum doesn't produce any particular pitch (it is not tuned percussion), but a kettledrum does. The sound of the bass drum may resemble a heartbeat and often has a strong influence on one's sense of the beat in a piece of music. Timpani are generally used to create impressive, grandiose effects, since their sound has a certain "large" quality to it.

Teaching Idea

Allow children the opportunity to play a variety of percussion instruments. Talk about ways that the percussion instruments are similar and different. Also, demonstrate the difference between the pitched and non-pitched percussion instruments. Ask children why the triangle or snare drum is not considered "pitched."

Xylophone

The xylophone is a tuned (pitched) percussion instrument, arranged almost like keyboard instruments, with the different pitches lined up in a row. Each pitch is created by a separate block of wood that the performer strikes with a fairly hard, padded mallet. The wooden sort of sound created by the xylophone is high-pitched, and each note lasts only a brief time. Xylophones are often used to create a zany, comic effect, though they can also be used to add a harsh, intense quality to the orchestral sound.

Wood Blocks

The wood block is exactly what it sounds like: a partially hollowed-out block of wood that is struck with a hard wooden stick to create a very sharp wooden "clack!" In some ways, it has a similar effect to the xylophone, but as an unpitched instrument, its use is much more limited.

Maracas

Maracas are an instrument mainly associated with Latin American music. They are hollowed-out pieces of wood or gourds that contain a small amount of coarse sand, which creates a rhythmic "swoosh" sound. The player holds one maraca in each hand and shakes each instrument in rhythm. Often, when maracas are used, their purpose is to set up an underlying sense of rhythm in a piece, and they play quietly throughout. They can also be used for individual effects: rattlesnake-like shuffling, for example.

Cymbals

Cymbals are large, thin metal plates designed to vibrate when struck. Like drums, they vary widely in size, shape, and effect. Some cymbals ("crash cymbals") are played as a pair: the performer pushes the two cymbals against one another to create a dramatic smashing sound, a sort of musical lightning effect. Other cymbals, like those in most popular bands, are mounted on stands and struck with hard sticks. Cymbals are used for many kinds of dramatic effects, some sudden and some gradual. They are unpitched.

Triangle

The triangle is named for its shape. It is a metal rod bent into a triangle, which the performer suspends from above and strikes with a small metal beater. The triangle has a very high, bright sound and can sometimes sound almost like a telephone ringing. It is often used in the orchestra to add a sparkling quality to higher pitched sounds, though the triangle itself has no modifiable pitch.

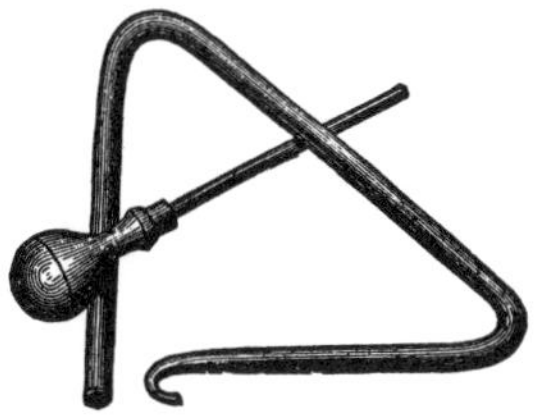

Tambourine

The tambourine is an instrument with several possibilities. It is built like a drum, with a tight, resonant surface pulled over a round frame—but in the rim of the frame, there are several tiny sets of cymbals, designed to make a jangling sound when the instrument vibrates. A tambourine player can simply shake the tambourine to create the jangling cymbal sound, or strike the surface of the tambourine to add a drum-like effect. Complicated tambourine parts involve these and other techniques in combination.

Carlos Chavez: *Toccata for Percussion*

Since only a few percussion instruments are tuned and capable of playing melodies, it is extremely rare that a piece is written for percussion instruments alone—it was completely unheard of until the 20th century. Traditionally, percussion instruments were used to add color and emphasis to the music being played by the rest of the orchestra. However, some composers have given percussion instruments their own chance to be heard.

Carlos Chavez (1899–1978), a 20th-century Mexican composer and conductor, wrote a toccata for percussion alone. A toccata is a piece of music with a relatively free construction, meant to sound a bit like an improvisation. The term *toccata* comes from the Latin word for "touching" or "striking," and most toccatas are written for the piano. The musician must play, or touch, the keys quickly and with great skill. In Chavez's toccata, percussion instruments are skillfully played with a rapid tempo. Children will learn more about toccatas when studying Bach's Toccata and Fugue in D Minor. Before listening to *Toccata for Percussion*, you and the children might wish to brainstorm ways to compose an interesting piece using only percussion instruments. Perhaps the class could experiment and try to compose its own *Toccata for Percussion* with classroom instruments. Review the elements of music—such as tempo, rhythm, and timbre—as you lead this activity. You may find that it is a challenge to make something musical from only the sounds of percussion instruments. On the other hand, you may also discover the pleasures of playing with pure rhythm.

Now listen to Chavez's answer to the challenge. His orchestra includes most of the instruments mentioned above, plus a few others. How does he combine different sets of percussion instruments to create different overall effects? Are some sections violent? Lighthearted? Exciting? How does the choice of rhythm affect the character of the music? How does it affect the character of each instrument? Do you miss the other families of the orchestra, or can the percussion stand alone?

B. Keyboard Instruments

One major category of musical instrument that rarely appears in the orchestra is keyboard instruments. Keyboard instruments are so named because they are played from a keyboard, which is an array of many keys, where each key controls a different note. The piano is the best-known keyboard instrument. When a piano key is depressed, it swings a small mallet at a string to produce a tone. Other keyboard instruments, however, such as the organ and harpsichord, operate differently and produce completely different sorts of timbres. Nonetheless, because they all are controlled from a keyboard, these instruments can all be played in approximately the same way.

Teaching Idea

Children will also study Bach's Toccata and Fugue in D Minor (discussed in the next section, on p. 323) this year. Once children have heard both pieces, you could compare the style of the toccatas and have children identify and describe the free, improvisational nature of the toccatas and the speed of the tempo.

Teaching Idea

Have posters of various instruments visible in the room so that children may become familiar with their appearances and look at them while listening to the selections. You may use Instructional Master 40, *Name That Instrument!*, to reinforce understanding.

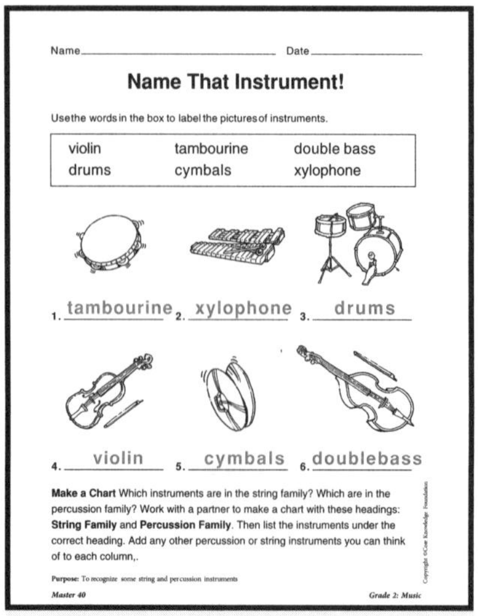
Name______ Date______

Name That Instrument!

Use the words in the box to label the pictures of instruments.

violin	tambourine	double bass
drums	cymbals	xylophone

1. tambourine 2. xylophone 3. drums

4. violin 5. cymbals 6. doublebass

Make a Chart Which instruments are in the string family? Which are in the percussion family? Work with a partner to make a chart with these headings: **String Family** and **Percussion Family**. Then list the instruments under the correct heading. Add any other percussion or string instruments you can think of to each column.

Purpose: To recognize some string and percussion instruments

Master 40 Grade 2: Music

Use Instructional Master 40.

A unique characteristic of keyboard instruments is that they are capable of producing many different tones at the same time. Since each finger can play a different key, a keyboard player could theoretically produce 10 different notes at once. Most other instruments can play only one note at a time. In this way, a keyboard instrument can approximate the complexity of orchestral music with only a single player. Because of this special capability, a large amount of music, from almost all eras of music history, has been written for solo keyboard instruments.

Teaching Idea

This would be a good time to remove the front board or open the top of a piano, if one is available, to let children have a look inside. It is a wonderful experience for children to see how each key has three strings and to watch and feel the strings vibrate after each key is stroked.

Piano

The piano is one of the largest instruments, and it is usually treated like a piece of furniture, since it can be difficult to move. It is in the stringed family of instruments, though the many strings are not visible when the piano lid is closed. The strings are struck by mallets, mechanically controlled from the piano keyboard, which the performer plays using all 10 fingers. This means that the piano is capable of producing many different pitches at once, and in any combination that the 10 fingers can manage. It also has a much wider range than most other instruments. As a result, the piano is one of the instruments best suited for solo performance (performance without any accompaniment). The piano appears only occasionally in the symphony orchestra, but it is one of the most commonly heard instruments in almost every other style of music. It produces clearly defined notes that, because of the way the strings are struck, gradually grow quieter when they are drawn out.

Wolfgang Amadeus Mozart: "Rondo alla Turca" from Piano Sonata K. 331

Wolfgang Amadeus Mozart [VOLF-gong ah-mah-DAY-oos MOTES-art] (1756–1791) is generally regarded as one of the greatest composers of all time. He was a child prodigy and had already begun composing by the age of five. He became widely famous several years later, when his father took him and his sister on a tour to perform for royalty throughout Europe. Even though Mozart lived to be only 35 years old, he composed steadily throughout his life and produced more than 600 works, nearly all of which are still played today. He made significant contributions in almost every music genre, including solo keyboard and chamber music, orchestral music, opera, and religious works. Though many of his great works are profoundly serious, Mozart's music is often of a stylish and elegant nature. This approach to music was characteristic of the era in which Mozart lived and was particularly admired among the European nobility for whom he composed.

The famous "Rondo alla Turca" is the final movement of the Piano Sonata K. 331. This catchy, spirited melody was originally intended to evoke the exotic sounds of a Turkish band, particularly in the second section, which has rolled effects in the left hand (or lower bass part of the piano) that imitate the distinctive Turkish percussion section. During Mozart's lifetime, there was a fascination with Turkish percussion among European composers, and the choice to write a rondo "alla turca" ("in the Turkish style") reflects that. It may seem odd now to hear that these "exotic" percussion instruments were, in fact, simply bass drums, cymbals, and triangles, instruments that have long since been incorporated into

Teaching Idea

Allow children the opportunity to explore a piano and to compose their own short melodies.

the Western symphony orchestra. Consider, though, that instead of actually scoring music for these percussion instruments, Mozart simply imitated them in a solo keyboard composition. In many ways, keyboard instruments provided the most convenient, efficient, and flexible way for a composer to explore new ideas and sounds.

Ludwig van Beethoven: *Für Elise*

Ludwig van Beethoven's [LOOD-vig fan BAIT-hofen] *Für Elise*, a short and somewhat uncharacteristic piano work, has become one of his most well-known pieces, primarily because it is not too difficult to play and is thus learned by many beginning piano students. The famous flowing melody occurs at the beginning, middle, and end of the piece, but in the two intervening sections, new melodies are used that have quite different characters. Keyboard instruments, because they can be played by a single performer, often encourage a personal, self-expressive way of performing. Listen to a performance of *Für Elise* and think about what you can tell about the performer's emotions. Do they change as the piece goes on? How is music like talking? How is it different? What kinds of things does this piece say to you? Popular legend has it that Beethoven composed this piece for Therese Malfatti, a woman he hoped to marry. There is much speculation that Beethoven's handwriting was illegible and that instead of "Für Elise" he actually wrote the title "Für Therese," which means "for Therese."

For more information about Beethoven, see Section II C on page 319, "Composers and Their Music."

Felix Mendelssohn: "Spring Song" from *Songs Without Words*

Felix Mendelssohn [MEN-del-son] (1809–1847) was one of the great German composers of the 19th century. His compositional style often combined dramatic and literary inspiration with classical ideals of clarity and elegance. His best works often have a light touch in dealing with sentimental or lyrical conceptions.

The melody of Mendelssohn's "Spring Song" (from *Songs Without Words*, 1829) has become famous in popular culture as a way of indicating carefree innocence. Originally it was meant to suggest the charms of nature in spring. The piece is scored like a voice singing with accompaniment: the smooth, song-like tune is surrounded by lightly tripping figures that almost sound as though they're coming from a different instrument entirely.

The Big Idea in Review

Exploring string and percussion instruments helps children learn the composition of an orchestra. Keyboard instruments rarely appear in the orchestra.

Review

The best time to ask questions about a musical piece is usually immediately after children have listened to it, or even in the middle of the piece. Below are some ideas for ongoing assessment and review activities. These are not meant to constitute a comprehensive list.

- Give children an opportunity to play some of the various instruments discussed in this section. Make simple maracas by providing the class with dried beans and jars or cans with lids. Have children experiment with putting different amounts of beans in the containers to see what different sounds they can create. When the class has made their maracas, have them play simple pieces.

• Review the families of instruments by making a class chart with a section for each family (strings, brass, woodwinds, percussion). Provide a variety of pictures of instruments, and have each child select a picture. Then, have children come forward and place the picture of the instrument in the correct section. Have each child state his or her reason for putting that instrument in each section, and then ask the class to double-check each choice.

• If possible, have the class attend a performance of an orchestra to hear the different instruments. Since the focus in second grade is strings and percussion, you may want to see if a local musical group plays either of these instruments and could provide a concert for the class. After the concert, have the class write thank-you notes and share with the musicians something that they have learned about the orchestra pieces. If it's not possible to attend an actual performance, obtain a videotape of a symphony playing.

• Make a class set of cards with pictures of the different instruments in the string family and the percussion family. Distribute the cards to the class, and then have each child identify the instrument and the family to which it belongs and pantomime what it would look like to play that instrument. For example, for a violin, the child would demonstrate pulling a bow across the strings. If the instrument was the cymbals, the child would demonstrate banging them together. There will be some instruments that are played with the same types of motions, but see what children can invent when they pantomime.

• Play recordings of the pieces from this section at different times during the day. What do children notice about the music? Is there a better time of day to play one piece over another? Do certain instruments make them feel more calm or more energetic? Provide a time for children to listen to the pieces and to identify the instruments as well as the mood of the pieces. Have each child keep a listening journal for the music during the year. Children can record observations about the pieces in this journal, which may be kept during the year to respond to music pieces or identify characteristics about each piece. Also provide a time to read selections aloud during a music sharing time.

• You may also ask the following questions at the end of this section:

1. List the four main string instruments in order from smallest to largest.

   The four main string instruments in order from smallest to largest are the violin, viola, cello, and double bass.

2. Why are the string instruments different sizes?

   The string instruments are different sizes in order to play in different ranges (lower or higher).

3. Name a percussion instrument that plays definite pitches.

   A timpani or xylophone plays a definite pitch.

4. What are two different ways of playing a string instrument?

   Two different ways of playing a string instrument are bowing and plucking (pizzicato).

5. What are some advantages of composing for a keyboard instrument?

   Keyboard instruments can play many notes at the same time, and they only require one player.

More Resources

The titles listed below are offered as a representative sample of materials and not a complete list of everything that is available.

For children —

These books are generally intended to be read aloud, though some children may be able to read parts or all of the simpler texts.

• *The Core Knowledge Music Collection: Grades 1 and 2* (Core Knowledge Foundation). A multi-CD set including works listed in the *Sequence* for Grade 2, such as Beethoven's Sixth Symphony and Vivaldi's *The Four Seasons.*

• *Carnival of the Animals: By Saint-Saëns (Classical Music for Kids),* by Barrie Carson Turner and illustrated by Sue Williams (Henry Holt & Company, 1999). Includes a CD with tracks to match the text of the book. Library binding, 48 pages, ISBN 0805061800.

• *I Can Make Music: Simple-to-Make and Fun-to-Play Musical Instruments for Young Children,* by Michael Purton (Lorenz Books, 2000). Simple musical instruments to make out of everyday objects. Paperback, 48 pages, ISBN 075480223X.

• *Ludwig van Beethoven (Getting to Know the World's Great Composers),* by Mike Venezia (Children's Press, 1996). Paperback, 32 pages, ISBN 0516200690. See also the title on Mozart in this series.

• *Max Found Two Sticks,* by Brian Pinkney (Aladdin, 1997). A young boy finds a way to make music. This story can spark discussion of homemade musical instruments and the joy of musical "invention." Paperback, 40 pages, ISBN 068981593X.

• *Mozart,* by Wendy Lynch (Heinemann, 2000). A simple biography for young readers. Library binding, 24 pages, ISBN 1575722194.

• *Percussion (Musical Instruments),* by Wendy Lynch (Heinemann, 2002). A straightforward introduction. Paperback, 32 pages, ISBN 0431129096. See also titles on string instruments and keyboards in this same series.

• *Zin! Zin! Zin! a Violin,* by Lloyd Moss (Aladdin, 2000). An introduction to the orchestra. Received the Caldecott Honor Award for excellence in children's book art. Paperback, 32 pages, ISBN 0689835248.

For teachers —

• Essentials of Music Theory 2.0 (Alfred, 2002) is interactive software that starts at the beginning and can take interested students through the equivalent of a one-year high school course. For more information, go to www.alfred.com/sub_software/emtcdrom_v2.html. You may also wish to get the accompanying book by the same title (Alfred Publishing, 1999). Spiral-bound, book and CD, ISBN 0882848976. Both can be ordered through The Mustard Seed, 711 Washington Avenue, Suite 11, Chestertown, MD, 21620 or phone 410-778-6707.

• Finale Notepad is free, downloadable software from the makers of the acclaimed music software, Finale. With this intuitive software, you and your class can create your own compositions with one or more instruments. Go to www.finalemusic.com to download a version for Windows or Mac.

• Meet the Instruments: Multimedia Kit (available through Music in Motion, www.musicmotion.com or 1-800-445-0649). Complete kit contains 25 posters of the instruments of the symphony orchestra and band, a package of 20 hole-punched student charts of these same instruments, and a teacher's guide. Also available as separate components. See the website or catalog for biographies of composers, posters of composers and families of instruments, games, software, and much more.

• *The Story of the Incredible Orchestra: An Introduction to Musical Instruments and the Symphony Orchestra,* by Bruce Koscielniak (Houghton Mifflin, 2000). "Informed and lively, Koscielniak's fact-filled excursion through music history is just the ticket for budding musicians and music-lovers at large" (*Publishers Weekly*). A little advanced for second graders, but an excellent overview nonetheless. Hardcover, ISBN 0395960525.

• Creating Music, www.creatingmusic.com, is an interactive website for children that teaches the basics of musical patterns. Children can write music using the mouse and hear it played back.

Text Resources

(67) *Who Was Ludwig van Beethoven?*

(68) *Bach: Never to Be Forgotten*

The Big Idea

Exploring several composers, including Vivaldi, Bach, and Beethoven, and listening to representative works, can broaden children's musical literacy.

What Students Should Already Know

Students in Core Knowledge schools should be familiar with

Kindergarten and Grade 1

- the music of Grieg, Herbert, Rodgers, Saint-Saëns
- composers: Mozart, Prokofiev, Humperdinck, Dukas, and Tchaikovsky

What Students Need to Learn

- **Vivaldi and *The Four Seasons***
- **Bach and Minuet in G Major; "Jesu, Joy of Man's Desiring"; Toccata and Fugue in D Minor**
- **Beethoven and Symphony No. 6 (*Pastoral*): first movement, and from "Thunderstorm" to end of symphony**

What Students Will Learn in Future Grades

In future grades, students will review and extend their learning about composers.

Grade 3

- Tchaikovsky, "Suite" from *Swan Lake*
- Sousa, *Stars and Stripes Forever*
- Copland, *Fanfare for the Common Man*; "Hoedown" from *Rodeo*; "Simple Gifts" from *Appalachian Spring*

Grade 4

- Handel, "Hallelujah Chorus" from *The Messiah*
- Haydn, Symphony No. 94 ("Surprise")
- Mozart, *The Magic Flute,* selections

Grade 5

- Beethoven, Symphony No. 5
- Mussorgsky, *Pictures at an Exhibition*

Materials

Instructional Master 52

Venn Diagram, p. 325

record, CD, audiotape, or videotape of the following:

The Four Seasons, Vivaldi, *p. 321*

Minuet in G Major; Jesu, Joy of Man's Desiring; Toccata and Fugue in D Minor, Bach, *pp. 322–323*

Symphony No. 6 (Pastoral), Beethoven, *p. 323*

class K-W-L chart on chart paper, p. 324

books or other materials about Vivaldi, Bach, and Beethoven, p. 324

variety of art materials, such as markers, crayons, or paints, p. 324

a large piece of paper for each child, p. 324

world map for each child, p. 324

pictures of each composer, p. 324

some instrumental pieces that have been composed recently (such as Thomas Newman's original score for *Finding Nemo*), p. 325

Vocabulary

Student/Teacher Vocabulary

Baroque: classical music of the 17th century (T)

concerto: a piece that sets a solo performer in relationship to a larger group of performers (T)

fugue: a kind of piece in which a single melody is juggled among several different independent voices within the music (T)

minuet: an elegant dance with three-beat groupings (T)

Pastoral: Beethoven's Symphony No. 6, which was reminiscent of the outdoors (S)

toccata: a piece of music with a relatively free construction, meant to sound a bit like an improvisation (T)

Domain Vocabulary

Vivaldi, The Four Seasons, *and associated words:*
Italian, baroque, Venice, teach, school, composer, orchestra, priest, red hair, violin, opera, classical, concerto, score, wind, rain, lightning, thunder, mystery, soloist, joy, breeze, bagpipe, celebrate, heat, sun, birds, calm, storm, repeat, strong, guns, horns, dogs, fire, warmth, snow, ice

Bach, Minuet in G Major, and associated words:
composer, Western music, German styles, clear, voice, counterpoint, religious, math, enormous, music director, Leipzig, keyboard, play, minuet, dance, popular, cantatas, hymns, graceful, organ, pedals, heavy, low, fugue, mood

Beethoven, Symphony No. 6, and associated words:
influential, classical, romantic, symphonies, nature, outdoors, wind, water, sun, sky, sheep, thunder, rain, lightning, horns, day, bright, pipes, shepherd, gentle, soft, lilting

In the Text Resources for this section, words are bolded that should be included as part of Domain Vocabulary.

Cross-curricular Connections

Science

Cycles in Nature

Seasonal Cycles
- *The Four Seasons*

The Water Cycle
- "Thunderstorm" from Symphony No. 6

At a Glance

The most important ideas for you are:

- Antonio Vivaldi was a major Italian composer of the Baroque era.
- *The Four Seasons* is a collection of violin concertos, each containing impressions of a particular season.
- Johann Sebastian Bach was a prolific German composer who is considered by many to have been the greatest composer in Western music history.
- Ludwig van Beethoven was an extremely influential composer who continued to write music even after going deaf.

What Teachers Need to Know

C. Composers and Their Music

Background

As you introduce the composers to the class, it is important to play their pieces, or parts of their pieces, for children.

Antonio Vivaldi: *The Four Seasons*

Antonio Vivaldi

Antonio Vivaldi [on-TONE-ee-oh vi-VAUL-dee] (1678–1741) was a major Italian composer of the Baroque era. He lived in Venice, where he spent most of his life teaching music at a school for orphaned girls. Part of his duties there included composing several pieces a month for the girls' orchestra to perform. As a result, his total compositional output is enormous. He was also an ordained Catholic priest and served in this role at the school, where he was known as "The Red Priest" because of his striking red hair. Vivaldi was a master violinist and wrote many works that would showcase his violin performance. He also composed several operas and some religious music.

The Four Seasons, by far Vivaldi's most famous work, is in fact one of the most popular pieces in all of classical music. It is a collection of four concertos, which each represent one of the four seasons. The pieces were originally published with four sonnets, one on each season, apparently written by Vivaldi himself. In fact, he even placed excerpts from these sonnets directly into the score, over the sections of the music that he felt specifically corresponded to them. In these pieces, the driving rhythms and repeated notes that Vivaldi was fond of using in his writing are put to good effect as depictions of natural phenomena like wind, rain, lightning, and thunder.

A concerto is a piece that sets a solo performer in relationship to a larger group of performers. These concertos, like many of Vivaldi's works, are for the violin as soloist. Listen to the interplay between the solo violin and the rest of the instruments. Each of the four concertos can stand alone as a musical work; each has three movements with a fast-slow-fast structure.

Cross-curricular Teaching Idea

Teach Vivaldi's *The Four Seasons* in conjunction with learning about the seasons in science. Children may also enjoy guessing which season is being represented based on the music alone. (It isn't always obvious without an explanation!) Have them explain what seasonal qualities made them guess as they did.

"Spring" is announced with a joyful melody, while the solo violin imitates the singing of birds. The second movement depicts the restful breeze over a meadow. The third movement is a celebratory, bagpipe-like dance beneath the clear spring sky.

"Summer" begins with an evocation of the oppressive heat of the sun, followed by an intense depiction of fierce winds. In the middle of the movement, the solo violin can once again be heard imitating birdcalls. The second movement is mostly placid and calm, but at the end of each phrase, a musical rumble of thunder warns of things to come. In the third movement, the storm breaks out, with thunder and lightning depicted by fast, repeated notes, and strong winds by fast, forceful scales.

The first movement of "Autumn" is a peasant dance that celebrates a successful harvest. After the vigorous dancing, the second movement shows the peasant farmers peacefully asleep. The third movement depicts a hunt with horns, guns, and dogs, which eventually is successful in tracking down and capturing its prey.

"Winter" begins with an impression of shivering caused by the bitter cold. The second movement contrasts the warmth of the fire indoors with the falling rain outdoors; the rain is represented by pizzicato playing. The third movement begins with a nervous walk on the slippery ice and builds up to a vigorous finale portraying the rushing wind.

Johann Sebastian Bach

Johann Sebastian Bach

Johann Sebastian Bach [YO-honn se-BAST-ian BOCKH] (1685–1750) is considered by many to have been the greatest composer in the history of Western music. Though he was German, his music incorporated elements from many different European styles of his time, achieving great variety while maintaining a clear, personal voice. His unrivaled craftsmanship, particularly in handling counterpoint, combined with the deep religious feeling in much of his work, gives his music a sense of profound, almost mathematical perfection. His output was truly enormous, in part because of his regular composing duties in his role as music director at a church in Leipzig. Though much of his music is religious, he also wrote many secular instrumental works, a body of work by which he is probably best known today.

Minuet in G Major

The Minuet in G Major (from the *Anna Magdalena Notebook*) is a particularly simple example of Bach's keyboard work. The piece was written for Bach's second wife to play and is often used today as a student piece. If you listen carefully, you can hear the two hands playing the two distinct lines that make up the piece. A minuet is an elegant dance with three-beat groupings. During the 18th century, the minuet was one of the most popular dance forms. Because of the simplicity of this particular composition, the form of the minuet can be clearly heard: listen and follow the AABABA construction. Think about this construction as being similar to poetry phrasing. The "A" sections are similar, and the "B" section is different from "A." When you go back to the "A" section, you can hear a contrast with section "B."

"Jesu, Joy of Man's Desiring"

"Jesu, Joy of Man's Desiring" is actually an excerpt from one of Bach's many cantatas, the long, elaborate sacred works he composed regularly for church services. The famous flowing melody provides a contrast and link between sections of the traditional hymn-tune that can be heard in slower notes. To Bach's audience, the chorale melody was most likely already known, and so this piece was, to them, a beautiful elaboration and expansion of a familiar hymn. Listen to the stately grace of the way Bach's musical lines unfold and lead into one another.

Toccata and Fugue in D Minor

Toccata and Fugue in D Minor is perhaps Bach's best-known piece for solo organ, an instrument for which he wrote many outstanding works. The piece shows off many of the characteristic abilities of the organ: huge, impressive masses of sound; sudden, mechanically controlled changes of volume and timbre; lines played simultaneously on two keyboards of the same instrument, and, in some passages, also on a large "keyboard" of pedals, played by the feet of the performer. A toccata, in Bach's time, was a piece of music with a relatively free construction, meant to sound a bit like an improvisation. A fugue is a kind of piece where a single melody is juggled among several different independent voices within the music. In contrast to a toccata, the construction of a fugue must be very carefully controlled by the composer to make it work out properly. Because of the contrast in the spirit of the two pieces (one free, one controlled), the combination of toccata and fugue was often used to form a satisfying whole.

The famous opening figures of the toccata establish the ominous mood of the piece. Some parts of the toccata seem to hint at the fugue to come, while others explore the sounds of the organ in unexpected ways. The fugue begins, as all fugues do, with a clear solo statement of the theme that will run through the rest of the piece. You can recognize this theme because of its distinctive back-and-forth motion, with every other note restating the pitch where the theme began. As the piece progresses, listen to the way that figure is passed down and up through the voices and used in different ways. It may disappear from the texture for brief sections, but it always returns, seeming to grow more powerful every time, until the impressive finish. (68)

> **Teaching Idea**
>
> **Think about how contrast serves an important role in Toccata and Fugue in D Minor: for instance, there is a contrast between the toccata and the fugue, between the different sections of the fugue, between the different sounds of the organ, etc. Why might contrast be satisfying?**

Ludwig van Beethoven: Symphony no. 6

Ludwig van Beethoven [LOOD-vig fan BAIT-hofen] (1770–1827) is one of the central figures in Western musical history and perhaps the most influential composer of all time. His body of work led the way from the Classical style of the late 18th century to the Romantic style of the 19th, introducing extremes of emotional expression in compositions more personal and adventurous than anything that had come before. His nine masterful symphonies are in many ways the core of the orchestral repertoire, with the Fifth, Sixth, and Ninth among the most well-known works in the classical music literature. Beethoven's hearing began to deteriorate while he was in his 20s, and, for the last 10 years of his life, he was completely deaf. During that time, despite his deafness, he continued to compose, working from the sound he could imagine in his mind and the skills he had learned from a lifetime of composing. It is poignant to think that he himself was never able to hear the great works of his late period, including the Ninth Symphony, which is often held to be his masterpiece.

Ludwig van Beethoven

Beethoven's Symphony no. 6 is known as the *Pastoral* Symphony because Beethoven made it clear that it represented his love of the outdoors. In fact, he gave descriptive titles to the different movements, suggesting scenes of country life.

Teaching Idea

Before revealing Beethoven's titles for each movement, have children listen to the movements and suggest their own titles. The first and last movements' titles describe different types of feelings. Ask children what types of feelings they hear in the music, and what elements in the music might make them feel that way.

The first movement was called "Awakening of Cheerful Feelings on Arriving in the Country." Listen carefully to hear one of Beethoven's favorite techniques at work: everything in the entire movement is built out of ideas taken from the tune that we hear right at the beginning. Sometimes the bits of the tune sound gentle, at other times they are grand and impressive, but the entire piece flows naturally from one section to another because the segments are all based on the same material. The tune itself seems to capture the emotion of the title: cheerful and exuberant, yet also relaxed by the peaceful beauty of the countryside.

The last two movements, which are played continuously without a break, portray a "Thunderstorm" followed by a "Shepherd's Song," which takes the subtitle "Happy, Thankful Feelings After the Storm." The storm begins with distant rumbles of thunder and a few drops of rain, but it's not long before the thunder and lightning break out at full force in vivid musical illustration. After the storm rages for a few minutes, it finally begins to subside, and, as the final movement begins, we can almost imagine the sun coming out again. The "Shepherd's Song" is represented by horn-call-like figures, which anticipate the full melody. Imagine the shepherds, after the storm, emerging into the daylight and playing their pipes and horns to celebrate the return of the good weather. (67)

The Big Idea in Review

Exploring several composers, including Vivaldi, Bach, and Beethoven, and listening to representative works, can broaden children's musical literacy.

Review

The best time to ask questions about a musical piece is usually immediately after children have listened to it, or even in the middle of the piece. Below are some ideas for ongoing assessment and review activities. These are not meant to constitute a comprehensive list.

- Construct a class K-W-L chart about the composers. Draw a column for what children may already know about each composer (K), what facts they would like to learn (W), and what they learned while reading or hearing about the composers (L). Choose some books about each composer from the resource section to share with children, or you may also ask your school media specialist to provide some books or magazines about each composer. Provide time to read the books, and then make a class chart to list some facts that children learned.
- Give children an opportunity to respond to the music in this section through art. Provide each child with a variety of art materials, such as markers, crayons, or paints, and a large piece of paper. Explain to the class that you are going to play one of the selections from this section, and you would like them to draw a picture about how the music makes them feel. Review the concepts of line and color from Visual Arts. For example, if the music is very fast, they may draw a lot of sharp lines and corners or use bold colors. If the music is slower, their lines may be curvier or the colors more muted. Let them explore the use of lines and color and how they relate to the music. When the pieces are completed, have each child write about his or her piece. Children should include the name of the composer and the piece to which they responded and also an explanation of what they drew and why.
- Make a connection between the composers and their home countries. Provide a map to each child, and have them identify the composers' countries and continents. On a class map, place pictures of the composers on their home countries. Review with the class what they know about those continents.

• Make a class time line with the dates when each composer lived and their pictures. Consider adding other historical figures from second-grade study to the time line to make a connection to when the composers lived.

• Bring in some pieces that have been composed recently and compare them to the pieces by Vivaldi, Bach, and Beethoven. Thomas Newman's original score for *Finding Nemo* is an excellent choice of a recent composition. He makes great use of strings and unusual percussion, as well as the piano. The music is uplifting, yet also contains some very dramatic parts, giving children a good feel for the range of string instruments and orchestration in general. What can the children identify in each piece of music? Use **Instructional Master 52,** *Venn Diagram,* to compare and contrast the pieces of music. Discuss what it takes to compose music.

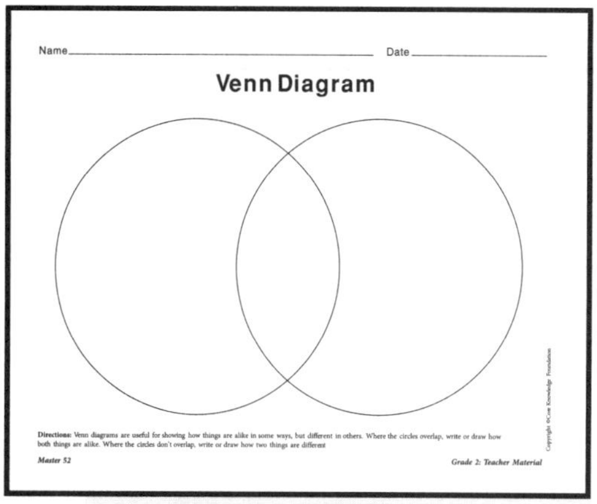
Name______ Date______

Venn Diagram

Directions: Venn diagrams are useful for showing how things are alike in some ways, but different in others. Where the circles overlap, write or draw how both things are alike. Where the circles don't overlap, write or draw how two things are different

Master 52 *Grade 2: Teacher Material*

Copyright ©Core Knowledge Foundation

Use Instructional Master 52.

• Have children listen to the music from this section and try to identify some of the instruments in each piece. Make a connection between these pieces of music and the instruments from the previous section.

• You may also ask the following questions at the end of this section:

1. Can you name one of the composers from this section and something that you have learned about him?

   Children should name Vivaldi, Bach, or Beethoven, and the answers may vary depending on what children have learned.

2. Who composed Toccata and Fugue in D Minor?

   Bach composed Toccata and Fugue in D Minor.

3. Why is Beethoven's Symphony No. 6 called *Pastoral*?

   Beethoven's Symphony No. 6 is called **Pastoral** ***because it represents scenes from the countryside.***

4. Who composed *The Four Seasons*?

   Vivaldi composed **The Four Seasons.**

5. Who is your favorite composer from this section and why?

   Answers may vary.

More Resources

The titles listed below are offered as a representative sample of materials and not a complete list of everything that is available.

For children —

These books are generally intended to be read aloud, though some children may be able to read parts or all of the simpler texts.

- *The Core Knowledge Music Collection: Grades 1 and 2* (Core Knowledge Foundation). A multi-CD set including works listed in the *Sequence* for Grade 2, such as Beethoven's Sixth Symphony and Vivaldi's *The Four Seasons.*
- *Bach (Famous Children),* by Ann Rachlin (Barron's Juveniles, 1992). Paperback, 24 pages, ISBN 0812049918.
- *Bach's Big Adventure,* by Sallie Ketcham and Timothy Bush (Orchard Books, 1999). Hardcover, 32 pages, ISBN 0531301400.
- *Ludwig van Beethoven (Getting to Know the World's Great Composers),* by Mike Venezia (Children's Press, 1996). Paperback, 32 pages, ISBN 0516200690.
- *Sebastian: A Book About Bach,* by Jeanette Winter (Silver Whistle, 1999). Library binding, 40 pages, ISBN 015200629X.

For teachers —

- *Finding Nemo: An Original Soundtrack,* composed by Thomas Newman (Disney, 2003). A fine example of contemporary orchestral composition. Forty tracks feature a wide range of sounds from both string and percussion instruments. Children will also recognize several piano interludes. CD, approximately 60 minutes, ASIN B000095J94.
- Meet the Instruments: Multimedia Kit (available through Music in Motion, www.musicmotion.com or 1-800-445-0649). Complete kit contains 25 posters of the instruments of the symphony orchestra and band, a package of 20 hole-punched student charts of these same instruments, and a teacher's guide. Also available as separate components. See the website or catalog for biographies of composers, posters of composers and families of instruments, games, software, and much more.
- *The Story of the Incredible Orchestra: An Introduction to Musical Instruments and the Symphony Orchestra,* by Bruce Koscielniak (Houghton Mifflin, 2000). "Informed and lively, Koscielniak's fact-filled excursion through music history is just the ticket for budding musicians and music-lovers at large" (*Publishers Weekly*). A little advanced for second graders, but an excellent overview nonetheless. Hardcover, ISBN 0395960525.
- Creating Music, www.creatingmusic.com, is an interactive website for children that teaches the basics of musical patterns. Children can write music using the mouse and hear it played back.

III. Songs

Text Resources
Lyrics

- (69) *Casey Jones*
- (70) *"Do-Re-Mi"*
- (71) *The Erie Canal*
- (72) *Follow the Drinking Gourd*
- (73) *Good-Bye, Old Paint*
- (74) *John Henry*
- (75) *Old Dan Tucker*
- (76) *This Land Is Your Land*
- (77) *When Johnny Comes Marching Home*

Sheet Music

- (78) *Buffalo Gals*
- (79) *Clementine*
- (80) *Dixie*
- (81) *Home on the Range*
- (82) *I've Been Working on the Railroad*
- (83) *The Star-Spangled Banner*
- (84) *Swing Low, Sweet Chariot*

The Big Idea

Learning traditional American songs can help children develop an understanding of elements of music and raise their cultural awareness and appreciation.

What Students Should Already Know

In Kindergarten and Grade 1, students in Core Knowledge schools should have become familiar with and sung many songs. (See the *Sequence* for a list of titles.)

What Students Need to Learn

- **The lyrics and melodies of the songs in this section**

What Students Will Learn in Future Grades

In Grades 3, 4, and 5, students will review and extend their learning about traditional songs.

Vocabulary

Student/Teacher Vocabulary

ballad: a song that tells a story (S)

forty-niner: a way of referring to the people who made the trip west in 1849 in search of gold (T)

"old paint": an old spotted horse (T)

spiritual: a religious song, most often from the African-American tradition (T)

work song: a song sung by workers to help pass the time (S)

Domain Vocabulary

Songs and associated words:
performance, verse, round, melody, harmony, singing, listening, lyrics, voice, rounders, engineer, wheeler, promised land, shrill, switchman, throttle, poppa, canal, barges, low bridge, mule, navigated, quail, gourd, pegfoot, little bitty baby, hammer, lawdy, gimme, rumbling, miller, toothache, redwood forest, diamond, chanting, grumblin', lads, lassies, jubilee, stirrup, hay, reins, range, graze, deer, antelope, discouraging, seldom, zephyr, brow, gay, *plus other words in song lyrics*

III. Songs

Cross-curricular Connections

Language Arts

Fiction

American Tall Tales

- "Casey Jones"
- "John Henry"

History and Geography

American: The War of 1812

American: Westward Expansion

Pioneers Head West

- Transcontinental railroad
- The Erie Canal

American: The Civil War

- The Underground Railroad

American: Geography of the Americas

North America

American: Symbols and Figures

- The U.S. flag

Visual Arts

Kinds of Pictures: Landscapes

Materials

Instructional Masters 41–42

The Erie Canal, p. 329

Home on the Range, p. 329

audiotape or CD of any of the songs listed in the *Sequence*, pp. 328–332

videotape of *The Sound of Music*, p. 329

chart paper, p. 332

pointer, p. 332

overhead projector, p. 332

At a Glance

The most important ideas for you are:

- Many American songs capture or reflect periods in American history.
- Songs often incorporate different elements of music.
- Singing can be a learning activity that is fun and encourages movement.

What Teachers Need to Know

Background

This year's songs are almost all popular American songs that became famous during the 19th century and are now considered traditional. Many of them can and should be taught in connection with the historical era from which they came. The Text Resources contain the lyrics and sheet music for this year's songs.

Buffalo Gals

This song was first published in 1844, but it is believed to have been sung even earlier. The "Buffalo" in the title simply refers to the city in New York. During the 19th century, the song was sung with the name of the singer's city substituted, but now we know it only as "Buffalo Gals."

Many people believe that this song became popular with men working to build the Erie Canal, a canal that provided a water route from Albany, New York, a city on the Hudson River, to Buffalo, New York, a city on the shores of Lake Erie. There is some speculation that the "Buffalo gals" referenced in the song were prostitutes who worked in the Buffalo Canal District. While it is not appropriate to share this infomation with your class, this story has become part of the popular legend about the song and the construction of the Erie Canal. (78)

Casey Jones

"Casey Jones" is an example of a ballad, or a song that tells a story. The story is based on a real event, and Casey Jones was a real person. Jones was a respected railway conductor who was killed in a collision in April 1900. The event inspired several songs, the first of which was originally written by Wallace Saunders, an engine wiper who had worked with Jones. (69)

Clementine

A sentimental ballad telling the tale of a girl who drowns, this song is often associated with the gold rush of 1849. The song itself was actually written around 1880 by Percy Montross, but the prospector in the lyrics, the "miner, forty-niner," is one of the thousands of people who traveled west in search of gold. "Forty-niner" was a way of referring to the people who had made the trip in 1849. (79)

Dixie

This catchy tune of the American South was written for a stage show by songwriter/performer Dan Emmett in 1859 and almost immediately became immensely popular. During the Civil War, it was used as a marching tune by both the North and South, but, by the end of the war, it had become strongly associated with the Confederacy, to the great dismay of Emmett, who was a Northerner and who came from a family of strict abolitionists. In its original form, the song was merely meant as a joke about a Northerner's longing for the warmth of the South on a rainy day. "Dixie" and "the land of cotton" are two names for the South. (80)

"Do-Re-Mi"

This song, originally from the musical *The Sound of Music* (Richard Rodgers and Oscar Hammerstein, 1959), has become a popular children's song in its own right. In the musical, it is used to teach children to sing solfège, and it actually works. Notice that, though the melody moves around freely in between the "do re mi" syllables, the song is written so that whenever a solfège syllable appears, it is being sung on the appropriate pitch. (70)

The Erie Canal

Though many songs about canal life were sung along the Erie Canal from the time it opened in 1825, this, the most famous of the canal songs, actually dates from the 20th century. Written by Thomas Allen in 1905, the song's lyrics describe the experience of passing under the many low bridges that span the canal. Originally, the canal barges were pulled by mules like Sal; this song was written as a response to the first mechanized barges being introduced to the canal. (71)

Cross-curricular Teaching Idea

Introduce "Casey Jones" and "John Henry" when you teach the tall tales "Casey Jones" and "John Henry."

Cross-curricular Teaching Idea

Teach "Clementine" and "the Erie Canal" in connection with the Westward Expansion section and as a preview of fifth-grade topics.

Cross-curricular Teaching Idea

Teach "Dixie" in connection with the Civil War section, along with "Follow the Drinking Gourd," "Swing Low, Sweet Chariot," and "When Johnny Comes Marching Home."

Teaching Idea

Show children the scene from *The Sound of Music* that features the song "Do-Re-Mi." Encourage them to sing along with the videotape.

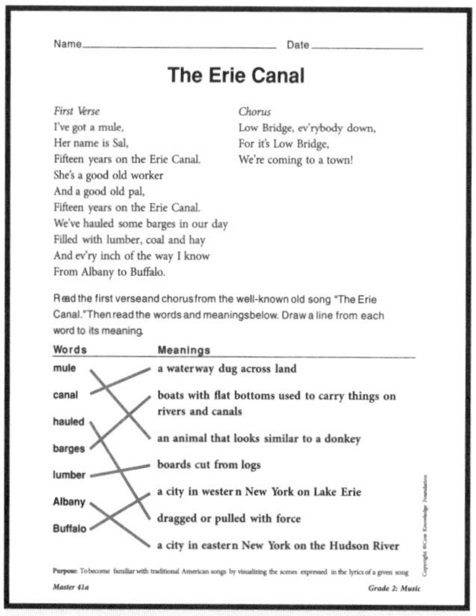

Name________ Date________

The Erie Canal

First Verse
I've got a mule,
Her name is Sal,
Fifteen years on the Erie Canal.
She's a good old worker
And a good old pal,
Fifteen years on the Erie Canal.
We've hauled some barges in our day
Filled with lumber, coal and hay
And ev'ry inch of the way I know
From Albany to Buffalo.

Chorus
Low Bridge, ev'rybody down,
For it's Low Bridge,
We're coming to a town!

Read the first verse and chorus from the well-known old song "The Erie Canal." Then read the words and meanings below. Draw a line from each word to its meaning.

Words	Meanings
mule	a waterway dug across land
canal	boats with flat bottoms used to carry things on rivers and canals
hauled	an animal that looks similar to a donkey
barges	boards cut from logs
lumber	a city in western New York on Lake Erie
Albany	dragged or pulled with force
Buffalo	a city in eastern New York on the Hudson River

Purpose: To become familiar with traditional American songs by visualizing the scenes expressed in the lyrics of a given song

Master 41a *Grade 2: Music*

Copyright ©Core Knowledge Foundation

Use Instructional Masters 41a and 41b.

Name________________ Date________

Home on the Range

First Verse
Oh, give me a home
Where the buffalo roam,
Where the deer and the antelope play,
Where seldom is heard
A discouraging word
And the skies are not cloudy all day.

Chorus
Home, home on the range,
Where the deer and the antelope play,
Where seldom is heard
A discouraging word
And the skies are not cloudy all day.

Read the first verse and chorus from "Home on the Range." Then answer the questions.

1. If you don't know what a **range** is, what context clues help you to figure it out? Possible answer: "Where the buffalo roam" and "Where the deer and the antelope play"

2. This song was originally called "The Western Home." Why do you think the narrator wants a home in the west? Possible answer: probably because of thee wide open spaces, the animals, and the blue sky

3. How can you tell that the narrator does not expect to hear people complain about life on the range? Possible answer because "a discouraging word" is seldom heard

Purpose: To become familiar with traditional American songs by analyzing the concepts and vocabulary in the lyrics of a given song

Copyright ©Core Knowledge Foundation

Master 42a *Grade 2: Music*

Use Instructional Masters 42a and 42b.

Teaching Idea

You may wish to have a "cowboy sing-along" of songs like "Good-Bye, Old Paint," "Home on the Range," "Clementine," and others. Children can pretend to be cowboys sitting around a fire on the open prairie.

Cross-curricular Teaching Idea

Once children have learned about the construction of the railroad, have them pretend to swing hammers while singing "I've Been Working on the Railroad" and "John Henry" in order to feel how the rhythm of the work goes along with the song. Teach "I've Been Working on the Railroad" in connection with the Westward Expansion section in History and Geography.

Follow the Drinking Gourd

The "drinking gourd" in the song is actually the constellation of the Big Dipper, which can be used to locate the North Star; this song was sung by slaves to remember how to find their way north if they were able to escape. A true remnant of the Underground Railroad, the song originally had several verses that contained more coded information about making the trip to freedom. What does this lyric mean: "Dead trees to show you the way"? Is that a reference to the moss that grows on one side of the tree, or is it a secret message? (72)

Good-Bye, Old Paint

This is one of the most enduring of the true cowboy songs, sung in the American West since before the 1870s. The song's lyrics show us a cowboy's attachment to his horse, the "old paint" of the title, to whom he is bidding a fond farewell as he heads to a new job. A "paint" is a spotted horse. (73)

Home on the Range

The lyrics to "Home on the Range" were written in 1872 by Dr. Brewster Higley, a physician from Indiana who moved to the plains of Kansas as part of the Homestead Act of 1862. The song began as a poem he had written celebrating the beauty of the newly settled land. The poem was set to music by a local fiddler named Dan Kelley, creating what is perhaps the most widely known of all American popular songs. "Home on the Range" is now the official state song of Kansas. (81)

I've Been Working on the Railroad

The exact origins of this popular song are unknown, but it clearly comes from the mid-19th-century era of railroad building, when it probably served, in some earlier form, as a work song. The "horn" in the song is the call to lunch that the weary workers are eagerly awaiting. (82)

John Henry

This song is another example of a ballad, or a song that tells a story. The song and the story come from West Virginia in the 1870s and describe the workers who cut holes for dynamite as they carved out a long railroad tunnel. John Henry, a legendary folk hero, shows that he and his hammer are more powerful than the steam drill, an invention that was starting to take away jobs as it replaced some of the railroad workers. The song is also a form of "work song," or a song sung by workers to help pass the time. The steel-drivers would all sing songs like this one as they worked, swinging their hammers in rhythm. (74)

Old Dan Tucker

In the 1840s, this silly song was the first big hit of Dan Emmett, the composer of "Dixie." Emmett is also often credited with the famous fiddle-tune "Turkey in the Straw." In his stage show, he would amuse audiences by acting out the character of Old Dan Tucker. (75)

The Star-Spangled Banner

The lyrics to "The Star-Spangled Banner" were written as a poem in 1814 by the lawyer Francis Scott Key, after he witnessed the successful defense of Fort McHenry, near Baltimore, during the War of 1812. (See pp. 166–174.) The poem soon became extremely popular and was set to an existing tune believed to have been written by British composer John Stafford Smith. The song has officially been the national anthem of the United States since 1931. (83)

Swing Low, Sweet Chariot

Like many of the slave-era spirituals that survive today, "Swing Low, Sweet Chariot" was collected and arranged (in 1917) by Harry T. Burleigh, an African-American musicologist and composer who was one of the first people to recognize the cultural importance of the spiritual. The song itself dates from around the time of the Civil War.

Many slaves sang these spirituals to express both their spiritual beliefs and their desire for freedom. Spirituals sometimes contained coded messages, which were used by slaves to communicate with one another or to help slaves escape on the Underground Railroad. "Swing Low, Sweet Chariot" is one of the most popular spirituals from this era. Many believe that the lyrics expressed the hope of slaves that after death they would be carried to heaven, where they would be free from the oppression they faced as slaves. The lyrics may have also communicated the hope that the Underground Railroad would "carry" slaves to the North, across the Mississippi or Ohio Rivers (instead of the "Jordan River") with the help of the "angels," or the people working on the Underground Railroad. Regardless of its meaning, "Swing Low, Sweet Chariot" remains one of the most-loved spirituals of the era. (84)

This Land Is Your Land

Folk singer/songwriter Woody Guthrie wrote this well-known song in 1940. In its original version, the lyrics contrasted the bounty of the American landscape with the poverty of the Depression era. However, today, long after the Depression, we still sing the first few verses of the song, which celebrate the natural beauty of America. (76)

When Johnny Comes Marching Home

Also known in a version with the title "Johnny, I Hardly Knew Ye," this song was adapted from Irish folk melodies and made popular during the Civil War by Union army bandleader Patrick Gilmore, a man known as "the father of the American band." It describes the hopeful anticipation of the day when the war would be over and friends and loved ones could return from battle. (77)

Cross-curricular Teaching Idea

You may wish to use the book *The Star-Spangled Banner* to read the words of the song to the children. (See More Resources.) Have them pay special attention to the illustrations in the book. When finished, have children write about Frances Scott Key's experience creating the song. What happened to make him write the song? Have they had experiences that could move them to write a song? Teach this song in connection with the War of 1812.

Teaching Idea

While learning "This Land Is Your Land," use the lyrics as an opportunity to review and extend childrens' knowledge of American geography. Where are the redwood forests? Where is the Gulf Stream? You can also reinforce the section "Kinds of Pictures: Landscapes" from Visual Arts while learning this song.

The Big Idea in Review

Learning traditional American songs can help children develop an understanding of elements of music and raise their cultural awareness and appreciation.

Review

The best time to ask questions about a musical piece is usually immediately after children have listened to it, or even in the middle of the piece. Below are some ideas for ongoing assessment and review activities. These are not meant to constitute a comprehensive list.

- Use the songs from this section to reinforce the study of musical elements in Section I. Take the songs from this section and write the lyrics on chart paper for children to use while singing. Give a volunteer a pointer to allow children to follow along while you sing. You may also enlarge the words from the songs on an overhead or provide children with copies to use while singing. Have children recognize the elements of music, such as changes in tempo, notes, scales, etc.
- You may also use the songs from this section to practice reading and recognizing sounds. Make a connection between the poems from Language Arts and the words to the music. What are the similarities? The language in songs is often poetic. Select one of the songs from this section, and ask children to respond to the lyrics in writing. For example, have children listen to "The Star-Spangled Banner" and then write about how this song makes them feel. How do they think that Francis Scott Key felt when he wrote the song?
- As an extension to listening to the songs, have children try to compose new verses that apply to their own lives. For example, listen to "This Land Is Your Land," and then have children write a verse about where they live. They can then try to sing their verse with the music. They will have to pay attention to the details of the music and also the words that they choose. Write the additional verses on chart paper with children so they can share them with visitors.
- Make a connection between songs such as "Follow the Drinking Gourd" and "Swing Low, Sweet Chariot" and the historical events that occurred during that time. Read the words of the songs aloud to the class, and ask them to illustrate the scenes depicted in the lyrics. Play the music while children are creating their pictures, and then have them write a paragraph describing what they drew. Post these pictures and play the music while another class visits the room. Have children present their pictures and read their paragraphs.
- One way to help children understand the music is to have them perform the songs. Select some of the songs from this section, and have children sing the songs to another class. Have children write pieces to read between songs, explaining the historical significance of the song or telling about the kinds of songs from this section (work songs, ballads).
- You may also ask the following questions at the end of this section:

1. What is a work song?

   A work song is sung by people doing hard work (such as plantation slaves or railroad workers) to help pass the time.

2. What is a ballad?

   A ballad is a song that tells a story, such as "Clementine" or "Casey Jones."

3. When was "The Star-Spangled Banner" written?

   "The Star-Spangled Banner" was written during the War of 1812.

4. What does it really mean to "Follow the Drinking Gourd"?

   "Follow the Drinking Gourd" means to head north, using the Big Dipper to find the North Star.

More Resources

The titles listed below are offered as a representative sample of materials and not a complete list of everything that is available.

For children —

These books are generally intended to be read aloud, though some children may be able to read parts or all of the simpler texts.

- *Casey Jones,* by Allan Drummond (Farrar, Straus & Giroux, 2001). This legend is hard to find in picture-book form, so this book is a jewel. Whimsical pictures in pen-and-ink and watercolor. Rhyming text creates a rhythm symbolic of a train on a track. Hardcover, 32 pages, ISBN 0374311757.
- *Follow the Drinking Gourd,* by Jeanette Winter (Knopf, 1992). Paperback, 48 pages, ISBN 0679819975.
- *The Star-Spangled Banner,* by Francis Scott Key and illustrated by Peter Spier (Yearling Books, 1992). The text of the national anthem accompanied by Caldecott medalist Peter Spier's wonderfully detailed, full-color drawings. Includes a facsimile of Key's original manuscript. Paperback, 56 pages, ISBN 0440406978.
- *This Land Is Your Land,* words and music by Woody Guthrie and illustrated by Kathy Jakobsen (Little, Brown & Co., 1998). Hardcover, 32 pages, ISBN 0316392154.
- *Wee Sing Sing-Alongs Series,* by Price Stern Sloan, includes CD formats of a number of titles, including *Wee Sing America* (featuring "Dixie," "Erie Canal," "Good-Bye, Old Paint," "I've Been Workin' on the Railroad," "John Henry," "The Star-Spangled Banner," and "When Johnny Comes Marching Home") and *Wee Sing Fun 'n' Folk* (featuring "Buffalo Gals" and "Old Dan Tucker"). For more information, see their website at www.weesing.com.
- *When Johnny Comes Marching Home: A Song About a Soldier's Return,* by Patrick S. Gilmore and illustrated by Todd Ouren (Picture Window Books, 2003). Library binding, 24 pages, ISBN 1404801715. See also *Clementine* and *I've Been Working on the Railroad* in this same series.

For teachers —

- *From Sea to Shining Sea: A Treasury of American Folklore and Folk Songs,* edited by Amy L. Cohn and illustrated by Molly Bang (Scholastic, 1993). Diverse and delightful collection of stories, poems, and songs. Includes a very useful subject index and suggestions for further reading. Illustrated by 11 Caldecott-winning artists. Textbook binding, ISBN 0590428683.
- *I Hear America Singing: Folksongs for American Families,* collected and arranged by Kathleen Krull and illustrated by Allen Garns (Random House, 2003). Illustrated collection of 62 American folk songs with easy arrangements for guitar and piano. Includes "Casey Jones," "Clementine," "Follow the Drinking Gourd," "I've Been Working on the Railroad," "This Land Is Your Land," and many more. Originally published as *Gonna Sing My Head Off! American Folk Songs for Children,* this new edition includes a brand-new, 23-song CD. Hardcover, 160 pages, ISBN 0375825274.
- John Henry: The Steel Driving Man, www.ibiblio.org/john_henry. A rich website for adults and children to enjoy. Contains discussions on the legend of John Henry as well as 17 musical interpretations of the famous African-American legend. Teachers are advised to review the songs and lyrics.
- Water Valley Casey Jones Railroad Museum, www.watervalley.net/users/caseyjones/casey.htm#cj, offers a historical account of what happened to Casey Jones and his train on the night of August 29, 1900. Includes several versions.

Mathematics

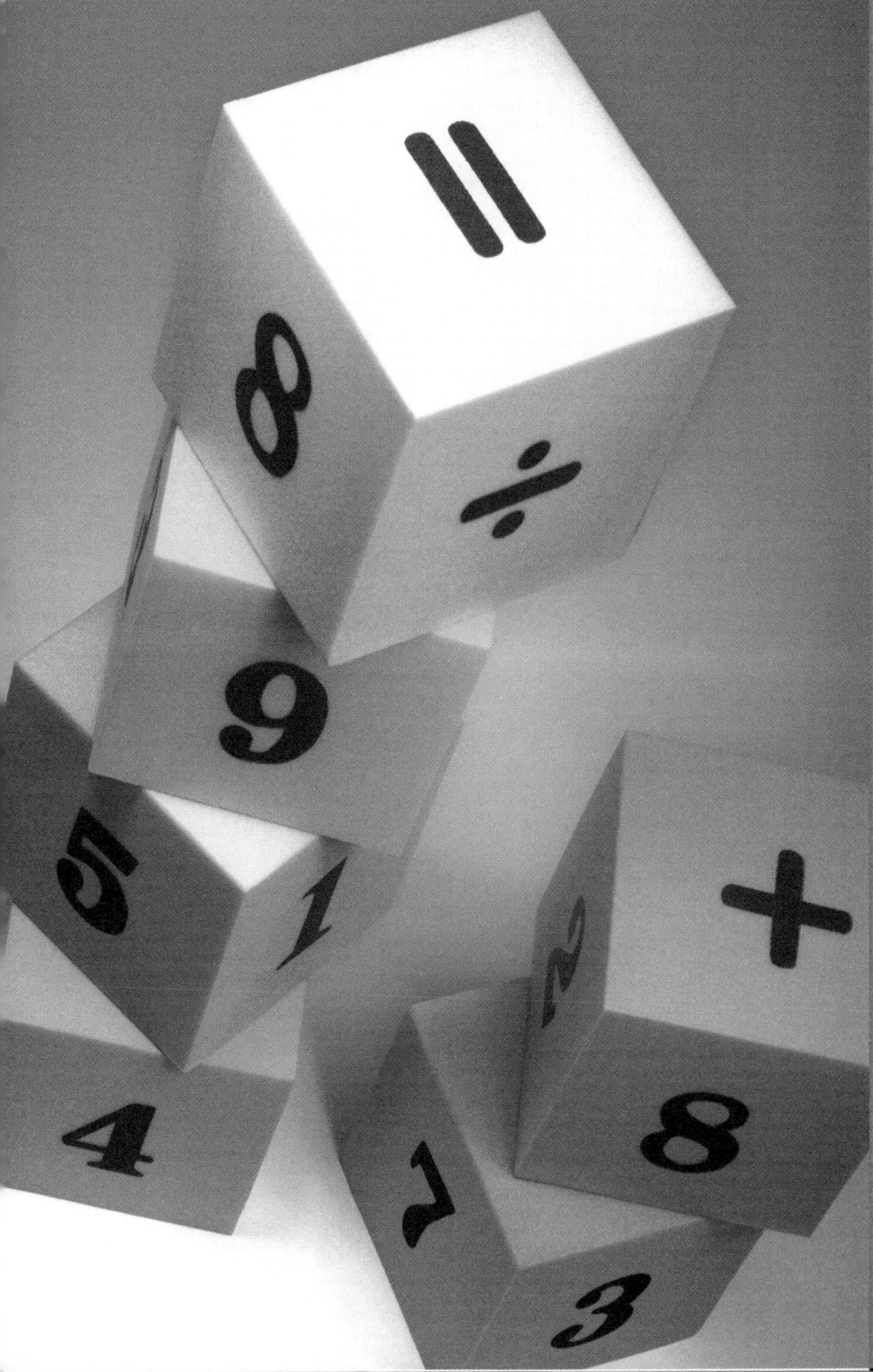

Follow your math program for time allotments, adding additional time for Sequence *topics not covered.*

Mathematics in Second Grade

The purpose of this chapter is to provide background information in mathematics for second-grade teachers. It is not intended to be a complete curriculum. For that purpose, an already-existing, sound, commercial mathematics program that coordinates topics for all of the elementary school grades is the best bet. Some suggestions for instruction are given in this chapter, but its main purpose is to provide mathematical insights at the adult level, and to illuminate the meaning of the second-grade mathematics content guidelines in the *Core Knowledge Sequence*.

In mathematics, there is a close interconnection between mathematical ideas and basic skills. Research has shown that children's success in mathematics depends upon mastery of both concepts and operations in the early grades. Giving children multiple concrete examples of concepts and ample opportunities to practice their skills will enable them to experience success in mathematics.

Children in second grade who have had the benefit of the *Core Knowledge Sequence* in Kindergarten and Grade 1 will have a good working knowledge of the topics introduced in this grade. However, if children don't already have mastery of one-digit addition and subtraction facts (fact families) or counting by twos, fives, and tens, this is the grade where they should gain it.

In the area of **Numbers and Number Sense**, second graders will learn to recognize, count, and write numbers to 1,000. They should also recognize place values: ones, tens, hundreds, and thousands. Children will write numbers up to hundreds in expanded form. And a new topic for children will be rounding to the nearest ten.

In **Fractions**, children will recognize the following fractions and write their corresponding numerical symbols: $\frac{1}{2}$, $\frac{1}{3}$, $\frac{1}{4}$, $\frac{1}{5}$, $\frac{1}{6}$, $\frac{1}{8}$, $\frac{1}{9}$, $\frac{1}{10}$. They will also identify fractions that are equal to 1.

In **Money**, children will be able to write amounts of money using both dollar ($) and cents (¢) signs, and the decimal point. Adding and subtracting amounts of money will be a natural offshoot of adding and subtracting two-and three-digit problems.

Knowing how to add in any order and check a sum by changing the order of the addends, as well as being able to estimate sums, are topics presented in **Computation** for the first time in Grade 2. Achieving timed mastery of both addition and subtraction facts is very important at this grade level. Children also need to understand the inverse relation between addition and subtraction and be able to use addition to check subtraction problems. Multiplication is another new topic in second grade, and children should learn the products of single-digit numbers through five. Writing and solving simple equations and solving basic word problems help children to realize the importance of mathematics in the everyday world.

In **Measurement**, children will learn to measure and draw line segments to the nearest $\frac{1}{2}$ inch and in centimeters. They'll compare weights using a balance scale and estimate and measure liquid volume in cups, pints, quarts, and gallons.

They will measure and record temperatures in degrees Fahrenheit. Using a clock face to tell time to five-minute intervals and distinguishing AM and PM are both introduced at this level.

Finally, in the area of **Geometry**, children learn to describe basic plane figures according to the number of sides they contain, and they learn to measure the perimeter of rectangles and squares. They identify lines as horizontal, vertical, perpendicular, and parallel, and name lines and line segments.

I. Numbers and Number Sense

The mathematics concepts outlined in the *Core Knowledge Sequence* do not constitute a complete second-grade mathematics program. The second-grade mathematics section of the *Core Knowledge Sequence* provides a comprehensive set of guidelines as to the mathematical concepts and skills that ought to be taught in Grade 2. The Core Knowledge Foundation recommends that you choose a structured, well-sequenced mathematics program (one that allows for distributed practice of fundamental math operations) and then compare the scope and sequence of this program with the *Core Knowledge Sequence* second-grade topics. In this way, you can identify any content gaps in the program that you have chosen and be certain to make any needed additions to the instructional program. Contact the Foundation for a list of mathematics programs that have been used with success in Core Knowledge schools.

The Big Idea

Counting and comparing numbers and data are fundamental parts of developing number sense.

What Students Should Already Know

Students in Core Knowledge schools should be familiar with

Kindergarten

- establish concepts of likeness and difference by classifying and sorting objects according to various attributes: size, shape, color, amount, function, etc.
- define a set by the common property of its elements
- in a given set, indicate which item does not belong
- recognize patterns and predict the extension of a pattern using concrete objects and pictorial representations
- extend a sequence of ordered concrete objects
- using concrete objects and pictorial representations, compare sets: same as (equal to), more than, less than, most, least
- count: forward from 1–31; backward from 10; from 1–10 by twos; by fives and tens to 50
- recognize and write numbers 1–31
- identify ordinal position, first (1st) through sixth (6th)
- identify pairs
- interpret simple pictorial graphs
- identify ½ as one of two equal parts of a region or object and find ½ of a set of concrete objects

Grade 1

- recognize and write numbers 0–100 and count: from 0–100 by ones, twos, fives, and tens; by tens from a given single-digit number; forward and backward; use tallies
- identify ordinal position, first (1st) through tenth (10th)
- identify dozen; half-dozen; pair
- recognize place value: ones, tens, hundreds
- given a number, identify one more and one less; ten more and ten less
- compare quantities using the signs <, >, and =
- recognize fractions as part of a whole: ½, ⅓, ¼
- create and interpret simple pictorial graphs and bar graphs

What Students Need to Learn

- **Recognize and write numbers to 1,000; read and write words for numbers from one to one-hundred**
- **Order and compare numbers to 1,000, using the signs <, >, and =**
- **Count: by threes; by hundreds to 1,000; by fifties to 1,000; forward and backward**
- **Use a number line**
- **Identify ordinal position, 1st through 20th, and write words for ordinal numbers, first to twentieth**
- **Identify even and odd numbers**
- **Recognize place value up to thousands**
- **Write numbers up to hundreds in expanded form (for example, 64 = 60 + 4; 367 = 300 + 60 + 7)**
- **Round to the nearest ten**
- **Identify and extend numerical and symbolic patterns**
- **Record numeric data systematically (for example, tossing a die) and find the lowest and highest values in a data set**

What Students Will Learn in Future Grades

The *Core Knowledge Sequence* for mathematics emphasizes the importance of reviewing and building on prior knowledge. Related topics from the Grade 3 *Sequence* are listed below, and subsequent grades will continue to focus on strengthening and expanding these skills.

Grade 3

- read and write numbers (in digits and words) up to six digits
- recognize place value up to hundred thousands
- order and compare numbers to 999,999, using the signs <, >, and =
- identify ordinal position, 1st through 100th
- round to the nearest hundred
- identify perfect squares (and square roots) to 100, and recognize the square root sign: $\sqrt{\quad}$
- identify Roman numerals from 1 to 20 (I–XX)
- understand what negative numbers are in relation to familiar uses (such as temperatures below zero)
- locate positive and negative whole numbers on a number line
- create and interpret line graphs
- record outcomes for a simple event (for example, tossing a die) and display the results graphically

I. Numbers and Number Sense

Materials

a variety of manipulatives, including sticks, color cubes, tiles, and other objects that can be counted, pp. 341–350

base ten blocks, strips, and squares, p. 343

number line (classroom and individual), p. 343, pp. 346–348, p. 350

yardstick or pointer, p. 343

hundreds chart, p. 344, p. 347, p. 350

thermometer, p. 347

pictorial graph, p. 349

bulletin board, p. 350

masking tape or strips of white paper for desks, p. 350

chart with columns, for each child, p. 350

newspapers and magazines, p. 350

paste, p. 350

laminated place value charts made with file folders, p. 350

crayons, p. 350

sentence strips, p. 350

Vocabulary

Student/Teacher Vocabulary

bar graph: a graph that uses bars, or wide lines, to represent data (T)

base ten system: a number system that groups numbers in sets of ten (T)

count: to determine how many there are of something (S)

dozen: a set of 12 items (S)

equal: the same amount (S)

fraction: a number that represents parts of a whole (S)

inequality: a mathematical statement that compares two unequal values (T)

number line: a line that uses equally spaced marks to represent numbers (T)

numeral: a symbol, e.g., 6, used to represent a number (T)

ordinal number: any number that expresses position in a series, such as first, second, third (T)

pair: two equal or corresponding things (T)

pattern: a consistent arrangement of objects (T)

place value: the value of the position of a digit in a number (T)

tally: a mark used to keep track of an item as it is counted or named (S)

whole number: any number in the infinite set {0, 1, 2, 3, 4, . . .} (T)

Domain Vocabulary

Numbers and number sense and associated words:
digit, inequalities, order, compare, count, forward, backward, tallies, even numbers, odd numbers, dozen, half-dozen, pair, place value, expanded form, one more, one less, ten more, ten less, round, bar graph, numeric pattern, symbolic pattern, data, lowest, highest

Cross-curricular Connections

Visual Arts	Music
Architecture	**Elements of Music**
• Patterns	• Rhythms and patterns

At a Glance

The most important ideas for you are:

- Counting in different ways helps children develop a deeper understanding of numbers and related concepts.
- Quantities can be compared using the signs <, >, and =.
- Place value is a system that assigns a value to the position of a digit in a number.
- Tally marks can be used to keep track of items being counted.
- Number lines can be used to compare values, round numbers, and strengthen children's understanding of place value.
- Ordinal numbers are used to tell the order of things.
- Sets of items can be labeled as a dozen, half-dozen, or pair depending on the number of items in the set.
- Learning how to round numbers helps children when measuring or performing mental calculations.
- Children can interpret data in bar graphs by measuring the height of a bar.

What Teachers Need to Know

Background

Since the dawn of civilization, people have struggled to find efficient and reliable ways to count and calculate. A landmark in that struggle was the introduction of place value in numeration systems such as the base ten system of numbers. This system, used throughout the world today, originated in India and was introduced to Europe through contact with Islamic culture. The operations of arithmetic are based fundamentally on place value, and it is impossible to understand how and why these procedures work without a thorough understanding of the base ten system of numbers.

Whole Numbers

The set of whole numbers is the set of all counting numbers together with the number zero. In other words, a whole number is any number in the collection {0, 1, 2, 3, . . .}. The way we write whole numbers uses the idea of place value. Place value in the base ten system of numbers is the fundamental ingredient for understanding arithmetic. (See the subsection "The Base Ten System and Place Value," on pp. 346–347.) Only ten different digits are needed to write any whole number. They are:

0, 1, 2, 3, 4, 5, 6, 7, 8, 9

When writing words for numbers, there are slightly different conventions. However, there are a few helpful guidelines. A commonly accepted convention is the use of the hyphen or dash (-) for number words that follow these words: *twenty, thirty, forty, fifty, sixty, seventy, eighty, ninety*. For example, the dash is used in these expressions:

twenty-one fifty-six ninety-nine

A standard convention is to avoid using the word *and* in expressions for whole numbers. Following this convention, it would not be correct to write *eight hundred* ***and*** *twenty-six*. Instead, the way to write this number is:

eight hundred twenty-six

As another example, the number 103 should be written as *one hundred three* rather than *one hundred and three*. The word *and* is reserved for writing words for numbers that include digits to the right of the decimal point, or a fraction. For example, the number 32.1 (which is the same number as $32\frac{1}{10}$) is written using the word *and* as *thirty-two and one-tenth*. However, this is a topic for later grades.

Another item to remember is that commas are generally used in number words in the same locations as in figures. For example, the number 35,426 is written:

thirty-five thousand, four hundred twenty-six

Notice the location of the comma after the word *thousand*.

Comparing Whole Numbers

> **Teaching Idea**
>
> **Children sometimes confuse the two inequality symbols (>, <) and forget which one means "is greater than" and which means "is less than." It might help children to think of these symbols as arrowheads that always point to the smaller number. An arrow that is well aimed hits the *small* circle in the middle of the target. Another way to remember is that both symbols > and < *open up* toward the larger number. A story to go with this could involve a hungry fish that knows that it gets more to eat when it opens its mouth toward the larger number.**

The symbol < is read aloud as "is less than," and the symbol > is read aloud as "is greater than." Mathematical statements using these symbols to compare two unequal values are called inequalities. For example, the statement "2 is less than 5" may be expressed as the inequality

2 < 5

Likewise, the statement "12 is greater than 0" may be written more concisely as

12 > 0

The base ten structure helps compare the size of numbers. (See the subsection "The Base Ten System and Place Value," on pp. 346–347.) Read each number from left to right. The first place value where the digits are different determines which number is larger. The reason is that any single (nonzero) digit in a placeholder to the left is worth more than all the digits beyond it (i.e., to its right) put together. The 1 in 199 represents 100, and that is greater than the value of 99 from all of the digits to the right of the 1.

As an example, compare 3,249 to 3,251. The 3 in the thousands place is the same for both numbers, as is the 2 in the hundreds place. Reading from left to right, the digits in the next placeholder, the tens column, are different; in one case there is a 4 and in the other a 5. Since 4 > 5,

3,249 < 3,251

Notice that the digits in the ones column did not play any role in deciding which of these two numbers is greater than the other.

As another example, compare 1,234 to 987. A possible mistake children might make is to compare the first digits that appear in the two numerals and conclude incorrectly that 987 is greater than 1,234 because 9 > 1. Why is this wrong and what is the correct way to compare digits? The 1 is in the thousands place while the 9 is in the hundreds place. The number 987 may be thought of as having a zero in the thousands place, so that for purposes of this comparison, 987 may be thought of as 0,987.

Now, looking at the corresponding place values of 1,234 and 0,987 from left to right, we see that 1 > 0 and, therefore,

1,234 > 987

Counting

Counting is a fundamental skill that is developed in Kindergarten and Grade 1. Second graders should continue to develop counting skills in more sophisticated ways.

A number line is a powerful teaching tool. It is important at many levels of mathematics, including the university level. Number lines can help children count forward and backward, as well as get started with counting by twos and threes. In the number line below, the whole numbers are represented in color.

Counting by twos amounts to choosing every other number. In the classroom, a teacher can simply point to every other number on the classroom number line as children count. Counting by threes can be done similarly. Children may also benefit from having a copy of a number line at their desk. They can move their fingers along the line, use tokens, or make marks on the paper to keep track of numbers while counting. They can compare numbers, realizing that the larger number is always to the right. Eventually, children should be able to count easily by twos and threes and compare numbers without looking at a number line.

Counting by twos, starting with zero, produces the even numbers. Starting with 0, the even numbers less than 10 are: 0, 2, 4, 6, 8. The next even number is 10 and the pattern repeats in the ones column: 10, 12, 14, 16, 18, 20, 22, 24, 26, 28, etc.

The even numbers continue this pattern, always with 0, 2, 4, 6, or 8 in the ones place. An even number may be defined as a whole number that is equal to some whole number added to itself. For example,

$$0 = 0 + 0 = 2 \times 0$$
$$2 = 1 + 1 = 2 \times 1$$
$$4 = 2 + 2$$
$$6 = 3 + 3$$
$$8 = 4 + 4$$
$$10 = 5 + 5$$

Children also can be asked to count by twos starting with 1 instead of 0:

1, 3, 5, 7, 9, 11, 13, 15, 17, 19, 21, . . .

These numbers are examples of odd numbers. Any whole number that is not an even number is an odd number. Notice that an odd number of objects, unlike an even number, cannot be divided into two equal parts consisting of whole objects.

Counting by twos, threes, fours, and fives from zero helps to lay the groundwork for the multiplication tables. Multiplication begins in Grade 2 and is discussed in the section "Computation" (pp. 364–381).

Counting beyond nine relies on the base ten structure of numbers. This is especially true when counting by tens from any number. For example, starting with the number 7, we proceed as:

7, 17, 27, 37, 47, 57, 67, 77, 87, 97

Teaching Idea

Make a number line that begins with zero for the front of your classroom. The space between tick marks and the size of the writing should be large enough so that children can read the number line from any seat in the classroom. Some teachers place the number line on the wall about a foot below the ceiling and let it wrap around the room so that it includes large numbers. Make sure that you can point to any number using a yardstick or a pointer.

Teaching Idea

A "hundreds chart" is a ten-by-ten array of the counting numbers ordered from 1 to 100, with ten consecutive counting numbers in each row. The numbers in the top row are 1 through 10; the numbers in the second row are 11 though 20; and so on, with the bottom row consisting of the numbers 91 through 100. It is a good idea for children to use and refer to a hundreds chart for these activities. Teach children what the numbers represent using concrete models, and then transfer this learning to the chart. Then, look at patterns of numbers in the chart. Eventually, children's understanding of numbers will be automatic, but this visual chart will help them make the transfer from the concrete (manipulatives) to the abstract (numbers without the chart).

1	2	3	4	5	6	7	8	9	10
11	12	13	14	15	16	17	18	19	20
21	22	23	24	25	26	27	28	29	30
31	32	33	34	35	36	37	38	39	40
41	42	43	44	45	46	47	48	49	50
51	52	53	54	55	56	57	58	59	60
61	62	63	64	65	66	67	68	69	70
71	72	73	74	75	76	77	78	79	80
81	82	83	84	85	86	87	88	89	90
91	92	93	94	95	96	97	98	99	100

The ones column remains unchanged and only the tens column increases (underlined here for emphasis only). Notice that proceeding further beyond 100 continues the count in the tens and hundreds columns:

107, 117, 127, 137, 147, etc.

The underlined digits above count from 10 to 14, but they are counting tens, not ones. After 9 tens comes 10 tens, but 10 tens is one hundred and so the 1 is placed in the hundreds column with a 0 in the tens column.

Counting by fives is closely related to using tallies. Tallies are useful for keeping track of categories one by one. For example, during a roll call of the children in class, you might keep track of the numbers of girls and boys through tallies for instructional purposes. As you call the names of the children, you place a tally mark in the row for *Boys* or for *Girls,* as follows. After four tally marks in either row, the fifth tally mark crosses the bundle of four to indicate a bundle of five altogether. The result of such a process might look like this:

Boys ⵝⵝ ⵝⵝ IIII
Girls ⵝⵝ ⵝⵝ II

Children can count the crossed bundles by fives, followed by counting the unbundled tallies by ones. The tally count indicates 14 boys and 12 girls, so there are 26 children in the class altogether.

Counting by tens and by hundreds reinforces understanding of place value. If you have counting blocks or other manipulatives that can be grouped by tens, have children experiment counting with them. You can use these concrete models to help children notice the similar patterns that arise from counting by ones, tens, and hundreds:

1	2	3	4	5	6	7	8	9	10
10	20	30	40	50	60	70	80	90	100
100	200	300	400	500	600	700	800	900	1,000

The similar appearance of these rows is not mere coincidence. It is part of the design of the base ten system of numbers. In the second row, the zeros are placeholders for the ones column. The tens column counts the number of tens. In the third row, the zeros are placeholders for the ones and the tens columns, and the hundreds column increases as we count by hundreds.

Notice that there is a relationship between counting by ones, counting by tens, and counting by hundreds. If every number in the first row of the previous chart is multiplied by 10, the result is the second row. Likewise, if every number in the second row is multiplied by 10, the result is the third row. Adults can understand this intuitively, but most children will need to use concrete models before they can grasp this abstract idea. The second row is counting groups of ten. Multiplying each number in the first row by 10 changes the counting by ones to tens. Similarly, 100 is 10 groups of ten, so multiplying each number in the second row by 10 changes the count from tens to hundreds.

Counting by fives and fifties produces a similar pattern:

5	10	15	20	25	30	35	40	45	50	etc.
50	100	150	200	250	300	350	400	450	500	etc.

Again, the similar appearance of these two rows is not coincidence. It is a consequence of the base ten system of numbers. Fifty means five groups of tens.

The first row is counting ones, five at a time, and the second row is counting tens, five at a time. Allow children to use concrete manipulatives to explore these relationships between numbers and develop a strong understanding of the base ten system.

Words for Numbers: Ordinal Numbers, Dozen, Half-Dozen, and Pairs

Another skill for second graders is learning to read and write ordinal numbers. Ordinal numbers refer to order. Ordinal numbers are not really numbers; they are adjectives that use the names of numbers. The first 31 ordinal numbers are:

1st	**first**	**17th**	**seventeenth**
2nd	**second**	**18th**	**eighteenth**
3rd	**third**	**19th**	**nineteenth**
4th	**fourth**	**20th**	**twentieth**
5th	**fifth**	**21st**	**twenty-first**
6th	**sixth**	**22nd**	**twenty-second**
7th	**seventh**	**23rd**	**twenty-third**
8th	**eighth**	**24th**	**twenty-fourth**
9th	**ninth**	**25th**	**twenty-fifth**
10th	**tenth**	**26th**	**twenty-sixth**
11th	**eleventh**	**27th**	**twenty-seventh**
12th	**twelfth**	**28th**	**twenty-eighth**
13th	**thirteenth**	**29th**	**twenty-ninth**
14th	**fourteenth**	**30th**	**thirtieth**
15th	**fifteenth**	**31st**	**thirty-first**
16th	**sixteenth**		

The numerical abbreviations always consist of counting numerals and the letters *st, nd, rd,* or *th* as suffixes. Other examples of ordinal numbers are thirty-third or 33rd, forty-fifth or 45th, and ninety-ninth or 99th. The ordinal numbers up to the 31st are important in communicating dates using days of the months, but children in Grade 2 are only required to know ordinal numbers up to twenty.

There are some specialized number words in the English language that second graders should understand and use. They should know the terms *dozen, half-dozen,* and *pair.* The *Core Knowledge Sequence* includes the same guidelines for these terms as for Grade 1, so children may already know these terms. However, they may need to be reminded and develop more familiarity with these words. A dozen objects means twelve objects, as in a dozen balls. A pair of objects means two objects, as in a pair of shoes. Children should realize that some things typically come in dozens, such as eggs, and that other things usually come in pairs, such as eyes and mittens. A half-dozen objects means six objects. The explanation of this term should include the fraction idea of one-half. Since $12 = 6 + 6$, one-half of twelve is six.

Teaching Idea

Practice using ordinal numbers anytime there is an appropriate opportunity to do so. For example, have children line up for recess or lunch with Sam first in line, Laura third, Nate eighth, and Quin ninth. Then have the other children arrange themselves so that these children are in the correct order.

The Base Ten System and Place Value

Children entering Grade 2 should have already been exposed to the fundamentals of the base ten system for three-digit numbers. The first example of a number expressed using place value is 10. The 1 signifies one ten and the 0 signifies zero ones. The 1 is in the tens place (or tens column), and the 0 is in the ones place (or ones column). The numeral 67 *means* 6 tens and 7 ones, all added together. Use concrete manipulatives to allow children to review and explore these concepts.

Numbers larger than 99 require the hundreds place. The meaning of the numeral 743 is 7 hundreds, 4 tens, and 3 ones. Children can see this more directly by writing 743 in expanded form:

$$743 = 700 + 40 + 3$$

Use a chart to explain the role of place value. The chart that follows demonstrates another way to exhibit the meaning of 6,572.

1,000s	100s	10s	1s
6	5	7	2

Include, as examples, numbers with zero placeholders, such as 7,068. The zero in this numeral is a placeholder for the hundreds position. In expanded form,

$$7{,}068 = 7{,}000 + 60 + 8$$

It is a good habit for children to include a comma after the 1,000s digit as in 7,068. Second-grade children are not expected to learn place value beyond four digits, but commas are a valuable aid for reading much larger numbers. The rule is to group the digits in a numeral by threes from the right to the left. For example, the commas help clarify that 6,572 is read as *six thousand, five hundred seventy-two.*

The number 10 plays a special role in the base ten number system. Each place value is 10 times greater than the next lower place value. This relationship for the first four placeholders, ones, tens, hundreds, and thousands, may be written as:

$$10 = 10 \times 1$$

$$100 = 10 \times 10$$

$$1{,}000 = 10 \times 100$$

This fundamental relationship between place values is true even for decimals, as children will learn in later grades.

Number lines can help children identify numbers that are one more and one less than a given number. This is a preliminary skill for addition and subtraction of two- and three-digit numbers, and it strengthens children's understanding of place value. To show how to add 1 to a number, point to that number on the number line and then move to the right one more number. To subtract 1 from a number, move to the left one unit instead. Here is a specific example:

60 – 1 = 59

This subtraction statement can be illustrated by using a portion of the number line like this:

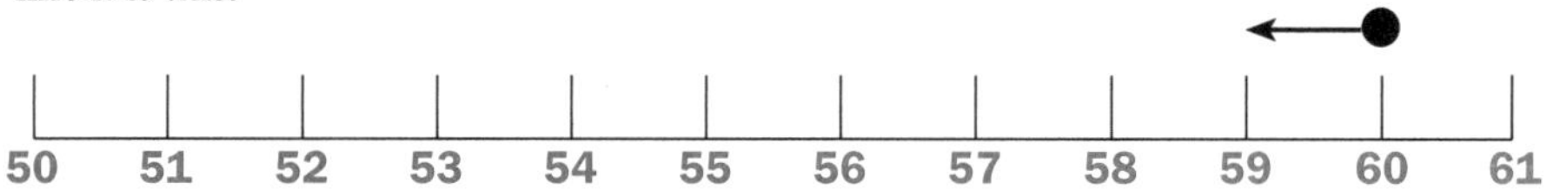

Children can use a number line to understand other examples such as these:

29 + 1 = 30

30 – 1 = 29

389 + 1 = 390

800 – 1 = 799

Teaching Idea

If a thermometer is posted just outside the classroom, children can read the thermometer directly and gain practical experience noticing how numbers move up and down. Seasonal temperatures can be compared and this can help to reinforce understanding of both temperature and the calendar.

Examples for which the addition or subtraction of 1 changes both the ones and the tens column of the original number will later help children with *regrouping* (that is, "borrowing" and "carrying"). Regrouping is discussed in the section "Computation" (pp. 364–381).

Adding or subtracting 10 from a number relies on place value and is preparatory for understanding the standard procedures for addition and subtraction. Why is it easy to see that 47 – 10 = 37? The answer is that 47 *means* 4 tens and 7 ones, so if 1 ten is taken away, there are 3 tens and 7 ones left. This is written as 37. Adding ten uses similar reasoning and place value.

A complication arises when 10 is subtracted from a number whose tens column is zero, or when 10 is added to a number whose tens column is nine, as in:

107 – 10 = 97

392 + 10 = 402

Teaching Idea

A hundreds chart can be used to help children add or subtract 10. To add 10 to a number, just move down one row to the number directly below the first number. To subtract 10, move directly up one row.

How can second graders deduce these addition and subtraction results? The key is to recognize explicitly that 100 is 10 tens. The number 107 is 1 hundred and 7 ones. Since 1 hundred is 10 tens, the number 107 is 10 tens and 7 ones. Removing one of those tens leaves 9 tens and 7 ones. Therefore, 107 – 10 = 97. Use manipulatives that have hundreds, tens, and ones to show this to children in a concrete manner and then move to the more abstract explanation.

There is more than one way for beginning second graders to use mathematical reasoning to deduce that 392 + 10 = 402. A method that later supports the addition algorithm is to recognize that 392 means 3 hundreds, 9 tens, and 2 ones. Adding one more ten gives 3 hundreds, 10 tens, and 2 ones. But 10 tens is 100. Therefore, the sum is 4 hundreds and 2 ones. That is, 392 + 10 = 402. Again, children should use concrete models to explore these types of problems.

Rounding

Rounding is an important number sense skill. It is useful in measurements and for mental estimations of arithmetic calculations.

There are two issues to focus on with regard to rounding: presenting a simple rule to round a number to the nearest ten and understanding the concept behind this rule.

Rounding can be explained through the use of the number line. Rounding a number to the nearest ten, except in one special case, means finding the closest multiple of 10 to that number. When rounding 56 to the nearest ten, the question that needs to be answered is "To which multiple of 10 is 56 the closest? Which of these numbers is 56 the closest to: 0, 10, 20, 30, 40, 50, 60, 70, etc.?" On the number line that follows, the multiples of 10 are in color and the number to be rounded, 56, is in black.

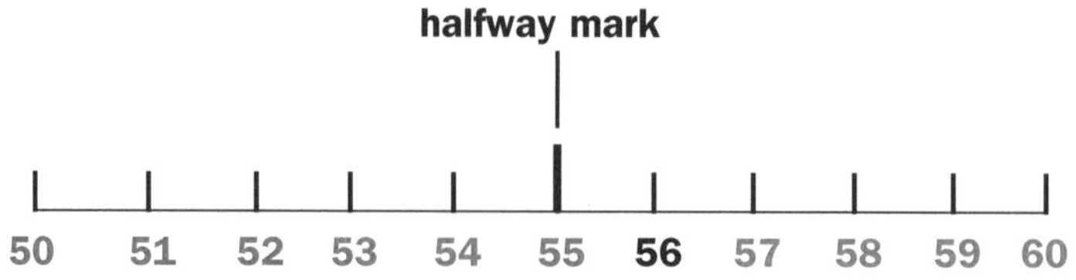

Since 56 lies between 50 and 60, these are the two candidates for the answer. The number, 56, lies to the right of the halfway mark, 55, and is closer to 60. Therefore, 56 rounded to the nearest ten is 60.

Instead of rounding 56, suppose we want to round 55 to the nearest 10. To which multiple of 10 is 55 the closest? It is an equal distance from both 50 and 60; it is exactly halfway between them. The usual convention is to round "halfway numbers" like 55 *up* to the larger of the two closest multiples of 10. Following this convention, 55 rounded to the nearest ten is 60. Notice that any number with a 5 in the ones column is halfway between two multiples of 10.

Once children understand the concept of rounding to the nearest ten using the number line, they can use a rule that only requires them to look at the digit in the ones column of the number to be rounded.

Graphs, Patterns, and Data

Recognizing patterns is a skill that is useful not only in mathematics, but in other subjects, such as art, music, and poetry. As an example, it is valuable for children to be able to recognize that, by filling in the blank below with the number 6, the following pattern is part of the sequence of even numbers:

2, 4, __, 8, 10, 12, . . .

Another example is to recognize the sequence of odd numbers and to be able to continue it:

1, 3, 5, 7, __, __, __, __, . . .

Repeating patterns may involve symbols, numbers, or pictures, as in:

ABCD ABCD ABCD . . .

78787878 . . .

▲■●▲■●▲■● . . .

Being able to organize, interpret, and display data are also useful skills. The first step in creating a graph, such as a bar graph, is to collect the information needed for the graph. One good way to collect the information is through a chart that uses tallies. Pose a classroom problem, such as favorite food preferences, allowing for four or five categories. Once the information has been collected, it can then be displayed in a simple horizontal or vertical bar graph.

Children were introduced to bar graphs in Grade 1. A bar graph uses bars, or wide lines, to represent a number. The vertical axis has an incremental scale used to indicate amounts of data. The horizontal axis lists items or categories of data, with a bar drawn above each item or category. The height of the bar indicates the quantity of data, using the scale on the vertical axis.

A good way to review bar graphs is to show children a pictorial graph and then create a bar graph with the same information. Pictorial graphs are made with pictures of objects that can be easily counted. By showing both types of graphs, children can compare and discuss the differences between each.

The bar graph below shows the results of a poll of favorite fruits among four fruits, conducted in a second-grade class.

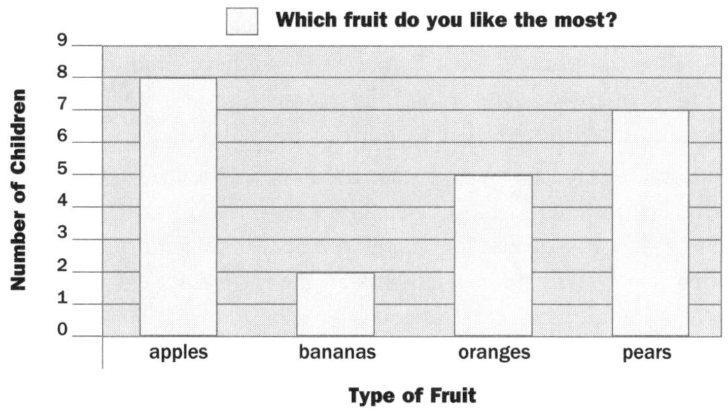

Questions about data displays like the one above can also reinforce addition and subtraction skills. Here are some sample questions related to this graph:

How many children liked apples the most? (8)
Bananas? (2) Oranges? (5) Pears? (7)

How many more children chose apples as their favorite fruit than children who chose oranges as their favorite fruit? (8 – 5 = 3 more children)

If all the children chose a favorite fruit, how many children were there in this classroom? (8 + 2 + 5 + 7 = 22 children)

When examining a set of data values, second graders should be able to determine the lowest and highest values in the set. Statisticians sometimes refer to the *range* of a list of numbers. The range of a list of numbers is the maximum value minus the minimum value. Children in Grade 2 do not need to identify the range or know the term, but you may be able to spark interesting discussion when reviewing data values and ranges of sets as a class. For example, you might ask children to identify the highest and lowest temperature recorded in a month or to find the continents with the greatest and least populations.

The Big Idea in Review

Counting and comparing numbers and data are fundamental parts of developing number sense.

Review

Below are some ideas for ongoing assessment and review activities. These are not meant to constitute a comprehensive list.

- Celebrate the one-hundredth day of school with the class. You will need to start on the first day of school by counting the days and keeping track of them on a hundreds chart or on a bulletin board. Each day, gather the class together to discuss what day it is in the countdown. Have children write the number on a chart with a tens and ones column. On the one-hundredth day, have children write about what they have learned about numbers.
- When making certain class decisions, allow the class to vote on choices and then have children show results using tally marks. Then, have children create a simple bar graph to represent the data. Have children construct bar graphs as a group using different colors to represent different choices.
- In addition to placing a number line on the wall of the classroom, have children make individual number lines for their desks on masking tape or strips of white paper. Check the number line for accuracy, and then attach it to the child's desk. Pose problems and have counting activities for the entire class, encouraging children to refer to their number line if necessary.
- Make a chart with columns to distribute to each child with the headings *One Dozen, Half-dozen,* and *Pair.* Provide newspapers and magazines and see if children can find pictures of items that are typically grouped in this way (i.e., eggs, socks, shoes) to cut out and paste in each column. Have children share their charts with the class and discuss any inaccuracies.
- Make place value charts on file folders with four columns labeled *Ones, Tens, Hundreds,* and *Thousands.* Give children numbers and have them write each digit in the appropriate column. For example, 2,256 would have a 2 in the thousands column, a 2 in the hundreds column, a 5 in the tens column, and a 6 in the ones column. If you laminate the file folders, children can write with crayons and then erase their numbers to use the chart again.
- Have children write number patterns with missing numbers on sentence strips. Children can trade strips with another classmate and fill in the missing numbers.

More Resources

A good mathematics program follows sound cognitive principles and allows many opportunities for thoughtful and varied practice to build mastery of important skills. For advice on suitable mathematics programs, contact the Foundation.

The titles listed below are offered as a representative sample of materials and not a complete list of everything that is available.

For children —

These books are generally intended to be read aloud, though some children may be able to read parts or all of the simpler texts.

- *Discovering Patterns (Math for Fun),* by Andrew King (Copper Beech, 1998). Library binding, 32 pages, ISBN 0761307249. See also *Plotting Points and Position* in the same series.

More Resources continued

• *The Grapes of Math,* by Greg Tang and illustrated by Harry Briggs (Scholastic, 2001). Hardcover, ISBN 043921033X. See also *Math Fables,* by the same author.

• *Pattern Bugs,* by Trudy Harris (Millbrook Press, 2001). "[A]n intelligent math tool that can be used by an individual child or with groups . . . . By using the sounds in the poems, the details of the pictures, and the various blocks of color that frame the initial spread, children can find and identify repetitive patterns" (*School Library Journal*). Library binding, 40 pages, ISBN 0761321071. See also *Pattern Fish,* by the same author.

• *What Comes In 2's, 3's and 4's?* by Suzanne Aker and illustrated by Bernie Karlin (Aladdin, 1992). Paperback, 32 pages, ISBN 0671792474.

For teachers —

• *About Teaching Mathematics: A K–8 Resource,* by Marilyn Burns (Math Solutions Publications, 1992). Paperback, 296 pages, ISBN 0941355055.

• ETA Cuisenaire carries the very useful and popular math manipulatives, Cuisenaire Rods, as well as many resources for using the rods and other products. Cuisenaire Rod activities can be used to supplement your current math program, or may be already integrated with published curricula (for example, Miquon Math, published by Key Curriculum Press). Contact ETA Cuisenaire at www.etacuisenaire.com or 1-800-445-5985 for a free catalog to peruse their complete product line.

• *Family Math,* by Jean Kerr Stenmark, Virginia Thompson, and Ruth Cossey (Equals, 1986). This generous, helpful book provides clear directions for fun, yet substantative, math activities that parents can do with children from 5 to 12 years old. Includes word problems, measurement, geometry, estimation, arithmetic, and lots of ideas for things to make. Provides a great way to supplement (not replace) math instruction in school. Paperback, ISBN 0912511060.

• *Mental Math in the Primary Grades,* by Jack Hope and others (Pearson Learning, 1997). "Builds mental math skills by promoting understanding of the base ten system through patterns" (from the publisher). Paperback, 128 pages, ISBN 0866514341.

• A+ Math, www.aplusmath.com, among its other offerings, lets you create printable flash cards online.

• AAA Math, www.aaamath.com, features hundreds of pages of basic math skills with interactive practice arranged by grade level and topic. Includes challenge activities. These activities plus additional ones are also available on a CD-ROM.

• Ask Dr. Math, www.mathforum.com/dr.math, has a number of interesting question-and-answer items on such topics as "Why does 2 + 2 = 4?" and "How many seconds are there in 1,000 years?" You can also search the site for answers to particular questions or submit your own.

• Houghton Mifflin MathSteps, www.eduplace.com/math/mathsteps/index.html, is a teacher support site with lesson plans, background information, and helpful tips.

II. Fractions

The Big Idea

Fractions express a relationship between a part and a whole.

What Students Should Already Know

Students in Core Knowledge schools should be familiar with

Kindergarten

- identify $\frac{1}{2}$ as one of two equal parts of a region or object
- find $\frac{1}{2}$ of a set of concrete objects

Grade 1

- recognize fractions as part of a whole: $\frac{1}{2}$, $\frac{1}{3}$, $\frac{1}{4}$

What Students Need to Learn

- **Recognize these fractions as part of a whole set or region and write the corresponding numerical symbols: $\frac{1}{2}$, $\frac{1}{3}$, $\frac{1}{4}$, $\frac{1}{5}$, $\frac{1}{6}$, $\frac{1}{8}$, $\frac{1}{10}$**
- **Recognize fractions that are equal to 1**

What Students Will Learn in Future Grades

The *Core Knowledge Sequence* for mathematics emphasizes the importance of reviewing and building on prior knowledge. Related topics from the Grade 3 *Sequence* are listed below, and subsequent grades will continue to focus on strengthening and expanding these skills.

Grade 3

- recognize fractions to $\frac{1}{10}$
- identify numerator and denominator
- write mixed numbers
- recognize equivalent fractions (for example, $\frac{1}{2} = \frac{3}{6}$)
- compare fractions with like denominators, using the signs $<$, $>$, and $=$
- know and write decimal equivalents to $\frac{1}{4}$, $\frac{1}{2}$, $\frac{3}{4}$

Vocabulary

Student/Teacher Vocabulary

denominator: the number on the bottom of a fraction, or the number of pieces a whole, region, or group has been divided into (S)

fraction: a number that represents parts of a whole, region, or group (S)

numerator: the number on the top of a fraction, or the number of pieces being considered (S)

Domain Vocabulary

Fractions and associated words:
fraction, whole, part, region, group

Cross-curricular Connections

Music

Elements of Music

- Half note
- Quarter note

Materials

paper plates, p. 354

materials such as cardboard, foam board, or plastic to create fraction manipulatives, p. 354

plastic coffee can lids in different colors, p. 354

colored blocks, p. 354

two-color counters, p. 354

painted lima beans, p. 354

carton of a dozen eggs, p. 355

one-color counters, p. 355

math journal or notebook, p. 355

index cards, p. 355

pictures of whole objects, regions, or sets divided into fractional parts, p. 355

colored fraction tiles, p. 355

At a Glance

The most important ideas for you are:

- Fractions consist of a numreator and a denominator.
- Fractions can be used to show part of a whole thing, region, or set.
- Children in Grade 2 should be able to identify seven common fractions.
- When the numerator and the denominator of a fraction are the same (nonzero) number, the fraction equals 1.

What Teachers Need to Know

Background

Fractions occupy a small but important place in the Grade 2 Core Knowledge curriculum. As children progress through the grades, the arithmetic of fractions becomes increasingly more important. In Grade 2, children will review the fractions learned in Grade 1 and learn other common fractions. They will also explore how to make fractions from whole objects, regions, or sets. Using familiar objects to teach fractions will help children develop a deeper understanding of the concepts.

Fractions as Part of a Whole, Region, or Set

Review with children the parts of a fraction. The numerator of a fraction is the number above the fraction bar (i.e., the number on top), and it describes the number of pieces being considered. The denominator of a fraction is the number below the fraction bar (i.e., the number on the bottom), and it tells the number of parts a whole, region, or set has been divided into. For example, the numerator of the fraction $\frac{1}{4}$ is 1, and the denominator of the fraction $\frac{1}{4}$ is 4. When reading fractions aloud, the numerator is read as a counting number, while the denominator is read as an ordinal number.

In Grade 2, children will extend their knowledge of fractions by learning more of the most common fractions. Exposure to a wide variety of pictures and manipulatives helps children visualize these fractions. It is worth emphasizing that whatever objects or pictures are used to illustrate fractions of a whole thing or a region should be divided into equal parts. For example, to illustrate the fraction $\frac{1}{3}$, divide an object or picture into 3 identical parts. Each of these parts represents $\frac{1}{3}$ of the whole. Both of these pictures represent the fraction $\frac{1}{3}$:

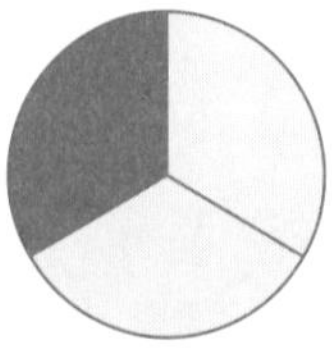

$\frac{1}{3}$

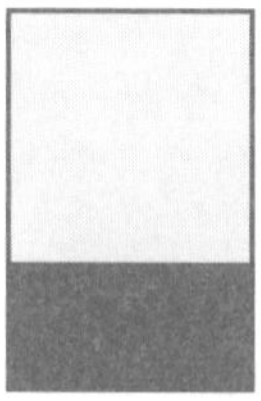

$\frac{1}{3}$

The concept of "equal parts" can be explained to children by using the notion of dividing an item into "fair shares." For example, if there is only one cookie left but two friends both want it, the fairest way to split the cookie is to divide it into two equal parts, or half. By exploring the idea of dividing things into fair shares, children will make logical connections to common fractions made up of equal parts.

Children can find examples of larger regions that are divided into fractional parts in their everyday lives. For example, encourage children to identify lines on basketball courts or soccer fields that divide the regions into equal parts.

When teaching children to recognize fractions as part of a set, it is helpful to use concrete objects, manipulatives, and pictures. These tools help illustrate the more difficult concept of how fractions can name part of a group of items. For example, you could give children three blocks: one red, one blue, and one yellow. Ask children to identify what fraction of the blocks is blue. The denominator will name the number of parts the set is broken into. Since the set consists of three blocks, or parts, the denominator of the fraction is 3. The numerator will name the number of parts being considered. In this case, children must identify the fraction of blue blocks in the set, so the numerator will be 1. In other words, $\frac{1}{3}$ of the blocks are blue. Children will benefit from using concrete examples such as this to explore and gain a better understanding of forming common fractions as parts of sets.

Teaching Idea

Use a drawing of a pizza to teach fractions. Draw circles on the board, and divide each into the fractions you are teaching, for example, $\frac{1}{3}$ and $\frac{1}{2}$. Then shade in one "piece" of each pizza. For distinguishing which is larger, $\frac{1}{3}$ or $\frac{1}{2}$, ask children to create models of $\frac{1}{3}$ and $\frac{1}{2}$ using paper plates, compare them, and demonstrate which is larger, $\frac{1}{2}$ or $\frac{1}{3}$. You can repeat this procedure with a variety of fractions.

Teaching Idea

Any sturdy material, such as cardboard, foam board, and plastic, can be used to create fraction manipulatives. One inexpensive idea is to collect plastic coffee can lids in different colors. Use one coffee lid as a base, and then remove the rims of different-colored lids and cut them into halves, fourths, etc. Children can manipulate the fraction pieces inside the inverted lid to explore fractional relationships.

Teaching Idea

Use two-color counters to help children explore fractions as parts of sets. The entire set can begin as one color to represent the whole set, or one, and children can flip counters over to allow the different-colored side to represent fractional parts of a set. Inexpensive counters can be made from sturdy cardboard, foam board, or even painted lima beans. Similarly, children can also draw Xs and Os on paper to represent fractional parts of sets.

Fractions Equal to 1

To illustrate how fractions can equal one, provide children with many visuals of sets, regions, or objects that have all of their parts present. For example, you can show children a carton with a dozen eggs inside. Children will understand that *one* dozen eggs is the same as twelve eggs. The fractional representation of a dozen eggs is $^{12}/_{12}$. There are twelve units in the set of a dozen, so the denominator is 12; and all twelve eggs are present, so the numerator is also 12. When the numerator and the denominator of a fraction are the same (nonzero) number, the fraction equals 1. Have children use many different concrete strategies to explore this concept, such as shading in all of the squares on a grid, having all fractional pieces present in a fractional model, or using counters or other objects of all one color to show that the numerator and the denominator are the same number. When the set is complete, or whole, it is equal to 1.

Teaching Idea

To teach fractions, use whole circles and circles divided into equal segments. For example, if a circle is divided into 8 equal segments, one segment equals $^1/_8$. An uncut circle is not divided into any segments. It is equal to $^1/_1$. And the whole circle with eight equal segments can be expressed as $^8/_8$.

Review

Below are some ideas for ongoing assessment and review activities. These are not meant to constitute a comprehensive list.

- After teaching about fractions, brainstorm with the class ways that we use fractions in our lives. How do we use fractions every day? Why are they important? You can discuss dividing up a pizza or cake, how a sports game is divided into quarters or halves, as well as how we measure rain or snowfall. Discuss with the class, and then have children record their observations in a math notebook or journal.
- Have each child make a personal set of flash cards on index cards with pictures of whole objects, regions, or sets divided into fractional parts on the front and the corresponding fractional number on the back. After you check for accuracy, children can use their cards to quiz a partner.
- Provide children with colored fraction tiles, and have them find a partner. Have one child represent a fraction with the tiles, and ask the other child to identify the fractional number. Have children fold paper to construct fractional parts. For example, you can have children fold a paper into halves, thirds, fourths, etc. Creating halves, fourths, and eighths is easiest for young children, but with some guidance they can also create thirds and sixths.

The Big Idea in Review

Fractions expess a relationship between a part and a whole.

More Resources

A good mathematics program follows sound cognitive principles and allows many opportunities for thoughtful and varied practice to build mastery of important skills. For advice on suitable mathematics programs, contact the Foundation.

The titles listed below are offered as a representative sample of materials and not a complete list of everything that is available.

For children —

These books are generally intended to be read aloud, though some children may be able to read parts or all of the simpler texts.

- *The Doorbell Rang,* by Pat Hutchins (HarperTrophy, 1989). It's not hard to divide a dozen cookies evenly between two kids, but every time the doorbell rings, someone else shows up who wouldn't mind having a share, too. Paperback, 24 pages, ISBN 0688092349.
- *Eating Fractions,* by Bruce McMillan (Scholastic, 1992). "Math was never so much fun or so wholesomely delicious. Recipes and suggestions for how children can use their new math skills to measure ingredients and prepare these kid-tested treats are included" (*Publishers Weekly*). Paperback, ISBN 0590437712.
- *Fraction Fun,* by David A. Adler (Holiday House, 1997). Simple, intuitive activities. Includes reinforcement on understanding money. Paperback, ISBN 0823413411.
- *Inchworm and a Half,* by Elinor J. Pinczes (Houghton Mifflin, 2003). On measuring and fractions. Paperback, 32 pages, ISBN 0618311017.
- *Jump, Kangaroo, Jump!,* by Stuart J. Murphy (HarperCollins, 1999). Twelve campers must be divided into different-sized groups to compete. Paperback, ISBN 006446721X.

For teachers —

- *About Teaching Mathematics: A K–8 Resource,* by Marilyn Burns (Math Solutions Publications, 1992). Paperback, 296 pages, ISBN 0941355055.
- ETA Cuisenaire carries the very useful and popular math manipulatives, Cuisenaire Rods, as well as many resources for using the rods and other products. Cuisenaire Rod activities can be used to supplement your current math program, or may be already integrated with published curricula (for example, Miquon Math, published by Key Curriculum Press). Contact ETA Cuisenaire at www.etacuisenaire.com or 1-800-445-5985 for a free catalog to peruse their complete product line.
- *Family Math,* by Jean Kerr Stenmark, Virginia Thompson, and Ruth Cossey (Equals, 1986). This generous, helpful book provides clear directions for fun, yet substantative, math activities that parents can do with children from 5 to 12 years old. Includes word problems, measurement, geometry, estimation, arithmetic, and lots of ideas for things to make. Provides a great way to supplement (not replace) math instruction in school. Paperback, ISBN 0912511060.
- AAA Math, www.aaamath.com, features hundreds of pages of basic math skills with interactive practice arranged by grade level and topic. Includes challenge activities. These activities plus additional ones are also available on a CD-ROM.
- Ask Dr. Math, www.mathforum.com/dr.math, has a number of interesting question-and-answer items on such topics as "Why does 2 + 2 = 4?" and "How many seconds are there in 1,000 years?" You can also search the site for answers to particular questions or submit your own.

III. Money

The Big Idea

Money has a relative value, which can be written, added, and subtracted.

What Students Should Already Know

Students in Core Knowledge schools should be familiar with

Kindergarten

- identify pennies, nickels, dimes, quarters, and the one-dollar bill
- identify the dollar sign ($) and cents sign (¢)
- write money amounts using the cents sign

Grade 1

- recognize relative value of a penny, nickel, dime, quarter
- recognize and use dollar ($) and cents (¢) signs
- show how different combinations of coins equal the same amounts of money

What Students Need to Learn

- **Recognize relative value of a dollar**
- **Write amounts of money using the decimal point**
- **Add and subtract amounts of money**

What Students Will Learn in Future Grades

The *Core Knowledge Sequence* for mathematics emphasizes the importance of reviewing and building on prior knowledge. Related topics from the Grade 3 and Grade 4 *Sequence* are listed below. Subsequent grades will continue to focus on strengthening and expanding these skills.

Grade 3

- make change, using as few coins as possible
- multiply and divide amounts of money by small whole numbers

Grade 4

- solve problems involving making change in amounts up to $100.00
- solve multiplication and division problems with money

III. Money

Materials

real or play coins and bills, pp. 359–362

base ten blocks, p. 359

chart paper, p. 361

coin bingo cards, p. 362

Vocabulary

Student/Teacher Vocabulary

money: coins and paper bills that people use to pay for things (S)

Domain Vocabulary

Money and associated words:
quarter, dime, penny, nickel, coin, dollar, buy, sell, change, decimal

Cross-curricular Connections

Language Arts

Poetry

- "Smart" (money and math)

At a Glance

The most important ideas for you are:

- Pennies, nickels, dimes, quarters, and dollars each have a relative value and model the base ten system of counting and writing numbers.
- The dollar sign ($) is used to represent dollars in written form, and the cents sign (¢) is used to represent cents in written form.
- Different combinations of coins can equal the same amount of money.
- Amounts of money can be added and subtracted using a variety of strategies.

What Teachers Need to Know

Background

Children should be familiar with the basic units of money, and in Grade 2 they will learn how to add and subtract amounts of money. Money can be studied throughout the school year by incorporating it into other math topics, such as patterns, place value, the base ten number system, counting, and computation. Whenever possible, children should have opportunities to use realistic play or actual money in class.

Relative Value of Coins and Bills

Children should already know the relative value of the penny (1¢), nickel (5¢), dime (10¢), and quarter (25¢). In Grade 2, children will also learn the value of one dollar (100¢), which can be represented by a one-dollar bill or coin. Children can use money manipulatives to compare the values of each type of coin and bill. For instance, a child could stack five pennies next to one nickel to show that the two amounts are equal, or stack four quarters next to one dollar to show that their values are also equal.

The advantage in giving special focus to pennies, dimes, and dollars in early lessons about money in Kindergarten and Grade 1 is that these denominations model the base ten system of counting and writing numbers up to 999. For example, 3 dimes and 2 pennies have the same value as 32 pennies and correspond in a natural way to the number 32. Remember, the symbol 32 means 3 groups of 10 (think of dimes) and 2 ones (think of pennies).

The dollar bill or dollar coin, which is studied in more depth in this grade, can play the role of the hundreds place. For example, \$2.34 is the same as 234¢ or 234 pennies. This amount may be directly represented by two one-dollar coins or bills, three dimes, and four pennies.

Teaching Idea

To make the value of coins concrete to children, first have them show the number 32 with base ten blocks and then again with pennies and dimes. Show children how a base ten block represents the same amount as a dime and how the "ones" are the same as pennies.

Money Symbols

Both of the money symbols ¢ and \$ are important. It is possible to write money amounts using either symbol. For example, 5¢ may be written as \$.05, and \$1.25 can be written as 125¢. However, the two symbols, ¢ and \$, should not be used at the same time. It is incorrect to write \$.05¢ or \$1.25¢. It is also incorrect to write .05¢ unless it is intended to mean five one-hundredths of one cent. Notice that .05¢ ≠ 5¢ because .05 ≠ 5.

Combining Coins

Different combinations of coins can equal the same amount of money, and questions about this are practical and serve to develop number sense skills. Children can be asked questions such as:

How can I make 25¢ using three coins?
(two dimes and one nickel)

How can I make 25¢ using five coins? (five nickels)

How can I make 25¢ using eight coins?
(one dime, two nickels, and five pennies)

Children can also combine coins to reinforce other math concepts. For example, children can be asked questions such as:

How many pennies make one dime? (ten)

How many dimes make one dollar? (ten)

How can I make 35¢ using three coins? (one quarter and two nickels)

How can I make \$1.25 using five coins? (five quarters)

The first two questions reinforce base ten relationships of placeholders. Money relationships can also enhance children's understanding of fractions. A key vocabulary word for this purpose is *quarter*. One quarter means one-fourth. A quarter hour will be discussed in the subsection "Time," on pp. 387–388. In the context of money, a quarter refers to the 25¢ coin because one-fourth of a dollar (100¢) is 25¢. Four quarters make a dollar and one-fourth of a dollar is a quarter. Likewise, the 50¢ piece, or 50¢ coin, is sometimes called a half-dollar because 50¢ is one-half of 100¢. Ten dimes make one dollar, so one dime is one-tenth of a dollar. These examples can be incorporated into fraction lessons.

Writing Amounts of Money Using the Decimal Point

Once children have learned the value of one dollar (100¢), you can introduce writing amounts of money using the decimal point. The decimal point is introduced in connection with money in Grade 2 *Sequence* and is explored more fully in connection with fractions in Grade 3 *Sequence*. Children will not learn how to add and subtract decimals until Grade 4.

In Grade 2, it is important to demonstrate different ways to write amounts of money, using amounts less than one dollar. For example, three dimes and two pennies can be written as 32¢ or as $0.32. You may wish to create a place value chart, showing children how the tenths and hundredths places fall to the right of the decimal point. Use money manipulatives to show the meaning of each column. Allow children ample opportunities to practice writing money amounts using both the cents sign and the decimal point. Children will explore decimal numbers in greater detail in Grade 3 and should become more comfortable with writing amounts of money using the decimal point at that time.

Adding and Subtracting Money

Adding and subtracting money amounts have practical applications in everyday life. Simple money calculations introduced in Grade 2 will help prepare children for decimal calculations in later grades.

Addition and subtraction money calculations in this grade should involve whole dollar amounts or amounts under a dollar. You might want to teach this topic in conjunction with the computation goals for this grade (see the "Computation" section, pp. 364–381).

Money manipulatives such as plastic coins should be used when teaching this topic. Begin with simple problems, such as adding one nickel and three pennies. Children can solve this problem by counting the coins or by using their addition facts to determine that $5 + 3 = 8$. Subtraction of simple money amounts can be done in the same way. If children have ten pennies and take two away, they can count the coins or use their facts to determine that there are 8 pennies remaining. Allow children to explore simple addition and subtraction calculations such as these until they are comfortable.

Next, introduce children to two-digit addition problems with money. It may be best to wait until you have introduced two-digit addition problems without money, which is discussed in further detail in the "Computation" section (see pp. 364–381).

With coin manipulatives, show children 11 cents using one dime and one penny. Then, show children 14 cents using one dime and four pennies. Ask children to add the two amounts using the manipulatives. At first, children may find the sum by counting the coins. Encourage them to group the dimes together and the pennies together when counting. This sorting will help children focus on the place value of each coin. In order to prepare children to add with decimals in later grades, you should also have children add the amounts using the following format:

dimes	pennies
1	1
+ 1	4
2	5

Explain that the tens column gives the number of dimes and the ones column gives the number of pennies, and relate this example to two-digit addition without money. As children become more proficient, the labels *pennies* and *dimes* can be discarded. You can follow this example with other calculations that add up to less than a dollar.

To introduce two-digit subtraction with money, follow a similar strategy. With coin manipulatives, show children 22 cents using two dimes and two pennies. Then, show children 11 cents using one dime and one penny. Ask children to subtract the two amounts using the manipulatives. At first, children may find the sum by taking away coins and then counting the remaining ones. In order to prepare children to subtract with decimals in later grades, you should also have children subtract the amounts using the following format:

dimes	pennies
2	2
– 1	1
1	1

Review that the tens column gives the number of dimes and the ones column gives the number of pennies, and relate this example to two-digit subtraction without money. You can follow this example when subtracting other amounts that are less than a dollar.

Cross-curricular Teaching Idea

You may wish to teach Shel Silverstein's poem "Smart," which focuses on math and money. The poem is included in the Language Arts section of the Text Resources for Grade 2. You can also extend this activity by discussing who some of the people on the coins are—children should already know Washington, Lincoln, and Jefferson.

Review

Below are some ideas for ongoing assessment and review activities. These are not meant to constitute a comprehensive list.

- Review the value of a quarter, dime, nickel, and penny with the class. Give children an amount, such as 50 cents, and ask children to use plastic coins to find as many combinations as they can to make 50 cents. Have children record their combinations on a piece of paper. Then, share the combinations and make a class chart of all of the possible ways to make that amount.
- Provide the class time to write about and discuss how they solve problems with money. For example, ask children to determine how much two nickels, one quarter, and three dimes equal. Have children find the total and write about the process they used to count the money. Did they skip count? Did they add certain numbers? Have them share their process with the class.

The Big Idea in Review

Money has a relative value, which can be written, added, and subtracted.

• Teaching about money can provide a way to review skip counting. Give each child some plastic nickels and dimes and then review skip counting by fives and tens. For example, have children count by fives to 35, placing plastic nickels in a row as they count by fives.

• Play a game of coin bingo with the class. Make bingo cards for each child with money amounts in the squares. Call out a letter, but instead of giving a number or amount, show the children a combination of plastic coins. Children must add the coins together to see if they have that amount listed in the appropriate column on their card.

More Resources

A good mathematics program follows sound cognitive principles and allows many opportunities for thoughtful and varied practice to build mastery of important skills. For advice on suitable mathematics programs, contact the Foundation.

The titles listed below are offered as a representative sample of materials and not a complete list of everything that is available.

For children —

These books are generally intended to be read aloud, though some children may be able to read parts or all of the simpler texts.

• *26 Letters & 99 Cents,* by Tana Hoban (HarperTrophy, 1995). "Hoban's crisp photo-essay presents images of upper- and lower-case letters beside objects beginning with that letter; reverse the book, and numerals are shown alongside coins that total that amount" (*Publishers Weekly*). Paperback, 32 pages, ISBN 068814389X.

• *The Coin Counting Book,* by Rozanne Lanczak Williams (Charlesbridge Publishing, 2001). Paperback, 32 pages, ISBN 0881063266.

• *Follow the Money,* by Loreen Leedy (Holiday House, 2002). Follow George Washington (a quarter) as he leaves the mint and travels around town on a busy journey. Some of the math problems will be too difficult for second graders, but the concept of how money changes hands will probably be interesting. Library binding, ISBN 0823415872.

• *The Penny Pot (MathStart, Level 3),* by Stuart Murphy (HarperTrophy, 1998). Paperback, 40 pages, ISBN 0064467171. See also *Slugger's Car Wash,* by the same author.

For teachers —

• *About Teaching Mathematics: A K–8 Resource,* by Marilyn Burns (Math Solutions Publications, 1992). Paperback, 296 pages, ISBN 0941355055.

• ETA Cuisenaire carries the very useful and popular math manipulatives, Cuisenaire Rods, as well as many resources for using the rods and other products. Cuisenaire Rod activities can be used to supplement your current math program, or may already be integrated with published curricula (for example, Miquon Math, published by Key Curriculum Press). Contact ETA Cuisenaire at www.etacuisenaire.com or 1-800-445-5985 for a free catalog to peruse their complete product line.

• *Family Math,* by Jean Kerr Stenmark, Virginia Thompson, and Ruth Cossey (Equals, 1986). This generous, helpful book provides clear directions for fun, yet substantative, math activities that parents can do with children from 5 to 12 years old. Includes word problems, measurement, geometry, estimation, arithmetic, and lots of ideas for things to make. Provides a great way to supplement (not replace) math instruction in school. Paperback, ISBN 0912511060.

• A+ Math, www.aplusmath.com, has online money "flash cards" that include currency and coins. From the home page, click on "Flashcards," and on the page that follows scroll down to "Money" under the "Non-Java Flashcards." Since the flash card answers are entered in dollar amounts, demonstrate to children how a decimal point goes before all "cents" amounts, whether or not they have any whole dollars preceding them. You may also show them how to put a "zero" before the decimal point to clearly indicate amounts less than a dollar, e.g., $0.47.

More Resources continued

- AAA Math, www.aaamath.com, features hundreds of pages of basic math skills with interactive practice arranged by grade level and topic. Includes challenge activities. These activities plus additional ones are also available on a CD-ROM.
- Ask Dr. Math, www.mathforum.com/dr.math, has a number of interesting money problems, such as "How can you make up one dollar using 50 coins?" Search the archive for the word *money*.
- Startwrite is a computer software program that allows you to create individualized money counting problems with a special money font. Both PC and Mac versions are available. To download a free trial, visit their website at www.startwrite.com.

IV. Computation

The Big Idea

Achieving mastery of addition and subtraction facts and learning to multiply are essential components of computation.

What Students Should Already Know

Students in Core Knowledge schools should be familiar with

Kindergarten

- add and subtract to 10, using concrete objects
- understand the plus sign (+)
- subtraction: the concept of "taking away"; understand the minus sign (–)

Grade 1

- know what a sum and a difference are
- know addition facts to 10 + 10 and corresponding subtraction facts (untimed mastery)
- add in any order
- know that when you add three numbers, you get the same sum regardless of grouping of addends
- know what happens when you add zero
- write addition and subtraction problems horizontally and vertically
- solve two-digit addition and subtraction problems with and without regrouping
- mentally subtract 10 from a two-digit number
- write an addition or subtraction equation to solve basic one-step story and picture problems in the form of ___ – 2 = 7; 5 + ____ = 7

What Students Need to Learn

- **Achieve timed mastery of addition facts (2 seconds) and master subtraction facts**
- **Know addition and subtraction fact families**
- **Estimate the sum and the difference**
- **Solve two-digit and three-digit addition and subtraction problems with and without regrouping; add three two-digit numbers**
- **Practice doubling (adding a number to itself)**
- **Understand addition and subtraction as inverse operations; use addition to check subtraction**
- **Recognize the "times" sign (x) and know what factor and product mean**
- **Understand that you can multiply numbers in any order**
- **Multiplication facts: know the product of any single-digit number x 1, 2, 3, 4, 5 and know what happens when you multiply by 1, by 0, and by 10**
- **Solve simple word problems and equations with addition, subtraction, or multiplication**

What Students Will Learn in Future Grades

The *Core Knowledge Sequence* for mathematics emphasizes the importance of reviewing and building on prior knowledge. Related topics from the Grade 3 *Sequence* are listed below, and subsequent grades will continue to focus on strengthening and expanding these skills.

Grade 3

- mentally estimate sums and differences, and estimate products
- use mental computation strategies
- addition and subtraction with and without regrouping: find the sum (up to 10,000) of any two whole numbers and find the difference given two whole numbers of 10,000 or less
- master basic multiplication facts to 10 x 10 and mentally multiply by 10, 100, and 1,000
- multiply two whole numbers, with and without regrouping, in which one factor is 9 or less and the other is a multi-digit number up to three digits
- write numbers in expanded form using multiplication, for example: 9,278 = (9 x 1,000) + (2 x 100) + (7 x 10) + 8
- solve two-step word problems and solve word problems involving multiplication
- know basic division facts to 100 ÷ 10 and the meaning of dividend, divisor, and quotient
- know that you cannot divide by 0 and that any number divided by 1 = that number
- divide two- and three-digit dividends by one-digit divisors; solve division problems with remainders
- understand multiplication and division as inverse operations; check division by multiplying (and adding remainder)
- solve equations in the form of ___ x 9 = 63; 81 ÷ __ = 9
- solve problems with more than one operation, as in (43 – 32) x (5 + 3) = ___
- read and write expressions that use parentheses to indicate order of multiple operations

IV. Computation

Materials

flash cards of single-digit addition problems, p. 367

base ten blocks, pp. 369–370, pp. 373–374

counting sticks, pp. 369–370, pp. 373–374

rubber bands, pp. 369–370, pp. 373–374

real coins, plastic replicas, or pictures of coins, p. 369, p. 374

colored blocks, p. 372

manipulatives such as blocks, pp. 376–378

index cards, p. 380

progress chart for each child, p. 380

math notebooks, p. 380

chart paper, p. 380

Vocabulary

Student/Teacher Vocabulary

add: to find the sum of two or more numbers (S)

addends: the numbers that are added in an addition problem (T)

algorithm: a standard mathematical procedure that shows each step in a process (T)

difference: the answer to a subtraction problem (S)

equation: a statement that two mathematical expressions are equal (T)

estimate: (noun) a number close to an exact amount (T)
(verb) to find a number close to an exact amount (T)

fact family: a group of three numbers that work together to form addition and subtraction equations (S)

factors: the numbers multiplied in a multiplication problem (S)

product: the answer to a multiplication problem (S)

subtract: to determine the difference between two numbers (S)

sum: the answer to an addition problem (S)

Domain Vocabulary

Computation and associated words:
associative property, horizontally, vertically, estimate, regrouping, commutative property, add, subtract, plus sign, minus sign, sum, difference, take away, addition facts, zero, addends, digit, equation, additive identity, property, more, less, fewer, base ten

At a Glance

The most important ideas for you are:

- Addition and subtraction facts must be mastered in order for children to successfully solve more complicated computations, including two- and three-digit addition and subtraction.
- The commutative properties of addition and multiplication show that numbers can be added or multiplied *in any order* and the sum or product will be the same. The associative property of addition shows that addends can be *grouped* in any way and the sum will be the same.
- In a subtraction problem, the order numbers are written in is important.
- Fact families show the relationship between addition and subtraction facts.
- Estimation can be used to find answers that are close to an exact amount.
- Algorithms offer children a procedure for solving more difficult problems.
- Multiplication can be introduced as repeated addition.
- Learning to write and solve simple equations is an important early step in a child's mathematical development.

What Teachers Need to Know

Background

Learning to calculate is an important second-grade mathematics topic. The Grade 2 Core Knowledge curriculum introduces multiplication and continues the development of the addition and subtraction algorithms from Grade 1. It is important for children to learn both basic math concepts and operations simultaneously, because one cannot really be understood or mastered without the other. That is why it is so important to provide numerous examples and practice for each concept and operation that is covered in Grade 2 mathematics. Because children have many different approaches to learning, the use of concrete objects and manipulatives can help many in grasping such basic concepts as addition, subtraction, and multiplication.

A. Addition

Basic Facts

Mastery of single-digit addition facts is perhaps the most important basic skill in the mathematics curriculum for children in the lower grades. Without automatic recall of these facts, children will be handicapped in their attempts to master the standard arithmetic procedures. As an example, children should be able to answer 30 single-digit addition problems in one minute (2 seconds per problem).

> **Teaching Idea**
>
> **Some second graders will have difficulty writing fast enough to solve 30 single-digit addition problems in one minute. As an intermediary step for these children, use flash cards and solicit correct verbal answers on an individual basis. As you show a child a card, urge him/her to answer as rapidly as possible.**

Fundamentals of Addition

The sum of two or more numbers is the answer you get from adding them. Each number being added is called an addend. Take a look at this example:

$$1 + 2 + 3 = 6$$

The numbers 1, 2, and 3 are addends, and the number 6 is the sum.

Children should compute sums when the numerals are written horizontally and when they are written vertically. For example, they should be able to write correct answers to calculations posed in either of these forms:

$$5 + 7 + 46 = \_\_\_ \quad \text{or} \quad \begin{array}{r} 5 \\ 7 \\ +\ 46 \\ \hline \end{array}$$

Encountering the horizontal form helps to prepare children for the kinds of equations they will see later in algebra. When a problem presented horizontally is difficult to calculate mentally, second graders should recognize that they can simply rewrite the problem in vertical form in order to use the addition algorithm.

Commutative and Associative Properties of Addition

Children in Core Knowledge schools should have been introduced to the commutative property of addition. The commutative property says that two numbers can be added in either order. Here are some examples:

$$9 + 8 = 8 + 9$$

$$21 + 53 = 53 + 21$$

Children do not need to know this property by name, but they should be aware that numbers can be added in any order. An example children might encounter is $1 + 2 = 3$ and $2 + 1 = 3$.

The associative property of addition is another fundamental principle of numbers. Children aren't required to know this property by name until Grade 5, but they should be aware of the idea. The associative property of addition says that the sum of three numbers is the same regardless of where the parentheses are placed. More specifically, the associative property of addition says that for any three numbers A, B, and C,

$$(A + B) + C = A + (B + C)$$

For example, when A = 3, B = 4, and C = 5,

$$(3 + 4) + 5 = 3 + (4 + 5)$$

That is,

$$7 + 5 = 3 + 9$$

The numbers 9 and 7 come from adding the numbers inside the parentheses first. Since both sides of the equation equal 12, the associative property of addition is verified for this particular example. The associative property holds for any choice of numbers substituting for A, B, and C.

Because of the associative property, it doesn't matter where parentheses are placed. Therefore, sums of three or more numbers usually appear without any parentheses, and this is particularly true for materials used in Grade 2.

Teaching Idea

Rearranging numbers to simplify addition helps children perform mental calculations. Consider the following:

$$9 + 8 + 1 + 5 + 2 = ?$$

In this example, adding 9 + 1 and 8 + 2 gives 10 + 10. The remaining addend is 5, so the total is 2 groups of ten and 5 ones. The sum is 25.

Why is it so helpful for children to understand the basic principles of these properties? Used together, the commutative and associative properties of addition allow you to change the order of addends and regroup them in whatever way makes a calculation easier. For example, consider

$$\underline{9} + 8 + \underline{1}$$

You may add left to right, or in any order, but the calculation is a little easier if you add the two underlined numbers first. The advantage is that $9 + 1 = 10$ and it is easy to add 10 to another number. Instead of trying to explain this technique to children using the terms "commutative property" and "associative property," teachers could call this the "any order property." Children can use this strategy to add numbers in any order necessary to make calculations easier.

Estimating Sums

To estimate is to find a number close to an exact amount. Estimation is a useful skill for everyday commerce, and it can be used as a rough check of exact calculations of sums and differences. The ability to make good estimates and knowing when to use them builds a kind of common sense with numbers. Talk to children about when to use estimation to find an answer that is close to, but not exactly the same as, the sum. For example, if you wanted to guess about how many jellybeans are in a large jar, you would use estimation. The word *about* is a clue that an exact answer is not needed. Other words that indicate an exact answer is not needed are *around, approximately, nearly,* and *roughly.*

Rounding is a valuable tool in estimation (see the subsection "Rounding," on pp. 347–348). For example, to estimate the sum for 87 + 26, you could round both numbers to the nearest ten and then add them. An estimate for the sum is then

90 + 30 = 120. The exact sum is 113. Since both of the original addends, 87 and 26, were rounded up, you know even without calculating the exact sum that the estimate is larger than the exact sum.

Estimation can also be used to check to see if sums are reasonable. Using the example above, you could add 87 + 26 and then use estimation to make sure your sum of 113 is close to your estimation of 120. This is a good strategy to introduce in the early grades.

The Addition Algorithm

Children entering Grade 2 who have followed the Core Knowledge curriculum will already be able to add two-digit numbers without regrouping ("carrying"), and some may have learned to perform addition of two-digit numbers with regrouping. However, it is quite possible that children will have forgotten how to do these calculations, or, in some cases, never learned how.

Reviewing the basic ideas for two-digit addition without regrouping is a good idea before proceeding to larger numbers. Children may use manipulatives, such as base ten pieces or groups of ten counting sticks bundled with rubber bands and individual counting sticks, to add the ten pieces and one pieces to find a sum. Explorations with base ten models are extremely helpful to children in gaining a more intuitive understanding of the meaning of addition and will be helpful to use as a review as well.

Children should also review the addition algorithm. An algorithm is a step-by-step procedure for performing a calculation. Here is a sample calculation for the addition algorithm that does not involve regrouping:

$$\begin{array}{r} 21 \\ +\ 53 \\ \hline 74 \end{array}$$

The calculation 21 + 53 = 74 is carried out in two steps: adding 1 + 3 in the ones column and 2 + 5 in the tens column. This algorithm reduces the problem of calculating 21 + 53 to two single-digit additions. For this reason and others, learning the single-digit addition facts is crucial. Why does this algorithm work and how can it be explained? The main ingredient is the base ten structure of the number system.

21 = 2 tens + 1

53 = 5 tens + 3

In order to add these numbers, add the ones and add the tens:

$$\begin{array}{r} 2 \text{ tens} + 1 \\ +\ 5 \text{ tens} + 3 \\ \hline 7 \text{ tens} + 4 \end{array}$$

Then, 7 tens + 4 = 74 because of the meaning of 74.

Many children try to add the tens column before adding the ones column, but part of the step-by-step procedure they must learn is to begin with the ones column and move to the left. This step becomes critical when adding numbers that require regrouping.

Teaching Idea

Another approach is to use representations of dimes and pennies. Plastic replicas of these coins are available, but sometimes it is enough to use pictures of the coins or eventually to ask children to imagine the coins. One possible format looks like this:

dimes	pennies
2	1
+ 5	3
7	4

The tens column gives the number of dimes, and the ones column gives the number of pennies from this addition of money. As children become more proficient, the labels *pennies* and *dimes* can be discarded.

Teaching Idea

An explanation of the addition algorithm for two- or three-digit numbers can be given with the help of manipulatives such as counting sticks bundled with rubber bands in groups of ten, along with individual sticks, or by using base ten blocks.

The generalization of the addition algorithm for three-digit numbers, without regrouping, follows in a natural way. Using manipulatives first to introduce the idea of adding three-digit numbers, follow by asking children to think of a way to apply the addition algorithm to solve these kinds of problems. Children may be able to discover the technique on their own, but you should also use the same models as described previously to show children the algorithm steps to add three-digit numbers without regrouping.

The case of adding two-digit numbers with regrouping should be reviewed before adding three-digit numbers with regrouping is introduced. Consider the addition problem 26 + 57 = ? Again, children will benefit from first using manipulatives to review how to add these numbers. How does the addition algorithm deal with this problem?

Here is an explanation:

26 = 2 tens + 6

57 = 5 tens + 7

These numbers can be added in this form:

2 tens	**+**	**6**
5 tens	**+**	**7**
7 tens	**+**	**13**

To complete the calculation, write 13 = 1 ten + 3. This is where the regrouping occurs. 13 ones is the same as 1 ten and 3 ones. Then 7 tens + 13 can be calculated as:

7 tens + 0

1 ten + 3

8 tens + 3 = 83

This calculation can be streamlined and written more concisely in the form of the standard addition algorithm. The digit 8 in 83 comes from adding 2 tens and 5 tens to the 1 ten from 13.

$$\begin{array}{r} ^{1}\\ 26 \\ +\,57 \\ \hline 83 \end{array}$$

The small numeral 1 above the 2 comes from the 1 in 13.

When three-digit numbers are added, regrouping a sum from the ones column works in the same way. It is also sometimes necessary to regroup the sum from the tens column and carry a one to the hundreds column. Consider as an example 450 + 270 = ? To focus attention on the tens column and hundreds column, the numbers in this example have zeros in the ones column.

The usual format for the addition algorithm looks like this:

$$\begin{array}{r} ^{1}\\ 450 \\ +\,270 \\ \hline 720 \end{array}$$

Regrouping can occur for more than one column, as in this example:

$$\begin{array}{r} {\scriptstyle 1\,1} \\ 468 \\ +\ 275 \\ \hline 743 \end{array}$$

In the calculation above, starting in the ones column, the sum is 13. The 13 ones are regrouped into 1 ten and 3 ones. The 1 ten is placed in the tens column, leaving the 3 as the placeholder for the ones column of the sum. The tens column is calculated by adding 1 + 6 + 7 to get 14. This group of 14 tens is regrouped into 1 hundred and 4 tens. The 1 hundred is placed in the hundreds column, leaving the 4 as the placeholder in the tens column. Finally, the hundreds are added: 1 + 4 + 2 = 7, indicating that there are 7 hundreds in the sum.

When teaching regrouping to children, it is important to remain consistent in using the term *regrouping* versus *carrying* because it more accurately represents what is happening.

Doubling

In those cases where children have not yet memorized the addition facts, they might start by memorizing the doubling facts:

$$1 + 1 = 2$$
$$2 + 2 = 4$$
$$3 + 3 = 6$$
$$4 + 4 = 8$$
$$5 + 5 = 10$$
$$6 + 6 = 12$$
$$7 + 7 = 14$$
$$8 + 8 = 16$$
$$9 + 9 = 18$$

The missing doubling fact, 10 + 10 = 20, deserves special consideration. It is valuable to use this example to stress the importance of place value. By its very definition, 20 is two groups of ten and zero ones. In other words, by its very meaning, 20 = 10 + 10.

Memorizing these doubling facts also helps children memorize the multiplication tables for the 2s. For example,

$$2 \times 7 = 7 + 7 = 14$$

Once children have committed the doubling facts to memory, they can use them to calculate other sums. For example, 7 + 8 may be thought of as 7 + 7 + 1, or 14 + 1, which is 15.

It is important that these kinds of methods not replace systematic memorization of all of the addition facts. Research in cognitive psychology points to the value of automatic recall of basic facts so as to free the working memory to deal with more challenging conceptual problems. A summary of some of that research appears on pp. 150–151 and 224 of *The Schools We Need: Why We Don't Have Them*, by

E. D. Hirsch, Jr. Children need to memorize the single-digit addition facts because doing so will free up "mental space" needed to master the arithmetic procedures and to tackle applications of mathematics.

B. Subtraction

Fundamentals of Subtraction

Just as the word *sum* means the answer that results from adding numbers, there is an analogous word for the answer to a subtraction problem. The answer to a subtraction problem is called a *difference*. The difference of two numbers is the number that results from subtracting the smaller one from the larger. For example, the difference between 9 and 7 is 2 because $9 - 7 = 2$. Later in this section, we will discuss how second graders can use the subtraction algorithm to calculate differences between multi-digit numbers.

First-grade children who have followed the *Core Knowledge Sequence* will have already made substantial progress toward computational fluency before they enter Grade 2. However, some children may have fallen behind the *Sequence*, moved to a Core Knowledge school only recently, or simply need review.

It is essential that children have a clear conceptual understanding of the meanings of addition and subtraction. If necessary, two piles of objects may be combined into one pile to illustrate addition; and from a given collection of objects, some may be taken away to illustrate subtraction in concrete terms. Learning addition and subtraction fact families bolsters the understanding of addition and subtraction and underscores the relationship between them.

Addition and subtraction facts can naturally be grouped into fact families. As an example, consider $3 + 4 = 7$. The fact family for $3 + 4 = 7$ has four members:

$$3 + 4 = 7$$
$$4 + 3 = 7$$
$$7 - 3 = 4$$
$$7 - 4 = 3$$

How can second-grade children understand why these four equations make a family? How are they related? The first two equations say that you can add 3 and 4 in either order and the result is still 7. In adult language, this is an example of the commutative property of addition (see the subsection "Commutative and Associative Properties of Addition," on pp. 367–368). For Grade 2 children, you can call this an example of the "any order property."

The subtraction statement $7 - 3 = 4$ says that 3 less than 7 is 4, or in other words, 7 is 3 more than 4. Now say this slightly differently: 3 more than 4 is 7. In symbols, this is: $4 + 3 = 7$. So the addition fact and the subtraction fact are really saying the same thing. The other subtraction statement, $7 - 4 = 3$, is related in the same way to $3 + 4 = 7$. It is very helpful to teach children to think of a related addition fact when they are learning subtraction facts.

The idea behind the addition and subtraction fact families applies to multi-digit numbers, too. Any addition calculation can be checked by performing a subtraction calculation, and any subtraction problem can be checked by performing an addition calculation. Here is an example:

Teaching Idea

For second graders having difficulty with fact families, concrete objects can be used to help them understand how addition and subtraction are related. For example, put three red blocks to one side and four blue blocks nearby. Ask children to count the blocks in each pile. Ask, "When I push these two piles together, how many blocks will there be?" The children should agree that there will be seven blocks. Push the blocks together and let the children count. Test their understanding by asking, "What is four plus three?" They should answer seven. Ask, "What is three plus four?" Again, the answer is seven. Next say, "If I take away all of the red blocks now, how many blocks will be left?" Let the children predict the answer first, then take away all of the red blocks and ask them to count. Test their understanding by asking, "What is seven take away three?" Then ask, "What is seven minus three?" This is really the same question but with the word *minus*. Once this subtraction is understood, put all of the red blocks back together with the blue blocks again. Ask children, "How many blocks will there be if I take away all of the blue blocks this time?" Again, ask the children to predict the answer and then take away the blue blocks. Ask them, "What is seven minus four?" Once this demonstration is understood, review the fact family. Ask them for the answers to: 3 + 4 = ?, 4 + 3 = ?, 7 – 3 = ?, 7 – 4 = ?

Check this subtraction problem using addition:

$$\begin{array}{r} 86 \\ -\ 45 \\ \hline 41 \end{array}$$

To check that the difference is correct, we must verify that 45 + 41 = 86:

$$\begin{array}{r} 45 \\ +\ 41 \\ \hline 86 \end{array}$$

Memorizing the subtraction facts is essential for second graders. Children who cannot accurately recall the basic subtraction facts will find the subtraction algorithm more difficult than those children who have learned them. Even children who have successfully memorized the subtraction facts will need some periodic review and practice with them.

The Subtraction Algorithm

The basic concept of subtraction as "taking away" may, in principle, be applied to any number. For example, 74 – 21 may be calculated by removing 21 objects from 74 objects and counting the 53 objects that remain. It is also possible to calculate 74 – 21 by counting backward 21 units, starting with 74: 73, 72, 71, . . . , 55, 54, 53. The answer is 53.

However, these counting procedures are awkward and time-consuming, especially for larger numbers. The subtraction algorithm takes advantage of the base ten structure of numbers to provide a more efficient way to calculate differences.

> **Teaching Idea**
>
> **As with addition, manipulatives, such as sticks bundled with rubber bands in groups of ten, along with individual sticks, or base ten blocks, can be used to illustrate subtraction.**

First-grade children following the Core Knowledge curriculum are expected to calculate differences of two-digit numbers, and some may have even learned how to regroup (or "borrow") in order to perform these calculations. However, some second graders may not have been exposed to the subtraction algorithm and others will benefit from a review of the fundamental ideas.

Here is the subtraction algorithm applied to 74 – 21, an example that does not require regrouping:

$$\begin{array}{r} 74 \\ -\ 21 \\ \hline 53 \end{array}$$

This algorithm reduces the subtraction problem 74 – 21 into two simple, single-digit subtractions: 4 – 1 = 3, the digit in the ones column, and 7 – 2 = 5, the digit in the tens column. The value of learning the single-digit subtraction facts can be seen already in this example, but the need for memorization increases when regrouping is involved. If children must struggle to calculate subtractions like 7 – 2, they are more likely to be confused by increasingly elaborate procedures of arithmetic algorithms (step-by-step procedures) as they progress in elementary school.

Why does the subtraction algorithm work, and how can it be explained to children? As with the addition algorithm, the subtraction algorithm relies on the base ten structure of numbers.

74 = 7 tens + 4

From this number, we want to take away 21.

21 = 2 tens + 1

That is, we want to take away 2 tens from 7 tens, and take away 1 one from 4 ones.

$$\begin{array}{r} \text{7 tens} \\ -\ \text{2 tens} \\ \hline \text{5 tens} \end{array} \quad \text{and} \quad \begin{array}{r} \text{4 ones} \\ -\ \text{1 one} \\ \hline \text{3 ones} \end{array}$$

This leaves 5 tens + 3 ones, or 53. The same calculation can be presented this way:

$$\begin{array}{r} \text{7 tens} + 4 \\ -\ \text{2 tens} + 1 \\ \hline \text{5 tens} + 3 \end{array}$$

Without regrouping, the extension of the subtraction algorithm to three-digit numbers follows in a natural way. As with addition, manipulatives, such as individual counting sticks and sticks bundled with rubber bands in groups of ten, or base ten blocks, can be used to illustrate subtraction while teaching the algorithm.

The extra step of regrouping is sometimes required to perform a subtraction calculation. Here is an example:

$$\begin{array}{r} 53 \\ -\ 28 \\ \hline \end{array}$$

Starting with the ones column, children are confronted with 3 – 8 = ? It is not possible to take 8 ones away from only 3 ones, so something else must be done. One may still take advantage of the base ten system of numbers for this problem by regrouping 53.

53 = 5 tens + 3 ones

One of the groups of ten is the same as 10 ones. So 53 is the same as 4 tens and 10 + 3 ones. That is,

53 = 4 tens + 13 ones

Now the subtraction can be done by columns for ones and tens; 53 – 28 can be calculated this way:

$$\begin{array}{r} \text{4 tens} + 13 \\ -\ \text{2 tens} + 8 \\ \hline \text{2 tens} + 5 \end{array}$$

This procedure can be streamlined like this:

$$\begin{array}{r} {\scriptstyle 4\ \ 1} \\ \not{5}\ 3 \\ -\ 2\ 8 \\ \hline 2\ 5 \end{array}$$

Crossing out the 5 and writing 4 above it indicates 4 tens. The extra ten becomes the 1 in front of the 3 indicating 13 in the ones column. Notice that adding 10 to a digit in the ones column is the number one gets by putting a 1 to the left of it, as above. By using manipulatives before and during the instruction of the subtraction algorithm with regrouping, you will help children gain a clear conceptual understanding of the procedure.

Teaching Idea

Dimes and pennies, or their replicas and pictures, can be used to explain regrouping for two-digit subtraction problems. Start with 53¢ in the form of 5 dimes and 3 pennies. The problem is to find what is left after taking away 28¢. "Cash in" one of the dimes for ten pennies. Now from the 53¢ in the form of 4 dimes and 13 pennies, remove 28¢ by removing 2 dimes and 8 pennies. Count the 2 dimes and 5 pennies that remain. The answer is 25¢. To help children believe that regrouping actually "works," they can solve the problem again by starting with 53 pennies and removing 28 of them, one at a time. They should compare results.

For three-digit numbers, it is sometimes necessary to regroup 1 hundred into 10 tens.

Regrouping in subtraction problems for three-digit numbers can involve all three columns. The most complicated situation occurs when 0 is a placeholder in the tens column as in a subtraction problem like this:

```
  9 0 2
- 3 5 4
-------
```

It is not possible to regroup or "borrow" directly from the tens column in order to carry out the subtraction in the ones column. This is because the placeholder in the tens column of the number 904 is zero. There are no tens available to regroup. The first step is therefore to regroup one of the hundreds into 10 tens so that the subtraction becomes:

```
  8
    1
  9̶ 0 2
- 3 5 4
-------
```

The superscript above the zero indicates that there are now 10 tens in the tens column. As with the earlier examples, the notation signifies that 902 has been regrouped as follows:

902 = 9 hundreds + 0 tens + 2 = 8 hundreds + 10 tens + 2 ones

Now start over and look at the tens and ones columns again. In the above form, the tens and ones columns may be regrouped without involving the hundreds column further.

The calculation can be streamlined this way:

```
  8 9
    1̶ 1
  9̶ 0̶ 2
- 3 5 4
-------
```

The notation now means that 902 has been regrouped further:

902 = 8 hundreds + 10 tens + 2 = 8 hundreds + 9 tens + 12 ones

The subtraction may now be carried out column by column. The difference has 12 – 4 ones; 9 – 5 tens; and 8 – 3 hundreds.

```
  8 9
    1̶ 1
  9̶ 0̶ 2
- 3 5 4
-------
  5 4 8
```

The calculation shows that 902 – 354 = 548. Children can check this answer by using the addition algorithm to compute 354 + 548 and verify that the sum is 902.

Children should compute differences when the numerals are written horizontally and when they are written vertically. When a problem presented horizontally is difficult to calculate mentally, second graders should recognize that they can simply rewrite the problem in vertical form.

Estimating Differences

Just as when estimating sums, rounding can also be used to estimate differences. For example, 86 – 27 can be estimated by rounding each of these numbers to the nearest ten and mentally computing the difference. After rounding, we have the estimate 90 – 30 = 60. The exact difference is 59. For more information, see the subsection “Rounding,” on pp. 347–348.

Just as when estimating sums, children should learn when to estimate to find an answer that is close to, but not exactly, the same as the difference. Some words in problems that indicate an exact answer is not needed are *about, around, approximately, nearly,* and *roughly.*

Estimation can also be used to check to see if differences are reasonable. Using the example above, you could subtract 87 – 26 and then use estimation to make sure your difference of 59 is close to your estimation of 60. Second-grade children may not use this strategy often, but it is a good one to introduce in the early grades.

C. Introduction to Multiplication

Elementary school children following the *Core Knowledge Sequence* are introduced to multiplication for the first time in Grade 2. It is important that they start on the right foot with a clear understanding of the meaning of multiplication.

Multiplication by 1 and by 0 are discussed below. Multiplication by other whole numbers is simply shorthand notation for repeated addition. For example,

3 x 4 *means* 4 + 4 + 4

Think of 3 groups of 4 objects. Notice that the meaning of 4 x 3 is 3 + 3 + 3 + 3, and this is different from the meaning of 3 x 4, even though the result is the same (see the commutative property of multiplication on p. 377).

A concrete way to represent multiplication to children is to create an array, or a rectangle, that shows numbers being multiplied. Using the example above, create a rectangle that has 3 rows of 4 squares each. The array would look like this:

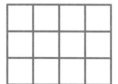

3 x 4

Children can draw or make their own arrays using blocks or other objects. If you turn the rectangular array 90 degrees, you can also show children that the rectangle now has 4 rows of 3 squares each. This can be linked to the discussions of the commutative property of multiplication (see p. 377).

Multiplication can be thought of as repeated addition even for larger numbers. However, larger numbers demonstrate how much easier it is to multiply instead of add. Think of 5 groups of 72 objects.

5 x 72 *means* 72 + 72 + 72 + 72 + 72

Multiplying a number by two is the sum of that number with itself.

2 x 7 *means* 7 + 7

The multiplication of any number by 1 is just that number. For example,

1 x 6 = 6

A good way to introduce multiplication to children is to pose a problem, such as this one:

Five children each brought two books to return to the library. How many books will be returned to the library?

Ask children to think of a way to solve the problem, and give them manipulatives to use. Most children will probably use repeated addition to find a solution, by adding

2 + 2 + 2 + 2 + 2 = 10

Encourage children to record their strategy on paper. Then show them how you can change the addition problem to a multiplication problem:

5 x 2 = 10

Just as the answer to an addition problem is called a *sum,* and the answer to a subtraction problem is called a *difference,* the answer to a multiplication problem is called a *product.* When numbers are multiplied, the answer is the product of those numbers. Each of the multiplied numbers is called a *factor.* For example, in the number sentence 3 x 4 = 12, the numbers 3 and 4 are each factors, and 12 is the product.

Two factors can be multiplied in either order and the product will be the same. This is true not only for whole numbers, but also for fractions and decimals. Because of its importance, this property of multiplication is given a name, the *commutative property of multiplication.* Here is what it says:

For any two numbers A and B, it is always true that

A x B = B x A

For example, if A = 5 and B = 3, the commutative property of multiplication says that 5 x 3 = 3 x 5. This means that 5 groups of 3 added together gives the same sum as 3 groups of 5 added together. A concrete way to demonstrate this concept to children is to have them make or draw rows of objects to represent these numbers and verify that the product is the same. They will see that 5 rows of 3 is the same as 3 rows of 5. See the example below:

★★★	★★★★★
★★★	★★★★★
★★★	★★★★★
★★★	
★★★	
5 rows of 3 = 15	**3 rows of 5 = 15**

Children should use this strategy with many different numbers to prove to themselves that changing the order of factors does not change the product.

Second-grade children should not be expected to know the commutative property of multiplication by name, but they do need to know that two factors can always be multiplied in either order with the same result. Knowing this is especially useful when memorizing multiplication tables. It is not until Grade 5 that students following the Core Knowledge curriculum are expected to know this basic property and others by name. In Grade 2, teachers can refer to this as the "any order property."

Initially, children can learn the multiplication tables by calculating sums, or counting by twos, threes, fours, and fives. However, during Grade 2, children should memorize these multiplication tables.

x	0	1	2	3	4	5
0	0	0	0	0	0	0
1	0	1	2	3	4	5
2	0	2	4	6	8	10
3	0	3	6	9	12	15
4	0	4	8	12	16	20
5	0	5	10	15	20	25

This requires practice and repetition. Children should also solve word problems involving multiplication. Further discussion of word problems is given in the subsection "Solving Problems and Equations," on pp. 378–380.

Multiplication by 0 is easy in the sense that the answer is always the same; the answer is always 0. Whenever at least one factor is zero, the product is zero. This is part of the definition of multiplication. For example,

0 x 3 = 0, 796 x 0 = 0, and 0 x 0 = 0

This can be demonstrated to children by using manipulatives such as blocks. Ask children to make zero groups of three blocks. They will quickly realize that if you have zero groups of three, you do not need to group any blocks.

Multiplication by 10 should be explained in terms of place value and the base ten structure of numbers. A representative problem is 3 x 10:

3 x 10 = 10 + 10 + 10

This is 3 groups of 10, and that is exactly what the numeral 30 means. Recall that 30 means 3 tens + 0 ones. So,

3 x 10 = 3 tens = 30

Children might also benefit by counting by tens in order to calculate 3 x 10: ten, twenty, thirty. Notice the important fact that multiplication by ten is accomplished by writing a zero to the right of the other whole number factor. For example, the product of 3 with 10 is three followed by a zero, i.e., 30.

Teaching Idea

The multiplication algorithm for multi-digit numbers is introduced in Grade 3. However, you can challenge children with a problem like 2 x 431 as part of a classroom discussion. Children's responses to a problem like this can give you an idea of how well children understand the concept of multiplication. Since 2 x 431 means 431 + 431, second graders can solve this problem by addition.

D. Solving Problems and Equations

Problem solving and the practice of skills are crucially important in the mathematical education of children. No mathematics curriculum is complete without those components, and Grade 2 Core Knowledge curriculum is no exception.

Problems can be used to promote understanding of the relationship between addition and subtraction, and for practice of basic number facts. What number minus 9 equals 7? The answer is the same as the answer to: 7 + 9 = what? Another sample problem asks, 7 + what = 16? The answer is the same as the answer to: 16 – 7 = what?

Recognizing the connections between addition and subtraction in these contexts deepens children's understanding of arithmetic. These problems are also early steps toward algebra. Problems such as 4 X ___ = 8 can be used to help children learn the multiplication tables. This type of problem also helps pave the way for the concept of division, which is introduced in Grade 3.

Number sentences like those above arise naturally in the solutions of basic word problems. Here are some examples:

Some children were riding a bus. When the bus stopped, 9 children got off the bus, and 7 children stayed on the bus. How many children were on the bus before it stopped?

You might first want to try a similar problem that involves numbers smaller than 7 and 9. Children might also find it helpful to draw pictures. Eventually, their solutions should be linked to one of these statements:

a) ___ – 9 = 7

b) ___ – 7 = 9

c) 7 + 9 = ___

d) 9 + 7 = ___

A child could reasonably connect any one of these number statements directly to this word problem. Notice that when the blanks are replaced by 16, these equations form a fact family (see the subsection "Fundamentals of Subtraction," on pp. 372–373).

A teacher had 7 pencils. She found some more and then had 16. How many did she find?

Here again, when the blanks below are replaced by 9, each member of a fact family may be directly connected to this word problem:

a) 7 + ___ = 16

b) ___ + 7 = 16

c) 16 – ___ = 7

d) 16 – 7 = ___

Here is a related type of problem:

I have 3 oranges and 7 apples. How many more apples than oranges do I have?

Children see the phrase *many more* and sometimes want to add 3 and 7 instead of subtract 3 from 7. Understanding fact families can help to clarify misconceptions like this one.

Word problems help children understand practical applications of mathematics, and they can help clarify fundamental concepts.

There are 8 elephants in a zoo. They are standing in groups. How many groups of elephants are there if each group has 4 elephants?

This word problem may be associated with the number sentence 4 X ___ = 8.

These sample problems represent only a limited portion of the kinds of problems appropriate for Grade 2. Good mathematics programs include liberal doses of word problems throughout the school year. Children should solve word problems involving multiplication and word problems involving multi-digit addition and subtraction, including money amounts. In some cases, word problems can involve more than one step. Many standardized exams, including Core Knowledge tests, include problems whose solutions require more than one step.

Maria had 3 quarts and 2 cups of milk.
How many cups can she pour?

Children need to recall that there are 4 cups in one quart and, therefore, 3 x 4 cups or 12 cups in 3 quarts. Then, they need to add 2 cups to 12 cups, for a total of 14 cups.

Mike had 35 pieces of candy. He had 6 friends and gave 3 pieces of candy away to each of them. How many pieces of candy did he have left?

To solve this problem, children must find 3 x 6 and subtract the product from 35. A child who has memorized the multiplication tables will find problems like this one easier to solve than a child who needs to spend time calculating 3 x 6, while perhaps losing track of his or her strategy for solving the original problem.

Second graders can solve some basic fraction word problems associated with Core Knowledge guidelines (see the section "Fractions," on pp. 352–356). Here are three examples:

1. If a pizza is divided into thirds, how many pieces make one whole pizza?

2. Fill in the missing numerals

$1 = \frac{?}{5} \qquad \frac{4}{?} = 1$

3. Which fraction is larger, $\frac{1}{3}$ or $\frac{1}{10}$?

For this last problem, it might be helpful for children to have access to some picture representations of fractions, such as those mentioned in the section "Fractions."

The Big Idea in Review

Achieving mastery of addition and subtraction facts and learning to multiply are essential components of computation.

Review

Below are some ideas for ongoing assessment and review activities. These are not meant to constitute a comprehensive list.

- Children can make addition and subtraction fact flash cards. Have them write problems on index cards and take turns quizzing each other on the addition and subtraction facts.
- After the class has become proficient in addition and subtraction facts, have drills in the mornings as a warm-up. You may also want to record scores on individual charts to help the children see their progress. After practicing the drills without timing them, introduce timed drills to see how many facts children can correctly name in one minute.
- Each morning, have a word problem of the day for the class to solve in their math notebooks. Ask children to solve the problem and then write about the strategy they used to solve it.
- Have the class create their own word problems to accompany a simple addition or subtraction problem, such as 22 + 45. For example, a farmer planted 22 rows of corn and 45 rows of bean plants. How many rows did he plant? Have the class work together to create word problems that you write on chart paper, and then have children write and share their own problems with the class.

More Resources

A good mathematics program follows sound cognitive principles and allows many opportunities for thoughtful and varied practice to build mastery of important skills. For advice on suitable mathematics programs, contact the Foundation.

The titles listed below are offered as a representative sample of materials and not a complete list of everything that is available.

For children —

These books are generally intended to be read aloud, though some children may be able to read parts or all of the simpler texts.

- *Anno's Mysterious Multiplying Jar,* by Masaichiro and Mitsumasa Anno (Puffin, 1999). Paperback, 48 pages, ISBN 0698117530.
- *Each Orange Had 8 Slices,* by Paul Giganti (HarperTrophy, 1999). A clever takeoff on the "As I was going to St. Ives" riddle—"On my way to Grandma's I saw two fat cows. Each cow had two calves. Each calf had four skinny legs . . . . How many fat cows . . . calves . . . legs were there in all?"(from the book). Paperback, 32 pages, ISBN 068813985X.
- *The Grapes of Math,* by Greg Tang and illustrated by Harry Briggs (Scholastic, 2001). Hardcover, ISBN 043921033X.
- *If You Hopped Like a Frog,* by David M. Schwartz and illustrated by James Warhola (Scholastic, 1999). "If you hopped like a frog, you could jump from home plate to first base in one mighty leap" (from the book). Several examples like this encourage children to multiply their own height, weight, etc., to see what they could do if they had proportionally the same abilities as animals. Some of the math will be too challenging, but the concept will be intriguing. Library binding, 32 pages, ISBN 0590098578.
- *Too Many Kangaroo Things to Do (MathStart: Multiplying, Level 3),* by Stuart J. Murphy and illustrated by Kevin O'Malley (Scott Foresman/Pearson K–12, 1996). Paperback, 40 pages, ISBN 0064467120. For more MathStart books, such as *Shark Swimathon,* a lesson in double-digit subtraction, go to www.harperchildrens. com/teacher and search for them by series title. For Stuart Murphy titles by other publishers, check with any bookstore or library.

For teachers —

- *About Teaching Mathematics: A K–8 Resource,* by Marilyn Burns (Math Solutions Publications, 1992). Paperback, 296 pages, ISBN 0941355055.
- ETA Cuisenaire carries the very useful and popular math manipulatives, Cuisenaire Rods, as well as many resources for using the rods and other products. Cuisenaire Rod activities can be used to supplement your current math program, or may already be integrated with published curricula (for example, Miquon Math, published by Key Curriculum Press). Contact ETA Cuisenaire at www.etacuisenaire.com or 1-800-445-5985 for a free catalog to peruse their complete product line.
- *Family Math,* by Jean Kerr Stenmark, Virginia Thompson, and Ruth Cossey (Equals, 1986). This generous, helpful book provides clear directions for fun, yet substantive, math activities that parents can do with children from 5 to 12 years old. Includes word problems, measurement, geometry, estimation, arithmetic, and lots of ideas for things to make. Provides a great way to supplement (not replace) math instruction in school. Paperback, ISBN 0912511060.
- *Mental Math in the Primary Grades,* by Jack Hope and others (Pearson Learning, 1997). Paperback, 128 pages, ISBN 0866514341.
- A+ Math, www.aplusmath.com, among its other offerings, lets you create printable flash cards online.
- AAA Math, www.aaamath.com, features hundreds of pages of basic math skills with interactive practice arranged by grade level and topic. Includes challenge activities. These activities plus additional ones are also available on a CD-ROM.
- Ask Dr. Math, www.mathforum.com/dr.math, has a number of interesting question-and-answer items on such topics as "Why does 2 + 2 = 4?" and "How many seconds are there in 1,000 years?" You can also search the site for answers to particular questions or submit your own.
- Houghton Mifflin MathSteps, www.eduplace.com/math/mathsteps/index.html, is a teacher support site with lesson plans, background information, and helpful tips.

V. Measurement

The Big Idea

Length, height, weight (mass), capacity (volume), temperature, and time can all be estimated and measured by instruments.

What Students Should Already Know

Students in Core Knowledge schools should be familiar with

Kindergarten

- identify familiar instruments of measurement, such as ruler, scale, thermometer
- compare objects according to linear measure, weight (mass), capacity (volume), and temperature
- sequence and compare duration of events and orient them in time
- read a clock face and tell time to the hour
- name the days of the week and the months of the year

Grade 1

- measure length using nonstandard units, inches, feet, and centimeters
- compare weights of objects using a balance scale, and measure weight in nonstandard units and in pounds
- estimate and measure capacity in cups; identify quart, gallon
- associate temperature in degrees Fahrenheit with weather
- read a clock face and tell time to the half-hour
- know the days of the week and the months of the year, both in order and out of sequence

What Students Need to Learn

- **Know that one foot = 12 inches and the abbreviations: ft., in.**
- **Measure and draw line segments in inches to ½ inch**
- **Estimate linear measurements, then measure to check estimates**
- **Estimate and measure weight in pounds, and know abbreviation: lb.**
- **Measure liquid volumes in pints, quarts, gallons**
- **Compare U.S. and metric liquid volumes: quart and liter (one liter is a little more than one quart)**
- **Measure and record temperature in degrees Fahrenheit to the nearest two degrees and know the degree sign: °**
- **Read a clock face and tell time to five-minute intervals, and know how to distinguish time as AM or PM; understand noon and midnight**
- **Solve problems on elapsed time (how much time has passed?)**
- **Using a calendar, identify the date, day of the week, month, and year**
- **Write the date using words (for name of month) and numbers**

What Students Will Learn in Future Grades

The *Core Knowledge Sequence* for mathematics emphasizes the importance of reviewing and building on prior knowledge. Related topics from the Grade 3 *Sequence* are listed below, and subsequent grades will continue to focus on strengthening and expanding these skills.

Grade 3

- make linear measurements in yards, feet, inches, centimeters, and meters
- know that one yard = 36 inches; 3 feet = 1 yard;
  1 meter = 100 centimeters; 1 meter is a little more than 1 yard
- measure and draw line segments in inches (to ¼ inch), and in centimeters
- estimate and measure weight in pounds and ounces; grams and kilograms
- know abbreviations: oz., g, kg
- estimate and measure capacity in liters
- know that 1 quart = 2 pints; 1 gallon = 4 quarts
- measure and record temperature in degrees Celsius
- identify freezing point of water as 32°F = 0°C
- read a clock face and tell time to the minute as either AM or PM; tell time in terms of both "minutes before" and "minutes after" the hour
- write the date using only numbers

V. Measurement

Materials

rulers, p. 385, p. 388
balance scale, pp. 386
cup, pint, and quart containers, p. 386
water, rice, sand, salt, or dried beans, p. 386
containers of various sizes and shapes, p. 386
measuring cups, p. 386
thermometer, p. 387
demonstration clock, or paper plates and brads, pp. 387–389
calendars, p. 387
time line, p. 388
number line, p. 388
various liquid containers from home, p. 388
math journals or notebooks, p. 388
chart paper, p. 388
various objects from around the room to weigh, p. 388
self-sticking notes, p. 389

Vocabulary

Student/Teacher Vocabulary

capacity: the volume of a solid shape expressed in units of liquid measurement (T)

mass: a measure of the quantity of matter (T)

measure: (noun) the length, dimensions, capacity, or quantity of something (T)
(verb) to find the length, dimensions, capacity, or quantity of something (S)

ruler: a tool used to measure length (S)

scale: a tool used to measure weight (S)

temperature: the degree of hot or cold of an object or space (S)

thermometer: a tool used to measure temperature (S)

volume: the amount of space inside a solid shape (T)

weight: the force of gravity on an object, or a measure of the heaviness of an object (S)

Domain Vocabulary

Measurement and associated words:
ruler, scale, thermometer, inch, foot, centimeter, short, long, tall, line segment, weight, pound, kilogram, heavy, light, cup, pint, quart, gallon, ounce, liter, glass, can, bottle, Fahrenheit, Celsius, calendar, clock, hour, minute, second, noon, midnight, elapsed time, week, month, year

At a Glance

The most important ideas for you are:

- The length of an object can be measured using a ruler with units of inches, feet, or centimeters.
- Weight can be compared or measured using a scale, and in the United States the pound is the common unit of measurement for weight.
- The concept of capacity (volume) can be illustrated through the use of containers for fluids or substances like rice or sand. Cups, pints, quarts, and gallons are common units of capacity in the United States.
- Length, weight (mass), and capacity (volume) can all be estimated.
- Temperature is measured with a thermometer, and the Fahrenheit scale is commonly used to measure weather temperatures in the United States.
- Time is measured with clocks and calendars. The duration of events can be compared using these tools.
- Time can be distinguished as AM or PM, with noon and midnight as important benchmarks.

What Teachers Need to Know

Background

In Kindergarten and Grade 1, children in Core Knowledge schools should have been introduced to the fundamental concepts of measurement. This year, children will learn how to estimate measurements and how to measure more accurately. Practical experience with making measurements and an understanding of various units of measurement give children a valuable foundation for applications in mathematics, science, and everyday life.

A. Linear Measure

Children following the *Sequence* are introduced to feet, inches, and centimeters in Grade 1. In Grade 2, they should continue working with these standard units of measurement but to greater precision, measuring lengths to the nearest half-inch instead of only the nearest inch. Standard units are important because they allow people to communicate unambiguously about measurements. Feet, inches, and centimeters are examples of standard units of measurement.

Children need practice choosing the appropriate unit of measurement to use. For example, which unit makes the most sense when measuring the length of a paper clip, a book, or a classroom wall? Although more than one unit could be used to measure any of these items, there is usually a unit that is most appropriate.

Many one-foot rulers have demarcations for centimeters on one edge and inches on the other. A centimeter is about the width of a child's finger. A quarter is about an inch wide. Being able to associate a standard unit with a familiar object can help children estimate lengths in terms of that unit.

When children first learn how to estimate measurements, it may be easier for them to make comparisons than to take a wild guess at a measurement. For example, ask children if their teacher is taller, shorter, or about the same as 6 feet. Is their math book taller, shorter, or about the same as 12 inches? You can also ask children to estimate something longer, such as the length of a board, and provide a 12-inch ruler as a visual cue. As children get better at estimating, frequently pose challenges such as estimating about how many centimeters long a pencil is, or about how many feet wide a basketball court is. Encourage children to discuss how they chose the unit and how they estimated the number of units it would take to measure an item. This awareness of the thought process is an important part of gaining a conceptual understanding of how to estimate measurements.

Second-grade children should practice measuring distances to the nearest half-inch and to the nearest centimeter. Reinforce the fact that there are 12 inches in a foot. Use abbreviations for feet (ft.), inches (in.), and centimeters (cm). One inch is about 2.54 centimeters. There are 100 centimeters in one meter. The prefix *centi* is a reminder; think of 100 cents in one dollar. A meter is approximately 39 inches. A yard is 3 feet, which is exactly 36 inches.

Teaching Idea

Discuss with children the importance of measurement skills in both mathematical and scientific applications. Children will use these skills in both subjects throughout their studies as well as in their everyday lives.

Teaching Idea

Divide your class into teams. Have each group make estimates of the length of a series of items. Allow children to choose the most appropriate unit of measurement, and have them record their estimates. When everyone is finished, have the teams compare and discuss their findings. Did some teams use a different strategy to estimate? Were the estimations consistent across the class? What would each team do differently next time, if anything?

B. Weight (Mass)

Weights can be compared by placing them in opposite trays of a balance scale like the one pictured. The tray with the lighter weight will rise, while the tray with the heavier weight will fall.

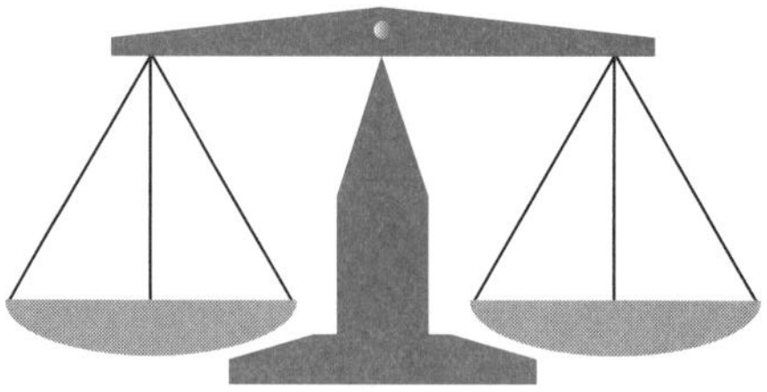

Make sure children know that the standard unit of weight in the United States is the pound and that the abbreviation for pound is lb. It is helpful to point out common items that weigh about one pound. For example, some books or two oranges weigh about one pound.

When teaching children how to estimate weight, it is again helpful to begin with comparisons. Does their math book weigh more, less, or about the same as one pound? Does their desk weigh more, less, or about the same as ten pounds? As children get better at estimating weight, you can have them estimate and then use a scale to compare the weight of objects.

Teaching Idea

Label a cup, a pint, and a quart container and show them to children. Have a child volunteer to put the containers in order from smallest to largest. Ask children how they could find out whether the containers are in the correct order. Demonstrate by filling each container and pouring it into another.

C. Capacity (Volume)

It is handy to remember that standard liquid volume measurements increase by doubling. There are:

2 cups in a pint

2 pints in a quart

2 quarts in a half-gallon

2 half-gallons in a gallon

Milk containers of various sizes will be familiar to many children. Some children may only need to see the different containers (cup, pint, quart, half-gallon, and gallon) to conceptualize the relationships among them. Others may need to pour a liquid or other substance from one container into another to understand these relationships. Water, rice, sand, salt, and dried beans can be easily poured from one container into another to compare capacities. It is helpful to use a wide variety of containers of different shapes and sizes when making comparisons.

Volume can be difficult for many children to conceptualize, and they will benefit from many hands-on experiences when learning how to estimate. Children can use a measuring cup or a container with a known volume to estimate and then measure the volume of another container by pouring units of water or another substance into the container until it is full. You can also ask children to compare the size of containers. Does the milk container hold more, less, or about the same amount as the jar?

In the metric system, widely used outside of the United States and for scientific purposes generally, a standard unit of volume is called a liter. One liter is slightly more than a quart (1 liter = 1.057 quarts). Soda sometimes comes in liter bottles.

D. Temperature

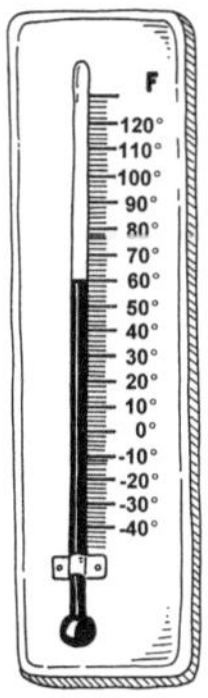

It is useful to remember that there are two widely used temperature scales, Fahrenheit and Celsius. The Fahrenheit scale is more commonly used in the United States. In this scale, water freezes at 32 degrees, more frequently written as 32° or 32°F. The superscript is the symbol (°) for degrees and *F* stands for *Fahrenheit*. Water boils at 212°F, and room temperature is about 72°F. It may happen that a second-grade classroom includes children from countries other than the United States, and they might think in terms of the Celsius temperature scale. To help them learn the Fahrenheit temperature scale, it is useful to know some corresponding temperatures in degrees Celsius. In the Celsius scale, water freezes at 0°C and it boils at 100°C (where *C* stands for *Celsius*). The room temperature of 72°F expressed in degrees Celsius is about 22°C. While children do not need to know these specific measurements in Grade 2, you may find it interesting to discuss briefly.

Reading a temperature from a thermometer may require children to count by twos, depending on the thermometer. For example, in the thermometer depicted here, each tick mark represents a temperature 2° higher than the tick mark below it. In Grade 2, children should learn how to measure and record temperature in degrees Fahrenheit to the nearest 2 degrees.

If a thermometer is posted outside the classroom, call attention to the outside temperature from time to time, and ask children to read the thermometer directly. Seasonal temperatures can be compared, and this can help to reinforce understanding of both temperature and the calendar.

Teaching Idea

Have children record the temperature daily during journal time or during math. Children will benefit from the practice, and interesting classroom discussions can occur when you compare changes and trends in temperature.

E. Time

Time is measured by clocks and calendars. The *Core Knowledge Sequence* expands on skills learned in the earlier grades. Second graders need to understand the meanings of the initials AM and PM. Placing "AM" after a clock time indicates that the time is after midnight and before noon, that is, in the morning. Placing "PM" after a clock time indicates that the time is after noon but before midnight. The letters in AM and PM are abbreviations for Latin words; AM stands for *ante meridian*, which means before noon, while PM stands for *post meridian*, which means after noon. There is no reason to confuse second graders unnecessarily with the Latin words, but if a curious second grader asks about the initials, it's good to have an answer. The changes between AM and PM occur at noon and midnight. Officially, noon is designated as 12:00 PM, and midnight is written as 12:00 AM.

Teaching Idea

Telling time on a clock is an important practical skill. In spite of the prevalence of digital clocks, it is still important to learn how to read conventional clocks. If a demonstration clock with a large face is not already available for classroom use, it is easy to write the numbers 1 to 12 along the circumference of a paper plate, cut out hour and minute hands from colored paper, and attach them with a brad.

Reading clock times in five-minute intervals relies heavily on being able to count by fives and understanding that there are 60 minutes in an hour. A diagram like the one on this page can serve as a stepping-stone in helping children learn to read clock times. Many commercial mathematics programs for Grade 2 include systematic treatments for teaching children how to tell time.

Children will have a chance to review ordinal numbers (see the subsection "Words for Numbers," on p. 345) when saying dates out loud. For example, the date May 21, 2005, is usually read as *May twenty-first, two thousand five,* rather than *May twenty-one, two thousand five*. Second graders should learn to use calendars to find the day of the week corresponding to a particular date and to be able to write and verbalize dates.

Teaching Idea

Post a time line in your room to review the idea of historical events happening before and after one another. Having a time line posted along with a number line will help the children identify passage of time when events happen, reviewing the concept of "before" and "after" and then connecting it to the idea of "greater than" and "less than"—moving up and down the line of dates and numbers.

Lessons on telling time may include discussions of duration so that children learn to compare lengths of time. Which lasts longer, the lunch period or recess? Look at how much the clock changes during each of these periods. A half-hour is the length of some television shows, and an hour is two of those. The duration of a half-hour television show is the time it takes a clock to go 30 minutes.

Children should be challenged with problems asking for the elapsed time between two times, such as from 3:15 PM to 3:45 PM, or 11:00 AM to 1:30 PM. For example, questions similar to the following can be asked:

If we leave the classroom at 2:15 PM to go to recess and return at 3:00 PM, how long will we be gone?

For children in Grade 2, it is helpful to provide a picture of a clock to use when determining elapsed time. Children may color in the portion of the clock between two times and use the clock markings to count the amount of time that passed. You can also teach children how to use tally marks for each increment of five minutes that passes. Be sure to discuss strategies used by children in solving these kinds of problems.

Review

The Big Idea in Review

Length, height, weight (mass), capacity (volume), temperature, and time can all be estimated and measured by instruments.

Below are some ideas for ongoing assessment and review activities. These are not meant to constitute a comprehensive list.

- Have children draw three lines of varying lengths on a piece of paper and measure each line with a ruler. Children should record their measurements next to each line. Then, have children trade papers with a partner and measure each other's lines to check for accuracy.
- Have the class conduct a scavenger hunt at home and bring in three empty containers that hold liquid. Make a class collection of these containers, and discover how much liquid each one can hold. Some liquid containers may have a capacity printed on the label. Explore whether the unit of measurement used is cups, pints, quarts, or gallons. If there is no capacity given, what unit of measurement could be used? What kinds of discoveries did the class make about liquid measurement and these containers? Have children record their discoveries about liquid measurement and containers in their math journals.
- On chart paper, make a list of pairs of common classroom objects. For example, list "a pencil and a crayon" and "a bottle of glue and a stapler." As a class, have children predict which object in each pair will weigh more. Record their predictions on the chart paper. Divide the class into groups, and give each group a pair of objects listed on the chart paper and a balance scale. Have each group compare their objects and record which one was heavier. Then, gather back together and share results, listing them on the class chart. Were the predictions correct?
- Post a daily schedule listing the times that the class will be in certain places, such as at lunch or during specialty classes. After reviewing this schedule with the class, have children make a personal schedule of activities for the rest of the day, when they are not at school. Children should record the time and name of each activity or event, such as brushing their teeth, catching the bus, or going to bed. Have children share their schedules with the class.

• One way to review the time on a clock and how to count by fives is to put self-sticking notes around the clock face counting by fives. The self-sticking note by the number 1 on the clock would show 5, the note by the number 2 would show 10, and so on, around the clock.

More Resources

A good mathematics program follows sound cognitive principles and allows many opportunities for thoughtful and varied practice to build mastery of important skills. For advice on suitable mathematics programs, contact the Foundation.

The titles listed below are offered as a representative sample of materials and not a complete list of everything that is available.

For children —

These books are generally intended to be read aloud, though some children may be able to read parts or all of the simpler texts.

• *Eating Fractions,* by Bruce McMillan (Scholastic, 1992). "Math was never so much fun or so wholesomely delicious. Recipes and suggestions for how children can use their new math skills to measure ingredients and prepare these kid-tested treats are included" (*Publishers Weekly*). Paperback, ISBN 0590437712.

• *How Big Is a Foot?* by Rolf Myller (Random House Children's Books, 1991). Humorously explains the "origin" of our basic measurement of length. Paperback, 48 pages, ISBN 0440404959.

• *Inchworm and a Half,* by Elinor J. Pinczes (Houghton Mifflin, 2003). On measuring and fractions. Paperback, 32 pages, ISBN 0618311017.

• *Measuring Penny,* by Loreen Leedy (Henry Holt & Company, 2000). From the author of *Mapping Penny's World,* another child's-eye perspective. In addition to traditional or standard measurements, Leedy also introduces children to nonstandard units, like "waist-high." Covers height, weight, volume, time, temperature, and money. Paperback, 32 pages, ISBN 0805065725.

• *Me Counting Time: From Seconds to Centuries,* by Joan Sweeney and illustrated by Annette Cable (Dragonfly, 2001). "A little girl approaching her seventh birthday introduces children to the elements of time from seconds to minutes, hours, days, weeks, months, and years, using concrete examples from her life to illustrate the concepts" (*School Library Journal*). Another excellent title by Joan Sweeney, author of *Me on the Map*. Paperback, 32 pages, ISBN 0440417511.

• *Telling Time with Big Mama Cat,* by Dan Harper and illustrated by Barry and Cara Moser (Harcourt, 1998). Mama Cat walks, naps, and stretches through her "busy" day. Clock with movable hands helps children learn how to read a traditional clock dial. Wonderful story and illustrations. Library binding, 36 pages, ISBN 0152017380.

For teachers —

• *About Teaching Mathematics: A K–8 Resource,* by Marilyn Burns (Math Solutions Publications, 1992). Paperback, 296 pages, ISBN 0941355055.

• ETA Cuisenaire carries the very useful and popular math manipulatives, Cuisenaire Rods, as well as many resources for using the rods and other products. Contact ETA Cuisenaire at www.etacuisenaire.com or 1-800-445-5985 for a free catalog.

• *Family Math,* by Jean Kerr Stenmark, Virginia Thompson, and Ruth Cossey (Equals, 1986). This generous, helpful book provides clear directions for fun, yet substantative, math activities that parents can do with children from 5 to 12 years old. Includes word problems, measurement, geometry, estimation, arithmetic, and lots of ideas for things to make. Paperback, ISBN 0912511060.

• *Pretend Soup and Other Real Recipes,* by Ann Henderson and Mollie Katzen (Tricycle Press, 1994). This cookbook, designed for and used with very young children, has a number of healthy recipes and provides a fun, practical way to teach measuring skills. Hardcover, 96 pages, ISBN 1883672066. See also *Honest Pretzels,* by Mollie Katzen.

• AAA Math, www.aaamath.com, features hundreds of pages of basic math skills with interactive practice arranged by grade level and topic. Includes challenge activities. These activities plus additional ones are also available on a CD-ROM.

• Ask Dr. Math, www.mathforum.com/dr.math, has a number of interesting question-and-answer items on such topics as "Why does 2 + 2 = 4?" and "How many seconds are there in 1,000 years?" You can also search the site for answers to particular questions or submit your own.

VI. Geometry

The Big Idea

Plane and solid figures can be identified and compared based on their size and shape. Lines can be classified and named.

What Students Should Already Know

Students in Core Knowledge schools should be familiar with

Kindergarten

- identify left and right hand; top, bottom, middle
- know and use terms of orientation and relative position, such as closed, open; on, under, over; in front, in back (behind); between, in the middle of; next to, beside; inside, outside; around; far from, near; above, below; to the right of, to the left of; here, there
- identify and sort basic plane figures: square, rectangle, triangle, circle
- identify basic shapes in a variety of common objects and artifacts (windows, pictures, books, buildings, cars, etc.)
- recognize shapes as the same or different
- make congruent shapes and designs
- compare size of basic plane figures (larger, smaller)

Grade 1

- draw basic plane figures: square, rectangle, triangle, circle
- describe square, rectangle, and triangle according to number of sides
- identify basic solid figures: sphere, cube, cone

What Students Need to Learn

- **Measure perimeter in inches of squares and rectangles**
- **Identify solid figures—sphere, cube, pyramid, cone, cylinder—and associate solid figures with planar shapes: sphere (circle), cube (square), pyramid (triangle)**
- **Identify lines as horizontal, vertical, perpendicular, parallel**
- **Name lines and line segments (for example, line *AB*; line segment *CD*)**
- **Identify a line of symmetry, and create simple symmetric figures**

What Students Will Learn in Future Grades

The *Core Knowledge Sequence* for mathematics emphasizes the importance of reviewing and building on prior knowledge. Related topics from the Grade 3 *Sequence* are listed below, and subsequent grades will continue to focus on strengthening and expanding these skills.

Grade 3

- polygons: recognize vertex (plural: vertices); identify pentagon, hexagon, and octagon (regular)
- identify angles by letter names (for example, ABC); identify a right angle; know that there are four right angles in a square or rectangle
- compute area in square inches (in^2) and square centimeters (cm^2)
- recognize and draw congruent figures; create symmetric figures
- identify solid figure: rectangular solid

Vocabulary

Student/Teacher Vocabulary

circle: the set of all points in a plane that are the same fixed distance from a single point (S)

cone: a solid figure with a circular base and a vertex that is not on the base (S)

congruent figures: figures with the same shape and size (S)

cube: a solid figure with six square faces at right angles with each other (S)

cylinder: a three-dimensional figure with two parallel and congruent circles as bases (S)

horizontal line: a line that is parallel to the ground (S)

line of symmetry: a line that divides a figure such that the two halves can be folded and match exactly (S)

parallel lines: two lines in the same plane that have no point in common (S)

perimeter: the distance around a plane figure (S)

perpendicular lines: two lines that meet to form four right angles (i.e., four 90-degree angles) (S)

pyramid: a three-dimensional figure that often has a square base and whose other faces are triangles (S)

rectangle: a four-sided figure with four right angles (S)

sphere: the set of all points in space that are a fixed distance from a particular point in space called the center (S)

square: a rectangle with all sides the same length (S)

triangle: a three-sided figure (S)

vertical line: a line that is perpendicular to the ground or perpendicular to any line parallel to the ground (S)

Domain Vocabulary

Geometry and associated words:
square, rectangle, triangle, circle, perimeter, sphere, cube, pyramid, cone, cylinder, horizontal, vertical, line, line segment, line of symmetry, symmetric, two-dimensional, three-dimensional, figure, surface, base, sides, faces

Materials

common objects that are solid figures: sphere, cube, cone, pyramid, and cylinder, p. 395

cutouts of congruent shapes, p. 396

copies of symmetric shapes, p. 398

scissors, pp. 398–399

chart paper with 4 columns labeled *Square, Rectangle, Triangle,* and *Circle,* p. 399

newspapers and magazines, p. 399

one or more art pieces from the Grade 2 Visual Arts section, p. 399

self-sticking notes, p. 399

construction paper, p. 399

index cards, p. 399

chart paper, p. 399

VI. Geometry

Cross-curricular Connections

History and Geography

World: Geography

- Spatial Sense
- Maps and globes

Visual Arts

Architecture

- Symmetry
- Patterns

Science

The Human Body

- Taking Care of Your Body: A Healthy Diet

At a Glance

The most important ideas for you are:

- Plane figures, such as squares, rectangles, triangles, and circles, are two-dimensional and can be identified by their shape.
- Perimeter is the distance around a plane figure such as a square or rectangle.
- Spheres, cubes, cones, and pyramids are solid three-dimensional figures that can be associated with planar shapes.
- Two geometric figures are congruent if they have the same size and shape.
- Lines can be identified as horizontal, vertical, perpendicular, or parallel.
- Lines and line segments can be named using the names of their points.
- Figures with a line of symmetry can be folded so that the two halves match exactly.

What Teachers Need to Know

Background

The vocabulary for locating an object in space is a prerequisite for geometry, geography, and the visual arts, as well as for everyday communication. Children following the Core Knowledge Sequence *should have already learned the meanings of many words and phrases describing orientation and position. Their studies in Grade 2 will continue to focus on identifying elements of space and shape. Encourage children to explore and find these geometric figures in objects they encounter in their everyday lives.*

Basic Plane Figures

A rectangle is a four-sided figure with four right angles.

rectangle

Notice that opposite sides of a rectangle are parallel, and adjacent sides are perpendicular.

A square is a special kind of rectangle whose sides all have the same length. In particular, every square is a rectangle, but not every rectangle is a square. Squares will become important when children learn about area.

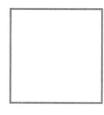

square

A triangle is a three-sided figure.

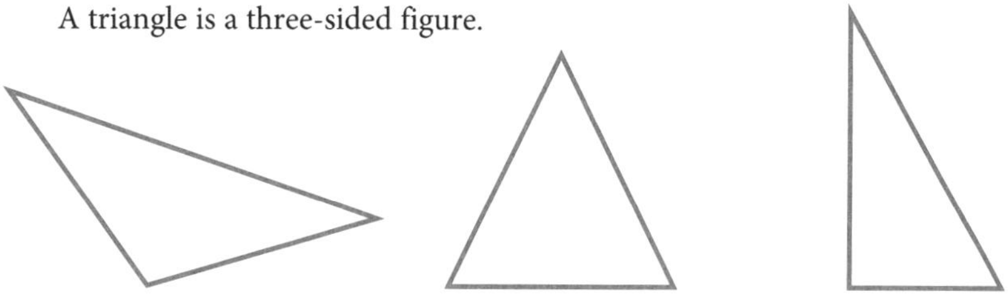

triangles

A circle is the set of all points in a plane that are a fixed distance from a particular point in the plane called the center of the circle. The distance from any point on the circle to the center of the circle is called the radius of that circle.

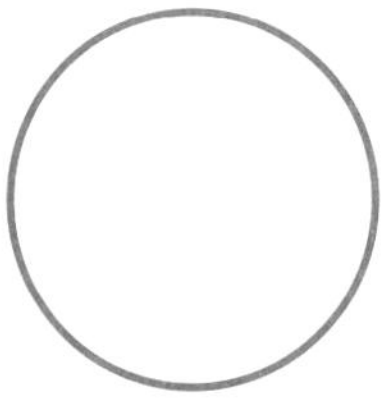

circle

Perimeter

The perimeter of a plane figure is the distance around it. Since a rectangle has four sides, its perimeter is the sum of the lengths of its four sides. For example, you can find the perimeter of the rectangle that follows by adding the lengths of all the sides:

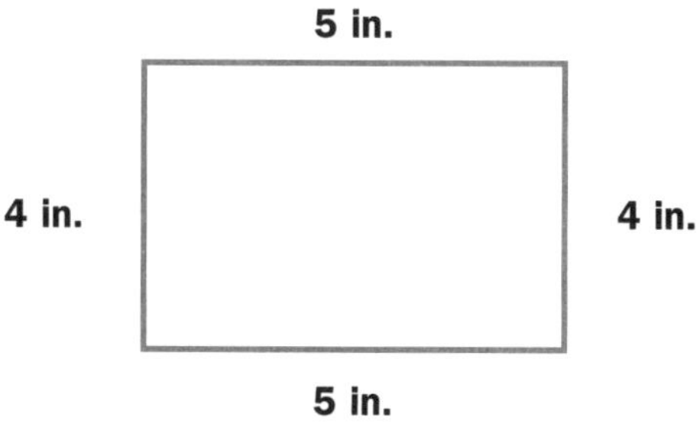

perimeter = 5 in. + 4 in. + 5 in. + 4 in. = 18 in.

Children might think of the perimeter as the distance that a small creature, like an ant, would have to crawl to go all the way around a figure, such as a rectangle, without ever leaving the figure itself. In the case of a square, either addition or multiplication can be used to find the perimeter.

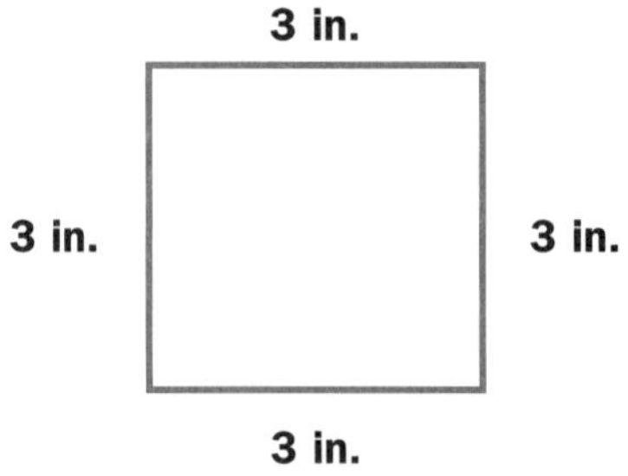

perimeter = 3 in. + 3 in. + 3 in. + 3 in. = 12 in.

or

perimeter = 4 x 3 inches = 12 inches

Although it goes beyond the Core Knowledge curriculum for Grade 2, it is a good idea to keep in mind that other geometric figures also have perimeters, not just rectangles and squares. For example, the perimeter of a triangle is the sum of the lengths of its three sides, and the perimeter of a pentagon is the sum of the lengths of its five sides.

Solid Figures

A sphere is the surface of a ball and is analogous to a circle. A sphere is the set of all points in space that are a fixed distance from a particular point in space called the center of the sphere.

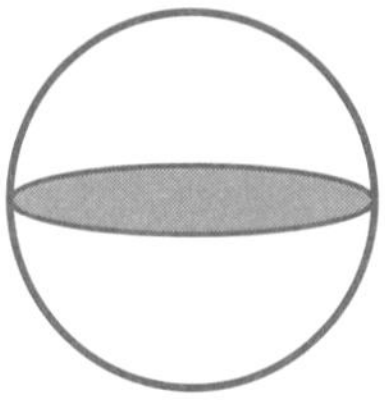

sphere

A cube has six faces (or "sides"), including the top and bottom. Each face is a square, and the adjacent faces make right angles with each other. Cubes will become more important as children begin to measure volume in various units in later grades.

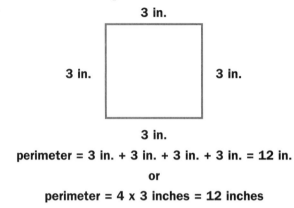

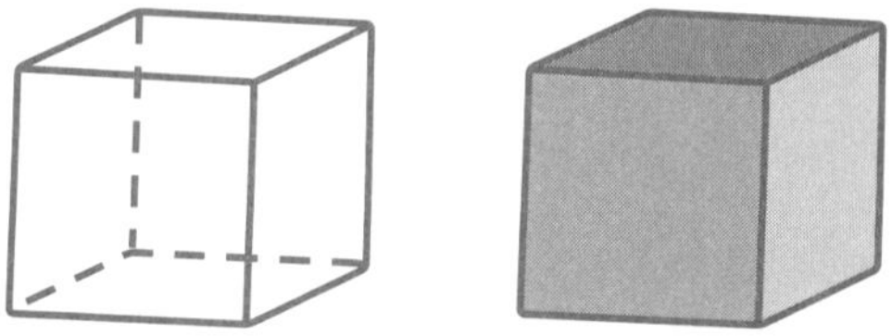

cubes

There is more than one kind of pyramid. The most important example of a pyramid is one with a square base, like the great pyramids in Egypt, which Core Knowledge children study in Grade 1. All of the faces of a pyramid, except for the base, are triangles.

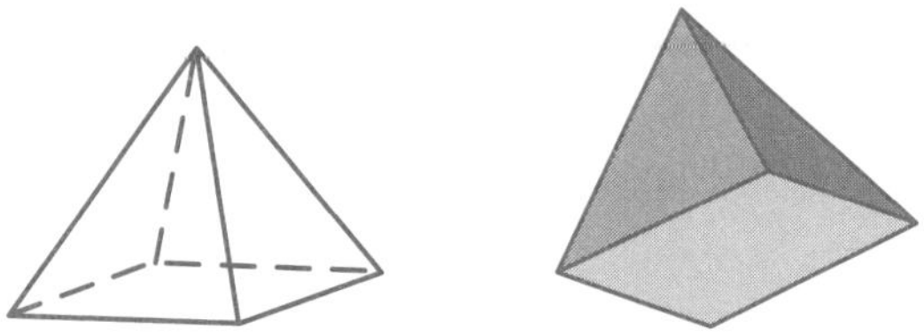

two views of a pyramid

Cones are like pyramids, but instead of a square base, a cone has a circular base. Funnels and ice cream cones have conical shapes.

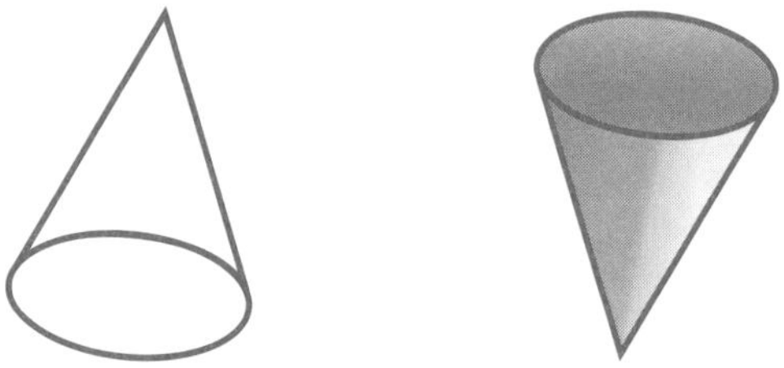

cones

Another common geometric figure is the cylinder. A cylinder has two circular bases. A soup can has the shape of a cylinder.

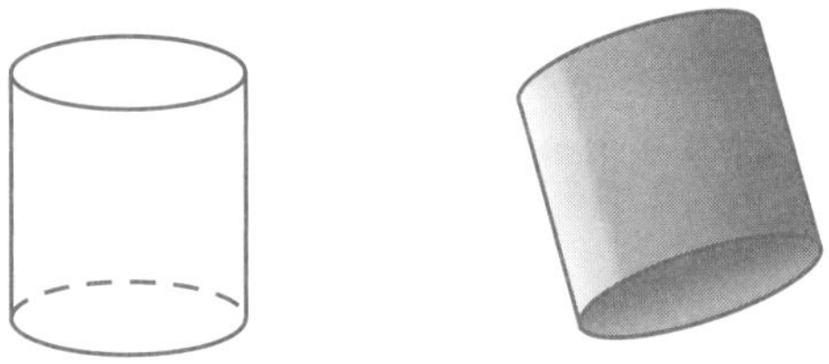

cylinders

Children should be able to associate each of these solid shapes with their related plane shapes, but they should have a clear understanding that solid figures are three-dimensional, while plane figures are two-dimensional.

Teaching Idea

Have children identify basic shapes in a variety of common objects and artifacts (balls, cans, windows, pictures, books, buildings, cars, etc.).

Congruent Figures

Two geometric figures are congruent if they have the same size and shape. This means that two figures are congruent if one of them could be placed on top of the other with an exact fit. For example, the pairs of figures that follow are congruent. Notice that while congruent figures may be oriented differently, they always have the same size and shape.

Teaching Idea

Have children experiment with congruent shapes by giving them paper cutouts of various shapes. Encourage children to place shapes on top of one another to see if they can find a perfect match, or two congruent shapes.

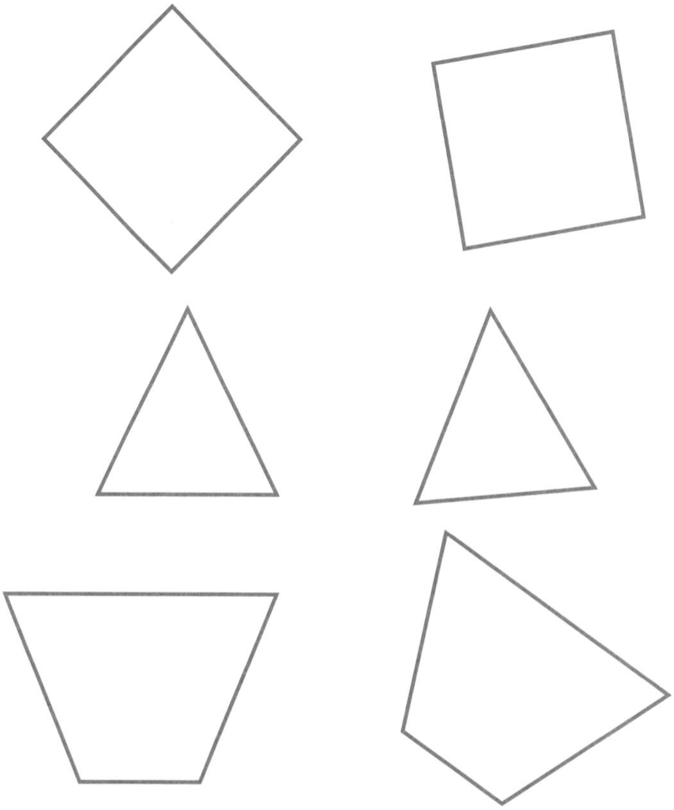

Lines and Line Segments

One important idea of geometry is that two points determine a line. That means that there is one and only one line that passes through two different, specific points. Think of a point as an exact location in space. Points are sometimes labeled with capital letters of the alphabet, A, B, C, D, etc., as shown.

There are two points indicated. One is called *A*, and the other is called *B*. There is only one (straight) line that contains both A and B.

line *AB*, or $\overleftrightarrow{AB}$

The arrows in the drawing serve as a reminder that a line must go on forever in both directions. You can identify, or name, a line by any two points that it contains. Since the line in this picture contains the two points A and B, we can call the line *line AB*. Line *AB* is sometimes written this way: $\overleftrightarrow{AB}$. This same line could just as well be described as *line BA*, or $\overleftrightarrow{BA}$. The part of a line that lies between the two points A and B is called a line segment. A line segment can be labeled or named by its two endpoints. The line segment below is called *line segment AB* and is sometimes written this way: $\overline{AB}$. This line segment can also be called *line segment BA*, or $\overline{BA}$.

line segment *AB*, or $\overline{AB}$

A plane is a flat surface that extends forever. Think of an infinite tabletop that extends forever in all directions, except the vertical directions. Two lines in the same plane are parallel if they have no point in common, that is, if they don't "touch," no matter how far they are extended in either direction.

two parallel lines

Two lines are perpendicular if they intersect to form four right angles (i.e., four 90-degree angles).

two pairs of perpendicular lines

A line or line segment that is parallel to the ground is called horizontal. If a line or line segment is perpendicular to the ground (or perpendicular to a horizontal line), it is said to be vertical. These are practical terms used to describe the orientation of objects. For example, a telephone pole is vertical, and telephone wires may be described as horizontal.

Symmetry

Another geometric concept is called symmetry. Symmetry is important in art. Our sense of aesthetics is tied in some ways to symmetry. Symmetry is also important in some of the sciences, such as biology.

What is meant by a line of symmetry for a figure? Think of a figure drawn on a sheet of paper, and imagine a line drawn through the figure. Now imagine folding the paper along that line. If the two sides of the figure folded over on top of each other exactly fit, then the line is a line of symmetry. Here is an example:

line of symmetry

The line drawn through the figure above is a line of symmetry. If the figure is folded along the line, the two sides, one on top of the other, match each other exactly. Another way to say this is that one side is the same as the other side reflected across the line. Some figures, like these, have more than one line of symmetry:

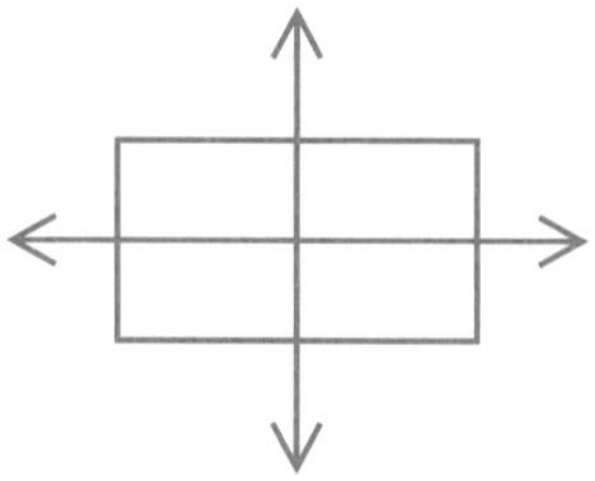

two lines of symmetry

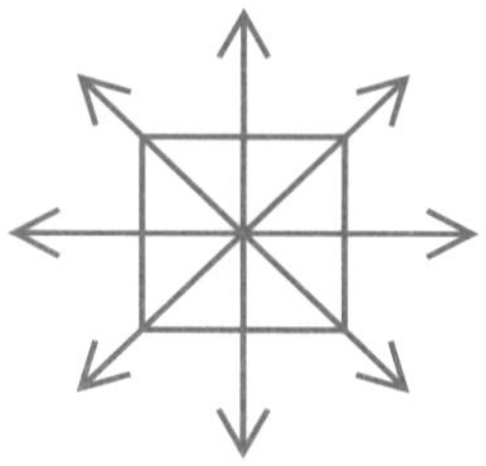

four lines of symmetry

A square has four lines of symmetry, and a rectangle that is not a square has two lines of symmetry. A circle has infinitely many lines of symmetry. Any line containing the center of a circle is a line of symmetry for the circle. In Grade 2, children are expected to identify and create only simple symmetric figures.

Teaching Idea

Give children photocopies of shapes that are symmetric. Have children cut out the shapes and then fold them to find a line of symmetry.

Review

Below are some ideas for ongoing assessment and review activities. These are not meant to constitute a comprehensive list.

- Develop a class chart with four columns. Label the columns with the categories *square, rectangle, triangle,* and *circle*. Remind the class of the characteristics of each shape and have groups of children search magazines and newspapers for pictures to put under each heading. Come together as a class, and post the shapes under each heading. Check for accuracy as a class.
- The study of geometry can be nicely integrated with the study of visual arts. Post one or more of the pieces from the Visual Arts section in front of the class. Provide each child with a self-sticking note with the name of a plane figure, such as a square, rectangle, triangle, or circle, or the name of a solid figure, such as a sphere, cube, pyramid, or cone. Have each child come forward and place his or her self-sticking note on an art print where they see the plane or solid figure named on his or her self-sticking note.
- Play the "congruency game" with the class. Make two sets of congruent shapes by stacking one sheet of construction paper on top of another and cutting out various types of polygons. Give each child a shape, and have him or her find the classmate with the matching congruent shape. After children have found each other, have them discuss what strategies they used to find a congruent pair.
- To help children associate plane figures with solid figures, make a set of flash cards out of index cards. On one side, name and draw a picture of a plane figure, and on the other side, name and draw a picture of the related solid figure. Children can take turns quizzing each other to review the relationships between the figures.
- Review the study of horizontal and vertical lines by having the class identify letters in the alphabet that have horizontal lines, vertical lines, and both kinds of lines. Make a class chart with a column for each category. For example, letters with horizontal lines would include A, Z, and F. Some letters with vertical lines would be K, N, and R. Letters that have both kinds of lines are T, E, and H. See what other letters the children can identify, and add them to the chart. Extend this activity by asking similar questions about parallel and perpendicular lines.
- After reviewing symmetry, have children take a walk around the school, and see if they can find examples of things that are symmetrical. Then, take a nature walk and look for other items in nature that are symmetrical. When you return to the room, have the class draw some pictures of items that they identified as symmetrical and explain why they believe this.

The Big Idea in Review

Plane and solid figures can be identified and compared based on their size and shape. Lines can be classified and named.

More Resources

A good mathematics program follows sound cognitive principles and allows many opportunities for thoughtful and varied practice to build mastery of important skills. For advice on suitable mathematics programs, contact the Foundation.

The titles listed below are offered as a representative sample of materials and not a complete list of everything that is available.

For children —

These books are generally intended to be read aloud, though some children may be able to read parts or all of the simpler texts.

- *Color Zoo,* by Lois Ehlert (HarperCollins, 1989). A very imaginative cutout book. Basic geometric shapes form different animal faces when placed on top of one another. Hardcover, ISBN 0397322593.
- *Exploring Shapes (Math for Fun),* by Andrew King (Copper Beach, 1998). Easy-to-make projects for fun math games. Library binding, 32 pages, ISBN 0761308512. See also *Discovering Patterns* and *Plotting Points and Position,* by the same author.
- *Let's Fly a Kite,* by Stuart J. Murphy (HarperCollins, 2000). A lesson in symmetry. Paperback, 32 pages, ISBN 0064467376. See also *Circus Shapes,* by the same author.
- *The Shape of Things,* by Dayle Ann Dodds and illustrated by Julie Lacome (Scott Foresman, 1996). Encourages children to look for basic geometric shapes around them. The big, colorful shapes may also encourage their artwork. Paperback, ISBN 1564026981.
- *Shapes, Shapes, Shapes,* by Tana Hoban (HarperTrophy, 1996). Intriguing, full-color photography encourages children to look for shapes in the world around them. A wordless book that will surely capture children's attention and interest. Paperback, 32 pages, ISBN 0688147402. See also *So Many Circles, So Many Squares,* by the same author.
- *The Wing on a Flea: A Book about Shapes,* by Ed Emberley (Little, Brown and Company, 2001). Ed Emberley, author of *Ed Emberley's Drawing Book of Animals,* uses three basic shapes—triangles, rectangles, and circles (and a few lines and scribbles!)—to create a wonderful collection of everything from make-believe fleas to a circus train. Library binding, ISBN 0316234877.

For teachers —

- *About Teaching Mathematics: A K–8 Resource,* by Marilyn Burns (Math Solutions Publications, 1992). Paperback, 296 pages, ISBN 0941355055.
- ETA Cuisenaire carries the very useful and popular math manipulatives, Cuisenaire Rods, as well as many resources for using the rods and other products. Cuisenaire Rod activities can be used to supplement your current math program, or may already be integrated with published curricula (for example, Miquon Math, published by Key Curriculum Press). Contact ETA Cuisenaire at www.etacuisenaire.com or 1-800-445-5985 for a free catalog to peruse their complete product line.
- *Family Math,* by Jean Kerr Stenmark, Virginia Thompson, and Ruth Cossey (Equals, 1986). This generous, helpful book provides clear directions for fun, yet substantative, math activities that parents can do with children from 5 to 12 years old. Includes word problems, measurement, geometry, estimation, arithmetic, and lots of ideas for things to make. Provides a great way to supplement (not replace) math instruction in school. Paperback, ISBN 0912511060.
- AAA Math, www.aaamath.com, features hundreds of pages of basic math skills with interactive practice arranged by grade level and topic. Includes challenge activities. These activities plus additional ones are also available on a CD-ROM.
- Ask Dr. Math, www.mathforum.com/dr.math, has a number of interesting question-and-answer items on such topics as "Why does 2 + 2 = 4?" and "How many seconds are there in 1,000 years?" You can also search the site for answers to particular questions or submit your own.

Supplemental Essay #1

Math and the Magical Number Seven

by E. D. Hirsch, Jr.

One of the most famous articles in modern psychology is "The Magical Number Seven—Plus or Minus Two" by George A. Miller. It's famous because it brought to people's attention a crucial absolute limit in the human mind that constrains both math geniuses and ordinary mortals. Seven is the approximate number of separate things that we can hold in mind before they start to evaporate into oblivion. We have to put those things together quickly in some meaningful way before they disappear, or else we will lose the opportunity to make sense of them. This small, momentary storage place of the mind is called working memory or short-term memory. It's where all of our conscious mental operations first take place. One of the reasons that novices in math have a hard time with some of the simplest problems is not that they lack understanding but that they lack the ability to put together one step of a multistep problem quickly before they forget what it is they were trying to do.

Take for instance the simple problem of adding 4 and 8 and 9. Very young beginners know the principle of how to add things. If you ask them to add one and one, they can do it without a mistake. But if you ask them to add 4 and 8 and 9 they may get the answer wrong not because they don't understand but because they have run up against the limits of short-term memory. Think of a five-year-old who still adds by finger counting. "One, two, three, four, that's four and then five, six, seven, eight, nine, ten, eleven, twelve, thirteen, that's four plus nine. And then what was I supposed to add to that? Oh, dear, I have to start over again!" So the child may give up or give a wrong answer, not because he or she doesn't understand, but because the underlying processes are too slow, making one part of the problem evaporate from memory before the problem is complete.

How is this limit overcome? Not by gaining a deeper understanding of addition, which children (and some animals) are born with but rather by using a faster processing method. Processing speed is what makes the big difference between novices and experts in any subject, and processing speed is increased not by making the mind work faster, which none of us can do, but by using two other devices: making some of the procedures unconscious and automatic, and by already knowing in advance certain facts such as 4 plus 8 is 12. Experts do the underlying math processes very fast (and partly unconsciously). This allows them to overcome the limits of short-term memory by using shortcuts like just knowing that 4 plus 8 is 12, and 12 plus 9 is 21. By having these already-familiar elements quickly available, the expert can keep all the elements in mind with ease.

In this respect, doing math is like reading. To understand the phrase "When in the course of human events it becomes necessary for one people to dissolve the political bands which have connected them with another," you have to be able to turn those letters into sounds and words very fast and automatically so you can hold in mind all the words of the phrase. Otherwise, some of them will drift out of memory. That's why gaining "automaticity," that is, being able to do the underlying processes fast and unconsciously, is the key to reading and the key to understanding math at all levels, and going on to gain still deeper understanding and achievement. That's why the education war between proponents of drill and proponents of deep understanding is a very big mistake. These two sides should get together. You can't have deep understanding in math without enough drill to make the basic math processes fast and automatic.

Supplemental Essay #2

Math Fluency and Familiarity Versus Math Phobia

by E. D. Hirsch, Jr.

A lot of people think that math is a subject that you are innately good at or you hate.

Some math experts have said that one of the great barriers to American achievement in math is a vicious cycle whereby elementary teachers themselves have math phobia and math aversion, and this rubs off on children and also causes teachers to spend less time on math, which in turn causes children to dislike math even more and fail to fulfill their potential. These same experts say that these children have much greater math potential than we may believe, and that this is proved by the fact that *all* young children perform rather well in math in those countries that have a tradition of math emphasis in the early grades.

In "Math and the Magical Number Seven" we explained why familiarity and speed are important in understanding math problems and getting them right. Fluency is equally important in avoiding math phobia and bringing out the math potential in our children.

Think of how important familiarity is in reading. Suppose I wrote a sentence using Cyrillic letters. You would have trouble reading it:

СУППОЗ АЙ

РОТ а СЭНТЭНС

ЮЗИН СЫРИЛИК

ЛЭТРС.

I wrote: "Suppose I wrote a sentence using Cyrillic letters." Yet what I wrote was easy to understand when it was presented in familiar letters.

The same is true in math. We have to make our children *familiar* with the symbols and with the operations of math, and as they become truly familiar, their pleasure in the subject will increase. And so will their understanding. Believe it or not, drill is the friend of taking pleasure in math, because drill is the road to fluency and familiarity.

We teachers who were not given the math education we deserve need to break the cycle of math aversion for our children. In doing so, we may very well find that we have an ever-greater liking for the subject ourselves.

Supplemental Essay #3

How to Help Children Understand Why They Make Math Errors

Think back to when you were a child in elementary school. Your answers to a worksheet of math problems have just been returned—or maybe a classmate has graded them in class—and you're dismayed to see that certain types of problems have stumped you again. Maybe it's addition problems that require regrouping. Or maybe it's subtraction when you must borrow from the tens column—that operation always gives you trouble. Or maybe the difficulty centers on (as it did for this writer) the mysterious "zero." When is it only a placeholder? And why can't you subtract 5 from zero? Won't the answer be 5?

As a teacher, you probably see errors like these committed by your children again and again. Some children seem to have a mental block about a particular operation. And because they tend to miss the same type of problem, they begin to give up—"I just don't get it!" You sympathize with their angry face-rubbing and frustration, but when a math answer is wrong, it's just wrong—isn't it?

Actually, an effective way of helping children "get it" springs from understanding how they think. The old proverb "Practice makes perfect" is true in some circumstances; but if children don't recognize the math errors they make again and again, the saying might as well be "Practicing mistakes can make them permanent."

Overlapping Waves Theory

How our thinking becomes more sophisticated as we grow—or the process of cognitive development—has been the subject of intense research for nearly a century. The Swiss psychologist and historian Jean Piaget (1896–1980) devoted his long and influential career, for example, to answering the question: How does knowledge grow? His answer was that gaining knowledge is a series of progressive steps. Lower, less powerful logical thoughts are folded into, and gradually overtaken by, higher and more powerful ones up to adulthood. Therefore, children's logic and modes of thinking start out entirely different from those of adults.

More recently, Robbie Case's book *The Mind's Staircase* (1992) uses a simple image to expand on Piaget's explanation about knowledge-building. According to Case, children think a particular way for a while (a tread on a staircase); then their thinking undergoes a breakthrough—"Oh, I get it!" (the riser on a staircase); then they think on a different and higher plane for another extended period (the next tread), and so on. Often, specific stages of cognitive development are said to be typical of a child's age level, too. Five-year-olds tend to solve simple addition problems by counting from 1; seven-year-olds by counting from the larger addend; and nine-year-olds by coming up with the answer from memory.

But studies by Robert S. Siegler at Carnegie Mellon University, and his colleagues, have pointed out a simple fact that most veteran teachers already know: children will use different strategies to figure out what they want to know. On a trial-by-trial basis, children will approach a problem in different ways—whether the task is reasoning, language, memory, attention, or motor activity—and whether they are infants, toddlers, preschoolers, elementary children, teenagers, or later, adults. Although called "variable strategies," these attempts are not random. Children *adapt* and *refine* their strategies as they go, sometimes falling back and rehearsing the old approaches, not discarding them quite yet, before trying a new strategy. This means that the staircase image of children going "up and up" in knowledge and learning does not describe what children really do (but if you think about it, many math textbooks take the "up and up" approach in the way they present material). A better image would be that knowledge and learning in a child's mind are like a tide coming in: the waves fall back (old strategies), then curl forward and fall on the shore (new strategies), and the waterline surges higher and higher up the beach. In fact, this explanation of cognitive change is called "overlapping waves theory."

Studies conducted to explore overlapping waves theory indicate that children gradually select strategies that ultimately result in rapid and accurate solutions. As they discover more successful strategies, they learn more about the problem at hand. Correct solutions become more strongly linked with problems, and children opt for the most efficient strategy. Often, they first must rely on a more time-consuming technique before they discover a faster way. But many factors—including practice, reasoning, tasks with new challenges, and adult help—contribute to improved problem solving.

So for you, the classroom teacher, the question is: How can I get children to experiment with different strategies for finding the right answer to a division problem, for instance?

Go Fly a Kite

First, to show that trying different strategies is a necessary step in learning, let's create an activity outside the classroom. Imagine this: you take your children outside and give a kite to teams of three children. All the kites are exactly the same. Then you state the problem and give instruction about solving it: "Get the kite to fly. Kites fly by going against the wind." (You demonstrate.) "You can check the direction of the wind by tossing a few blades of grass in the air." (You demonstrate.) "The goal is to get the kite to fly higher until your string runs out." This is basically similar to putting a math problem on the board and giving instruction about getting the answer (the goal) by steps you recommend.

As you would expect, in both kite-flying and math problem situations, children will take different approaches and use different strategies. As Siegler writes, "Children who are presented the same instructional procedure often construct quite different strategies." To solve the kite-flying problem, some children will pull their kite behind a bike; some will go around the building in search of more wind; others will shorten the kite's tail. They may go back and adapt a strategy that seemed promising and combine it with a new one, say, shortening the kite's tail but using a bike to pull it this time.

And this is important: you'll hear them *talk through what they're doing*—suggesting reasons, offering new ideas, recommending new approaches. Siegler and his colleagues call this "self-explanations." Self-explanations are inferences about the connections between objects and events—the "hows" and "whys" events happen. The kite keeps nose-diving? Maybe the tail's too heavy. Or the string could be too slack, too. Try keeping the string stretched tight this time. Let's try it. Moreover, when the kite does fly, the team can explain what did or didn't work and why.

Making Connections

The ability to make causal connections—to explain the causes of events—seems to be a fundamental trait of human beings. Even very young children can do it. Consequently, math teachers—and science teachers, too—can become exasperated when children's ability to make connections suddenly seems to have vanished. As if they were blindly following a recipe, children can perform a procedure in math and have no idea why it works—or doesn't. Siegler calls such situations "failures of self-explanation." Siegler explains, "For example, children often borrow [regroup] across a zero without decrementing the number from which the borrowing was done. On 704 – 377 = ___, this would produce the answer 477. Such procedures may reflect children knowing the superficial form of the long subtraction algorithm but not understanding why it generates the answers that it does." Self-explanation has the power to reveal to the child where he or she went wrong—or right. It's the key to *error analysis.*

In a number of studies, the difference between better and worse learners has been shown to come down to the degree to which they try to explain what they are learning. Studies of textbook reading, for example, indicate that how often children explain to themselves the logic of statements in a textbook is positively related to learning the material. In Japan, classroom discussions about logic often revolve around why some math procedures only slightly different yield the same answer, while procedures that make sense on the surface result in incorrect answers. Drawing on the research of some of his colleagues, Siegler writes, "Encouraging children to explain why the procedures work appears to promote deeper understanding of them than having the [teacher] describe the procedures, provide examples of how they work, and tell children to practice them—the typical approach to mathematics instruction in U.S. classrooms."

Specifically, self-explanation helps children learn in these ways:

- Encouragement to explain increases the likelihood that the learner will seek an explanation at all. When children are told an answer is wrong, they simply accept the fact without thinking about why it's wrong.
- Encouragement to explain increases the depth of children's search for an explanation. Children in experiments who were asked to explain both correct and incorrect answers worked harder at finding reasons why.
- Children asked to explain correct and incorrect answers drop their old strategies more rapidly. Realizing why a certain path of reasoning is faulty, they tend to abandon it faster.
- The more time a child spends thinking about why one answer is correct and another isn't, the more likely the child is to be learning.
- Learning is more enjoyable when the act of making connections becomes a motivator.

How You Can Help

Bringing the benefits of research-based teaching strategies into your classroom may require some changes in your teaching. You may even find yourself going against your instincts.

For example, when children respond incorrectly to a math problem, many teachers instinctively encourage children to "try again" to figure out the correct answer on their own. A study by Siegler involving 45 children, however, suggests that there may be other, more constructive responses that a teacher might make.

Children were divided into three groups and individually shown two parallel rows of blocks. Then the experimenter changed a row by lengthening it spatially, shortening it, or removing a block. The experimenter asked whether the child thought the transformed row had more objects, fewer objects, or the same number.

The first group of children was given feedback only: "That's right," or "No, look again." The second group was given feedback, and then the experimenter asked the child to explain his or her answer. The third group gave their answers and received feedback concerning the correct answer; then the experimenter asked, "How do you think I knew that?"

The results of the experiment indicated that the third approach was most successful. Providing the correct answer and then encouraging the children to explain the reasoning behind the answer led to greater learning—more than receiving the feedback "to look again" or feedback and a request to explain their own answer. Gains were largest, in fact, with more difficult problems. What this indicates is that children must be led on a path of discovering reasons, finding out why something happened without being told how to do so. As children grow older, they will be able to use self-explanation to lead themselves toward discovery.

- So here is one way to bring the benefits of research-tested teaching strategies to your classroom: If a child provides an incorrect response to a math problem or question, provide the correct response AND then immediately ask the child to show or explain why your answer is correct. For example, if a child states that $3 + 2 = 4$, you could say, "The correct answer is that $3 + 2 = 5$. Can you use these counting blocks to show me how I knew that the correct answer was 5, instead of 4?" You can also have the children explain other children's correct and incorrect answers.

Another finding from the experiment involving three groups of children has to do with the concept of "variability of reasoning." Careful observation revealed that children showed a variety of ways of thinking about the block problem, both before and during the test. In other words, "thinking through"—adapting and refining explanations, discarding old strategies in favor of better ones, as overlapping waves theory predicts would happen—was part of the process of learning.

- So another way to bring the benefits of research to your classroom is this: Recognize and encourage various ways of thinking through a problem. Model how to "talk through" your thought process out loud as you figure out a problem and encourage children to do the same. For example, "The question is what is $3 + 4$. Hmmm, well, I know that $4 + 4 = 8$, and 3 is one less than 4, so $3 + 4$ must be one less than 8. That means $3 + 4 = 7$." Recognize that other children may solve the same addition problem correctly using different strategies and encourage them to share these strategies as well.

- Listen carefully to children's explanations when they have provided incorrect answers to see if there is a fundamental misunderstanding that contributed to their error. For example, if a child has answered that $7 - 5$ is 3 and then explains that it's 3 by stating, "You have to count backward from 7. See—7 (shows 1 finger)—6 (shows 2 fingers)—5 (shows 3 fingers)—4 (shows 4 fingers)—3 (shows 5 fingers)," you know that the child understands the process of subtraction as counting backward on a mental number line but needs to be taught to *start counting* backward only *after* saying the first number—in this case, starting to count backward with 6 . . . 5—4—3—2.

Finally, as a practical way of measuring whether children's learning is surging further and further "up the beach," so to speak, you need to become familiar with typical math errors children make. One way to accomplish this is to administer a pretest and note the types of mistakes children make. It may also be helpful to familiarize yourself with what research says about the various strategies that children typically use to solve math problems.

For Teachers:

Alibali, M. W. 1999. How children change their minds: Strategy change can be gradual or abrupt. *Developmental Psychology* 35 (January): 127.

Chen, Z., and R. S. Siegler. 2000. Across the Great Divide: Bridging the gap between understanding of toddlers' and older children's thinking. *Monographs of the Society for Research in Child Development* 65.

Griffin, S., and R. Case. 1997. Re-thinking the primary school math curriculum: An approach based on cognitive science. *Issues in Education* 3.

Siegler, R. S. 2002. Microgenetic studies of self-explanation. In *Microdevelopment: Transition Processes in Development and Learning,* N. Granott and J. Parziale, eds. Cambridge, England: Cambridge University Press.

______. 2000. The rebirth of children's learning. *Child Development* 71 (January/February): 26.

Further Readings:

Bower, B. 1999. Minds on the move. *Science News* Vol. 155 No. 12 (March 20): 184.

______. 1999. Math discoveries catch kids unawares. *Science News* Vol. 155 No. 1 (Jan. 2): 5.

______. 1995. Kids take mental aim at others' goals. *Science News* 148 (Sept. 16): 181.

Kuhn, D. 1995. Microgenetic study of change: What has it told us? *Psychological Science* 6 (May): 133.

______. 2000. Metacognitive development. *Current Directions in Psychological Science* 8 (October): 178.

Miller, P. H., and T. R. Coyle. 1999. Developmental change: Lessons from microgenesis. In *Conceptual Development: Piaget's Legacy,* E. K. Scholnick, K. Nelson, S. A. Gelma, and P. H. Miller, eds. Mahway, NJ: Erlbaum.

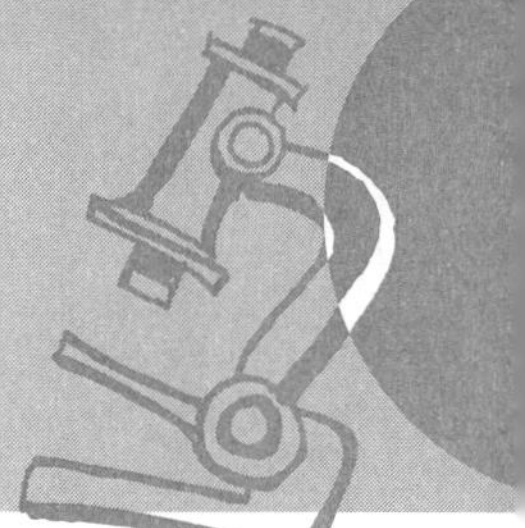

Science

Percentages beside major topics provide a rough guide for allocating time for Science during the year.

Science in Second Grade

Whether wondering about the weather, observing the change of seasons, or watching the work of insects, you are dabbling in science. Science is a pursuit for knowledge about the world in which we live. Through continuous and systematic observation, we begin to hypothesize about and classify observed phenomena so that we may better understand our universe. Science is not only the process of gaining knowledge, it is also the knowledge obtained from that process. The information we have gained over the centuries about the broad-ranging phenomena of our world, such as mountains, earthquakes, weather, plants, animals, gravity, and magnetism, is included in the realm of science.

In Grade 2, children will continue their explorations in science by broadening and building on courses of study undertaken in previous grades. This year, children will increase their knowledge of cycles in nature by learning more about seasonal cycles, beginning their study of life cycles, and studying the importance of the water cycle. They will learn about the effect of the seasonal changes on both plants and animals. A deeper study of precipitation will help children understand the importance of the water cycle to their own health and well-being.

A new classification of animals—insects—is introduced in Grade 2. Children will learn about the parts of insects, their life cycles, what distinguishes them from other animals, and how some can be helpful and others harmful. Children will learn about social insects and should be given an opportunity to observe some insect behaviors.

Children will also review and expand their knowledge about the body systems, learning about the digestive and excretory systems. They will learn about the many organs that make up both systems and how food is transformed from what they eat into nutrients for the body. They will review the importance of good nutrition.

In Grade 2, children will return to the intriguing study of magnets as they extend their understanding of magnetic forces. They will have an opportunity to experiment with magnets and develop an understanding of how they work. Their knowledge of Earth and the use of maps and globes is enhanced by learning more about compasses and how to use them.

Children will also learn about the six simple machines that have helped humans do work for thousands of years. In Grade 2, they will learn how many of the items they use are actually machines, and should have the opportunity to experiment with them, building their own simple machines from everyday classroom materials.

In learning about the scientific endeavors and contributions of Anton van Leeuwenhoek, Elijah McCoy, Florence Nightingale, and Daniel Hale Williams, children will continue to see science as a human endeavor and will be able to connect their studies of science, which often include abstract concepts, to human faces.

I. Cycles in Nature

The Big Idea

There are many natural cycles that occur on Earth that make life on Earth possible.

Remember that each subject you study with children expands their vocabulary and introduces new terms, thus making them better listeners and readers. As you study about cycles in nature, use read alouds and discussions to build children's vocabularies.

What Students Should Already Know

Students in Core Knowledge schools should be familiar with

Kindergarten

- seasons and weather

Grade 1

- life cycles
- habitats, the food chain

What Students Need to Learn

- **Seasonal Cycles**
  - **The four seasons and Earth's orbit around the sun (one year)**
  - **Seasons and life processes**
    - **Spring: sprouting, sap flow in plants, mating and hatching**
    - **Summer: growth**
    - **Fall: ripening, migration**
    - **Winter: plant dormancy, animal hibernation**
- **Life Cycles**
  - **The life cycle: birth, growth, reproduction, death**
  - **Reproduction in plants and animals**
    - **From seed to seed with a plant**
    - **From egg to egg with a chicken**
    - **From frog to frog**
    - **From butterfly to butterfly: metamorphosis**
- **The Water Cycle**
  - **Most of Earth's surface is covered by water.**
  - **The water cycle**
    - **Evaporation and condensation**
    - **Water vapor in the air, humidity**
    - **Clouds: cirrus, cumulus, stratus**
    - **Precipitation, groundwater**

I. Cycles in Nature

As a general rule of thumb, when choosing projects to do with your children, they should be well-thought-out and relate directly to the unit objectives and time allotments outlined in the beginning of each section. Projects have an important place, especially in the early grades when they help reinforce vocabulary and content and don't serve purely as time fillers. Throughout this subject, we have added teaching ideas with fun and purposeful extensions to further children's understanding.

What Students Will Learn in Future Grades

In future grades, students will review and extend their learning about cycles in nature.

Grade 3

- the food chain

Grade 4

- the water cycle and meteorology

Grade 5

- photosynthesis
- the life cycle and reproduction

Vocabulary

Student/Teacher Vocabulary

axis: a straight line around which a body rotates (T)

condensation: the process in which vapor or gas turns into a liquid (S)

deposition: something that is deposited, or the process in which something is deposited (T)

dormancy: a state of inactivity or rest, such as the state of plants in winter (S)

evaporation: the process in which a liquid changes to a gas (S)

groundwater: all water found under the surface of the ground, in and saturating soil (S)

hibernation: a state of inactivity in some animals, in which they are partly or totally insensible, usually in winter (S)

humidity: the amount of water vapor in the air (S)

metamorphosis: a change or transformation from one form to another, e.g., from a caterpillar to a butterfly (S)

migrate: to move from one region to another periodically (S)

orbit: a path in space along which one celestial body revolves around another (S)

precipitation: any form of water that falls from clouds to Earth's surface, e.g., rain, snow, hail (S)

sprout: to cause to grow and give off shoots or buds; to germinate (S)

vernal pools: small bodies of water that form from spring rains and runoff, but which generally dry up as temperatures rise (T)

water vapor: the gaseous state of water (S)

Domain Vocabulary

Cycles in nature and associated words:
cycle, recycle, seasonal, annual, solstice, angle, tilt, parallel, equinox, revolution, variation, fluctuate, intensify, diminish, increase, decrease, increment, incremental, organism, species, embryo, embryonic, birth, immature, mature, juvenile, metamorphosis, reconstitution, change, alter, rudimentary, fruit, ovary, legume, deciduous, evergreen, conifer, cone, scale, cotyledon, seed leaf, root, leaf, stem, flower, seed, node, pollen, pollinate, fertilize, anther, stamen, stigma, ovule, endosperm, seed coat, photosynthesis, synthesis, produce, reproduce, offspring, nourish, nutrient, fertile, infertile, spawn, hatch, larva, larval, caterpillar, tadpole, gill, lung, herbivorous, carnivorous, internal, external, molt, pupa, pupate, chrysalis, cocoon, atmosphere, gaseous, substance, particle, hydrologic, circulate, circulation, saturate, cirrus, stratus, cumulus, collide, collision, combine, dissolve, strata, layer, pore, fissure, vent

Cross-curricular Connections

Language Arts

Poetry

- "Bed in Summer" (seasons)
- "Bee! I'm expecting you!" (seasons)
- "Caterpillars" (life cycle)
- "Something Told the Wild Geese" (seasons)

Music

Listening and Understanding

The Orchestra

- Antonio Vivaldi, *The Four Seasons*

Mathematics

Measurement

Time

- Calendars

At a Glance

The most important ideas for you are:

- The four seasons are caused by Earth's orbit and axial tilt.
- The seasonal cycle affects the life processes of most organisms.
- The main stages of the life cycle are birth, growth, reproduction, and death.
- The water cycle is responsible for the redistribution of water between Earth's surface and the atmosphere.

Materials

Instructional Masters 43–45

The Seasons, p. 416

Butterfly—From Egg to Adult, p. 418

What's the Weather?, p. 418

lima beans, p. 416

water, pp. 416–417, 419

plastic knife, p. 416

seeds, assorted fresh or dried, that are used as food or spices, p. 416

large flower, such as a lily or rose, p. 417

cotton swab, p. 417

tadpoles, p. 417

aquarium tank with breathable lid, p. 417

rocks or twigs, p. 417

2 empty baby food jars per each pair of children, p. 419

markers, p. 419

electrical tape, p. 419

ice cubes (1 per each pair of children), p. 419

chart paper, p. 420

science company information about caterpillars, p. 420

science journals, p. 420

cotton balls, p. 420

What Teachers Need to Know

Background

Earth orbits the sun tilted at an angle, which causes different seasons to recur in an annual cycle. Organisms' rates of growth and development change in relation to the seasonal cycle. All organisms go through the developmental stages of birth, growth, reproduction, and death, called the life cycle. Water on Earth is continuously recycled, which is essential to the survival of all living hings.

A. Seasonal Cycles

What Causes Seasons

Earth orbits, or follows a path, around the sun in a period of one year. Earth's axis of rotation is inclined at an angle of 23.5 degrees from the plane of its orbit. This tilt remains at the same angle and points in the same direction throughout Earth's entire orbital period, which causes the seasons.

When the Northern Hemisphere is tilted toward the sun, it receives more radiation from the sun and at a more direct angle. On about June 21, the sun reaches its maximum angle overhead, the summer solstice. On the same day, the Southern Hemisphere is tilted away from the sun and experiences the winter solstice, with the sun at its minimum angle in the sky. On about December 22, the angles are reversed, which means it is winter in the Northern Hemisphere and summer in the Southern Hemisphere. When Earth is halfway between the two solstices in its orbital path, the axis of rotation is parallel with the sun, so both hemispheres receive the same amount of radiation from the sun. The hours of daylight and of darkness are of equal duration on these days, called equinoxes. Equinoxes occur on or near March 21 and September 23.

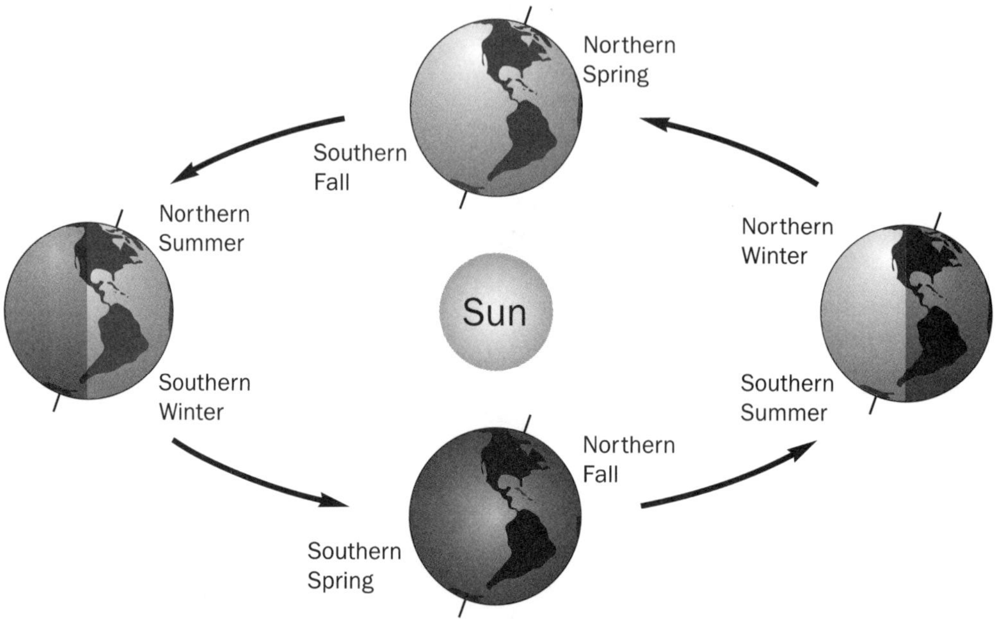

The motion of Earth as it orbits the sun is a revolution. The time Earth takes to make one complete revolution of the sun and return to the same position in space is 365.25 days, designated as one year. The 0.25 explains why we have a leap year, with one additional day, every fourth year. As Earth orbits the sun, it also rotates, or spins on its axis, once every 24 hours. Earth's axis is an imaginary line that runs through the center of Earth from the North Pole to the South Pole. In Grade 1, children learned that this axial rotation brings about the phenomena of sunrise and sunset. For instance, the apparent motion of the sun across the sky begins to be observable as a part of Earth reaches a point in its eastward spin where it faces into the sun. The moment the edge of Earth comes into view of the sun is known as sunrise. Daytime continues as Earth rotates across the sunlit face. Then sunset occurs as that side of Earth turns away from the sunlit side and plunges into night on the dark side.

Cross-curricular Teaching Idea

You may wish to listen to the applicable musical piece from Antonio Vivaldi's *The Four Seasons* when teaching about each of the four seasons.

Life Through the Seasons

Because of Earth's axial tilt, both the proportion of daylight to darkness and the intensity of solar radiation vary over the course of a year. Living organisms react to the variations of sunlight and temperature. As these conditions fluctuate, life processes for growth and development in their environment accelerate or decelerate. For example, many plants grow more rapidly during the summer, when there is more sun, and more slowly, or not at all, during the winter. Some organisms develop to maturity (the ability to reproduce) within one year, but many other organisms require multiple years to develop fully into a mature adult.

Cross-curricular Teaching Idea

You may wish to teach some poems in conjunction with your study of seasons. Emily Dickinson's poem "Bee! I'm expecting you!" describes a springtime scene in which the insects return after the winter. "Bed in Summer" describes how the days get longer in the summer and shorter in the winter. "Something Told the Wild Geese" deals with the geese and their sense of seasons.

Spring

During the spring months, daylight hours increase quickly and the sun's rising angle in the sky intensifies and directs light, heating the ground incrementally. The process of plant growth and development begins as temperature and daylight increase. Two of the most important conditions that must be met for plant seeds to germinate, or sprout into a new plant, are proper temperature and sufficient water. Once germinated, all green plants begin to photosynthesize, or make their own food, which requires light. Water absorbed in the spring by a plant begins to circulate up the stem to the leaves, where it can be used along with sunlight to manufacture food in the form of glucose, a simple carbohydrate, or sugar. Glucose is carried back down the stem with the water to feed the plant's roots. This sugar water is the sap of growing plants.

Warming spring conditions are also more favorable for animals. Spring is when many animals bear their offspring. Animals give birth either by bearing live young, which were nourished first in the mother's body, or by laying eggs, which have a yolk to provide nourishment, that will hatch with emergent young. Warmer temperatures and longer days increase the availability of food, in the form of plants or other animals, to nourish the young so their bodies are provided with enough energy to grow and develop properly. Animals that usually have babies in the spring, summer, or early fall include most mammals, e.g., rabbits, horses, and squirrels.

Cross-curricular Teaching Idea

Connect the sequencing of the seasons with the passage of time and calendars in Mathematics.

Summer

Summer provides months of sufficient light and heat for conditions that promote growth and development of living organisms. Plant parts grow and new parts form and develop toward maturity and reproduction. Young animals grow and develop to become more like their parents. In many types of animal organisms, a reconstitution of the individual's appearance may be involved, called metamorphosis (see the Life Cycles section, pp. 416–418).

Fall (Autumn)

As the amount and intensity of sunlight diminishes and temperatures decrease, growth and development begin to slow. Seeds may be produced by plants over the summer. Some seeds, such as those from conifers, are produced on the scales of cones and require very little food inside the seed coat. Other seeds are surrounded by a dry or fleshy fruit that develops from the ripened ovary of the plant. Examples of dry fruits include nuts, pods, and legumes. Fleshy fruits that ripen in the fall include apples, watermelons, tomatoes, pumpkins, and cucumbers. Another result of lessening hours of daylight is the shedding of leaves on deciduous plants. Leaves are shed to help prepare the plant for cooler, less ideal conditions. When plants receive insufficient amounts of sunlight, the process of photosynthesis ceases. As the temperature and amount of daylight diminish, food sources are consumed and become less abundant. At this time, animals whose food source becomes less or completely unavailable migrate, or travel to warmer climates where food continues to be available.

Winter

Temperature and sunlight are at their minimum intensity during winter. Conditions are least favorable for living organisms, and the processes of growth and development slow considerably. Many organisms enter a period of rest and inactivity. Most plants enter this state, called dormancy, in winter, when many of the plant parts cease functioning. Some animals, such as chipmunks, bats, and bears, enter an inactive state called hibernation.

B. Life Cycles

All organisms pass through a sequence of developmental stages called a life cycle. The four main stages of the cycle are birth, growth, reproduction, and death. An individual organism is born as a newly formed immature member of its species with the potential of becoming a mature adult. An organism reaches physical maturity when it has fully developed and become able to reproduce. For some species, the adult stage may be as brief as a few hours; for others, it may last many years. The adult, reproductive stage allows individuals to reproduce themselves in their offspring. At the end of the adult stage for all organisms comes death. Death is the final stage of an individual life cycle. However, if the individual organism has reproduced, the offspring begin the cycle again.

Life Cycle of a Plant

A typical flowering plant begins its life cycle as a seed. When temperature and moisture conditions are favorable, the seed splits open and begins germination. Normally, the embryonic root, called the radicle, emerges first, pushing down into the soil. The rudimentary stem, or plumule, grows upward above the ground, toward light. Cotyledons, the first leaves, also called seed leaves, fold open to allow photosynthesis to begin. The plant continues to grow; the stem lengthens, and true leaves emerge. When the plant matures, flower structures appear at the nodes, where a leaf base grows from the stem.

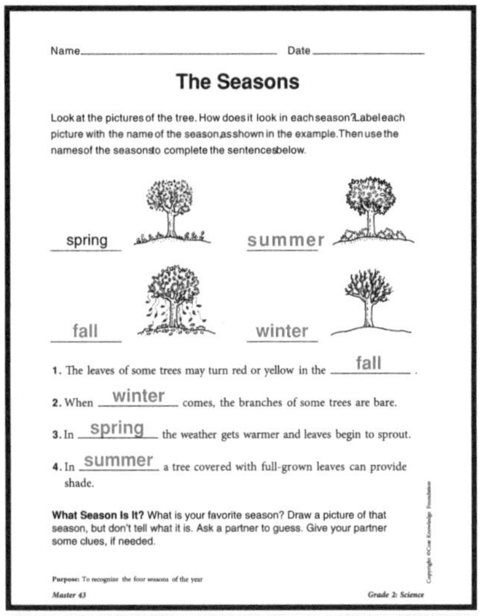
Name________________ Date__________

The Seasons

Look at the pictures of the tree. How does it look in each season? Label each picture with the name of the season, as shown in the example. Then use the names of the seasons to complete the sentences below.

spring — summer — fall — winter

1. The leaves of some trees may turn red or yellow in the fall.
2. When winter comes, the branches of some trees are bare.
3. In spring the weather gets warmer and leaves begin to sprout.
4. In summer a tree covered with full-grown leaves can provide shade.

What Season Is It? What is your favorite season? Draw a picture of that season, but don't tell what it is. Ask a partner to guess. Give your partner some clues, if needed.

Purpose: To recognize the four seasons of the year

Master 43 — *Grade 2: Science*

Copyright ©Core Knowledge Foundation

Use Instructional Master 43.

Teaching Idea

Bring in some dried lima beans to class and have children soak them in water overnight. The next day, split apart the halves of the beans using your fingers or a small plastic knife. Children can then observe plant embryos, the baby plants that can germinate.

Teaching Idea

Bring samples of fresh and dried foods and spices to the classroom to investigate some seeds that humans use for food. Examples include sunflower seeds, pomegranates, mustard seed, cloves, and cinnamon. (Be sure to consult with the school nurse about children's allergies and school policy before bringing any plants, animals, or food into the classroom.)

Flowers contain the reproductive parts of the plant. Flowers are pollinated either by wind or by animal pollinators, like bees, who visit the flower to consume nectar. Pollination occurs when pollen, the male reproductive element in flowering plants, is transferred from the anther, the sac at the top of the stamen, to the stigma, the top of the female reproductive part. The pollen then travels to the ovule where pollen fertilizes the egg, which develops into a seed. A seed is comprised of an embryo (baby plant), a tough, protective seed coat, and an endosperm. The endosperm is the food source for the embryo so it may begin to develop. The food source varies in different types of seeds.

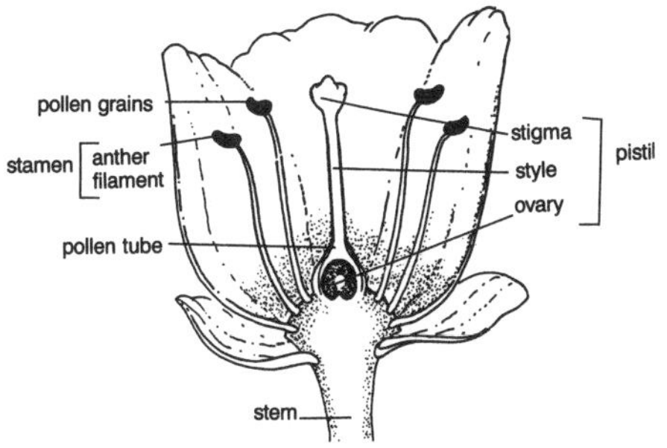

A Typical Flower and Its Parts

> **Teaching Idea**
> **Bring in one or more large flowers to the classroom to allow children to examine the reproductive parts of a plant. Use a cotton swab to collect pollen from an anther and hand-pollinate the stigma, a method that plant propagators may use if they wish to ascertain and control the breeding of particular plants. (Be sure to consult with the school nurse about children's allergies and school policy before bringing any plants, animals, or food into the classroom.)**

Life Cycle of a Chicken

A chicken egg consists of a yolk, which is comprised mainly of fat that will be absorbed by the embryo; an albumen, or white of the egg; and an eggshell that forms a barrier and protects the egg contents. After the female chicken, or hen, has laid a fertilized egg, the embryo begins to grow and develop rapidly and dramatically. In approximately 21 days, the chick breaks through the shell and hatches. A chick can see, walk, and feed itself almost immediately upon hatching. Juvenile chicks grow to maturity in about 20–22 weeks. At this adult stage, young females, called pullets, are ready to begin producing eggs. The lifespan of a chicken is normally 1–3 years.

Life Cycle of a Frog

Frog eggs are laid in large masses called spawn, usually in the shallow water of streams, ponds, and pools. Within about 3–25 days, depending on the species and temperature, the eggs hatch and the juvenile tadpoles emerge in an aquatic larval stage as fishlike animals with a tail used for swimming, and external gills, but no limbs. Tadpoles are herbivorous, or plant-eating, feeding primarily on algae and decaying vegetation in the water. Within the next few weeks to months, tadpoles' external gills disappear, developing into internal gills, which eventually are supplanted by lungs. Hind legs first start as small buds, which grow and develop into fully grown legs. Front legs then grow, and the mouth structure changes by becoming broader and shorter. The lower jaw develops, and from the upper jaw, teeth grow. The final change in a frog's metamorphosis occurs in the gradual and total disappearance of the tail in the adult frog. At this stage, the frog leaves the water to live on land. Frogs generally mate in the spring, when a female lays her eggs in water and the male releases sperm over the eggs. The lifespan of a frog can be between 5 and 15 years, depending on the species.

> **Teaching Idea**
> **If possible, collect tadpoles from a local body of water, or order them from a science catalog, for children to examine and observe their metamorphosis into adult frogs. Prepare an aquarium tank with some water and rocks or branches that protrude above the surface of the water for tadpoles to climb on as they develop. Make sure to have a tight-fitting, but permeable, cover to prevent frogs from jumping out of the tank. (If you collected tadpoles locally, return the adult frogs to the same area. Check a field guide on amphibians for frogs native to your region, before ordering from a science supplier. If you cannot use native species, don't try this activity since you will not have a place to let the frogs go once they have matured.)**

Cross-curricular Teaching Idea

You may wish to teach "Caterpillars" from the Poetry section (on p. 64) in conjunction with the life cycle of the butterfly.

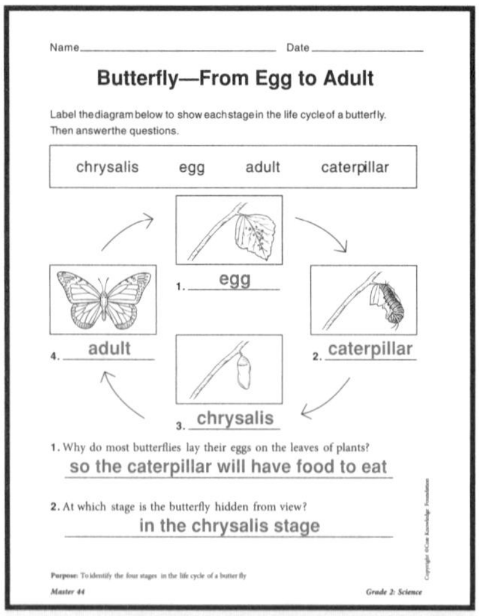
Name Date

Butterfly—From Egg to Adult

Label the diagram below to show each stage in the life cycle of a butterfly. Then answer the questions.

chrysalis egg adult caterpillar

1. egg
2. caterpillar
3. chrysalis
4. adult

1. Why do most butterflies lay their eggs on the leaves of plants?
so the caterpillar will have food to eat

2. At which stage is the butterfly hidden from view?
in the chrysalis stage

Purpose: To identify the four stages in the life cycle of a butter fly

Master 44 Grade 2: Science

Copyright ©Core Knowledge Foundation

Use Instructional Master 44.

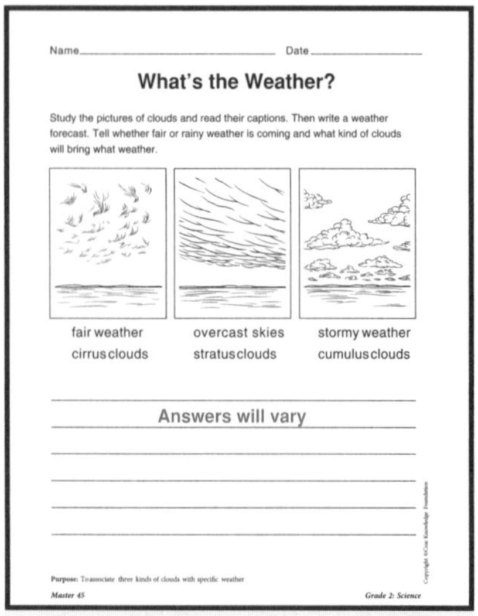
Name Date

What's the Weather?

Study the pictures of clouds and read their captions. Then write a weather forecast. Tell whether fair or rainy weather is coming and what kind of clouds will bring what weather.

fair weather cirrus clouds | overcast skies stratus clouds | stormy weather cumulus clouds

Answers will vary

Purpose: To associate three kinds of clouds with specific weather

Master 45 Grade 2: Science

Copyright ©Core Knowledge Foundation

Use Instructional Master 45.

Life Cycle of a Butterfly

Butterflies usually lay their eggs on the leaves of plants on which they feed. Generally within one week, the eggs hatch as larvae in the form of caterpillars. For the next one or more weeks, the caterpillar feeds on the leaves. As the caterpillar grows, it molts, or sheds its skin, several times to allow for more growth, until it finally molts to form a pupa, or chrysalis, the final developmental stage before reaching adulthood. The skin splits and the chrysalis wriggles out; then the chrysalis dries and hardens, and an outwardly inactive period begins. During this stage, the larval cells break down and completely new groups of cells begin to proliferate, feeding off the larval tissues. Generally within 1 to 2 weeks, the metamorphosis is complete and the adult butterfly emerges from the chrysalis. Butterflies then mate and die soon afterwards, the adult stage often lasting only a few days.

C. The Water Cycle

More than two-thirds of Earth's surface is covered with water. Most of this water is in the oceans. The remaining 3% is divided in lakes, ponds, streams, and rivers; some is frozen as glaciers and polar ice; and some is always found in the atmosphere as water vapor and clouds. Water is one of relatively few substances on Earth that naturally and commonly exists in all three states of matter: solid, liquid, and gas. Uneven heating and cooling of Earth account for the natural changes from one state to another. The water cycle, or hydrologic cycle, is the continuous natural circulation of water between the surface of Earth and the atmosphere. This circulation, or movement of water, has three main phases: evaporation, condensation, and precipitation.

Evaporation and Condensation

Heat from the sun evaporates water, or turns liquid water into a vapor, or gaseous state. Gaseous water molecules rise in the air. The miniscule water vapor particles float in the air and are blown around by wind and circulate through the atmosphere. Water vapor in the air is called humidity. When there is a lot of water

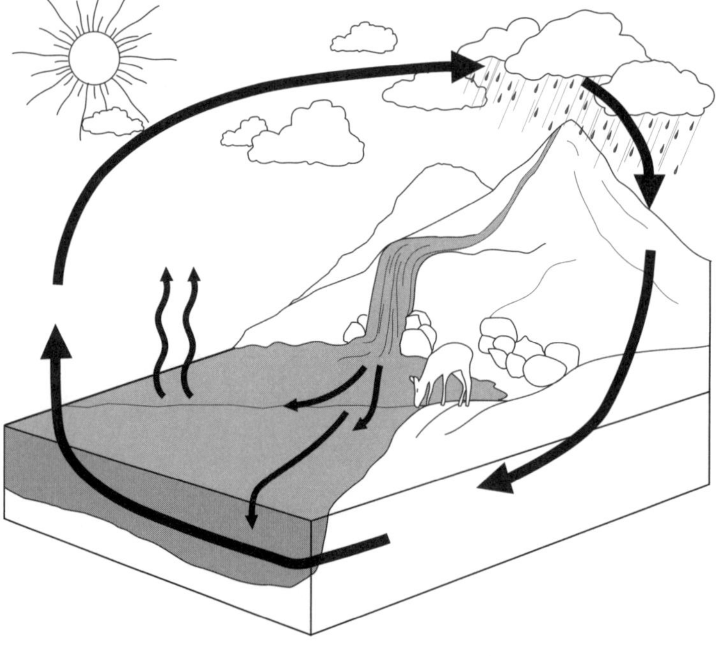

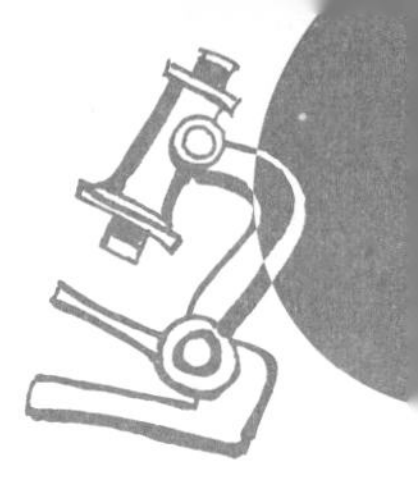

in the air, we say it is "humid." The amount of water vapor that air can hold is determined partly by temperature. Generally, warm air is able to hold more water vapor than cold air. When there is more water vapor present than the air can hold, the excess vapor condenses, or returns to the liquid state. As air cools, water vapor contained in it condenses around tiny dust particles to become liquid or frozen water droplets in the air, forming clouds.

Clouds

Clouds come in many shapes and sizes. Scientists classify clouds according to their shape and altitude, or height in the sky. Each type of cloud is associated with certain weather conditions. There are three main types of clouds—cirrus, stratus, and cumulus. Cirrus clouds appear wispy and thin or feathery. They form at high altitudes from ice crystals. Cirrus clouds are usually a sign of good weather. Stratus clouds form lower in the atmosphere as blanket-like layers. They often appear with an even, gray color and tend to cover the sky and block the sun. Stratus clouds are usually associated with overcast skies and can signal light rain. Cumulus clouds are puffy, dense, cotton-like clouds that appear to rise up from a flat bottom. Cumulus clouds tend to signal fair weather. However, when cumulus clouds get larger and dark on the bottom, they signal thunderstorms. If rain or snow falls from a cloud, the term *nimbo* or *nimbus*, for rain, is added to the cloud's name.

Precipitation

When water droplets in a cloud collide as they move through the atmosphere, they combine to form bigger drops. While rising air currents can suspend small drops, the drops eventually grow too large and heavy to be held aloft, and they fall as a form of precipitation. This precipitation can be liquid or solid, depending on the temperature of the air at different levels. Precipitation is the deposition of moisture from the atmosphere to Earth's surface. Most commonly, precipitation is in the form of rain or snow, but other rarer forms are possible, such as hail, sleet, etc.

Groundwater

Groundwater is liquid water that has seeped into Earth and circulates through the ground. Groundwater nourishes plant life, and it assists in dissolving minerals in rock, transporting and redepositing mineral matter. Groundwater flows down through strata, or layers, of rock, passing through pores and fissures in the rock until the water reaches a layer where all the pore spaces are saturated, or water-filled. The top of this layer is the groundwater table.

Wells are formed by digging down below this layer. Water flows into the excavation and can then be pumped out for use as a water source.

Teaching Idea

Have children work in pairs to make models of the water cycle. Provide each pair with 2 equal-size baby food jars (without the lids). Then, instruct them to fill one jar about a quarter of the way with water and to use a marker to note the level of water on the outside of the jar. Take the other jar, turn it upside down, and secure it on top of the first jar with electrical tape. Ask the pairs to draw a picture of the model and to predict what will happen when they place the jars outside in a warm, sunny location. (The water will begin to evaporate, and the top jar will fill with water vapor.) After letting the jars sit outside, bring the jars inside and observe the changes in the water. Have children record and draw their observations and make a prediction about what will happen when they put an ice cube on top of the top jar. (The water vapor will condense and drops of water will fall back to the bottom jar.) Have children observe and record results. After letting the jars sit inside for several hours, how does the level of water compare to the original level? Encourage children to use the vocabulary words for this process (*evaporation, condensation, precipitation*) when they are recording and discussing their observations.

The Big Idea in Review

There are many natural cycles that occur on Earth that make life on Earth possible.

Review

Below are some ideas for ongoing assessment and review activities. These are not meant to constitute a comprehensive list.

- After studying about the seasonal cycle, life cycle, and water cycle, make a large drawing of each cycle on chart paper showing the stages. Post these drawings in your classroom for children to view. Ask children why all of these events in nature are called cycles. Have them verbally describe what happens during each cycle. Children may reference the charts for help with the details. You may extend this activity by having children write about these science topics.
- There are science companies that will send your class caterpillars that will then develop into butterflies. Check with your school district to see if it has this information, or search the Internet. This is a wonderful way to actually watch the life cycle of a butterfly in action. Incorporate writing activities with this project, and have the class record and draw daily observations of the caterpillars in a science journal. When the butterflies emerge, release them outside the classroom. If you cannot use a native species, don't try this activity since you will not have a place to let the butterflies go once they have matured.
- The class will enjoy studying the different types of clouds during a study of the water cycle. Take the class outside and have them observe the clouds. Return to the classroom, and have children write a paragraph describing the clouds that day. The class may also use cotton balls to make pictures illustrating the clouds that day. For one week, have children observe the clouds and then make observations about the weather. Have them draw conclusions about what types of clouds cause different weather. At the end of the week, children can write a summary of their observations.
- Have the class perform a "water cycle dance." Children will pretend that they are going through the steps of the water cycle. First, the raindrops in the cloud will start to condense, so children will need to squeeze together. Then, when they are gathered in a circle, tell children that the cloud is too heavy and cannot hold the water any longer, so the rain will fall. Have children fall to the ground. Then, the sun will come out and the water drops on the ground will need to rise to the sky, like the raindrops when they evaporate. Repeat the water cycle dance to review the terms that label each of their parts in the dance *(condensation, precipitation, evaporation).* Ask the class to write about their dance and how they interpret each of the steps. Which is their favorite part of the water cycle to perform?
- You may also ask the following questions at the end of this section:

1. What are the four seasons, in order?

   The four seasons in order are spring, summer, fall, winter.

2. What causes parts of Earth to experience summer?

   The part of Earth that is tilted toward the sun experiences summer.

3. What are three of the most important conditions that seeds need to sprout and grow?

   The most important conditions are proper temperature, water, and sunlight.

4. Why do some animals migrate in the fall?

   Some animals migrate to places where they are able to find food.

5. What is a metamorphosis?

A metamorphosis is a dramatic change in an animal from one form to another, e.g., from a caterpillar to a butterfly.

6. Where do butterflies prefer to lay their eggs?

Butterflies prefer to lay their eggs on the leaves of plants on which they feed.

7. How do clouds form?

Clouds form when water vapor condenses into water droplets.

8. What are three kinds of clouds?

Cirrus, stratus, and cumulus are three kinds of clouds.

9. When the water in a cup evaporates, where does it go?

It turns to gas, or water vapor, and goes into the air.

10. What are some kinds of precipitation?

Kinds of precipitation include snow, rain, sleet, and hail.

More Resources

The titles listed below are offered as a representative sample of materials and not a complete list of everything that is available.

For children —

These books are generally intended to be read aloud, though some children may be able to read parts or all of the simpler texts.

- *Disappearing Lake: Nature's Magic in Denali National Park,* by Debbie Miller (Walker & Company, 1996). A lake in Alaska appears and disappears each year, helping to create an unusual and dynamic ecosystem. Winner of 1998 IRA-CBC Teachers' Choice Award. Hardcover, ISBN 0802784747.
- *Down Comes the Rain (Let's-Read-and-Find-Out Science, Stage 2),* by Franklyn M. Branley and illustrated by James Graham Hale (HarperTrophy, 1997). A look at the water cycle. Paperback, 32 pages, ISBN 0064451666. See also several other books in this series, including: *Sunshine Makes the Seasons, What Makes Day and Night, How Do Birds Find Their Way?, How do Apples Grow?,* and *Why Do Leaves Change Color?* For more, go to http://www.harperchildrens.com/teacher. From the drop-down menu in the bottom right corner, select "Let'sReadAndFindOut.com."
- *From Tadpole to Frog (Start to Finish),* by Shannon Zemlicka (Lerner, 2003). Clear, "dual-text" book provides a single, large-font sentence with a slightly more detailed explanation beneath it. Great photographs in a handy format. Library binding, 24 pages, ISBN 0822503999.
- *The Gift of the Tree,* by Alvin Tresselt and illustrated by Henri Sorensen (HarperCollins, 1992). Beautiful illustrations and text chronicle the life and death of a great oak tree. Over half the story occurs after the tree dies, showing how even the rotting tree stump contributes to the cycle of life in the forest. Hardcover, 32 pages, ISBN 0688106846.
- *I Get Wet,* by Vicki Cobb (HarperCollins, 2002). "[I]ntroduces a single, simple concept [why water gets you wet] through words, pictures, and experimentation" (*Booklist,* starred review). Hardcover, 40 pages, ISBN 0688178383.
- *A Log's Life,* by Wendy Pfeffer and illustrated by Robin Brickman (Simon & Schuster, Inc., 1997). The habitat of an oak tree while it is standing and after it falls to the ground. An excellent book. Honored by the Orbis Pictus Awards program for excellence in children's nonfiction and winner of the 2000 Giverny Award for best children's science picture book. Library binding, 32 pages, ISBN 0689806361.
- *A Pill Bug's Life (Nature Upclose),* by John Himmelman (Children's Press, 1999). A 2000 CBC/NSTA Outstanding Trade Book for Young People. Library binding, ISBN 051621165X. One of many books in the *Nature Upclose* series, which includes the life cycle of a dandelion, a monarch butterfly, a ladybug, a luna moth, a hummingbird, a slug, and a house spider.
- *The Reasons for Seasons,* by Gail Gibbons (Holiday House, 1996). Paperback, ISBN 0823412385.

More Resources continued

• *This Is the Ocean,* by Kersten Hamilton (Caroline House, 2001). A simple, attractively illustrated book that explains the water cycle. Provides a nice tie-in with the unit on oceans as well as elements of the Kindergarten and Grade 2 science curriculum. Hardcover, ISBN 1563978903.

• *Water,* by Aaron Frisch (Smart Apple Media, 2002). Good pictures accompany an advanced text. Reviews physical states of water and discusses the water cycle. Will need to be read aloud. Note that the information regarding the Grand Canyon's formation is now in question. Hardcover, 24 pages, ISBN 1583400761.

For teachers —

• BrainPop, www.brainpop.com. Although intended for slightly older children, this website contains a number of short animations that illustrate topics such as seasons, clouds, autumn leaves, metamorphosis, and the water cycle. Anyone visiting the site is allowed to watch two animations per day free of charge. School subscriptions are available for more frequent users.

II. Insects

Remember that each subject you study with children expands their vocabulary and introduces new terms, thus making them better listeners and readers. As you study about insects, use read alouds and discussions to build children's vocabularies.

The Big Idea

Insects, like other animals, have specific identifying features. Some insects are considered either beneficial or detrimental from a human perspective.

What Students Should Already Know

Students in Core Knowledge Schools should be familar with

Grade 1

- Living Things and Their Environments
  - Habitats

What Students Need to Learn

- **Distinguishing characteristics**
  - **Exoskeleton, chitin**
  - **Six legs and three body parts: head, thorax, and abdomen**
  - **Most but not all insects have wings.**
- **Life cycles: metamorphosis**
  - **Some insects look like miniature adults when born from eggs, and they molt to grow (examples: grasshopper, cricket).**
  - **Some insects go through distinct stages of egg, larva, pupa, adult (examples: butterflies, ants).**
- **Social insects**
  - **Most insects live solitary lives, but some are social (such as ants, honeybees, termites, wasps).**
  - **Ants: colonies**
  - **Honeybees: workers, drones, queen**
- **Insects can be helpful and harmful to people.**
  - **Helpful: pollination; products like honey, beeswax, and silk; eat harmful insects**
  - **Harmful: destroy crops, trees, wooden buildings, clothes; carry disease; bite or sting**

What Students Will Learn in Future Grades

In future grades, students will review and extend their learning about insects.

Grade 3

- Ecology; the food chain

Grade 5

- Reproduction

II. Insects

Materials

Instructional Masters 46, 50, 52

K-W-L Chart, p. 425

How Does a Bee Become a Bee?, p. 427

Venn Diagram, p. 429

books about insects, p. 425

chart paper, p. 425

paper wasp nest, if available, p. 426

ant colony, p. 426

information about local resource for viewing beehives, videotape about bees or local beekeeper, p. 426

CD or audiotape of Rimsky-Korsakov's "Flight of the Bumblebee," p. 427

silk fabric, p. 428

honey, with honeycomb, if available, p. 428

magnifying glasses or microscope, and insects, if available; or magnified pictures of insects in books or on the Internet, p. 428

information about local insects, p. 429

Vocabulary

Student/Teacher Vocabulary

abdomen: the hind part of an insect, containing digestive organs (S)

chitin: [KYE-tun] a hard material that makes up the exoskeleton of an insect (S)

drone: a male bee who mates with the queen bee (S)

exoskeleton: the external or outside skeleton of some animals, which is used for support and protection of the body (S)

larva: the first immature stage after hatching from an egg for many insects (S)

mastication: chewing in order to soften or break down a substance (T)

metamorphosis: a change or transformation from one form to another (S)

pupa: an inactive development stage that occurs between the larva and adult stages in an insect that undergoes complete metamorphosis (S)

regurgitate: to cause to surge back or cast up; to vomit (T)

thorax: the middle part of an insect, to which the legs are attached (S)

vestigial: a small or degenerate form or remaining part (T)

Domain Vocabulary

Insects and associated words:
crawl, fly, hatch, bite, itch, colony, chew, characteristic, feature, segment, segmented, division, divide, head, antenna, wing, leg, immature, mature, invertebrate, vertebrate, internal, external, molt, shed, nymph, bee, wasp, hornet, flea, beetle, grasshopper, cricket, ant, cockroach, lightning bug, ladybug, grub, maggot, caterpillar, sequence, stage, complete, incomplete, social, colony, forage, worker, queen, fertilized, unfertilized, secrete, gland, nectar, pollen, honey, coexist, beneficial, harmful, malignant, predator, prey, crops, decimate, destroy, damage

Cross-curricular Connections

Language Arts

Poetry

- "Bee! I'm expecting you!" (insects)
- "Caterpillars" (insects)

At a Glance

The most important ideas for you are:

- All insects have specific distinguishing characteristics.
- Life cycles of insects can include incomplete or complete metamorphosis.
- Social insects are those that live together in a group, or colony.
- Some insects may be helpful to people and some might be harmful.

What Teachers Need to Know

Background

Insects comprise the largest group in the animal kingdom; in fact, over half of the animal species on Earth are insects. Insects are distributed throughout the world and can be found on all seven continents. They are so successful at surviving and reproducing that many scientists have described insects as the closest rivals of human beings in the struggle for domination of the planet.

Distinguishing Characteristics of Insects

Characteristic features of an insect include a segmented body with three divisions: head, thorax, and abdomen. On the head is one pair of antennae. Three pairs of jointed legs are attached to the thorax. Most adult insects have two pairs of wings, also attached to the thorax. In some insects, wings never evolved; in others, such as fleas and lice, wings have become vestigial or have been lost altogether from disuse. Insects are invertebrate animals; that is, they have no internal backbone structure, or spine. Insect bodies are usually soft, but they are protected by an external skeleton, or exoskeleton. This hard, horny coating is made of chitin, which is comprised of proteins and carbohydrates.

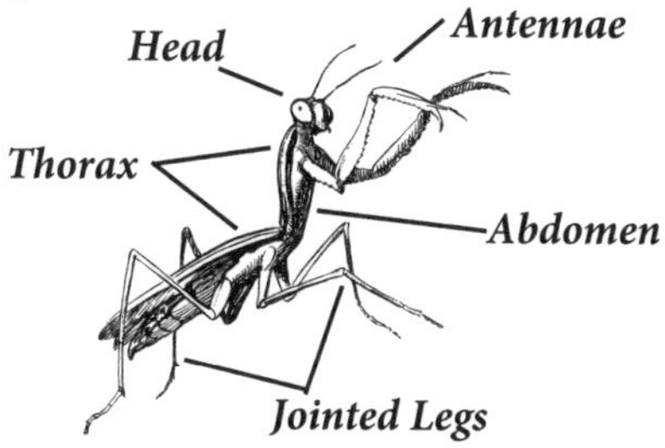

Life Cycles

As insects grow from egg to adult, they change not only in size, but often in form, a process known as metamorphosis. In some species, the young resemble miniature adults, although sexually immature. Immature insects undergo a series of growth spurts. They form a new, soft exoskeleton underneath the old one, then shed, or molt, the old exoskeleton. The young molt several times until they attain full size. Other insects, such as grasshoppers, have no wings when they hatch, but wings begin to appear and grow in later immature stages. The immature forms of these types of insects are called nymphs and undergo what is known as incomplete metamorphosis. Almost 90% of insects go through a complete metamorphosis, in which the adult form is drastically different from the immature forms, passing through four different forms in the course of its life. The egg hatches into a larva, which may be in the form of a grub, maggot, or caterpillar. The larva is often the only form that eats, both for its growth and for storing reserves for the adult stage in which it may not feed. The larva grows and molts several times until it reaches its growth capacity, then molts once more to become a pupa, an outwardly resting stage, in which the insect's larval cells break down and are completely reorganized. When the transformation is complete, the adult, which is sexually mature, emerges.

Teaching Idea

Use a K-W-L chart as you begin the study of insects. Go to the school or local library and collect a variety of books about insects. On chart paper, list the questions that children might have about specific insects and their behaviors, and collect them in the "What students WANT to know" column of the chart. Then, challenge the class to find the answers to the questions, and record them in the "What students LEARNED" column on the class chart. Designate a time each day to gather and share information. After you have gathered all of the answers, have children write a paragraph about what they have learned, using information from the chart.

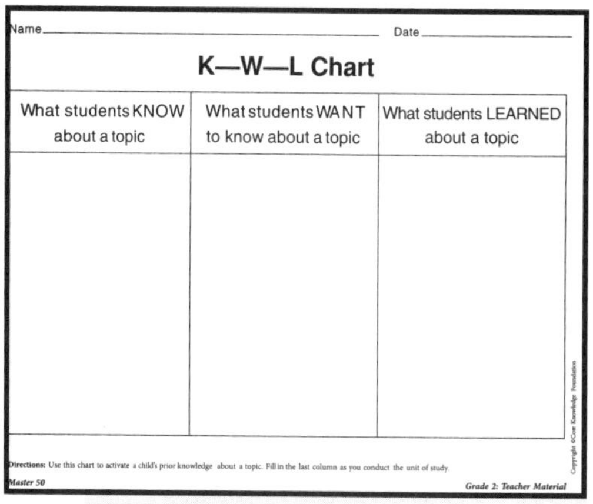

Name______ Date______

K—W—L Chart

What students KNOW about a topic	What students WANT to know about a topic	What students LEARNED about a topic

Directions: Use this chart to activate a child's prior knowledge about a topic. Fill in the last column as you conduct the unit of study.

Master 50 *Grade 2: Teacher Material*

Copyright ©Core Knowledge Foundation

Use Instructional Master 50.

Cross-curricular Teaching Idea

Read "Caterpillars" in the Poetry section (on p. 64), and connect the poem to the life cycle of a butterfly.

Teaching Idea

If possible, bring in an abandoned paper wasp nest, commonly found after leaves have fallen in bushes, trees, or in overhangs on buildings. Cut the nest open to observe the chambers within the nest. (Note: Wasps make a nest to use for only one generation, then they leave. Also, to assure that the nest is abandoned, check if the temperature in the area has dropped below 45°F— wasps cannot live below this temperature, even briefly.)

Teaching Idea

Go for a walk outside with children to search for ant colonies. Note locations ants have used, and observe workers coming and going from a particular colony. If you do not live in an area where these are easy to find, purchase and observe an "ant colony" kit.

Teaching Idea

For a fun extension, sing "The Ants Go Marching" while studying ant colonies.

Teaching Idea

Make a class visit to a science museum, nature center, or other place that keeps hives of bees, if possible. Most human-made hives allow for viewing inside to observe bee activity, behavior, and hive structure. If you don't have a local resource, watch a short videotape about bees and observe their behavior, or locate a local beekeeper who would be willing to visit your class.

Social Insects

Most insects lead individual lives except to mate, but some species have evolved to have a social structure, or colony, whose members help maintain and protect the colony. In truly social colonies, such as those of ants, termites, and some wasps and bees, each colony is actually a family. All the members are descended from one queen. These social insects cooperate in caring for their young, and they also have a division of labor and are specialized in performing different functions.

Ant Colonies

An ant colony is begun when a female and one or more males from an old colony (one that is several years old) are capable of reproducing. These become winged adult ants that leave their colony and mate in the air. The mating flight is the only time the wings are used, after which they break off. The males die shortly after mating. The female locates an existing crevice, such as under a rock, or she digs a chamber and begins to lay her eggs in this new nest. When the eggs hatch, the larvae are voracious eaters. After the larval stage, the young enter the pupa stage in the nest. Some species spin silk to wrap themselves in a cocoon; others hide in a chamber. Adults emerge as wingless, infertile females, called workers. The workers begin to excavate tunnels to expand the nest for later generations. Workers also find food and care for the young of succeeding generations. The queen can continue to lay eggs for several years. During this time, the colony goes through a growing phase in population, nest size, and foraging area. An ant colony may grow to contain over a million individuals. Generally after several years, the queen produces a generation of sexuals—fertile males and females that will be able to reproduce. These ants mature and take flight to start new colonies elsewhere. When the queen of a colony dies, she is seldom replaced, as workers cannot reproduce. Without the queen, the colony usually does not survive more than a few months.

Honeybees

Honeybees live in a hollow tree or other shelter, in colonies of about 30,000 individuals, comprised mostly of workers, one queen, and a few hundred drones. A queen bee mates once with one or more males, the drones, whose sperm she then retains to fertilize her eggs as she lays them for the rest of her life, which may be from five to seven years. Fertilized eggs develop into females, and unfertilized eggs develop into males. Each egg is deposited in a separate wax cell. The eggs hatch into eyeless, legless, grublike larvae, which need to be fed continually for almost a week. The diet in the larval stage determines whether a female will become a worker or a queen. Most larvae are fed a high carbohydrate diet primarily of honey and pollen. Those larvae chosen to become queens are fed a more nutritious, higher protein diet. When a larva has grown to fill the cell, it is sealed inside with a wax cap on the cell. Here, the pupa transforms, over the course of about 21 days, into an adult bee.

Most females become workers that do all the tasks necessary for the survival of the hive. At first the worker becomes a nurse, bringing honey and pollen from storage cells to the queen, larvae, and drones. After a period of time, she begins to produce wax, secreted by glands in the abdomen, which, after mastication, is used to enlarge the hive. The worker also cleans refuse and any dead bodies out of the hive, guards the hive entrance, and eventually goes out of the hive to forage for nectar and pollen. Worker bees generally live about six weeks, and are continually replaced by later generations over the course of the year. In late summer or early fall, the drones are driven out or killed by the workers. Drones cannot feed themselves and their only function is for mating. Since mating occurs in the spring, they become a liability to the colony once they have performed their function. Honeybees are able to survive the winter by clustering themselves densely together to maintain their temperature inside the hive. The queen bees emerge in the spring and begin building new nests.

In spring, when supplies of nectar are abundant, too many young may be raised—more than can be sustained by the colony. Then, the old queen leaves the hive with about half the worker bees, founding a new colony at a new site. Before the old queen leaves the hive, several of the larvae are prepared to develop into queens. When the first new adult queen emerges and goes out on her mating flight, the rest of the new queens are destroyed. The new queen returns to the hive and begins laying her eggs.

Bees make honey by gathering nectar from flowers and bringing it back to the nest. The nectar is carried in a bee's stomach. The bee digests the nectar and adds special enzymes that turn the nectar into honey. When the bee gets back to the hive, the honey is regurgitated into the cells of the honeycomb. The honeycomb cells are left open while the honey thickens. Then the bees seal up the cells with wax to keep the honey from drying out and thickening any more.

When a worker honeybee finds an exciting new source of food, it flies back to the hive and lets the other bees taste the nectar. Then the bee does a special dance by vibrating its wings. The speed and length of the dance provide information about where the food is, how to get there, and how much food is available.

People who keep bees for their honey are known as beekeepers. They wear masks and special clothing to protect them. Beekeepers build special wooden houses for their bees. Inside these houses, the beekeepers place frames that the bees can use as foundations in building their combs.

Helpful and Harmful

Insects can be helpful and harmful to humans. One way in which they are helpful is by pollinating plants. As many plants evolved, some insects also evolved to coexist with the plants. The plants produce sugary nectar on which the insects can feed. The insects in turn transfer pollen from one plant to another, so the plants are able to reproduce. These insect pollinators are responsible for pollinating many plant species, and without their assistance plants would not reproduce and grow the fruits that humans and other animals use as food sources. If insects did not exist to pollinate crops, we would be left without many of the crops that make our lives better. Apples, pears, and many other fruits are pollinated by insects, as are many vine vegetables, including tomatoes and cucumbers. Almonds, chocolate, coffee, and tea also come from plants that are pollinated by insects.

Bees benefit humans by producing honey from the nectar of flowers. Silkworm larva produce a very strong silk that is used to weave into fabrics. Dragonflies eat mosquitos. Some insects are predators that eat other animals that would otherwise damage or destroy plants. For example, ladybugs prey on aphids that suck

Cross-curricular Teaching Idea

Read the poem "Bee! I'm expecting you!" In the Poetry section (on p. 63), and discuss its relevance to the study of bees.

Teaching Idea

For a fun extension, listen to the "Flight of the Bumblebee" by Nikolai Rimsky-Korsakov and discuss why the piece got its name.

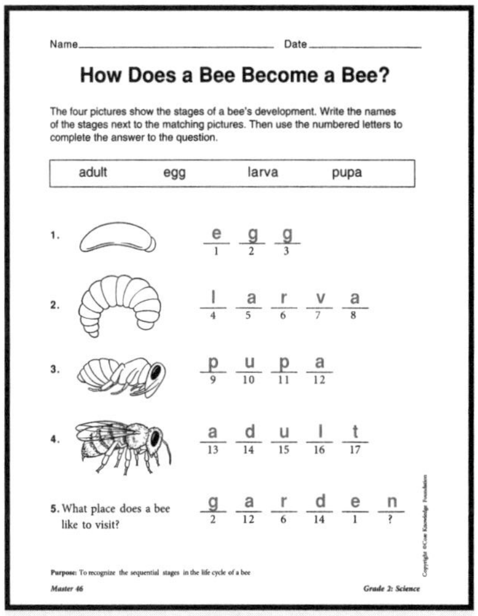
Name________________ Date__________

How Does a Bee Become a Bee?

The four pictures show the stages of a bee's development. Write the names of the stages next to the matching pictures. Then use the numbered letters to complete the answer to the question.

adult	egg	larva	pupa

1. e(1) g(2) g(3)
2. l(4) a(5) r(6) v(7) a(8)
3. p(9) u(10) p(11) a(12)
4. a(13) d(14) u(15) l(16) t(17)
5. What place does a bee like to visit? g(2) a(12) r(6) d(14) e(1) n(?)

Purpose: To recognize the sequential stages in the life cycle of a bee

Master 46 Grade 2: Science

Copyright ©Core Knowledge Foundation

Use Instructional Master 46.

Teaching Idea

Bring into class some silk fabric or honey (with honeycomb, if possible) to demonstrate for children a product made by insects. Many locally produced honeys will name the flower source on their labels and can be compared by their scent and color.

Teaching Idea

Children will enjoy looking at dead insects under magnifying glasses or microscopes. If you don't have access to magnifying devices or insects, look for magnified pictures of insects in books, or on the Internet. A simple search for an insect name, e.g., "fly" and "magnified," will turn up many images.

plant sap. Insects are also important because they provide food for other animals humans like to eat, such as fish.

Insects can also be harmful to humans in various ways. Locusts can decimate entire fields of crops, trees, and any other plant material in their path. Termites and carpenter ants can carve tunnels through dead timber and weaken wooden beams and other wooden structural materials. Moths eat clothing made from animal products, like fur and wool. Cockroaches get into food. Fire ants in Texas and other southern states have a nasty sting. Mosquitos drink blood and can transfer many diseases to the animals and humans they bite. Throughout history, mosquitos have been responsible for the transmission of such deadly diseases as malaria and yellow fever. During the Middle Ages, fleas were responsible for the Bubonic Plague, or Black Death, which is believed to have wiped out as much as a quarter of the population of Europe. Other insects, like bees and wasps, bite or sting as a defensive mechanism when they feel they or their colony is in danger.

One of the most famous harmful insects is the so-called "killer bee." Killer bees were created in the 1950s in South America, as part of a genetic experiment to make better honeybees. An insect scientist crossed African bees with European honeybees, but the new bees turned out to be very aggressive, and some of them escaped. They bred in the forests of Brazil and multiplied rapidly. In the years since, the killer bees have migrated out of Brazil in swarms, stinging small animals and several hundred people to death. Although killer bees have reached the United States, only a handful of Americans have died from them.

Because insects can be harmful—or just annoying—human beings have developed pesticides to kill insects. However, pesticides and other poisons need to be used with care, lest they contaminate the environment.

Creepy, Crawly, But Not an Insect

Children sometimes assume that all small, creepy-crawly animals are insects. In fact, many of these animals—such as ticks, centipedes, worms, scorpions, and spiders—are not classified as insects.

Spiders are an interesting case that you can discuss with children. Help children see that, whereas insects have six legs and three body parts, spiders have eight legs and two body parts. Spiders are classified as arachnids.

Review

Below are some ideas for ongoing assessment and review activities. These are not meant to constitute a comprehensive list.

- Ask children to invent their own insect. Instruct the class that the insect should have all of the defining characteristics studied for this section. Post a list of distinguishing characteristics of insects for children to reference. Instruct them to illustrate their insects, label the parts, name their insect, and write a paragraph describing this newly discovered insect. Share with the class.
- Make a local connection to the study of insects by focusing on some of the varieties commonly found in your area. You may want to have a local entomologist from a university, museum, or high school visit the class and share facts about local insects. Have the class observe these insects and identify the common characteristics that they have studied about all insects.
- Have the class write insect poems to illustrate what they have learned in class. You may give them a form to follow, such as haiku or cinquain, or you may let them create their own poetic form. One way to start thinking about writing the poems would be to brainstorm a list of words that the class associates with insects. These words can be vocabulary words from this section, sounds that insects make, adjectives describing them, or other words. Then, children can choose from this list to write their poems. Have an insect poetry reading in your classroom, and invite another second-grade class.
- When focusing on the study of social insects, talk about the composition of ant colonies and beehives. Both of these groups have a social structure with specific jobs for each insect. See if the class can draw parallels between the two insect communities. Make a class Venn diagram to illustrate the similarities and differences. Have the class compare and contrast the roles of the insects in these communities to jobs in our communities. How are they alike and different? What kinds of jobs do the insects do that we also have in our communities?
- You may also ask the following questions at the end of this section:

1. What are some features that all insects have?

   Insects share the following features: a body with three parts—the head, thorax, and abdomen; three pairs of jointed legs; and one pair of antennae.

2. What stages do most insects go through during their life cycle?

   Most insects go from egg to larva to pupa to adult.

3. What is a colony?

   A colony is a group in which all members work together for survival.

4. What is the most important bee in a beehive?

   The queen bee is the most important.

5. What are some ways in which insects are helpful to people?

   They accomplish tasks that are beneficial to people, such as pollinating flowers and plants, or eating other, destructive insects.

6. What are some ways in which insects are harmful to people?

   They eat houses, clothes, and plants; spread diseases; bite; and sting.

The Big Idea in Review

Insects, like other animals, have specific identifying features. Some insects are considered either beneficial or detrimental from a human perspective.

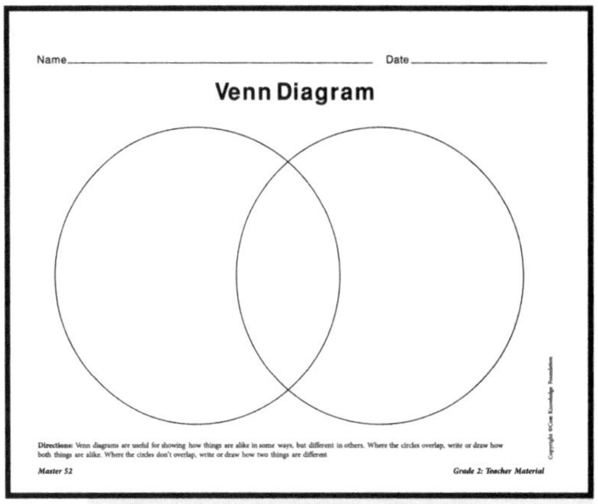

Use Instructional Master 52.

More Resources

The titles listed below are offered as a representative sample of materials and not a complete list of everything that is available.

For children —

These books are generally intended to be read aloud, though some children may be able to read parts or all of the simpler texts.

• *About Insects: A Guide for Children*, by Cathryn Sill (Peachtree Books, 2000). A fine overview with realistic watercolor illustrations. An easy-to-read text is followed by detailed notes on each illustration. Hardcover, 48 pages, ISBN 1561452076.

• *Ant Cities (Let's-Read-and-Find-Out Science, Stage 2),* by Arthur Dorros (HarperTrophy, 2000). Explores the fascinating and complex ways in which these industrious insects work together to keep their ant cities alive. A Reading Rainbow selection. Paperback, 32 pages, ISBN 0064450791. See also *Chirping Crickets,* in this same series.

• *Are You a Bee? (Backyard Books),* by Judy Allen and Tudor Humphries (Kingfisher, 2001). Hardcover, 32 pages, ISBN 0753453452. See also *Are You a Ladybug?; Are You a Dragonfly?*

• *Beetles (Insects),* by Cheryl Coughlan (Pebble Books, 1999). Easy text and good photography. Library binding, 24 pages, ISBN 0516218239. Other titles in this series cover ants, bumblebees, crickets, dragonflies, fireflies, flies, grasshoppers, ladybugs, and mosquitos. For much more detail, consider *Beetles (A True Book),* by Ann O. Squire (Children's Press, 2004). Paperback, 47 pages, ISBN 0516293583. Intended for children in Grades 3–5, books in this series also cover ants, bees, cicadas, cockroaches, crickets, grasshoppers, flies, praying mantises, and termites.

• *Caterpillar (Bug Books),* by Karen Hartley and others (Heinemann, 1999). A well-written book full of fun facts and great photography. Good introduction to basic vocabulary. Library binding, 32 pages, ISBN 1575727951. Other titles in this series cover ants, bees, ladybugs, mosquitos, cockroaches, termites, and grasshoppers.

• *Creepy, Crawly Baby Bugs*, by Sandra Markle (Walker & Co., 2003). "Extraordinary, full-color close-ups reveal 20 kinds of insect 'babies' in intimate detail. This beautifully photographed, well-written, and organized title will be a welcome resource on insect development" *(School Library Journal,* starred review). Paperback, 32 pages, ISBN 0802776590.

• *Ladybugs: Red, Fiery, and Bright*, by Mia Posada (Carolrhoda Books, 2002). Library binding, 32 pages, ISBN 0876143346.

For teachers —

• *An Extraordinary Life: The Story of a Monarch Butterfly*, by Laurence Pringle with paintings by Bob Marstall (Orchard Books, 1997). "[C]aptures the amazing story of one monarch butterfly's migration across a continent" (from the publisher). Hardcover, 64 pages, ISBN 0531300021.

• *Janice VanCleave's Play and Find Out about Bugs: Easy Experiments for Young Children*, by Janice VanCleave (John Wiley & Sons, 1999). "Contains instructions for more than 50 simple, hands-on experiments inspired by questions from real kids" (author's preface). Hardcover, 121 pages, ISBN 0471176648.

• Hall Kids Science, www.HallKidsScience.com, bills itself as "the most comprehensive Kids Science portal." Search for microscopes, books, kits on bug collecting or ant farms, and many more topics.

• Insect Lore, www.insectlore.com, has classroom kits, activities, and plenty of information. Call 1-800-LIVE-BUG (1-800-548-3284) to receive a catalog.

III. The Human Body

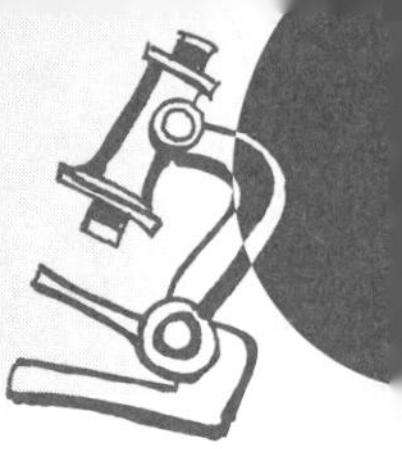

Remember that each subject you study with children expands their vocabulary and introduces new terms, thus making them better listeners and readers. As you study about the human body, use read alouds and discussions to build children's vocabularies.

The Big Idea

The human body is made up of microscopic cells that group together in highly organized fashions to form tissues, organs, and systems.

What Students Should Already Know

Students in Core Knowledge schools should be familiar with

Kindergarten

- the five senses and associated body parts
- taking care of your body

Grade 1

- skeletal, muscular, digestive, circulatory, and nervous systems
- vaccinations

What Students Need to Learn

- **Cells**
  - **All living things are made up of cells.**
- **The digestive and excretory systems**
  - **Salivary glands and taste buds**
  - **Teeth: incisors, bicuspids, molars**
  - **Esophagus, stomach, liver, intestines**
  - **Kidneys, urine, bladder, urethra, anus, appendix**
- **Taking care of your body: a healthy diet**
  - **Vitamins and minerals**
  - **The food pyramid**

What Students Will Learn in Future Grades

In future grades, students will review and extend their learning about the human body.

Grade 3

- muscular, skeletal, and nervous systems
- vision and hearing

Grade 4

- circulatory and respiratory systems

Grade 5

- cells: organization into tissues, organs, and systems
- changes in human adolescence
- endocrine and reproductive systems

III. The Human Body

Materials

Instructional Masters 47, 50

Digestive System Matchup, p. 435

K-W-L Chart, p. 436

piece of skin, section of onion membrane, or drop of blood on slide, p. 434

microscope, p. 434

mirror, p. 434

food labels from children's favorite breakfast foods and snacks, p. 437

magazines, p. 437

scissors, p. 437

nutritional information from a variety of restaurants, p. 437

paper for a flap book, p. 437

chart paper, p. 438

index cards, p. 438

list of student vocabulary from this section written on chart paper, p. 438

Vocabulary

Student/Teacher Vocabulary

balanced diet: a diet that includes a mixture of foods from a variety of food categories—grains, fruits, vegetables, dairy, meats and fish, and fats (S)

bladder: a saclike muscle that stores urine (T)

blood: a liquid that travels through the body as a way to move nutrients, oxygen, and waste to and from all parts of the body (S)

blood vessel: a passageway through which blood circulates throughout the body; arteries, veins, and capillaries (T)

body system: a group of body parts that work together to perform a specific function in the body (T)

cell: the smallest unit of life that can carry out all the jobs of a living thing (S)

circulatory system: the body system that pumps blood and brings oxygen and nutrients to all parts of the body (S)

digestion: the process by which food is broken down so it can be used by the body (S)

digestive system: the body system that processes food (S)

esophagus: a stretchy, tunnel-like organ about 10 inches long. The walls of the esophagus contain muscles that push food toward the stomach. (T)

exercise: movement that keeps the body healthy and fit (S)

heart: the organ that pumps blood through the body (S)

kidneys: the primary organs of excretion. They are bean-shaped organs that both prepare wastes to be removed from the body and maintain homeostasis in the body. (T)

large intestine: the organ where water is removed and solid food waste, called feces, is formed (T)

minerals: substances that keep your teeth and bones strong and also help your body do special jobs (S)

muscle: tissue that allows your body to move (S)

muscular system: the body system that makes it possible for you to stand and move (S)

nervous system: the body system that helps you take in information about the world and respond to stimuli (S)

nutrients: substances, like proteins, minerals, and vitamins, that let your muscles move and your body work and grow (S)

organ: a part of the body, made up of groups of tissue that have a certain job (S)

small intestine: the organ where food is further broken down and usable nutrients and water are absorbed into the bloodstream (T)

stomach: the organ where food is broken down into a paste-like consistency by the gastric juices (T)

tissue: a group of similar cells that have a specialized job, e.g., muscle tissue (S)

urethra: the organ through which urine eventually leaves the body (T)

vitamins: substances, such as vitamins B and C, that help your body do special jobs and keep you healthy (S)

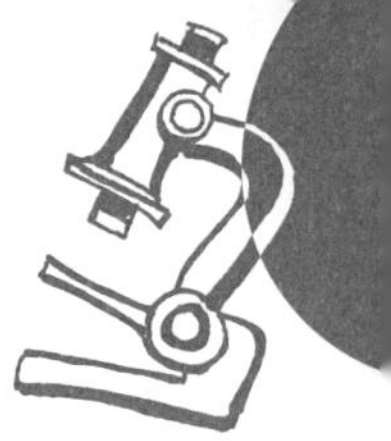

Domain Vocabulary

The human body and associated words:
system, function, groupings, tissues, specific, specialized, process, substance, matter, material, absorb, distribute, incisor, bicuspid, canine teeth, premolar, molar, dentition, masticate, salivate, saliva, drool, bite, chew, crush, grind, taste, taste bud, flavor, smell, odor, scent, enzyme, catalyst, swallow, gulp, gastric, gastritis, excrete, expel, anus, feces, urine, urinate, perspire, perspiration, sweat, gland, toxic, toxin, poison, poisonous, metabolize, metabolism, homeostasis, protein, carbohydrate, fat, mineral, variety, category

At a Glance

The most important ideas for you are:

- The human body is made up of cells that are too small to be seen unaided.
- Cells group together to form tissues; tissues group together to form organs; organs work together in systems to perform specific functions in the body.
- The digestive system is responsible for breaking down food into substances the body can use.
- The excretory system is responsible for removing waste products from the body.
- Eating a healthy diet is an important component to maintaining health.

What Teachers Need to Know

Background

The human body works like a complex machine. It consists of a network of systems that together keep you healthy and alive and allow you to perform countless tasks. The skeletal and muscular systems give your body shape and allow you to stand and move; the circulatory system pumps blood through your body, bringing oxygen and nutrients to all parts of your body, enabling you to function and grow; the digestive system is responsible for processing energy-giving food; the excretory system is responsible for removing waste products from your body and helps to regulate your body temperature; and the nervous system enables you to take in information about the world and respond to stimuli. Each body system is made up of different body parts that work together to perform a specific function in the body.

You demand a lot from your body. You expect your mind to stay alert through the workday and evening. Your muscles stay active and keep you moving, and your senses continually take in information about the environment—and you expect them not to tire. Even when you are asleep, your body is working hard to meet the demands of health and survival. While your body systems work naturally and do not require conscious instruction, you must play an active role in your health to ensure the continual functioning of the body systems. Exercise, eating healthy foods, and getting plenty of rest are essential for the high-level functioning you expect from your body.

Teaching Idea

As an introduction to this section, activate children's prior knowledge of the human body by reviewing body systems that children in Core Knowledge schools should have learned about in Grade 1. You may also wish to review with children ways to maintain good health: exercise, a healthy diet, rest, and grooming.

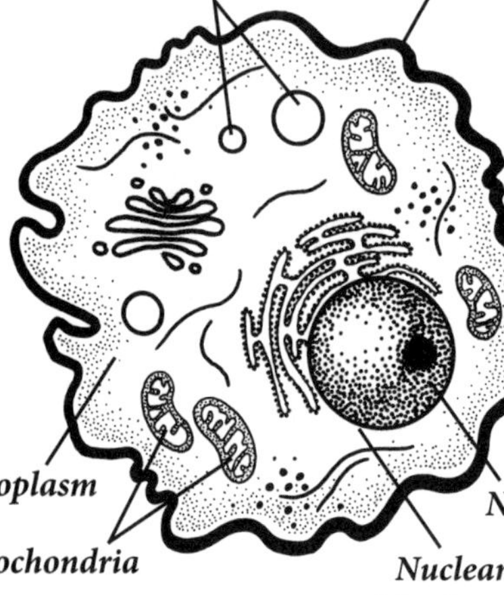

A. Cells

All your body's parts are made up of tiny units called cells. In fact, all living things are made up of one or more cells. A cell is the smallest unit of life that can carry out all the functions of a living thing. Most cells are too small to be seen unaided—smaller even than the period at the end of this sentence. Cells come in a variety of shapes and sizes. Your body is a collection of different types of cells. Amazingly, all the information that a living thing needs to survive is contained in each of that organism's cells.

Tissues

Cells of a similar type and function group together and form tissues. Your body's cells are organized into four main types of tissue—connective tissue, muscle tissue, epithelial tissue, and nervous tissue. Each type has a specialized function. Muscle tissue, for example, is tissue that contracts in response to signals from the brain and spinal cord. Your heart, stomach, and skeletal muscles all contain muscle tissue. Epithelial tissue covers and protects your body and organs. Skin contains epithelial tissue.

Organs

Your heart, stomach, skeletal muscles, and skin are all organs. Organs are functional units of the body and are made up of groups of tissue. Organs may be made up of a combination of different types of tissue. Your stomach is made up of all four of the main types of tissue listed above. Organs work together in systems to carry out specific functions in the body.

B. The Digestive and Excretory Systems

The Digestive System

Your digestive system is an example of a body system. It is a network of organs, which is responsible for processing food into substances your body can use. Your body needs nutrients for your muscles to move and for your body to function and grow, and nutrients come from food. It is the job of the digestive system to turn food into useable substances for the body. During digestion, food is broken down and prepared for distribution throughout the body.

Teeth

Digestion begins when you first bite into food. When you chew, your teeth break apart food into smaller pieces. First, your incisors, the front teeth on the top and bottom of your mouth, cut and tear apart food when you bite into it. Your bicuspids, the teeth between your canines and molars, help to crush and break apart food. Your molars help to grind food into small pieces.

Taste Buds

Food is transferred between the teeth and moved around in your mouth by your tongue. Your tongue also allows you to taste food. Taste buds on the tongue respond to flavors in food so that you can both recognize and enjoy meals. Taste buds also warn you of danger. Poisons may be detected by the action of the taste buds in identifying bitter-tasting food.

Teaching Idea

Children may enjoy looking at cells through the lens of a microscope. Place a small piece of skin, a section of onion membrane, or a drop of blood on a slide, and place it under the microscope. Invite children to describe and draw what they see.

Teaching Idea

You may wish to teach about Anton van Leeuwenhoek, discussed on pp. 457–458 in Science Biographies, in conjunction with the study of cells.

Teaching Idea

Invite children to look at their teeth with a mirror and to observe the different shapes of their teeth. Explain that the shapes of teeth have evolved to break apart different types of food. Explain to children that teeth are important for more than just chewing. Teeth are essential for speaking, too. Invite children to say the word *tooth*. Explain that their teeth help them pronounce the "th" sound.

Salivary Glands

Salivary glands in your mouth produce saliva, which mixes with food and moistens it as you chew to aid with swallowing. Saliva contains an enzyme that begins to break down some of the substances in food before it even leaves your mouth. When you are ready to swallow, the tongue helps to push food to the back of the throat.

Throat, Stomach, Intestines

When food is swallowed, it passes through the throat and enters the esophagus. The esophagus is a stretchy, tunnel-like organ about 10 inches long. The walls of the esophagus contain muscles that push food toward the stomach, a small pouchlike organ in the upper abdomen. Once food travels through the esophagus to the stomach, it is broken down into a paste-like consistency by the stomach's gastric juices. Food then passes from the stomach to the small intestine, where it is further broken down. Here, usable nutrients and water are absorbed into the bloodstream through fingerlike projections, known as villi, in the inner wall of the small intestine. The liver, pancreas, and gallbladder produce enzymes that are transported into the small intestine and aid in digestion.

Food and water not absorbed in the small intestine travels to the large intestine, where water is removed and solid food waste, called feces, is formed. Feces are expelled from the body through the anus in the final stage of digestion. The complete digestive process takes approximately 20 hours.

The Excretory System

Although they may seem like a nuisance at times, perspiring and urinating are two very important body processes. Perspiration and urine are two examples of excretory products. They are each involved in removing waste products from the body. Your body produces toxic wastes during certain activities. When you metabolize proteins, for example, ammonia is produced as a by-product. Ammonia is a very toxic substance and cannot be tolerated by the body. Ammonia is converted and stored in the body as urea, a substance that is more easily tolerated by the body, until it can be removed from the body as a component of urine. Without a system that removes such wastes, wastes would build up in your body causing illness and possibly even death. The excretory system is responsible for removing these waste products from the body. Excretion includes the removal of excess water, salts, and nitrogen wastes—primarily as urea.

The kidneys are the primary organs of excretion. They are located at the bottom of the ribcage. In addition to preparing wastes to be removed from the body, the kidneys help to maintain homeostasis (a state of balance) in the body. They regulate the amount of salt, water, and nutrients in the blood and extracellular fluid surrounding the cells.

As blood passes through the kidneys, waste products are filtered from the blood and are collected by each kidney as urine. Urine passes from each kidney through the ureters to the urinary bladder. The urinary bladder is a saclike muscle that stores urine. It expands and contracts as it is filled with and emptied of urine. Urine eventually leaves the body through the urethra, a tube at the bottom of the urinary bladder.

Teaching Idea

Invite children to make a flow chart to show the sequence of steps in digestion. As an extension, give children a topic sentence, and have them write a paragraph about the sequence of the digestive system using time-order words.

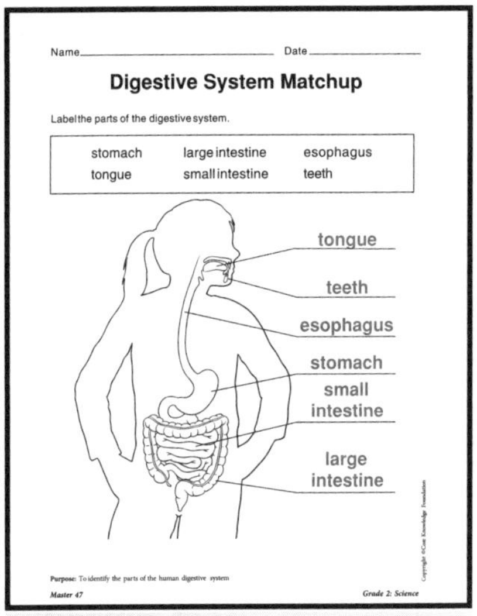
Name Date

Digestive System Matchup

Label the parts of the digestive system.

stomach	large intestine	esophagus
tongue	small intestine	teeth

Purpose: To identify the parts of the human digestive system

Master 47 — Grade 2: Science

Use Instructional Master 47.

Skin, your body's largest organ, is also involved in excretion. Sweat glands below the surface of your skin help rid the body of waste through perspiration, or sweat. When you perspire, water, salt, and other waste products, such as urea, are excreted from the body.

Teaching Idea

Children should have studied ways they can care for their body in Kindergarten and Grade 1. Introduce the concept of eating a healthy diet by inviting children to recall information they previously learned, read about, or heard or saw on television. A K-W-L chart can be used with this activity.

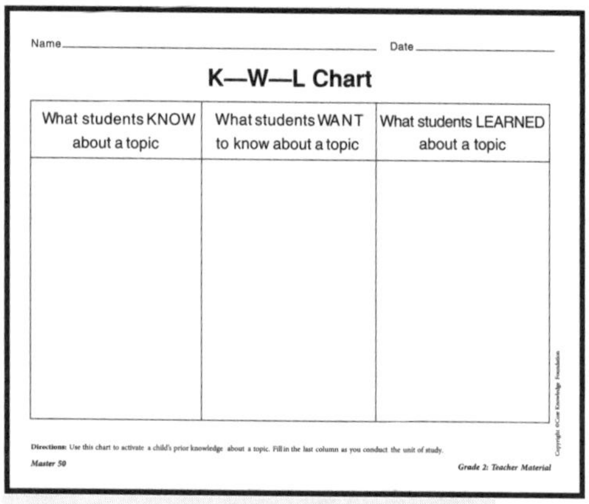

Name ________ Date ________

K—W—L Chart

What students KNOW about a topic	What students WANT to know about a topic	What students LEARNED about a topic

Directions: Use this chart to activate a child's prior knowledge about a topic. Fill in the last column as you conduct the unit of study.

Master 50

Grade 2: Teacher Material

Copyright ©Core Knowledge Foundation

Use Instructional Master 50.

C. Taking Care of Your Body: A Healthy Diet

Providing your body with the nutrients it needs is an essential component of staying healthy. You need a variety of nutrients that come from a variety of food sources. Water is one of the most important nutrients that your body needs. It aids in digestion, cell growth, body-temperature stabilization, and excretion of wastes. Proteins are another important nutrient. Proteins are used to build muscle and are important for cell growth and repair. Carbohydrates are nutrients that provide the body with its main source of energy. Fats provide insulation for the cells and act as an important source of stored energy. Vitamins, such as the C and B vitamins, help your body perform specific functions. Minerals, such as iron, calcium, and sodium, keep your teeth and bones strong and also help your body perform specific functions. The following chart lists a few vitamins and minerals and tells some of the roles each plays in the body:

Vitamins and Minerals	Role in Body	Source
Vitamin A	keeps skin and eyes healthy needed for cell growth promotes a healthy immune system	spinach, broccoli, carrots milk, eggs
Vitamin C	keeps blood vessels, gums, and teeth healthy helps build tissue	citrus fruits, tomatoes, strawberries
Fluoride	helps prevent tooth decay	fish, gelatin
Iron	protects against infection helps blood carry oxygen throughout the body	beef, pork, soybeans, oatmeal

How can you be sure you are getting all the nutrients you need in the right amounts? Eating a well-balanced diet that includes a mixture of foods from a variety of food categories—grains, fruits, vegetables, dairy, meats and fish, and fats—ensures that you get all the nutrients your body needs. Each food category listed above contains different nutrients that you need daily. Grains, such as pasta, rice, bread, and cereal, are rich in carbohydrates. Fruits and vegetables are also a source of carbohydrates and are rich in vitamins and minerals. Meats and fish provide your body with proteins.

Explain to children that many different food guides exist, each outlining the amounts and kinds of food that are best to eat. The USDA Food Guide Pyramid is one guideline that has traditionally been widely cited, although it has come under attack in recent years. The Food Guide Pyramid shows a range for the number of servings of

each food group that you should eat on a daily basis. Reading food labels printed on most packaged foods can help you make sure you are eating healthfully. Food labels tell you how big a serving is, which essential nutrients are provided in each serving, and the quantities of each nutrient. Instead of focusing on a specific food guide, you may prefer to discuss with children the importance of eating a variety of foods and making healthy meal and snack choices. Healthful eating habits start when children are young. Explain to children that breakfast is one of the most important meals of the day. After a full night of rest, they need to replenish their body with nutrients so that they can be ready for the demands of a new day.

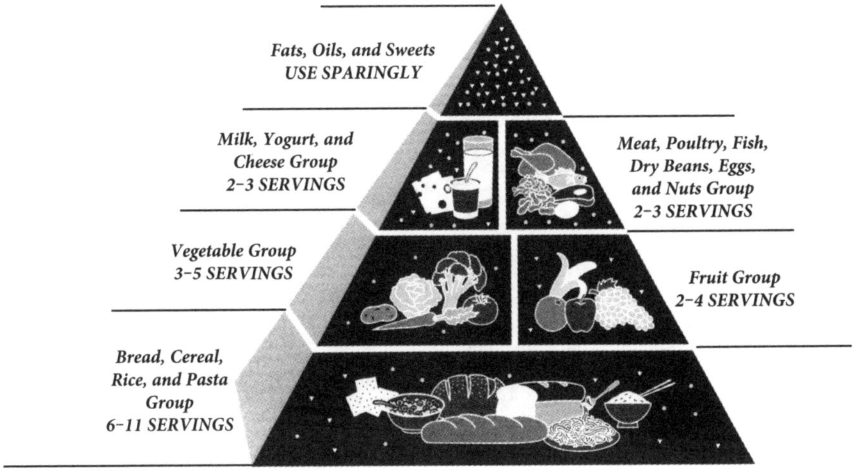

Teaching Idea

Provide children with a variety of food labels, or invite them to bring food labels in for their favorite breakfast foods and snacks. Read the labels with them, and help them understand the information that is provided on the labels. Compare the labels for two breakfast meals or snacks, for example, donuts and cereal, or raisins and cookies. Ask questions such as these: "Which has more sugar? Which has a greater number of nutrients? What food groups do they belong to?" Challenge children to determine which food would make a healthier food choice.

Teaching Idea

Invite children to cut out pictures from magazines of different types of foods. Encourage children to classify each picture according to the food group in which it belongs. Children can then use their pictures to construct their own "food guide chart" that shows examples of foods that belong in each of the six food groups.

Review

Below are some ideas for ongoing assessment and review activities. These are not meant to constitute a comprehensive list.

- In addition to having the class plan a healthy meal at home, also have them think about food that they can eat while dining in a restaurant. You can find nutritional information for a variety of restaurants, from fast-food restaurants to dining establishments. Bring in these materials and help the class read the nutritional information of the food. What observations can they make? Are there more healthy restaurants to choose from? Have the class write about this experience.
- In order to understand the parts of the digestive system, have the children make a simple flap book with four flaps. Label each flap with one of the following words: *cell, tissue, organs,* and *systems.* On top of the flap, have children draw a simple picture to illustrate the meaning of the word. Then, have children write under each flap what that part does and how they build on each other. The class can see the progression from the smallest part to the biggest part.

The Big Idea in Review

The human body is made up of microscopic cells that group together in highly organized fashions to form tissues, organs, and systems.

• Make a connection between Anton van Leeuwenhoek and the study of cells if you taught these topics jointly. Ask each child to make up one question to ask Leeuwenhoek about his study of the microscope. Make a class list of these questions on chart paper, and then make a trip to the library to see if you can find the answers. When the answers are discovered, write them on the chart.

• Create sets of digestive system index cards labeled *teeth, tongue, esophagus, stomach, small intestine,* and *large intestine.* Make enough sets of cards so that everyone in the class has one card. Depending on the number of children in your class, you may need to have some children pair up. Pass out the cards and have children group themselves to form a complete digestive system, with each part of the system represented. Again, depending on the number of children in your class, there may be several complete digestive system groups in the class. Then, have children take turns briefly describing the part of the system on their card.

• Plan a writing activity to focus on some of the vocabulary in this section. Post a list of words from the student vocabulary section on a piece of chart paper, and instruct children to write a paragraph using a set number of words from the list. For example, you may ask them to use five of the words correctly in sentences. You may structure the writing activity around a journal question, or you may let the class make up their own stories. After finishing, share the pieces aloud and have children raise their hands when they hear a vocabulary word from the list.

• You may also ask the following questions at the end of this section:

1. What is the basic unit that makes up all living things?

   The cell is the basic unit that makes up all living things.

2. What is an organ?

   An organ is made up of a group of tissues. It works with other organs as a system to perform a job in the body.

3. What happens during digestion?

   Food is broken down into substances the body can use, and waste is removed from the body.

4. What are some of the organs involved in digestion?

   Organs involved in digestion include the stomach, intestines, etc.

5. What is the main job of the excretory system?

   The main job of the excretory system is to remove liquid waste from the body.

6. How can you have a healthy, well-balanced diet?

   Be sure to eat a variety of foods and make healthy meal and snack choices.

More Resources

The titles listed below are offered as a representative sample of materials and not a complete list of everything that is available.

For children —

These books are generally intended to be read aloud, though some children may be able to read parts or all of the simpler texts.

- *Good Enough to Eat: A Kid's Guide to Food and Nutrition,* by Lizzy Rockwell (HarperCollins Juvenile Books, 1999). Designed for early readers. Also includes information on the digestive system. Note that the scientific basis for the USDA Food Guide Pyramid has been challenged. Hardcover, 40 pages, ISBN 0060274344.
- *Looking into My Body,* by Nigel Nelson and illustrated by Simon Able (Reader's Digest, 1996). "Features simple, scientifically correct illustrations on specially designed 'see-through' windows" (from the publisher). Hardcover, 12 pages, ISBN 1575840340. For a more advanced text, see *The Human Body: A Fascinating See-Through View of How Bodies Work,* by Lawrence T. Lorimer and others, also published by Reader's Digest (ISBN 1575842483).
- *What Happens to a Hamburger? (Let's-Read-and-Find-Out Science, Stage 2),* by Paul Showers and illustrated by Edward Miller (HarperTrophy, 2001). A journey through the human digestive system. Paperback, 40 pages, ISBN 0064451836.

For teachers —

- *DK Guide to the Human Body: A Photographic Journey through the Human Body,* by Richard Walker (Dorling Kindersley, 2001). Hardcover, 64 pages, ISBN 0789473887.
- *Janice VanCleave's Play and Find Out About the Human Body: Easy Experiments for Young Children,* by Janice VanCleave (John Wiley & Sons, 1998). Paperback, 122 pages, ISBN 0471129356. See also *Janice VanCleave's Food and Nutrition for Every Kid,* which has many simple hands-on activities that will need to be teacher-directed for younger children. Note that the USDA Food Guide Pyramid is currently under review.
- *Watch Me Grow: Fun Ways to Learn about Cells, Muscles, Bones, and Joints—Activities for Children 5 to 9,* by Michelle O'Brien-Palmer (Chicago Review Press, 1999). Paperback, 142 pages, ISBN 155652367X. See also *Healthy Me,* by the same author.

IV. Magnetism

The Big Idea

Magnets exert forces of attraction on certain materials.

Remember that each subject you study with children expands their vocabulary and introduces new terms, thus making them better listeners and readers. As you study about magnetism, use read alouds and discussions to build children's vocabularies.

What Students Should Already Know

Students in Core Knowledge schools should be familiar with

Kindergarten

- Introduction to Magnetism
  - identifying familiar everyday uses of magnets (for example, in toys, in cabinet locks, in "refrigerator magnets," etc.)
  - classifying materials according to whether they are or are not attracted by a magnet

What Students Need to Learn

- **Magnetism demonstrates that there are forces that act upon objects but cannot be seen.**
- **Most magnets contain iron.**
- **Lodestones: naturally occurring magnets**
- **Magnetic poles: north-seeking and south-seeking poles**
- **Magnetic field (strongest at the poles)**
- **Law of magnetic attraction: unlike poles attract, like poles repel**
- **Earth behaves as if it were a huge magnet: north and south magnetic poles**
- **Orienteering: use of a magnetized needle in a compass, which will always point to the north**

Vocabulary

Student/Teacher Vocabulary

attract: to draw to (S)

magnet: a body that attracts certain materials by its surrounding field of force (S)

magnetic field: the region around a magnet in which a magnetic force is exerted (T)

magnetic pole: the region where a magnet produces a force (T)

magnetism: an invisible force that attracts most materials made of iron, nickel, or cobalt (S)

north pole: one of the magnetic poles of a magnet (S)

repel: to push away (S)

south pole: one of the magnetic poles of a magnet (S)

Domain Vocabulary

Magnetism and associated words:
exert, invisible, force, iron, nickel, cobalt, steel, pull, push, power, strength, move, effect, attraction, repulsion, oppose, resist

At a Glance

The most important ideas for you are:

- Magnetism is an invisible phenomenon: we cannot see it but we can observe its effects on objects.
- Lodestone, or magnetite, is a naturally occurring magnetic rock.
- The regions that interact magnetically are called magnetic poles. Magnets have north and south poles.
- Magnets exert a force of attraction on most materials made of iron, nickel, or cobalt.
- The region around a magnet in which a magnetic force is exerted is called a magnetic field.
- Earth acts as a huge magnet.
- Compasses can be used for orienteering.

Materials

world map or globe, p. 442

magnets of various shapes and sizes, pp. 442–446

everyday objects: paper clips, coins, nails, plastic bottle caps, corks, etc., p. 442

bar magnets, p. 443

piece of paper or cardboard, p. 443

iron filings, p. 443

safety goggles, p. 443

transparency and overhead projector, p. 443

nail and 10 metal paper clips, p. 443

needle, p. 444

small bowl and water, p. 444

tissue paper or facial tissue, p. 444

magnetic compass, pp. 444–445

NO MAGNETS! signs with tape, p. 445

individual chart for each child with two columns, one labeled *attract* and one labeled *don't attract*, p. 445

science journals, pp. 445–446

writing journals, p. 445

chart paper, p. 445

lunch bags filled with small "treasures" (pencils, erasers, stickers), 1 bag for each group of children, p. 445

compass directions for treasure hunt, 1 set for each group of children, p. 445

paper clips, p. 446

Cross-curricular Teaching Idea

Connect this section to children's study of history and world geography by locating Turkey and China on a world map. Review with children what they have learned about ancient Greek and Asian cultures. Explain that the geographic boundaries of these countries were different thousands of years ago. Discuss how long ago these early discoveries of magnetism were made and why they were of great importance to these cultures.

Teaching Idea

Introduce the topic of magnetism by providing opportunities for children to observe magnets. Distribute magnets of various shapes and sizes, along with everyday objects, such as paper clips, coins, nails, plastic bottle caps, corks, etc. Allow children to experiment. Be sure to discuss their observations, and relate them to the magnetic forces they are observing.

Teaching Idea

Invite children to experiment with attraction and repulsion. Have them take 2 magnets of the same size and shape and then bring the 2 south poles together. Encourage them to describe what happens and what they feel. Invite them to predict what will happen when they bring the two north poles together and what will happen when they bring a north pole and a south pole together. Encourage children to use the terminology introduced in this section, e.g., *attract* and *repel*.

What Teachers Need to Know

Background

More than 2,000 years ago, Greeks living in a region of Turkey known as Magnesia discovered that certain black rocks attracted materials that contained iron. They named these rocks magnetite, in honor of their homeland. The Greeks also called these rocks lodestones, meaning "leading stones." This name was the result of an important observation the Greeks made: Whenever the stones (or rocks) were hung from a string and allowed to swing freely, the same parts of the stones would always point in the same direction. That direction was toward a certain star in the north called the leading star, or lodestar. Based on this property, magnetite came to be known as lodestone.

People in China also knew about the properties of magnetite. In the 12th century, they used lodestones for navigating ships. By rubbing small, flat pieces of iron over lodestones, the pieces became magnetized. The magnetized iron pointed in a north-south direction when hung by a silken thread. These pieces of magnetized iron were the first compasses!

What the Greeks and Chinese did not know then was that they were observing and using an important physical property of matter called magnetism.

The Nature of Magnets

Magnets are fascinating objects! If you've ever experimented with them, you know how hard it can be to pull them apart or push them together. Magnets will stick to certain objects (the refrigerator door, a metallic bulletin board) but not to others (an aluminum pan). Magnets make popular toys and are essential to the operation of common devices, such as doorbells, telephones, audiotape and videotape units, motors, and generators. Compasses are magnets. Magnets come in a variety of shapes and sizes, yet they all exert the same magnetic forces.

Magnetic Poles

All magnets exert forces on one another. The regions where the magnetic forces are exerted are called magnetic poles. All magnets have two poles—a north pole and a south pole. (However, magnets can have more than just a pair of poles. For example, a sheet refrigerator magnet has dozens of north and south poles. Only the simplest magnets have a single pair. In fact, the poles don't even have to come in pairs: you can have two south poles and one north pole, as long as the sum of north pole character is equal to the sum of south pole character; that is, the two souths have to be weaker than the one north.) The simplest kind of magnet is a bar magnet. Its poles are located at the two ends. A horseshoe magnet, which is a bar magnet that has been bent, also has its poles at the two ends.

When two magnets are brought together, the north poles of two magnets repel, or push away, each other. The south poles of two magnets also repel each other. The north pole and south pole of two magnets attract, or pull, each other. This phenomenon of like poles repelling and unlike poles attracting is often called the "law of magnetic attraction."

Magnetic poles usually appear in pairs—a north pole and a south pole. It might seem logical to think that the two poles of a magnet can be separated if the

magnet is cut in half. But this is not the case. If a bar magnet is cut in half, each half behaves as a complete magnet. If those two smaller magnets are cut in half, four even smaller complete magnets result. No amount of cutting will ever produce an isolated single pole.

Magnetic Fields

Magnetic forces are exerted on the poles of a magnet, but that magnet's influence extends beyond the poles themselves. The magnet can exert magnetic forces on other poles located all around the magnet. The region around a magnet in which a magnetic force is exerted is called a magnetic field. The shape of a magnetic field is represented by lines of force that extend from one pole to the other. They are most numerous and closest together at the poles—the places where the field strength is the strongest.

Magnetic Materials

If a magnet is brought near a piece of plastic, wood, glass, aluminum, or cloth, there is no action—attraction or repulsion—between the magnet and these nonmagnetic materials. None of these materials can be magnetized. But materials such as iron, nickel, cobalt, and steel react to a magnet and are easily magnetized. Why are some materials magnetic and others not magnetic?

The magnetic properties of a material depend on its atomic structure. The electrons in all atoms spin as they move around the nucleus. A spinning electron produces a magnetic field with both a north pole and a south pole. Thus, an atom acts like a tiny magnet.

In most materials, the atoms are arranged so that the magnetic fields of individual atoms cancel each other. Nonmagnetic materials have absolutely no magnetic order inside because of this perfect cancellation.

In some materials, however, groups of atoms can cluster in such a way that their magnetic fields are all arranged in the same direction, or aligned. These clusters of aligned atoms are called magnetic domains. In a magnet, most of the domains are aligned. In unmagnetized materials, the domains are arranged randomly, hiding a magnetic order. Materials that are easily magnetized have magnetic domains that are readily aligned in the presence of a magnet. Here's an example. When a magnet is brought near an unmagnetized object, such as a paper clip, the magnet's field causes the domains in the paper clip to align. The paper clip becomes a temporary magnet. Its south pole faces the north pole of the permanent magnet. It is attracted to the magnet. When the permanent magnet is removed, however, the domains in the paper clip become random again and the paper clip is no longer magnetized.

Objects made of soft iron like paper clips are easy to magnetize, but they lose their magnetism easily. They make good temporary magnets. Permanent magnets are made of materials that are more difficult to magnetize, but permanent magnets tend to stay magnetized. Most permanent magnets are made from alloys containing iron, nickel, cobalt, and aluminum in various proportions. Permanent magnets can also be made from ceramic products containing barium, iron, cobalt, and nickel. Dropping or heating a permanent magnet will jar some of its domains into randomness, and the magnet will become weaker. Explain to children that some magnets are very strong and always exhibit magnetism (permanent magnets). Other magnets are not as strong and tend to lose their magnetism (temporary magnets).

Teaching Idea

Magnetic lines of force can be demonstrated by sprinkling iron fillngs on a sheet of paper or piece of cardboard placed on top of a bar magnet. The filings will form an orderly pattern of lines around the magnet, going in complete loops from a north pole to a south pole. This can also be done on a transparency and projected onto a screen or wall. It is important when using filings to follow science safety procedures. Many schools require children to wear goggles when experimenting with iron filings.

Teaching Idea

Invite children to brainstorm a list of familiar objects that contain magnets. After a list has been compiled, "amaze" children with the following information: credit cards, computer discs, radios, subway tickets, medical diagnostic instruments, and even light itself involve magnets/magnetism.

Cross-curricular Teaching Idea

Use your study of magnetism to reinforce counting and measuring skills learned in math. Children can "make a magnet" by obtaining a nail, a bar magnet, and about 10 metal paper clips. Instruct them to stroke the nail with the magnet in the same direction about 20 times and to determine how many (if any) paper clips their nail magnet will pick up. Have children stroke the nail again 40 and then 60 times and determine how many paper clips their nail magnet will pick up now. Encourage children to record their results and state a conclusion. You could even chart this information on a class bar graph.

Earth as a Magnet

Why does one pole of a bar magnet suspended from a string always point north and the other pole always point south? Why does a compass always point northward? The answer is that Earth itself is a huge magnet. Thus, it has magnetic poles, exerts magnetic forces, and is surrounded by a magnetic field.

The magnetic poles of Earth do not coincide with the geographic poles, however. The geographic North Pole and South Pole identify Earth's axis (or the imaginary line about which Earth rotates). The magnetic poles are about 1,300 miles from the geographic poles. The angle between magnetic north and true north is called the magnetic declination.

The actual origin of Earth's magnetic field is not completely understood. Scientists believe, however, that it is related to the motion of molten metals (mainly iron and nickel) in Earth's core. As these molten metals move, they create convection currents. Such currents may be responsible for Earth's magnetic field. While the idea is theoretically reasonable, it has yet to be proven.

Teaching Idea

You can demonstrate how to make a floating compass similar to ones used in early days of navigation. (Note: You can make this a class demonstration by using a glass bowl and placing the setup on an overhead projector.)

Magnetize a needle by stroking it with one end of a magnet (the north pole, preferably; if one end of the magnet is clearly marked with an "N" or with red paint, this will avoid any confusion). Stroke the magnet along the needle in the same direction at least 50 times. Add water to a small bowl until it is nearly full. Tear a small piece of tissue and carefully place it on the water so that it floats. Then gently place the magnetized needle on the tissue. After a few moments, the needle will stop moving and will end up pointing in a northerly direction. You have constructed a simple compass. If you have a commercial compass, you can use it for comparison.

Magnetic Compasses and Orienteering

As we noted earlier, because Earth is a huge magnet, there is a magnetic field all around it. Therefore, magnetic material is attracted to Earth's magnetic poles, the points of strongest attraction. A magnetic compass is an instrument made of a magnet that can pivot, or turn freely, and, in so doing, can show direction relative to compass points. A magnetic compass needle pivots until it lies along the magnetic lines of force in Earth's magnetic field. So, one end always points in a northerly direction.

You can determine your position and make your way, or navigate, through unfamiliar territory by using a magnetic compass. This method of getting from one place to another is called orienteering. Orienteering also usually involves the use of a map along with a compass to help you pinpoint, or zero in on, your destination. Geographical maps show a key that gives the orientation, or the arrangement, of different locations on the map, usually with north at the top of the map. If you align a compass with the orientation of the map you are using, you can easily make your way to the desired location.

Commercial compasses generally are designed with a backing plate or card that shows an arrow, which you can use to point out the direction you wish to travel. There is also an inner arrow pointing to north on a disk that marks the degrees of a circle. To use a map and compass together, first line up the compass with the needle pointing north, then align the map in the same position, so that the compass points to the top of the map. Note your starting location on the map, and place the compass over that point. Next find the location on the map of the destination to which you wish to travel. Move the back plate of the compass so that the outer arrow points to your destination. Note the degree marking, for instance, 100 degrees, or just past due east. If you then travel in the direction of that outer arrow, and keep the inner arrow aligned with the needle, you will reach your destination. If you have a watch and know your rate of travel, you can use the distance key on the map to determine the approximate length of time needed to traverse the distance.

Knowing the destination's degree angle is helpful if the ground you are traveling over is uneven or has obstacles around which you may have to detour, such as a mountain or a canyon. You can make the detour and then get back on track by using the compass markings to compensate for any changes in direction you may need to make. For example, if you must head due south to avoid a canyon, the simplest way to navigate is to use a watch; note the time, first when you started the deviation south, and then again when you get past the canyon, and then walk due north for the same period of time. After the correct period of time (assuming you are traveling at the same rate of speed all the way), you can once again pick up your original direction, east, and still arrive at your desired destination. It is most useful to keep notes of all times and directions in a small notebook. More experienced navigators may also recalculate angles, as necessary, to correct for deviations and shorten the journey when traveling around obstacles.

Review

The Big Idea in Review

Magnets exert forces of attraction on certain materials.

Below are some ideas for ongoing assessment and review activities. These are not meant to constitute a comprehensive list.

- When brainstorming about magnets and reviewing the material from Kindergarten, remind children that magnets can damage some materials. Since you will be working with magnets in this section, prepare some signs with tape on the back that say, "NO MAGNETS!" Ask the class to see if they can remember areas where magnets should not be used. Upon giving correct answers, let the children hang the signs on those areas. Possible examples would include areas near the computers, videotapes, computer discs, televisions, video recorders, DVD players, telephones, compact discs, stereos, or radios.
- When letting the class experiment with magnets, have them categorize materials into two groups: those that attract and those that don't attract. Make a chart for each child with two columns, one labeled *attract* and one labeled *don't attract*. When experimenting with magnets and materials, have children record their observations in each chart. After working with the materials, have them write in a science journal about their observations and conclude why some materials are attracted to magnets and others are not.
- Pose a journal question to the class about magnets and how they might be helpful in our daily lives. What uses are there for magnets? Have children write about a situation in which they might use a magnet and then read it aloud to the class. As each child shares his or her journal response, make a class chart listing all of the different situations in which magnets may be used.
- Take the class outside to conduct an orienteering treasure hunt activity. Divide the class into groups, and give each group printed directions. They will use these directions to find a bag of goodies labeled with their group name. Each group will use a compass to follow their directions. (For example, the directions might begin by saying to take four steps north from the basketball net and two steps east.) You may wish to have each group start from a different location. Be sure to test the compasses and the instructions before you give them to the children. After each group has found its bag, follow up with a writing activity in which children describe the experience of orienteering.

• To explore the concept of a magnetic field, have the class experiment using a magnet and a paper clip in small groups. Ask them to predict what will happen when they move the magnets closer to the paper clips. Does the magnet have to be touching the paper clip to attract it, or does the magnet draw the paper clip to it? How close does the magnet need to be to attract the paper clip? This is the magnetic field in action. Ask children to record their results in their science journals.

• You may also ask the following questions at the end of this section:

1. What are some properties common to all magnets?

   All magnets have north poles and south poles, have a magnetic field, and exert a force on most objects made of iron, nickel, and cobalt.

2. What is the law of magnetic attraction?

   Like poles repel; unlike poles attract.

3. Where on a magnet is the magnetic field the strongest?

   The magnetic field is strongest around the poles of a magnet.

4. What is the connection between magnets and compasses?

   A compass uses a magnet to determine which way is north.

5. How does a compass work?

   A compass works because Earth is like a huge magnet. The magnetic needle of a compass aligns with Earth's magnetic field, thereby showing us the direction of north.

More Resources

The titles listed below are offered as a representative sample of materials and not a complete list of everything that is available.

For children —

These books are generally intended to be read aloud, though some children may be able to read parts or all of the simpler texts.

• *Science with Magnets (Usborne Science Activities),* by Helen Edom (EDC Publications, 1992). Full-color activity book with simple and safe experiments and games. Paperback, ISBN 0881106372. A Science with Magnets Kid Kit (compass, corks, magnets, nail, wire, non-hardening clay, paper clips) is also available.

• *What Magnets Can Do,* by Allan Fowler (Children's Book Press, 1995). Paperback, 32 pages, ISBN 051646034X.

• *What Makes a Magnet? (Let's-Read-and-Find-Out Science),* by Franklyn M. Branley and illustrated by True Kelley (HarperTrophy, 1996). Paperback, 32 pages, ISBN 0064451488. See also *Mickey's Magnet,* by the same author.

For teachers —

• *Janice VanCleave's Magnets: Mind-boggling Experiments You Can Turn into Science Fair Projects,* by Janice VanCleave (John Wiley & Sons, 1993). Some experiments may be too difficult for this age group. Paperback, 96 pages, 0471571067.

• *The Magnet Book,* by Shar Levine and Leslie Johnstone (Sterling, 1997). Contains a number of very interesting experiments using relatively simple materials. Hardcover, 80 pages, ISBN 0806999438.

• *Mudpies to Magnets,* by Robert A. Williams, Robert E. Rockwell, and Elizabeth A. Sherwood (Gryphon House, 1990). Originally written as a "preschool science curriculum," this book and its sequel, *More Mudpies to Magnets,* contain experiments that can be enjoyed by children up to age 10, according to *The Science Spiders Newsletter.* Covers a wide range of topics, including good cross-curricular connections with art and math. Paperback, 156 pages, ISBN 0876591128.

• Magnet Man, http://my.execpc.com/~rhoadley/magindex.htm, has numerous experiments you can do with magnets.

V. Simple Machines

The Big Idea

Simple machines help us do work.

Remember that each subject you study with children expands their vocabulary and introduces new terms, thus making them better listeners and readers. As you study about simple machines, use read alouds and discussions to build children's vocabularies.

What Students Need to Learn

- **Simple machines**
  - **Lever**
  - **Pulley**
  - **Wheel and axle (gears: wheels with teeth and notches; how gears work, and familiar uses [for example, in bicycles])**
  - **Inclined plane**
  - **Wedge**
  - **Screw**
- **Friction, and ways to reduce friction (lubricants, rollers, etc.)**

V. Simple Machines

Materials

Instructional Masters 48a–48b

Simple Machine Crossword, p. 452

ruler, p. 449

yarn, p. 450

empty spool of thread, 1 per pair of children, p. 450

blocks or other small classroom objects, p. 450

can opener, p. 451

scissors, p. 451

writing journals, p. 453

chart paper, p. 453

2 half-pints of whipping cream, p. 453

1 jar with a screw-on lid, p. 453

clear glass bowl, p. 453

manual eggbeater, p. 453

stopwatch, p. 453

science journals, p. 453

hammer, p. 453

screw, p. 453

screwdriver, p. 453

toy car with wheels, p. 453

pulley and rope, p. 453

wheel with notched teeth, p. 453

Vocabulary

Student/Teacher Vocabulary

force: a push or a pull (T)

friction: a phenomenon in nature that exerts forces that oppose motion (S)

inclined plane: a simple machine that consists of a flat, slanted surface (S)

lever: a simple machine with a bar that is free to pivot around a fixed point (S)

pulley: a simple machine that has a rope, belt, or chain that is wrapped around a grooved wheel (S)

screw: an inclined plane wrapped around a central cylinder (S)

wedge: an inclined plane (S)

wheel and axle: a simple machine that has two circular objects of different sizes. The larger circle is known as the wheel, and the smaller circle is known as the axle. (S)

work: the transfer of energy that occurs when an object is moved in the direction of a force applied to it (T)

Domain Vocabulary

Simple machines and associated words:

machine, device, tool, distance, direction, speed, change, alter, increase, decrease, reduce, limit, efficient, inefficient, direct, indirect, proportional, pivot, swivel, swing, pry, lift, fixed, unfixed, movable, balance, imbalance, unbalance, fulcrum, resistance, load, effort, ramp, slant, angle, spiral, circle, circular, upward, downward, touch, rub, slide, push, pull, exert, gear, smooth, slick, slippery, rough, coarse

At a Glance

The most important ideas for you are:

- In science, work is defined as applying a force over a distance.
- Machines can be used to make work easier.
- The six simple machines are the lever, pulley, wheel and axle, inclined plane, wedge, and screw.
- Friction is a force in nature that exists between two objects that are touching or moving against one another.

What Teachers Need to Know

Background

What images come to mind when you see the word machine*? Do you think of large tractors and cranes or cars and jets? You may not realize it, but such simple items as scissors, pencil sharpeners, hammers, and bicycles are all machines, too. A machine is any device or tool that helps you do work. You do work when you apply a force on an object and it moves a distance in the*

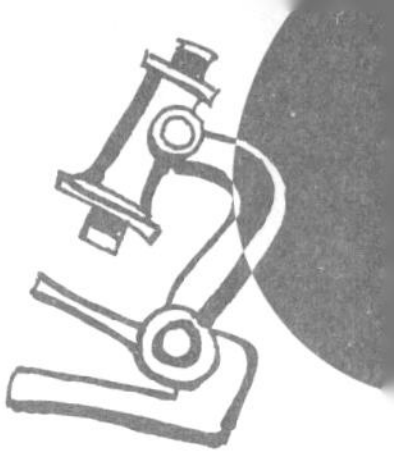

direction of your force on it. When you lift a stack of books, hammer a nail into the wall, or push a baby stroller, you are doing work.

People have been using tools since ancient times to help them with activities, such as hunting, gardening, gathering food, cooking, and lifting and moving heavy objects. Although we are unsure exactly when the first machines were used, the simplest and oldest machines are the lever, pulley, wheel and axle, inclined plane, wedge, and screw. These machines are known as simple machines—they each consist of just one or two parts.

Remember that work is the transfer of energy that occurs when an object is moved in the direction of a force applied to it. Work can be measured by multiplying the force exerted on an object by the distance the object moved in the direction of that force. These six simple machines help you do work by changing the direction of force you must apply to move an object, decreasing the amount of force required to move an object, or decreasing the distance through which you must apply a force. It is important to note that the amount of work required to move something a particular distance does not change whether or not you use a machine. The same amount of work is done when you use a machine as when you do not use the help of a machine.

Simple machines merely change the way in which work is done. Force and distance are indirectly proportional. That means when the use of a machine decreases the amount of force you must apply, it increases the distance through which the force must be applied. Likewise, when a simple machine decreases the distance through which you must apply a force, it increases the amount of force that is required.

The Lever

If you have ever removed a bottle cap from a container of soda with a bottle opener, or if you have removed a nail from a piece of wood with a hammer or crowbar, then you have used a lever. Wheelbarrows, boat oars, baseball bats, and seesaws are some other examples of levers that you may commonly encounter. A lever is a simple machine that is comprised of a bar that is free to pivot around a fixed point.

The fixed, pivotal point of a lever is known as the fulcrum. The item that must be moved (the bottle cap and nail in the first examples) is the resistance, or load. The force that must be applied to move the load is called the effort force. When a force is applied to the bar, the bar swings around the fulcrum to move the load. A lever helps you do work by either decreasing the effort force you must apply to move an object or decreasing the distance through which you must apply a force. Levers may also help you do work by changing the direction of the force required to move a load.

Teaching Idea

It is important for children to understand the concept of work in studying this section. Explain that, in science, work is done when you push or pull on something and it moves in the direction of your push or pull. Invite children to brainstorm a list of activities that require work. To further exemplify the concept, invite one child to push very hard against the wall or floor. Ask the class if the child did any work. (No: although a force was applied, the floor did not move.) Invite another child to push a chair. Again ask the class if the child did any work. (Yes: a force was applied, and the chair moved.)

Teaching Idea

Invite children to experiment with levers. Instruct them to collect a pencil, a ruler, and 3 or 4 books. Have children place the ruler on top of the pencil, and invite them to press down on one end of the ruler. Explain that this is a model of a lever; the ruler (bar) pivots around the pencil (fulcrum)—when one side is pressed down, the other side goes up. Encourage them to experiment with their lever by adding books and moving the pencil closer to and further from the books. How many books can they lift when the pencil is very close to the books? How many can they lift when the pencil is further from the books? How does the pencil's location affect the way the lever works? Talk about how the lever system can make work easier.

Levers can be grouped into three classes, depending on the position of the fulcrum in relation to the effort force and load. When the fulcrum is located between the load and effort force, the lever is called a first-class lever. Seesaws and boat oars are first-class levers. When the fulcrum is located at the far end of the lever, and the effort force is at the opposite end, the lever is called a second-class lever. Wheelbarrows are second-class levers. When the effort force is between the fulcrum and load, the lever is called a third-class lever. Shovels are examples of third-class levers.

Teaching Idea

Invite pairs of children to make a pulley system with 2 pieces of yarn and an empty spool of thread. Have children make a "handle" for their pulley by threading one piece of yarn through the hole of the spool and tying it in a loop. Have children tie the other piece of yarn to a classroom object, such as a small block or book. They should wrap the free end of the yarn around the groove of the spool. While one child holds the pulley by the handle, the other child should pull down on the free end of the yarn to lift the object. Encourage children to take a turn doing both the holding and the lifting. Talk about how the pulley system can make work easier.

Teaching Idea

If your school raises the flag every morning, you can show children how this is typically done by using a pulley: the person pulls down and the flag goes up.

The Pulley

If you have ever raised or lowered a window shade, then you have used another type of simple machine—the pulley. A pulley is comprised of a rope, belt, or chain that is wrapped around a grooved wheel. Pulley systems can be found in a variety of places, such as the top of cranes, the sails of sailboats, in sports exercise equipment, and ski lifts.

Pulleys that are attached to a structure are called fixed pulleys. Fixed pulleys help you do work by changing the direction of the force you need to apply to lift a load. Imagine trying to lift a filing cabinet in your home. You would have to apply a great upward force to get the cabinet off the floor. If the cabinet were tied to a rope that ran through a fixed pulley—such as a pulley attached to the ceiling, for example—you would have an easier time lifting the object. It is much easier to pull down on the rope than to lift the object directly. Fixed pulleys do not decrease the effort force that must be applied—they simply change the direction of the force; for example, a pulley allows you to lift something *up* by pulling *down*.

Movable pulleys are a second type of pulley system. With a movable pulley, the pulley is attached to the load and is able to move freely along a rope that is attached to a structure. Movable pulleys help you do work by decreasing the amount of force you must apply to move an object. With single movable pulleys, the direction of the effort force does not change.

Fixed and movable pulleys can be used together in pulley systems to both change the direction and decrease the amount of force required to move an object.

The Wheel and Axle

Doorknobs, Ferris wheels, steering wheels, and screwdrivers are examples of the simple machine known as the wheel and axle. A wheel and axle is comprised of two circular objects of different sizes. The larger circle is known as the wheel, and the smaller

circle is known as the axle. A wheel and axle helps you do work by decreasing either the effort force or the distance through which a force must be applied.

Try to turn a doorknob by the small circular axle that runs through the door. You probably cannot turn it far enough to open the door with ease. You can probably turn the knob quite easily, however. Why is this? Because the wheel is larger than the axle, it always moves a greater distance than the axle. Therefore, the force applied to the wheel is multiplied when it is transferred to the axle. You apply less force over a greater distance to turn the knob, making it easier to open the door.

A gear is a special type of wheel and axle. The wheel of a gear has teeth and notches. The teeth of one gear may be made to fit in the teeth of another, so that by turning one gear, both gears move. Gears can be found in watches, clocks, and can openers.

The Inclined Plane

Imagine that you have to load a 200-pound box full of books onto a truck. How would you do it? Would you lift it straight up? This would require a great deal of force. Pushing the box up a ramp would make the job much easier. A ramp is an example of an inclined plane. An inclined plane consists of a flat, slanted surface. This simple machine helps you do work by decreasing the amount of force required to move a load. Although the force is decreased, the distance you must move the load increases. The longer and less slanted the inclined plane, the less force (but greater distance) required to move a load.

The Wedge

Zippers, knives, and axes are some examples of the simple machine known as the wedge. A wedge is actually an inclined plane. However, instead of the load moving while the machine remains stationary, as is the case with an inclined plane, the wedge moves across a load. A wedge helps you do work by decreasing the amount and changing the direction of the effort force required to act on an object. When you use an axe to chop wood, you hit the wood with a downward force to split apart the wood. The wedge in a zipper is a small triangular piece of metal moved by the handle, known as a slide, used to pull a zipper open or closed. The wedge forces the two tracks of teeth in a zipper to come together or pull apart, depending on the direction in which the slide is moved.

Teaching Idea

The inclined plane, consisting of one nonmoving part, is the simplest of the simple machines. Ancient Egyptians used the inclined plane over 4,500 years ago as a means for transporting stones in building the pyramids. Inclined planes can be found today in many modern buildings as handicapped accessible ramps. Inclined planes make it easier for people with handicaps to get around. Go on an "inclined plane hunt" around the school, noting which places have them and why, and which places could possibly use one.

Teaching Idea

Most machines are compound machines. A compound machine is a machine comprised of 2 or more simple machines. Scissors, can openers, and pencil sharpeners are examples of compound machines. Challenge children to find a few of the simple machines that are used in a can opener or a pair of scissors. In a can opener, the handle works as a lever, the knob works as a wheel and axle, and the cutting wheel works as a wedge. In a pair of scissors, the handle works as a lever and the cutting edge works as a wedge.

The Screw

Nuts, bolts, corkscrews, and wood screws are some examples of the simple machine known as the screw. A screw, like a wedge, is a type of inclined plane. A screw consists of an inclined plane wrapped around a central cylinder. A screw decreases the amount of effort force required to do work. Since a screw is an inclined plane wrapped around a cylinder, the force required to go up and down the screw is much less than going "straight up and down." Compare this to climbing straight up a hill or following a road that makes its way to the top of the hill by circling around it: the road around the hill is easier in the same way that the windings on a screw make the work easier. The finer the screw's threads are, the less force is required. To make up for what is gained in force, however, you lose in distance.

Teaching Idea

To give children a concrete idea of friction, have them rub their hands together quickly. The warmth is a result of friction.

Friction

Suppose you were driving or riding a bicycle and you stopped pressing on the gas pedal or stopped pedaling. What would happen? You would eventually slow to a stop. This occurs as a result of friction. Friction is a phenomenon in nature that exerts forces that oppose motion. Friction exists between objects that are touching or rubbing against one another, and between the moving parts of machines. There is friction between the teeth of gears, for example. Friction works against motion—it slows you down when you are moving, or keeps you still when you are not. Whether already moving or standing still, a great deal of work is required to overcome friction.

Friction between objects varies. The amount of friction between two smooth or slick surfaces is lower than that between two rough surfaces. When ice-skating, you experience little friction between the ice and blade of your skate. When rubbing two pieces of coarse sandpaper against each other, you experience a great deal of friction. The greater the friction between two objects, the greater the amount of work required to overcome friction.

Because friction exists between the moving parts of a machine, a certain amount of work put into the machine is lost to overcome this friction. (You do not get out all the energy that you put in.) Most of this lost work becomes thermal energy, or heat. The more gears and moving parts a machine has, the more friction and the more work lost. Machines are most efficient when friction is reduced or limited.

Keeping the parts of machines clean and well-oiled is important—these activities reduce friction. Rust and dirt increase friction. If you have ever tried to turn a rusty doorknob or ride a rusty bike, you know how great friction caused by rust can be. Taking care of machines ensures that they will continue to work and function properly and efficiently.

Teaching Idea

Use Instructional Masters 48a and 48b, *Simple Machine Crossword,* to help reinforce the different types of simple machines. As an extention, have children try to find an example of each type of machine in their school.

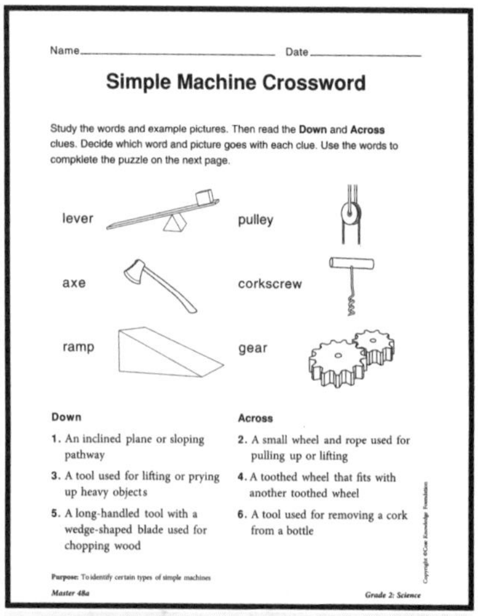

Name________ Date________

Simple Machine Crossword

Study the words and example pictures. Then read the **Down** and **Across** clues. Decide which word and picture goes with each clue. Use the words to compkiete the puzzle on the next page.

lever
pulley
axe
corkscrew
ramp
gear

Down

1. An inclined plane or sloping pathway
3. A tool used for lifting or prying up heavy objects
5. A long-handled tool with a wedge-shaped blade used for chopping wood

Across

2. A small wheel and rope used for pulling up or lifting
4. A toothed wheel that fits with another toothed wheel
6. A tool used for removing a cork from a bottle

Purpose: To identify certain types of simple machines

Master 48a *Grade 2: Science*

Copyright ©Core Knowledge Foundation

Use Instructional Masters 48a and 48b.

Review

The Big Idea in Review

Simple machines help us do work.

Below are some ideas for ongoing assessment and review activities. These are not meant to constitute a comprehensive list.

- Incorporate a journal topic into the study of simple machines. Pose a question to the class about how simple machines simplify our lives. What are some ways that children use simple machines in their lives? Write about what would happen if we did not have simple machines.
- Make a class chart with the name of each type of simple machine at the top of each column (*lever, pulley, wheel and axle, inclined plane, wedge,* and *screw*). Brainstorm a list of objects that use the simple machine in each column. Have children draw pictures on the chart to illustrate each type of simple machine.
- Send children home for the weekend with an assignment to be on the lookout for simple machines. On Monday, ask them to tell about what they saw and which simple machines were involved.
- As a way to review the section on simple machines, name a task for children to perform, and discuss how to make the task easier and more efficient. For example, explain how butter is made, and ask children if they think it would be faster to make butter by shaking a jar of whipping cream or by stirring whipping cream using a manual eggbeater. Record the predictions. To begin, pour one half- pint of cream into a jar and screw the lid on tightly. Ask children to take turns shaking the jar, and use a stopwatch to time how long it takes to make butter. Then, pour another half-pint of cream into a bowl, and have children take turns using the eggbeater to stir the cream. Again, time them to see how long it takes to make butter. After finishing, have the class discuss the activity and record their results and observations in their science journals.
- Once children have studied all of the simple machines, describe a "problem" situation and invite children to come up with a solution based on one or more simple machines. For example, you need to move a heavy appliance across a floor, but you are having trouble lifting it. What kind of simple machine could help? Possible solutions include using a pulley to lift it or putting roller wheels underneath it.
- Bring the following examples of simple machines into class: a hammer, a screw, a screwdriver, one toy car with wheels, one pulley and rope, and a wheel with notched teeth. Set up stations with each example of a simple machine, and have the class rotate through stations to observe each tool and write in a science journal about how that tool makes jobs easier. How do we use each one? Have children record the characteristics that make each tool useful.
- Have the class imagine examples of inventions that use some combination of simple machines. As a class, brainstorm and discuss possible ideas; encourage children to use their imagination to invent machines that could improve their lives. Ask each child to write about their favorite machine idea, draw a picture of it, and write about the use of the machine. How will it make our lives easier? Then, have children share their writing and pictures with the class.
- You may also ask the following questions at the end of this section:

1. Why do we use machines?

   We use machines because they help us do work.

2. What are the six simple machines?

   The six simple machines are the lever, wheel and axle, pulley, inclined plane, wedge, and screw.

3. What is a gear?

   A gear is a special type of wheel and axle. The wheel of a gear has teeth that can fit into the teeth of another gear.

4. What is friction?

   Friction is a phenomenon in nature that exerts forces that oppose motion.

More Resources

The titles listed below are offered as a representative sample of materials and not a complete list of everything that is available.

For children —

These books are generally intended to be read aloud, though some children may be able to read parts or all of the simpler texts.

- *Experiments with Simple Machines (A True Book),* by Salvatore Tocci (Children's Press, 2003). Library binding, 48 pages, ISBN 0516226045.
- *How Do You Lift a Lion?,* by Robert E. Wells (Albert Whitman & Co., 1996). Paperback, ISBN 0807534218.
- *Levers (Early Bird Physics),* by Sally M. Walker and Roseann Feldmann (Lerner, 2002). A terrific hands-on book. Library binding, 48 pages, ISBN 0822522187. Other titles in the series are *Screws, Wheels and Axles, Pulleys,* and *Inclined Planes and Wedges.*
- *Levers (Understanding Simple Machines),* by Anne Welsbacher (Bridgestone Books, 2001). Library binding, 24 pages, ISBN 0736806113. Other titles in this series are *Inclined Planes, Pulleys, Screws, Wedges,* and *Wheels and Axles.*
- *Machines We Use (It's Science!),* by Sally Hewitt (Children's Press, 1998). Paperback, 32 pages, ISBN 0516263927.
- *Science Experiments with Simple Machines,* by Sally Nankivell-Aston and Dorothy Jackson (Franklin Watts, 2000). Paperback, 32 pages, ISBN 0531154459.
- *Simple Machines (Rookie Read-About Science),* by Allan Fowler (Children's Book Press, 2001). Paperback, 32 pages, ISBN 0516273108.

For teachers —

- *Awesome Experiments in Force and Motion,* by Michael DiSpezio (Sterling Publishing, 1999). Hardcover, 160 pages, ISBN 0806998210.
- *Janice VanCleave's Machines,* by Janice VanCleave (John Wiley & Sons, 1993). Paperback, 96 pages, ISBN 0471571083.
- *The New Way Things Work,* by David Macaulay (Houghton Mifflin, 1998). The revised edition of the book that stayed on the *New York Times* bestseller list for 50 weeks. Macaulay, a former architect and junior high school teacher, gives clear, humorous, and detailed explanations of the workings of many ordinary items. The text is too complicated for younger children, but this is a great addition to your resource shelf. Hardcover, 400 pages, ISBN 0395938473.
- *Science Experiments with Simple Machines,* by Sally Nankivell-Aston and Dorothy Jackson (Franklin Watts, 2000). ISBN 0531145794.

VI. Science Biographies

The Big Idea

Science is built on the careful observations and creative contributions of individuals.

Remember that each subject you study with children expands their vocabulary and introduces new terms, thus making them better listeners and readers. As you study about the contributions of individuals to science, use read alouds and discussions to build children's vocabularies.

Text Resources

(85) *Anton van Leeuwenhoek*
(86) *Elijah McCoy*
(87) *Florence Nightingale*
(88) *Daniel Hale Williams*

What Students Should Already Know

Students in Core Knowledge schools should be familiar with

Kindergarten

- George Washington Carver: scientist who helped Southern farmers by teaching them to plant new crops and by inventing new uses for peanuts, sweet potatoes, and soybeans
- Jane Goodall: animal behavior scientist who observed chimpanzees and discovered that they are intelligent, social, and emotional animals
- Wilbur and Orville Wright: invented the first airplane and had the first successful powered flight from a level surface

Grade 1

- Rachel Carson: wrote many books and articles about the environment and the harmful effects human actions can have on the environment, revealing the devastating effects of DDT on the environment and setting the stage for the modern environmental movement
- Thomas Edison: one of the most prolific inventors of the past two centuries who invented the electric light and the phonograph and formed the foundation for many of the machines and devices we use today
- Edward Jenner: developed a vaccine for smallpox and essentially began the field of immunology
- Louis Pasteur: established the scientific field of microbiology, developed the process of pasteurization, and discovered the vaccination for rabies

What Students Need to Learn

- **Anton van Leeuwenhoek**
- **Elijah McCoy**
- **Florence Nightingale**
- **Daniel Hale Williams**

VI. Science Biographies

Materials

Instructional Master 49

Name That Scientist!, p. 461

microscope, p. 458

water, p. 458

poster board, p. 462

magazines and newspapers, p. 462

index cards, p. 462

pictures of items associated with each scientist, p. 462

writing journals, p. 462

What Students Will Learn in Future Grades

Students will review and extend their learning about scientists and inventors in each year of the Core Knowledge curriculum.

Grade 3

- Alexander Graham Bell
- Copernicus
- Mae Jemison
- John Muir

Grade 4

- Benjamin Banneker
- Elizabeth Blackwell
- Charles Drew
- Michael Faraday

Grade 5

- Galileo Galilei
- Percy Lavon Julian
- Ernest Just
- Carolus Linnaeus

Vocabulary

Student/Teacher Vocabulary

antiseptic: something that prevents or reduces infection, often by stopping the growth of microorganisms (T)

aptitude: a natural skill (S)

hone: to intensely develop something (T)

lens: a piece of glass, or another transparent object, which forms an image through the refraction of light that passes through it (S)

lubricate: to make slippery (S)

mortality rate: the rate at which people of a place or region are dying (T)

patent: the legal right to own or sell an invention (T)

plaque: a buildup of bacteria, on the gums and teeth, which can cause gum disease (T)

sanitary: clean and free from disease (S)

sterilize: to rid of germs and bacteria (S)

Domain Vocabulary

Science biographies and associated words:
apprentice, master, microscope, microscopic, experiment, test, trial, magnify, enlarge, textile, fabric, thread, determine, distinguish, density, examine, observe, sharpen, expand, structure, feature, characteristic, bacteria, protist, organism, living thing, machine, machinery, mechanics, skill, preference, engineering, engineer, engine, motor, maintain, revolutionize, industrial, industrialize, device, tool, instrument, automatic, factory, efficient, minimize, maximize, social, pursue, menial, privileged, aspiration, casualty, unsanitary, sanitation, neglect, statistic, data, calculate, surgeon, physician, medical, medicine, reputation, sterile, sterilization, anatomy, infection, inflate, deflate, improvise, technique, meticulous

In the Text Resources for this section, words are bolded that should be included as part of Domain Vocabulary.

What Teachers Need to Know

Anton van Leeuwenhoek (1632–1722)

Anton van Leeuwenhoek [LAY-vun-huke] was born in Delft, Holland, on October 24, 1632. It is believed that his last name is derived from where he lived—on the corner (*hoek*) of Lion's (*leeuw*) Gate. At age 16, Leeuwenhoek moved to Amsterdam and got a job as an apprentice to a textile (fabric) merchant. After some time, he took the Cloth Worker's Guild exam—the Master's exam for his trade. Typically, this exam took three years to pass, but Leeuwenhoek completed his exam in only six weeks. He returned to his native Delft when he was 21 years old and opened up his own textile shop. In his spare time, Leeuwenhoek began to experiment with microscopes and lenses.

Leeuwenhoek was probably introduced to magnifying lenses during his apprenticeship in Amsterdam. It was common for fabric merchants to use lenses to more closely examine cloth and determine thread density. These experiences may have led to Leeuwenhoek's interest in microscopes and the microscopic world.

Anton van Leeuwenhoek

Although Leeuwenhoek was not trained as a scientist, he was curious and began experimenting with grinding lenses and developing simple microscopes of his own. Unlike compound microscopes of the day, Leeuwenhoek's simple microscopes were made with only one lens. His lenses were very strong, magnifying objects from 50 to 200 times their natural size; this was a much greater magnification than that of even the very best compound microscopes available then. Objects seen through Leeuwenhoek's microscopes were brighter and clearer as well. However, his lenses were very small, some the size of a pinhead, and had to be held very close to the eye. For these reasons, using simple microscopes was very difficult, requiring excellent eyesight and a lot of patience. Luckily, Leeuwenhoek had both!

Leeuwenhoek honed his skills at grinding lenses and became completely immersed in looking at anything and everything through his microscopes. One of his greatest talents was his ability to describe in great detail the tiny structures he saw with his microscopes. Any modern scientist would instantly recognize the microbes that he described. In 1673, Leeuwenhoek began writing to the Royal Society of London, a prestigious scientific academy, about the amazing things he was discovering with his microscopes. His first letter included his observations of bee stingers. In 1674, he examined the green, slimy matter on the surface of a lake near his home and found tiny little creatures. He called these tiny creatures "animalcules" and described them as spiral strings of small green globules joined together, what we now commonly call algae.

Ever curious, Leeuwenhoek delved into his own mouth, and those of several other people, to examine plaque under his microscope. In the plaque from his own mouth he found "many very little living animalcules, very prettily a-moving." The plaque from the mouths of two old men (who supposedly never brushed their teeth) revealed "an unbelievably great company of living animalcules." Leeuwenhoek commented that the fluid "seemed to be alive." These were

Teaching Idea

Science doesn't always have the answer! Explain to children the concept of spontaneous generation—the belief that living organisms could form spontaneously from nonliving things; a maggot could form from a piece of decaying meat, for example. It sounds ridiculous today, but, for many years, this theory was commonly accepted. Use this concept as an example to point out to children that scientific ideas build and change as new discoveries are made.

> **Teaching Idea**
> **Invite children to look at slides of a drop of water and other items under a microscope so that they might share the fascination Leeuwenhoek experienced when looking through his own microscopes. Children will see a world of microscopic organisms alive with activity in just a single drop of water!**

among the first recorded observations of bacteria and protists, single-celled organisms that have characteristics of plants, animals, or both.

Leeuwenhoek went on to challenge the commonly accepted idea of spontaneous generation—the belief that life could arise spontaneously from dirt or sand. Through his careful observations, Leeuwenhoek proved that animals breed as humans do to produce young. In fact, he was the first person to describe the spermatozoa (sperm cells) of humans, animals, and insects.

It is believed that Leeuwenhoek made between 400 and 500 microscopes, of which fewer than a dozen still exist. He never told anyone how he made his lenses, and it was over 100 years before anyone could match or surpass their quality. (85)

Elijah McCoy (1843–1929)

Elijah McCoy

Elijah McCoy was born in 1843 in Ontario, Canada. His parents, George and Mildred, had escaped from slavery in Kentucky by way of the Underground Railroad, a network of safe houses organized by opponents to slavery in the United States. As a young boy, McCoy was fascinated with tools and machinery. Recognizing their son's aptitude and interest in mechanics, the McCoys sent their son to Edinburgh, Scotland, to study engineering when he was 15 years old. After completing his studies and earning the title "master mechanic and engineer," McCoy returned to Canada, and the family then moved to Michigan after the Civil War. Despite his training, he could not find employment as an engineer; it was still very difficult for African Americans to find professional work in the United States. He finally settled for a job on the Michigan Central Railroad, working as a fireman/oilman, stoking the train engine's fires and oiling the axles.

> **Cross-curricular Teaching Idea**
> **Review with children the Civil War and the Underground Railroad. Remind children of what life in America was like during this time period. Explain the risk Elijah McCoy's parents had to take to gain their freedom from slavery.**

The period from 1865 to 1900 is often referred to as the "machine age," a time when engines and heavy machinery were rapidly being developed and employed for all types of work, from farming to the mass production of goods. Advances in science and materials had made steam engines an economical and reliable source of power. However, these complex machines had many moving parts that required lubrication, and inventors had not figured out how to lubricate the parts without shutting the machinery down. This problem made traveling by train very difficult and timely, because trains would have to be stopped regularly to allow the engine to be oiled—the job McCoy was hired to do. Inspired to discover a more effective way of lubricating machines, McCoy invented a small, oil-filled container that would automatically drip oil on the machine's parts while the machine was moving. This simple device revolutionized the industrial world. Machinery could now run continuously, without stopping for lubrication. McCoy patented his automatic lubricating device in 1872. The high demand for his invention prompted many competitors to develop similar products. However, McCoy's device was so reliable that buyers would ask for "the real McCoy" to ensure they got the real thing. His invention was used for many years on trains, steamships, and in factories around the world, and we still use the expression "the real McCoy" today to distinguish an original from an imitation.

> **Teaching Idea**
> **As part of their study of language arts, children learn idiomatic sayings. "The real McCoy" is a perfect example of another saying. See that children understand that it stands for authenticity or the genuine article. The biography also shows that such sayings derive from real events and people in history.**

McCoy spent the rest of his life inventing things, including the lawn sprinkler and the folding ironing board. In 1920, he founded the Elijah McCoy Manufacturing Company, in Detroit, Michigan, where he developed and sold

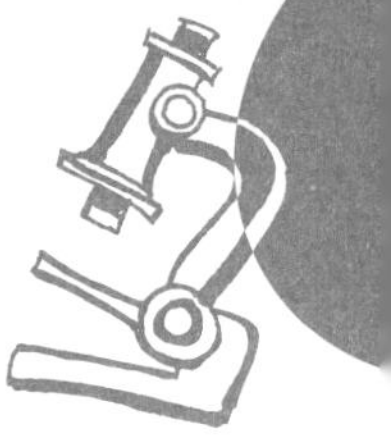

his inventions, and where he made a point of hiring young African-American men. McCoy would also show his inventions to the young children in his neighborhood and encourage them to attend school. Elijah McCoy died in 1929 at the age of 86. (86)

Florence Nightingale (1820–1910)

Florence Nightingale was born on May 12, 1820, in Florence, Italy, while her parents traveled in Europe on a two-year honeymoon. Her older sister, Parthenope (the Greek name for Naples), had been born one year earlier. The Nightingales were a wealthy English family, and Florence and her sister were raised in a life of privilege. The girls were taught at home by their father, who provided them with an education that was usually reserved for young men. Florence excelled at math, philosophy, history, and languages. She believed that she had a mission. In fact, when she was 17 years old she said she heard the voice of God summoning her to work; however, she was not sure what that work was.

Nightingale grew interested in the social issues of the time and began visiting the sick in the local hospital. It was during this time that she met Elizabeth Blackwell (see Grade 4 Science Biographies), the first woman to qualify as a doctor in the United States, who encouraged her to pursue her interest in nursing. However, during the Victorian Age, nursing was considered a menial job not fit for educated people, and Nightingale's parents opposed the idea of their daughter becoming a nurse. Hospitals were known to be dirty, dreary places for poorer people. In 1849, Nightingale's parents sent her on a trip to tour Europe in the hopes of discouraging their daughter's aspirations. However, the trip only served to strengthen her resolve. Her parents finally capitulated, and the following year Nightingale began training as a nurse in Alexandria, Egypt. Upon her return to England in 1853, she took a position as the Superintendent of the London Establishment for Gentlewomen during Illness.

In 1854, the Crimean War began. Britain, France, and Turkey declared war on Russia. Word of horrific casualties filtered back to Great Britain, and the British were criticized for their poor medical facilities for the wounded. The British Minister of War, Sir Sidney Herbert, arranged for Nightingale and about 40 other nurses to be sent to Scutari, near Constantinople. Nightingale was charged with the introduction and direction of the nursing operations at the front. When the nurses arrived at the hospital in Scutari they were met with an appalling sight—the unsanitary and neglected condition of the wounded.

Nightingale quickly went to work. She imposed strict rules of cleanliness and sanitation, which helped to significantly reduce the mortality rate. She became known as the "Lady with the Lamp." While she conducted her nursing duties, Nightingale also introduced systematized record keeping and began collecting data on hospital conditions, mortality rates, and other such statistics. Using the data, Nightingale calculated that the army hospital mortality rate could be greatly decreased by imposing improved sanitary measures. She presented her statistical analysis in a report titled "Notes Affecting the Health, Efficiency, and Hospital Administration for the British Army." Through this work, she helped to change the conditions of military hospitals and influenced the development of the Army Statistical Department.

Teaching Idea

Connect children's study of Elijah McCoy to their study of simple machines and friction. Challenge children to explain why the parts of machines need lubricating. Explain that lubrication decreases the friction between the many moving parts of a complex machine and that minimizing friction means the machine can work more efficiently.

Florence Nightingale

Cross-curricular Teaching Idea

If children have already studied the Civil War, you can connect Florence Nightingale with Clara Barton: both were early female pioneers in nursing, and both were active around the same time in treating battlefield victims.

When Nightingale returned home after the war, she turned her attention to England's hospitals and began advocating for reform in the public health field. In 1859, she published her *Notes on Hospitals,* which advocated for a new hospital design with separate pavilions, each providing abundant fresh air and sunlight. Nightingale mistakenly believed that infections were spontaneously generated in dirty, airless surroundings; nevertheless, her analysis of hospital statistics demonstrated that improving sanitary conditions was essential to ensuring healthy environments. In 1860, she published her most recognized work, *Notes on Nursing,* which outlines the principles of nursing. That same year, she also established the Nightingale Training School for Nurses.

Although Nightingale's health slowly deteriorated due to an illness she had contracted in Crimea, she continued to work, and her influence was widespread. She consulted with the U.S. government during the Civil War, and advocated for public health care reforms in England and its colonies. Florence Nightingale died in 1910 at the age of 90. (87)

Daniel Hale Williams (1856–1931)

Daniel Hale Williams

Daniel Hale Williams was born January 18, 1856, in Hollidaysburg, Pennsylvania, the fifth of seven children born to Daniel and Sarah Williams. Williams's father, who worked as a barber, died when Williams was only nine years old. After his father's death, Williams's mother realized she could not raise her large family alone, so she sent some of the children to live with relatives. Williams was apprenticed to a shoemaker in Baltimore, where he lived for three years before moving to Wisconsin to live with his sister. He worked repairing shoes and studied to become a barber (like his father). By the time he was 17 years old, he had completed high school and had become a successful barber.

While working at the local barbershop, Williams met Dr. Henry Palmer, Wisconsin's surgeon general. Dr. Palmer saw a lot of promise in Williams, and arranged for him to become his apprentice. In 1880, Williams was accepted into a three-year medical training program at the Chicago Medical School, which was considered to be one of the best medical schools in the country (now Northwestern University Medical School). Williams graduated in 1883 with an M.D. and set up a private practice, which grew quickly, and established his reputation as a skilled surgeon. He often had to conduct surgical procedures in his patients' homes and, consequently, utilized a variety of emerging sterilization and antiseptic procedures. His insistence on stringent sanitary conditions reinforced his good reputation as a surgeon. He also worked at the South Side Dispensary and taught anatomy classes at the Chicago Medical School.

Williams began his medical practice at a time when African-American doctors had difficulty practicing medicine and many African-American people were not provided with adequate health care. Williams was very aware of the limited opportunities for African-American physicians, and the inferior treatment that African-American patients often received. When he was appointed to the Illinois State Board of Health in 1889, he worked to influence medical standards and hospital rules. In 1890, Emma Reynolds, a young African-American woman who aspired to a career in nursing but had been refused entrance to nursing schools in Chicago because of her color, approached Williams for help. He set up a hospital and training school

where Reynolds and other African-American women could study nursing. In 1891, Provident Hospital and Nurses Training School opened its doors to all who lived in the Chicago community.

In July 1893, a young man named James Cornish, who had suffered a stab wound to his chest, was brought to Provident Hospital. Although the external bleeding had stopped, the young man's condition continued to deteriorate—the signs indicated that he was bleeding internally. At the time, surgeons did not open up the chest of a living person, for infection and death were almost certain. However, Williams determined that he had no choice but to open the young man's chest and operate internally. He identified the internal injury, a tear in the pericardium (the sac surrounding the heart) and performed a first-of-its-kind surgery to repair the torn membrane. During the surgery, assistants had to breathe for the patient, and his lungs were reinflated after his chest was closed. All of the techniques that were used to keep the patient alive were improvised. Williams's commitment to meticulous and sterile procedures prevented infection, and James Cornish recovered completely and went on to live a long life. This was the first successful open-chest surgery that did not result in infection and death. The procedures Williams used during this surgery set the standard for future internal surgeries.

In 1894, Williams was appointed Surgeon-in-Chief of Freedmen's Hospital in Washington, D.C., by President Grover Cleveland. During his tenure, Williams worked tirelessly to reorganize the hospital and implement a variety of improvements that helped increase efficiency and reduce the patient mortality rate. He also helped to organize the National Medical Association, the only national organization open to African-American physicians at the time. In 1898, Williams returned to Chicago and Provident Hospital, where he continued his work as a surgeon. He wrote frequently for the Chicago Medical Record, correcting fellow surgeons' false medical opinions that were often based on race rather than science. In 1900, he joined the faculty at Meharry Medical College and then went on to become the staff surgeon at St. Luke's Hospital, where he worked until 1926, when he suffered a stroke. Over his lifetime, he received many honors and awards. He was named a Fellow in the American College of Surgeons and was awarded an honorary degree from Howard University. His work helped expand the opportunities for African-American children interested in pursuing a career in medicine. Dr. Daniel Hale Williams died in 1931. (88)

Cross-curricular Teaching Idea

You may want to introduce children to Daniel Hale Williams when you discuss civil rights in History and Geography. Explain to children that Williams lived during a time when African Americans had fewer choices and opportunities than they do today.

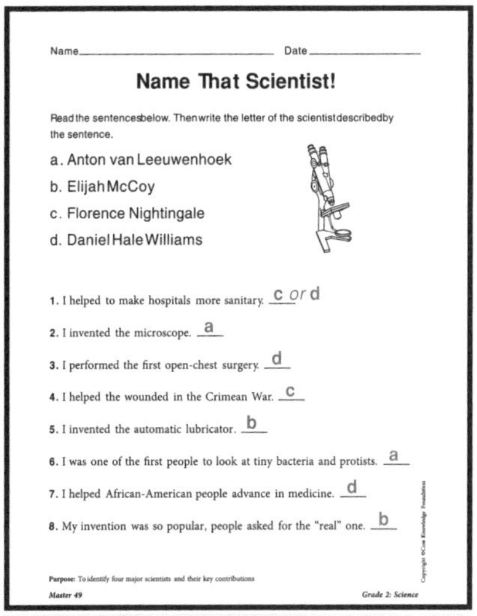

Name________________ Date__________

Name That Scientist!

Read the sentences below. Then write the letter of the scientist described by the sentence.

a. Anton van Leeuwenhoek

b. Elijah McCoy

c. Florence Nightingale

d. Daniel Hale Williams

1. I helped to make hospitals more sanitary. c or d
2. I invented the microscope. a
3. I performed the first open-chest surgery. d
4. I helped the wounded in the Crimean War. c
5. I invented the automatic lubricator. b
6. I was one of the first people to look at tiny bacteria and protists. a
7. I helped African-American people advance in medicine. d
8. My invention was so popular, people asked for the "real" one. b

Purpose: To identify four major scientists and their key contributions

Master 49 *Grade 2: Science*

Copyright ©Core Knowledge Foundation

Use Instructional Master 49.

VI. Science Biographies

The Big Idea in Review

Science is built on the careful observations and creative contributions of individuals.

Review

Below are some ideas for ongoing assessment and review activities. These are not meant to constitute a comprehensive list.

- Make a poster to illustrate each scientist's accomplishments. For example, take a piece of poster board and post the name of the scientist and that person's picture. Then, have the class find relevant pictures or words from magazines and newspapers to add to the poster (e.g., "wounded soldiers" and "nurses" for Florence Nightingale). When you have completed the study of each individual, select a child to stand and share knowledge about that scientist, explaining the significance of the words and pictures from the poster.
- After the study of each scientist, have the class write an interview with that person. Ask children to write questions to illustrate what they have learned about each scientist. For example, they might ask where that person was from and why he or she was famous. Then, ask the class to write their questions on one index card and the answers on another card. Perform the interview for the class, having one child play the role of interviewer and one play the role of the scientist.
- Play an association game in which you hold up a picture of something associated with each scientist and the class has to guess which person you are talking about. For example, you may hold up a picture of a microscope for Anton van Leeuwenhoek or a picture of a nurse for Florence Nightingale. You may challenge the class by finding pictures that describe the lives of each scientist as well as their discoveries.
- After the study of each scientist, ask the class to brainstorm a list of adjectives to describe that person and to explain why they chose those adjectives. After you have studied all of the scientists, have a journal writing activity in which children write about the most important characteristics of a successful scientist. Children can refer to the adjectives from each list while they are writing.
- You may also ask the following questions at the end of this section:

1. What did Anton van Leeuwenhoek see through the lens of his microscopes?

   He saw microscopic organisms.

2. What is Elijah McCoy known for?

   Elijah McCoy is known for his inventions, including the automatic lubricator.

3. Why was Elijah McCoy's automatic lubricator important?

   It allowed machines to be lubricated automatically while they continued to run, which saved time.

4. What did Florence Nightingale do to improve hospitals?

   She worked to make them more sanitary.

5. Why was the surgery performed by Daniel Hale Williams considered a breakthrough?

   No one had successfully performed an open-chest surgery before.

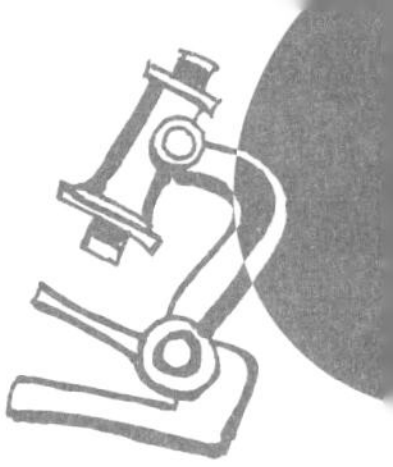

More Resources

The titles listed below are offered as a representative sample of materials and not a complete list of everything that is available.

For children —

These books are generally intended to be read aloud, though some children may be able to read parts or all of the simpler texts.

- *Florence Nightingale: An Animated Hero Classic* (Nest Entertainment, 2001). Distributed by Schlessinger Media, a division of Library Video.com, www.libraryvideo.com or 1-800-843-3620. DVD, approximately 30 minutes.
- *A Picture Book of Florence Nightingale,* by David Adler (Holiday House, 1992). ISBN 0823409651. See also *Florence Nightingale,* by David and Patricia Armentrout (Rourke, 2002). Library binding, 24 pages, ISBN 1589521692.
- *The Real McCoy: The Life of an African-American Inventor,* by Wendy Towle and illustrated by Wil Clay (Scholastic, 1995). Paperback, ISBN 0590481029.
- *What Is a Scientist?,* by Barbara Lehn (BT Bound, 2001). A simply worded explanation of what scientists do. Hardcover, ISBN 061321031X.

For teachers —

- *Notes on Nursing: What It Is, and What It Is Not,* by Florence Nightingale (Dover, 1969). Paperback, 140 pages, ISBN 048622340X. Also available online at the University of Michigan's Making of America website, www.hti.umich.edu/m/moagrp. Select "Other Searches in MoA," and limit search by title.
- *One Doctor: Daniel Hale Williams* (History on Video, 1997). Distributed through Library Video, www.libraryvideo.com or 1-800-843-3620. Suggested for Grades 7 and up. VHS, 45 minutes.
- Black Inventor.com, www.blackinventor.com/pages/danielwilliams.html, has a brief biography of Daniel Hale Williams. (See also the website of the Provident Foundation, www.providentfoundation.org/williams.htm, which seeks to preserve the historical legacy of Provident Hospital, founded by Williams.) Black Inventor.com also has a page on Elijah McCoy, www.blackinventor.com/ pages/elijahmccoy.html.
- Selected Correspondence of Florence Nightingale can be found at http://clendening.kumc.edu/dc/fn/flochron.html, posted by the Clendening History of Medicine Library and Museum at the University of Kansas Medical Center. The site features both facsimiles of the originals as well as transcriptions.
- Van Leeuwenhoek microscopes, including the original specimens observed, have been extensively researched by Brian J. Ford, a British scientist. You can view many of his findings at his website, www.sciences.demon.co.uk/whistmic.htm.